U0542540

2021年江苏省高等学校重点教材（编号：2021-1-030）

教育部基础学科拔尖学生培养计划2.0基地建设成果
国家级一流本科专业建设点建设成果
江苏高校品牌专业建设工程二期项目建设成果

西方马克思主义原著选读

［第3版］

张 亮 孙乐强 主编

南京大学出版社

目　录
CONTENTS

第一章　西方马克思主义哲学的奠基之作
——《历史与阶级意识》选读

教学目的与要求

理解“马克思主义的正统是方法”这一命题的含义及其在西方马克思主义哲学发展史上的意义；了解总体性范畴的三重内涵，认识总体性辩证法在马克思主义辩证法发展史上的地位；掌握物化理论的来源、本质及其与马克思的异化、物化学说的联系与差别；正确认识卢卡奇的无产阶级学说。

一、历史背景

（一）作者介绍

1885年，格奥尔格·卢卡奇（Georg Lukács）出生于匈牙利布达佩斯的一个犹太家庭，1909年获得布达佩斯大学的哲学博士学位，1918年12月加入匈牙利共产党，此后以马克思主义者的形象活跃在20世纪的思想史舞台上。[①] 卢卡奇加入匈牙利共产党这一“人生中最大的转折”之所以会发生，外在原因是他当时重新认真研究了马克思主义，而更为根本的内在原因则

① 参见[美]罗伯特·戈尔曼编《“新马克思主义”传记辞典》，赵培杰等译，重庆出版社1990年版，第540页。

是卢卡奇已经找到了证明共产主义与自己早期反资本主义立场的一致性的理论基础和政治基础。[①] 在此之后，卢卡奇积极投身匈牙利革命，并在革命失败后于 1919 年 9 月底流亡维也纳。流亡期间，他坚信无产阶级革命高潮很快会出现并将席卷全世界。基于这种认识，他开始怀着以救世主自居的乌托邦主义，思考马克思主义的哲学本质及党的组织路线等重大理论和现实问题，其最终成果就是 1923 年出版的《历史与阶级意识——关于马克思主义辩证法的研究》。该书是"作为弄清作者本人及其读者头脑中的革命运动的理论问题的尝试而写出的"，基本上体现了卢卡奇自 1918 年底加入共产党以来的哲学思想和政治思想的发展成果。该书出版后在马克思主义阵营中得到了截然不同的对待：在 1924 年夏季于莫斯科召开的共产国际第五次会议上，它引起了巨大争论，并遭到共产国际主要领导人季诺维也夫的严厉批评；而在德国左派知识分子中，它却得强烈共鸣，成为人们重新认识、理解马克思主义的新典范，许多人（包括后来成为法兰克福学派主要成员的霍克海默、马尔库塞、阿多诺、本雅明等）在它的影响下转向马克思主义，西方马克思主义哲学传统就此在客观上形成。卢卡奇于 1929 年至 1933 年在柏林居住，期间曾短暂住在莫斯科的马克思-恩格斯研究院。当时他迫于形势，暂时放弃了激进的政治活动，撰写了一系列文学批评类的文章，以及两部重要著作：1937 年发表的《历史小说》与 1938 年完成的《青年黑格尔》。这一时期，卢卡奇奋战在马克思主义文艺理论、德国俄国文学史、青年黑格尔研究这三个马克思主义者未曾深耕过的领域，最终扭转了马克思主义在这些领域少有作为的局面。1945 年，卢卡奇回到匈牙利，开启了新的理论与实践之路：在实践上，他担任议会议员和纳吉政府的文化部部长；在理论研究方面，他回归哲学，在布达佩斯大学担任美学和文化哲学教授，频繁参加各类文化政治活动，发表了大量文学及通俗哲学文章，形成了大众化文化创作和实践方式。这一时期，卢卡奇先是致力于对现代资产阶级哲学当代发展的马克思主义批判，创作了《理性的毁灭》，继而转向马克思主义哲学体系的正面建构，在以出版《美学的特殊性质》为标志而成功构建马克思主义美学体系之后，又力图建构马克思主义伦理学体系，最终回到马克思主义哲

---

① Georg Lukács, *Record of a Life: An Autobiographical Sketch*, trans. Rodney Livingstone, Verso, 1983, p. 159.

学的基础问题，留下了《关于社会存在的本体论》这一宏大残篇。1971 年，卢卡奇在匈牙利逝世。

（二）时代背景

1. 现代资本主义的新变化

随着资本主义生产方式的矛盾运动，十九世纪末二十世纪初，西方主要资本主义国家陆续从自由资本主义阶段进入垄断资本主义阶段，也就是列宁所说的帝国主义阶段。由此，现代资本主义呈现了一些新变化。首先，经济高速发展，生产力水平显著提高，工人阶级的绝对贫困化趋势得到扭转，物质生活水平不断改善。其次，政治现代化进程加速进行，资产阶级民主政治在不同程度上得到实现，无产阶级与资产阶级的阶级斗争的主战场从经济领域开始向政治领域转移。最后，随着科学技术与教育的发展、文化的繁荣，资产阶级意识形态迅速扩张，对包括工人阶级在内的普通人民群众的控制能力日益增强。

2. 国际共产主义运动的新变化

按照马克思恩格斯原来的构想，无产阶级革命将在若干发达资本主义国家同时发生并陆续取得胜利。不过，随着现代资本主义发展，国际共产主义运动的形势也随之发生了相应的变化。首先，在英国、法国、德国等发达资本主义国家，随着工人阶级陆续取得普选权，合法的议会政治斗争逐渐成为无产阶级斗争的主要形式，马克思恩格斯原来所设想的无产阶级革命迟迟没有能够出现。其次，伴随着资本主义经济政治的不平衡发展，相对落后的俄国率先发动革命并取得胜利。

3. 匈牙利国内形势的新变化

虽然《历史与阶级意识》是卢卡奇在维也纳流亡期间创作的，但是，当时匈牙利复杂的国内形势以及社会发展的新变化，也构成了他思考的重要社会背景。在俄国十月革命的激励下，1918 年至 1919 年间，德国、匈牙利均爆发了无产阶级革命，并先后成立了匈牙利苏维埃共和国和巴伐利亚苏维埃共和国。尽管这些革命运动最后均以失败告终，但是，匈牙利国内爆发的无产阶级革命使得卢卡奇支持激进思潮，反对任何主张维护传统权力体系的宗派主义。

（三）思想背景

1. 二十世纪初德语知识界的基本思想走向

二十世纪初的德语知识界非常活跃，新思想、新观点层出不穷，有一种“乱花渐欲迷人眼”的感觉。不过，透过这种纷繁芜杂的现象，我们可以捕捉到两条基本的思想发展轴线。第一条轴线是对资本主义的浪漫主义批判和反思。资本主义工业的飞速发展导致传统价值观和精神世界的解体，知识分子突然发现自己正处于一种“无灵魂的世界”中。对于这种状况，知识分子一方面是强烈的憎恨，另一方面是对前资本主义传统的共同体生活产生了绵长的乡愁。于是，从滕尼斯的《共同体与社会》(1887 年)开始，浪漫主义的反资本主义情绪在知识界迅速蔓延，并在从狄尔泰、席美尔到韦伯的德国经典社会理论主流中得到深刻体现。第二条轴线是对资本主义的总体性本质的理解与把握。资本主义的高速发展导致人们的日常社会生活剧烈膨胀，从而使得人们越来越难以把握到它的总体性本质，甚至开始怀疑这种本质是否存在。这种倾向引发了一些哲学家和社会学家们的忧虑。1912 年至 1915 年居留海德堡期间，卢卡奇甚至成为韦伯圈子中的重要成员。他这一阶段的思想经历基本上就是一个融入德国主流思想圈，进而成为其中有影响的思想家的过程。从新康德主义到新黑格尔主义，当时的德国思想家都努力对这一问题做出肯定的回答，而韦伯的合理化理论则代表了德国思想家当时在这一问题上的最高水平。① 用卢卡奇晚年的话来说，他当时的世界观是“左”的伦理(浪漫主义的反资本主义立场)和“右”的认识论与本体论(韦伯的类型学和狄尔泰的精神科学)融合的产物，它因为深刻反映了同时代激进青年们的心声，而对后来的德国左翼思想界产生了巨大影响。②

---

① [匈]格奥尔格·卢卡奇:《卢卡奇早期文选》,张亮、吴勇立译,南京大学出版社 2004 年版,第Ⅳ页。

② [匈]格奥尔格·卢卡奇:《卢卡奇早期文选》,张亮、吴勇立译,南京大学出版社 2004 年版,第Ⅷ-Ⅸ页。

2. 二十世纪初国际共产主义理论的发展状况

二十世纪初，国际共产主义运动接连遇到阻碍，列宁的探索为运动提供了新的思路。卢卡奇曾经在不同的版本中都强调了列宁的论述对他写作《历史与阶级意识》产生的最直接的影响。一方面，列宁的批评引导卢卡奇开始脱离宗派主义；另一方面，列宁为卢卡奇展示了马克思主义作为一种方法论的“决定性的意义”。除了列宁，卢卡奇接触最多的社会主义思想，一个来自德国社会民主党，以考茨基的思想为主；另一个则是来自罗莎·卢森堡，两者之间的矛盾立场也为当时卢卡奇的理论创作提供了重要的素材。同时，卢卡奇本人还提到，兰德列尔·耶诺的反官僚主义和冒险主义的立场为他树立起反宗派主义的路线奠定了重要基础。

二、篇章结构

《历史与阶级意识》的正文由 8 篇论文构成，其中的 6 篇是卢卡奇创作于 1919 年至 1922 年间的旧作，另外两篇即《物化和无产阶级意识》与《关于组织问题的方法论》则是他专为该书而创作的，不过它们也都有以前的即兴之作作为基础。

对于《历史与阶级意识》，读者通常不考虑它的编排顺序，直接进入那些在理论上最具创造性的部分。这种做法的问题在于容易忽略卢卡奇创作该书时的真实意图，因为该书不具有“系统的科学的完整性”，却具有“一定的实际联系”，“这也表现在论文的编排顺序上。因此读者最好按照这个顺序来阅读它们”①。

《什么是正统马克思主义？》最初写作于 1919 年 3 月。在这篇论文中，卢卡奇主要针对第二国际教条主义的马克思主义观，阐发了自己对马克思主义本质的理解。就像柯尔施后来在《马克思主义和哲学》中所批评的那样，第二国际思想家片面地理解恩格斯的论述，宣称马克思主义从本质上讲和哲学没有任何关系，是一种真正的科学。他们因此以教条主义的态度对

① [匈]格奥尔格·卢卡奇：《历史与阶级意识——关于马克思主义辩证法的研究》，杜章智、任立、燕宏远译，商务印书馆 1999 年版，第39 页。

待马克思主义，认为正统马克思主义就必须接受马克思的一切结论。卢卡奇坚决反对这种教条主义立场，认为马克思主义的正统就是辩证法。在他看来，辩证法的核心是理论和实践的关系，即理论通过掌握群众，变成一种改造世界的物质力量。恩格斯没有能够正确理解马克思的辩证法的本质，仅仅在概念的相互作用、相互转化的意义上来理解它，根本没有意识到辩证法的核心是主体和客体之间的辩证关系。正是这种理解导致第二国际思想家的思想混乱。第二国际的修正主义者反对辩证法，推崇所谓的事实。他们没有意识到他们赖以得到纯粹事实的所谓科学方法不过是一种资产阶级意识形态，因为它从根本上忽略了事实的历史性。事实上，只有在历史的总体中，对事实的认识才能成为现实的认识。辩证法与各种所谓的"批判"方法之间的冲突本身是一个社会问题，其实质是资本主义社会力图用拜物教假象来掩盖自己的过渡的、暂时的性质，而辩证法的任务就是要摧毁这种假象。马克思的辩证法来源于黑格尔，又超越了黑格尔。他正确地指出，人是社会历史过程的主体和客体，但只有在资本主义社会中，无产阶级才真正意识到自己是主体和客体的统一，理论和实践的统一即改变世界是自己的历史地位的一个方面。

《作为马克思主义者的罗莎·卢森堡》创作于 1921 年 1 月。这篇论文在逻辑上是《什么是正统马克思主义?》的一个例证。它通过阐述卢森堡对伯恩斯坦、庸俗经济学家、奥地利马克思主义者等的经济学思想和政治观点的批判，表明卢森堡是一名真正的马克思主义者，因为她基本正确地领会了马克思主义辩证法的实质，把理论与实践在实践基础上的统一作为自己毕生追求的事业。

《阶级意识》创作于 1920 年 3 月。通过剖析资产阶级的阶级意识的虚假性，卢卡奇指出，在前资本主义社会，由于阶级利益还没有以清晰的经济利益的形式表示出来，而是和政治的、宗教的等因素不可分割地结合在一起，因此，它们的阶级意识既不可能具有清晰的形式，也不可能有意识地影响历史进程。随着资本主义的出现、纯粹的经济划分的社会的建立，阶级意识进入了一个可能被意识到的时期。与以往不同，资产阶级的阶级利益促进了资产阶级的阶级意识的发展，但是，随着无产阶级的出现，资产阶级的阶级意识陷入了一种悲剧性的灾难即自我否定之中。当资产阶级意识到这种灾难之后，它进行了自觉的反抗，从虚假意识变成了虚伪意识，从而在资产阶级统治全社会的过程中发挥了客观的维护功能。历史唯物主义在无产阶级与资产阶级的阶级意识斗争中发挥了决定性的作用。正是历史唯物主义使无产阶级明白，如果不废除阶级社会，自己作为阶级就不可能解放自己。这使无产阶级的阶级意识具有了与以往的阶级意识不同的特殊功能。无产阶级的阶级意识存在着眼前利益和最终目标的内在对立。只有超越这种内在对立，无产阶级才可能取得外部阶级斗争的胜利。各种机会主义的根子就在于没有能够正确对待这种内在对立，而是将无产者实际的心理意识状态和无产阶级的阶级意识混为一谈，从而给无产阶级革命实践带来致命的伤害。就此而言，无产阶级不仅要和资产阶级进行斗争，而且要和自身进行斗争，和资本主义制度对无产阶级的阶级意识的破坏和腐蚀的影响做斗争。

《物化和无产阶级意识》是卢卡奇专为《历史与阶级意识》一书新写的一篇长文。该文的中心思想就是要回答《阶级意识》一文已经提出的一个命题，即无产阶级必须要和资本主义制度对自己的阶级意识的破坏和腐蚀的影响做斗争，而所有破坏和腐蚀的影响归结为一个根本就是物化现象。《物化和无产阶级意识》一文有三个部分。第一部分"物化现象"首先从商品结构的本质出发，指出它的基础是人与人之间的关系获得了物的性质，从而获得了一种"幽灵般的对象性"。随着资本主义商品经济的不断发展，根据计算即可加以调节的合理化原则发挥了最重要的作用。它一方面破坏了经济过程中的客体即产品本身的有机的质的统一；另一方面导致经济过程中的主体的孤立化和原子化。而个人的原子化现象所反映的不过是人的自我客体化，即人的功能变成商品这一事实。当所有使用价值都成为商品后，事物就获得了一种新的客观性，即一种新的物性，而它们原来的真正的物性却消失了。在现代资本主义社会里，物化不仅仅存在于经济过程中，还渗透到现代官僚政治乃至人的肉体和心理的最深处。专门化是合理化的一个必然结果。正是由于工作的专门化，任何整体景象都消失了，而资产阶级的各专门科学也因此放弃了对整体的认识。《物化和无产阶级意识》的第二部分"资产阶级思想的二律背反"是对从康德到黑格尔的德国古典哲学的再阐释。卢卡奇肯定，德国古典哲学的目的是希望把握物化世界的总体本质，从而在思想上克服资产阶级社会，思辨地复活在这个社会中并被这个社会毁灭了的人。但是，由于它们是从意识的物化结构中产生出来的，所以，它们最终只是把它们生存于其中的资产阶级社会的所有二律背反都推到了思想中的极致，而没有解决和不可能解决它们。《物化和无产阶级意识》的第三部分“无产阶级的立场”着重论证了一个命题：无产阶级是德国古典哲学的真正继承人，它有能力从自己的生活基础出发，找到同一的主体-客体，即改变世界、创造世界的主体，从而解决二律背反。卢卡奇指出，资产阶级和无产阶级同样生活在物化世界之中，资产阶级由于满足于直接性而没有能力把握历史，而无产阶级则从对自身现实的阶级地位的认识出发，最终认识到了历史的必然性。这意味着只有从物化关系的直接性出发并且消除了这种直接性后，人们才能认识到作为物化关系的核心和基础的人。作为历史的同一的主体-客体，无产阶级只有按照辩证法的客观要求，认识到自己的历史使命后，才能真正成为这种主体-客体，它的实践才能改造现实。

《历史唯物主义的功能变化》一文是 1919 年 6 月卢卡奇在布达佩斯历史唯物主义研究所成立会上所做的报告。在该报告中，卢卡奇指出，历史唯物主义是无产阶级在其受压迫的时代里最强大的武器之一，现在，随着匈牙利革命的胜利，无产阶级需要把历史唯物主义运用于这个新的时代，服务于社会的重建和文化的重建。在他看来，在新的历史条件下，历史唯物主义最重要的任务就是对资本主义社会制度做出准确的判断，揭露资本主义社会制度的本质。同时，在与资产阶级关于社会领导权的斗争中，无产阶级需要运用历史唯物主义这一最重要的武器，像其他意识形态一样去发展和瓦解资本主义。

《合法性和非法性》是一篇完成于 1920 年 7 月的短文。在该文中，卢卡奇针对十月革命前后国际共产主义运动内部关于革命问题的争论，表达了自己的看法：无产阶级革命的合法性和非法性问题纯粹是策略问题，只要条件具备了，就应当发动革命，必须既摆脱合法性的呆小病又摆脱非法性的幼稚病。

《对罗莎·卢森堡〈论俄国革命〉的批评意见》一文写于 1922 年 1 月，是卢卡奇对卢森堡后期有机论思想的集中批评。在卢卡奇看来，虽然卢森堡是一名真正的马克思主义者，但是，她在临终前的残稿《论俄国革命》中在暴力、制宪议会、苏维埃制度、党的组织化建设等一系列重大问题上得出和列宁截然不同的观点，而这些观点已经被苏俄的革命与社会主义建设实践证明是错误的。她之所以会犯这些错误，非常重要的一点就在于她过高估计了历史发展的有机性质，对党的组织建设存在某种偏见。

《关于组织问题的方法论》一文创作于 1922 年 9 月。它体现了卢卡奇在列宁的影响下所形成的党的组织建设理论。在这个问题上，他反对卢森堡等人的自发论，肯定党组织的重要性，认为它是理论和实践之间的中介形式，对于解决理论问题具有决定性意义。无产阶级的阶级意识是革命运动的前提条件，党组织的关键任务就是要把无产阶级的阶级意识从自发的水平提升到自觉的高度。党是领导人民走向自由王国的组织形式，在当前阶段，党必须依靠纪律，实现有限的自由，通过革命逐步达到真正的自由。虽然党在组织上是与阶级分开的，但作为一种为革命利益服务的无产阶级阶级意识的独立形式，党与阶级更是统一的。

三、研究前沿

《历史与阶级意识》是卢卡奇早期的著作，虽然卢卡奇之后反思和纠正了该书中的一些观点与立场。但是，正如他本人也指出的，这部书已经“提出一种典型的观点，并因而获得某种历史的合法性”。[①] 国内学界在开展西方马克思主义研究的过程中，将解读《历史与阶级意识》作为一项重要的工作，相关研究始终能够掀起新的热潮。在此基础上，卢卡奇作为一个真正的马克思主义“思想家”的地位进一步得到确立。近年来，学界从多元路径推动卢卡奇研究，取得了重要突破。

第一，以《历史与阶级意识》为基础，重新评估卢卡奇在西方马克思主义中的历史地位。学者们普遍认为，能否科学对待《历史与阶级意识》关系到我们能否正确评价西方马克思主义。当然，学界针对该著作的评价也存在着较大分歧。一种观点认为，这部著作标志着马克思主义在西方实现了巨大跨越，应当将卢卡奇作为西方马克思主义的真正开创者；另一种观点认为，卢卡奇在这部著作中的许多认识是错误的，因此不应予以过高评价。学术界之所以产生这种分歧，一方面是卢卡奇在 1967 年“序言”中的论述；另一方面是他在书中对部分概念的阐述与马克思有所差别。不过，学界仍然

① ［匈］格奥尔格·卢卡奇：《历史与阶级意识——关于马克思主义辩证法的研究》，杜章智、任立、燕宏远译，商务印书馆 1999 年版，第 21 页。

达成了一个普遍共识，那就是卢卡奇对马克思思想的理解的确达到了很高的水平，研究《历史与阶级意识》对理解卢卡奇走向马克思主义和发展马克思主义的历程具有重要意义。

第二，对《历史与阶级意识》中的重要范畴和理论的深化解读。《历史与阶级意识》是卢卡奇的天才创作，他的一系列创造性思考对理解马克思的部分思想具有重要的参考价值。因此，学界重点探讨了卢卡奇在这部著作中论及的重要范畴，包括总体性、主体性、物化等，相对而言，学者们更加集中于研究总体性概念，研究成果也相对更丰富。此外，学界还对卢卡奇的一些重要理论，包括阶级意识理论、革命理论、现代性话语等进行了富有深度的考察，为进一步研究卢卡奇对资本主义社会的批判奠定了重要基础。在深入研究这些概念和理论的过程中，学者们采用了多元化的研究方法，包括词源考证、思想史考证、比较性研究等等。

第三，对《历史与阶级意识》的方法论探究。卢卡奇在《历史与阶级意识》中运用的方法论，以及对马克思辩证法、恩格斯自然辩证法的重要探索也成为学者们重点讨论的对象。有学者指出，卢卡奇对辩证法的研究，体现在其对马克思辩证法的黑格尔渊源的论述上，其证明了马克思的辩证法是深入历史现实的方法。因此，有学者认为，卢卡奇找到了马克思主义方法论的内核，并进一步用于对资本主义现实的批判。只不过，卢卡奇借助“总体”视野，力图尽可能囊括对社会和人类整体发展的描述，但是，这反而令他只能停留在一种整体形式之上，而将考察的所有内容抽象化，从而对马克思辩证法的理解产生了偏差。

第四，对《历史与阶级意识》现实意义的重新挖掘。有学者专门梳理了卢卡奇思想的生成过程以及学界对其的研究历程，认为对卢卡奇及《历史与阶级意识》的研究是西方马克思主义研究的重要组成部分，对真正理解马克思主义哲学的真理性，真正把握人类社会发展的内在机理都具有重要意义。也有学者提出，《历史与阶级意识》能够为当前政治意识形态建设提供重要方法指导，在当代，卢卡奇的阶级理论以及由此延伸出的政党建设理论依然具有参考价值。

四、文本节选

What is Orthodox Marxism?

... Orthodox Marxism, therefore, does not imply the uncritical acceptance of the results of Marx's investigations. It is not the "belief" in this or that thesis, nor the exegesis of a "sacred" book. On the contrary, orthodoxy refers exclusively to *method*. It is the scientific conviction that dialectical materialism is the road to truth and that its methods can be developed, expanded and deepened only along the lines laid down by its founders. It is the conviction, moreover, that all attempts to surpass or "improve" it have led and must lead to over-simplification, triviality and eclecticism.

1

Materialist dialectic is a revolutionary dialectic. This definition is so important and altogether so crucial for an understanding of its nature that if the problem is to be approached in the right way this must be fully grasped before we venture upon a discussion of the dialectical method itself. The issue turns on the question of theory and practice. And this not merely in the sense given it by Marx when he says in his first critique of Hegel that "theory becomes a material force when it grips the masses". Even more to the point is the need to discover those features and definitions both of the theory and the ways of gripping the masses which convert the theory, the dialectical method, into a vehicle of revolution. We must extract the practical essence of the theory from the method and its relation to its object. If this is not done that "gripping the masses" could well turn out to be a will o' the wisp. ...

... Only when consciousness stands in such a relation to reality can theory and practice be united. But for this to happen the emergence of consciousness must become the *decisive step* which the historical process must take towards its proper end (an end constituted by the wills of men, but neither dependent on human whim, nor the product of human invention). The historical function of theory is to make this step a practical possibility. Only when a historical situation has arisen in which a class must understand society if it is to assert itself; only when the fact that a class understands itself means that it understands society as a whole and when, in consequence, the class becomes both the subject and the object of knowledge; in short, only when these conditions are all satisfied will the unity of theory and practice, the precondition of the revolutionary function of the theory, become possible.

——Georg Lukács, *History and Class Consciousness*: *Studies in Marxist Dialectics*, trans. Rodney Livingstone, The MIT Press, 1971, pp. 1 - 3.

2

... If such methods seem plausible at first this is because capitalism tends to produce a social structure that in great measure encourages such views. But for that very reason we need the dialectical method to puncture the social illusion so produced and help us to glimpse the reality underlying it. The "pure" facts of the natural sciences arise when a phenomenon of the real world is placed (in thought or in reality) into an environment where its laws can be inspected without outside interference. This process is reinforced by reducing the phenomena to their purely quantitative essence, to their expression in numbers and numerical relations. Opportunists always fail to recognise that it is in the nature of capitalism to process phenomena in this way. Marx gives an incisive account of such a "process of abstraction" in the case of labour, but he does not omit to point out with equal vigour that he is dealing with a *historical* peculiarity of capitalist society. ...

... The fetishistic character of economic forms, the reification of all human relations, the constant expansion and extension of the division of labour which subjects the process of production to an abstract, rational analysis, without regard to the human potentialities and abilities of the immediate producers, all these things transform the phenomena of society and with them the way in which they are perceived. In this way arise the "isolated" facts, "isolated" complexes of facts, separate, specialist disciplines (economics, law, etc.) whose very appearance seems to have done much to pave the way for such scientific methods. It thus appears extraordinarily "scientific" to think out the tendencies implicit in the facts themselves and to promote this activity to the status of science.

——Georg Lukács, *History and Class Consciousness*: *Studies in Marxist Dialectics*, trans. Rodney Livingstone, The MIT Press, 1971, pp. 5 - 6.

Only in this context which sees the isolated facts of social life as aspects of the historical process and integrates them in a *totality*, can knowledge of the facts hope to become knowledge of *reality*. This knowledge starts from the simple (and to the capitalist world), pure, immediate, natural determinants described above. It progresses from them to the knowledge of the concrete totality, i. e. to the conceptual reproduction of reality. This concrete totality is by no means an unmediated datum for thought. ...

... the vulgar materialists, even in the modern guise donned by Bernstein and others, do not go beyond the reproduction of the immediate, simple determinants of social life. They imagine that they are being quite extraordinarily "exact" when they simply take over these determinants without either analysing them further or welding them into a concrete totality. They take the facts in abstract isolation, explaining them only in terms of abstract laws unrelated to the concrete totality. ...

The crudeness and conceptual nullity of such thought lies primarily in the fact that it obscures the historical, transitory nature of capitalist society. Its determinants take on the appearance of timeless, eternal categories valid for all social formations. This could be seen at its crassest in the vulgar bourgeois economists, but the vulgar Marxists soon followed in their footsteps. The dialectical method was overthrown and with it the methodological supremacy of the totality over the individual aspects; the parts were prevented from finding their definition within the whole and, instead, the whole was dismissed as unscientific or else it degenerated into the mere "idea" or "sum" of the parts. With the totality out of the way, the fetishistic relations of the isolated parts appeared as a timeless law valid for every human society.

Marx's dictum: "The relations of production of every society form a whole" is the methodological point of departure and the key to the *historical* understanding of social relations. All the isolated partial categories can be thought of and treated—in isolation—as something that is always present in every society. (If it cannot be found in a given society this is put down to "chance" as the exception that proves the rule.) But the changes to which these individual aspects are subject give no clear and unambiguous picture of the real differences in the various stages of the evolution of society. These can really only be discerned in the context of the total historical process of their relation to society as a whole.

3

This dialectical conception of totality seems to have put a great distance between itself and reality, it appears to construct reality very "unscientifically". But it is the only method capable of understanding and reproducing reality. Concrete totality is, therefore, the category that governs reality. The rightness of this view only emerges with complete clarity when we direct our attention to the real, material substratum of our method, viz. capitalist society with its internal antagonism between the forces and the relations of production. ...

But we maintain that in the case of social reality these contradictions are not a sign of the imperfect understanding of society; on the contrary, they belong to *the nature of reality itself and to the nature of capitalism*. When the totality is known they will not be transcended and *cease* to be contradictions. Quite the reverse, they will be seen to be necessary contradictions arising out of the antagonisms of this system of production. When theory (as the knowledge of the whole) opens up the way to resolving these contradictions it does so by revealing the *real tendencies* of social evolution. For these are destined to effect a *real* resolution of the contradictions that have emerged in the course of history.

...

Thus with the rejection or blurring of the dialectical method history becomes unknowable. This does not imply that a more or less exact account of particular people or epochs cannot be given without the aid of dialectics. But it does put paid to attempts to understand history *as a unified process*. ... Whatever the epoch or special topic of study, the question of a unified approach to the process of history is inescapable. It is here that the crucial importance of the dialectical view of totality reveals itself. For it is perfectly possible for someone to describe the essentials of an historical event and yet be in the dark about the real nature of that event and of its function in the historical totality, i. e. without understanding it as part of a unified historical process.

...

We repeat: the category of totality does not reduce its various elements to an undifferentiated uniformity, to identity. The apparent independence and autonomy which they possess in the capitalist system of production is an illusion only in so far as they are involved in a dynamic dialectical relationship with one another and can be thought of as the dynamic dialectical aspects of an equally dynamic and dialectical whole. ...

But even the category of interaction requires inspection. If by interaction we mean just the reciprocal causal impact of two otherwise unchangeable objects on each other, we shall not have come an inch nearer to an understanding of society. ... The interaction we have in mind must be more than the interaction of *otherwise unchanging objects*. It must go further in its relation to the whole: for this relation determines the objective form of every object of cognition. Every substantial change that is of concern to knowledge manifests itself as a change in relation to the whole and through this as a change in the form of objectivity itself. ...

Thus the objective forms of all social phenomena change constantly in the course of their ceaseless dialectical interactions with each other. The intelligibility of objects develops in proportion as we grasp their function in the totality to which they belong. This is why only the dialectical conception of totality can enable us to understand *reality as a social process*. For only this conception dissolves the fetishistic forms necessarily produced by the capitalist mode of production and enables us to see them as mere illusions which are not less illusory for being seen to be necessary. These unmediated concepts, these "laws" sprout just as inevitably from the soil of capitalism and veil the real relations between objects. They can all be seen as ideas necessarily held by the agents of the capitalist system of production. They are, therefore, objects of knowledge, but the object which is known through them is not the capitalist system of production itself, but the ideology of its ruling class.

Only when this veil is torn aside does historical knowledge become possible. For the function of these unmediated concepts that have been derived from the fetishistic forms of objectivity is to make the phenomena of capitalist society appear as supra-historical essences. The knowledge of the real, objective nature of a phenomenon, the knowledge of its historical character and the knowledge of its actual function in the totality of society form, therefore, a single, undivided act of cognition. ...

——Georg Lukács, *History and Class Consciousness*: *Studies in Marxist Dialectics*, trans. Rodney Livingstone, The MIT Press, 1971, pp. 8 - 14.

Reification and the Consciousness of the Proletariat

Before tackling the problem itself we must be quite clear in our minds that commodity fetishism is a *specific* problem of our age, the age of modern capitalism. ...

...

... The commodity can only be understood in its undistorted essence when it becomes the universal category of society as a whole. Only in this context does the reification produced by commodity relations assume decisive importance both for the objective evolution of society and for the stance adopted by men towards it. Only then does the commodity become crucial for the subjugation of men's consciousness to the forms in which this reification finds expression and for their attempts to comprehend the process or to rebel against its disastrous effects and liberate themselves from servitude to the "second nature" so created.

...

What is of central importance here is that because of this situation a man's own activity, his own labour becomes something objective and independent of him, something that controls him by virtue of an autonomy alien to man. There is both an objective and a subjective side to this phenomenon. *Objectively* a world of objects and relations between things springs into being (the world of commodities and their movements on the market). The laws governing these objects are indeed gradually discovered by man, but even so they confront him as invisible forces that generate their own power. The individual can use his knowledge of these laws to his own advantage, but he is not able to modify the process by his own activity. ...

——Georg Lukács, *History and Class Consciousness: Studies in Marxist Dialectics*, trans. Rodney Livingstone, The MIT Press, 1971, pp. 84 - 87.

We are concerned above all with the *principle* at work here: the principle of rationalisation based on what is and *can be calculated*. The chief changes undergone by the subject and object of the economic process are as follows: (1) in the first place, the mathematical analysis of work-processes denotes a break with the organic, irrational and qualitatively determined unity of the product. Rationalisation in the sense of being able to predict with ever greater precision all the results to be achieved is only to be acquired by the exact breakdown of every complex into its elements and by the study of the special laws governing production. Accordingly it must declare war on the organic manufacture of whole products based on the *traditional amalgam of empirical experiences of work*: rationalisation is unthinkable without specialisation.

The finished article ceases to be the object of the work-process. The latter turns into the objective synthesis of rationalised special systems whose unity is determined by pure calculation and which must therefore seem to be arbitrarily connected with each other. ...

(2) In the second place, this fragmentation of the object of production necessarily entails the fragmentation of its subject. In consequence of the rationalisation of the work-process the human qualities and idiosyncrasies of the worker appear increasingly as *mere sources of error* when contrasted with these abstract special laws

functioning according to rational predictions. Neither objectively nor in his relation to his work does man appear as the authentic master of the process; on the contrary, he is a mechanical part incorporated into a mechanical system. He finds it already pre-existing and self-sufficient, it functions independently of him and he has to conform to its laws whether he likes it or not. As labour is progressively rationalised and mechanised his lack of will is reinforced by the way in which his activity becomes less and less active and more and more *contemplative*. The contemplative stance adopted towards a process mechanically conforming to fixed laws and enacted independently of man's consciousness and impervious to human intervention, i. e. a perfectly closed system, must likewise transform the basic categories of man's immediate attitude to the world: it reduces space and time to a common denominator and degrades time to the dimension of space.

...

Thus time sheds its qualitative, variable, flowing nature; it freezes into an exactly delimited, quantifiable continuum filled with quantifiable "things" (the reified, mechanically objectified "performance" of the worker, wholly separated from his total human personality): in short, it becomes space. In this environment where time is transformed into abstract, exactly measurable, physical space, an environment at once the cause and effect of the scientifically and mechanically fragmented and specialised production of the object of labour, the subjects of labour must like-wise be rationally fragmented. On the one hand, the objectification of their labour-power into something opposed to their total personality (a process already accomplished with the sale of that labour-power as a commodity) is now made into the permanent ineluctable reality of their daily life. Here, too, the personality can do no more than look on helplessly while its own existence is reduced to an isolated particle and fed into an alien system. On the other hand, the mechanical disintegration of the process of production into its components also destroys those bonds that had bound individuals to a community in the days when production was still "organic". ...

...

2

This rational objectification conceals above all the immediate—qualitative and material—character of things as things. When use-values appear universally as commodities they acquire a new objectivity, a new substantiality which they did not possess in an age of episodic exchange and which destroys their original and authentic substantiality. ...

...

... It is obviously not possible here to give an analysis of the whole economic structure of capitalism. It must suffice to point out that modern capitalism does not content itself with transforming the relations of production in accordance with its own needs. It also integrates into its own system those forms of primitive capitalism that led an isolated existence in pre-capitalist times, divorced from production; it converts them into members of the henceforth unified process of radical capitalism. (Cf. merchant capital, the role of money as a hoard or as finance capital, etc.)

These forms of capital are objectively subordinated, it is true, to the real life-process of capitalism, the extraction of surplus value in the course of production. They are, therefore, only to be explained in terms of the nature of industrial capitalism itself. But in the minds of people in bourgeois society they constitute the pure, authentic, unadulterated forms of capital. In them the relations between men that lie hidden in the immediate commodity relation, as well as the relations between men and the objects that should really gratify their needs, have faded to the point where they can be neither recognised nor even perceived.

For that very reason the reified mind has come to regard them as the true representatives of his societal existence. The commodity character of the commodity, the abstract, quantitative mode of calculability shows itself here in its purest form: the reified mind necessarily sees it as the form in which its own authentic immediacy becomes manifest and—as reified consciousness—does not even attempt to transcend it. On the contrary, it is concerned to make it permanent by "scientifically deepening" the laws at work. Just as the capitalist system continuously produces and reproduces itself economically on higher and higher levels, the structure of reification progressively sinks more deeply, more fatefully and more definitively into the consciousness of man. ...

...

The divorce of the phenomena of reification from their economic bases and from the vantage point from which alone they can be understood, is facilitated by the fact that the [capitalist] process of transformation must embrace every manifestation of tilt life of society if the preconditions for the complete self-realisation of capitalist production are to be fulfilled.

Thus capitalism has created a form for the state and a system of law corresponding to its needs and harmonising with its own structure. ...

——Georg Lukács, *History and Class Consciousness*: *Studies in Marxist Dialectics*, trans. Rodney Livingstone, The MIT Press, 1971, pp. 88 - 95.

The transformation of the commodity relation into a thing of "ghostly objectivity" cannot therefore content itself with the reduction of all objects for the gratification of human needs to commodities. It stamps its imprint upon the whole consciousness of man; his qualities and abilities are no longer an organic part of his personality, they are things which he can "own" or "dispose of" like the various objects of the external world. And there is no natural form in which human relations can be cast, no way in which man can bring his physical and psychic "qualities" into play without their being subjected increasingly to this reifying process. ...

...

This rationalisation of the world appears to be complete, it seems to penetrate the very depths of man's physical and psychic nature. It is limited, however, by its own formalism. That is to say, the rationalisation of isolated aspects of life results in the creation of—formal—laws. All these things do join together into what seems to the superficial observer to constitute a unified system of general "laws". But the disregard of the concrete aspects of the subject matter of these laws, upon which disregard their authority as laws is based, makes itself felt in the incoherence of the system in fact. This incoherence becomes particularly egregious in periods of crisis. At such times we can see how the immediate continuity between two partial systems is disrupted and their independence from and adventitious connection with each other is suddenly forced into the consciousness of everyone. ...

——Georg Lukács, *History and Class Consciousness*: *Studies in Marxist Dialectics*, trans. Rodney Livingstone, The MIT Press, 1971, pp. 100 - 101.

4

...

... But this semblance is enough to dissipate wholly the attempt of the classical philosophers to break out of the limits imposed on formal and rationalistic (bourgeois, reified) thought and thereby to restore a humanity destroyed by that reification. Thought relapses into the contemplative duality of subject and object.

Classical philosophy did, it is true, take all the antinomies of its life-basis to the furthest extreme it was capable of in thought; it conferred on them the highest possible intellectual expression. But even for this philosophy they remain unsolved and insoluble. Thus classical philosophy finds itself historically in the paradoxical position that it was concerned to find a philosophy that would mean the end of bourgeois society, and to resurrect in thought a humanity destroyed in that society and by it. In the upshot, however, it did not manage to do more than provide a complete intellectual copy and the *a priori* deduction of bourgeois society. It is only the *manner* of this deduction, namely the dialectical method that points beyond bourgeois society. And even in classical philosophy this is only expressed in the form of an unsolved and insoluble antinomy. This antinomy is admittedly the most profound and the most magnificent intellectual expression of those antinomies which lie at the roots of bourgeois society and which are unceasingly produced and reproduced by it—albeit in confused and inferior forms. Hence classical philosophy had nothing but these unresolved antinomies to bequeath to succeeding (bourgeois) generations. The continuation of that course which at least in method started to point the way beyond these limits, namely the dialectical method as the true historical method was reserved for the class which was able to discover within itself on the basis of its life-experience the identical subject-object, the subject of action; the "we" of the genesis: namely the proletariat.

——Georg Lukács, *History and Class Consciousness*: *Studies in Marxist Dialectics*, trans. Rodney Livingstone, The MIT Press, 1971, pp. 148 - 149.

6

Reification is, then, the necessary, immediate reality of every person living in capitalist society. It can be overcome only by *constant and constantly renewed efforts to disrupt the reified structure of existence by concretely relating to the concretely manifested contradictions of the total development*, *by becoming conscious of the immanent meanings of these contradictions for the total development*. But it must be emphasided that (1) the structure can be disrupted only if the immanent contradictions of the process are made conscious. ...

(2) Inseparable from this is the fact that the relation to totality does not need to become explicit, the plenitude of the totality does not need to be consciously integrated into the motives and objects of action. What is crucial is that there should be an aspiration towards totality, that action should serve the purpose, described above, in the totality of the process. ...

Hence (3) when judging whether an action is right or wrong it is essential to relate it to its function in the total process. ... This pudding, however, is the making of the proletariat into a class: the process by which its class consciousness becomes real in practice. This gives a more concrete form to the proposition that the proletariat is the identical subject-object of the historical process, i. e. the first subject in history that is (objectively) capable of an adequate social consciousness. It turns out that the contradictions in which the antagonisms of the mechanics of history are expressed are only capable of an objective social solution in practice if the solution is at the same time a new, practically-won consciousness on the part of the proletariat. Whether an action is functionally right or wrong is decided ultimately by the evolution of proletarian class consciousness.

The eminently practical nature of this consciousness is to be seen (4) in that an adequate, correct consciousness means a change in its own objects, and in the first instance, in itself. ...

——Georg Lukács, *History and Class Consciousness*: *Studies in Marxist Dialectics*, trans. Rodney Livingstone, The MIT Press, 1971, pp. 197 – 199.

But it must never be forgotten: *only the practical class consciousness of the proletariat* possesses this ability to transform things. Every contemplative, purely cognitive stance leads ultimately to a divided relationship to its object. Simply to transplant the structure we have discerned here into any stance other than that of proletarian action—for only the class can be practical in its relation to the total process—would mean the creation of a new conceptual mythology and a regression to the standpoint of classical philosophy refuted by Marx. ...

...

Even the proletariat can only overcome reification as long as it is oriented towards practice. And this means that there can be no single act that will eliminate reification in all its forms at one blow; it means that there will be a whole host of objects that at least in appearance remain more or less unaffected by the process. This is true in the first instance of nature. But it is also illuminating to observe how a whole set of social phenomena become dialecticised by a different path than the one we have traced out to show the nature of the dialectics of history and the process by which the barriers of reification can be shattered. ...

... It would be necessary to set forth the whole system of these qualitative gradations in the dialectical character of the different kinds of phenomena before we should be in a position to arrive at the concrete totality of the categories with which alone true knowledge of the present is possible. The hierarchy of these categories would determine at the same time the point where system and history meet, thus fulfilling Marx's postulate (already cited) concerning the categories that "their sequence is determined by the relations they have to each other in modern bourgeois society."

——Georg Lukács, *History and Class Consciousness: Studies in Marxist Dialectics*, trans. Rodney Livingstone, The MIT Press, 1971, pp. 205 - 206.

五、观点解读

1. 总体性概念是马克思方法论的核心

卢卡奇在《历史与阶级意识》一书的新版(1967 年)“序言”中对自己的总体性辩证法做了两个评论:一是认为它重新恢复了总体性范畴在马克思著作中一向占有的方法论的核心地位;二是导致对马克思的方法的黑格尔主义式的歪曲,即将总体性辩证法的核心地位与经济优先性对立起来。应当说,他的评价是中肯的。当时第二国际思想家由于受新康德主义和实证主义的深刻影响,满足于对具体的局部的科学的事实的追求,放弃了对资本主义社会的本质及其未来的总体把握。虽然此前列宁已经在《哲学笔记》中恢复了马克思的辩证法,但《历史与阶级意识》的出版才使与卢卡奇同时代的马克思主义者第一次认识到了总体性辩证法及其在马克思的方法论中的核心地位。卢卡奇把总体范畴看作马克思取自黑格尔并独创性地改造成为一门全新科学的基础的方法的本质。这种总体性概念包含两个方面的规定性:第一,它是共时性结构中相对于部分的整体,这种总体性消解的现象的片面性,使孤立的事物获得了普遍的联系;第二,它是历时性视角中相对于有限历史存在的全程总体,这使社会生活的具体发展显示出特殊的定在性。卢卡奇认为,现实的总体性是指历史运动中主体与客体的直接统一,历史总体性的实现就是主体性和历史的真正统一。在卢卡奇看来,总体性就是无产阶级运动的最终目标,他希望以总体性的逻辑张力作为批判现实资本主义的出发点,通过设定总体性规定,来重新引出对资产阶级现实力量极为强大的西方资本主义现实的批判。同时,他认为马克思将总体性确定为认识的总体性和被认识的总体性,即理论和实践的总体性。应当说,卢卡奇的这一论断恢复了马克思主义辩证法的本真精神,将基于无产阶级革命实践的主体-客体关系重新确立为辩证法的核心。但也应看到,卢卡奇的总体性辩证法与马克思的思想存在着不可忽视的区别,其核心就在于马克思在社会历史领域解剖生产方式的历史时,一方面把社会关系的异己性(物化、异化)社会作为历史的产物,另一方面在强调消除这一历史特征的实质性历史行动时,除了主体的自觉性外,还需要生产力发展的前提,但青年卢卡奇在讨论中不仅没有把总体性建立在工业文明之上，而且把理论批判的矛头指向了生产力本身，这就造成了二者理论走向的不同。卢卡奇的总体性辩证法思想得到了同时代以及后来的西方马克思主义者的肯定与继承，并作为一条基本哲学原则而不断得到再阐释和发展。但在近半个世纪以后，青年卢卡奇这个批判资本主义现实的总体性遭到来自萨特和阿多诺不同方面的批判。

2. 物化理论是卢卡奇对马克思思想研究的天才发现

青年卢卡奇的物化理论应当可以被看作他早期哲学中最为突出的理论贡献。他在既没有读过青年马克思建构人本主义劳动异化史观的《1844年经济学哲学手稿》，也不曾看过马克思后来具体建构自己物化理论的《1857—1858年经济学手稿》的情况下，仅从马克思的《政治经济学批判》和《资本论》等文献的大量经济学批判中就体会到了马克思的批判性物化理论。卢卡奇的物化理论认为，在商品生产过程中的人与人的关系具有了物的性质，成为一种不依赖人的客观的东西，并通过自己的自律性来控制人。以韦伯的合理化学说为论说工具，卢卡奇试图证明，物化已经渗透到现代资本主义商品生产的各个方面，并导致两个基本后果：客体的有机整体性的丧失和主体的孤立化与原子化。进而，卢卡奇指出，社会存在决定社会意识，物化现实最终导致物化意识。在现代资本主义社会中，物化意识已经由官僚政治发展到科学和哲学，渗透到现代资本主义社会的各个方面，其最终结果是导致各种二律背反，从而使得人们无法正确认识资本主义的本质及其未来，妨碍了理论与实践、主体与客体的统一。正是基于这种判断，卢卡奇把物化意识的消除作为物化现实的消除、理论与实践的统一、主体与客体的统一的前提，从而把无产阶级与资产阶级在阶级意识领域中的斗争与领导权的争夺提高到了一个前所未有的高度。但是更值得注意的是，卢卡奇的物化理论实际上存在着双重逻辑：从表面语义来看，他的物化理论继承了马克思的物化思想，是马克思意义上商品结构（生产关系）之上的物化；但从理论实质来看，却受到了以合理性思想为主的马克斯·韦伯的“物化”理论的深刻影响。总体说来，青年卢卡奇的物化理论是有重要意义的，其理论用马克思对资本主义经济过程的否定尺度来颠倒韦伯的合理性指认，在生产技术层面开创了一种对工具理性（科学技术）的资本主义文明批判。这开启了后来法兰克福学派的“启蒙辩证法”新的批判逻辑。但卢卡奇以德国古典哲学的思考方式将异化理解为资本主义工业生产过程中的社会关系的工具理性和技术理性化，过分简化了马克思含义极为丰富的“异化”概念，同时远离了“经济剥削”这个经典的马克思的理论语境，这直接导致了他对马克思异化理论的混淆理解。

3. 作为历史主体—客体的无产阶级

卢卡奇认为，随着资本主义制度下经济利益的日益显现，从社会的主体来看，第一次出现了资产阶级与无产阶级这两种“纯粹的阶级”。但由于资产阶级意识形态的二律背反始终无法化解，无法达成主客体的同一，使得资产阶级在其巅峰之时就跌入了无法挣脱的泥淖，社会矛盾得不到解决。因此，卢卡奇将希望寄托于无产阶级。在他看来，无产阶级是行为的主体，能够在自己身上找到同一的主体—客体，依靠无产阶级的力量就能够把辩证法当作历史的方法来完成革命实践。无产阶级具有不同于其他阶级的优越性，这个阶级在产生之时就被历史赋予了自觉改造社会的使命，它是历史的主体-客体，因此它的实践能够改造现实，从而推翻资本主义制度。应当说，在《历史与阶级意识》中，卢卡奇不是从无产阶级的现实出发，而是从自身的理论逻辑出发，把无产阶级定义为历史的主体和客体的同一。通过这种极为思辨的方式，他着力突出了人、主体在历史发展过程中的重要作用，有力反击了第二国际的历史宿命论，西方马克思主义中的人本主义道路由此得以开启。

4. 阶级意识是卢卡奇理论的落脚点

由于青年卢卡奇的物化理论建立在生产的对象化之上，只要物质生产存在一天，物化也会发生一天，这种残酷的现实逼得他只能转向浪漫主义的意识解放以寻求解脱，因此他的理论逻辑终结点落在了阶级意识上。卢卡奇把客观可能性看作是无产阶级阶级意识的核心，并将其作为欧洲革命的希望所在。以马克思的历史唯物主义原则为基础，卢卡奇把阶级意识看作与一定社会存在相关联的“总体的阶级”的意识，他以一种与社会发展特定状况相关的“客观可能性”为尺度，希望通过对作为整体的社会关系的具体研究，更准确地认识与客观状况相符的思想和情感。同时，他也指出，由于人们无法跳出自己生活于其中的社会构架，因此阶级意识从另一个层面讲也是一种受阶级制约的对人们自己的社会的、历史的经济地位的无意识。在卢卡奇看来，只有到了资本主义时期，阶级意识才具有历史可能性。对于资产阶级来说，他们的阶级意识与自身的阶级利益是出于一种相互对立的、辩证的矛盾关系之中的。因此，资产阶级的意识形态就具有上升时期的虚假意识和与无产阶级斗争时期的虚伪意识两种表现形式。但资本主义难以克服的矛盾现实导致了其意识形态出现了无法解决的二律背反，透过黑格尔的哲学逻辑，卢卡奇把目光投向了无产阶级。在他看来，不同于资产阶级意识形态的直接性，无产阶级意识形态最重要的本质就是具有中介性，借助中介性的批判方法，资本主义现实被扬弃了。然而，这一从观念出发的解放理论在现实中没能找到出路，因此仅能算是一种浪漫主义式的理论追寻。

六、进一步阅读指南

1．[匈]格奥尔格・卢卡奇：《历史与阶级意识——关于马克思主义辩证法的研究》，杜章智、任立、燕宏远译，商务印书馆 2004 年版。

2．[匈]格奥尔格・卢卡奇：《卢卡奇早期文选》，张亮、吴勇立译，南京大学出版社 2004 年版。

3．[英]G. H. R. 帕金森：《格奥尔格・卢卡奇》，翁绍军译，上海人民出版社 1999 年版。

10．[日]初见基：《卢卡奇：物象化》，范景武译，河北教育出版社 2001 年版。

4．《马克思恩格斯全集》第 39 卷，人民出版社 1974 年版。

5．孙伯鍨：《卢卡奇与马克思》，南京大学出版社 1999 年版。

6．张一兵：《文本的深度耕犁(第一卷)》第 1 章，中国人民大学出版社 2004 年版。

7．张翼星：《为卢卡奇申辩——卢卡奇哲学思想若干问题辨析》，云南人民出版社 2001 年版。

8．张西平：《历史哲学的重建——卢卡奇与当代西方社会思潮》，三联书店 1997 年版。

9．杜章智编：《卢卡奇自传》，社会科学文献出版社 1986 年版。

10．Lee Congdon, *The Young Lukács*, University of North Carolina

Press，1983.

11. Michael Löwy，*Georg Lukács*：*From Romanticism to Bolshevism*，NLB，1979.

12. Victor Zitta，*Georg Lukács' Marxism Alienation*，*Dialectics*，*Revolution*：*A Study in Utopia and Ideology*，Martinus Nijhoff，1964.

七、问题与思考

1. 卢卡奇对马克思主义正统的理解是否符合马克思主义的本质？
2. 应当如何正确理解卢卡奇的物化学说与马克思的异化、物化学说的异同？
3. 应当如何理解卢卡奇总体性辩证法及其与马克思辩证法的关系？

第二章　人本主义马克思主义哲学的先声——《乌托邦精神》选读

教学目的与要求

正确理解"人'尚未'存在"的命题；认识社会革命和灵魂革命的关系；掌握"乌托邦"概念及其与卢卡奇的"总体性"概念的联系和区别；正确理解马克思的"自由王国"和基督教的"千年王国"之间的关系。

一、历史背景

（一）作者介绍

1885年，恩斯特·布洛赫(Ernst Bloch)出生于德国新兴工业城市路德维希港城的一个犹太家庭。他在青年时期就受到众多哲学思潮影响，初步形成了乌托邦意识。1914年第一次世界大战爆发，布洛赫对帝国主义战争和德国人狂热的民族情绪十分反感，因而设法去了瑞士，同时期冀帝国主义战争成为德国社会变革的契机。他在1918年写的小册子《军事失败对德国是利是弊?》中，他对标题中的问题给出了肯定的回答，认为承受战争的"不幸"后果是这个国家摆脱军事独裁的前提。尽管他对德国革命抱有热情，却不赞成俄国的十月革命。1918年2月27日，布洛赫为瑞士《自由报》撰稿的题目就是《列宁，红色沙皇》。在这篇文章中，他尖锐地指责布尔什维克是"恐怖统治”。布洛赫一方面欢迎革命，一方面又害怕“红色沙皇”的独裁结果。

1921年，布洛赫出版了《革命神学家托马斯·闵采尔》一书。这是他在德国十一月革命的影响下转向马克思主义之后的初次思想亮相。在1923年为卢卡奇的《历史与阶级意识》撰写的书评中，布洛赫力图把自己的乌托邦哲学与马克思主义系统地结合到一起。从此，布洛赫开始以马克思主义者自居。1923年，布洛赫对《乌托邦精神》进行了大幅度修订，试图用马克思主义哲学去补充和发展他自己的哲学体系。布洛赫一方面支持苏联的社会主义，一方面坚持自身探索，到二十世纪中叶，他进一步推动了马克思主义的哲学化发展，尝试站在马克思主义的立场上，对黑格尔哲学进行重新阐释，探索一条更加具有开放性的马克思主义道路。显然，这一尝试同当时苏联主导的“正统马克思主义”格格不入，因而遭受到巨大的阻碍。苏共二十大召开后，布洛赫进一步呼吁各国探索各自的社会主义道路，对苏联的社会主义道路进行反思。不过，布洛赫的主张受到了社会主义阵营内部极为严厉的批判，被视为修正主义、唯心主义的典型。

晚年时期，布洛赫对社会主义进行了全面反思，其研究作品也得到了普遍传播，并赢得了应有的声誉。布洛赫积极支持社会主义政治运动，但又对苏联社会主义模式持保留立场。他始终反对将人类历史单纯看作是脱离热情的程序性推进，致力于将乌托邦精神注入马克思主义乃至整个人文社会科学之中，因而成为西方马克思主义阵营里面一位独特的“形而上学”主义者。

(二) 时代背景

1. 德国动荡的政治革命局势

《乌托邦精神》一书的直接背景是第一次世界大战和流产的德国十一月革命，其中，德国十一月革命是历时数月的一系列事件。1918年11月3日，基尔水兵起义吹响了十一月革命的号角。11月9日，柏林工人和士兵举行总罢工和武装起义，推翻了霍亨索伦王朝。斯巴达克派领导人李卜克内西在皇宫阳台宣布“一个包括全体德国人的自由的社会主义德意志共和国成立了”。随后，社会民主党人谢德曼则宣布“德意志共和国”成立了。11月10日，德国社会民主党和独立社会民主党联合组成了以艾伯特为首的资产阶级临时政府。工兵代表苏维埃将立法权和行政权全部交出。1919 年 1 月 4 日，艾伯特政府解除独立社会民主党左翼埃希霍恩的柏林警察局长职务，激起柏林工人的愤怒。1 月 5 日，15 万工人走上街头，1 月 6 日，部分武装工人占领了火车站、《前进报》社、警察局、电报局等战略要地。李卜克内西宣布艾伯特政府已被推翻。但柏林工人没有准备好夺权，士兵缺乏明确的政治立场，小资产阶级迷恋刚开始的“民主时代”，农村还处在沉寂状态，外省的工人尚未行动起来，革命成为“大量工人群众在柏林街头的乱七八糟的运动”。1 月 11 日，残酷的镇压开始了。1 月 15 日，李卜克内西和罗莎·卢森堡被杀害，一月起义失败。但带有无产阶级革命性质的斗争仍不断出现。1919 年 4 月 7 日，德国南方的巴伐利亚成立了苏维埃共和国。艾伯特政府及其同伙纠集武装，进攻巴伐利亚首府慕尼黑。5 月 1 日，攻入慕尼黑。5 月 5 日，战斗结束，500 多名共产党人和革命群众惨遭杀害，6 000 多人被捕。巴伐利亚苏维埃共和国的失败，标志着德国十一月革命的结束。

德国的十一月革命是俄国十月革命以后在欧洲爆发的最大的一次革命，是战后欧洲革命浪潮的重要组成部分。它推翻了帝制，建立了共和政体。德国共产党成立了，并奋不顾身地努力使革命向社会主义方向发展，但终究被社会民主党右派所扼杀。作为德国人，布洛赫对十一月革命的感受当然远远超过了对俄国十月革命的感受，也正因为十一月革命，布洛赫转向了马克思主义的立场。

2. 德国经济困境和民众的艰难处境

随着巴伐利亚苏维埃共和国在 1919 年 5 月的失败，魏玛共和国于同年 8 月 11 日成立。但是这个共和国并不像布洛赫想象的那样进步，而是经济危机不断，通货膨胀居高不下。从 1919 年开始，魏玛共和国失业的人数就快速上升，特别是到 1923 年，失业人数跃升到 1922 年的近 4 倍，失业率接近 10%。雪上加霜的是，当时德国的社会保险制度已经破产。1923 年，德国有 660 万人在领取劳工部的社会福利救济，约占当时德国总人口的 10%，如果再加上接受乡村济贫福利的人数，数字就更为庞大。[①] 德国人民的饥饿和贫穷不仅导致了社会道德的败坏，还使得整个德国社会笼罩在失

① 邢来顺、吴友法主编：《德国通史》第五卷，江苏人民出版社 2019 年版，第 125—136 页。

望和幻灭的情绪之下,引发种族主义情绪的高涨。因此,布洛赫在二十世纪二十年代撰写了大量的政治和文化评论,抨击魏玛共和国的资产阶级文化,批判资本主义生活的功利主义、虚无主义和市侩主义,希望苏联的社会主义革命能在德国爆发。

(三)思想背景

1. 多元的社会文化思潮

布洛赫在早期受到了不同思潮的影响,令《乌托邦精神》中凝聚了非常复杂的文化形态。二十世纪初期,随着现代化的推进,德意志民族的文化和哲学形态呈现为多元且复杂的特点。其一是在政治上,资产阶级的自由主义模式与改革派的社团、运动主张之间形成尖锐对立,背后反映的是现代性和反现代性的矛盾。其二是在主流哲学思想上,整个社会受到以费尔巴哈为代表的传统唯物主义、以马克思恩格斯为代表的辩证唯物主义、以黑格尔为代表的一元论唯心主义和以尼采为代表的非理性主义哲学等的影响,整个社会充斥着巨大的理论张力,为布洛赫的马克思主义创作提供了重要的思想氛围。从布洛赫早期的作品中可以找到多元思潮的印记,所以他也被称作"一位马克思主义的预言家""一位马克思主义的谢林""最后一位马克思主义形而上学者"等,这也充分反映了布洛赫复杂的思想理论背景。其三是在艺术形式上,当时的表现主义依旧影响巨大。因此,由现代性所带来的现代主义也为布洛赫哲学思路的拓展提供了重要动力。

2. 马克思主义的时代召唤与时代活力

在《乌托邦精神》中,布洛赫提到了当时德意志复杂多变的社会存在形式,以及多元思想文化的冲撞。在布洛赫看来,当时德意志民族被表现主义的庸俗氛围环绕着,整个社会充满了不切实际的谄媚和虚伪氛围。同时,由于缺乏正确的路线,社会革命也往往无果而终,并未取得应有的效果,反而造成社会乱象频发。布洛赫目睹了战争和社会动荡,看到了不同阶层、不同文化思潮在社会中的实际表现和影响,因而更加坚定了马克思主义立场。布洛赫说:"马克思彻底净化掉所有简单、虚伪、松散与抽象的类似于雅各宾主义热情中的社会主义逻辑,我们也一定不会忘记建立在现实政治之上的康德和巴德精神，它们在近期行动中体现出的浪漫主义没有继承任何真实的东西，不是客观的、狂热的，也不是普世性的，而仅仅是愚蠢的、孤立的，无灵魂和去基督的，这种'本土'能力的悲怆，只会导致西方文明的衰落，直至动物化的麻木和非宗教化的闭塞。"①在布洛赫看来，与其他理论思潮相比，马克思主义具备更加彻底的革命性，是能真正带领德意志民族实现社会变革的理论，也是具有最强实践性的运动纲领。因此，布洛赫创作《乌托邦精神》的直接目的，就是要在当时混乱不堪的德国社会中，为马克思主义呐喊，为德国社会提供一条可行的发展道路，真正帮助德意志民族摆脱那个时代的泥潭。

二、篇章结构

《乌托邦精神》写作于 1915 年到 1916 年，首次出版于 1918 年，是布洛赫哲学思想的基础和出发点，奠定了他哲学探讨的基本主题。1923 年，布洛赫对此书进行了比较大的删减和修改。现在普遍使用的《乌托邦精神》就是 1923 年的版本，该版本收录于《布洛赫全集》第 3 卷，而 1918 年版的《乌托邦精神》收于《布洛赫全集》的第 16 卷。《乌托邦精神》第一版出版后，特别是在德国十一月革命失败后，布洛赫对列宁和十月革命的态度发生了变化，他日益演变为一个马克思主义者。这也是布洛赫在 1923 年修订《乌托邦精神》的一个重要原因。

《乌托邦精神》这一散文风格的著作囊括了布洛赫早期的所有兴趣点，它混合了犹太教神秘主义、基督教异端神学、改造过的黑格尔主义和马克思主义、社会主义等思想。布洛赫在大学期间曾对犹太教神秘主义产生了浓厚的兴趣。后来他指出，犹太教神秘主义中包含着浓厚的乌托邦精神。1911 年，布洛赫结识了卢卡奇。他们精神相通，都赞同黑格尔关于建立一个总体系的愿望，当然这必须是一个不断被辩证的矛盾所打断的体系；他们都被一种末世论的希望所打动，并将救赎的基础放置在一个依靠博爱建立起来的社会主义社会秩序中。布洛赫通过卢卡奇熟悉了陀思妥耶夫斯基、

① Ernst Bloch, *The Spirit of Utopia*, trans. Anthony A. Nassar, Stanford University Press, 2000, p. 2.

克尔凯郭尔和德国神秘主义大师埃克哈特。布洛赫在1974年说:"《乌托邦精神》的有些内容来自我和卢卡奇的谈话。"1913年6月,布洛赫和一位来自拉脱维亚的雕塑家艾尔莎·冯·斯特里茨基(Else von Stritzky)结婚,艾尔莎的诺斯替主义[①]思想对布洛赫影响甚大。1918年,布洛赫把《乌托邦精神》题献给艾尔莎。在1963年新版的《乌托邦精神》的后记里,布洛赫承认此书包含着"革命的浪漫主义"和"革命的诺斯",后者就是指诺斯替主义。

布洛赫所说的"革命的浪漫主义"则是来自犹太教和基督教传统的弥赛亚主义(或译为"救世主义")。弥赛亚在希伯来文中的意思是"受膏者",意指上帝所派遣和封立的民族领袖和救主。众所周知,犹太民族是一个历经艰辛、苦难和不幸的民族。犹太民族最为辉煌的时代就是以色列王国的大卫王及其儿子所罗门王(约公元前973—前933年在位)时期,其他时代均生活在分裂或被异族奴役之中。犹太人长期沦落为无家可归的流浪民族,信仰上帝的犹太人把这些苦难视为上帝对他们的惩罚,同时也坚信自己是上帝最优秀的选民,虽遭惩罚,但只要改过自新,按照上帝的意旨行事,他们必得上帝的拯救。犹太人相信,在适当的时候,上帝将派他所膏立的"弥赛亚"(救世主)降生。一旦弥赛亚降临,正义就会得到伸张,邪恶就会得到惩处。在弥赛亚的国度里,犹太人就会享受一千年的幸福,这就是千年王国。弥赛亚主义也因此叫作千禧年主义。弥赛亚主义本来是一种世俗政治的主张,但是弥赛亚左等也不来,右等也不来,对弥赛亚的期盼就渐渐地成为一种宗教信仰。这种信仰表现在《圣经·新约全书》的《启示录》中。核心思想就是:历史会有一种终结(末日审判),然后就是千年王国。就这样,弥赛亚主义又跟末世论扯上了干系。总而言之,弥赛亚主义有三个最基本的特征:(1)对"救赎"(千禧年王国)的热切企盼是弥赛亚观念的核心;(2)作为救赎事件的千年王国在历史中从未出现,因此是"乌托邦";(3)末世论和启示录哲学,救赎需要彻底破坏旧秩序,"暴力"和"灾难"不可或缺。

在《乌托邦精神》里,布洛赫同样表露出明显的弥赛亚主义的思想倾向。《乌托邦精神》是布洛赫为第一次世界大战后的欧洲、为人类文明下的诊断

① 诺斯替主义是基督教的一个古老的异端派别。根据诺斯替主义,创造这个世界的上帝(造物主上帝)是无知的、邪恶的,而真正的上帝是神圣的、神秘的存在。人必须凭借自己的精神获得真正的知识(诺斯),才能够摆脱恶,从而重返光明(得救)。作为一种反世界主义,其首要原则是"恶的第一性"原则,认为这个世界本质上是邪恶的、黑暗的。人凭借着精神才能拯救这个恶的世界。

书，开的药方。其表层文字是“战争”和“革命”，深层的含义却是“灾难”和“救赎”这两个弥赛亚主题。第一次世界大战不仅带来了巨大的灾难，也导致了欧洲人精神上的颓废，造成整个欧洲文明的自我怀疑和否定。欧洲文明死了，“人”死了，是当时弥漫在欧洲人心灵的集体情绪。施宾格勒的《西方的没落》(1919)就是这种心态的反应。第一次世界大战似乎标志着西方文明的总崩溃，但它促使布洛赫走向了激进的弥赛亚主义路线。布洛赫相信，战争是“黎明前的黑暗”，没有死亡、没有痛苦的世界是战争经历后的乌托邦内容。只有先经历毁灭，才能永远埋葬旧秩序。整个欧洲文化，不论宗教文化还是世俗文化，都能在旧秩序的废墟上得到救赎，实现一种新文化。

《乌托邦精神》得到了许多左派思想家(阿多诺、马尔库塞等人)的推崇和喜爱，连不喜欢这本书的本雅明也认为《乌托邦精神》是“当代著作中少有的几个精品之一”，“时代的真正表达”。其理由是：当时的哲学著作过分面对现实，思想却因循守旧，没有条理，但布洛赫能够“独自一人”站在哲学的层面高瞻远瞩[①]。《乌托邦精神》之所以能成为“时代的真正表达”，正是由于布洛赫紧扣了时代的脉搏。透过战争的创伤，布洛赫看到了现代人的生存困境在于乌托邦精神的丧失，或者说是“超越维度的丧失”。

布洛赫在《乌托邦精神》的《题旨》中提出，唯有唤醒我们内在的乌托邦精神才能拯救欧洲、拯救人类，正文部分则要回答如何唤醒乌托邦精神的问题。这包括两个要点或两个步骤：先是人的内在方面对乌托邦的意识，然后把内在的东西外在化。与之对应，《乌托邦精神》的主要内容包括两大块。第一块叫《自我相遇》，布洛赫从旧瓦罐、装饰艺术谈起，然后花费了一百多页的篇幅讲音乐的理论和历史，几乎占了全部著作的一半篇幅[②]。这一块讲的是人通过与自我深处对“当下瞬间的黑暗”体验以及“作为绝对问题的讶异”(Staunen，或译为“惊讶”“惊奇”“惊异”)体验，达成心灵与弥赛亚的“自我相遇”(“相遇”一词很容易让人想到马丁·布伯说的“我”与“你”的神圣相遇)，这是“唤醒乌托邦精神”的第一个方面，即内在的方面。第二块的标题是《卡尔·马克思、死亡和启示录》，副标题叫作“在这世界上能让内在

---

① 本雅明1919年9月19日致舍恩的信，见 Gershom Scholem, Theodor W. Adorno, *The Correspondence of Walter Benjamin, 1910—1940*, trans. Manfred R. Jacobson and Evelyn M. Jocobson, The University of Chicago Press, 1994, p. 148.

② 出版商出于商业考虑，《乌托邦精神》才没有以《音乐和启示录》的书名出版。

成为外在、外在宛如内在的道路”。这是“唤醒乌托邦精神”的第二个方面，即人们在黑暗和讶异中觉醒，在乌托邦精神的神奇力量引领下走向外部世界，力图使内在的乌托邦东西成为外在的实现，变革世界，使之成为我们的“家园”。简单说来，第一个方面（内在的“自我相遇”）即人本主义的方面，第二个方面（外在的实现）即马克思主义（社会主义）的方面。当然，布洛赫的人本主义乃是一种宽泛意义上的人本主义立场。

三、研究前沿

布洛赫在西方马克思主义阵营中的位置比较特殊，因此，国内学界虽然对其始终保持着一定的关注，但是与其他西方马克思主义思想家相比，研究成果的总量相对较少。从成果发表时间来看，从二十世纪七八十年代开始就有少数学者开展了研究，但成果数量并不算多。二十一世纪以来，部分学者开始全面研究布洛赫，后者的思想在国内逐步得到深层次阐发和审视。

第一，对布洛赫哲学思想的整体研究。国内学界对布洛赫的思想研究中有相当数量是分析后者的整个理论形态和理论特征，对于他的乌托邦思想也往往是基于其一生的整体立场进行概括和评价。对于布洛赫来说，《乌托邦精神》是他的成名作，但是他的学术成就远不止于这部书，之后的其他著作，特别是《希望的原理》等，也蕴含了乌托邦思想在内的大量创新思想。由此，学界形成了普遍共识，即不能将布洛赫不同时期的乌托邦思想孤立起来看待，而是要结合更多的人类学、社会学、历史学、哲学、文学、政治学、宗教、艺术和人性等方面予以分析，还要注意以本体论和存在论为起点，对其思想进行系统性理解。有学者认为，布洛赫思想的当代价值是为马克思主义赋予了更加现实的指引作用，并且去除了“正统马克思主义”对马克思主义开放性的限制。但是，这些特性也带来了反面作用，就是会过度重视价值和意识的作用，容易导致对真理客观性的忽视，同时，也会导致对人本主义的过度强调，进而片面化理解共产主义目标。

第二，对《乌托邦精神》及乌托邦思想的专门研究。学界一般认为，布洛赫对乌托邦的认知是从最为基础的哲学认知开始的，所以有学者从“尚未”“形象”“功能”等概念出发，解读布洛赫对乌托邦的开放性构想，将马克思主义与乌托邦的关系进行深刻阐发，并认为布洛赫笔下的马克思主义是对乌托邦的更加现实化的阐释，为乌托邦的实现提供了更加开放但又更加具有引领性的道路。此外，《乌托邦精神》虽然是布洛赫早期的著作，但是，这部著作对他一生的影响也是十分巨大的，学界普遍认为，这部著作预示了他之后的哲学旨趣，开启了其一系列著作的思想主题。因此，只有理解了布洛赫的乌托邦思想，才能够理解他之后的哲学和神学思想。有学者就此将布洛赫称为“无神论的革命神学家”，认为他的这一身份特征是由无神论、革命、神学家这三种维度共同构成的，而马克思主义则是革命与神学的黏合剂。作为一部思想激进的著作，《乌托邦精神》体现出浓厚的巴洛克风格，极富表现力，能够对现实开展强烈的批判，却又形成了一种新的形而上学哲学思维，是一部能够面向心灵深处的作品。因而有学者指出，布洛赫在当时受到黑格尔、谢林的影响更大，并没有完全摆脱唯心主义和克尔凯郭尔的宗教思维，并因此体现出浓厚的犹太神秘主义信念。所以，布洛赫构建的这一条乌托邦精神之路只适用于精英们，并且只可能体现在少数领袖身上，缺乏大众的普遍实践基础。

第三，对相关概念的发散性研究。《乌托邦精神》产生的影响是广泛而深远的，这部著作确立了布洛赫马克思主义者的身份，其中的核心概念“乌托邦精神”则是他构建其他重要哲学观点的前提。要全面理解布洛赫的思想，需要同时处理好存在与意识、人与世界、必然性的现实与超越性“尚未”和“希望”、市民社会与乌托邦、希望与失望等重要范畴之间的关系。因此，学者们发现，要研究布洛赫的希望哲学在多大程度上基于并发展了马克思主义，就必须将马克思主义的“具体乌托邦”同“抽象乌托邦”“恶乌托邦”“传统乌托邦”等从本质上区分开来，还要警惕“敌乌托邦”的侵蚀。还有学者发掘了布洛赫的哲学之于中国特色社会主义的价值，包括对新时代马克思主义信仰的意义、对实现中国梦的意义和对美好生活的启示等。我们看到，布洛赫的美好生活观点与其具体和抽象的乌托邦观点高度对应：美好生活既包括真实的美好生活，又包括虚幻的美好生活。由此，布洛赫认为，只有真实的美好生活才具有现实可能性，这种理解与马克思对于共产主义的阐释是有一致性的。此外，布洛赫还有志于呼吁加强“马克思主义热流”研究，建立属于马克思主义的新的美学、宗教哲学、伦理学、美学和教义学。因此，学界普遍认为，布洛赫为马克思主义的发展进一步打开了空间，赋予了后者史无前例的广度和多样性，为探讨人的权利的实现提供了新的向度。

四、文本节选

The Socialist Idea

So we need ourselves first, above all. For that, however, the outer path must be cleared.

But will not everything inward in particular already be far too much then? Does not a great inwardness, which traversed the self-encounter in ever rising loops, ever higher levels of integration, reduce precisely the simple power to turn back *socially*, to do right in politics, and to think? Thus we also step back here somewhat at first. But it is no less already essential that we kindle a light before our feet. Precisely the one who was a thousand steps ahead can help more easily and closely than someone who blindly gasps along or adds his voice to the currently feasible.

So we repeat: What just was will probably soon be forgotten. Only an empty, horrible memory hangs in the air. Who was defended? Foul, wretched, profiteers were defended. What was young had to fall, forced to die for ends so alien and hostile to the spirit, but the despicable ones were saved, and sit in their warm drawing rooms. Not one of them was lost, but those who waved other flags, so much flowering, so much dream, so much spiritual hope, are dead. The artists defended the middlemen and kept the home front warm for the instigators; the clerics in the churches and in literature however betrayed their Lord for the sake of a uniform, an enlisted one, more cheaply than Esau, more cheaply than Judas. There has never been a more dismal military objective than imperial Germany's: plunder and brutality, the enslavement of all and the arsenal of the reaction; a stifling coercion, imposed by mediocrities, tolerated by mediocrities; the triumph of stupidity, guarded by the gendarme, acclaimed by the intellectuals who did not have enough brains to supply slogans.

We repeat again: And of course, as though one had not been burned badly enough, this is how it remains even today. The War ended, the Revolution began and with it, seemingly, the open doors. But correct, these soon closed again. The black-marketeer moved, sat back down, and everything obsolete drifted back into place. The profiteering farmer, the mighty *grand bourgeois* truly put out the fire in places, and the panicked *petit bourgeois* helps to enfeeble and encrust, as always. Nonproletarian youth itself is more coarse and stupid, has its head thrown further back than any youth before; the universities have become true burial mounds of the spirit, hotbeds of "Germany, awaken!" and filled with the stink of rigidity, corruption and gloom. So those who have apparently been restored completely reenact what the reaction of a century ago auditioned, as Hegel's friend Niethammer already lamented: "Just as worms, frogs, and other vermin often follow the rain, so do Kajetan von Weiller and his crowd follow the dark day spreading across the entire civilized world." They reenact that Restoration's recuperation, when the cloddish slogans, the corporative state were recalled; when the traditionalism of *Vaterland* was rampant against the truly Christian, indeed even quite properly medieval idea of humanity; when that insensible Romanticism appeared that forgot Münzer yet revered the junk of heraldry, that ignored the true German popular tradition, the Peasant's War, and saw only knights' castles rising into enchanted, moonlit nights. Once again, predictably, the writer helps apply the brakes; indeed, Expressionism's former priests—incinerating what they had just recently exalted—rush to help incompetent literary homesteaders patch together misrepresentations from the tasteful ruins of the past, in order to bar the way for the vitally formative sensation of the future, of the city, of the collective; in order to insert the reaction's black market deception into a better ideology; in order to make their lamentable hygiene, their doubly imitative Romanticism absolute.

Instead of this petty generation being ashamed of itself for mostly failing before a principle of which it had nevertheless had a presentiment, the postulate of the very dawning of creative Expression, it now in addition to all that slanders even the presentiment, the historical-philosophically overdue principle itself, because to its misfortune it found only this petty generation. Meanwhile the West with its millions of proletarians has not yet spoken; meanwhile there stands, unbowed, a Marxist republic in Russia; and the eternal questions of our longing, of our religious conscience still burn, undiminished, unbent, unredeemed in their absolute claims. What is more: we Socialists have at least learned from the same outlook on reality that came a century ago; Marx thoroughly purified Socialist planning of every simple, false, disengaged and abstract enthusiasm, of mere Jacobinism, and we have especially not forgotten the spirit of Kant and Baader above. Whereas the Romanticism of the latest reaction has inherited absolutely nothing proper, is simply coarse and backward, is neither factual nor enthusiastic nor universalist, but simply numb, obstinate, withdrawn, soulless and un-Christian; so with its pathos of the autochthonous it can elicit only the decline of the West, in completely animalistic stupidity, irreligious extinction: faded blossom and for today only civilizational atrophy, a navy, and the pessimism of historiographical registration as the only goal, but for Europe only prompt, eternal death.

Consequently the inner glow won for us elsewhere may certainly not glimmer only on high here, but must move back far into the medial life all around. From this place of the self-encounter, so that it may become one for everyone, there consequently also springs, inevitably, the arena of political-social leadership: toward real personal freedom, toward real religious affiliation. Here, then, a *second* point has been attained, where the "soul", the "intuition of the We", the content of its "Magna Carta", streams responsibly into the world. To be practical in this way, to help in this way on everyday life's structural horizon and put things into place, precisely to be political-social in this way, is powerfully near to conscience, and is a revolutionary mission absolutely inscribed in utopia.

Certainly its light fears becoming somewhat feebler thereby. However, even if its luminosity darkens at first, one has to persist: this light must be moved from the inner sanctum onto a broader domain. To some, certainly, even this restriction is not yet enough of a renunciation, and they become indignant whenever some concept cannot immediately be resold or exchanged, in other words whenever the nevertheless inextinguishable ultraviolet of the genuine, great thought does not absolutely immediately describe party appeals and statutes. But for this reason the seemingly more remote revolutionary *concept* is not "rootless" after all, or "impossible" or "abstract" in the capitalist age; rather, since the thinking subject is located not only in its time, and the collective from which it speaks is not only socially collective, it can be achieved absolutely eccentrically to time as the inventory of Oughts (that is, of our tasks even beyond the historically given) and thus in a suprahistorically concrete way, as an absolutely constitutive presentiment of the goal, knowledge of the goal. As a whole, in any case, we have here reached the place to strive—instead of for the mere self-way, the pure soul-expanse of the self-encounter, even the most direct shape of the moment and the question—for another, practical-exemplary level of concretion. To shape a path from the lonely waking dream of the inner self-encounter to the dream that goes out to shape the external world at least to alleviate it, at least as *locus minoris resistentiae* or even as the instrumentation for the goal. And just this, the explication of "glossolalia" as "prophecy" of the metapsychological as the socially, ultimately cosmically metaphysical system, distinguishes the passage to the "world" of the soul, which is neither of this world nor of that, but is nonetheless not simply acosmic and closed to the cosmos, but turned toward the new, all-pervading power of the subject-object space.

Accordingly this passage, precisely as such, turns back, gains height precisely by flattening out, gains the resonant energy of utopia precisely by sinking in level, gains the cosmic element reverberating throughout its hitherto only vertical salvific intention precisely by also confronting the state of society; for how could there be an inwardness, and how would it notice that it was one, whether as sorrow or as truly paradoxical joy, if it stopped being rebellious and desperate against everything given? If here too, then, in glossolalia's transition into a still unelaborated, provisionally social part of a "world system," we are working in a different metal than has been customary in the domain of self-invention: only when the goal-invention is added, after all, does the ore of the social world begin a ferment and a process that will open a passage for glossolalia itself from Kant to Hegel, and on the other hand, for the natural "Hegelianism" of the state of the world, the passage to "Kant", to the absolute Ought, to the problem of a Kingdom of moral beings.

...

Until now everything has usually been brought down to dollars and cents, while on the other side the soul could always only shine in from above. The businessman laughs during his *earthly* business, and the levers are in his hands; a misunderstood Jesus offers encouragement in the *ideal* domain, seeks in vain to shame us by not resisting evil himself. Marx on the other hand finally sensitized us against the external method, which by itself so readily makes us inflexible, and then, separately, against the good man who thinks freedom already comes with him, in order finally to unite both; his conduct is guided so to speak by the Jesus of the scourge and the Jesus of fraternal love simultaneously. Sometimes the conquest of evil may succeed more quietly, as the rider on Lake Constance succeeded through heedlessness, and, more deeply, the saint in special situations succeeds through the kiss of righteousness, through a creative disregard; but as a rule the soul must assume guilt in order to destroy the existing evil, in order not to assume even more guilt by an idyllic retreat, a hypocritical connivance in injustice. Dominance and power in themselves are evil, but it is necessary to confront power in terms of power, as a categorical imperative with revolver in hand, wherever and as long as power cannot otherwise be destroyed, wherever and as long as everything diabolical still balks so violently at the (undiscovered) amulet of purity, and thereafter finally discharge authority, the "power" even of the good, the lie of vengeance and its right, as methodically as possible. Hence Marx provides, as this *third* term, a sufficiently complicated sensibility and a variation of the identical revolutionary concept: in order to be able to think purely economically alongside capital, against its injustices, just as the detective is homogeneous with the criminal—where nothing but the economic aspect has to be considered; and only afterward to imagine a higher life, as soon as the space and the liberation of the idea have been won, and the measureless lies, as well as the unwitting embellishments, excuses, superstructures, variables of purely economic functions, can be destroyed in favor of the always and finally genuine idea of society. Here a separate procedure is operative that wants to define economic relations not with spiritual means, with a "league of the just," but rather places the economy outside of spirituality, and deduces the spiritual from the economic; or, as Marx himself similarly defined the proper maxim of the scientific socialism gained through him: it is not our consciousness that determines our being, but on the contrary our economic being that determines our consciousness, the breeding ground of ideas.

Ultimately, of course, this alone can not make the sober view fruitful; man does not live by bread alone. As extensively important as the external may be, and must be attended to, it still only suggests, it does not create, for human beings, not things, not their powerful process, outside of us and wrongly turned over onto us, invent history. What must still come economically, the necessary economic-institutional change, is defined by Marx, but the new man, the leap, the power of love and of light, morality itself, has not yet been allotted the desirable degree of autonomy in the definitive social order. Put differently: if primitive accumulation, the feudal and then the capitalistic modes of production successively determined particular moral and cultural systems, at least in terms of sphere, then the obsolescence of every discrete economic element, in other words the finally triumphant socialist mode of production, must bring in its train certain moral and cultural consequences, an equally "correct," aprioristic kind of sensibility and of culture, which can not just be defined as free thinking or a banal atheism, in accordance with the Philistine cultural ideals socialism has taken over from the bourgeoisie. Certainly socialism could not have been grounded if Marx had been submissively devout, if he had insisted on an Arcadian state of the world where rational distribution gives everyone what he needs, if in other words Marx had organized only consumption and not above all production: with his practical eye toward an inexorable industrialization, with his unromantic coldness and his materialism as a powerfully demystifying rigor. But precisely when this narrowness persists too long, man is simply saddled again, precisely in economic terms; oppression is only curtailed and not lifted. In just this way production is finally taken out of the hands of the subjects again, and a phantasmal process of the general, of economic developments in themselves, goes its own way: like an idol, occasionalistic, detached and even in the future indestructible. This is consistent with the fact that Marx, by really aiming his thrust, even where he did not weaken it into a "revolutionary development," only against capitalism—a relatively recent, derivative kind of decadence—and not also against the ceaseless, primordial locus of all enslavement, brutality and exploitation: against militarism, feudalism, a world from the top down as such; here the ancient socialist movement had already been reduced, misdirected and trivialized just by its opponent. Similarly there can be no doubt (from a religious viewpoint, closely related to the foregoing) that the indiscriminate ideology-critical distrust of every idea, without the need to exalt an idea oneself, does not encourage anything brighter; that even when Engels took up a dialectical-synthetic reconstruction of the condition of liberty, equality, and fraternity predominating in the ancient communistic *gentes*, the social-constructive labor he expended was not confronted by a particularly clear and impressive ideal-constructive emphasis. Heart, conscience, spirituality, the communion of all the living, fraternity, *philadelphia* and the end of all isolation, found in the French Revolution, this truly not just "bourgeois" breakthrough of heretical history, its *closer* earthly reflection. And in this age, where God's desperate red sunset is already sufficiently in all things and neither Atlas nor Christ holds up his heaven, it finally appears that Marxism is no special philosophical accomplishment if it remains aesthetically fixed in the status quo in order to posit nothing but a more or less eudaemonistically instituted "heaven" on earth—without the music that ought to resound out of this effortlessly functioning mechanism of the economy and of social existence. One can thus say that precisely the acute emphasis on all (economically) determining moments, and on the latency of all transcendent moments, existing but remaining in mystery, *moves Marxism close to a critique of pure reason, for which a corresponding critique of practical reason has not yet been written*. Here the economy has been sublated, but soul, faith, for which room must be made, are lacking; the actively intelligent gaze has destroyed everything, certainly often justly, all the private idylls and uncritical reveries of socialism's hermits and secessionists, who wanted to distill just for themselves a beautiful parallel earth from what is best on this earth, and dismissed the rest of the globe's phlegmatism; certainly the all too Arcadian, the abstract-utopian kind of socialism—appearing since the Renaissance as the secular mode of the thousand-year Kingdom [*Reich*], and often merely as insubstantial draping, as the ideology of extremely sober class objectives and economic revolution—has been disavowed on good grounds. But then the utopian tendency in all these things is neither comprehended, nor is the substance of their miraculous images located or redirected, nor is even the primordially religious wish rescinded which in every movement or objective of a reconstruction of the world absolutely wanted to make room for life, in order divinely to essentialize itself, finally chiliastically to install itself into goodness, freedom, the light of the *telos*.

Only then will the deceivers truly tremble; what is right will appear. Magicians will no longer invoke the spirit, which will no longer lead beyond the light. But more than just a partial enlightenment is necessary, more than the kind that neglects the old heretical dreams of a better life rather than investigating and inheriting them. Only in this way, and not by means of the wretchedness of a vulgar atheism, can the ideological oxygen be cut off from the businessmen as the heroes, the negotiators and leaders, and their storehouse of beautifications be barred. Only someone who speaks not just for the earth but also for the wrongly surrendered heaven will truly be able to demystify the fabrications of bourgeois-feudal state ideology, namely unseductively, and the "enthusiasm for an equal share in enjoyment" will no longer be what it seemed to the Prussian state theologian Stahl, the sole stimulating aspect of communist social theories. Certainly we will no longer work out of necessity, indeed we will work much better and more productively, our boredom and wretchedness is a sufficient guarantee of that, and there—as is already true for the teacher, official, politician, artist and scientist—pleasure in one's ability will replace the profit motive as a sufficient motivation, at least for practical occupations. Especially for the social valuation of this motive, in accordance with the tremendous, intensifying potential—fully capable of replacing the monetary stimulus—of contempt or esteem, of honor and of glory. Only very extrinsically do dangerous alliances appear in this hardly

Manchesterian "state of the future": as Hegelian correlations to Prussia, especially to the universal state, to the very principle of organization—the more readily, more urgently does the duty thus arise of placing Marx into the higher space, into the new, most real adventure of disclosed life, into the What For of its society. That is: of bringing the usually all too truncated construal of society back into Weitling's, Baader's, Tolstoy's utopianly superior world of love, into the new force of the human encounter in Dostoevsky, into the Adventism of heretical history. Hence utopia's distant totality offers the image of a structure in no way still economically profitable: everyone producing according to his abilities, everybody consuming according to his needs, everyone openly "comprehended" according to the degree of his assistance, his moral-spiritual lay ministry and humanity's homeward journey through the world's darkness. Only thus can the new life, now radical as well as orthodox, be understood; only thus may the most exact economic logic and austerity be linked to political mysticism, and legitimate itself thereby. This logic removes every hateful sort of impediment in order, under the sublation of the economic private sphere, to hand it over to a communitarian society, but in return it lets the true privacy, and the entire, socially unsublatable problematic of the soul, step forward stronger than ever, in order—at the height of a structure that will only become reliable and orderly under socialism—to affiliate it to the Church, one necessarily and a priori posited after to socialism, oriented toward the new content of revelation. Only in this way will the community, freely electing itself, have space *above* a society that merely disburdens and a communistically restructured social economy, in a structure without violence because without classes. But a transfigured Church is the bearer of the furthest discernible purposes; in life she stands beyond labor, is the conceivable space of a continuously flowing tradition and of a connection to the end, and no social order, however successful, can do without this final link in the correlative series between the We and the final problem of the What For. Then human beings will finally be free for those concerns and questions which alone are practical, which otherwise only await them at their hour of death after their entire restless life up to then had done nothing but seal them off from everything essential. It is as the Baal Shem says: the Messiah can only come when all the guests have sat down at the table; this table is first of all the table of labor, beyond labor, but then at the same the time the table of the Lord—in the philadelphian Kingdom the organization of the earth finds its ultimately coordinative metaphysics.

——Ernst Bloch, *The Spirit of Utopia*, trans. Anthony A. Nassar, Stanford University Press, 2000, pp. 234 - 246.

五、观点解读

1. 人"尚未"存在

1907年,布洛赫撰写了《论"尚未"范畴》("Über die Kategorie Noch-Nicht")一文,他自称为"人生道路上的一次突破"。这篇手稿从心理学方面探讨了某种主观上还未被意识到的东西,而在这种东西背后正隐藏着与那些客观上尚未形成的东西之间应有的一种相互关系——当然是具体的和乌托邦的。手稿中的基本思想成了布洛赫毕生思考的一个确定不移的方向。表征生成性和开放性的"尚未"范畴后来被布洛赫称为"我的哲学的起源"。这个哲学范畴成为布洛赫的"乌托邦精神"的核心范畴。在布洛赫眼中,人的"类本质"是他的尚未完成性。在《乌托邦精神》的"低人一等的生活"一节中,布洛赫指出人之为人的根本,就在于对光明的向往。布洛赫不仅把人定义为"以未完成为特征的存在""最后一个也是第一个的存在",也把人叫作"制造工具的动物""迂回前行的动物":"他不能仅仅依靠天生的反射和以前的信号。随着时间的推移,在筑巢和相关活动中,他更多地依靠自觉的计划:完全的人为创作,并向前拓展。"布洛赫这里把人的类本质说成是"计划"

“创作”，实际上就是“劳动”的哲学说辞。当然，这种劳动不是哪个具体社会生产方式中的劳动，而是对人创造历史的主体性的一种抽象规定。布洛赫关于人的“尚未存在”的思想和青年卢卡奇相当接近。但布洛赫还有不同于卢卡奇的思想特色。他不仅从“类本质”的高度描述人的历史性生存，还从个人的经验出发描述当下直接的生存状态。布洛赫在《乌托邦精神》中叙述了现代人生存的黑暗状态：我活着，却“体验不到我自己，不拥有我自己”。布洛赫称之为“当下瞬间的黑暗”；尽管我们活着，却体会不到自己活着。不过，在黑暗之中同时也蕴藏着希望，希望指向了我们想要的完满状态。这种希望是以“讶异”的形式体现的。我们在讶异中与弥赛亚相遇，与最后的救赎相遇，与这个世界的“不可避免的终结”相遇。我们是在“为我们无限的潜在可能性而讶异”。换言之，我们的希望和讶异指向了一个尚未存在的、在未来将要出现的乌托邦。布洛赫认为哲学的作用就在于表达唯一真实的现实——乌托邦现实。布洛赫的《乌托邦精神》就是要在现实中寻找这一乌托邦现实的蛛丝马迹，然后像禅宗说佛那样，用手（语言文字）指向了明月——人尚未完全达到的乌托邦。

2. 社会革命是灵魂革命的先决步骤

在布洛赫看来，魏玛共和国的精神枯萎状况只能招致“西方的没落”、文明萎缩症和悲观主义，只能导致欧洲迅速和永远的死亡。“战争结束了，革命开始了，随着革命，大门似乎打开了。然而，很快又合上了。”如何把很快关上的大门重新打开呢？布洛赫求助于马克思主义。然而，布洛赫并不把社会主义革命理解为单纯的经济革命和政治革命，而是视之为灵魂革命的一个先决步骤。他认为，为了获得不断上升的“自我相遇”乃至更高层面的内在性，必须先要后退一步，即回到社会的政治行动和思考上来，因为“内在火焰一定不会仅仅在高处闪耀，而必须回到周围的普通生活，以便它成为每一个人的火焰”。为了到达“真正的个人自由”，走向“政治领袖们角逐的舞台”是不可避免的。这样一来，布洛赫就从“自我相遇之心灵”的外在化问题转向了社会历史问题。布洛赫认为，马克思主义“开启了一条从内在的自我相遇中的孤独醒梦通向塑造（起码是缓解）外部世界的梦想的道路”。但布洛赫也有所保留地说，这条道路“至少是作为达到目标的工具使用”。换言之，布洛赫的真正目标还是“绝对的应该和道德人的王国”，与之相比，马克思主义也好，社会主义革命也好，都不过是一种手段。在布洛赫那里，此岸世界的社会主义革命不过是乌托邦的灵魂救赎计划的第一部分。说到底，布洛赫试图把他的人本主义哲学和马克思主义混合起来。这就是布洛赫对马克思主义的“工具性使用”。

3. 马克思主义接近于一种纯粹理性批判

布洛赫的《乌托邦精神》(1923年版)和青年卢卡奇同年出版的《历史和阶级意识》一样，都是在批判第二国际对马克思主义哲学的经济决定论解释。布洛赫认为，如果过于强调马克思主义的经济学方面，强调经济因素的决定作用，就会使马克思主义“接近于”一种纯粹理性批判，而相对应的《实践理性批判》还没有写出来。也就是说，本应在马克思主义当中占据一席之地的“灵魂和信仰”缺席了。

布洛赫把马克思主义理解为一种抗议，由资本主义社会中的剥削和压迫引发的伦理抗议。布洛赫相信，社会主义并不单纯建立在经济的基础上。相反，“用意志的共同体来定义作为革命阶级利益的意志，不但在道德上更容易，而且较为明确”。这就用“共同意志”(类似于青年卢卡奇的“阶级意识”概念)代替了“利益”，用“道德”替代了经济来解释马克思主义了。在经济和伦理中间，布洛赫看似不偏不倚，其实站在了伦理这一边。他坚持马克思“是同时由拿鞭子的耶稣和博爱的耶稣所引导的”。因此，布洛赫认为，如果马克思坚持“按需分配”的“理性桃花源”，如果社会主义仅仅是“接管资产阶级的市侩文化理想”，那么，社会主义就是没有根据的。在那样的社会主义中，人只是再次承受了经济的压迫，“国家转变为控制消费和生产的国际性工具组织”。布洛赫较为准确地把握了马克思对资本主义社会的历史性批判。经济对人的压迫只是一种特殊的社会历史形态，而不是历史的必然性。第二国际和德国社会民主党把历史看作生产力的发展所决定的自然过程，这种经济决定论的解释恰恰是非历史的。就此而言，布洛赫的批判有相当的合理性。要注意的是，布洛赫并不认为马克思主义“根本没有”《实践理性批判》，也不是“不应该有”，更不是“不可能有”，只是“还没有”。正如青年卢卡奇一样，布洛赫不是在批判马克思，相反，是在“保卫马克思”，是在捍卫他心目中的那个马克思——人本主义的马克思。既然布洛赫认为马克思主义缺少形而上学，他当然要给马克思补课。因此，布洛赫的《乌托邦精神》实际上是在给马克思主义补写一本马克思本人没有写出来的《实践理性批判》——经济学之外的“形而上学”。

4. 必须强调乌托邦精神对于未来共产主义社会的重要性

在《乌托邦精神》中，布洛赫十分强调社会主义革命的乌托邦维度。布洛赫提出，虽然马克思预言了经济制度的变革，但在马克思界说的社会秩序中，“新的人类、飞跃、爱的力量和光明的力量、道德本身，还没有取得应有的独立性”。因此，“紧迫的任务是把马克思放入更高的空间”——也就是把过于狭隘的马克思主义经济学理论放回到“乌托邦”的世界。只有这样，未来的社会主义才能获得合法性。布洛赫十分强调未来共产主义社会的乌托邦精神方面。他认为，社会主义社会（布洛赫的“社会主义”其实指的是共产主义）不仅是满足人的物质需求，更是满足人的精神需求。“人并不只是靠面包活着”，还得有音乐。布洛赫强调，共产主义社会否定了经济的私人领域，但反过来，它让真正的私人领域，即社会不能否定的“灵魂”问题阔步前进了。他甚至认为共产主义社会必然设立一个新的“教会”。布洛赫就这样把马克思说的自由王国和基督教的千年王国论连通了起来，把马克思主义和宗教连通了起来。总之，布洛赫用“乌托邦”统一了经济和伦理（灵魂）两个方面。布洛赫所强调的“乌托邦”与青年卢卡奇的“总体性”观念有明显的互文关系。正如布洛赫所说，“创造历史的是人，而不是物”，历史不是一个“外在于我们、并错误地交给我们的强大物质过程”。

六、进一步阅读指南

1. 习近平：《在纪念马克思诞辰200周年大会上的讲话》，人民出版社2018年版。

2. 习近平：《习近平谈治国理政》第一卷，外文出版社2018年版。

3. 《中共中央关于党的百年奋斗重大成就和历史经验的决议》，人民出版社2021年版。

4. [德]恩斯特·布洛赫等：《德国著名哲学家自述（上册）》，张慎等译，东方出版社2002年版。

5. 邢来顺、吴友法主编：《德国通史》第四、五卷，江苏人民出版社2019

年版。

6. 童庆炳主编:《文化与诗学》(第一辑),上海人民出版社 2004 年版。

7. 刘小枫:《走向十字架上的真》,三联书店 1994 年版。

8. 金寿铁:《真理与现实——恩斯特·布洛赫哲学研究》,同济大学出版社 2007 年版。

9. 夏凡:《乌托邦困境中的希望:布洛赫早中期哲学的文本学解读》,中央编译出版社 2008 年版。

10. Ernst Bloch, *The Spirit of Utopia*, Meridian, 1998.

11. Jack Zipes, "Introduction: Toward a Realization of Anticipatory Illumination", in Ernst Bloch, *The Utopian Function of Art and Literature*: *Selected Essays*, trans. Jack Zipes and Frank Mecklenberg, MIT Press,1988.

12. Vincent Geoghegan, *Ernst Bloch*, Routledge, 1995.

13. Jamie Owen Daniel, Tom Moylan, eds., *Not Yet*: *Reconsidering Ernst Bloch*, Verso, 1997.

14. Leszek Kolakowski, *Main Currents of Marxism*: *The Breakdown*, Clarendon Press, 1978, Chapter 12, "Ernst Bloch: Marxsim as a Futuristis Gnosis".

七、问题与思考

1. 为什么说布洛赫的《乌托邦精神》是一种人本主义哲学?

2. 试论布洛赫的"乌托邦"概念与卢卡奇的"总体性"概念的联系和区别。

3. 如何理解马克思的"自由王国"和基督教的"千年王国"之间的关系?

第三章　马克思主义精神实质的时代反思
——《马克思主义和哲学》和《卡尔·马克思》选读

教学目的与要求

理解柯尔施关于马克思主义和哲学关系的论述；掌握柯尔施总体性社会革命理论的科学内涵；了解柯尔施关于马克思主义发展史三阶段的划分；重点掌握柯尔施关于哲学批判与政治经济学批判内在关系的认识；把握柯尔施关于商品拜物教批判理论的历史定位；系统理解柯尔施对成熟时期唯物主义理论实质的论述。

一、历史背景

（一）作者介绍

1886年，卡尔·柯尔施（Karl Korsch）出生于德国汉堡附近的托斯泰特，父亲是一位银行职员。不久，举家迁到迈宁根，他在那里上了中学，之后就读于慕尼黑、柏林、日内瓦和耶拿等大学，主要学习法学、经济学和哲学。这一时期，他的思想非常活跃，积极参加了“自由学生运动”这一组织，致力于建立大学知识界与社会运动之间的联系。1910年，他在耶拿大学获得法学博士学位。1912年，他在英国伦敦从事博士后研究工作，在那里，他加入了费边社，受到了“工团主义运动”的强烈影响。1914年，第一次世界大战爆发，柯尔施回到德国，应征入伍。战争结束后，他开始走上自己的政治生涯，于1917年加入了“独立的德国社会民主党”，这是从官方的“德国社会民主党”中分化出来的左派组织。1919年3月，他出版了《什么是社会化？》一书，主张用社会主义公社取代资本主义私人经济，在思想上逐渐接近马克思主义。在十月革命的影响下，柯尔施渐渐转向马克思主义，并于1920年正式加入德国共产党。在入党后，面对革命形势的衰退和资本主义的稳定发展，柯尔施力图从理论上总结革命斗争的经验教训。1922年，他完成了《工厂委员会的劳动法》一书，强调工厂委员会是无产阶级斗争的中坚力量。同年，他还为党内同志写了三本阐发马克思主义基本思想的宣传册：《唯物史观原理》《马克思主义的精髓》和《〈哥达纲领批判〉导言》。这些思想在1923年的《马克思主义和哲学》中得到了进一步阐发。然而，这一著作的出版也改变了柯尔施的命运。他于1926年被开除党籍。在这一时期，虽然柯尔施提出了不同于列宁的一些见解，但在总体上，他还是支持列宁主义的。但是在此之后，柯尔施开始转变对列宁主义的态度。1929年，他就考茨基1927年的主要著作《唯物主义历史观》写了一篇措辞激烈的抨击文章；1930年，他再版了《马克思主义和哲学》，并写了一篇《反批判》序言；1931年，他新写了一篇论述马克思主义危机的文章，但未发表；1932年，他再版了马克思的《资本论》，并附加了一篇导言。在整个三十年代，他自认为是一个马克思主义者，但始终对考茨基和列宁的思想持公开批判态度，这些观点在他的《卡尔·马克思》(1938)、《我为什么是一个马克思主义者》(1935)、《马克思主义的主要原则：再论述》(1937)等文中得到重要体现。我们看到，《马克思主义和哲学》(1923)、《卡尔·马克思》(1938)是柯尔施一生中最具原创性的两部著作，分别探讨了马克思主义与德国古典哲学以及英国古典政治经济学之间的内在关系，系统批判了第二国际马克思主义以及列宁对马克思主义的理解，并从独特的视角阐述了马克思主义的精神实质，对后来的西方马克思主义产生了巨大影响。由于希特勒上台，1936年，柯尔施移居美国，1943—1945年在图拉纳大学教社会学，1945—1950年在纽约国际社会研究所工作，同时发表了一些关于马克思主义理论的文章。二十世纪五十年代初期，柯尔施始终为自己的孤独处境和悲观思想而苦恼，并在绝望中最终放弃了马克思主义，成为一名自由的批判理论家。五十年代后期，他又对苏联和中国的马克思主义产生了兴趣，并为选编的《毛泽东文集》写了一篇导言，强调后者在理论上的独创性。1961 年 10 月，柯尔施病逝于美国马萨诸塞州。

（二）时代背景

1. 十月革命之后国际工人运动的新形势

《马克思主义和哲学》第一版是柯尔施在俄国十月革命的推动下，对第二国际马克思主义的一种理论反思。自十九世纪七八十年代以来，资本主义在政治、经济、文化、意识形态等领域均发生了重大变化，特别是随着资产阶级民主化进程的加快，资本主义进入相对平稳的发展时期。在此背景下，如何理解马克思主义的精神实质，并以此来指导工人的革命实践，就具有极其重要的战略意义。然而，令人遗憾的是，第二国际没有完成这一历史使命，在内部出现了重大分歧，形成了各种不同倾向的理论思潮，走向了马克思主义的反面。正统马克思主义者大多忽视了马克思主义的革命-批判本性，将它诠释为一种实证主义或经济决定论，把唯物辩证法混同于一般进化论。这不可避免地导致了理论与实践、科学与社会主义、工人运动的直接实践与社会主义根本目标的分离和对立。而新康德主义的流行和伯恩施坦修正主义的出现，则是这种冲突外化的产物：前者用康德的思想来补充马克思主义，将科学社会主义诠释为一种伦理学；后者则公开抛弃马克思主义，主张用合法的议会斗争和改良主义路线来代替马克思的革命理论。这种分裂导致了双重后果：一方面，在理论上，使马克思主义遭遇重大危机；另一方面，在实践中，导致一些无产阶级政党公开抛弃马克思主义指导纲领，走上了资产阶级改良主义路线，给世界范围内的无产阶级革命运动带来了极为严重的消极影响。这双重后果最终导致第二国际的破产。因此，如何基于工人革命运动实践和马克思主义发展史来系统反思第二国际失败的内在根源，就是一项极其重要的研究课题。而第一次世界大战的爆发和俄国十月革命的胜利，为这一课题的研究奠定了客观基础。也是在此背景下，柯尔施以十月革命为现实支撑，以马克思主义和德国古典哲学的关系为突破口，对这一问题做出了深入探讨，于 1923 年完成了《马克思主义和哲学》这一长文，并首次发表在《社会主义和工人运动史文库》上。

2. 第一次世界大战后德国和西欧政局的动荡与分裂

在《马克思主义和哲学》与《卡尔·马克思》发表期间,也是整个欧洲形势发生剧烈变化的阶段。当时,德国国内的社会状况随着政治、经济和阶级状况的变化而发生了激烈的冲突,对德国和整个欧洲及世界都产生了深远影响。其一,1918 年魏玛共和国成立后,德国政局始终处于极为动荡的阶段。当时德国虽然建立了新的议会制政体,但是整个社会非但迟迟不能够稳定下来,反而频繁发生各类突发性政治事件。革命派与保守派和大资产阶级之间的矛盾也愈加尖锐。其二,在第一次世界大战后形成的新的世界格局下,德国始终受到以法国为代表的反德势力的针对,导致国际地位不断下降,同时,整个国家背负着沉重的战争赔偿,不断激起德国人强烈的抵触情绪。其三,剧烈的社会变动令德国民众的生活受到极大影响。德国国内的通货膨胀愈发严重,大量劳工失业,整个社会对魏玛政府的不满也与日俱增。这些因素为极端民族主义掌权埋下了伏笔,直到德意志民族社会主义工人党(纳粹党)走上前台。

(三) 思想背景

1. 二十世纪二三十年代德国社会主义阵营的思想倾向

《马克思主义和哲学》的发表,预示着柯尔施悲剧性命运的开始。德国社会民主党、德国共产党都公开批判柯尔施,将其视为党内的唯心主义者和修正主义者;季诺维也夫在 1924 年的共产国际第五次代表大会上谴责了他和卢卡奇,在 1926 年 2—3 月召开的共产国际执行委员会第六次会议上,季诺维也夫进一步指责他为“疯狂的小资产阶级”。不过,面对同样的批判,柯尔施走了一条与卢卡奇不同的道路:后者选择了妥协,做了一个一半出于策略一半出于真诚的自我批判,继续留在了共产主义运动之中;而柯尔施则始终坚持自己的立场,拒不妥协。于是,在 1926 年 4 月,他被开除党籍。随后,1928 年,《共产主义政治》杂志停刊。这预示着,他作为一个政治组织成员的时期彻底宣告结束,从此成为一名独立的马克思主义者。在这一系列事件的影响下,他的立场出现了一些变化,开始公开批判列宁的思想,成为一位反列宁主义的马克思主义者。而《马克思主义和哲学》第二版就是在这一背景下出场的，为此，他还专门写了一篇名为《反批判》的序言。在接下来的整个二十世纪三十年代，他都始终坚持这一立场，并在1938年的《卡尔·马克思》中得到了集中体现。

2. 二十世纪二三十年代德国国内的其他思潮

在魏玛共和国时期，虽然德国国内的社会局势始终动荡不安，但是，这一独特的时代却给德国人文社会科学的发展提供了适宜的"土壤"。当时，以马堡学派（逻辑学派）为代表的新康德主义学派拥有一个较为短暂的活跃期。他们的主要立场是将康德思想中的唯物主义剔除出去，并且用唯心主义的内容包装自然科学，因而更加强调纯粹主观化的逻辑思维，避免对现实世界的纠缠。在这一时期，胡塞尔的现象学完全成熟。在完成《逻辑研究》之后，胡塞尔继续创作了《形式的与先验的逻辑》《笛卡尔的沉思》等重要作品，开创了现代哲学的一个重要门类。同时，雅斯贝尔斯和海德格尔在现象学的基础上，进一步丰富了存在主义的道路。他们将人和事物的存在状态作为研究的对象，实现了欧洲哲学研究的一个重大突破。同时，在宗教哲学方面，舍勒、巴尔特等人也将德国的宗教哲学研究推上了一个新的高度。总之，在经历了第一次世界大战之后，包括德国在内的西欧各国虽然经济状况遭到严重破坏，但是，包括左派思想在内的人文社会科学却在这一时期迎来了突破式的发展，为西方马克思主义的形成和发展起到了重要推动作用。

二、篇章结构

1923年，《马克思主义和哲学》以德文首次出版；1930年，柯尔施再版时新写了一篇序言《关于〈马克思主义和哲学〉问题的现状——一个反批判》（以下简称《反批判》）。1966年，欧洲出版社以1930年版为稿本，重印了这一著作。1970年，每月评论出版社出版了这一著作的英文版，不过，在内容上与1930年版略有不同：此版删除了1930年版收录的三篇小论文，新增了两篇重要论文《〈哥达纲领批判〉导言》（1922）和《第一国际的马克思主义》（1924）。1938年，《卡尔·马克思》以英文首次出版，1963年再版，1967年在充分吸收巴黎稿本和美国稿本的基础上，出版了德文版。与英文版相比，虽然著作的整体格局（分三大部分）没有发生变化，但在具体章节的编排和标题上均出现了较大变动,特别是第三部分,由原来的 7 节变成了 15 节;更为重要的是,这一版在文后列出了详细的英文参考资料,为读者清晰把握这一著作的写作过程提供了文献依据。

由于版本不同,《马克思主义和哲学》收录的文章也有所不同。本教材主要选编自 1970 年的英文版。因此,在篇章介绍上,主要以这一版为准。这一版主要收录了 4 篇文章:《马克思主义和哲学》(1923)、《反批判》(1930)、《〈哥达纲领批判〉导言》(1922)和《第一国际的马克思主义》(1924)。

在柯尔施看来,在工人运动史上,有两个重大问题是无法回避的:一是马克思主义与国家的关系问题,二是马克思主义和哲学的关系问题。列宁成功地解决了第一个问题,写下了专门的研究著作即《国家与革命》,并最终取得了十月革命的胜利。而柯尔施则力图解决第二个问题,这也是《马克思主义和哲学》的核心议题。在这篇论文中,柯尔施从理论与实践的辩证关系入手,集中批判了资产阶级思想家、第二国际正统马克思主义者、修正主义者以及中间派对马克思主义和哲学关系的错误解读,从根本上揭示了马克思主义与哲学的内在关系。在他看来,马克思主义不仅是无产阶级革命运动的思想反映,而且也是黑格尔哲学的继承者。在此基础上,他集中阐发了马克思主义的精神实质,即以理论和实践的辩证统一为核心的、总体性的社会革命理论,并以此为据,将整个马克思主义发展史划分为三个阶段(1843—1848、1848—1900、1900 年以来)。更为重要的是,他系统诠释了马克思恩格斯从早期的哲学批判到后期的政治经济学批判的发展历程,并着重强调了后者在理论和实践上的重要性。这些论点对后来马克思主义的发展产生了重大影响,当然也遭到了巨大非议。

《反批判》是柯尔施对《马克思主义和哲学》一文发表七年来所遭遇到的各种批评意见的反驳,也是这些年他重新思考这一问题的理论结晶。这篇文章包括四个部分:第一部分柯尔施从总体上概述了七年来资产阶级思想家和正统马克思主义者对这篇文章的各种曲解和批判,认为这些批评或曲解始终没有抓住这篇文章的核心,而是纠缠于两个次要问题:一是马克思主义本身的概念问题,二是马克思主义的意识形态问题,进而将最根本的一个问题即马克思主义和哲学的关系问题丢掉了。第二部分主要围绕第一个方面展开论述,重申了马克思主义的内在本质,即一种总体性的社会革命理论,肯定了《马克思主义和哲学》将马克思主义发展史划分为三阶段的正确性，进一步揭示了教条主义马克思主义的内在缺陷，并从正面一一反驳了资产阶级思想家和正统马克思主义对他的批判。第三部分主要围绕第二个方面展开论述。在这里，柯尔施集中批判了列宁的哲学思想。他指出，列宁很想成为一名真正的马克思主义者，但实际上，他仍像他的老师普列汉诺夫一样停留在黑格尔的立场之中，曲解了马克思主义唯物辩证法的科学内涵，割裂了理论与实践、存在与意识的辩证关系，陷入灌输论、知识论和抽象认识论的窠臼之中，为后来的"意识形态专政"埋下了祸根。这些缺陷表明，列宁在根本上并没有真正摆脱资产阶级哲学的影响，也注定了他的哲学不可能满足当时阶级斗争的实际需要。在第四部分，柯尔施进一步批判了第三国际的列宁主义，认为它像第二国际一样完全割裂了意识形态与工人革命实践之间的辩证关系，是一种历史的倒退。在结尾部分，柯尔施澄清了《马克思主义和哲学》中的"意识形态专政"概念与当时俄国在"无产阶级专政"的名义下建立起来的"意识形态专政"的本质区别。他指出：第一，前者是一种无产阶级的专政，而不是凌驾于无产阶级之上的专政；第二，前者是一种阶级的专政，而不是一个政党或党的领袖的专政；第三，前者是一种革命的专政，是向更高阶段的一种过渡，而不是一种虚假的模仿。

在最后两篇文章中，柯尔施分别以《哥达纲领批判》和第一国际为例，从理论和实践双重维度入手，系统阐发了马克思主义的总体性原则，进一步批判了德国社会民主党以及第二国际马克思主义的内在缺陷，总结了无产阶级革命的经验教训。

如果说《马克思主义和哲学》是柯尔施运用马克思主义方法论来分析马克思主义发展史的一次理论尝试，那么，《卡尔·马克思》则是他运用这一方法来研究马克思本人思想发展过程的一次理论结晶。这一著作共包括三个紧密相关的部分，不过，由于版本不同，相关内容存在较大差异，本教材主要以德文版为准，对每一部分内容逐一展开介绍。

第一部分以"资产阶级社会"为题，共包括 8 节，旨在澄清资产阶级与无产阶级社会理论的区别，力图从根本上诠释马克思社会理论的基本原则及其方法论本质。柯尔施指出，资产阶级社会学家的共同缺陷，就是他们观察和分析问题时往往采取非历史主义的态度，把资产阶级社会当成永恒不变的自然制度。因此，他们在理解社会发展时，往往拘泥于资产阶级社会的特殊范畴，把以前的社会形态看成是资产阶级社会的"预备阶段"，而把未来社会视为资产阶级社会的进化发展和历史延续，反对社会革命。柯尔施将这种发展观称为虚假的发展观。他指出，与此相反，在马克思看来，社会科学中的普遍规律只存在于发展之中，即从过去的特殊状况过渡到当前的特殊状况，并从后者再过渡到新的社会形态。就此而言，社会科学中唯一真正的规律就是发展的规律，这是一种彻底的历史主义。也是在此基础上，柯尔施从革命的批判、革命的理论和革命的实践三个方面，系统阐发了马克思的社会发展理论，揭示了它与资产阶级社会理论的本质区别。

第二部分以“政治经济学”为题，共包括 11 节，主要分析了马克思的政治经济学批判及其第二个伟大发现的科学意义。柯尔施首先梳理了政治经济学的发展史，揭示了马克思对古典政治经济学的批判继承关系，并基于文本，将马克思的经济学发展历程划分为几个不同时期。柯尔施指出，在《1844 年经济学哲学手稿》中，马克思虽然批判了资产阶级经济学，但这种批判还停留在哲学层面上，并没有真正克服黑格尔唯心主义的影响。在此之后，通过对黑格尔之后的资产阶级哲学的批判，马克思克服了前期的唯心主义，建立了科学的历史观。在这一立场的指导下，马克思开始将唯物史观与政治经济学嫁接起来，力图建构自己独特的政治经济学批判（《哲学的贫困》）。然而，令人遗憾的是，在经济学内容上，此时马克思并没有真正超越资产阶级经济学，而是站在李嘉图的肩膀之上来反抗蒲鲁东。这一点到了《雇佣劳动与资本》中有所推进。在这一著作中，马克思实现了对资本本质的内在解剖，并力图通过经济范畴来全面阐述作为阶级斗争基础的经济关系。然而，随着 1848 年二月革命的爆发，这种探索不得不中断，这也决定了此时他关于历史唯物主义与政治经济学批判关系的研究还是初步的、不完整的。进入十九世纪五十年代，马克思重新回到这一课题上来，使他的研究迈入一个全新的阶段，从而制定出最完善、最充分的唯物主义理论，即政治经济学批判，它的最终结晶就是《资本论》。就此而言，这一著作不仅是古典经济学最后的伟大成果，而且也是将政治经济学批判与无产阶级革命立场完美结合的历史产物，更是无产阶级革命科学的第一部伟大著作。由此出发，柯尔施以 1850 年为界，将马克思主义经济学划分为两大阶段：前者是一种哲学批判，与其相对应的革命模式是主体逻辑；而后者是一种科学批判，与其相对应的则是一种强调生产力反叛的客观逻辑。接下来，柯尔施分别从商品拜物教、价值规律、剩余价值理论、资产阶级意识形态等方面逐一阐述了《资本论》的科学价值，再次重申了马克思主义作为一种总体革命理论的本真内涵。

第三部分以“历史”为题，共包括 15 节，主要阐述了马克思的第一个伟大发现即唯物史观。在这部分中，柯尔施详细考察了十七世纪至十八世纪英法早期唯物主义者、黑格尔、费尔巴哈等人对马克思恩格斯思想的影响，揭示了他们从唯心主义向唯物主义、革命民主主义向共产主义的转变过程。然后，围绕生产力与生产关系、经济基础与上层建筑概念本身的内涵以及它们之间的相互作用，开辟了 6 个小节专门论述。柯尔施指出，马克思提出的客观机制绝不是一种宿命论或机械论，虽然生产力决定生产关系、经济基础决定上层建筑，但这并不是说它们是自行发展的，相反，必须依靠主体的力量，深入现存制度的基础即物质生产领域，才能从根本上彻底推翻整个社会的经济结构和上层建筑。就此而言，马克思所说的客观公式即“生产力与生产关系的矛盾运动”与《共产党宣言》提出来的主观公式即阶级斗争，并不是对立的，而是同一事物的不同表达。在此基础上，柯尔施将马克思的革命理论划分为两个阶段：1850 年之前，马克思主要强调以主体力量为核心的阶级斗争逻辑，突出直接革命行动的重要性；而在 1850 年之后，马克思则强调以生产力与生产关系矛盾运动为基础的、只是间接地针对革命目标的运动。柯尔施将这种转变概括为从工人主体力量的反叛到生产力的反叛，并着重分析了后者与革命唯意志论、机械决定论的本质区别。在最后一小节中，柯尔施概括了成熟时期的马克思主义的精神实质。他指出，构成马克思主义新科学基础的，既不是黑格尔主义也不是李嘉图的学说，既不是资产阶级哲学也不是资产阶级经济学，而是现实的革命运动与经验。就此而言，成熟时期的唯物主义不再像前期那样是一种“哲学”方法，而是转化为一种严格意义上的经验科学方法。

三、研究前沿

同对卢卡奇、布洛赫等早期西方马克思主义者的研究工作相比，国内学界对柯尔施的研究成果数量更少，且起步也相对更晚，学者们起初一般是在对西方马克思主义的整体研究中顺带开展柯尔施的相关讨论，鲜有专门对其展开分析解读。虽然从二十世纪九十年代起，有部分学者开始讨论柯尔施的相关论著，但是他们涉讨论的主题仅仅局限在柯尔施一些非代表性的立场和范畴上。直到二十一世纪，学者们才开始较为全面地开展研究。近年来，国内的柯尔施研究总体来说保持较为稳定的数量和质量，只是就柯尔施在西方马克思主义发展史中的地位来说，还显得很不相称。不过，整体来看，国内学者的柯尔施研究已经具备了相当的学术深度和学术广度，在三个方面取得了重要成果。

第一，阐释柯尔施以总体观为代表的重要观点。总体性作为柯尔施最具代表性的概念，是学者们普遍聚焦的范畴。有学者认为，柯尔施在《卡尔·马克思》中阐发的马克思主义观是对早期《马克思主义和哲学》的继承和改变，体现在他坚持将马克思主义的哲学批判、政治经济学批判和文化意识形态批判作为一种"总体性理论"。也有学者认为，柯尔施提出的总体性理论，本质上是一种认识论、历史观和革命观，强调了马克思主义理论是唯物主义哲学和历史观的高度统一，主要目的是要维护马克思主义的哲学性，突出哲学在马克思主义中应当起到的重要作用。

第二，阐释柯尔施的马克思主义哲学观。有学者围绕柯尔施针对各种错误理解马克思主义的理论形态展开论述。还有学者提出应当从柯尔施所处的理论背景和时代背景去理解其哲学观，要正确看待马克思主义理论批判性与实证性之间的关系，不能忽略柯尔施在阐述唯物辩证法过程中展现的革命精神，以及在当时社会情境下为推介历史唯物主义进行的重新启蒙的努力。有学者得出结论，提出柯尔施在《卡尔·马克思》一书中把马克思主义理论分为唯物主义的哲学和历史观，柯尔施对马克思政治经济学批判与唯物史观的关系、马克思主义中理论与实践的关系等问题均做出了重要的探索，而认为柯尔施在后期背离了马克思主义的立场是根本错误的。因此，有学者注意到柯尔施对列宁哲学的批评，并指出，应当把握柯尔施的理论出发点，而不能简单将其当作一名反列宁主义者加以对待。

第三，阐释柯尔施在西方马克思主义发展史中的地位和作用。虽然目前学界关于柯尔施在西方马克思主义中的地位问题讨论还较少，但是，由于他在西方马克思主义历史中的重要作用，学界在开展西方马克思主义研究过程中注定无法绕开这个人物。学者们在分析西方马克思主义的过程中，普遍把柯尔施作为重要的理论奠基者，特别是充分重视柯尔施研究之于考察整个西方马克思主义的作用，认为只有通过界定他和其他几位具有代表性的西方马克思主义学者的思想观点，才能够正确评价西方马克思主义之于整个马克思主义的地位。因此，学界对柯尔施的研究不仅仅停留在其理论本身，而且将之融入对整个西方马克思主义的认知上来。

四、文本节选

Marxism and Philosophy

Until very recently, neither bourgeois nor Marxist thinkers had much appreciation of the fact that the relation between Marxism and philosophy might pose a very important theoretical and practical problem. For professors of philosophy, Marxism was at best a rather minor sub-section within the history of nineteenth-century philosophy, dismissed as"The Decay of Hegelianism". But "Marxists" as well tended not to lay great stress on the "philosophical side" of their theory, although for quite different reasons. ...

During that period, therefore, however great the contradictions between Marxist and bourgeois theory were in all other respects, on this one point there was an apparent agreement between the two extremes. Bourgeois professors of philosophy reassured each other that Marxism had no philosophical content of its own—and thought they were saying something important *against* it. Orthodox Marxists also reassured each other that their Marxism by its very nature had nothing to do with philosophy—and thought they were saying something important in favour of it. There was yet a third trend that started from the same basic position; and throughout this period it was the only one to concern itself somewhat more thoroughly with the philosophical side of socialism. It consisted of those "philosophizing socialists" of various kinds who saw their task as that of "supplementing" the Marxist system with ideas from *Kulturphilosophie* or with notion from Kant, Dietzgen or Mach, or other philosophies. Yet precisely because they thought that the Marxist system needed philosophical supplements, they made it quite clear that in their eyes too Marxism in itself lacked philosophical content.

Nowadays it is rather easy to show that this purely *negative* conception of the relation between Marxism and philosophy, which we have shown to be held in apparent unanimity by bourgeois scholars as well as by orthodox Marxists, arose in both cases from a very superficial and incomplete analysis of historical and logical development. However, the conditions under which they both came to this conclusion *in part* diverge greatly, and so I want to describe them separately. It will then be clear that in spite of the great difference between the motives on either side, the two sets of causes do coincide in *one* crucial place. Among *bourgeois scholars* in the second half of the nineteenth century there was a total disregard of Hegel's philosophy, which coincided with a complete incomprehension of the relation of philosophy to reality, and of theory to practice, which constituted the living principle of all philosophy and science in Hegel's time. On the other hand *Marxists* simultaneously tended in exactly the same way increasingly to forget the original meaning of the dialectical principle.

...

Neither the development of philosophical thought *after* Hegel, nor the preceding evolution of philosophy *from* Kant *to* Hegel, can be understood as a mere chain of ideas. Any attempt to understand the full nature and meaning of this whole later period—normally referred to in history books as the epoch of "German idealism"—will fail hopelessly so long as certain connections that are vital for its whole form and course are not registered, or are registered only superficially or belatedly. These are the connections between the "intellectual movement" of the period and the "revolutionary movement" that was contemporary with it.

...

Viewed in this perspective, the revolutionary movement in the realm of ideas, rather than abating and finally ceasing in the 1840s, merely underwent a deep and significant change of character. Instead of making an *exit*, classical German philosophy, the ideological expression of the revolutionary movement of the bourgeoisie, made a *transition* to a new science which henceforward appeared in the history of ideas as the general-expression of the revolutionary movement of the proletariat: the theory of "scientific socialism" first founded and formulated by Marx and Engels in the 1840s. Bourgeois historians of philosophy have hitherto either entirely ignored this essential and necessary relation between German idealism and Marxism, or they have only conceived and presented it inadequately and incoherently. To grasp it properly, it is necessary to abandon the normal abstract and ideological approach of modern historians of philosophy for an approach that need not be specifically Marxist but is just straightforwardly dialectical, in the Hegelian *and* Marxist sense. If we do this, we can see at once not only the interrelations between German idealist philosophy and Marxism, but also their internal necessity. Since the Marxist system is the theoretical expression of the revolutionary movement of the proletariat, and German idealist philosophy is the theoretical expression of the revolutionary movement of the bourgeoisie, they must stand intelligently and historically (i.e. ideologically) in the same relation to each other as the revolutionary movement of the proletariat as a class stands to the revolutionary movement of the bourgeoisie, in the realm of social and political practice. There is one unified historical process of historical development in which an "autonomous" proletarian class movement emerges from the revolutionary movement of the third estate, and the new materialist theory of Marxism "autonomously" confronts bourgeois idealist philosophy. All these processes affect each other reciprocally. The emergence of Marxist theory is, in Hegelian-Marxist terms, only the "other side" of the emergence of the real proletarian movement; it is both sides together that comprise the concrete totality of the historical process.

This dialectical approach enables us to grasp the four different trends we have mentioned—the revolutionary movement of the bourgeoisie, idealist philosophy from Kant to Hegel, the revolutionary class movement of the proletariat, and the materialist philosophy of Marxism—as four moments of a single historical process. This allows us to understand the real nature of the new science, theoretically formulated by Marx and Engels, which forms the general expression of the independent revolutionary movement of the proletariat. This materialist philosophy emerged from the most advanced systems of revolutionary bourgeois idealism; and it is now intelligible why bourgeois histories of philosophy had either to ignore it completely or could only understand its nature in a negative and—literally—inverted sense.

——Karl Korsch, *Marxism and Philosophy*, trans. Fred Halliday, Monthly Review Press, 1970, pp. 29 - 46.

... Hitherto we have only used the dialectical method, which Hegel and Marx introduced into the study of history, to analyse the philosophy of German idealism and the Marxist theory that *emerged* from it. But the only really "materialist and therefore scientific method" (Marx) of pursuing this analysis is to apply it to the *further development* of Marxism up to the present. This means that we must try to understand every change, development and revision of Marxist theory, since its original emergence from the philosophy of German Idealism, as a necessary product of its epoch (Hegel). More precisely, we should seek to understand their determination by the totality of the historico-social process of which they are a general expression (Marx). We will then be able to grasp the real origins of the degeneration of Marxist theory into vulgar-Marxism. We may also discern the meaning of the passionate yet apparently "ideological" efforts of the Marxist theorists of the Third

International today to restore "Marx's genuine doctrine".

If we thus apply Marx's principle of dialectical materialism to the whole history of Marxism, we can distinguish three major stages of development through which Marxist theory has passed *since* its birth—inevitably so in the context of the concrete social development of this epoch. The first phase begins around 1843, and corresponds in the history of ideas to the *Critique of Hegel's Philosophy of Right*. It ends with the Revolution of 1848—corresponding to the *Communist Manifesto*. The second phase begins with the bloody suppression of the Parisian proletariat in the battle of June 1848 and the resultant crushing of all the working class's organizations and dreams of emancipation "in a period of feverish industrial activity, moral degeneration and political reaction", as Marx masterfully describes it in his *Inaugural Address* of 1864. We are not concerned here with the social history of the working-class as a whole, but only with the internal development of Marxist theory in its relation to the general class history of the proletariat. Hence the second period may be said to last approximately to the end of the century, leaving out all the less important divisions (the foundation and collapse of the First International; the interlude of the Commune; the struggle between Marxists and Lassalleaner; the Anti-socialist laws in Germany; trade unions; the founding of the Second International). The third phase extends from the start of this century to the present and into an indefinite future.

Arranged in this way, the historical development of Marxist theory presents the following picture. The first manifestation of it naturally remained essentially unchanged in the minds of Marx and Engels themselves throughout the later period, although in their *writings* it did not stay entirely unaltered. In spite of all their denials of philosophy, this first version of the theory is permeated through and through with philosophical thought. It is a theory of *social development* seen and comprehended as a living totality; or, more precisely, it is a theory of *social revolution* comprehended and practised as a living totality. At this stage there is no question whatever of dividing the economic, political and intellectual moments of this totality into separate branches of knowledge, even while every concrete peculiarity of each separate moment is comprehended analysed and criticized with historical fidelity. Of course, it is not only economics, politics and ideology, but also the historical process and conscious social action that continue to make up the living unity of "revolutionary practice" (*Theses on Feuerbach*). The best example of this early and youthful form of Marxist theory as the theory of social revolution is obviously the *Communist Manifesto*.

...

... A dialectical conception comprehends every form without exception in terms of the flow of this movement, and it necessarily follows from it that Marx's and Engels's theory of social revolution inevitably underwent considerable changes in the course of its further development. When Marx in 1864 drafted the *Inaugural Address* and the *Statutes of the First International*, he was perfectly conscious of the fact that "time was needed for the reawakened movement to permit the old audacity of language". This is of course true not only for language but for all the other components of the theory of the movement. Therefore the scientific socialism of the *Capital* of 1867 - 1894 and the other later writings of Marx and Engels represent an expression of the general theory of Marxism, which is in many ways a different and more developed one than that of the direct revolutionary communism of the *Manifesto* of 1847 - 1848—or for that matter, *The Poverty of Philosophy*, *The Class Struggles in France* and *The Eighteenth Brumaire*. Nevertheless, the central characteristic of Marxist theory remains essentially unaltered even in the later writings of Marx and Engels. For in its later version, as scientific socialism, the Marxism of Marx and Engels remains the inclusive whole of a theory of social revolution. The difference is only that in the later phase the various components of this whole, its economic, political and ideological elements, scientific theory and social practice, are further separated out. We can use an expression of Marx's and say that the umbilical cord of its natural combination has been broken. In Marx and Engels, however, this never produces a multiplicity of independent elements instead of the whole. It is merely that another combination of the components of the system emerges developed with greater scientific precision and built on the infrastructure of the critique of political economy. In the writings of its creators, the Marxist system itself never dissolves into a sum of separate branches of knowledge, in spite of a practical and outward employment of its results that suggests such a conclusion. For example, many bourgeois interpreters of Marx and some later Marxists thought they were able to distinguish between the historical and the theoretico-economic material in Marx's major work *Capital*; but all they proved by this is that they understood nothing of the real method of Marx's critique of political economy. For it is one of the essential signs of his dialectical materialist method that this distinction does not exist for it; it is indeed precisely a theoretical comprehension of history. Moreover, the unbreakable interconnection of theory and practice, which formed the most characteristic sign of the first communist version of Marx's materialism, was in no way abolished in the later form of his system. ...

... All these deformations and a row of other less important ones were inflicted on Marxism by its epigones in the second phase of its development, and they can be summarized in one all-inclusive formulation: a unified general theory of social revolution was changed into criticisms of the bourgeois economic order, of the bourgeois State, of the bourgeois system of education, of bourgeois religion, art, science and culture. These criticisms no longer necessarily develop by their very nature into revolutionary practice; they can equally well develop, into all kinds of attempts at *reform*, which fundamentally remain within the limits of bourgeois society and the bourgeois State, and in actual practice usually did so. ... Eventually, at the start of the twentieth century, the first signs of the approaching storm heralded a new period of conflicts and revolutionary battles, and thereby led to the decisive crisis of Marxism in which we still find ourselves today.

...

... Therewith purely theoretical orthodox Marxism—till the outbreak of the World War the officially established version of Marxism in the Second International—collapsed completely and disintegrated. This was, of course, an inevitable result of its long internal decay. It is in this epoch that we can see in many countries the beginnings of *third period of development*, above all represented by Russian Marxists, and often described by its major representatives as a "restoration" of Marxism.

This transformation and development of Marxist theory has been effected under the peculiar ideological guise of a return to the pure teaching of original or true Marxism. Yet it is easy to understand both the reasons for this guise and the real character of the process which is concealed by it. What theoreticians like Rosa Luxemburg in Germany and Lenin in Russia have done, and are doing, in the field of Marxist theory is to liberate it from the inhibiting traditions of the Social Democracy of the second period. They thereby answer the practical needs of the new revolutionary stage of proletarian class struggle, for these traditions weighed "like a nightmare" on the brain of the working masses whose objectively revolutionary socio-economic position no longer corresponded to these evolutionary doctrines. The apparent revival of original Marxist theory in the Third International is simply a result of the fact that in a new revolutionary period not only the workers' movement itself, but the theoretical conceptions of communists which express it, must assume an explicitly revolutionary form. This is why large sections of the Marxist system, which seemed virtually forgotten in the final decades of the nineteenth century, have now come to life again. It also explains why the leader of the Russian Revolution could write a book a few months before October in which he stated that his aim was "in the first place to *restore* the correct Marxist theory of the State." Events themselves placed the question of the dictatorship of the proletariat on the agenda as a practical problem. When Lenin placed the same question theoretically on the agenda at a decisive moment, this was an early indication that the internal connection of theory and practice within revolutionary Marxism had been consciously re-established.

——Karl Korsch, *Marxism and Philosophy*, trans. Fred Halliday, Monthly Review Press, 1970, pp.55 - 68.

... German idealism from Kant to Hegel did not cease to be philosophical when it affirmed this universal role (which is anyway what is colloquially thought to be the essence of *any* philosophy). Similarly it is incorrect to say that Marx's materialist theory is no longer philosophical merely because it has an aim that is not simply theoretical but is also a practical and revolutionary goal. On the contrary, the dialectical materialism of Marx and Engels is by its very nature a philosophy through and through, as formulated in the eleventh thesis on Feuerbach and in other published and unpublished writings of the period. It is a revolutionary philosophy whose task is to participate in the revolutionary struggles waged in all spheres of society against the whole of the existing order, by fighting in one specific area—philosophy. Eventually, it aims at the concrete abolition of philosophy as part of the abolition of bourgeois social reality as a whole, of which it is an ideal component. In Marx's words: "Philosophy cannot be abolished without being realized." Thus just when Marx and Engels were progressing from Hegel's dialectical idealism to dialectical materialism, it is clear that the abolition of philosophy did not mean for them its simple rejection. Even when their later positions are under consideration, it is essential to take it as a constant starting point that

Marx and Engels were dialecticians before they were materialists. The sense of their materialism is distorted in a disastrous and irreparable manner if one forgets that Marxist materialism was dialectical from the very beginning. It always remained a historical and dialectical materialism, in contrast to Feuerbach's abstract-scientific materialism and all other abstract materialisms, whether earlier or later, bourgeois or vulgar-Marxist. In other words, it was a materialism whose theory comprehended the totality of society and history, and whose practice overthrew it. It was therefore possible for philosophy to become a less central component of the socio-historical process for Marx and Engels, in the course of their development of materialism, than it had seemed at the start; this did in fact occur. But no really dialectical materialist conception of history (certainly not that of Marx and Engels) could cease to regard philosophical ideology, or ideology in general, as a material component of general socio-historical reality—that is, a real part which had to be grasped in materialist theory and overthrown by materialist practice.

...

Given this situation, any theoretical attempt to restore what Marx regarded as the only scientific, dialectical materialist conception and treatment of *ideological* realities, inevitably encounters even greater theoretical obstacles than an attempt to restore the correct Marxist theory of the State. The distortion of Marxism by the epigones in the question of the *state* and *politics* merely consisted in the fact that the most prominent theoreticians of the Second International never dealt concretely enough with the most vital political problems of the revolutionary transition. However, they at least agreed in abstract, and emphasized strongly in their long struggles against anarchists and syndicalists that, for materialism, not only the economic structure of society, which underlay all other socio-historical phenomena, but also the juridical and political superstructure of Law and the State were *realities*. Consequently, they could not be ignored or dismissed in an anarcho-syndicalist fashion: they had to be overthrown in reality by a political revolution. In spite of this, many *vulgar-marxists* to this day have never, even in theory, admitted that intellectual life and forms of social consciousness are comparable realities. Quoting certain statements by Marx and especially Engels they simply explain away the *intellectual* (*ideological*) *structures of society* as a mere *pseudo-reality* which only exists in the minds of ideologues—as error, imagination and illusion, devoid of a genuine object. At any rate, this is supposed to be true for all the so-called "higher" ideologies. For this conception, political and legal representatives may have an ideological and unreal character, but they are at least related to something real—the institutions of Law and the State, which comprise the superstructure of the society in question. On the other hand, the "higher" ideological representations (men's religions, aesthetic and philosophical conceptions) correspond to no real object. This can be formulated concisely, with only a slight caricature, by saying that for vulgar-Marxism there are *three degrees of reality*: (1) the economy, which in the last instance is the only objective and totally non-ideological reality; (2) Law and the State, which are already somewhat less real because clad in ideology, and (3) pure ideology which is objectless and totally unreal ("pure rubbish").

To restore a genuine dialectically materialist conception of intellectual reality, it is first necessary to make a few mainly terminological points. The key problem to settle here is how in general to approach the relationship of consciousness to its object. Terminologically, it must be said that it never occurred to Marx and Engels to describe social consciousness and intellectual life merely as ideology. Ideology is only a false consciousness, in particular one that mistakenly attributes an autonomous character to a partial phenomena of social life. Legal and political representations which conceive Law and the State to be independent forces above society are cases in point. In the passage where Marx is most precise about his terminology, he says explicitly that within the complex of material relations that Hegel called civil society, the social relations of production—the economic structure of society—forms the real foundation on which arise juridical and political superstructures and to which determinate forms of social consciousness correspond. In particular, these forms of social consciousness, which are no less real than Law and the State, include commodity fetishism, the concept of value, and other economic representations derived from them. Marx and Engels analysed these in their critique of political economy. What is strikingly characteristic of their treatment is that they never refer to this basic economic ideology of bourgeois society as an ideology. In their terminology only the legal, political, religious, aesthetic or philosophical forms of consciousness are ideological. Even these need not be so in all situations, but become so only under specific conditions which have already been stated. The special position now allotted to forms of economic consciousness marks the new conception of philosophy which distinguishes the fully matured dialectical materialism of the later period from its undeveloped earlier version. The theoretical and practical criticisms of philosophy is henceforward relegated to the second, third, fourth or even last but one place in their critique of society. The "critical philosophy" which the Marx of the *Deutsch Französische Jahrbücher* saw as his essential task became a more radical critique of society, which went to the roots of it through a critique of political economy. ... Consequently the critique of political economy is theoretically and practically the first priority. Yet even this deeper and more radical version of Marx's revolutionary critique of society never ceases to be a critique of the *whole* of bourgeois society and so of *all* its forms of consciousness. It may seem as if Marx and Engels were later to criticize philosophy only in an occasional and haphazard manner. In fact, far from neglecting the subject, they actually developed their critique of it in a more profound and radical direction. ...

——Karl Korsch, *Marxism and Philosophy*, trans. Fred Halliday, Monthly Review Press, 1970, pp. 75 – 86.

The Fetishism of Commodities

Marx had, however, emphasized as early as this, the real economic and social facts underlying that Hegelian philosophical term. Much more clearly than Feuerbach and the other philosophizing Hegelians he had recognized that the various forms in which that philosophical category enters into present-day society—as "property, capital, money, wage-labour, etc." are by no means a kind of self-created "idealistic figment of our imagination." On the contrary, all those "alienated forms" actually exist in present society as "very practical, very material things." For example, the fact that one of the worst cases of that "self-alienation of humanity" appears in present-day bourgeois society as the contrast of the *haves* and the *have-nots* is by no means the outcome of a mere conceptual or spiritual process. "Not *having* is the most desperate *spiritualism*, an entire negation of the reality of the human being, a very positive *having*, a having of hunger, of cold, of sickness, of crimes, of debasement, of imbecility, of all forms of inhumanity and abnormality." And in striking contrast to the "idealistic" dialectics of Hegel who had endeavoured to annihilate the existing self-alienation of man in society merely by an imaginary philosophical annihilation of the objective form, in which it is reflected within the human mind, Marx denounced the utter insufficiency of a mere effort of thought to handle the real forms of that self-alienation which exist in the present-day bourgeois order of society and of which the "alienated" concepts of the bourgeois economists are only an outward expression. It is, for this purpose, above all necessary to abolish, by the practical effort of a social act, its underlying real conditions. Marx had also called by name the social force which was to perform that revolutionary action: "the communist workers in the workshops of Manchester and Lyons" and the "associations" founded by them.

The later Marxian criticism of the "fetish-character" inherent in the commodity "labour-power" and, indeed, in all "economic" categories differs from that earlier criticism of the economic "self-alienation" mainly by its scientific and no more philosophical form.

Modern capitalistic production both historically and theoretically rests on the separation of the real producers from their material means of production. Thus it is but a juridical illusion that the workers either as individuals or as members of an amalgamated group of labour-power owners freely dispose of their property. The common assumptions underlying the "fetishistic" concept of an individual, and even of a collective, "bargaining" with regard to the commodity "labour power" are still derived entirely from the dreamland of the free and equal individuals united within a self-governed society. The propertyless wage labourers selling through a "free labour contract," their individual labour powers for a certain time to a capitalistic "entrepreneur" are, as a class, from the outset and for ever a common property of the possessing class which alone has the real means of labour at its disposal.

It is, therefore, only one part of the truth that was revealed by Marx in the *Communist Manifesto* when he said that the bourgeoisie had "resolved personal worth into exchange value," and thus replaced the veiled forms of exploitation applied by the "pious, chivalrous, ecstatic, and sentimental middle ages" by an altogether *unveiled exploitation*. The bourgeoisie replaced an exploitation embroidered with religious and political illusion, by a new and more refined system of concealed exploitation. Whereas in medieval society even the utterly material tasks of production were performed under the spiritual disguise of "faith" and of an "allegiance" due by the "servant" to his "master," in the new era of "Free Trade," conversely, the continuing exploitation and oppression of the labourers is hidden under the pretext of the "economic necessities of production." The scientific method of concealing this state of affairs is called *Political Economy*.

From the critical exposure of the fetishism inherent in the commodity "labour-power" there was but one step to the discovery of the most general form of the "economic" delusion appearing in the "commodity" itself. Just as the classical economists had derived all other terms of their science from the "value" appearing in the exchange of commodities, so Marx now traced back the delusive character of all other economic categories to the fetish-character of the "commodity." Though even now that most obvious and direct form of the "self-alienation of the human being" which occurs in the relation between wage-labour and capital, keeps its decisive importance for the practical attack on the existing order of society, the fetishism of the *commodity* labour-power is at this stage for theoretical purposes regarded as a mere derivative form of the more general fetishism which is contained in *commodity* itself.

Thus the Marxian criticism of the existing order is transformed from a particular attack on the class character into a universal attack on the fundamental deficiency of the capitalistic mode of production and the structure of society based upon it. By revealing *all* economic categories to be mere fragments of one great fetish did Marx ultimately transcend all preceding forms and phases of economic and social theory. Political Economy itself had in its later development rectified such primitive misconceptions as that by which the adherents of the so-called "monetary system" had regarded *money*, in the form of gold and silver, as a product of nature, endowed with some peculiar social qualities, or the physiocratic illusion that *rent* grows out of the earth, not out of society. It had at its highest point of development theoretically interpreted "*interest*" and "*rent*" as mere fractions of the industrial "profit."

However, even the most advanced classical economists remained under the spell of that same fetish which they had already practically dissolved by their own theoretical analysis, or fell back into it, because they had never succeeded in extending their critical analysis to that general fundamental form which appears in the *value-form* of the labour products and in the form of commodity itself. The great theoretical art of classical Political Economy here met its his historical barrier. "The value form of the labour product is the most abstract but also the most general form of the bourgeois mode of production which is thereby historically characterized as a particular kind of social production. By misconceiving it as an eternal and natural form, he will overlook the particular character of the value form and thus also that of the commodity form, which appears further developed as money form, capital form, etc." Marx was the first to represent that fundamental character of the bourgeois mode of production as the particular historical stage of material production, whose characteristic social form is reflected reversedly, in a "fetishistic" manner, both in the practical concepts of the ordinary man of business and in the scientific reflection of that "normal" bourgeois consciousness — Political Economy. Thus the theoretical exposure of "the fetish character of the commodity and its secret" is not only the kernel of the Marxian *Critique of Political Economy*, but, at the same time the quintessence of the economic theory of *Capital* and the most explicit and most exact definition of the theoretical and historical standpoint of the whole materialistic science of society.

The theoretical disclosure of the fetishistic appearance of commodity production has a tremendous importance for the practical struggle carried on by those who are oppressed in present-day society and who as a class are rebelling against this oppression. In view of the "good intentions" and scrap of paper proclamations constantly repeated by the official spokesmen of present-day economics and politics that "*the worker shall no more be regarded as being a mere article of commerce*," the very statement of the existing fact that under present conditions *the worker is and remains an article of commerce*, becomes an open rebellion against the paramount interest of the ruling class in keeping intact both the fetishistic disguise and the underlying actual conditions. It forcibly re-establishes the responsibility of the ruling bourgeois class for all the waste and hideousness which by the "fetishistic" device of bourgeois economics had been shifted from the realm of human action to the so-called immutable, nature-ordained relations between things. For this reason alone, any theoretical tendency aiming at an unbiassed criticism of the prevailing economic categories, and the corresponding practical tendency to change the social system of which they are an ideological expression, is opposed from the outset by the overwhelming power of the classes privileged by the present social order and interested in its maintenance. The ultimate destruction of capitalistic commodity-fetishism by a direct social organization of labour, becomes the task of the revolutionary proletarian class struggle. A theoretical expression of this class struggle and, at the same time, one of its tools, is the revolutionary *Critique of Political Economy*.

——Karl Korsch, *Karl Marx*, Russell and Russell, 1963, pp.131 - 137.

Conclusions

Marx's most important contributions to social research are that he:

(1) related all phenomena of the life process of society to economics;

(2) conceived of economics itself as a social science;

(3) defined all social phenomena historically and, indeed, as a revolutionary process which results from the development of the material forces of production and is realized by the struggle of the social classes.

These three general results of the Marxian science of society include as particularly important partial results:

(4) an exact definition of the relation between economics and politics;

(5) a reduction of all phenomena of the so-called "mind" to definite forms of social consciousness pertaining to a definite historical epoch.

A detailed analysis of topics (4) and (5) is beyond the scope of this work.

To arrive at these results, Marx used a conceptual framework of his own, which he composed largely of philosophical elements reshaped from Hegel, but into which he absorbed as well all the new tendencies of the social knowledge of his time. In conscious opposition to Hegel's idealistic system, he called this new set of ideas his *materialism*. As against the various other materialism tenets, he described it more precisely by the addition of one or more such adjectives as historical, dialectical, critical, revolutionary, scientific, or proletarian.

Historical materialism is in its main tendency no longer a philosophical, but rather an empirical and scientific, method. It contains the premises for a real solution of the task which naturalistic materialism and positivism had only apparently solved by an eclectic application to the science of society of the highly specialized methods which, through centuries of study, the natural scientists had invented and meticulously adapted to their particular fields of investigation. Instead of transferring those scientific methods ready-made to the new sphere of society, Marx developed specific methods of social research, a *Novum Organum* which would permit the investigator in this newly opened field to penetrate the "*eidola*" standing in the way of unbiassed research, and to determine "with the precision of natural science" the real subject-matter hidden behind an interminable confusion of "ideological" disguises. This is the kernel of Marxian materialism.

Just as positivism could not move with freedom in the new field of social science, but remained tied to the specific concepts and methods of natural science, so Marx's historical materialism has not entirely freed itself from the spell of Hegel's philosophical method which in its day overshadowed all contemporary thought. This was not a materialistic science of society which had developed on its own basis. Rather it was a materialistic theory that had just emerged from idealistic philosophy; a theory, therefore, which still showed in its contents, its methods, and its terminology the birthmarks of the old Hegelian philosophy from whose womb it sprang. All these imperfections were unavoidable under the circumstances out of which Marx's materialistic social research arose. With all these faults, it was far and away in advance of the other contemporary schools of social thought. It remains superior to all other social theories even now, in spite of the comparatively negligible progress which Marxists have in the meantime made in the formal development of the methods discovered by Marx and Engels. In a partly philosophical form, it has yet achieved a great number of important scientific results which hold good to this day.

Through Hegel, the new proletarian materialism linked itself to the sum of bourgeois social thought of the preceding historical period. It did so in the same antagonistic manner in which, during the same period, the historical movement of the bourgeoisie was continued by the new revolutionary movement of the proletarian class.

The philosophical idealism of Hegel corresponded to a further advanced stage of the material development of society than did the old bourgeois materialism. Hegel had embodied in his "idealistic" system a greater number of elements that could be used by the new historical materialism. He had also presented them in a more highly developed form than had any of thc 18th century materialists. We have seen in a former chapter how loosely Hegel's doctrine of "civil society" was connected with the whole of his idealistic system. Similarly, many other sections of Hegel's system can without difficulty be read materialistically instead of idealistically.

The fact that the new proletarian theory had incorporated in its methods and contents some important results of Hegel's philosophy, did not in any way infer an obligation. Marx and Engels disrupted the elements which in Hegel had been bound up in an idealistic system. They welded together the parts which they found suitable for their purpose, with elements taken from other sources into the new whole of a materialistic science.

Hegel had been in his time an encyclopaedic thinker, a genius at annexation, a "philosopher" hungry both for theory and reality, who brought within the scope of his system an incomparably greater field of experience than anyone since Aristotle. The mass of thought-material stored up in Hegel's philosophy is, nevertheless, only one of the tributaries which Marx and Engels directed into the broad stream of their new materialistic doctrine of society. They took from all sides. From the bourgeois historians of the French Restoration they took the historical importance of class and class struggle; from Ricardo, the conflicting economic interests of the social classes; from Proudhon, the description of the modern proletariat as the only revolutionary class; from the feudal and Christian assailants of the new political order born of the 18th century revolution, the ruthless unmasking of the liberal ideas of the bourgeoisie, the piercing invective full of hatred. Their ingenuous dissection of the unsolvable antagonisms of the modern mode of production they took from the petty-bourgeoisie socialism of Sismondi; the accents of humanism perceptible even in their later materialistic writings from earlier companions among the left Hegelians, especially from Feuerbach; the relevance of politics to the struggle of the working class from the contemporary labour parties, French Social Democrats and English Chartists; the doctrine of the revolutionary dictatorship from the French Convention, and from Blanqui and his followers. Finally, they took from Saint-Simon, Fourier, and Owen the ultimate goal of all socialism and communism, the complete overthrow of existing capitalistic society, abolition of all classes and class oppositions, and transformation of the political State into a mere management of production. These were the annexations they had made from the beginning. During the further development of their theory, they made others, adopting, for instance, at one stroke the results of that first age of discovery in primaeval research which began early in the 19th century and concluded with Morgan.

Just as Marx's new science is in its form above all a strictly empirical investigation and critique of society, so in its content it is, above all, economic research. Marx, who had begun his materialistic investigation of society as a critic of religion, of philosophy, of politics, and of law, later concentrated more and more upon economics. He did not thereby narrow down the realm of his all-comprehensive social science. The critique of Political Economy as embodied in *Capital* deals with the State and the law, and with such "higher," i.e., still more ideological, social phenomena as philosophy, art, and religion only in occasional remarks which light up, in sudden flashes, extensive fields of social activity; yet it remains a materialistic investigation into *the whole of existing bourgeois society*. It proceeds methodically from the view that when we have examined the bourgeois mode of production and its historical changes we have thereby examined everything of the structure and development of present-day society which can be the subject-matter of a strictly empirical science. In this sense, Marx's materialistic social science is not sociology, but economics.

For the other branches of the so-called social science there remains then, according to the materialistic principle of Marxism, a scale of phenomena which become in proportion to their increasing distance from the economic foundation, less and less accessible to a strictly scientific investigation, less and less "material," more and more "ideological," and which, finally, cannot be treated in a theoretical manner at all, but only critically and in the closest connection with the practical tasks of the revolutionary class war.

The last foundation of the new Marxian science is neither Hegel nor Ricardo, neither bourgeois philosophy nor bourgeois economy. Marx's materialistic investigation into the movement of modern bourgeois society received its decisive impulses from the reality of historical development, that is, from the great bourgeois revolutions of the 17th and 18th centuries and from the historical movement of the 19th century, the revolutionary rise of the proletarian class. A genetic presentation would show with what precision and at the same time with what weight every new phase of the real history of society, every new experience of the proletarian class struggle, is reflected in each new turn of the theoretical development of Marx's doctrine. This close connection between the real history of society and Marx's materialistic science does not rest upon a mere passive reflection of reality in theory. What Marx and Engels gained in theoretical views and concepts from their study of the real history of the proletarian movement, they gave back immediately in the form of direct participation in the class conflicts of their time and of powerful impulses which historically continue to enlarge and stimulate the proletarian movement up to the present day.

To be instrumental in the historical movement of our time is the great purpose of Marx. This revolutionary principle which shapes all his later theoretical work he had formulated in his earliest youth when he concluded his violent criticism of Feuerbach's politically insufficient materialistic philosophy with a last mighty hammer stroke: "Philosophers have only *interpreted* the world differently; the important thing, however, is to *change it*."

——Karl Korsch, *Karl Marx*, Russell and Russell, 1963, pp. 230 - 235.

五、观点解读

1. 马克思主义和哲学的关系问题涉及马克思主义的精神实质

在柯尔施看来，截至二十世纪早期，不论是资产阶级思想家还是马克思主义理论家，始终没有澄清一个核心问题，即马克思主义和哲学（特别是黑格尔哲学）的关系问题。前者始终将马克思主义当作黑格尔哲学的余波不予考虑，否认马克思主义存在任何哲学内容；第二国际马克思主义者则反复强调马克思主义是一种实证科学，否认它与哲学之间存在任何联系；而其他理论家则主张用康德、狄慈根、马赫等人的思想来补充马克思主义，实际上，这也就等于否认了马克思主义的哲学性质。虽然他们的立场是根本对立的，但在这一问题上出奇地一致，即都否认马克思主义和哲学之间存在任何关系。在柯尔施看来，他们之所以会得出这种结论，根本原因在于他们都不理解哲学与现实、理论与实践之间的辩证关系。哲学的演变绝不是观念自我运动的结果，而是现实运动的产物，只有全面理解思想发展与革命运动的辩证法，才能真正理解马克思主义与黑格尔哲学之间的内在关系。作为资产阶级革命时期的思想反映，黑格尔哲学体现资产阶级的进步性和革命性，因此，当资产阶级处于上升时期时，黑格尔哲学无疑顺应了时代潮流，产生了广泛影响。然而，到了十九世纪中叶，资产阶级全面走向反动，黑格尔哲学自然不再适应时代发展的需要，最终只能走向没落，这是它作为一种意识形态反映的必然宿命。但这并不是说，它彻底退场了，而是在无产阶级革命的熔炉中得到了重生，转变为一种新的科学，这也就是由马克思恩格斯在十九世纪四十年代发现和系统阐述的“科学社会主义”理论。因此，要想准确理解马克思主义与哲学的关系，必须进入历史过程之中，将资产阶级的革命运动、从康德到黑格尔的唯心主义哲学、无产阶级的革命运动、马克思主义的唯物主义哲学当成历史过程的四种因素来把握。就此而言，马克思主义不仅是无产阶级革命运动的思想反映，而且也是资产阶级哲学的继承者，正是在后者（特别是黑格尔哲学）的胎胞中，马克思主义才一步一步地成长起来。因此，绝不能像资产阶级思想家或第二国际马克思主义者那样，彻底否认马克思主义的哲学性质，恰恰相反，在马克思恩格斯思想发展的早期形态中，到处都渗透着哲学，否认这一点，就无法准确理解马克思主义的精神实质。

2. 马克思主义是一种总体性的社会革命理论

在柯尔施看来，马克思主义在本质上是一种总体性的社会革命理论，这不仅是把握马克思主义和哲学关系的关键，而且也是理解马克思主义发展史的根本原则。由此出发，他将马克思主义发展史划分为三个重要阶段。第一阶段是从1843—1848年，起于《黑格尔法哲学批判》，结束于《共产党宣言》。这一时期，马克思主义完全表现为一种活的总体性的社会革命理论，它并没有被分解为经济的、政治的和精神的各种因素或各个知识的分支，即使在分门别类地对待各个分支时，仍然保持着整体性。不论是经济、政治、意识形态，还是社会行动，都共同构成了"革命的实践"的活的统一体。第二阶段始于1848年的六月起义，终于1900年。这一时期虽然经历了第一国际的建立和解散、巴黎公社、马克思主义和拉萨尔派之间的斗争、第二国际的建立等一系列重大事件，但总的来说，工人运动处于低潮期，因此，马克思恩格斯的社会革命理论不可避免地经历了重大变化。相较于1848年之前的著作，这一时期，马克思恩格斯的唯物主义理论更加趋于成熟，但它的核心特征即作为一种总体性的革命理论却没有丝毫改变，区别只是在于，在后一阶段，作为总体组成部分的经济、政治、意识形态因素逐渐与社会实践分离开来，但并没有产生一种代替总体的各个分支，相反，是在政治经济学批判的基础上得到了重新整合。然而，到了第二国际那里，这种总体性的革命理论被肢解了：一方面，理论与实践的统一被分裂了，另一方面，政治、经济、意识形态等因素也从总体中被分离了出来，成为一种碎片化的存在；结果，作为一种总体性的革命理论，被分解为对资产阶级经济秩序、资产阶级国家、资产阶级教育制度、资产阶级宗教、艺术和文化的批判。它们与无产阶级革命实践不再有任何关联，最终导致了马克思主义的危机。第三阶段是从1900年开始，延续到一个不确定的未来。在这一阶段，卢森堡和列宁从新的革命实践出发，力图将马克思主义从第二国际的封闭传统中解放出来，恢复了以理论和实践的统一为核心特征的马克思主义革命理论，因而适应了新时期无产阶级革命运动的实践需要，开启了马克思主义的新阶段。

3. 从哲学批判到政治经济学批判：总体革命理论的深化

柯尔施指出，马克思主义在本质上是一种总体性的社会革命理论，这一点不论在前期还是后期都没有丝毫的改变，但在表现形式上却出现了重大变化，即从前期的哲学批判转变为后期的政治经济学批判。柯尔施认为，要理解这一转变，必须澄清马克思"消灭哲学"思想的真实内涵。他指出，在早期，马克思恩格斯的确是从黑格尔哲学的胎胞中孕育出来的，就此而言，"马克思和恩格斯的辩证唯物主义按其基本性质来说，是彻头彻尾的哲学"。不过，这种哲学在本性上并不是一种单纯的思想批判，而是一种以颠覆整个资产阶级社会为根本目标的总体性革命，只有实现了后者，才能从根本上彻底扬弃哲学，这也就是马克思"不在现实中实现哲学，就不能消灭哲学"命题的真实内涵。但在十九世纪五十年代之后，柯尔施指出，随着马克思经济学研究的逐步深化，他在这一问题上获得了新的突破，从而打开了一片新天地。

如果说在早期，马克思更多地关注作为意识形态的哲学与现实的关系问题，那么，到了后期，这一问题则被拓展为整个精神生活与社会存在的关系问题。柯尔施指出，在1859年的《政治经济学批判。第一分册》的"序言"中，马克思明确区分了两种不同的社会意识：一是意识形态，包括法律、政治、宗教、艺术或哲学等多种形式；二是社会意识形式，包括商品拜物教、价值观念以及从它们派生出来的其他范畴，它们的真实性完全不亚于法和国家，并同后者一起，共同构成了整个社会的有机组成部分。这时，马克思才意识到，要想实现对资产阶级社会的整体批判，单纯停留在哲学层面还是不够的，毕竟后者作为一种意识形态，只是社会意识的一部分，要完成这一点，就必须将前期的哲学批判拓展为对整个社会意识的批判，而这恰恰就是政治经济学批判的出场语境。因此，在后期，马克思的重心不再像前期那样集中于哲学批判，而是转化为对经济学意识形式的理论和实践批判，即通过对资本主义物质生产关系的批判，来引出意识形式批判，从而实现对资产阶级社会的总体性批判。就此而言，政治经济学批判在本质上始终是对资产阶级社会及其全部意识形式的整体批判。基于此，柯尔施指出，从前期的哲学批判到后期政治经济学批判的转变，绝不是无关紧要的，而是马克思主义革命理论的系统深化和发展，只是到了这时，马克思的唯物主义理论才彻底成熟，才真正转化为一种更加彻底的社会批判；也只有立足于后者，才能全面揭示马克思唯物主义理论的精神实质。基于此，柯尔施强调，与前期的哲学批判相比，政治经济学批判不论在理论上还是实践上始终都是第一位的。

在此基础上，柯尔施进一步批判了庸俗马克思主义。他指出，就意识与存在的关系而言，庸俗马克思主义犯了两重错误：第一，完全扭曲了马克思的社会意识理论。在前者那里，社会现实被划分为三个等级：(1)经济，它被视为是整个社会中唯一客观的和非观念性的存在；(2)法和国家，它们是一种带有观念形态的、较不现实的存在；(3)纯粹意识形态，这是一种完全无用的、单纯观念性的存在。在这种解读中，庸俗马克思主义完全把社会意识混同于意识形态，忽视了其他社会意识形式的存在，恰恰阉割了政治经济学批判的革命意义。第二，忽视了意识形态的现实功能。庸俗马克思主义完全把意识形态当作一种幻象、错误或无用之物，似乎它只存在于空想家的头脑中，只要经过观念的变革就可以消除了。实际上，这是对马克思恩格斯意识形态理论的极大扭曲。柯尔施指出，马克思恩格斯的确将意识形态界定为一种虚假的观念体系，但这绝不是说意识形态就是一种"无用之物"，相反，它在人们的社会生活中起到极为重要的作用，是人们现实生活的重要组成部分。就此而言，要真正消除资产阶级意识形态，单纯依靠观念领域的变革是行不通的，必须彻底消除资产阶级意识形态得以存在的社会基础，即通过无产阶级革命彻底推翻资产阶级社会本身，才能从根本上彻底消灭资产阶级意识形态，这一点对经济意识形式同样适用。这也告诫马克思主义者们，在推翻资产阶级国家政权，建立无产阶级专政之后，也必须高度重视意识形态的现实功能，强化无产阶级的意识形态专政，绝不能像庸俗马克思主义那样，仅仅将其视为一种无用之物，否则的话，必将会对无产阶级政权产生不可估量的负面影响。

4. 商品拜物教批判是马克思政治经济学批判的核心

在《马克思主义和哲学》中，柯尔施初步分析了政治经济学批判在马克思思想发展中的历史地位，但由于主题和篇幅限制，这种探讨未能全面展开。而《卡尔·马克思》则弥补了这一缺憾，其中《商品的拜物教性质》一节就是这种思考的集中体现。柯尔施指出，在马克思看来，产品之所以能够取得价值量的形式，能够与别的商品相互交换，是由于生产这种物的劳动是一种无差别的社会劳动，后者是人类历史发展的特定产物，与产品的物理性质没有任何直接联系。然而，资产阶级及其代言人却天真地以为，这种社会劳动的形式就是劳动产品本身具有的物的属性，将原本作为社会发展的特定产物的社会关系，看作物本身固有的自然属性，结果，原本作为人类劳动产物的物，呈现为某种富有生命的、彼此发生关系并同人相互独立的东西，成了充满魔幻力量的物神，而真实的主人不得不跪倒在自己的创造物面前，成为后者的奴隶。另一方面，通过这种变形，社会关系丧失了它的特定的历史规定性，实现了与自然物质形态的合而为一，于是，资本主义就摆脱了社会的历史规定性，成为一种永恒的自然制度。

对此，柯尔施指出，马克思关于商品拜物教的分析彰显了一种全新的批判范式：首先，它系统深化了前期的异化批判理论。在《1844 年经济学哲学手稿》中，由于深受黑格尔和费尔巴哈的影响，马克思还在使用他们的异化范式来批判资产阶级社会，虽然他也认识到，构成异化基础的不是想象中的幻影，而是财产、金钱、资本、雇佣劳动等，但由于此时他的经济学水平的限制，致使他对这种异化的分析还停留在哲学的层面上，未能深入到资本主义制度的内在肌理之中。而到了这里，马克思通过对商品拜物教的批判分析，从根本上揭示了人类自我异化的根源，系统深化了早期的异化批判理论。其次，商品拜物教批判理论全面扬弃了资产阶级经济学的内在局限性。柯尔施指出，资产阶级经济学家错误地将资本主义视为一种永恒的自然制度，完全陷入拜物教的窠臼之中。而马克思通过对商品拜物教的批判分析，揭示了资本主义生产方式的历史性，实现了对资产阶级社会及其意识形式（政治经济学）的全面批判，建立了无产阶级的政治经济学理论。再次，商品拜物教批判理论系统诠释了政治经济学批判的精髓。柯尔施指出，意识形态虽然具有一定的现实功能，但它在本性上毕竟是一种虚假的观念体系。然而，与此不同，商品拜物教并不是一种虚假的意识，而是个人在资产阶级社会实践中生成的一种具有客观效力的社会意识形式，“这种种形式恰好形成资产阶级经济学的各种范畴。对于这个历史上一定的社会生产方式即商品生产的生产关系来说，这些范畴是有社会效力的、因而是客观的思维形式”①。因此，拜物教绝不是观念错认的结果，而是资本主义生产方式必然产生的客观颠倒形式。只要资本主义生产方式还存在，拜物教就必然存在。

① 《马克思恩格斯全集》第 44 卷，人民出版社 2001 年版，第 93 页。

因此，要扬弃拜物教，绝不能停留在单纯的思想层面，必须通过社会行动扬弃拜物教得以产生的社会基础，即资本主义生产方式。这种理论批判与现实革命相统一的总体性原则，恰恰构成了马克思唯物辩证法与黑格尔唯心辩证法的本质区别，也是政治经济学批判的内在精髓。

也是基于此，柯尔施得出结论说，马克思关于"商品的拜物教性质及其秘密"的研究，不仅构成了马克思政治经济学批判和《资本论》全部理论的核心，而且也是他的整个唯物主义理论和历史观的最精辟的表达。

5. 成熟时期的唯物主义理论是一种经验科学方法

在《结论》部分，柯尔施系统总结了马克思主义的发展过程及其最后形态的精神实质。他指出，马克思主义充分继承和吸收了资产阶级的一切优秀文化成果。具体而言，马克思恩格斯从黑格尔那里继承了批判的革命辩证法；从复辟时期的历史学那里吸收了社会阶级和阶级斗争概念；从李嘉图那里接受了从经济学的角度来论证阶级对立的思路；从蒲鲁东那里接受了现代无产阶级是唯一的革命阶级理论；从西斯蒙第那里吸收了对现代生产方式的矛盾分析；从费尔巴哈和赫斯那里获取了人道主义和行动哲学的思想；从布朗基那里获得了革命专政理论；从空想社会主义者那里吸收了共产主义学说。也正是在吸收和整合这些资源的基础上，马克思恩格斯才创立了自己的唯物主义。

不过，柯尔施指出，从马克思恩格斯思想发展的历程来看，这种整合并不是一蹴而就的，而是经过了一个漫长的过程。总体来看，分为两个阶段：一是早期的哲学阶段。在这一时期，马克思主义刚从资产阶级哲学的怀抱中挣脱出来，还没有建立自己的科学基础，因此，在内容、方法和用语方面仍然带有它的母体即黑格尔哲学的胎记，这些缺陷不能完全归咎于马克思，而是由当时的社会历史条件决定的。这一时期，马克思的唯物主义理论尚未达到科学的层次，而是表现为对哲学的理论和实践批判，还没有从根本上超越资产阶级哲学和政治经济学的内在缺陷。二是后期的科学阶段。经过系统的经济学研究，马克思建立了科学的政治经济学批判，并在此基础上，重新整合了各种资源，实现了对资产阶级哲学和经济学的全面超越。它不再像前期那样聚焦于哲学、宗教或法的批判，而是更多地集中于经济学研究，即通过对资产阶级社会经济结构的研究，系统解剖资本主义制度的生理机制及其运行规律，从而实现了对资产阶级社会及其意识形式的总体批判。只是到了这时，马克思的唯物主义才最终摆脱了哲学批判的形式，成为一门最充分、最成熟的科学理论。也是在此基础上，柯尔施指出，真正构成成熟时期马克思新科学基础的，既不是黑格尔也不是李嘉图，既不是资产阶级哲学也不是资产阶级经济学，而是现实的革命运动与经验，这才是马克思主义得以产生、发展并最终成为一门新科学的决定性源泉。

那么，这种新科学的精神实质是什么呢？柯尔施指出，与资产阶级社会学相比，马克思政治经济学批判的重要贡献在于：(1)把社会生活过程的一切现象都归结于经济；(2)把经济学理解为一种社会科学；(3)历史地界定一切社会现象，将其理解为由物质生产力发展推动并由社会阶级斗争实现的一种革命性过程。换言之，只有通过对社会和历史的经济学分析，才能真正把握社会关系的整体，也才能从根本上实现对社会和历史的科学解剖。基于此，柯尔施指出，如果说成熟时期的唯物主义理论是一种社会科学的话，那么，这种科学绝不是资产阶级所说的社会学，而是一种经济学；同样，这种社会研究方法也不再是一种“哲学”方法，而是转化为一种严格意义上的经验科学方法。

六、进一步阅读指南

1. [美]罗伯特·A.戈尔曼主编：《新马克思主义研究辞典》，中央编译局当代马克思主义研究所译，社会科学文献出版社 1989 年版。

2. [加]本·阿格尔：《西方马克思主义概论》，慎之等译，中国人民大学出版社 1991 年版。

3. 俞吾金、陈学明：《国外马克思主义哲学流派新编》，复旦大学出版社 2002 年版。

4. 黄浩：《马克思的哲学观——基于“柯尔施问题”的视角》，学习出版社 2014 年版。

5. 邢来顺、吴友法主编：《德国通史》第四卷，江苏人民出版社 2019 年版。

6. Karl Korsch, *Karl Korsch: Revolutionary Theory*, ed. Douglas Kellner, University of Texas, 1977.

7. John Rundell, "Karl Korsch: Historicised Dialectics", *Thesis Eleven*, 1981(3).

8. James Watson, "Karl Korsch: Development and Dialectic", *Philosophy & Social Criticism*, 1981(8).

七、问题与思考

1. 在柯尔施看来,马克思主义在何种意义上是一种哲学?
2. 试论述柯尔施对马克思主义发展史的理解。
3. 柯尔施是如何理解哲学批判与政治经济学批判的内在关系的?
4. 为什么说商品拜物教批判是马克思政治经济学批判的核心?
5. 柯尔施是如何理解成熟时期马克思唯物主义理论的精神实质的?

第四章　艰难的政治哲学探索
——《狱中札记》选读

教学目的与要求

了解传统知识分子与有机知识分子的差别与联系，正确理解有机知识分子在霸权建构中的作用；掌握霸权概念的总体性意蕴；了解阵地战的民族历史适用条件，正确评估它在夺取霸权过程中的重要作用；正确理解实践哲学的绝对历史主义本质。

一、历史背景

（一）作者介绍

1891 年，安东尼奥·葛兰西（Antonio Gramsci）出生于意大利南部撒丁岛的一个小职员家庭。受自己哥哥的影响，他在学生时代就接触到了使撒丁岛从意大利分离出来的撒丁主义。1911 年，他获得奖学金前往都灵大学学习。大学期间，他比较全面地研究了撒丁岛问题的历史以及关于解决撒丁岛农民贫困问题的各种观点，逐步认识到自己原先信奉的撒丁主义的狭隘性，最终转向了当时代表劳动人民利益的社会党。这是他思想发展中的第一次重要转折。从此以后，他感到要克服撒丁人在二十世纪初那种落后的思想和生活方式，接受民族的思想和生活方式。随着了解不断深入，葛兰西感受到社会党中存在的工团主义思想，并察觉到这是地方主义思想的另外一种表现，于是尝试了解其他思想与主张。他广泛阅读了克罗齐、马基雅维利、黑格尔、拉布里奥拉、马克思、索列尔等人的著作，其中，克罗齐的新黑格尔主义对他思想的影响最大。1914 年，葛兰西在《人民呼声》上发表了自己的第一篇政论文章“积极的有行动的中立”。该文呼应墨索里尼同名文章对社会党关于战争的看法的批评，从精神哲学的立场解释了无产阶级对战争的一种态度，强调通过战争为无产阶级革命创造条件。1915 年，作为社会党党员的葛兰西从大学毕业并成为一名新闻记者。

十月革命后，在列宁的影响下，葛兰西开始关注无产阶级的文化宣传问题。1919 年 5 月 1 日，他参与创办了《新秩序报》，之后更是直接投身到工人阶级的组织活动中。1919 年至 1920 年革命风暴的再一次失败使葛兰西深刻认识到了社会党改良主义的危害，于是，他于 1921 年 5 月参加了新成立的意大利共产党，并当选为中央委员。由于在共产国际第二次代表大会上，列宁赞扬了葛兰西，肯定了他对工厂委员会的工作以及对党与革命的理解，因此，他被任命为共产国际执委会代表，并于 1922 年 5 月前往莫斯科任职。1922 年 10 月 28 日，墨索里尼领导法西斯党发动政变。10 月 30 日，意大利国王任命墨索里尼为总理，法西斯主义就此正式登上了意大利的政治舞台。1924 年 5 月，葛兰西回到意大利，随后成为意大利共产党总书记，如何推翻法西斯主义统治成为葛兰西这一时期革命活动的根本主题。同时，他还在继续思考意大利的南方农民问题，并开始反思自己以前的工联主义倾向以及克罗齐的新黑格尔主义对自己的消极影响。不过，他的理论与实践活动很快就中断了。1926 年 11 月，社会党人暗杀墨索里尼未遂，墨索里尼随即得到国王的支持，开始逮捕一切反法西斯主义的政党与团体的人员；11 月 8 日晚上十点半左右，葛兰西被捕，开始了长达十余年的监狱生活。法西斯政府原本以为这样就可以让葛兰西停止思考。但艰难困苦的牢狱岁月并没有击倒葛兰西，在狱中，他一直努力争取进行阅读、思想、写作的权利和条件。1929 年 2 月，在终于争取到自己所需要的笔墨和书籍后，葛兰西立刻投入自己制定的研究和写作计划中。到 1935 年 8 月，葛兰西总共留下了 33 本《狱中札记》，其中 29 本是关于哲学、政治、历史、经济、文化等的读书笔记和片段札记，另外 4 本是从德文和俄文翻译过来的文学作品和其他文献。1937 年 4 月，葛兰西在罗马逝世。

(二) 时代背景

1. 福特制与资本主义社会的结构转型

1911 年,泰勒出版《管理原理》一书,系统阐述了自己的科学管理思想,即将人的劳动过程划分为具体相连的环节,以专业化的分工来促进生产率的提高。1914 年,亨利·福特将流水线引进到他的汽车工厂,完美实现了泰勒的管理思想。第一次世界大战结束后,福特制逐渐从美国传播到欧洲,最终使得机械化分工、大企业生产历史性地取代工厂手工业生产,成为垄断资本主义时代的主要生产组织形式。这种生产组织方式的转变一方面从根本上改变了人与机器的关系,使劳动者成为机器的附庸;另一方面,对生产的各个环节的组织化程度都提出了新的要求,逐渐使自由市场的竞争让位于有计划的生产与管理。在这种背景下,传统意义上的国家与市民社会之间的界限开始模糊起来,出现了哈贝马斯所说的"国家社会化"与"社会国家化"现象:"随着资本集中和国家干预,从国家社会化和社会国家化这一互动过程中,产生出一个新的领域。从这个意义上来说,公共利益的公共因素与契约的私法因素糅合在了一起。"①进入二十世纪三十年代以后,由福特制所导致的资本主义社会的结构转型已经变得相当清晰。葛兰西是西方马克思主义者中率先注意到这种转型,并开始思考这种转型的社会效应及其对无产阶级革命的影响的思想家。

2. 法西斯主义的兴起及其对意大利革命的影响

二十世纪初,与欧洲其他一些大国相比,意大利的经济和军事实力都相对落后。第一次世界大战后,帝国主义之间的矛盾更加激烈,而当时作为战胜国的意大利没有从中获得足够的好处,国内各阶层对政府都极为不满,政治局势处于动荡之中。此外,随着苏联的建立和发展,意大利的统治阶级"惧怕赤色",极需要一个敌视无产阶级政权及运动的政治团体。1921 年,墨索里尼建立了国家法西斯党。1922 年 10 月 28 日,墨索里尼领导法西斯

① [德]尤尔根·哈贝马斯:《公共领域的结构转型》,曹卫东等译,学林出版社 1999 年版,第 179 页。

党向罗马进军，10月30日，意大利国王任命墨索里尼为总理，法西斯主义就此正式登上了意大利的政治舞台。1925年1月，墨索里尼宣布国家法西斯党为意大利唯一合法政党，从而建立了意大利法西斯主义独裁的统治。作为意大利资产阶级从民主统治向专制统治转变的一个必然结果，国家法西斯党代表了大土地所有者和资产阶级的利益。虽然它从表面上看存在温和与保守之分，不过其实质是反无产阶级的反动统治。按照共产国际的正确分析，法西斯主义的兴起改变了意大利无产阶级革命的形势，意大利无产阶级必须建立统一战线，联合一切反法西斯主义的力量，率先推翻法西斯主义的暴力统治。在这种背景下，无产阶级的领导权问题、知识分子问题和南方农民问题就历史性地成为意大利革命的主要问题。

（三）思想背景

1. 多元的马克思主义理解方式

十月革命后，欧洲各国的马克思主义者都开始反思第二国际的马克思主义。马克思主义究竟有没有哲学？如果有，这种哲学的本质是什么？这些问题成为萦绕在当时许多马克思主义者心头的重大现实问题。关于马克思主义哲学，当时的意大利主要存在三种比较流行的理解方式。一种是在第二国际内部曾具有重要影响的新康德主义倾向。这种倾向以实证主义的方式来理解马克思主义哲学，倡导伦理社会主义，最终导致理论和实践的脱节，否定了历史发展的规律性。第二种是对马克思主义哲学的庸俗唯物主义理解。这种倾向在第二国际内部原本就存在，后来在斯大林主义中得到延续和发展。第三种是在意大利具有重要影响的克罗齐的新黑格尔主义倾向。克罗齐是意大利著名的新黑格尔主义哲学家。受拉布里奥拉影响，他曾从新黑格尔主义的立场出发对马克思的哲学进行过研究，并在意大利产生了相当大的影响。在他看来，马克思非常喜欢黑格尔主义，但这种传统现在丢失了，这导致马克思哲学具有了经济决定论的性质，内在地反对伦理。克罗齐认为，马克思哲学关于经济基础与上层建筑的学说，就是一种二元论的残余，这种残余将“目的论”引进到了马克思哲学中。由此，克罗齐认为，追踪人类的精神在历史中的变迁是一项重要任务，即在唯心主义的意义上强调理论与实践的统一。正是在克罗齐这种新黑格尔主义的基础上，葛兰西形成了对马克思主义哲学的最初理解。

2. 意大利主要左派的政治立场纷争

二十世纪二十年代初，随着资本主义的发展，带有天主教色彩的意大利人民党成立，在政坛里的影响逐渐扩大。与此同时，意大利的工人阶级运动也掀起了一波高潮。尽管工人运动最终失败了，但也为工人阶级政党的发展奠定了重要的基础。在工人运动的发展过程中，工人阶级政党不断面临新的革命斗争形势，因而也就不断涌现新的革命思想路线。当时，意大利存在着众多的左派政治思潮，既包括以葛兰西为代表的“文化派”或“工人委员会派”，也包括“改良派”“拥俄多数派”“共产主义派”等。这些左派政治思潮在一些重要斗争问题上，比如是否与资产阶级及其政府采取合作、如何对待当时的其他思想潮流，特别是列宁主义，以及是否坚持革命斗争等问题上，均产生了巨大分歧。当时，意大利各左派政治思潮之间，以及与共产国际和苏联的关系都异常微妙。在此情况下，葛兰西领导的派别与列宁主义站在了一起，与共产国际保持一致，坚持开展针对墨索里尼的斗争。

二、篇章结构

《狱中札记》有两个中文版。1983 年，人民出版社根据 1959 年俄文版《葛兰西选集》第三卷出版了国内第一个版本的《狱中札记》。这个版本分“历史唯物主义问题”“革命问题”“历史问题和政治问题”“文化生活问题”四个专题，总计有 37 万字，近 500 页。2000 年，中国社会科学出版社根据英国劳伦斯和威萨特出版社 1971 年出版的、在西方世界享有盛誉的《安东尼奥·葛兰西〈狱中札记〉选集》(*Selections from the Prison Notebooks of Antonio Gramsci*, edited and translated by Quintin Hoare and Geoffrey Nowell Smith)出版了第二版本的《狱中札记》。在目前国内学界，绝大多数人使用的都是这个版本。

《狱中札记》的第一章《历史文化问题》包含三节。在第一节“知识界”题为《知识界的形成》的札记中，葛兰西着重分析了知识分子的形成、类型、社会功能等。他指出，知识分子的形成是历史的、形式各不相同的，其中有两种最重要的形式：一是新兴的经济社会过程可以同时有机地制造出一个或多个知识分子阶层，如资本主义企业家同自身一起创造出工业技师、政治经济专家、新文化和新法律体系的组织者等；二是在过去的经济结构中形成的知识分子集团在历史中的连续发展，如教士阶层。不应当在知识分子活动的本质中，而应当在他们所处的社会关系总体中，去寻找区分不同知识分子的标准。因此，可以说所有的人都是知识分子，但并非所有的人在社会中都具有知识分子的职能。一个社会集团越是能成功地制造自己的有机知识分子，就能越成功地同化、征服传统知识分子，从而争取到自己的统治地位。知识分子是统治集团的管家，担当着服从于社会领导和政治管理任务的职能。在题为《城市型和乡村型知识分子的地位差别》札记中，葛兰西指出，城市型知识分子是标准化的，而乡村型知识分子则大多数是传统的，政党的责任就是把居于统治地位的集团的有机知识分子和传统知识分子结合起来。

在第一章第二节《论教育》中，葛兰西主要阐发了自己对教育问题的看法，认为教育是实现文化领导权的重要手段，教育必须重视理论联系实际，学校教育尤其应当注重实践能力的培养，为了实现文化领导权，必须扩大教育的层面和教育的方式，国家应该实现教育均衡，大力发展公立学校教育，公民意识教育应当从小抓起。他认为，知识分子的专门化是历史发展的一个趋势。任何在争取统治地位的集团中所具有的最重要的特征之一，就是要同化和在意识形态领域征服传统知识分子。在第三节《意大利历史随笔》中，葛兰西着重讨论了19世纪意大利民族和现代国家形成过程中政治领导权的转换、城乡关系的发展、知识分子问题以及特定政治人物的历史作用等问题。

第二章《政治随笔》包含《现代君主》与《国家和市民社会》两节。在第一节《现代君主》中，葛兰西首先对马基雅弗利的政治学观点进行摘录，认为其《君主论》的要点在于，它不是系统的论述，而是生动的作品，以艺术的形式体现出了"集体意志"。政治是一门自主科学，马基雅维利的政治科学的目的是建立民族的君主专制政体。政治的第一要素是存在着统治者和被统治者、领导者和被领导者。政党是培养领导者和领导权的最有效手段。现代君主不是个人只能是政党。政党的存在需要同时具备三个要素：群众、主要的凝聚力和中间要素。马克思的实践哲学被片面地理解为各种形式的经济主义，它们使得实践哲学丧失了在高级知识分子中的影响力。正确分析特定历史阶段的活跃力量及其相互关系，必须准确理解并解决经济基础和上层建筑的相互关系。分析局势就是要确立不同层次的力量关系。力量关系具有不同的阶段和层次：首先是与经济基础联系密切的社会力量关系，其次是政治力量关系，即评价不同社会阶级达到的同质性、觉悟高低和组织程度，最后是军事力量。对力量关系的分析不可能也不可以成为目的，只有用它们来正确说明某一特定的实践活动或意志的创举，才能获得一定的意义。官僚阶层的出现具有必然性，民主集中制和体力劳动及脑力劳动的统一是消除官僚主义的有效方式。人民群众的历史活动具有自发性，政治领袖应当教化、引导这种自发性，以建立有意识的霸权。不过，必须反对脱离具体的实践、为理论而理论的拜占庭主义。因为历史地看，战后工人阶级的意识水平已经得到发展，已经认识到自己是不仅属于一个工厂，而且属于更大意义上的国家与国际分工的集体工人。必须警惕随意发挥个人主动性、从群众中独立出来的志愿者，以及脱离群众的自愿主义。

第二章第二节《国家和市民社会》包含葛兰西对现代国家和市民社会的理论思考。他认为，随着历史的发展，政党具有脱离自己所代表的阶级的倾向，从而导致领导权危机，使得神奇领袖有可能利用神秘力量以暴力方式解决危机。在现代，恺撒主义之所以能够出现，是因为基本力量势均力敌。面对恺撒主义的崛起，各个政党都像海狸那样没有抵抗，这是因为不管是派系还是政党都没有能够形成政策。自复兴运动时期开始，意大利政党就出现了缺乏有机的连续、战术和战略不均衡等问题。政治斗争中存在三种形式的战争：运动战、阵地战和地下战。在第一次世界大战后的意大利，政治斗争的主要趋势是从机动战向阵地战转变。在现代国家中，国家组织和市民社会都已经成为政治的阵地战的总体因素。现代国家不仅仅是宪兵守夜人，还包括一些需要追溯到市民社会的观念，就此可以说：国家 = 政治社会 + 市民社会，换言之，以高压手段支持的领导权。在现代国家中，政党和国家发展出一定的世界观，这种世界观反过来又影响政党和国家本身。在进入自主的国家生活之前，市民社会是不可能出现的。

第三章《实践哲学》包含《哲学研究》和《马克思主义诸问题》两节。在第一节中，葛兰西主要围绕哲学与常识、宗教、科学的关系，谈了自己对哲学的认识。他认为，哲学是一种精神结构，无论常识或宗教都不能成为这种东西，因为它们无论在个人意识还是集体意识中都不能达到统一性和一贯性。不存在一般的哲学，只存在各种哲学和世界观，但总的说来有两类世界观：

一种是口头的，一种是事实的。哲学是对宗教和常识的克服。在第一节的"哲学与历史问题"部分中，葛兰西指出，哲学总是历史的、属于特定时代的。据此，他阐发了自己对于马克思主义哲学一些基本理论的理解。在第三章第二节《马克思主义哲学诸问题》中，葛兰西着重论述了自己对于实践哲学即马克思主义哲学的本质的理解。他认为，马克思主义哲学就是实践哲学。实践哲学的诞生是哲学史上的一场革命。马克思是新世界观的创造者，是一个历史时代的精神的创造者，只有新的社会建立起来之后，他的世界观才会被超越。实践哲学是最高的历史主义，它摆脱了任何一种抽象的观念论，是世界历史实在的成果，新的文明的开始。

三、研究前沿

葛兰西是西方马克思主义发展史上的一个重要人物，也是学界西方马克思主义研究的一个热点人物。可以说，学界对葛兰西的研究是始终伴随着对西方马克思主义的研究而同步进行的，也是后者研究中的一个重要组成部分。整体来看，学界对葛兰西的研究在二十一世纪走向系统化和深入化，就成果数量上来说，葛兰西是被研究最多的西方马克思主义者之一。近十多年来，成果的数量就一直保持在一个较高水平，特别是以葛兰西哲学为主题的学位论文在所有成果中占的比例较为突出。作为葛兰西的代表作，《狱中札记》也自然成为国内西方马克思主义研究的关注焦点。

第一，对文化领导权的专题研究。文化领导权是葛兰西思想中的一个重要话题，也是《狱中札记》的主题之一。学界的研究成果涵盖了学术论文、学位论文以及研究专著。学者们基于文本，阐述了葛兰西文化领导权概念的主要内涵、形成机理和理论意义，提出葛兰西文化领导权理论内核包括三个方面，即市民社会理论、有机知识分子理论和阵地战理论。有学者指出，葛兰西完整论述了无产阶级在革命胜利前后应当如何取得文化的领导权，阐释了文化领导权在不同革命阶段应当具有的不同形式和功能。近年来，部分学者从葛兰西的文化领导权论述中解读出新的意义，认为能够为巩固马克思主义的意识形态指导地位、瓦解西方资本主义的意识形态威胁提供重要借鉴意义。同时，有学者指出，这一理论对我国当前提升文化自信和民族自信也具有重要的参考价值；我们应当充分重视知识分子在意识形态建设过程中的角色，推动知识分子与群众的有机结合，进一步调动知识分子的积极作用。也有学者提出，从国家治理层面来看，当前我国社会主义经济政治体制在改革中不断发展，如何更好地建立起现代化强国，我们也可以从葛兰西的著作中获得一些有益启示。

第二，对《狱中札记》其他重要问题的研究。除了文化领导权问题，葛兰西还在《狱中札记》中深刻讨论了其他一些重要问题。比如，对实践哲学的研究就是一个重要组成部分。学者们认为，葛兰西的哲学观立足于哲学、历史学和政治学，他的实践哲学是一种在当时背景下的独特世界观，包含了多重意蕴，即包括当时的特殊时代背景、具有肯定及否定双重方法论意义以及本人独特的政治立场，也体现了他突出马克思主义的行动特征。葛兰西借助黑格尔的统一性哲学，提出和阐释了历史性和历史思维方式，对黑格尔哲学进行了扬弃，强调马克思主义的方法论和主体创造性，并且有助于打破第二国际时代的宿命论。还有学者依据葛兰西的人民阵线理论，讨论了当代西方左派学者关于民主革命的思想，指出后者们往往只停留在理论层面，却忽视了革命理论的现实可实践性，因而会导致理论与实践的脱节。同时，葛兰西哲学始终无法避免一些悖论，有学者主张通过重构其他西方马克思主义哲学家的概念以解决这些悖论。

第三，对《狱中札记》的历史地位及价值的评估。总体来说，学界对《狱中札记》在西方马克思主义和整个马克思主义发展过程中的价值予以了充分肯定。有学者认为，葛兰西虽然在《狱中札记》中一定程度上忽视了马克思主义哲学的出发点，但是他对唯物史观的贡献是不容否认的，这对开拓不同于第二国际马克思主义的阐释路径提供了重要基础。有学者研究了葛兰西在探讨意识形态领导权时涉及的语言学及其他方面的建构，认为即使是这些具体领域的建构，对之后西方马克思主义的发展也是有着深远意义的。还有学者从马克思主义的其他视角分析《狱中札记》的相关思想。比如，有学者运用政治经济学视角，对葛兰西的“实践哲学”进行阐述，认为葛兰西在《狱中札记》中基于政治经济学开展的相关讨论直接受到克罗齐等人的影响，这有助于理解葛兰西的文化领导权理论和国家理论。有学者考察了葛兰西之后其他西方马克思主义学者对葛兰西理论的批判，认为西方左派学者们对葛兰西的批判在一定层面上捍卫了马克思主义方法论，使后者避免被历史主义及其他错误立场侵蚀。还有学者通过反思国内意大利马克思主义研究的路径、成果，对未来葛兰西理论研究提出了新的思路。

四、文本节选

The Intellectuals

Are intellectuals an autonomous and independent social group, or does every social group have its own particular specialised category of intellectuals? The problem is a complex one, because of the variety of forms assumed to date by the real historical process of formation of the different categories of intellectuals.

The most important of these forms are two:

1. Every social group, coming into existence on the original terrain of an essential function in the world of economic production, creates together with itself, organically, one or more strata of intellectuals which give it homogeneity and an awareness of its own function not only in the economic but also in the social and political fields. The capitalist entrepreneur creates alongside himself the industrial technician, the specialist in political economy, the organisers of a new culture, of a new legal system, etc. ...

If not all entrepreneurs, at least an *élite* amongst them must have the capacity to be an organiser of society in general, including all its complex organism of services, right up to the state organism, because of the need to create the conditions most favourable to the expansion of their own class; or at the least they must possess the capacity to choose the deputies (specialised employees) to whom to entrust this activity of organising the general system of relationships external to the business itself. It can be observed that the "organic" intellectuals which every new class creates alongside itself and elaborates in the course of its development, are for the most part "specialisations" of partial aspects of the primitive activity of the new social type which the new class has brought into prominence.

... Thus it is to be noted that the mass of the peasantry, although it performs an essential function in the world of production, does not elaborate its own "organic" intellectuals, nor does it "assimilate" any stratum of "traditional" intellectuals, although it is from the peasantry that other social groups draw many of their intellectuals and a high proportion of traditional intellectuals are of peasant origin.

2. However, every "essential" social group which emerges into history out of the preceding economic structure, and as an expression of a development of this structure, has found (at least in all of history up to the present) categories of intellectuals already in existence and which seemed indeed to represent an historical continuity uninterrupted even by the most complicated and radical changes in political and social forms.

...

Since these various categories of traditional intellectuals experience through an "*esprit de corps*" their uninterrupted historical continuity and their special qualification, they thus put themselves forward as autonomous and independent of the dominant social group. This self-assessment is not without consequences in the ideological and political field, consequences of wide-ranging import. The whole of idealist philosophy can easily be connected with this position assumed by the social complex of intellectuals and can be defined as the expression of that social utopia by which the intellectuals think of themselves as "independent", autonomous, endowed with a character of their own, etc.

...

... One of the most important characteristics of any group that is developing towards dominance is its struggle to assimilate and to conquer "ideologically" the traditional intellectuals, but this assimilation and conquest is made quicker and more efficacious the more the group in question succeeds in simultaneously elaborating its own organic intellectuals.

...

The relationship between the intellectuals and the world of production is not as direct as it is with the fundamental social groups but is, in varying degrees, "mediated" by the whole fabric of society and by the complex of superstructures, of which the intellectuals are, precisely, the "functionaries". It should be possible both to measure the "organic quality" [*organicità*] of the various intellectual strata and their degree of connection with a fundamental social group, and to establish a gradation of their functions and of the superstructures from the bottom to the top (from the structural base upwards). What we can do, for the moment, is to fix two major super structural "levels": the one that can be called "civil society", that is the ensemble of organisms commonly called "private", and that of "political society" or "the State". These two levels correspond on the one hand to the function of "hegemony" which the dominant group exercises throughout society and on the other hand to that of "direct domination" or command exercised through the State and "juridical" government. The functions in question are precisely organisational and connective. The intellectuals are the dominant group's "deputies" exercising the subaltern functions of social hegemony and political government. These comprise:

1. The "spontaneous" consent given by the great masses of the population to the general direction imposed on social life by the dominant fundamental group; this consent is "historically" caused by the prestige (and consequent confidence) which the dominant group enjoys because of its position and function in the world of production.

2. The apparatus of state coercive power which "legally" enforces discipline on those groups who do not "consent" either actively or passively. This apparatus is, however, constituted for the whole of society in anticipation of moments of crisis of command and direction when spontaneous consent has failed.

——Antonio Gramsci, *Selections from the Prison Notebooks of Antonio Gramsci*, ed. and trans. Quintin Hoare and Geoffrey Nowell Smith, International Publishes, 1971, pp.5–12.

The most interesting problem is that which, when studied from this point of view, relates to the modern political party, its real origins, its developments and the forms which it takes. What is the character of the political party in relation to the problem of the intellectuals? Some distinctions must be made:

1. The political party for some social groups is nothing other than their specific way of elaborating their own category of organic intellectuals directly in the political and philosophical field and not just in the field of productive technique. These intellectuals are formed in this way and cannot indeed be formed in any other way, given the general character and the conditions of formation, life and development of the social group.

2. The political party, for all groups, is precisely the mechanism which carries out in civil society the same function as the State carries out, more synthetically and over a larger scale, in political society. In other words it is responsible for welding together the organic intellectuals of a given group—the dominant one—and the traditional intellectuals. The party carries out this function in strict dependence on its basic function, which is that of elaborating its own component parts—those elements of a social group which has been born and developed as an "economic" group—and of turning them into qualified political intellectuals, leaders [*dirigenti*] and organisers of all the activities and functions inherent in the organic development of an integral society, both civil and political. Indeed it can be said that within its field the political party accomplishes its function more completely and organically than the State does within its admittedly far larger field. An intellectual who joins the political party of a particular

social group is merged with the organic intellectuals of the group itself, and is linked tightly with the group. This takes place through participation in the life of the State only to a limited degree and often not at all. Indeed it happens that many intellectuals think that they *are* the State, a belief which, given the magnitude of the category, occasionally has important consequences and leads to unpleasant complications for the fundamental economic group which *really* is the State.

That all members of a political party should be regarded as intellectuals is an affirmation that can easily lend itself to mockery and caricature. But if one thinks about it nothing could be more exact. There are of course distinctions of level to be made. A party might have a greater or lesser proportion of members in the higher grades or in the lower, but this is not the point. What matters is the function, which is directive and organisational, i.e. educative, i.e. intellectual. ...

——Antonio Gramsci, *Selections from the Prison Notebooks of Antonio Gramsci*, ed. and trans. Quintin Hoare and Geoffrey Nowell Smith, International Publishes, 1971, pp.15 - 16.

The Modern Prince

One may term "Byzantinism" or "scholasticism" the regressive tendency to treat so-called theoretical questions as if they had a value in themselves, independently of any specific practice. A typical example of Byzantinism were the so-called Rome Theses, in which a kind of mathematical method was applied to each issue, as in pure economics. The problem arises of whether a theoretical truth, whose discovery corresponded to a specific practice, can be generalised and considered as universal for a historical epoch. The proof of its universality consists precisely 1. in its becoming a stimulus to know better the concrete reality of a situation that is different from that in which it was discovered (this is the principal measure of its fecundity); 2. when it has stimulated and helped this better understanding of concrete reality, in its capacity to incorporate itself in that same reality as if it were originally an expression of it. It is in this incorporation that its real universality lies, and not simply in its logical or formal coherence, or in the fact that it is a useful polemical tool for confounding the enemy. In short, the principle must always rule that ideas are not born of other ideas, philosophies of other philosophies; they are a continually renewed expression of real historical development. The unity of history (what the idealists call unity of the spirit) is not a presupposition, but a continuously developing process. Identity in concrete reality determines identity of thought, and not vice versa. It can further be deduced that every truth, even if it is universal, and even if it can be expressed by an abstract formula of a mathematical kind (for the sake of the theoreticians), owes its effectiveness to its being expressed in the language appropriate to specific concrete situations. If it cannot be expressed in such specific terms, it is a byzantine and scholastic abstraction, good only for phrasemongers to toy with. [1932]

——Antonio Gramsci, *Selections from the Prison Notebooks of Antonio Gramsci*, ed. and trans. Quintin Hoare and Geoffrey Nowell Smith, International Publishes, 1971, pp.200 - 201.

In a critical account of the post-war events, and of the constitutional (organic) attempts to escape from the prevailing state of disorder and dispersal of forces, show how the movement to valorise the factory by contrast with (or rather independently of) craft organisation corresponded perfectly to the analysis of how the factory system developed given in the first volume of the Critique of Political Economy. An increasingly perfect division of labour objectively reduces the position of the factory worker to increasingly "analytical" movements of detail, so that the complexity of the collective work passes the comprehension of the individual worker; in the latter's consciousness, his own contribution is devalued to the point where it seems easily replaceable at any moment. At the same time, work that is concerted and well organised gives a better "social" productivity, so that the entire work-force of a factory should see itself as a "collective worker". These were the premises of the factory movement, which aimed to render "subjective" that which is given "objectively". What does objective mean in this instance? For the individual worker, the junction between the requirements of technical development and the interests of the ruling class is "objective". But this junction, this unity between technical development and the interests of the ruling class is only a historical phase of industrial development, and must be conceived of as transitory. The nexus can be dissolved; technical requirements can be conceived in concrete terms, not merely separately from the interests of the ruling class, but in relation to the interests of the class which is as yet still subaltern. A compelling proof that such a "split" and new synthesis is historically mature is constituted by the very fact that such a process is understood by the subaltern class—which precisely for that reason is no longer subaltern, or at least is demonstrably on the way to emerging from its subordinate position. The "collective worker" understands that this is what he is, not merely in each individual factory but in the broader spheres of the national and international division of labour. It is precisely in the organisms which represent the factory as a producer of real objects and not of profit that he gives an external, political demonstration of the consciousness he has acquired. [1932]

——Antonio Gramsci, *Selections from the Prison Notebooks of Antonio Gramsci*, ed. and trans. Quintin Hoare and Geoffrey Nowell Smith, International Publishes, 1971, pp. 201 - 202.

State and Civil Society

The separation of powers, together with all the discussion provoked by its realisation and the legal dogmas which its appearance brought into being, is a product of the struggle between civil society and political society in a specific historical period. This period is characterised by a certain unstable equilibrium between the classes, which is a result of the fact that certain categories of intellectuals (in the direct service of the State, especially the civil and military bureaucracy) are still too closely tied to the old dominant classes. In other words, there takes place within the society what Croce calls the "perpetual conflict between Church and State", in which the Church is taken as representing the totality of civil society (whereas in fact it is only an element of diminishing importance within it), and the State as representing every attempt to crystallise permanently a particular stage of development, a particular situation. In this sense, the Church itself may become State, and the conflict may occur between on the one hand secular (and secularising) civil society, and on the other State/Church (when the Church has become an integral part of the State, of political society monopolised by a specific privileged group, which absorbs the Church in order the better to preserve its monopoly with the support of that zone of "civil society" which the Church represents).

Essential importance of the separation of powers for political and economic liberalism; the entire liberal ideology, with its strengths and its weaknesses, can be encapsulated in the principle of the separation of powers, and the source of liberalism's weakness then becomes apparent: it is the bureaucracy—i.e. the crystallisation of the leading personnel—which exercises coercive power, and at a certain point it becomes a caste. Hence the popular demand for making all posts elective-a demand which is extreme liberalism, and at the same time its dissolution (principle of the permanent Constituent Assembly, etc.; in Republics, the election at fixed intervals of the Head of State gives the illusion of satisfying this elementary popular demand).

Unity of the State in the differentiation of powers: Parliament more closely linked to civil society; the judiciary power, between government and Parliament, represents the continuity of the written law (even against the government). Naturally all three powers are also organs of political hegemony, but in different degrees: 1. Legislature; 2. Judiciary; 3. Executive. It is to be noted how lapses in the administration of justice make an especially disastrous impression on the public: the hegemonic apparatus is more sensitive in this sector, to which arbitrary actions on the part of the police and political administration may also be referred. [1930—1932]

——Antonio Gramsci, *Selections from the Prison Notebooks of Antonio Gramsci*, ed. and trans. Quintin Hoare and Geoffrey Nowell Smith, International Publishes, 1971, pp. 245 - 246.

In my opinion, the most reasonable and concrete thing that can be said about the ethical State, the cultural State, is this: every State is ethical in as much as one of its most important functions is to raise the great mass of the population to a particular cultural and moral level, a level (or type) which corresponds to the needs of the productive forces for development, and hence to the interests of the ruling classes. The school as a positive educative function, and the courts as a repressive and negative educative function, are the most important State activities in this sense: but, in reality, a multitude of other so-called private initiatives and activities tend to the same end—initiatives and activities which form the apparatus of the political and cultural hegemony of the ruling classes. Hegel's conception belongs to a period in which the spreading development of the bourgeoisie could seem limitless, so that its ethicity or universality could be asserted: all mankind will be bourgeois.

But, in reality, only the social group that poses the end of the State and its own end as the target to be achieved can create an ethical State—i.e. one which tends to put an end to the internal divisions of the ruled, etc., and to create a technically and morally unitary social organism. [1931—1932]

Hegel's doctrine of parties and associations as the "private" woof of the State. This derived historically from the political experiences of the French Revolution, and was to serve to give a more concrete character to constitutionalism. ... Marx was not able to have historical experiences superior (or at least much superior) to those of Hegel; but, as a result of his journalistic and agitational activities, he had a sense for the masses. Marx's concept of organisation remains entangled amid the following elements: craft organisation; Jacobin clubs; secret conspiracies by small groups; journalistic organisation.

——Antonio Gramsci, *Selections from the Prison Notebooks of Antonio Gramsci*, ed. and trans. Quintin Hoare and Geoffrey Nowell Smith, International Publishes, 1971, pp.258-259.

The following argument is worth reflecting upon: is the conception of the *gendarme*-nightwatchman State (leaving aside the polemical designation: *gendarme*, nightwatchman, etc.) not in fact the only conception of the State to transcend the purely "economic-corporate" stages?

We are still on the terrain of the identification of State and government—an identification which is precisely a representation of the economic-corporate form, in other words of the confusion between civil society and political society. For it should be remarked that the general notion of State includes elements which need to be referred back to the notion of civil society (in the sense that one might say that State = political society + civil society, in other words hegemony protected by the armour of coercion). In a doctrine of the State which conceives the latter as tendentially capable of withering away and of being subsumed into regulated society, the argument is a fundamental one. It is possible to imagine the coercive element of the State withering away by degrees, as ever-more conspicuous elements of regulated society (or ethical State or civil society) make their appearance.

The expressions "ethical State" or "civil society" would thus mean that this "image" of a State without a State was present to the greatest political and legal thinkers, in so far as they placed themselves on the terrain of pure science (pure utopia, since based on the premise that all men are really equal and hence equally rational and moral, i.e. capable of accepting the law spontaneously, freely, and not through coercion, as imposed by another class, as something external to consciousness).

It must be remembered that the expression "nightwatchman" for the liberal State comes from Lassalle, i.e. from a dogmatic and non-dialectical statalist (look closely at Lassalle's doctrines on this point and on the State in general, in contrast with Marxism). In the doctrine of the State as regulated society, one will have to pass from a phase in which "State" will be equal to "government", and "State" will be identified with "civil society", to a phase of the State as nightwatchman—i.e. of a coercive organisation which will safeguard the development of the continually proliferating elements of regulated society, and which will therefore progressively reduce its own authoritarian and forcible interventions. Nor can this conjure up the idea of a new "liberalism", even though the beginning of an era of organic liberty be imminent. [1930—1932]

——Antonio Gramsci, *Selections from the Prison Notebooks of Antonio Gramsci*, ed. and trans. Quintin Hoare and Geoffrey Nowell Smith, International Publishes, 1971, pp. 262 - 264.

Problems of Marxism

Production of new *Weltanschauungen* [world outlooks] to fertilise and nourish the culture of an historical epoch, and philosophically directed production according to the original *Weltanschauungen*. Marx is the creator of a *Weltanschauung*. But what is Ilich[Lenin]'s position? Is it purely subordinate and subaltern? The explanation is to be found in Marxism itself as both science and action.

The passage from utopia to science and from science to action. The foundation of a directive class [*classe dirigente*] (i. e. of a State) is equivalent to the creation of a *Weltanschauung*. How is the statement that the German proletariat is the heir of classical German philosophy to be understood? Surely what Marx wanted to indicate was the historical function of his philosophy when it became the theory of a class which was in turn to become a State? With Ilich this really came about in a particular territory. I have referred elsewhere to the philosophical importance of the concept and the fact of hegemony, for which Ilich is responsible. Hegemony realised means the real critique of a philosophy, its real dialectic. Compare here what Graziadei writes in the introduction to *Prezzo e sopraprezzo*: he puts forward Marx as a unit in a series of great men of science. Fundamental error: none of the others has produced an original and integral conception of the world. Marx initiates intellectually an historical epoch which will last in all probability for centuries, that is, until the disappearance of political society and the coming of a regulated society. Only then will his conception of the world be superseded, when the conception of necessity is superseded by the conception of freedom.

To make a comparison between Marx and Ilich in order to create a hierarchy is stupid and useless. They express two phases: science and action, which are homogeneous and heterogeneous at the same time.

Thus, historically, a parallel between Christ and St. Paul would be absurd. Christ—*Weltanschauung*, and St. Paul—organiser, action, expansion of the *Weltanschauung*—are both necessary to the same degree and therefore of the same historical stature. Christianity could be called historically "Christianity-Paulinism", and this would indeed be a more exact title. (It is only the belief in the divinity of Christ which has prevented this from happening, but the belief is itself an historical and not a theoretical element.)

——Antonio Gramsci, *Selections from the Prison Notebooks of Antonio Gramsci*, ed. and trans. Quintin Hoare and Geoffrey Nowell Smith, International Publishes, 1971, pp.381 - 382.

Historicity of the Philosophy of Praxis

That the philosophy of praxis thinks of itself in a historicist manner, that is, as a transitory phase of philosophical thought, is not only implicit in its entire system, but is made quite explicit in the well-known thesis that historical development will at a certain point be characterised by the passage from the reign of necessity to the reign of freedom. All hitherto existing philosophies (philosophical systems) have been manifestations of the intimate contradictions by which society is lacerated. But each philosophical system taken by itself has not been the conscious expression of these contradictions, since this expression could be provided only by the *ensemble* of systems in conflict with each other. Every philosopher is, and cannot but be, convinced that he expresses the unity of the human spirit, that is, the unity of history and nature. Indeed, if such a conviction did not exist, men would not act, they would not create new history, philosophies would not become ideologies and would not in practice assume the fanatical granite compactness of the "popular beliefs" which assume the same energy as "material forces".

In the history of philosophical thought Hegel represents a chapter on his own, since in his system, in one way or another, even in the form of a "philosophical romance", one manages to understand what reality is. That is to say, one finds, in a single system and in a single philosopher, that consciousness of contradictions which one previously acquired from the *ensemble* of systems and of philosophers in polemic and contradiction with each other.

In a sense, moreover, the philosophy of praxis is a reform and a development of Hegelianism; it is a philosophy that has been liberated (or is attempting to liberate itself) from any unilateral and fanatical ideological elements; it is consciousness full of contradictions, in which the philosopher himself, understood both individually and as an entire social group, not only grasps the contradictions, but posits himself as an element of the contradiction and elevates this element to a principle of knowledge and therefore of action. "Man in general", in whatever form he presents himself, is denied and all dogmatically "unitary" concepts are spurned and destroyed as expressions of the concept of "man in general" or of "human nature" immanent in every man.

But even the philosophy of praxis is an expression of historical contradictions, and indeed their most complete, because most conscious, expression; this means that it too is tied to "necessity" and not to a "freedom" which does not exist and, historically, cannot yet exist. If, therefore, it is demonstrated that contradictions will disappear, it is also demonstrated implicitly that the philosophy of praxis too will disappear, or be superseded. In the reign of "freedom" thought and ideas can no longer be born on the terrain of contradictions and the necessity of struggle. At the present time the philosopher—the philosopher of praxis-can only make this generic affirmation and can go no further; he cannot escape from the present field of contradictions, he cannot affirm, other than generically, a world without contradictions, without immediately creating a utopia.

——Antonio Gramsci, *Selections from the Prison Notebooks of Antonio Gramsci*, ed. and trans. Quintin Hoare and Geoffrey Nowell Smith, International Publishes, 1971, pp. 404 - 405.

If the philosophy of praxis affirms theoretically that every "truth" believed to be eternal and absolute has had practical origins and has represented a "provisional" value (historicity of every conception of the world and of life), it is still very difficult to make people grasp "practically" that such an interpretation is valid also for the philosophy of praxis itself, without in so doing shaking the convictions that are necessary for action. This is, moreover, a difficulty that recurs for every historicist philosophy; it is taken advantage of by cheap polemicists (particularly Catholics) in order to contrast within the same individual the "scientist" and the "demagogue", the philosopher and the man of action, and to deduce that historicism leads necessarily to moral scepticism and depravity. From this difficulty arise many dramas of conscience in little men, and in great men the "Olympian" attitude *à la* Goethe. This is the reason why the proposition about the passage from the reign of necessity to that of freedom must be analysed and elaborated with subtlety and delicacy.

As a result even the philosophy of praxis tends to become an ideology in the worst sense of the word, that is to say a dogmatic system of eternal and absolute truths. This is particularly true when, as happens in the "Popular Manual", it is confused with vulgar materialism, with its metaphysics of "matter" which is necessarily eternal and absolute.

——Antonio Gramsci, *Selections from the Prison Notebooks of Antonio Gramsci*, ed. and trans. Quintin Hoare and Geoffrey Nowell Smith, International Publishes, 1971, pp. 406 - 407.

五、观点解读

1. 必须重视有机知识分子与霸权建构的关系

在对知识分子的历史作用与现代作用进行历史性分析基础上，葛兰西形成了自己的知识分子理论。针对知识分子具有独立自主性这一传统假象，他指出，知识分子实际上是特定社会集团所生产出来的特定的经济与政治职能的承担者。社会历史阶段不同，知识分子范畴的含义也不同。正是在这个意义上，他区分出了有机知识分子与传统知识分子。传统知识分子指前工业社会的知识分子。有机知识分子主要指随着现代资本主义发展产生出来的知识分子。有机知识分子具有如下特征：第一，是具有专业特征的知识分子，他们渗透在经济生活的各个层面中，这种知识分子与资本主义社会联为一体。第二，有机知识分子通过其专业分工，承担起组织整个社会的职能，并使社会成为一个整体。第三，有机知识分子不再停留于言辞上的侃侃而谈，而是作为建设者、组织者和劝说者积极地参与实际生活，通过自己的批判性话语，使知识分子与肌肉-神经劳动之间的关系趋于平衡，通过对"共识"的批判，形成新的完整的世界观，并通过自己的实践，来改造世界。葛兰西认为，传统知识分子与有机知识分子的划分并不是截然对立的。传统知识分子可以被整合到新兴阶级集团之中，使之为自己服务。同样，有机知识分子如果不能随着历史情境的发展而发展自己，或者只是在言辞层面来适应历史发展，那么有机知识分子也会变成僵化的传统知识分子，走向保守主义。他还认为，现代社会的分工与技术在生产中的普遍化，为新的知识分子集团的兴起创造了前提条件：首先，随着工人劳动分工的细化和技术与生产过程的直接接合，工人通过生产过程学会了过去知识分子才能掌握的东西，这加深了对世界的理解和把握，对于打破传统知识分子在知识文化方面的垄断作用至关重要；其次，生产内部的分工和社会化，使得工人得到了纪律的训练，并通过相互的合作形成了较为统一的集体意志，才能形成"总体的人"。在他看来，知识分子要成功地建构霸权关系，就必须与其所体现的社会集团之间的关系达到有机性的统一，这种有机的统一就在于，代表者与被代表者之间获得了普遍的同意，知识分子作为代表者，体现的是普遍的利益，从而获得大众的认同，也就是说，知识分子最终要跳出专家意识形态，将大众的共同意志聚集起来，使之投向更高的目标，即获得霸权。就知识分子自身而言，要实现霸权的职能，必须同时具备三个条件：第一，传统知识分子与有机知识分子走向联合，但必须让有机知识分子占主导地位；第二，知识分子必须是“有机的”和“民族的”，而不是“分散的”和“国际化的”；第三，知识分子必须有能力在政治与市民社会中扮演领导角色。葛兰西对知识分子与霸权关系的讨论，不仅在马克思主义传统中实现了知识分子政治历史地位的自觉，而且开启了当代知识分子讨论的先河，他对知识分子与社会历史变迁内在关系的分析、他提出的有机知识分子概念、他对知识分子与霸权建构的内在理路的探讨，仍然是我们今天所处语境中的重要问题。

2. 霸权的总体性意蕴是对政治、经济、文化领导权的总体性建构

葛兰西的霸权学说是他在列宁的领导权思想的基础上，综合索列尔以及马基雅维利和克罗齐的相关思想形成的。在《狱中札记》中，他沿用马基雅维利的说法，认为必须结合无产阶级革命的当代境遇，写出一本《现代君主》，它由两个重要支点构成：“这里的两个基本点之一是民族人民集体意志的形成，在这方面，现代君主既是民族人民意志的组织者，又是这一意志积极主动的体现；第二个基本点是精神和道德改革，这两点应当构成全书的骨架。”这一解释是我们理解葛兰西霸权理论的主要文本依据。准确地说，葛兰西的霸权概念包含总体性意蕴，是对政治、经济、文化领导权的总体性建构。就思想的具体形成而言，他一开始关注的是霸权理论的经济生活层面，并将经济生活中的霸权提升为政治意义上的霸权，进入《狱中札记》的写作语境之后，结合意大利文化与政治运动史的分析，特别是对马基雅维利与克罗齐的批判思考，文化－道德意义上的霸权概念成为他思考的主要对象，但即使是在后一意义上讨论霸权理论时，经济与政治构成了文化霸权理论的支体，形成了政治斗争中的“阵地战”理论，即从总体上实现对资本主义社会的批判分析与革命改造。葛兰西认为，在统治的意义上，霸权具有三种组成方式。第一是绝对的支配状态，这是通过国家及其组织机器实现的，也正是传统马克思主义所强调的国家作为统治阶级压迫被统治阶级的工具。第二是政治合法性的建构，这种合法性不只是强制统治的问题，还涉及意识形态的建构问题。以上两个层面的霸权都涉及政治关系领域。第三是文化（道

德)合法性建构问题,霸权只有渗透到这个层次时,才能使人们自觉不自觉地遵从着统治者的霸权逻辑。他认为,作为统治者而言,这三种意义上的霸权都不可缺少,特别是文化霸权,非常重要。文化霸权是获得统治权的基本条件之一,而且也是获得政权之后还必须具有的领导能力。葛兰西认为,对于下层集团来说,要获得领导权,主要体现为三个环节:第一步,在受到强大外在束缚的时候,必须战胜外部的敌人,获得相对自治的权力,这是与外部敌人的斗争策略;第二步,经济上的重组对于缔造新型国家来说是至关重要的一步,特别是组织化资本主义,生产工具与人的结合,对于获得经济霸权来说是非常重要的;第三步,要获得各个历史阶层和历史集团的支持,从而获得统一的集体意志与政治、文化(道德)的自觉。在集体意志的形成过程中,知识分子与政党的作用就呈现出来了,因为人民群众只有在知识分子和政党的组织下,才能真正地发挥作用,因此建立政党构成了文化领导权自觉意识建构中的重要环节。

3. 阵地战是夺取文化领导权的重要手段

葛兰西认为现代政治斗争的形式具有多样性。既有敌对双方的正面交锋,用坦克、大炮、机枪迅速快捷地夺取政权的运动战,也有在敌强我弱的情况下,避免直接交锋,悄悄积累人力和物力资源的地下战;还有立足长期斗争,不以对国家政权的正面进攻为目标,而是向资产阶级的领导权机构提出挑战,对敌人思想阵地不断入侵,以最后取得意识形态上和文化上的领导权,从而达到"领导权的前所未有的高度集中"的阵地战。葛兰西清醒地看到,随着历史的发展,西欧发达资产主义依赖市民社会中的领导权,建立了稳固的政权合法性基础,这使得十月革命的运动战道路不再可能在西欧取得胜利。在这种条件下,他把阵地战确立为不同于东方的西方国家革命的策略,因为在俄国,国家就是一切,市民社会还处于原始的混沌状态;而在西方,在国家与市民社会之间有一定的联系,国家一有风吹草动,市民社会的坚固结构立即挺身而出。国家只是外围的壕沟,后面屹立着一个强大的碉堡工事网。他据此批评了罗莎·卢森堡从经济主义出发产生的自发论,认为后者低估了发达资本主义国家领导权机构的作用。西方革命应该采取灵活的战略战术,对资产阶级领导权巧妙地反其意而用之,首先在市民社会中进行"反领导权"斗争。这就要求新的历史集团必须在思想上更加成熟,必须有用来反对资产阶级人生观的另一种人生观，必须有新的道德、新的理想、新的生活方式和新的思想方法，并使之渗透到被统治者的意识中，以便取代他们从前的观念，减少对自由国家的赞同，确保新型国家有最广泛的支持作为基础。只有这样，新的历史集团领导下的新型国家在被领导者的赞同下才会诞生。

4. 实践哲学：对马克思主义哲学的绝对历史主义阐释

实践哲学是葛兰西在《狱中札记》中对马克思主义哲学的一种称谓，但同时也是对马克思主义哲学形态的一种探索，以便将自己所理解的马克思主义哲学同第二国际的正统解释区别开来。面对马克思主义哲学理解中流行的庸俗唯物主义与新康德主义的倾向，葛兰西从理论与实践相统一的立场出发，透视了马克思主义哲学理解中庸俗唯物主义与新康德主义的理论同质性，提出了一种绝对历史主义的哲学视野。在他看来，实践哲学具有四重特征。第一，实践哲学是一种合理意志的创造性哲学，没有这种能动的创造性，就无法超越机械唯物主义。第二，实践哲学的创造指的是能够在现实生活中得到实现的创造性，它使思想历史化，即把思想看成一种在许多人中间得以传播(要是没有合理性或历史性，这种传播就会是不可设想的)，并且是以使自身变成为一种积极的行为准则这样的方式进行传播的世界观和健全的见识。第三，实践哲学具有绝对的历史性。绝对历史主义是针对克罗齐的历史主义而言的。在葛兰西看来，真正的历史主义首先就需要打破这种观念第一性的思想，将观念放置于上层建筑之中加以定位，并从社会历史生活的过程中来分析观念的存在方式。由此，绝对历史主义将社会历史生活本身当作是历史性的存在。第四，实践哲学本身也适用于历史主义的规定性。这一规定对于理解马克思主义哲学来说非常重要，首先，它意味着马克思主义哲学并不是一个已经完成了的东西。其次，实践哲学自身的历史性，决定了任何超历史的普遍真理都是不存在的，每个国家在运用马克思主义指导自己的实践时，都必须从自身的历史情境出发，进行此时此地的研究。

六、进一步阅读指南

1. [意]安东尼奥·葛兰西:《狱中札记》,曹雷雨等译,中国社会科学出版社2000年版。

2. [意]安东尼奥·葛兰西:《狱中书简:1926—1937》,田时纲译,人民出版社2007年版。

3. [意]朱塞佩·费奥里:《葛兰西传》,吴高译,人民出版社1983年版。

4. [英]詹姆斯·约尔:《"西方马克思主义"的鼻祖——葛兰西》,郝其睿译,湖南人民出版社1988年版。

5. [德]尤尔根·哈贝马斯:《公共领域的结构转型》,曹卫东等译,学林出版社1999年版。

6. [意]萨尔沃·马斯泰罗内:《一个未完成的政治思索:葛兰西的〈狱中札记〉》,黄华光、徐力源译,社会科学文献出版社2000年版。

7. [英]唐纳德·萨松:《欧洲社会主义百年史——二十世纪的西欧左翼》,姜辉、于海青、庞晓明译,社会科学文献出版社、重庆出版社2017年版。

8. 毛韵泽:《葛兰西——政治家、囚徒和理论家》,求实出版社1987年版。

9. 仰海峰:《实践哲学与领导权:当代语境中的葛兰西哲学》,北京大学出版社2009年版。

10. Antonio Gramsci, *Pre-Prison Writings*, ed. Richard Bellamy, trans. Virginia Cox,中国政法大学出版社2003年影印版。

11. Esteve Morera, *Gramsci's Historicism: A Realist Interpretation*, Routledge, 1990.

12. Joseph V. Femia, *Gramsci's Political Thought: Hegemony, Consciousness, and the Revolutionary Process*, Oxford University Press, 1981.

七、问题与思考

1. 如何理解葛兰西的领导权学说及其当代价值?

2. 如何评价阵地战在夺取领导权过程中的重要作用?

3. 葛兰西的实践哲学是否符合马克思主义哲学的基本精神?

第五章　激进的现代艺术哲学之思——《机械复制时代的艺术作品》选读

教学目的与要求

正确掌握艺术品本身所固有的"灵氛"概念，了解艺术作品的膜拜价值与展示价值，对"灵氛"衰落的后果有一个清晰的认识；正确理解、评价艺术的政治化观念；理解救赎历史观及其与历史唯物主义的关系。

一、历史背景

（一）作者介绍

1892年，瓦尔特·本迪克斯·舍恩弗里斯·本雅明（Walter Bendix Schoenflies Benjamin）出生于德国柏林一个富裕的犹太人家庭。本雅明在中学时代参加了当时非常盛行的青年运动，并成为其中一个组织的核心成员。不过，1913年他即与这个组织决裂了。1912年到1915年间，他辗转于弗赖堡大学、柏林大学和慕尼黑大学的哲学课堂。除了哲学课，他还修读了艺术史和文学史课程。和当时许多在柏林求学的人一样，他也受到了社会学家和文化历史学家格奥尔格·席美尔的影响。第一次世界大战爆发后，本雅明的两位诗人朋友弗里茨·海因勒和里加·塞里希森以自杀的方式宣示了自己的反战立场，这两起悲惨事件对本雅明最初的战争经历触动颇大，从而使他接受了卢卡奇《小说理论》中的浪漫主义的反资本主义立场。在整个第一次世界战争期间，他都坚持反战原则，以各种方式逃避兵役。1917年，他携妻子去了中立国瑞士，在那里，他于1919年完成了关于康德和浪漫主义的博士学位论文《德国浪漫派的艺术批评概念》。获得博士学位后，本雅明决意成为“最伟大的德国文学批评家”。不过，他所理解的批评只能在艺术、宗教和哲学的形而上学交汇点这个意义上才能得到正确的理解。在他看来，艺术关注生活，哲学探索真理，宗教追问上帝的意义（或者上帝对于我们的意义：救赎），从作为其对象的艺术起步，再经哲学洞察的中介，批评将与被救赎的生活领域建立起最终的连接。对救赎持之以恒的渴望，代表了贯穿本雅明全部理论著作的内驱力。二十世纪二十年代初，本雅明借用浪漫派的“内在批评”方法完成了以《歌德的〈亲和力〉》为代表的一批出色的作品，在学术界初步确立了自己的地位。随后，为了获得大学的教职资格，他开始集中精力研究17世纪的德国悲苦剧，力图“将它的形式——悲苦剧——与悲剧做比较，从而揭示出作为文学形式的悲苦剧与作为艺术形式的寓言之间存在的亲缘性”。1925年，他完成了《德国悲剧的起源》一书的写作，深刻揭示了寓言的哲学本质：“思想领域中的寓言正如事物领域中的废墟。”但是，很不幸，当本雅明将《德国悲剧的起源》提交给法兰克福大学后，却因为它的思想超前性而遭到“大失败”。这迫使他放弃获得大学教职的努力，在自己生命的最后15年里，一直以自由撰稿人的身份过着颠沛流离的生活。

1924年春，本雅明前往意大利的卡普里岛度假。在那里，他认真阅读了卢卡奇的《历史与阶级意识》，同时还结识了来自拉脱维亚的女布尔什维克阿西娅·拉西斯，其思想开始转向马克思主义。1926年12月6日到1927年2月1日，本雅明造访莫斯科。虽然他对苏联社会主义的印象不甚完美，但莫斯科之行却决定性地推动了他向马克思主义的转变。从1927年开始，本雅明就筹划着一个大的写作计划，即“拱廊街计划”。在1940年9月去世以前，他一直都断断续续地忙于这项研究，但从最终完成的笔记和手稿看，“拱廊街计划”的完成情况非常差：他一共编制了600多个标题，但只讨论了其中的三分之一，而真正编入拱廊街著作的“笔记和材料”中的只有50个左右的标题。不过，在“拱廊街计划”的创作过程中，他却形成了两个非常重要的前期成果：一个是作为“拱廊街计划”的方法论预演的《机械复制时代的艺术作品》,另一个就是"拱廊街计划"中提前完成的《波德莱尔笔下第二帝国的巴黎》。这两部作品和1940年的《历史哲学论纲》共同构成了本雅明后期艺术哲学思想的最高峰。另外,本雅明在1932年创作的具有自传意义的回忆录《柏林纪事》和《1900年前后的柏林童年》中,追忆了自己的童年经历。这两部作品兼具文化批评和个人沉思的混合风格,充分展现了本雅明作品跨越学科界限、打破体裁常规的复杂性。1940年,本雅明在西班牙边境的一个小镇上自杀。

(二)时代背景

1. 现代电影技术的兴起

1839年,法国人路易·达盖尔发明了实用摄影术,令摄影开始走进人们的日常生活,并迅猛发展起来。最初,摄影只是被当作一种现代魔术,而到了19世纪末期,它逐渐变成了一种新兴的大众艺术,并对人们传统的艺术观念构成了重大冲击。作为摄影术的一种发展,电影在1895年正式诞生。在第一次世界大战前后,它从杂耍发展成为一门艺术,并获得了极为迅猛的发展,成为一种大众喜闻乐见的文化娱乐形式。电影技术的发展和成熟极大改变了大众的文化参与方式,也对文化产业和文化理论体系产生了巨大影响。电影成为一个社会性的文化形式和产业,主要体现在两个方面。一是体现在电影产业的整体规模。当时,德国的电影院和座位数量急速上升,电影市场迅速火爆,电影作品也超过欧洲其他国家的总和。二是体现在德国当时的电影作品呈现出明显的表现主义特征,这成为该段时期德国电影的总体特色。[①] 德国电影产业的发展为本雅明开展艺术作品机械复制模式的分析提供了鲜活素材。

2. 纳粹政府的独裁统治与反共产主义道路

德国纳粹党上台之后,始终推行"民族社会主义"的政策,强调全社会的一元性,企图通过加强极权统治,建立起一种"民族共同体",消除国家内部的各种对抗因素,维护全德意志民族的统一利益。这要求全德国的民族一

---

① 邢来顺、吴友法主编:《德国通史》第五卷,江苏人民出版社2019年版,第159—160页。

起维护这一利益，更是演化为要求维护雅利安-北欧日耳曼人的种族纯洁性。纳粹政府标榜的各种种族主义口号，实际上都是为实现希特勒的个人独裁服务的。他们强烈敌视马克思主义，将之视为“毒瘤”，对共产党进行全面的政治打压，取缔共产党的组织，镇压共产党的政治活动，销毁马克思主义的著作。但与此同时，纳粹政府又非常重视拉拢民众。他们抛出“消除失业、拯救工人和农民、解决失业和农业危机”等口号，赢得了德国广大中下层民众的支持。此外，纳粹政府借助增加公共支出、稳定物价、强制调整工人阶层结构和劳动形式等方法，在一定程度上缓解了德国的经济危机，又充分保障了大资产阶级企业主的利益。纳粹政府的一系列措施取得了一些短期效果，令德国民众感到“胜利”的希望，营造出真的要实行“社会主义”的假象。但这一假象的背后包藏了德国纳粹政府小资产阶级社会主义的政治野心。

3. 纳粹政府的文化宣传策略

纳粹政府实行了广泛、极端、单一的文化宣传工作。纳粹政府通过设立全社会性质的电影播放机制，大规模制作官方电影，让电影成为政治宣传的重要途径。这一措施使得纳粹的思想在社会中广泛传播开来，特别是对青少年群体产生了深远的影响。在具体文化内容方面，纳粹政府采取严格的审查制度，并且体现出强烈的保守倾向：对当时多元新潮的文化形式一律采取排斥和禁止措施，对“非德意志精神”的思想潮流，特别是现代主义、犹太主义和马克思主义文化进行了坚决打击，对文化工作者也采取严厉的监督和控制措施。在这种环境下，当时德国的文化呈现出强烈的民族性、政治性特征，造成文化创作枯竭，大量人才流失或遭到迫害。因此，虽然当时德国的文化和理论表面上看起来繁荣异常，但实质上丧失了应有的创作性和时代性，文化艺术形式高度单一化，同之前的水平都无法相提并论，造成了巨大的反差。比如，1933 年，曾与巴拉兹·贝拉合作拍摄过电影的德国女导演莱尼·里芬施塔尔(1902—2003)应邀为纳粹宣传部拍摄了一部反映当年纳粹党代会的新闻纪录片《忠诚的胜利》。次年，她又奉命拍摄了反映纳粹纽伦堡党代会的纪录片《意志的胜利》。该影片在艺术上完全符合纳粹当局的意图，因此，在 1935 年公映后，该片取得了巨大成功，被纳粹头目们称赞为“杰作”，这也使里芬施塔尔成为“国家社会主义自我标榜最有想象力的宣传员”。1936 年,里芬施塔尔拍摄了她最具代表性的影片《奥林匹亚》,全面记录了 1936 年柏林奥运会的举办经过,充分达到了纳粹政府美化法西斯主义的政治目的。

(三) 思想背景

1. 现代大众艺术的兴起

电影艺术的大发展、大繁荣成为当时社会文化发展的重要推动因素。从 20 世纪 20 年代开始,整个知识界尤其是左翼知识界开始思考作为艺术的电影的本质。在这个方面,最具代表性的就是左派学者巴拉兹·贝拉(1884—1949)和谢尔盖·米哈依洛维奇·爱森斯坦(1898—1948)。巴拉兹是卢卡奇同时代的匈牙利左派文艺理论家和电影理论家。作为曾有过电影实践的早期电影理论家,他目睹了电影这门新兴艺术的产生和成长,并始终关注它的发展,致力于不断发掘它的潜能,总结它的基本审美规律。在《可见的人——电影文化》(1924)和《电影精神》(1930)这两部早期著作中,他积极捍卫电影作为一门艺术的合法性,证明电影不仅是一门艺术,而且是一门与其他艺术存在差别的独立艺术;同时,他还比较全面地阐述了电影语言形式(特写、场面调度、蒙太奇)的独特性。爱森斯坦是苏联最重要的电影导演和电影理论家。基于自己卓越的电影实践,他发展了苏联的电影蒙太奇学说,提出了自己独特的理性蒙太奇理论,使人们对电影的艺术基础有了更为深刻的认识。

2. 大众艺术的政治功能与来自纳粹政府的艺术策略

随着大众艺术的兴起,20 世纪 20 年代末期,以布莱希特(1893—1956)为代表的一些左派艺术家开始思考使大众艺术服务于左派政治的问题。这些艺术家们主张借助马克思主义的历史观和唯物主义认知和反映社会生产生活,并且力主通过灵活多样的、富有个性的手法和内容,全面而又富有艺术气息地展现具体的内容。布莱希特的主张得到了本雅明的热情支持。在 1931 年出版的《作为生产者的作者》中,本雅明提出,以机械复制为代表的最先进的技术手段本身足以保证最进步的政治和艺术成果,也就是说,诸如蒙太奇、文学化、陌生化等技术在传统资产阶级艺术形式语境内中的结合,将反过来推翻资产阶级艺术形式。因此，文学、电影和戏剧等艺术不再能够服务于疲乏和冷漠的资产阶级美学幻想，相反，它们将启发接受者在面对自己的环境和命运时发挥积极的、批评的作用。不过，他们还没有来得及实验自己的主张，纳粹政府就上台了。纳粹政府上台后十分重视运用大众艺术来宣传自己的政治观念，但是，纳粹政府官方炮制的作品不仅缺乏思想性和理论性，也同当时德国人民的实际需求相距甚远。

3. 四种哲学力量的交错影响

在转向马克思主义后，本雅明在思想上始终处于四种思想力量的纠缠、争夺之中。第一种力量是他从青年时代起就一直坚持的乌托邦的末世论历史哲学思想。第二种力量是他青年时代的朋友、犹太教神秘主义学者朔勒姆(1897—1982)所倡导的犹太复国主义思想。第三种力量是他于 1929 年结识的布莱希特的那种比较粗犷的马克思主义文艺理论。第四种力量则是他 1930 年加入其中的法兰克福学派的早期批判理论。本雅明非常珍视自己与朔勒姆、布莱希特、阿多诺的友谊和理论合作，但是，他并不愿意因此放弃自己的理论立场。从某种意义上讲，1933 年以后，他之所以一直拒绝朔勒姆、布莱希特、阿多诺等人的安排，既不去以色列、丹麦，也不去美国，而是选择长期在巴黎流亡，非常重要的一个原因就是他希望在上述力量的冲突中寻求平衡。不过，仔细比较下来，他最终还是与法兰克福学派的早期批判理论更近一些。首先，在生命的最后 6 年里，他主要是依靠流亡中的社会研究所提供的津贴生活的，并且他最终接受了研究所的安排，决意前往美国。其次，尽管他与研究所的理论关系有时候相当紧张，但是，他在二十世纪三十年代中后期的主要研究活动都是在与霍克海默、阿多诺的协调、沟通和后者的支持下进行的。最后，他去世前明确表示要把自己的绝笔之作《历史哲学论纲》寄给在纽约的阿多诺。

二、篇章结构

《机械复制时代的艺术作品》有两个版本。第一个版本发表在 1936 年的《社会研究杂志》(第 5 卷，第 1 期)的法语译本上，因为本雅明与霍克海默都认为，由于戈培尔及其党羽已经从根本上废除了德国的自律文化这一事实，因此这篇文章的“宣传价值”的冲击效应在法国文化地平上应当更强烈。在法文版之后，本雅明又新写了一个德文版，因为他希望该文能在布莱希特等主编的德国流亡出版物《言语》上发表，但未果。1955 年，阿多诺夫妇编辑出版的两卷本《本雅明著作集》收录了这个版本的《机械复制时代的艺术作品》，后来阿伦特编辑的《启迪：本雅明文选》也正是依据这个版本进行了英译。

《机械复制时代的艺术作品》包含一篇序言、一篇后记和 15 段文字。在序言中，本雅明引证了马克思《政治经济学批判》序言中对历史唯物主义的经典表述，指出上层建筑的变革要比经济基础的变革缓慢得多，资本主义生产在十九世纪中叶就创造出来的复制技术用了半个多世纪才在所有文化领域中得到体现。就像在经济基础中一样，先进的复制技术必将深刻影响上层建筑的发展，从而为资本主义的灭亡创造相应的条件。在段落 1 中，本雅明简单追溯了复制技术的发展，指出摄影等机械复制技术的出现带来了两个重要的后果：一是艺术品复制技术的根本变革，二是电影艺术的出现，它们都反过来对传统艺术形式产生了影响。在段落 2 中，本雅明指出，尽管机械复制技术能够创造出比传统的手工复制技术高明得多的复制品，但这些复制品终究是赝品，它们并不能获得艺术品本身的唯一性和原真性，因为在它们中间艺术品本身固有的“灵氛”消失了。在段落 3 中，本雅明指出，人类的感知方式随着人类生存方式的变化而变化，这种变化的最新表现就是“灵氛”的消失。所谓“灵氛”就是在一定距离之外但感觉上如此贴近之物的独一无二的显现。人们从复制品中看到的和用肉眼目睹的形象是不同的，后者与唯一性和永久性紧密交叉，而前者与暂时性和可重复性紧密交叉，它意味着“灵氛”的消失。在段落 4 中，本雅明指出，艺术作品的唯一性与它置身于那种传统的联系相一致，它们在传统联系中的存在方式最初体现在其所具有的膜拜功能中。机械复制技术在世界历史上第一次把艺术品从它对礼仪的寄生中解放了出来。当艺术创作的原真性标准失灵之时，艺术的整个社会功能也就得到了改变。它不再建立在礼仪的根基上，而是建立在另一种实践上，即建立在政治的根基上。在段落 5 中，本雅明紧接着指出，随着艺术作品的“灵氛”、膜拜功能的消失，艺术作品的另外一种功能即展示功能极大地凸现出来。

在段落 6 至段落 11 中，本雅明主要分析了摄影和电影这两种机械复制的新兴艺术形式。他认为，在摄影中，展示价值压倒了膜拜价值，尽管膜拜价值在人像摄影中拉住了自己的最后防线。不过，进入二十世纪以后，随着人像在摄影中的消失，展示价值便决定性地超越了膜拜价值。照片、电影中的文字说明与绘画标题具有完全不同的性质。观赏者通过图片文字说明直接获知作者的意旨，而在电影中，好像对任何单个画面的理解都是由已消逝的所有先行展现的画面所规定好了的。整个十九世纪，人们都在为照相摄影是不是艺术而争论不休。这种争论体现了双方都未意识到的世界历史的变化：随着机械复制技术的出现，艺术失去了它的膜拜基础，因而它的自主性外观也就消失了。与舞台演员不同，电影演员所做出的艺术成就是由某种机械体现的，后者具有双重结果：第一，电影演员的成就受制于一系列视觉检测机械；第二，电影演员由于不是本人亲自向观众展现他的表演，因而，他就失去了舞台演员所具有的在表演中使他的成就适应观众的可能。对电影来说，关键之处更在于演员是在机械面前自我表演，而不是在观众面前为人表演。当代电影一般来说具有了一种革命贡献，即对传统的艺术观念进行革命的批判。此外，当代电影在某些独特情形中也对社会状况即对财产秩序进行了革命的批判。从文学的发展历程来看，几百年以来，文献中的情形都是很少的一部分作者与成千上万倍的读者相对峙。但十九世纪末期以后，随着新闻出版业的日益发展，不断地给读者提供了新的政治、宗教、科学、职业和地方的喉舌，促使越来越多的读者变成了作者。在苏联，从事文学的权力不再植根于专门的训练中，而是植根于多方面的训练中，因此，文学成了公共财富。与文学在几百年以来所经历的演变相比，电影的这种改变只经过十年就实现了。因为，在电影实践中——尤其在俄罗斯的电影实践中——这种演变已经部分地实现了。面对当代人希望自己被复现的正当要求，在西欧，那种对电影的资本主义开发却制止了对个体进行特殊的满足。在这样的情况下，电影工业就只有竭尽全力地通过幻觉般的想象和多义的推测来诱使大众参与进来。电影对现实的表现，在现代人看来就是无与伦比地富有意义的表现，因为这种表现正是通过其最强烈的机械手段，实现了现实中非机械的方面，而现代人就有权要求艺术品展现现实中的这种非机械的方面。

在段落 12 至段落 15 中，本雅明着重分析了电影的大众艺术特性。他指出，艺术作品的机械复制性改变了大众与艺术的关系。在电影院中，观众个人的批判态度和欣赏态度都化解了，这就是说，其主要特点在于，没有何处比得上在电影院中那样，个人的反应会从一开始就以眼前直接的密集化反应为条件的。个人反应的总和就组成了观众的强烈反应。个人的反应正由于表现了出来，因而，个人反应也就被制约了。电影的特征不仅在于人如何面对着摄影机去表演，而且还在于人如何借助摄影机去表现客观世界。功效心理学使人们明白了仪器检测的能力，而精神分析学则从另一角度说明了仪器的能力。电影实际上是用可以由弗洛伊德理论来解释的方法，丰富了人们的观照世界。电影在视觉世界的整个领域中，现在也在听觉领域中，导致了对统觉的类似的深化。电影所展示的成就比绘画或剧场所展示的成就精确得多，而且它能放在更多的视点中去加以分析，这只是以上那个事实所导致的另一面。较之于舞台，电影展示的成就所具有的更大的可分析性是以一个更高级的可剥离性为条件的，这个可剥离性的主要意义，在于它具有促进艺术和科学相互渗透的倾向。自古以来，艺术的最重要任务之一就是对时下尚未完全满足之问题的追求。每一种艺术形式的发展史都有一些关键阶段，在这些关键阶段中，艺术形式就追求着那些只有在技术水准发生变化的、即只有在某个新的艺术形式中才会随意产生的效应。如此所出现的艺术的无节制性和粗野性，尤其在所谓的衰落时代，实际上是产生于它的最丰富的历史合力中。电影凭借它的技巧结构获得了这种似乎仍被达达主义者包装于道德之中的官能上的震惊效果，也就从那种束缚中解放了出来。大众是促使所有现今面对艺术作品的惯常态度获得新生的母体。通过艺术所提供的消遣，人们可轻易检验属于统觉的新任务在怎样的范围内能被完成。此外，由于对单个人来说存在着逃避这些任务的诱惑，因此，艺术在唤起大众之处触及了那些最艰难和最重要的任务。目前，电影便展现了这一点。消遣性接受随着日益在所有艺术领域中得到推重而引人注目，而且它成了知觉已发生深刻变化的迹象。这种消遣性接受借助电影便获得了特有的实验工具。电影在它的震惊效果中迎合了这种接受方式。电影抑制了膜拜价值，这不仅是由于它使观众采取了一种鉴赏态度，而且还由于这种鉴赏态度在电影院中并不包括凝神专注。观众成了一位主考官，但这是一位心不在焉的主考官。

在后记中，本雅明点出了自己写作这篇论说文的政治目的：反对法西斯主义。他指出，现代人日益增长着的无产阶级化和大众联合是同一个事件的两个方面。法西斯主义试图去组织新产生的无产阶级大众，而不去触及他们要求消灭的所有制关系。法西斯主义把大众获得表达(绝不是获得他们的权力)视为其福祉。大众具有改变所有制关系的权力；而法西斯主义则试图在对所有制关系的维护中对此做出反应。法西斯主义一贯地使政治生活审美化。法西斯主义使对领袖伏地叩拜的大众所遭受的压制，与为法西斯主义创造膜拜价值服务的机器所遭受的压制是相一致的。面对法西斯主义的政治审美化，共产主义必须用艺术的政治化去应对。

《历史哲学论纲》是本雅明的天鹅之作。这篇手稿后来按照他的意愿寄给了当时在纽约的阿多诺。1942 年，流亡中的社会研究所以纪念刊的形式出版了这一手稿。在这篇由 18 段文字组成的文献中，本雅明比较完整地表达了他的救赎历史观。

三、研究前沿

国内学界对本雅明的研究大致是从二十世纪八十年代开始的，但是直到二十一世纪初才形成一定的规模，此后研究成果的数量保持相对稳定。同卢卡奇、阿多诺等西方马克思主义旗手相比，本雅明研究的主题相对集中，但由于他的过早离世，一定程度上导致他的作品价值还没有得到充分发掘。不过，学界对本雅明的相关探索依旧进行了深刻分析，解读研究工作也涵盖了本雅明思想的各个领域。同时，学界对本雅明相关思想的研究还有一个显著的特点，即研究者往往来自不同领域，包括哲学、马克思主义理论、新闻传播、艺术、中文等多个学科或专业，呈现出专业背景和研究话语的多元特征。由此，研究者从不同的理论旨趣和研究主题入手，对本雅明的哲学和艺术理论进行了卓有成效的探索。

第一，对《机械复制时代的艺术作品》的版本考订与总体性考察。《机械复制时代的艺术作品》再版多次，都与当时的时代环境密切相关，也能够在一定程度上反映本雅明的立场。有学者指出，该著作一共有三个版本，但是问世的第二版是被大量删减和篡改之后的版本，这种情况与当时的政治社会和思想文化形势紧密相关，而本雅明本人的态度也是其中一个很重要的原因。有学者认为，本雅明在该作品中表现出了一定程度上的妥协和犹豫，其立场并没有充分直白地展示出来。不过，学者们并没有因此否认本雅明的革命性。在《机械复制时代的艺术作品》中，本雅明虽然表达了一种悲观的立场，但是，他批判历史进步论、坚持发现革命契机以捍卫历史唯物主义的努力仍然是值得肯定的。

第二，对《机械复制时代的艺术作品》中重点概念的研究。作为该著作中的核心概念，有相当数量的学者专门研究"灵氛"概念。我们看到，本雅明充分运用"灵氛"概念，分析了现代艺术同以往传统的戏剧、绘画等艺术相比具有的独特模式和特点，也推动观众和艺术作品之间关系发生了更加深刻的变化。"灵氛"概念是本雅明针对电影艺术的思维逻辑起点，也是他揭示整个电影艺术形式的革命性贡献的重要支点。随着机械复制时代的来临，现代艺术原先具备的特点不断丧失，艺术文化丧失权威性，走向世俗化。有学者通过比较本雅明与其他左翼思想家，指出本雅明作品中体现出的悲观立场、政治权力、资本主义的商品拜物教等内在逻辑能够与其他学者的立场起到良好的互补作用，为思考现代社会提供重要的学理路径。另外，复制技术及其与艺术的关系也是该著作中的核心部分。有学者指出，随着技术的发展，作者与作品、作者与读者的关系会发生深刻转变，本雅明关于作品复制与需求的关系因此成为我们思考现代性危机的一个重要方面。

第三，对《机械复制时代的艺术作品》时代价值的研究。有学者对"灵氛"概念提出的价值和学理依据进行了讨论，认为"灵氛"概念是本雅明考察电影艺术的重要支点，而后者对于电影理论的贡献还应当超越"灵氛"概念的范畴，用更加广泛的视野来考察。本雅明包括"灵氛"概念在内的创造性发现是在当时纳粹专制独裁统治之下，德国本土思想家进行的难能可贵的重要探索，开创了与法兰克福学派其他学者相异的学理观点，体现出了预见性和前瞻性。有学者就此指出，本雅明的"灵氛"概念揭示了人与世界的互惠关系，随着当时人类艺术形式的改变，这种互惠关系不断消失，进而引发了艺术作品创造性的丧失。本雅明对艺术作品的现代经验空洞化、抽象化和被操纵化的批判，直接触及了文化发展的内核，这种批判对当前我们推进人类数字媒介时代的感知与交流方式的演进具有重要意义。随着交互、AR、VR 等新形式和技术的出现，极大促进了艺术带给人的全新的感官体验，公众的艺术接受和鉴赏能力也发生了改变，对媒介、图像形成了一种新的依赖，而传统的认识论和反映论则不断瓦解。因此，我们需要辨析好"机械复制"与创作艺术成果的关系，以及与民众艺术接受的关系，这对一些超越感官成果的培育,以及凸显这些成果的价值具有重要的意义。从这个意义上讲,我们需要着力发掘本雅明思想的时代意义与价值。

四、文本节选

The Work of Art in the Age of Mechanical Reproduction

I

In principle a work of art has always been reproducible. Man-made artifacts could always be imitated by men. Replicas were made by pupils in practice of their craft, by masters for diffusing their works, and, finally, by third parties in the pursuit of gain. Mechanical reproduction of a work of art, however, represents something new. Historically, it advanced intermittently and in leaps at long intervals, but with accelerated intensity. The Greeks knew only two procedures of technically reproducing works of art: founding and stamping. Bronzes, terra cottas, and coins were the only art works which they could produce in quantity. All others were unique and could not be mechanically reproduced. ...

... Around 1900 technical reproduction had reached a standard that not only permitted it to reproduce all transmitted works of art and thus to cause the most profound change in their impact upon the public; it also had captured a place of its own among the artistic processes. For the study of this standard nothing is more revealing than the nature of the repercussions that these two different manifestations—the reproduction of works of art and the art of the film—have had on art in its traditional form.

Ⅱ

Even the most perfect reproduction of a work of art is lacking in one element: its presence in time and space, its unique existence at the place where it happens to be. This unique existence of the work of art determined the history to which it was subject throughout the time of its existence. This includes the changes which it may have suffered in physical condition over the years as well as the various changes in its ownership. The traces of the first can be revealed only by chemical or physical analyses which it is impossible to perform on a reproduction; changes of ownership are subject to a tradition which must be traced from the situation of the original.

The presence of the original is the prerequisite to the concept of authenticity. Chemical analyses of the patina of a bronze can help to establish this, as does the proof that a given manuscript of the Middle Ages stems from an archive of the fifteenth century. The whole sphere of authenticity is outside technical—and, of course, not only technical—reproducibility. Confronted with its manual reproduction, which was usually branded as a forgery, the original preserved all its authority; not so *vis à vis* technical reproduction. The reason is twofold. First, process reproduction is more independent of the original than manual reproduction. For example, in photography, process reproduction can bring out those aspects of the original that are unattainable to the naked eye yet accessible to the lens, which is adjustable and chooses its angle at will. And photographic reproduction, with the aid of certain processes, such as enlargement or slow motion, can capture images which escape natural vision. Secondly, technical reproduction can put the copy of the original into situations which would be out of reach for the original itself. Above all, it enables the original to meet the beholder halfway, be it in the form of a photograph or a phonograph record. The cathedral leaves its locale to be received in the studio of a lover of art; the choral production, performed in an auditorium or in the open air, resounds in the drawing room.

...

One might subsume the eliminated element in the term "aura" and go on to say: that which withers in the age of mechanical reproduction is the aura of the work of art. This is a symptomatic process whose significance points beyond the realm of art. One might generalize by saying: the technique of reproduction detaches the reproduced object from the domain of tradition. By making many reproductions it substitutes a plurality of copies for a unique existence. And in permitting the reproduction to meet the beholder or listener in his own particular situation, it reactivates the object reproduced. These two processes lead to a tremendous shattering of tradition which is the obverse of the contemporary crisis and renewal of mankind. Both processes are intimately connected with the contemporary mass movements. Their most powerful agent is the film. Its social significance, particularly in its most positive form, is inconceivable without its destructive, cathartic aspect, that is, the liquidation of the traditional value of the cultural heritage. This phenomenon is most palpable in the great historical films. It extends to ever new positions. ...

Ⅲ

During long periods of history, the mode of human sense perception changes with humanity's entire mode of existence. The manner in which human sense perception is organized, the medium in which it is accomplished, is determined not only by nature but by historical circumstances as well. The fifth century, with its great shifts of population, saw the birth of the late Roman art industry and the Vienna Genesis, and there developed not only an art different from that of antiquity but also a new kind of perception. The scholars of the Viennese school, Riegl and Wickhoff, who resisted the weight of classical tradition under which these later art forms had been buried, were the first to draw conclusions from them concerning the organization of perception at the time. However far-reaching their insight, these scholars limited themselves to showing the significant, formal hallmark which characterized perception in late Roman times. They did not attempt—and, perhaps, saw no way—to show the social transformations expressed by these changes of perception. The conditions for an analogous insight are more favorable in the present. And if changes in the medium of contemporary perception can be comprehended as decay of the aura, it is possible to show its social causes.

The concept of aura which was proposed above with reference to historical objects may usefully be illustrated with reference to the aura of natural ones. We define the aura of the latter as the unique phenomenon of a distance, however close it may be. If, while resting on a summer afternoon, you follow with your eyes a mountain range on the horizon or a branch which casts its shadow over you, you experience the aura of those mountains, of that branch. This image makes it easy to comprehend the social bases of the contemporary decay of the aura. It rests on two circumstances, both of which are related to the increasing significance of the masses in contemporary life. Namely, the desire of contemporary masses to bring things "closer" spatially and humanly, which is just as ardent as their bent toward overcoming the uniqueness of every reality by accepting its reproduction. Every day the urge grows stronger to get hold of an object at very close range by way of its likeness, its reproduction. Unmistakably, reproduction as offered by picture magazines and newsreels differs from the image seen by the unarmed eye. Uniqueness and permanence are as closely linked in the latter as are transitoriness and reproducibility in the former. To pry an object from its shell, to destroy its aura, is the mark of a perception whose "sense of the universal equality of things" has increased to such a degree that it extracts it even from a unique object by means of reproduction. Thus is manifested in the field of perception what in the theoretical sphere is noticeable in the increasing importance of statistics. The adjustment of reality to the masses and of the masses to reality is a process of unlimited scope, as much for thinking as for perception.

Ⅳ

The uniqueness of a work of art is inseparable from its being imbedded in the fabric of tradition. This tradition itself is thoroughly alive and extremely changeable. An ancient statue of Venus, for example, stood in a different traditional context with the Greeks, who made it an object of veneration, than with the clerics of the Middle Ages, who viewed it as an ominous idol. Both of them, however, were equally confronted with its uniqueness, that is, its aura. Originally the contextual integration of art in tradition found its expression in the cult. We know that the earliest art works originated in the service of a ritual—first the magical, then the religious kind. It is significant that the existence of the work of art with reference to its aura is never entirely separated from its ritual function. In other words, the unique value of the "authentic" work of art has its basis in ritual, the location of its original use value. This ritualistic basis, however remote, is still recognizable as secularized ritual even in the most profane forms of the cult of beauty. The secular cult of beauty, developed during the Renaissance and prevailing for three centuries, clearly showed that ritualistic basis in its decline and the first deep crisis which befell it. With the advent of the first truly revolutionary means of reproduction, photography, simultaneously with the rise of socialism, art sensed the approaching crisis which has become evident a century later. At the time, art reacted with the doctrine of *l'art pour l'art*, that is, with a theology of art. This gave rise to what might be called a negative theology in the form of the idea of "pure" art, which not only denied any social function of art but also any categorizing by subject matter. (In poetry, Mallarmé was the first to take this position.)

An analysis of art in the age of mechanical reproduction must do justice to these relationships, for they lead us to an all-important insight:

for the first time in world history, mechanical reproduction emancipates the work of art from its parasitical dependence on ritual. To an ever greater degree the work of art reproduced becomes the work of art designed for reproducibility. From a photographic negative, for example, one can make any number of prints; to ask for the "authentic" print makes no sense. But the instant the criterion of authenticity ceases to be applicable to artistic production, the total function of art is reversed. Instead of being based on ritual, it begins to be based on another practice—politics.

V

Works of art are received and valued on different planes. Two polar types stand out: with one, the accent is on the cult value; with the other, on the exhibition value of the work. Artistic production begins with ceremonial objects destined to serve in a cult. One may assume that what mattered was their existence, not their being on view. The elk portrayed by the man of the Stone Age on the walls of his cave was an instrument of magic. He did expose it to his fellow men, but in the main it was meant for the spirits. Today the cult value would seem to demand that the work of art remain hidden. Certain statues of gods are accessible only to the priest in the cella; certain Madonnas remain covered nearly all year round; certain sculptures on medieval cathedrals are invisible to the spectator on ground level. With the emancipation of the various art practices from ritual go increasing opportunities for the exhibition of their products. It is easier to exhibit a portrait bust that can be sent here and there than to exhibit the statue of a divinity that has its fixed place in the interior of a temple. The same holds for the painting as against the mosaic or fresco that preceded it. And even though the public presentability of a mass originally may have been just as great as that of a symphony, the latter originated at the moment when its public presentability promised to surpass that of the mass.

With the different methods of technical reproduction of a work of art, its fitness for exhibition increased to such an extent that the quantitative shift between its two poles turned into a qualitative transformation of its nature. This is comparable to the situation of the work of art in prehistoric times when, by the absolute emphasis on its cult value, it was, first and foremost, an instrument of magic. Only later did it come to be recognized as a work of art. In the same way today, by the absolute emphasis on its exhibition value the work of art become a creation with entirely new functions, among which the one we are conscious of, the artistic function, later may be recognized as incidental. This much is certain: today photography and the film are the most serviceable exemplifications of this new function.

——Walter Benjamin, *Illuminations*, trans. Harry Zohn, Schocken Books, 1968, pp. 218 - 225.

XII

Mechanical reproduction of art changes the reaction of the masses toward art. The reactionary attitude toward a Picasso painting changes into the progressive reaction toward a Chaplin movie. The progressive reaction is characterized by the direct, intimate fusion of visual and emotional enjoyment with the orientation of the expert. Such fusion is of great social significance. The greater the decrease in the social significance of an art form, the sharper the distinction between criticism and enjoyment by the public. The conventional is uncritically enjoyed, and the truly new is criticized with aversion. With regard to the screen, the critical and the receptive attitudes of the public coincide. The decisive reason for this is that individual reactions are predetermined by the mass audience response they are about to produce, and this is nowhere more pronounced than in the film. The moment these responses become manifest they control each other. Again, the comparison with painting is fruitful. A painting has always had an excellent chance to be viewed by one person or by a few. The simultaneous contemplation of paintings by a large public, such as developed in the nineteenth century, is an early symptom of the crisis of painting, a crisis which was by no means occasioned exclusively by photography but rather in a relatively independent manner by the appeal of art works to the masses.

——Walter Benjamin, *Illuminations*, trans. Harry Zohn, Schocken Books, 1968, p. 234.

XIV

One of the foremost tasks of art has always been the creation of a demand which could be fully satisfied only later. The history of every art form shows critical epochs in which a certain art form aspires to effects which could be fully obtained only with a changed technical standard, that is to say, in a new art form. ...

...

From an alluring appearance or persuasive structure of sound the work of art of the Dadaists became an instrument of ballistics. It hit the spectator like a bullet, it happened to him, thus acquiring a tactile quality. It promoted a demand for the film, the distracting element of which is also primarily tactile being based on changes of place and focus which periodically assail the spectator. Let us compare the screen on which a film unfolds with the canvas of a painting. The painting invites the spectator to contemplation; before it the spectator can abandon himself to his associations. Before the movie frame he cannot do so. No sooner has his eye grasped a scene than it is already changed. It cannot be arrested. Duhamel, who detests the film and knows nothing of its significance, though something of its structure, notes this circumstance as follows: "I can no longer think what I want to think. My thoughts have been replaced by moving images." The spectator's process of association in view of these images is indeed interrupted by their constant, sudden change. This constitutes the shock effect of the film, which, like all shocks, should be cushioned by heightened presence of mind. By means of its technical structure, the film has taken the physical shock effect out of the wrappers in which Dadaism had, as it were, kept it inside the moral shock effect.

XV

...

... Distraction as provided by art presents a covert control of the extent to which new tasks have become soluble by apperception. Since, moreover, individuals are tempted to avoid such tasks, art will tackle the most difficult and most important ones where it is able to mobilize the masses. Today it does so in the film. Reception in a state of distraction, which is increasing noticeably in all fields of art and is symptomatic ofprofound changes in apperception, finds in the film its true means of exercise. The film with its shock effect meets this mode of reception halfway. The film makes the cult value recede into the background not only by putting the public in the position of the critic, but also by the fact that at the movies this position requires no attention. The public is an examiner, but an absent-minded one.

EPILOGUE

The growing proletarianization of modern man and the increasing formation of masses are two aspects of the same process. Fascism attempts to organize the newly created proletarian masses without affecting the property structure which the masses strive to eliminate. Fascism sees its salvation in giving these masses not their right, but instead a chance to express themselves. The masses have a right to change property relations; Fascism seeks to give them an expression while preserving property. The logical result of Fascism is the introduction of aesthetics into political life. The violation of the masses, whom Fascism, with its *Führer* cult, forces to their knees, has its counterpart in the violation of an apparatus which is pressed into the production of ritual values.

All efforts to render politics aesthetic culminate in one thing: war. War and war only can set a goal for mass movements on the largest scale while respecting the traditional property system. This is the political formula for the situation. The technological formula may be stated as follows: Only war makes it possible to mobilize all of today's technical resources while maintaining the property system. It goes without saying that the Fascist apotheosis of war does not employ such arguments. Still, Marinetti says in his manifesto on the Ethiopian colonial war: "For twenty-seven years we Futurists have rebelled against the branding of war as antiaesthetic. ... Accordingly we state: ... War is beautiful because it establishes man's dominion over the subjugated machinery by means of gas masks, terrifying megaphones, flame throwers, and small tanks. War is beautiful because it initiates the dreamt-of metalization of the human body. War is beautiful because it enriches a flowering meadow with the fiery orchids of machine guns. War is beautiful because it combines the gunfire, the cannonades, the cease-fire, the scents, and the stench of putrefaction into a symphony. War is beautiful because it creates new architecture, like that of the big tanks, the geometrical formation flights, the smoke spirals from burning villages, and many others ... . Poets and artists of Futurism! ... remember these principles of an aesthetics of war so that your struggle for a new literature and a new graphic art ... may be illumined by them!"

This manifesto has the virtue of clarity. Its formulations deserve to be accepted by dialecticians. To the latter, the aesthetics of today's war appears as follows: If the natural utilization of productive forces is impeded by the property system, the increase in technical devices, in speed, and in the sources of energy will press for an unnatural utilization, and this is found in war. The destructiveness of war furnishes proof that society has not been mature enough to incorporate technology as its organ, that technology has not been sufficiently developed to cope with the elemental forces of society. The horrible features of imperialistic warfare are attributable to the discrepancy between the tremendous means of production and their inadequate utilization in the process of production—in other words, to unemployment and the lack of markets. Imperialistic war is a rebellion of technology which collects, in the form of "human material", the claims to which society has denied its natural material. Instead of draining rivers, society directs a human stream into a bed of trenches; instead of dropping seeds from airplanes, it drops incendiary bombs over cities; and through gas warfare the aura is abolished in a new way.

"*Fiat ars—pereat mundus*," says Fascism, and, as Marinetti admits, expects war to supply the artistic gratification of a sense perception that has been changed by technology. This is evidently the consummation of "*l'art pour l'art*". Mankind, which in Homer's time was an object of contemplation for the Olympian gods, now is one for itself. Its self-alienation has reached such a degree that it can experience its own destruction as an aesthetic pleasure of the first order. This is the situation of politics which Fascism is rendering aesthetic. Communism responds by politicizing art.

——Walter Benjamin, *Illuminations*, trans. Harry Zohn, Schocken Books, 1968, pp. 237 - 242.

Theses on the Philosophy of History

I

The story is told of an automaton constructed in such a way that it could play a winning game of chess, answering each move of an opponent with a countermove. A puppet in Turkish attire and with a hookah in its mouth sat before a chessboard placed on a large table. A system of mirrors created the illusion that this table was transparent from all sides. Actually, a little hunchback who was an expert chess player sat inside and guided the puppet's hand by means of strings. One can imagine a philosophical counterpart to this device. The puppet called "historical materialism" is to win all the time. It can easily be a match for anyone if it enlists the services of theology, which today, as we know, is wizened and has to keep out of sight.

II

"One of the most remarkable characteristics of human nature," writes Lotze, "is, alongside so much selfishness in specific instances, the freedom from envy which the present displays toward the future." Reflection shows us that our image of happiness is thoroughly colored by the time to which the course of our own existence has assigned us. The kind of happiness that could arouse envy in us exists only in the air we have breathed, among people we could have talked to, women who could have given themselves to us. In other words, our image of happiness is indissolubly bound up with the image of redemption. The same applies to our view of the past, which is the concern of history. The past carries with it a temporal index by which it is referred to redemption. There is a secret agreement between past generations and the present one. Our coming was expected on earth. Like every generation that preceded us, we have been endowed with a *weak*

Messianic power, a power to which the past has a claim. That claim cannot be settled cheaply. Historical materialists are aware of that.

...

Ⅷ

The tradition of the oppressed teaches us that the "state of emergency" in which we live is not the exception but the rule. We must attain to a conception of history that is in keeping with this insight. Then we shall clearly realize that it is our task to bring about a real state of emergency, and this will improve our position in the struggle against Fascism. One reason why Fascism has a chance is that in the name of progress its opponents treat it as a historical norm. The current amazement that the things we are experiencing are "still" possible in the twentieth century is *not* philosophical. This amazement is not the beginning of knowledge—unless it is. the knowledge that the view of history which gives rise to it is untenable.

...

XⅥ

A historical materialist cannot do without the notion of a present which is not a transition, but in which time stands still and has come to a stop. For this notion defines the present in which he himself is writing history. Historicism gives the "eternal" image of the past; historical materialism supplies a unique experience with the past. The historical materialist leaves it to others to be drained by the whore called "Once upon a time" in historicism's bordello. He remains in control of his powers, man enough to blast open the continuum of history.

XⅦ

Historicism rightly culminates in universal history. Materialistic historiography differs from it as to method more clearly than from any other kind. Universal history has no theoretical armature. Its method is additive; it musters a mass of data to fill the homogeneous, empty time. Materialistic historiography, on the other hand, is based on a constructive principle. Thinking involves not only the flow of thoughts, but their arrest as well. Where thinking suddenly stops in a configuration pregnant with tensions, it gives that configuration a shock, by which it crystallizes into a monad. A historical materialist approaches a historical subject only where he encounters it as a monad. In this structure he recognizes the sign of a Messianic cessation of happening, or, put differently, a revolutionary chance in the fight for the oppressed past. He takes cognizance of it in order to blast a specific era out of the homogeneous course of history-blasting a specific life out of the era or a specific work out of the lifework. As a result of this method the lifework is preserved in this work and at the same time canceled; in the lifework, the era; and in the era, the entire course of history. The nourishing fruit of the historically understood contains time as a precious but tasteless seed.

XVIII

"In relation to the history of organic life on earth," writes a modern biologist, "the paltry fifty millennia of *homo sapiens* constitute something like two seconds at the close of a twenty-four-hour day. On this scale, the history of civilized mankind would fill one-fifth of the last second of the last hour." The present, which, as a model of Messianic time, comprises the entire history of mankind in an enormous abridgment, coincides exactly with the stature which the history of mankind has in the universe.

A

Historicism contents itself with establishing a causal connection between various moments in history. But no fact that is a cause is for that very reason historical. It became historical posthumously, as it were, through events that may be separated from it by thousands of years. A historian who takes this as his point of departure stops telling the sequence of events like the beads of a rosary. Instead, he grasps the constellation which his own era has formed with a definite earlier one. Thus he establishes a conception of the present as the "time of the now" which is shot through with chips of Messianic time.

——Walter Benjamin, *Illuminations*, trans. Harry Zohn, Schocken Books, 1968, pp. 253 - 263.

五、观点解读

1. "灵氛"的衰落导致了"膜拜价值"的丧失

"灵氛"是《机械复制时代的艺术作品》中用来分析艺术的社会史的核心范畴。它指的是艺术作品在传统社会形态的文化合法性中扮演的历史角色。本雅明把这个方面描述为艺术作品的仪式或膜拜功能。它指的是在整个文化历史上艺术作品都曾具有独立地位这一事实——就是说,它们把自己的根本存在归结为它们在社会整合过程中的含义。作为宗教顶礼膜拜的对象,艺术作品获得了一种独一无二的意义、一种纯真性和一种被敬为神圣的特征。于是,本雅明把"灵氛"定义为"一定距离外的独一无二的显现——无论它有多远"。"灵氛"证实了艺术作品在其膜拜形式中的权威性,地位无以模仿的独特性,以及在时空中的唯一性——这是它的真实性的特点。随着文艺复兴时期绘画的诞生,艺术产品的礼仪基础受到了挑战,对美的世俗膜拜盛行起来。在这一点上,艺术开始了争取自律地位的漫长而艰难的斗争,浪漫主义对它做了强有力的更新,唯美主义"为艺术而艺术"的理论——本雅明称之为"艺术神学"——则将它推到了顶峰。在本雅明看来,二十世纪艺术作品的生产和接受领域最重要的变化当属技术手段对这些过程日益强烈的干涉。结果就是"灵氛衰落"。本雅明认为,机械复制艺术用大堆的复制品取代唯一的原件,破坏了灵氛艺术作品生产非常重要的基础——作品的权威性和真实性所倚重的时空唯一性。当一件艺术作品被大批量生产时,它的独创性、个性就成了无关紧要的东西,因为每件作品现在都是可以被替换的。结果,艺术作品再也不能像过去那样,作为礼仪或膜拜对象获得人们的崇敬。它不再是宗教膜拜的对象,丧失了其"膜拜价值",取而代之的是一种新的功能,即"展示价值":注意力的核心从作为享有特权的实体的艺术作品本身转移到了作品与观众之间的交叉点。在本雅明看来,这一事实开启了艺术的政治运用之巨大的、至今尚未被触及的潜能。艺术的制作与接受的技术条件的变化与传统形成了具有世界历史性质的决裂,这一决裂有效地废除了艺术先前的礼仪或膜拜基础,为艺术的政治功能的优势发挥铺平了道路。这一过程体现了艺术本身内在定义中发生的质变:艺术原本是审美美学消遣或娱乐的对象,现在,其地位却让位于其作为交流工具的职能了。"膜拜价值"变成了"展示价值"。

2. 先进的艺术生产力与进步的艺术政治化是对抗资产阶级美学的有力武器

二十世纪三十年代中期,受布莱希特的影响,本雅明认为,如果艺术作品采用了最先进的艺术技术,那么,艺术作品就是进步的;如果它采用的是传统的、过时的艺术实践方式,那么,它就是退步的,且其政治倾向和质量都是退步的。他希冀在技术概念的基础上建立唯物主义批评的尝试完全依靠超越个人的"艺术生产力",这是一种艺术家个人只能够选择服从或不服从的机制,因为它似乎是完全独立于艺术家的意志之外发生作用的。他相信,作为先进艺术生产力的代表,机械复制的方法因此不加批评地与迄今未曾开发的、将沿着革命的路线被改造的巨大艺术潜能成为一体。只要一心一意地拥护这些新技术,艺术家的作品就能保证自己在正确的政治倾向上和美学质量上一道水涨船高。也就是说,诸如蒙太奇、文学化、陌生化等技术在传统资产阶级艺术形式语境中的结合,将使后者从内部被推翻。文学、电影和戏剧等艺术因此不再能够服务于接受者在疲乏和冷漠的资产阶级美学幻想中的被动吸收,相反,它们将启发接受者在面对自己的环境和命运时发挥积极的、批评的作用。在他看来,电影代表了超现实主义的蒙太奇技术的最终实现,因为电影从总体上看无非是对一系列单独拍摄的事件和场景的最后合成。此外，当我们从电影的制作与接受的最重要的集体立场来考虑时，就会发现，电影代表了对资产阶级自律艺术(例如小说和绘画)的制作与接受的最显著的私人性和唯一性地位的全面攻击，这使得它非常适合于政治内容的宣传。它在“捕捉”客观现实上的优越性使视觉艺术和小说陷入了一场突如其来的危机，迫使其另外寻找更为主体化的表现形式。不仅如此，通过应用蒙太奇原理，电影传达了一种震惊效果，该效果使电影与资产阶级灵氛艺术最为典型的被动性、冥思性状态变得不再相容。如果传统的资产阶级艺术的观赏者是被动地全神贯注于作品，那么，借助于其震惊特点，电影就会制造出一种异化或者离散的效果，迫使观赏者承担起一个积极的、批判的角色。由此，本雅明希望共产主义者能够充分利用电影这种艺术形式服务于自己进步的政治需要，以对抗法西斯主义谋求的政治审美化。

3. 透过停滞的辩证法实现历史的救赎

面对法西斯主义的不断胜利，本雅明对世界历史的前途变得日益悲观，作为一种反动，其思想中始终存在的神学救赎之维空前发展起来。因此，在《历史哲学论纲》中，他比较充分地阐发了自己由来已久的救赎历史观。他坚决反对第二国际历史主义的进化论历史观。这种历史观按照历史事件的因果必然性和线性进步观来看待解释历史，结果，它不仅对法西斯主义的崛起视而不见，反倒认为其是技术进步的必然。本雅明认为，过去、现在和未来并不是线性排列的，过去之中蕴含着现在得到救赎的信息，而现在则意味着时间的停顿和静止。在这种辩证的停滞中，历史唯物主义者发现了为受压迫的过去而斗争的革命机会。在这种现在观念中，过去、现在和未来融合在一起，是一种把现在看作透入了弥赛亚式时间的碎片的“当下时间”概念。这种当下是一种弥赛亚时间，通过它，人类历史不断得到救赎，由此进入千年王国——共产主义。

六、进一步阅读指南

1. [德]瓦尔特·本雅明：《本雅明文选》，陈永国、马海良编，中国社会科学出版社1999年版。

2. [德]瓦尔特·本雅明：《德国悲剧的起源》，陈永刚译，文化艺术出版社 2001 年版。

3. [德]瓦尔特·本雅明:《经验与贫乏》,王炳钧、杨劲译,百花文艺出版社 1999 年版。

4. [德]汉娜·阿伦特编:《启迪:本雅明文选》,张旭东、王斑译,三联书店 2008 年版。

5. [德]瓦尔特·本雅明:《发达资本主义时代的抒情诗人:论波德莱尔》,张旭东、魏文生译,三联书店 1989 年版。

6. [德]瓦尔特·本雅明:《机械复制时代的艺术作品》,王才勇译,中国城市出版社 2002 年版。

7. [美]理查德·沃林:《瓦尔特·本雅明:救赎美学》,吴勇立、张亮译,江苏人民出版社 2008 年版。

8. [英]特里·伊格尔顿:《沃尔特·本雅明,或走向革命批评》,郭国良、陆汉臻译,译林出版社 2005 年版。

9. [德]毛姆·布罗德森:《本雅明传》,国容等译,敦煌文艺出版社 2000 年版。

10. [英]戴维·弗里斯比:《现代性的碎片:齐美尔、克拉考尔和本雅明作品中的现代性理论》,卢晖临等译,商务印书馆 2003 年版。

11. [日]三岛宪一:《本雅明:破坏·收集·记忆》,贾倞译,河北教育出版社 2001 年版。

12. [英]唐纳德·萨松:《欧洲社会主义百年史——二十世纪的西欧左翼》(上册),姜辉、于海青、庞晓明译,社会科学文献出版社、重庆出版社 2017 年版。

13. 刘北成:《本雅明思想肖像》,上海人民出版社 1998 年版。

14. 于闽梅:《灵韵与救赎:本雅明思想研究》,文化艺术出版社 2008 年版。

15. 秦露:《文学形式与历史救赎:论本雅明〈德国哀悼剧起源〉》,华夏出版社 2005 年版。

16. Beatrice Hanssen, *Walter Benjamin's Other History: of Stones, Animals, Human Beings, and Angels*, Berkeley, University of California Press, 1998.

17. David S. Ferris, ed., *Walter Benjamin: Theoretical Questions*,

Stanford，Stanford University Press，1996.

七、问题与思考

1. 什么是“灵氛”？“灵氛”的衰落导致了什么样的后果？
2. 如何正确认识、评价本雅明艺术的政治化思想？
3. 如何看待本雅明的救赎历史观及其与历史唯物主义的关系？

第六章　用“总体人”的辩证法来反对斯大林主义——《辩证唯物主义》选读

教学目的与要求

了解列斐伏尔眼中马克思思想的发展过程；理解列斐伏尔对于历史唯物主义和辩证唯物主义之间的区分，以及列斐伏尔理解的辩证唯物主义与传统马克思主义所理解的辩证唯物主义之间的理论差别；认识列斐伏尔“总体人”的辩证法。

一、历史背景

（一）作者介绍

1901年，亨利·列斐伏尔(Henri Lefebvre)出生于法国西南部的朗德省，在当地度过了自己的青年时代。中学毕业后，他先是在普罗旺斯地区的爱克斯大学学习哲学，主攻奥古斯丁哲学和帕斯卡哲学，后转入巴黎的索邦大学继续深造。在这里，他结识了乔治·波利策、保罗·尼赞、诺伯特·古德曼和乔治·弗里德曼等人，并一同创立了“哲学家小组”。该小组是一个具有比较自觉的分工合作意识的学派性组织，小组成员们相信自己的工作将能为理解并重建世界提供基础。最初，他们坚信重建世界的真正基础在于神秘的个人体验，因此，他们对当时正方兴未艾的超现实主义运动产生了兴趣，双方曾多有合作。正是这段经历导致列斐伏尔以后一直对超现实主义保持着某种时断时续的兴趣。不过，他们随后就意识到神秘主义并不能为他们所构想的未来提供伦理和理论基础，于是，他们和同时代其他哲学家一样，将目光转向了德国。一开始，他们只是希望从以黑格尔哲学为代表的德国古典哲学那里获得启示，寻找到一种可以将个人、集体和绝对调和起来的理论工具，但是，随后的研究不仅使他们意识到了政治参与的必要性，而且最终将他们引导到了马克思哲学那里。最终，他们于 1928 年一同加入法国共产党，并出版了法国第一本严肃的马克思主义理论刊物《马克思主义评论》。

加入法国共产党后，列斐伏尔和“哲学家小组”的其他成员一起继续致力于德国哲学的研究。在此过程中，他们受到了刚刚兴起的海德格尔存在哲学的重要影响，列斐伏尔的某些观点甚至被认为已经预示了法国存在主义的诞生。1933 年马克思的《1844 年经济学哲学手稿》公开出版后，列斐伏尔等人即开始向法国理论界译介该著作。1934 年，“哲学家小组”合作完成了一部《马克思著作导读》，文集的导论是由列斐伏尔和古特曼合作撰写的。正是在这一过程中，列斐伏尔开始与古特曼密切合作，于 1936 年合作出版了《被神秘化的意识》，在 1938 年又连续推出了《黑格尔著作导读》和《列宁著作导读》。这一系列著作都强调通过理解黑格尔理论与实践统一的辩证法，从而重新解读马克思辩证法的精神实质。

列斐伏尔实际上在 1936 年就已经独立撰写出了《辩证唯物主义》，但是他直到 1938 年《黑格尔著作导读》和《列宁著作导读》出版后，方才将《辩证唯物主义》交付出版。之所以这么做，首先是因为他深知自己的观点与作为法国共产党官方意识形态的斯大林主义是格格不入、甚至是完全对立的，其次是因为他希望通过《马克思著作导读》《黑格尔著作导读》《列宁著作导读》为自己的“离经叛道”寻找到令人信服的思想史基础，以期减少该书可能受到的政治压力。但事与愿违，《辩证唯物主义》刚一出版，《论辩证唯物主义和历史唯物主义》的法文单行本就紧跟着出版了。在这种机缘巧合造就的独特语境中，《辩证唯物主义》得到了同时代人的广泛关注，在客观上促进了人本主义马克思主义在法国的传播与发展。只不过，列斐伏尔不出所料地受到了法国共产党领导层的质疑和批判。

但是第二次世界大战的爆发使得理论斗争让位于反法西斯斗争。列斐伏尔先是参加了反法西斯的地下抵抗运动，随后则在法国西南部流亡。在此期间，列斐伏尔从社会学的角度对《辩证唯物主义》中的观点进行了系统扩展，其最终成果就是1947年出版的《日常生活批判》第一卷。该书的出版使他成为法国共产党内最重要的理论家之一。此后，他被迫介入党内思想战线的斗争，结果于1957年被开除出党。在此之后，列斐伏尔加入了以《争鸣》期刊为代表的马克思主义研究圈子里，与符号学家罗兰·巴特、社会学家阿兰·图林纳等人共同致力于反思发展马克思主义和研究战后法国资本主义社会。二十世纪六十年代，列斐伏尔转向日常生活批判研究，拓展了经典马克思主义关于新资本主义时代下的消费问题的理论分析，以此开创了著名的日常生活批判思潮。列斐伏尔在日常生活批判研究中呼唤"节日"与"总体人"，以此预见了后来发生的法国1968年五月风暴。不过，五月风暴的失败导致列斐伏尔的亲密追随者散去。在二十世纪七八十年代，列斐伏尔转向都市主义、全球化、空间与资本主义再生产问题的研究，出版了影响深远的《空间的生产》。

同时期，列斐伏尔先后在斯特拉斯堡大学(1961—1965)、巴黎大学南特尔分校(1965—1971)、巴黎高等研究专科学校(1971—1973)任教。1991年6月，列斐伏尔与世长辞。

(二) 时代背景

1. 斯大林主义哲学体系的形成与广泛传播

列宁逝世后，斯大林成为苏联党和国家的最高领导人。在二十世纪二十年代中后期，因为忙于党内政治斗争，斯大林尚无暇顾及马克思主义哲学问题，尽管他实际上始终密切关注着苏联国内马克思主义哲学界的理论动向。随着斯大林绝对领导地位的确立，情况悄然发生了变化。1929年末，以米丁、尤金为代表的青年红色哲学家向占据苏联哲学界领导地位的德波林学派发动进攻，批评后者不关注斯大林领导下的社会主义建设事业及其伟大成就。此后，双方展开了长达一年的论战。1930年12月9日，就在论战进入高潮的时候，斯大林与青年红色哲学家们进行座谈，把论战定性为哲学战线上两条路线的斗争，即布尔什维克式的唯物主义和孟什维克式的唯心主义之间的路线斗争。随即，苏共中央发布文件，从组织上清算了德波林学派及其影响，从而使得代表斯大林意志的青年红色哲学家们成为苏联哲学的领导者。此后，苏联的马克思主义哲学研究完全统一到了斯大林所赞赏的辩证唯物主义和历史唯物主义体系中，并迅速出版了一批研究成果，借助第三国际的影响在各国共产党中广泛传播起来，这其中当然就包括法国共产党。也就是说，尽管《论辩证唯物主义和历史唯物主义》在 1938 年才面世，但是斯大林主义的哲学体系早在三十年代初就基本成型并对国际马克思主义哲学界产生广泛影响了，广泛传播的文本包括 1938 年出版的《联共(布)党史简明教程》，以及次年由各国共产党陆续翻译出版的，由斯大林撰写的《联共(布)党史简明教程》第四章第二节，即《论辩证唯物主义和历史唯物主义》的单行本。

2. 无产阶级运动发展的低谷

1920 年，法国共产党成立。但是，法国共产党的成立先天就缺乏科学理论的指引。就像阿尔都塞后来所说的那样，1789 年大革命之后的一百三十多年间，"法国的哲学史简直贫乏得可怜"，法国共产党就是在这种"理论空白"中诞生的。[①] 因此，成立以后的一段时期内，法国共产党在理论上长期追随斯大林主义，鲜有重大理论创新。另一个原因是，法国工人阶级的主要政治力量是法国社会党。这一政党在"一战"后法国的政治舞台上存在感较低，虽然人数要多于法国共产党，但缺乏成型的组织结构和意识形态纲领，极大制约了其发展。法国社会党在这一时期，虽然在形式上坚持马克思主义，在理念上致力于建设社会主义，然而在实际斗争中，却并没有寻找到一条切实可行的社会主义道路。在欧洲多国的法西斯上台后，第三国际在组织形式问题上的立场逐渐松动，推动了法国境内的多个左派政党和团体的合并。1935 年，法国社会党、法国激进社会党、法国共产党和工会组织联合成立了法国人民阵线。起初，法国人民阵线取得了一系列政治斗争成果，特别是在争取八小时工作制中取得了巨大进展。但是，随着运动和斗争的进一步开展，法国人民阵线遇到了强大阻力。一方面是来自国外的压力，面对法西斯政权不断对外扩张，以英国为代表的欧洲国家没有立刻进行遏制，反而对法国社会和法国人民阵线施加极大压力；另一方面，当时法国的资产

---

① [法]路易·阿尔都塞：《保卫马克思》，顾良译，商务印书馆 1984 年版，第 6 页。

阶级势力依旧强大，在涉及权力分配问题上寸步不让。加之法国人民阵线自身在经济管理、社会改革等方面缺乏经验，导致之后的运动和斗争黯然走向分裂和失败。

（三）思想背景

1. 两次世界大战之间法国哲学的发展趋势

法国思想界从二十世纪初开始探索摆脱绝对主体的牢笼、确立个别经验主体的主体地位的尝试，不过，由柏格森所开启的这个潮流的发展相当艰难、曲折。只是在俄国十月革命之后由马克思主义召唤出来的法国思想界的激进化趋势中，这一主题方才拨云见日：革命必须首先寻找到承担自身的革命主体，但这不应当是《历史与阶级意识》中的那种集体主体，而应是萨特后来所说的那种能够承担"自由"与"责任"的个人主体。为了寻找到这种个人主体，法国哲学家们纷纷将目光转向了邻近的德国，以期找到可资借鉴的思想资源。对于两次世界大战之间的法国思想界而言，最重要的两种德国思想资源分别是从胡塞尔到海德格尔的现象学和黑格尔《精神现象学》中的自我意识哲学。二十世纪三十年代初期，萨特等法国思想家先后前往德国，研究并引进了现象学，从而促成了存在主义在法国的传播和发展。与此同时，曾在德国研究现象学多年的科耶夫开始在法国讲授《精神现象学》，而其重点则是其中的自我意识哲学。经过他的不懈努力，黑格尔的自我意识哲学在当时的法国思想界产生了重要影响，有力促进了同时代许多法国思想家的思想发展。

2. 尼采生命哲学思想的传入

二十世纪三十年代，尼采的生命哲学被传入法国思想界。乔治·巴塔耶、让·瓦尔、列斐伏尔都撰文介绍了尼采哲学，特别强调了尼采对生命自主性的关注。比如，巴塔耶在1937年的《散论》中强调，尼采表达了人对生命的绝对自主性，第一次将长久以来压迫在人身上的形而上学的同质化暴力（无论是上帝还是善、道德等）驱除了出去。瓦尔在1937年的《尼采与上帝之死》中肯定，尼采颠覆了形而上学的先验存在后，人被赋予了无限的创造潜能。在此背景下，列斐伏尔也认为尼采重新阐释了人的存在根基，揭示了人类生命是为了生存而欲求着“权力意志”的存在，涌动着一股不断意欲突破现存境遇、自主创造价值的“超越的意志”。尼采对个体生命自主性的强调，与列斐伏尔参与翻译的马克思早期著作《1844年经济学哲学手稿》里的人本主义思想相近，直接促成了列斐伏尔“总体人”概念的形成。因为尼采对人内在具有的生命力量的强调，可将马克思主义的历史主体化为积极行动的个体主体。人不再是经济决定论下毫无主体意识的从属，而是一股蓬勃的生命冲力，不断克服限制生命存在的障碍；人不仅可以通过社会经济的客观运动获得解放，更可以在伦理的、审美的自主生命经验中超越资本主义的物化统治。

3.《1844年经济学哲学手稿》的人本主义哲学影响

在列斐伏尔参与翻译马克思早期著作《1844年经济学哲学手稿》中，列斐伏尔形成了一种具有某种存在主义倾向的人本主义马克思主义观念，异化、实践、总体人等概念被发掘出来。这引导着列斐伏尔逐步靠近黑格尔辩证法，以重新解读马克思主义。随后，列斐伏尔在与古特曼合作的《被神秘化的意识》《黑格尔著作导读》和《列宁著作导读》中，从《1844年经济学哲学手稿》中马克思的论断出发，揭示出了一个为马克思主义进行了理论准备的黑格尔。他们对辩证唯物主义即马克思主义哲学形成了与斯大林主义截然不同的理解，强调马克思主义哲学的本质是从黑格尔哲学那里批判继承而来的辩证法，这种辩证法一方面以理论和实践的统一即改造世界为目的，另一方面则为批判地理解资本主义社会关系的神秘化现实提供了科学的方法论。

4. 超现实主义的流行

第一次世界大战结束后，一批参加过战争的法国青年文学艺术家在反思战争的荒谬与破坏的过程中，对以理性为核心的传统文化及其价值观产生怀疑，着手探索一种新的理想来替代已然失去吸引力的传统信念。正是在这一背景下，二十年代初期，超现实主义运动勃然兴起，由文学而至绘画、音乐、电影等其他艺术领域，很快就成为一股风行法国波及欧美其他资本主义国家的文艺思潮。在理论上，超现实主义受到柏格森的直觉主义和弗洛伊德的无意识学说的深刻影响，否定理性的作用，强调人的无意识的作用，希望离开现实，返回原始。除了反思艺术创作的源泉、方法及目的等问题外，超现实主义者还对资本主义制度及人的生存条件等社会问题进行了某种思考，并表达了强烈的批判意识。正因为如此，超现实主义运动吸引了很多不满于现实的进步青年。同时，不少超现实主义者也积极向无产阶级运动靠拢，成为法国进步文艺阵营的成员。

二、篇章结构

《辩证唯物主义》一书正文分为两个部分。第一部分主要描述了马克思唯物主义辩证法的发展过程，重点探讨了马克思的辩证法与黑格尔辩证法之间的继承关系及其差异，同时正面阐述了马克思的历史唯物主义与辩证唯物主义的科学内涵及其对以往哲学的超越之处。第二部分则首先从人与自然的总体性实践关系出发来理解人类及存在物的起源与本质，继而探讨了科学和哲学中存在的决定论思想及其弊端，最后在分析了由劳动异化带来的人的全方面的异化现实的基础上，列斐伏尔提出了克服这种异化现实的“总体人”的革命理想。

第一部分标题为“辩证的矛盾”，其中又包含《对黑格尔辩证法的批判》《历史唯物主义》《辩证唯物主义》《学说的统一》四个小节。列斐伏尔开篇并没有直接批判黑格尔的辩证法，而是首先分析了古典的形式逻辑的弊端。列斐伏尔认为，在形式逻辑中形式和内容之间的关系存在着悖结。一方面，形式为了维持自身的纯洁性和真理性常常拒绝和放弃多样的、流动性的经验内容。另一方面，西方形而上学又总是试图从形式中榨取内容，从思想的存在中逻辑地推演出存在物和世界的存在。这种形式和内容的悖结到康德这里达到了顶峰。黑格尔发展出了辩证逻辑来试图解决这一困境，区别于古典的形式逻辑，理性的形式和流动多样的现实内容在辩证逻辑中、在精神的总体性的运动中得到了有机的统一。在过去，内容实体外在于思想，同时严格的思想保持着静止和虚空；而在黑格尔这里，观念和精神浸透在现实内容之中，思想的存在就是对内容的规定性。形式逻辑被吸纳至黑格尔的辩证法之中，成为辩证逻辑的一个特定阶段。

在第一部分第一小节《对黑格尔辩证法的批判》中，列斐伏尔认为黑格尔的辩证法虽然超越了形式逻辑，但依然存在众多缺陷，同样应该被批判。

首先，精神最终取消了现实内容。逻辑之思是一切事物的绝对基础，思想观念是内容的秘密来源，现实在黑格尔这里不过是理念为了完成自身的一个中介而已。因此，黑格尔不是将内容自由地提升为观念，而是在内容中发现一个已经确定了的思之规定性，在黑格尔那里太阳底下没有新鲜的事物。其次，黑格尔的辩证哲学取消了实践的内涵。黑格尔当然也强调“行动”，并且认为绝对理念是实践和知识、创造性的行动和思想的同一，然而行动在黑格尔的体系中处于从属的地位，它只是对精神的模仿，现实的行动在黑格尔这里被混同于关于行动的“思”。最后，黑格尔尽管看到了现实社会中存在的矛盾，但是这种矛盾被体系化到精神的发展过程之中，成为必要的恶，黑格尔的哲学因而失去了批判和改造世界的意向，陷入政治上的保守主义。此处列斐伏尔大费周章地分析黑格尔的辩证法，是在为下文讨论马克思和黑格尔的关系做铺垫。

接下来的《历史唯物主义》和《辩证唯物主义》两小节，正面阐述了马克思从历史唯物主义到辩证唯物主义的发展过程，以及黑格尔辩证法对于马克思思想发展过程的影响。列斐伏尔认为，从1843到1858年，马克思经历了一段对黑格尔方法“特别敌视”的时期：在马克思看来，黑格尔的哲学把一切具体的事物都变成了抽象的逻辑范畴，人的真实生活被剥夺和消解。黑格尔无视现实社会中人的生存的异化状态，而只是将其看作精神运动的必然外化过程，失去了批判精神。马克思（恩格斯）在批判黑格尔、费尔巴哈、青年黑格尔派的过程中，形成了带有经验主义特征的历史唯物主义。这种历史唯物主义反对将一切的现实过程纳入抽象的观念之中的黑格尔辩证法，强调必须从现实个人生活的生产方式出发，通过革命性的实践超越现存的异化。在列氏看来，历史唯物主义已经超越了传统的唯心主义和一般的唯物主义，走向了一种更高形态的唯物主义，然而此时辩证唯物主义并不存在，因为作为辩证唯物主义核心要素之一的辩证法被马克思明确地拒绝了。

直到1858年，马克思才对黑格尔辩证法不怀贬意。从此辩证的方法才被马克思纳入分析经济内容的历史唯物主义之中，这才有了辩证唯物主义。辩证的方法不再作为精神生成为历史存在与发展过程的唯心论的形式而存在，而是作为经济社会内容的现实表现方式而存在，它丢掉了唯心主义的思辨形式而成为社会历史的唯物主义辩证法。列斐伏尔明确反对将辩证唯物主义曲解为一种经济决定论，认为应当将经济因素作为一种具体的总体纳入整个社会的总体化运动中展开分析。马克思的历史辩证法的核心要素有三：(1) 必须从内容出发，强调内容对于辩证观念的首要地位。(2) 区别于经验主义的直观方法，强调必须通过具体的范畴和方法来对复杂具体的内容进行思维的整合，从而越来越达到具体的内容和具体的抽象，在这个意义上可以说，辩证法也是一种叙述的方法。(3) 在资本主义生产方式之中，人与人之间直接性的关系被抽象的物与物的关系所掩盖，商品、货币以及资本脱离了人的活动的外观，成为具有统治地位的抽象的独立存在。要克服拜物教意识形态必须依赖历史辩证法。

在第一部分的最后一节"学说的统一"中，列斐伏尔以自己的理论逻辑重新阐述了对"辩证唯物主义"的人道主义理解。在列斐伏尔看来，辩证唯物主义与历史唯物主义的统一基础，不是斯大林式的物质世界本体论，而是超越物质生产实践的、生命生活的总体性活动的本体论哲学。辩证法既不同于实证主义经验主义那样陷入一种抽象的直观之中，也不像黑格尔和其他观念论者那样将自身禁锢在一种既定的观念和图式之中，它总是在现实和范畴之间的矛盾运动中不断丰富和发展着自身。辩证法首先承认自己处于一定的、客观的历史条件之中，却也强调通过人的实践行为而超越它。辩证法既是一种理解生活总体性意义的哲学，也是一种改造现存世界的意志。实践是辩证唯物主义的出发点也是其落脚点，只有通过作为一种研究和行动的工具的辩证唯物主义，才可能实现人类真正的总体性的解放。

第二部分题为"人的生产"，其中又包含《存在物的分析》《整体的活动》《已被掌握的领域和尚未被掌握的领域》《物质决定论》《社会决定论》《总体的人》和《探索总体内容》七个小节。在进行"存在物的分析"之前，列氏首先探讨了人与自然的关系。受马克思《1844 年经济学哲学手稿》的影响，列斐伏尔认为，人首先是自然界中的一种生物体，具有生物性的本能、倾向和生命力；但是人类绝不只是自然界的附属物，他生活于自然界之中，又将自然界看作自身行动的对象而改造着自然界。紧接着，在《存在物的分析》一节中，列斐伏尔分析了"存在物"。在列氏看来，任何存在物都是从自然界中分离出来的，因而具有面向自然的一面；但是这些存在物之所以可以被分离出来，也正是由于人类的行动、语言等能力的作用，所以这些存在物又有面向人的一面。作为人类生产活动的必要因素的工具和技术，实际上也是在人类的实践活动中不断积累而成的。

在从人与自然的关系的角度分析了“人”和“存在物”之后，列斐伏尔在第二部分第二小节“整体的活动”中提出作为普通哲学和其他专门科学的基本方法的“整体化”的方法，他认为哲学的基本活动始终是再现整体。早期的哲学是通过“直觉”的思想方法来寻求整体的，这种方法抛开了问题的已知条件陷入了某种抽象之中；机械论将物体的分离定型看成是永恒的，将整个世界看成是相互分离的存在物的总和，这种整体同样也是一种简单抽象的总体，而不是局部和整体的具体结合；一般的自然科学和社会科学推崇整体，但又不懂得整体，他们孤立地承认基本现象，因而一脱离这些基本现象就看不到整体。在列氏看来，社会整体是作为一种实践的动态结构而存在的。整体化固然不是意识的、思辨的幻想，但是意识承担着不断再现整体的功能，意识的知性能力来源于人们的实践活动。

第二部分的第三小节题为“已被掌握的领域和尚未被掌握的领域”。列斐伏尔指出，人类处在不断的改造自然的总体实践之中，通过具体的实践也在不断地从事着对周围世界事物和关系的分析活动，由此自然界中的有些领域就可以为人类所掌握。在已被掌握的领域内，人们的生产活动的目的在于建立一个巩固的统一体，一个由许多确定了的因素组成的世界，这就形成了一定的“决定论”。决定论在确定人类的全部活动及其目的中占有地位，全部决定论叠加在一起构成了由人的活动控制的一个整体，人类的活动就处于各种决定论构成的统一体之中。在这个世界上，也同时存在许多人类尚未掌握的领域，这个领域对人类来说充满着必然性和未被认识的偶然性，人类活动至今还不能支配和巩固这一领域，人类也不能通过对这一领域进行生产、加工以便为人类服务。原来似乎十分强大的人类力量，在这种未知领域面前会变得极为脆弱并受到其威胁。区分了“已被掌握的领域”和“尚未被掌握的领域”之后，列斐伏尔分析了两种具体的决定论：“物质决定论”和“社会决定论”，这也就是第二部分第四、五两小节的内容。在列氏看来，这两种决定论首先是人类实践活动的必然结果，也是我们能够巩固既有成果以及在此基础上继续进步的必要前提；但是哲学与科学理论中的自然决定论与社会决定论常常有将这种决定论绝对化、凝固化的倾向，这其实是对周围世界的一种抽象孤立的静止的“实体化”的误认，是一种拜物教的思维方式。各种决定论的抽象思维幻觉，其实都可以在人的生产活动过程与生产的总体性联系中得到辩证合理地理解，并可以在具体的实践斗争中予以克服。

在“总体的人”和“探索总体内容”最后两小节中，列斐伏尔提出了“总体人”的革命理想，并认为哲学的任务应当是探索总体内容。列斐伏尔反对唯心主义对人性的抽象探讨，认为应当将人的本质放到人与自然的实际关系中去理解。人本来属于自然界，但是在与自然界斗争的过程中从自然界中分离出来，人通过劳动“使以人为中心的自然界人化”。然而，在人与自然的分化以及社会分工的作用下，人们开始不能在自己的活动的结果中认识自身，产品成了社会的抽象的产品，人也不再理解自己的本质和真实的价值。在以生产资料个人私有制为基础的社会结构中，人类的实在性比以往任何时候都更完全地被分离，全部生活对人来说变成一种外部的力量。这种异化扩展到全部生活，任何个人都无法摆脱这种异化。列斐伏尔认为在现代社会人的分散和矛盾达到了极端，但人的本质也许已经接近形成了，因为人的本质变得越复杂就越应当达到更高度的统一，矛盾越深就越迫切需要统一。要消除这种异化以及意识的神秘化，就必须消除作为其基础的经济结构和社会结构。“消除了异化”的人就是总体人，列斐伏尔为了区别于单纯的主体和单纯的客体而用了“主体—客体”的概念来描述这种“总体人”。总体人的集体结构消除了以往集体中的对立，个人和集体实现了统一，人的个性得到充分和多样性的发展。在这个全新的人类社会中，意识也克服了原来的拜物教形态，现实地探寻生产者和产品、个人和社会、自然生物与人类的统一。“总体人”结束了人的“自然历史”，迈进了“真正的人类时期”。

三、研究前沿

《辩证唯物主义》是列斐伏尔在重新发现了马克思《1844 年经济学哲学手稿》里的人本主义哲学后撰写的。在这部著作中，列斐伏尔希望在斯大林主义哲学体系对辩证法的经济决定论阐释之外，借用黑格尔理论与实践相统一的辩证法，为马克思的辩证唯物主义正名，强调辩证法是主体与外部世界进行矛盾斗争统一的实践哲学。基于此，在国内学界的研究中，《辩证唯物主义》的理论贡献、概念内容和理论影响都得到了充分研究与阐释。

第一，对《辩证唯物主义》理论贡献的准确定位。在国内学界的研究中，《辩证唯物主义》被视为西方马克思主义者依据资本主义新现实，发展马克思主义理论的重要作品。因此，国内学者基本都肯定，基于黑格尔—马克思—尼采三位一体的辩证法思想，列斐伏尔在《辩证唯物主义》中以人的实践为核心重构了能动的总体辩证法，将作为社会历史变革的物质生产实践改写为个体生命的自由创造活动，将以经济活动为基础的宏观辩证法诠释为以个体生命实践为核心的微观辩证法，拓宽了经典马克思主义的研究论域。但是，学界研究也指出，《辩证唯物主义》存在着理论缺陷，特别是它过多引入了黑格尔、尼采等人的思想资源，使得对马克思作品的解读并不符合马克思的真实思想，同时过多强调了人类主体意识与诗性创造的能力，忽视了现实经济活动、社会生产等的根本作用，陷入了抽象的人本主义。

第二，对《辩证唯物主义》概念内容的深化解读。《辩证唯物主义》产生于独特的社会历史语境之中，是列斐伏尔在对马克思《1844 年经济学哲学手稿》解读的基础上，尝试在斯大林主义哲学体系的经济决定论之外，寻找解答资本主义新现实的理论“突围”。因此国内学界都紧扣这一主题来阐释《辩证唯物主义》的概念与内容。一方面，国内学者重点阐释了《辩证唯物主义》中的关键理论范畴，包括异化、总体人等，区分了马克思基于劳动活动的异化概念与列斐伏尔基于抽象人性的异化概念，强调了列斐伏尔对《1844 年经济学哲学手稿》的创造性解读，即列斐伏尔将马克思的异化概念扩展到了资本主义社会的日常生活领域之中，以及在此基础上论述了克服日常生活异化的总体人思想。另一方面，国内学者也关注了《辩证唯物主义》中独特的马克思辩证法内涵，特别是强调在《1844 年经济学哲学手稿》中的人本主义思想的启发下，列斐伏尔从理论与现实、主体与客体相统一的视角来阐释马克思的辩证法思想，激活了抵抗资本主义现实统治的差异性与主体性。

第三，对《辩证唯物主义》理论影响的多元阐释。除了对《辩证唯物主义》的理论贡献与概念内容进行研究之外，国内学者还集中探讨了它对列斐伏尔后期思想发展的重要影响。比如，有学者认为，《辩证唯物主义》为日常生活批判理论提供了哲学方法论基础，它不仅提供了关于日常生活的最初界定与雏形，而且为揭穿资本主义伪自然性的日常生活与神秘化意识提供了异化批判的方法论指引。也有学者提出，《辩证唯物主义》为列斐伏尔的空间理论进行了理论准备，指出列斐伏尔在其中突破了黑格尔与马克思基于时间性分析的历史辩证法，将人类的矛盾与冲突延伸到了空间辩证法之中，进而在抽象、盲目的资本主义空间之外寻找到了属人的社会主义空间。

四、文本节选

Unity of the Doctrine

The recent publication of the 1844 *Manuscript* and *The German Ideology* has thrown a new light on the formation and objectives of Marxian thought.

The texts in question did not reveal Marx's humanism, which was already known from *The Holy Family*, *The Jewish Question* and the *Critique of Hegel's Philosophy of Right*, but they do show how the development of his ideas—his economic theory—did not destroy his concrete humanism but made it richer and explicit.

Dialectical materialism was formed and developed dialectically. Marxian thought began from Hegel's logic and first of all denied this logic in the name of materialism, that is, of a consequent empiricism. The discovery of the natural (material) man of flesh and blood was the first moment of this development. It seemed incompatible with Hegel's Idea and with his absolute method, which constructs its own abstract object. And yet this humanism went further than the materialism of the eighteenth century, which had been based on the early results of the natural sciences; it implied Hegel's theory of alienation and gave alienation a decisive scope, attributing to it both a good and a bad side and determining it as a creative process. In the 1844 *Manuscript*, the theory of alienation is still closer to Hegelian rationalism than to Feuerbach's naturalism. However, it demands that speculative philosophy be transcended, in the name of action and practice; practice is seen as both a beginning and an end, as the origin of all thought and the source of every solution, as a fundamental relation of the living man to Nature and to his own nature. The critical investigation into economics (whose importance Engels was the first to notice) then comes to be naturally integrated with humanism, as being an analysis of the social practice, that is of men's concrete relations with each other and with Nature. The most pressing human problems are determined as economic problems, calling for practical, that is for political solutions, politics being the supreme instance of the social practice, the only means of acting consciously on social relations.

As this humanism becomes more profound it next reveals the dialectical elements it had contained: a dialectic of historical contradictions and the economic categories, a dialectic of "reification" or alienation. Historical materialism, inasmuch as it is a science of economics, integrates the dialectical method with itself and, raised thereby to a higher level, appears as an application of the general method—the scientific dialectic—to a specific field. After having been denied by Marx, the dialectic joins up again with a more profound materialism; it has itself been freed from its momentary and congealed form: Hegelianism. It has ceased to be the absolute method, independent of the object, and has become the scientific method of exploration and exposition of the object. It discovers its truth by being united with the actual content.

In other words:

(a) The materialist dialectic accords the primacy explicitly to the content. The primacy of the content over the form is, however, only one definition of materialism. Materialism asserts essentially that Being (discovered and experienced as content, without our aspiring to define it *a priori* and exhaust it) determines thought.

(b) The materialist dialectic is an analysis of the movement of this content, and a reconstruction of the total movement. It is thus a method of analysis for each degree and for each concrete totality—for each original historical situation. At the same time it is a synthetic method that sets itself the task of comprehending the total movement. It does not lead to axioms, constancies or permanencies, or to mere analogies, but to laws of development.

(c) Thus understood, the dialectical method therefore constructs the historical and sociological object, while locating and determining its specific objectivity. A brute objectivity of history would be inaccessible, transcendent to the individual mind, the concept and discourse. It would be overwhelming and inexorable in character; allowing itself to be described indefinitely, but without our being able to glimpse any explanatory analysis or effectiveness in it. Conversely, without an object and without objectivity there is no science; every historical or sociological theory which sets out to be a science must establish the reality of its object and define the method which enables it to approach this object. Dialectical materialism satisfies this double requirement of the scientific mind. It establishes the economic objectivity without hypostatizing it, it locates the objective reality of history but straight away transcends it, as being a reality independent of men. It thus introduces living men—actions, self-interest, aims, unselfishness, events and chances—into the texture and intelligible structure of the Becoming. It analyses a totality that is coherent yet many-sided and dramatic.

Is not dialectical materialism therefore both a science and a philosophy, a causal analysis and a world-view, a form of knowledge and an attitude to life, a becoming aware of the given world and a will to transform this world, without any one of these characteristics excluding the other?

The movement and inner content of Hegel's dialectic, between rationalism and idealism, that is, are taken up again in dialectical materialism, which, in one sense, is more Hegelian than Hegelianism. A plurality of different and perhaps even incompatible meanings of the dialectic survived in the speculative dialectic. The dialectic as a method of analysis of the content excluded the dialectic as *a priori* construct, and these two meanings did not fit in very well with the theory of alienation. By positing a total, *a priori* object—absolute knowledge, the system—Hegel went against the content, against the Becoming, against living subjectivity and negativity. Dialectical materialism restores the inner unity of dialectical thought. It dissolves the static determinations attributed by Hegel to the Idea, to knowledge, to religion and to the State. It rejects any speculative construct, any metaphysical synthesis. Thus the different meanings of the dialectic become not only compatible but complementary. The dialectical method epitomizes the investigation of the historical development, it is the highest consciousness which living man can have of his own formation, development and vital content. Categories and concepts are elaborations of the actual content, abbreviations of the infinite mass of particularities of concrete existence. The method is thus the expression of the Becoming in general and of the universal laws of all development. In themselves these laws are abstract but they can be found in specific forms in all concrete contents. The method begins from the logical sequence of fundamental categories, a sequence by virtue of which we can recover the Becoming, of which they are the abridged expression. This method permits the analysis of particularities and specific situations, of the original concrete contents in the various spheres. It becomes the method that will guide the transformation of a world in which the form (economic, social, political or ideological) is not adequate to the content (to man's actual and potential power over Nature and his own artefacts) but enters into contradiction with it.

The Third Term is therefore the practical solution to the problems posed by life, to the conflicts and contradictions to which the praxis gives birth and which are experienced practically. The transcending is located within the movement of action, not in the pure time-scale of the philosophical mind. Wherever there is a conflict there may—but it is not inevitable—appear a solution which transforms the opposed terms and puts an end to the conflict by transcending them. It is up to the analysis to determine this solution, up to experience to release it, and up to action to realize it. Sometimes there is no solution: no social group was capable of putting an end to the economico-political contradictions of the Roman world in its decadence.

The relation between the contradictories ceases therefore to be a static one, defined logically and then found again in things—or negated in the name of a transcendent absolute. It becomes a living relation, experienced in existence. Several of Hegel's illustrations of the reciprocal determination of contradictories (*summum jus*, *summa injuria*—the way East is also the way West, etc.) become insufficient. The opposed terms are energies, or acts. The unity of the contradictories is not only an interpenetration of concepts, an internal scission, it is also a struggle, a dramatic relation between energies which are only by virtue of one another and cannot exist except one against the other. Thus Master and Slave or, if one prefers, the different species of animals. This struggle is a tragic relation, in which the contradictories are produced and support one another mutually, until either one of them triumphs and they are transcended or else they destroy each other. Taken in all its objectivity, the contradiction is fluid, and the logical relation is only its abstract expression. The transcending is action and life, the victory of one of the two forces which overcomes the other by transforming it, transforming itself and raising the content to a higher level.

The problem of man—or, more precisely, the problem of modern society, of the "social mystery" and its transcending—is central for dialectical materialism, which has appeared in this society at its appointed hour, as a scientific expression of its reality, its multiform contradictions and the potentialities it contains.

However, in order to elucidate modern industrial society, the analysis must go back to older societies. These it determines in their relation to the concrete totality as given today, inasmuch as they are original totalities that have been transcended, that is in the only historical reality that we can conceive of or determine. In the past this analysis finds, under specific forms, certain relations (such as that between Master and Slave for example, which Marx called "the exploitation of man by man") or else typical modes of thought or social existence, such as Fetishism. Dialectical materialism's field cannot therefore be restricted to the present day, it extends over the whole of sociology. But Nature itself exists for us only as a content, in experience and human practice. The dialectical analysis is valid for any content, it expresses the connection between the elements or moments of all Becoming. By incorporating the experimental sciences (physical, biological, etc.) and using them to verify itself, it can therefore discover, even in Nature, quality and quantity, quantity turning into quality, reciprocal actions, polarities and discontinuities, the complex but still analysable Becoming.

The sciences of Nature are specific. They recognize and study as such natural, physical, biological, etc., polarities or oppositions. They use the concept as a "trick" in order to study and modify qualities through the mediation of quantities, but they are never able to overcome these oppositions. Social science on the other hand examines the oppositions so as to overcome them. The sciences of Nature and the social sciences are specifically creative, each of them having its own method and objectives. However, the laws of the human reality cannot be entirely different from the laws of Nature. The dialectical chain of fundamental categories may therefore have a universal truth. It was only with great caution that Marx embarked on this path (as in his application of the dialectical method to economics). However, *Capital* shows how, in Marxian thought, the concrete dialectic is extended to Nature [K I], an extension carried on by Engels in *Dialectics of Nature*. Their *Correspondence* at this period (1873—1874) shows that Marx followed Engels's endeavour closely and approved of it.

Thus dialectical materialism is made universal and acquires the full dimensions of a philosophy: it becomes a general conception of the world, a *Weltanschauung* and hence a renewal of philosophy.

For the materialist dialectician, universal interdependence (*Zusammenhang*) is not a formless tangle, a chaos without structure. It is only the decline of speculative thought since Hegel that has dissociated the determinations and devalued the structural elements of the Becoming: quantity, discontinuity, relative nothingness. Dialectical materialism rescues the human mind from falling back into confusion and one-sidedness. The totality of the world, the infinite-finite of Nature, has a determinable structure, and its movement can become intelligible for us without our having to attribute it to an organizing intelligence. Its order and structure emerge from reciprocal action, from the complex of conflicts and solutions, destructions and creations, transcendings and eliminations, chances and necessities, revolutions and involutions. Order emerges from the Becoming; the structure of the movement is not distinct from the movement. Relative disorders prepare a new order and make it manifest.

All reality is a totality, both one and many, scattered or coherent and open to its future, that is, to its end. Between "moments" there cannot exist either a purely external finality or a purely internal one, either a harmony or mechanical collisions. Being elements of a totality, having been transcended and maintained within it, limited by each other and yet reciprocally determined, they are the "ends" one of another. There exist ends without finality. Each moment contains other moments, aspects or elements that have come from its past. Reality thus overflows the mind, obliging us to delve ever deeper into it—and especially to be ever revising our principles of identity, causality and finality and making them more thorough. Being determines our consciousness of Being, and the being of our thought determines our reflection on our thought. The reality is Nature, a given content, yet one that can be apprehended in its infinite richness by the mind which moves forward, based on the praxis, and becomes more and more penetrating and supple, tending as if towards a mathematical limit (to which we are for ever drawing nearer but have never reached), towards absolute knowledge, or the Idea.

The dialectic, far from being an inner movement of the mind, is real, it precedes the mind, in Being. It imposes itself on the mind. First of all we analyse the simplest and most abstract movement, that of thought that has been stripped as far as possible of all content. In this way we discover the most general categories and how they are linked together. Next, this movement must be connected up with the concrete movement, with the given content. We then become aware of the fact that the movement of the content or of Being is made clear for us in the laws of the dialectic. The contradictions in thought do not come simply from thought itself, from its ultimate incoherence or impotence, they also come from the content. Linked together they tend towards the expression of the total movement of the content and raise it to the level of consciousness and reflection.

Our quest for knowledge cannot be thought of as having been terminated by dialectical logic; quite the reverse, it must acquire a fresh impetus from it. The dialectic, a movement of thought, is true only in a mind that is in motion. In the form of a general theory of the Becoming and its laws, or of a theory of knowledge, or of concrete logic, dialectical materialism can only be an instrument of research and action, never a dogma. It does not define, it locates the two elements of human existence: Being and consciousness. It places them in order: Being (Nature) has priority, but consciousness comes first for man. Whatever has appeared in time can be erected, by man and for man, into a superior value. Nor, as a doctrine, can dialectical materialism be enclosed within an exhaustive definition. It is defined negatively, by being opposed to those doctrines which limit human existence, either from without or within, by subordinating it to some external existence or else by reducing it to a one-sided element or partial experience seen as being privileged and definitive.

Dialectical materialism asserts that the equalization of thought and Being cannot be reduced to an idea, but must be achieved concretely, that is in life, as the concrete power of the mind over Being.

Dialectical thinking has never ceased to evolve nor new aspects of it to appear, both in the lifetime and the writings of Marx and Engels, and since. Every truth is relative to a certain stage of the analysis and of thought, to a certain social content. It preserves its truth only by being transcended. We must go on constantly deepening our awareness of the content and extending the content itself. In the past as in the present, our knowledge has been limited by the limitation of the content and of the social form. Every doctrine, and this includes dialectical materialism, stems from this limitation, which is not that of the human mind in general but the limitation of man's present state. It is at the precise moment when it becomes aware of its own dialectical nature that thought must distinguish with the utmost care what, in the dialectical movement of ideas, comes from the actual content and what from the present form of thought. The exposition of dialectical materialism does not pretend to put an end to the forward march of knowledge or to offer a closed totality, of which all previous systems had been no more than the inadequate expression. However, with our modern awareness of human potential and of the problem of man, the limitation of thought changes in character. No expression of dialectical materialism can be definitive, but, instead of being incompatible and conflicting with each other, it may perhaps be possible for these expressions to be integrated into an open totality, perpetually in the process of being transcended, precisely in so far as they will be expressing the solutions to the problems facing concrete man.

For man, the relation of a particular reality to the total movement takes the form of a Problem. There is a problem whenever the Becoming carries thought and activity along and orientates them by forcing them to take account of new elements: at the moment when the Solution is tending, so to speak, to enter into reality and demanding the consciousness and the action which can realize it. It is in this sense that humanity only sets itself problems it is capable of solving. The resolution of contradictions in the transcending thus takes on its full practical significance.

The solution—the Third Term—is not an attitude of the mind. There is no substitute for practical contact with things, or effective cooperation with the demands and movements of the content.

In human terms, the energy of creation is extended and made manifest in and through the Praxis, that is the total activity of mankind, action and thought, physical labour and knowledge. The Praxis is doubly creative: in its contact with realities, hence in knowledge, and in invention or discovery. Dialectical materialism seeks to transcend the doctrines which reduce the mind's activity to becoming acquainted with what has already been achieved, or which recommend it to hurl itself into the void of mystical exploration. Experience and reason, intelligence and intuition, knowing and creating, conflict with one another only if we take a one-sided view of them.

The Praxis is where dialectical materialism both starts and finishes. The word itself denotes, in philosophical terms, what common sense refers to as "real life", that life which is at once more prosaic and more dramatic than that of the speculative intellect. Dialectical materialism's aim is nothing less than the rational expression of the Praxis, of the actual content of life—and, correlatively, the transformation of the present Praxis into a social practice that is conscious, coherent and free. Its theoretical aim and its practical aim—knowledge and creative action—cannot be separated.

In Hegel, the inferior moments had co-existed with the superior ones, in the eternity of the Idea and the system. In this way time, history and freedom had become unreal again, having allowed themselves to be arranged into a schema that included all the established forms of law, of customs and of consciousness. In dialectical materialism negativity is more profoundly positive and dynamic in character. The Third Term, the triumphant outcome of a conflict, transforms the content of the contradiction by re-assuming it; it lacks the conservative solemnity of the Hegelian synthesis. Only in this way can there be a real movement, a dramatic history and action, creation and development, liberation and liberty. The rectilinear schema of the Becoming is too simple, Hegel's triangular one too mechanical. In dialectical materialism the static representation of time is replaced by a vital and directly experienced notion of succession, of the action which eliminates and creates. Man can thus, perfectly rationally, set himself an objective which is both a transcending and a coming to fruition.

In Hegel, finally, the idea and the mind appear to produce themselves only because they already are. History comes to look like a bad joke. At the end of the Becoming all we find is the spiritual principle of the Becoming, which is thus only a repetition, an absurd illusion. The ordeal and misfortunes of consciousness have a ritual, magic action which causes absolute Mind to descend amongst us. But this Hegelian Mind always remains oddly narcissistic and solitary. In its contemplation of itself it obscures the living beings and dramatic movement of the world.

According to dialectical materialism men can and must set themselves a total solution. Man does not exist in advance, metaphysically. The game has not already been won; men may lose everything. The transcending is never inevitable. But it is for this precise reason that the question Man and of Mind acquires an infinite tragic significance, and that those who can sense this will give up their solitude in order to enter into an authentic spiritual community.

——Henri Lefebvre, *Dialectical Materialism*, University of Minnesota Press, 2009, pp. 88 - 101.

五、观点解读

1. 马克思的思想发展经历了从历史唯物主义到辩证唯物主义的上升过程

马克思主义在苏联思想界被简单化、同质化为一种名为"辩证唯物主义"的哲学，这种哲学在自然界表现为自然物质本体论，而在社会领域则表现为经济决定论。列斐伏尔无法接受这样的马克思主义，提出要为辩证唯物主义正名。他认为，马克思并不是一个天生的辩证唯物主义者，辩证唯物主义的形成有一个历史过程。经过对哲学、科学与政治经济学等诸多学科的持久研究，马克思恩格斯的思想经历了一个从德国古典唯心主义到历史唯物主义再到辩证唯物主义的发展演变过程。在列氏看来，马克思对黑格尔辩证法的接受过程深刻地影响了辩证唯物主义的形成和发展。青年马克思在对黑格尔唯心主义以及青年黑格尔派的批判过程中逐渐形成了历史唯物主义。列斐伏尔认为早期的马克思曾经经历了一段对黑格尔特别敌视的时期，这一时期代表性的著作是《1844 年经济学哲学手稿》《德意志意识形态》(以下简称《形态》)以及《哲学的贫困》。在马克思看来，黑格尔将一切具体的事物都变成了抽象的逻辑范畴；人的真实生活及其现实的异化则被消融在精神的抽象运动过程之中。在对黑格尔抽象的观念论体系的批判过程中，马克思发现了历史唯物主义。由于马克思对黑格尔思辨哲学的反感以及受经济学的熏染，马克思的历史唯物主义带有一定的经验主义和实证主义特征。历史唯物主义的基本命题在《形态》中得到了基本的理论表述。马克思反对思辨性的纯粹哲学态度，认为应当在现实个人的生产实践活动中去寻求具体的普遍性；马克思也反对黑格尔对人的异化生存状态的漠然态度，认为奴役、阶级斗争、国家等都是现实的异化形式，强调应当在具体的实践条件下现实地超越人的异化。列斐伏尔认为，1858 年左右马克思对黑格尔辩证法的态度经历了一次从拒斥到接受的转变，正是通过马克思对黑格尔辩证法的重新发现，历史唯物主义才超越了自身的经验主义态度，走向成熟形态的辩证唯物主义思想。列斐伏尔所理解的辩证唯物主义主要有三层内涵。第一，辩证唯物主义反对欧洲哲学史上一切形式主义的形而上学，坚持内容对于形式的第一性地位，坚持存在对于思想的决定性作用。第二，辩证唯物主义作为分析各种具体的总体性内容的辩证方法，并不打算终结认识的前进过程，或者提出一个封闭的总体性，辩证理性在其自身的运动过程中，必须将自身与实际内容以及思想的目前形式区分开来，从而不断加深对于世界总体性的理解。第三，辩证唯物主义是一种理解生活总体性意义的哲学以及基于这种理解之上的实践行动。列斐伏尔对辩证唯物主义的重新阐释对于打破苏东的理论教条具有重要的积极意义。但是我们也应该看到，由于列斐伏尔受马克思的《1844 年经济学哲学手稿》以及尼采思想的影响过重，同时忽视了政治经济学、空想社会主义等其他理论资源对于马克思的影响，因而他对历史唯物主义发展进程的某些论断并不符合马克思思想发展历程的真实面貌，这需要我们予以认真鉴别。

2. 列斐伏尔对辩证唯物主义进行了人学化改造

在列斐伏尔看来，苏联学界对于马克思主义的解释无疑陷入了一种机械的决定论之中，取消了辩证唯物主义原有的人道主义内涵。列斐伏尔通过对马克思思想发展过程的考察，得出马克思终其一生都没有放弃人道主义思想的结论。很多人认为，通过实证经济学的研究，马克思逐步放弃了早期的人道主义，列斐伏尔反对这种观点，认为马克思的经济理论非但没有破坏其具体的人道主义，反而使这种思想更加丰富和明晰。① 我们都知道经济学的研究对于《1844 年经济学哲学手稿》和《形态》的理论影响，列氏认为马克思的经济学研究并没有导致其走向经济决定论，相反，此时的马克思坚持一种人道主义立场，既批判黑格尔的逻辑学也批判国民经济学，因为在马克思看来两者都取消了“有血有肉的、自然的人”。列斐伏尔认为，正是通过“异化”逻辑，马克思将对经济学的批判性研究和人道主义思想自然地结合在了一起。在马克思后期的经济学研究中，人道主义依然没有被马克思所放弃。通过对黑格尔辩证法的重新发现，马克思成功超越了早期思想中的经验主义因素，分析具体经济内容的历史唯物主义吸收了辩证法的要素升级为科学的辩证唯物主义。辩证法一方面将世界的总体性把握为一个既定

① Henri Lefebvre, *Dialectical Materialism*, trans. John Sturrock, Jonathan Cape Ltd., 1968, p. 101.

的结构，但同时要求将这种结构纳入辩证的总体实践运动中去理解，强调通过人的革命实践现实地超越资本主义社会的物化结构，因此，晚期的马克思并没有放弃人道主义思想。观察列斐伏尔的论证，我们不难发现《辩证唯物主义》一书的理论实质并非对辩证唯物主义的"正本清源"，而是一次独特的、也是"过度的"人学化改造。列斐伏尔既反对将马克思辩证法解释成为一种斯大林式的自然物质本体论，也反对将马克思辩证法变成类似于黑格尔的绝对精神的发展与外化的哲学，而是"将辩证法理解成为人的精神与外部世界的矛盾—斗争—解决这样一种周而复始的追求绝对精神的实践哲学，将马克思的人的社会生产概念过度诠释成为一种总体性的人的生命辩证法本体论"①。列斐伏尔反对把马克思的历史观或社会学决定论化，强调一种总体性的生命实践辩证法。整体来说，我们认为列斐伏尔通过对人的实践和辩证法的强调，批判了传统的自然物质本体论和物质决定论，具有积极的思想史意义。但是列斐伏尔对辩证唯物主义的改造，脱离了马克思关于资本主义生产方式研究的经典语境，而陷入了一种抽象的人本主义。

3. 应当用"总体人"的辩证法克服现实的异化

"总体人"概念或"总体人"的辩证法占据着《辩证唯物主义》一书的核心地位，并且在一定程度上预示了列斐伏尔后来的日常生活批判哲学。我们首先考察一下列氏"总体人"辩证法的理论逻辑。列氏认为，当今世界的人处于全面的异化之中，任何个人都无法摆脱这种异化。列斐伏尔从以下三个角度论证了异化的来源：(1) 人从自然界中脱离出来以及人的社会分工是人类被抽象化、个体化与神秘化的开始。在今天，人的生产活动只是作为满足人类生存的物质需要的一种手段而存在，人类无意识地从事着这种生产活动而认识不到其中所蕴含的人的本质力量。(2) 人的类本质和现实个人之间的矛盾也是造成"异化"的根源之一。人的理想本质本来应该在同集体的牢固和明确的关系中获得，但是现代社会的个人颠倒地认为个人可以在孤立中认识自己。个人脱离了自己的社会基础，沦为理论的抽象或纯粹

---

① 刘怀玉：《现代性的平庸与神奇：列斐伏尔日常生活批判哲学的文本学解读》，中央编译出版社 2006 年版，第 70 页。

生物性的存在；而集体则陷入了更加严重的分裂和矛盾之中[①]。(3) 对应于以生产资料个人所有制为基础的社会结构，无产阶级构成了最基本的异化集团。那么如何克服这种异化呢？在列斐伏尔看来，克服与超越现代人的日常生活异化或全面的异化的根本途径正是马克思的总体人批判理想。总体人的内涵主要有两个方面。其一，实现了的总体人是消除了异化的人，它经历了支离破碎之后，成为"自由的自然界"。这与青年马克思关于共产主义是自然主义和人道主义的统一的理论表述基本一致。其二，总体人是自由集体中的自由的个人。它是在差别无穷的各种可能性的个性中充分发展的个性。而艺术则被当作脱离了工具性和异化特征的人的实践活动的价值典范。我们认为，列斐伏尔的"总体人"的社会理想既来自马克思，又区别于马克思，它具有明显的存在主义的"本真生存"理想色彩。"总体人"作为一种解放的艺术形式，是尼采式的"酒神精神"和马克思的"人的自由全面发展"思想的融合。由此，马克思的"总体人"或"人的自由全面发展"的理想，不再是建立在经济必然王国高度发展基础上的未来社会形态，而成了超越当下日常生活矛盾与冲突的永恒艺术的理想瞬间，是与历史、与生活具体内容无关的永恒形式。马克思哲学视野中需要历史地解决的问题，在列斐伏尔这里被转换成为一种永恒的日常生活的"终极关怀"问题[②]。列斐伏尔"总体人"的哲学理想无疑脱离了具体的历史语境，成为一种浪漫的人本主义乌托邦想象。

六、进一步阅读指南

1. 习近平：《辩证唯物主义是中国共产党人的世界观和方法论》，《求是》2019 年第 1 期。

2. 《习近平新时代中国特色社会主义思想三十讲》，学习出版社 2018 年版。

3. [法]亨利・列斐伏尔：《辩证唯物主义》(选译)，载《西方学者论

① 参见复旦大学哲学系现代西方哲学研究室编译：《西方学者论〈一八八四年经济学—哲学手稿〉》，复旦大学出版社 1983 年版，第 196 页。

② 刘怀玉：《现代性的平庸与神奇：列斐伏尔日常生活批判哲学的文本学解读》，中央编译出版社 2006 年版，第 91—92 页。

〈1844年经济学哲学手稿〉》，复旦大学出版社1983年版。

4. [法]亨利·列斐伏尔：《马克思主义的当前问题》，三联书店1966年版。

5. [法]亨利·列斐伏尔：《再谈异化理论》，载陆梅林、程代熙编选《异化问题》下卷，文化艺术出版社1986年版。

6. [法]亨利·列斐伏尔：《从黑格尔到毛泽东》，结构群文化事业公司1990年版。

7. 刘怀玉：《现代性的平庸与神奇：列斐伏尔日常生活批判哲学的文本学解读》，中央编译出版社2006年版。

8. 吴宁：《日常生活批判：列斐伏尔哲学思想研究》，人民出版社2007年版。

9. Henri Lefebvre, *Dialectical Materialism*, trans. John Sturrock, Jonathan Cape Ltd., 1968.

10. Henri Lefebvre, *Everyday Life in the Modern World*, trans. Sacha Rabinovitch, Transaction Publishers, 1994.

11. Henri Lefebvre, *Henri Lefebvre: Key Writings*, eds. Stuart Elden, Elizabeth Lebas, and Eleonore Kofman, Continuum, 2003.

12. Bud Burkhard, *French Marxism Between the Wars, Henri Lefebvre and the "Philophies"*, Humanity Books, 2000.

七、问题与思考

1. 在列斐伏尔眼中，马克思与黑格尔的思想之间有何内在关联？

2. 列斐伏尔是如何为"辩证唯物主义"正名的？他所理解的辩证唯物主义与传统马克思主义的辩证唯物主义之间存在着怎样的理论差别？

3. 马克思的《1844年经济学哲学手稿》对列斐伏尔的"总体人"辩证法有何影响？

第七章　现代性的哲学诊断
——《启蒙辩证法》选读

教学目的与要求

了解《启蒙辩证法》的成书原因及其在法兰克福学派发展史上的地位；正确理解启蒙与神话的关系；认识启蒙的概念，弄清启蒙是如何走向了自我毁灭；掌握文化工业理论，理解文化工业是如何使艺术丧失了超越精神，并使消费者成为与其主体本质相背离的物化存在的。

一、历史背景

（一）作者简介

1895 年，马克斯・霍克海默（Max Horkheimer）出生于德国斯图加特的一个富有的犹太商人家庭中。霍克海默的父亲原本希望儿子继承家里的事业，所以提前一年结束了霍克海默的高中学习生涯，让他在自己的公司中实习。1911 年，霍克海默结识弗里德里希・波洛克，开始学习哲学和社会科学。第一次世界大战结束后，霍克海默先后到慕尼黑大学、弗莱堡大学和法兰克福大学学习了哲学、心理学和经济学等科目。大学时期的霍克海默主要受到其导师科奈留斯的新康德主义的影响。1925 年，霍克海默以一篇关于康德《判断力批判》的论文通过了授课资格答辩，开始担任法兰克福大学的讲师一职。1930 年，霍克海默接任法兰克福社会研究所第二任所长。在霍克海默的带领下，研究所的影响越来越大。1933 年希特勒上台，德国的政治环境发生剧烈变化。由于社会研究所的许多成员是犹太血统，所以被纳粹政权以“敌视国家的倾向”的罪名封闭，但社会研究所并未解散。社会研究所先后辗转日内瓦、巴黎等地，最后在美国纽约的哥伦比亚大学落脚。二十世纪三十年代，霍克海默进入了创作的高产期，写下了《权威家庭》《传统理论与批判理论》和《独裁国家》等作品，其中，尤以 1937 年出版的《传统理论和批判理论》的影响最大。在这部著作中，霍克海默认为，传统形式理性主义忽视了现实的历史性构成这一特征，企图用所谓中立客观的立场和方法去研究现实，结果变成了对现实秩序的肯定和辩护，丧失了理论的批判和解放功能。与之相对，“批判理论”强调的是理论对现实的干预，是“使世界革命化”。流亡美国期间，霍克海默与阿多诺合写了《启蒙辩证法：哲学断片》。该书初版于 1944 年，再版于 1947 年。这部作品对大众文化、工具理性等问题做出了精彩的分析，从根源上否定了西方现代文明，大胆提出“启蒙倒退为神话”这一命题，使之成为西方马克思主义乃至整个现代西方思想的经典之作。1950 年，霍克海默应联邦德国政府邀请回国，重建社会研究所。次年，霍克海默担任法兰克福大学校长。这段时期霍克海默的主要任务是阐述对各种政治制度的思考。1973 年 7 月 7 日，霍克海默病逝于纽伦堡。

西奥多・阿多诺(Theodor Wiesengrund Adorno)，1903 年出生于德国法兰克福。父亲是一位德国犹太造酒企业家，母亲是一位歌唱家。受家庭环境影响，阿多诺在童年和少年时期专心于研究音乐，在音乐方面有很大的抱负。第一次世界大战后，阿多诺结识克拉考尔，开始研究康德的《纯粹理性批判》，同时期也阅读了卢卡奇的《小说理论》和布洛赫的《乌托邦精神》。1921 年，阿多诺考上歌德－法兰克福大学，学习哲学、心理学、社会学和音乐。1924 年在科奈留斯的指导下，阿多诺以一篇题为《胡塞尔现象学中事物和意向之先验性》的论文获得了哲学博士学位。阿多诺在二十世纪三十年初期受到本雅明《德国悲剧的起源》的重要影响，形成了自己独特的“崩溃的逻辑”思想，主要致力于“唯物辩证法”的重新阐释。1931 年，阿多诺凭借《克尔凯郭尔：美学的建构》一文获得法兰克福大学的执教资格。德国纳粹兴起后，阿多诺先是移居英格兰，尝试在牛津大学执教未果后于 1938 年受霍克海默之邀来到美国。他先是在普林斯顿广播研究所担任音乐指导，后受聘于纽约社会研究所。1941—1948年，阿多诺移居加利福尼亚，出任普林斯顿·拉杜克社会研究项目课题组组长，专门主持权力主义的研究，期间与霍克海默合作写下了《启蒙辩证法：哲学断片》。1950年，阿多诺同霍克海默一道返回西德重建社会研究所，并任法兰克福大学哲学与社会学教授。同年，阿多诺任社会研究所副所长，并在8年后接替霍克海默任所长。重返法兰克福大学后是阿多诺创作的鼎盛期，先后出版了《新音乐哲学》(1951)、《最低限度的道德》(1951)、《棱镜》(1955)、《主体与客体》(1960)等作品。在1961年，阿多诺同波普尔发生了激烈的"实证主义之争"，在德国学界产生巨大影响力，阿多诺也成了激进社会批判理论的代表人物。1966年，阿多诺发表了最具代表性的作品《否定辩证法》，集中反映了他学术思想的精华。但是在二十世纪六十年代末的学生运动中，由于阿多诺始终与学生运动保持距离，让造反的学生们感到极度失望和愤怒，因此他受到了大量谩骂、侮辱和人身攻击。1969年，阿多诺在瑞士度假时因突发心脏病离世。

(二) 时代背景

1. 凯恩斯主义成为拯救资本主义的"良药"

十月革命的成功震撼了整个资本主义世界，1929—1933年席卷全球的"大萧条"给了资本主义经济体系致命一击。为拯救摇摇欲坠的统治，资本主义国家不得不寻找一剂"良药"，凯恩斯主义应运而生。在1939年出版的《就业、利息和货币通论》中，凯恩斯强调扩大国家对经济的干预来保证解决就业等问题，以达到总需求和总供给的平衡。但实际上凯恩斯的理论只是资本主义内部寻求变革的一种表征。早在这本书出版之前，美国就通过"罗斯福新政"采取了许多强化国家垄断和调节的措施，呼应了凯恩斯提出的一些理论，凯恩斯主义正是这种倾向的系统理论表达。第二次世界大战的爆发刺激了国家权力的集中和战争动员的需要，催生了国家军事资本主义，进一步推动凯恩斯主义成为资本主义新的主导意识形态，一直维持到了二十世纪七十年代前后。

2. 社会生产力迅速发展，资本主义社会关系大幅调整

第二次世界大战结束后，科学技术的迅速发展给资本主义社会生产和生活带来了巨大变化。一方面，战后经济恢复产生巨大社会需要，战争时期积累的科学技术和人才资源迅速转移至各个生产部门，劳动生产率大幅提升，极大促进了社会生产力的快速发展；另一方面，凯恩斯主义的实施和经济复苏逐渐消除了普遍的物质匮乏状况，资本主义生产关系在调整中不断适应社会化大生产的要求，无产阶级获得相对丰裕的物质生活资料，生活水平得到大幅提升。与此同时，资本主义国家先后运用"福利国家"政策、让工人有限度的参政议政和管理经济等手段缓解阶级矛盾，试图将工人阶级"一体化"到资本主义制度中，资本主义社会关系出现新的特征。

3. 资本主义世界进入"被管理的社会"

随着国家垄断资本主义的深入发展，二十世纪三十年代开始流行的"管理革命"思潮逐渐从价值理念落实为现实的制度设计，资本主义国家对政治、经济、文化、科技和日常生活的控制越来越全面。过去赤裸裸的经济剥削和政治压迫逐渐让位于通过技术理性整合成的一种全方位的、更加隐性的心理压迫和文化精神控制，现代人受制于资本主义的新型统治而深陷意识麻痹、精神空虚和深度无根的状态。在这个社会体制中，"生产过程对人的影响，并不仅仅表现在直接的当代形式中，人们自己可以在其工作中体验到这种形式；而且还表现为被整合进诸如家庭、学术、教会、崇拜构制等一系列变化缓慢和相对稳定体制中的形式"。可以说，资本主义进入了一个总体上被管理的社会，而这种管理是与资本主义的生产变化相一致的。

（三）思想背景

1. 波洛克的政治经济学及其对批判理论的影响

在 1937 年霍克海默发表"传统理论和批判理论"之前，法兰克福学派并没有真正确立自己的理论传统，他们主要还是在卢卡奇《历史与阶级意识》所提供的逻辑框架中进行思考。当时，为学派提供政治经济学基础的是格罗斯曼(1881—1950)的危机理论。不过，1933 年以后，随着资本主义和苏

联社会主义的新发展，格罗斯曼的危机理论日益变得陈腐。弗雷德里希·波洛克（1894—1970）历史性地成为学派新的政治经济学理论的提供者。波洛克并不怀疑资本主义的必然灭亡，但他对当时资本主义是否已进入崩溃则深表怀疑。他认为，“大萧条”只是证明自由资本主义已经走到了自己的终点，但这并不意味着资本主义已经崩溃了，现状只是表明资本主义生产关系不再能够适应生产力的发展，它正期待着自己的计划经济，而在这种被管理的资本主义体制下，压迫将会更长久，繁荣将会更短暂但更旺盛，较之于“自由竞争”时代，危机也将更具毁灭性，但是其“自动的”毁灭不再能够被预期了。现实的发展趋势很快就证明了这种看法的真理性，从而迫使学派改变自己的理论定位、重新发明理论：1937 年“批判理论”概念的提出，“一方面，仅仅是霍克海默和马尔库塞为马克思主义理论传统引进的一个新名字；另一方面，它是学派自己的理论定位的名字，它最终阐明了学派关于陈述马克思主义传统的真正目的要求”[①]。作为政治经济学家，波洛克在二十世纪三四十年代最主要的成就是对国家社会主义的本质的研究。在 1941 年的《国家社会主义是一种新制度吗？》的演讲中，他针对关于纳粹德国的国家社会主义的本质的各种不同理解，阐明国家社会主义是资本主义当代发展的一种新的社会经济体系，其本质是垄断资本主义之后的国家资本主义。[②]而在同年的《国家资本主义：它的可能性及其界限》一文中，他则详细论证了自己的观点。[③] 波洛克的国家资本主义理论对批判理论的发展意义十分重大。因为正是在这一基础上，批判理论调整了自己对资本主义的理解方式，从而推动了批判理论的逻辑转型。所以，在体现这一时期批判理论基本立场的《启蒙辩证法》中，霍克海默和阿多诺在 1947 年版的“导论”和 1969 年版的“说明”中两次都专门致谢波洛克为他们的理论转型提供了坚实的政治经济学基础。具体地说，波洛克的影响主要表现在如下四个方面：第一，依据他的国家资本主义学说，法兰克福学派的其他成员对国家资本主义社会

① Helmut Dubiel, *Theory and Political*: *Studies in the Development of Critical Theory*, The MIT Press, 1985, p. 104.

② Friedrich Pollock, "Is National Socialism a New Order?", in *Studies in Philosophy and Social Science* Ⅸ, 3, 1941.

③ Friedrich Pollock, "State Capitalism: Its Possibilities and Limitations", in *The Essential Frankfurt School Reader*, ed. Andrew Arato, Urizen Books, 1978.

的政治法律结构、文化形式、社会心理等进行了深入分析；第二，他揭示了工具理性和非工具理性在历史哲学层面上的本质区别，促进了霍克海默等人对工具理性的批判；第三，他对有计划的资本主义的持久存在的悲观主义预言，极大地影响了霍克海默和阿多诺等人对资本主义的理解；第四，他对国家资本主义全面被管理的论述促进了阿多诺同一性观念的形成。

2. 批判理论的理论转型与法兰克福学派的研究蓝图

作为法兰克福学派的理论规划者，霍克海默承继了卢卡奇、柯尔施等人的总体性理念，力图实现跨学科的融合，对当下的社会生活进程进行全面认识和批判。《启蒙辩证法》源于学派对于学科间真正实现合作的构想，希望把经济学分析、政治分析和具体的、材料充实的理论全部纳入其中。霍克海默和阿多诺是这一蓝图的真正实践者，而对学派其他成员，如波洛克和韦尔等人来说，它一直都只是一种构想。成书后的《启蒙辩证法》，反映了法兰克福学派从早期以整合不同学科为旨趣的批判模式转型为主题集中的工具理性批判。在给洛文塔尔的信中，霍克海默规划了这一项准备性研究的大纲："第一章（当然，这现在还是严格保密的）将讨论启蒙这个哲学概念。在这里，启蒙就是指资产阶级思想，不仅如此，而且指一般的思想，因为最适合讨论的正是城市之中的思想。主要论题如下：启蒙与神话、启蒙与统治、启蒙与实践、启蒙的社会根源、启蒙与神学、事实和体系、启蒙及其与人道主义和野蛮的关系。第二章将包括对实证科学与各种大众文化现象的分析。这一章与你的研究是紧密相关的。一共可能五章，但是最后三章还非常不确定。"①根据霍克海默的蓝图，这项研究计划是一个综合性的整体，应该是探讨时代一般趋势的历史—唯物主义理论，所以，学科间的紧密合作是十分必要的。《哲学家们无法完成的洛杉矶研究计划的分工备忘录》说明了这项工作的总路线："研究计划作为一个整体，主要涉及对文化意识形态的全面批判。……这些分析要取得成功，从根本上取决于它们对哪些有关最新经济发展的具体洞见的判断。这项工作作为一个整体，其目标就是克服政治上

① "Horkheimer to Lowenthal", *Pacific Palisades*, 23 May 1942.

的停滞。”[①]霍克海默希望波洛克和菲利克斯·韦尔分别承担经济和政治部分。但现实情况是，两者更愿意投身于研究所的“外围”工作。波洛克和韦尔的离去，以及实际研究工作推行过程中的变化，使两位作者不得不承认，“我们错误地估计了自己的能力”。《启蒙辩证法》有了它的副标题——哲学断片，并体现出它的开放性和未完成品格。罗尔夫·魏格豪斯评价：“‘哲学断片’只是那些全部工作中的一些选段，只不过他们是以‘它们的内在关联性和语言统一性’为选择标准来选编出来的罢了。”[②]

3. 诊断资本主义的共同旨趣

《启蒙辩证法》的创作是当时社会上诸多文化形式交汇的产物，更是对当代意识的批判性反思。其中的重要动机，既有对当代启蒙的审视，也有对法西斯主义的警惕和反抗。正如阿多诺所讲：“我们必须放弃对当代意识的这种信任，对科学传统加以细心呵护和认真筛选”，“特别是当实证主义者指责科学传统如同无用的包袱而应当予以抛弃的时候，我们就更是应当对科学传统加以细心呵护和认真筛选”。[③] 在目睹了西方特别是德国境内由新兴科学技术带来的现代启蒙与专制的文化理论环境逐渐合流之后，从 1937 年底开始，霍克海默和阿多诺就计划写作“一本极有可能非常重要的关于辩证唯物主义的书”。从思想历程看，阿多诺是在他的音乐研究中走向启蒙辩证法的，而霍克海默则从他的批判理论建构走向启蒙辩证法。两者在反犹主义问题研究中取得了共鸣，并使他们走向对资本主义的共同诊断：资本主义这个被管理的社会已经成了一个同一性的整体。启蒙理性没有完成使人类走向自由自主的使命，反而成为资本主义意识形态的帮凶。法兰克福学派其他成员的既有研究成果也被充分纳入了《启蒙辩证法》中。比如，在创作过程中，霍克海默和阿多诺收到了本雅明寄来的天鹅之作《历史哲学论纲》，并深深地被后者所折服，进而将后者的核心思想，即历史的本质是神

① 转引自[德]罗尔夫·魏格豪斯：《法兰克福学派：历史、理论及政治影响》（上册），孟登迎、赵文、刘凯译，上海人民出版社 2010 年版，第 418 页。

② [德]罗尔夫·魏格豪斯：《法兰克福学派：历史、理论及政治影响》（上册），孟登迎、赵文、刘凯译，上海人民出版社 2010 年版，第 427 页。

③ [德]马克斯·霍克海默、西奥多·阿多诺：《启蒙辩证法：哲学断片》，渠敬东、曹卫东译，上海人民出版社 2006 年版，第 1 页。

话、是始终如此的永恒轮回,以及一些主要的思想和结论融入了《启蒙辩证法》之中。另外,齐格弗里特·克拉考尔对现代大众文化的审美形式研究,也是这本著作的一个重要思想来源。

二、篇章结构

从本质上讲,《启蒙辩证法》体现了法兰克福学派 1930 年代后期至 40 年代早期的基本思想成果,只不过最终是由霍克海默和阿多诺两人负责实现出来罢了。根据后人的分析,他们的具体分工大致如下:各版前言均由霍克海默撰写,阿多诺参与修改;《启蒙的概念》由霍克海默执笔完成,该文的第一篇附论《奥德修斯或神话与启蒙》由阿多诺执笔,第二篇附论《朱莉埃特或启蒙与道德》由霍克海默完成;《文化工业:作为大众欺骗的启蒙》由两人合作完成;《反犹主义要素:启蒙的界限》由阿多诺执笔;《笔记与札记》由霍克海默执笔。

《启蒙的概念》指出,启蒙的根本目标就是要使人们摆脱恐惧,树立自主。但是,被彻底启蒙的世界却笼罩在一片因胜利而招致的灾难之中。启蒙的纲领是要唤醒世界,祛除神话,用知识代替幻想。可实际上,启蒙始终是在神话中确认自身。任何抵抗所诉诸的神话,都通过作为反证之论据的极端事实,承认了它所要谴责的启蒙运动带有破坏性的理性原则。启蒙带有极权主义性质,就像一个独裁者对待人民一样对待万物。启蒙总是把神人同形论当作神话的基础,即用主体来折射自然界。启蒙的理想就是要建立包罗万象的体系。理性主义和经验主义对此的理解没有什么差别。从巴门尼德到罗素,同一性一直是一句口号,旨在坚持不懈地摧毁诸神和多质。然而,被启蒙摧毁的神话,却是启蒙自身的产物。神话因此变成了启蒙,自然则变成了纯粹的客观性。但这些都不能掩盖启蒙与神话的相似性。在文明世界中,神话进入了世俗领域。现实继承了神话及其概念的传统,表现出古典社会被归结为神灵的超自然特征。工业主义使人的精神客观化,甚至在总计划之前,经济设备就自动地使商品具有了决定人的行为的价值。从那时以后,随着自由交换的结束,商品失去了全部的经济特征,而只具有拜物教的特点。更重要的是,拜物教的影响已经扩大到了社会生活的一切方面。启蒙的本质是选择,而选择的根本特性在于控制。人们一向不得不在从属自然或从属于自我这两者之间进行选择。随着资产阶级商品经济的扩大,神话的黑暗地平线被可以计算的理性的光辉照耀。在这寒冷的光线下,新的野蛮的种子在发芽、开花、结果。在控制的压抑下,人的劳动永远摆脱了神话,但在控制中,劳动又永远回到了神话的范围中。启蒙具有毁灭性。就像它的敌人指出的那样,只有当启蒙与浪漫主义达到最后的和谐,并敢于超越虚假的绝对、盲目统治的原则时,启蒙才能成为启蒙。但是,面对这种可能性,在为现时代服务的过程中,启蒙就是对群众的全面欺骗。因为恐怖和文明是分不开的,我们不能抛弃恐怖而保留文明,因此,启蒙的发展变成了丧失理性,成为国际性的法西斯主义的危险。于是启蒙走向自我毁灭。

附论1《奥德修斯或神话与启蒙》通过解读古希腊神话《奥德塞》,分析了牺牲与放弃,即资产阶级的所得与所失。该附论认为,牺牲是一种象征性的等价交换,它在表面上是失去,但实质上是更多的获得,所以说,奥德塞这个冒险的英雄、"资产阶级个人的原型"的漂泊之旅实际上是一个不断"自我确证"其主体统治地位的过程。然而,小说时代与史诗时代根本不同的地方就在于,如今是有复数的奥德塞在确证自我,因此,这必然是一种相互欺骗和相互谋求统治的"虚假的社会"。在这里,"社会要求(试图逃避普遍的、不平等的、非正义的交换,试图断绝然而却只能直接抓住那不能遏止的整体的)人必须因此失去一切——即使是自我保存所应允给他的可怜的逃离也不例外。这个广大的然而却过剩的牺牲被要求反对牺牲自身"。也就是说,牺牲是为了获得,但它最终走到了反对自己获得的境地。所以,奥德塞这个不断确证自我的自我"也是那种总是限制自身、遗忘自己的生活的自我,他希望挽救自己的生活,然而只能在流浪中回忆"。该文由此揭示出了资产阶级的历史哲学宿命:在牺牲中放弃,在得到对自然的支配的同时失去进行完整生活的权力,资产阶级的所得就是他的所失。这种"启蒙辩证法"实际上是被统治的自然对人展开的报复。更重要的是,这种报复其实才刚刚开始。

附论2《朱莉埃特或启蒙与道德》指出,奥德修斯击败塞壬仅仅象征工具理性的萌芽,它的极致是二十世纪的新野蛮主义。但从康德走向尼采的旅途中有一中介环节,这就是法国作家萨德侯爵。他的色情小说《朱莉埃特》是工具理性的典范,宣告了康德理性的破产。之所以如此,是因为萨德受二元论支配,造成灵与肉的分离。大革命中,朱莉埃特成了"启蒙的女儿"。她以科学为信条,像实证主义者那样操纵逻辑。其姊妹篇更是无情地颠覆了康德的知识系统:它反抗压抑,鼓吹放纵,嘲笑道德。启蒙貌似支持妇女解放,实则还原其为交配工具,直至“没有一个器官被闲置”。

《文化工业:作为大众欺骗的启蒙》指出,发达资本主义国家的文化具有大工业的特征,而不同于前资本主义时代的个体劳动者的精神劳动。那时,文化是少数“天才”的特权,所造就的文化一般也表现为所谓的精英文化、贵族文化。而今天由于科技的发展,文艺作品制作的手段日渐普及,文艺创作转变为以建立在科学技术之上的机械化、自动化生产为前提,进行大规模成批生产和复制,是为“文化工业”。文化工业的产品,是一种适合于大众口味的、方便面式的精神消费品即大众文化。文化工业尽管表现出一种符合需求的表象,实际上仍然是由不合理的社会力量所控制的。金钱是文化工业运转的枢纽和动力,是它存在的目的和根源。商人的力量在文化工业的背后巍然屹立着,他们为了自己的利益,必须有意识地为广大消费者提供适宜于心理机制的作品。文化工业立足于世俗的基础,已丧失了艺术的超越性精神。精英文化不可避免地带有乌托邦的色彩和超越的意识,一般都与社会保持一定的距离而对社会进行审美的审视。

《反犹主义要素:启蒙的界限》在对各种解释反犹太主义何以会出现的观点进行评析后,从弗洛伊德那里引入病态投射观念,对反犹太主义进行了新的解释。该文认为,反犹主义建立在一种虚假投射基础上,是被压抑的模仿行为的病态表现。就模仿行为而言,外在世界是内在世界必须努力加以遵从的一种模式,模仿的目的是把陌生的事物变成熟悉的事物,而虚假投射则把内在世界和外在世界混淆在一起,并把最熟悉的事物说成是敌对的事物。虚假投射是启蒙的必要组成部分:因为反思被剔除了,所以病态的客体被看作符合现实的,疯狂的制度变成了合理的规范。就此而言,反犹主义的非理性主义不过是启蒙理性的自我毁灭趋势在现实中的一种表现而已。

《笔记与札记》中收录的是霍克海默和阿多诺与正文主题密切相关的一些思想断片。

三、研究前沿

自《启蒙辩证法》的第一个中译本于1990年出版后,国内学界便对这一经典之作陆续开展了一些研究,对其理论内容已经有了比较全面的认识。

随着研究的深入和积累，这部著作在学界更加全面的考察视角下获得了更为丰富的内涵，其意义和价值得到了进一步揭示。

第一，由表及里，深度挖掘了《启蒙辩证法》背后的政治经济学批判基础。对《启蒙辩证法》乃至整个法兰克福学派的既有研究，大多着眼于从哲学视域来理解和评价，并未充分意识到它的政治经济学批判基础。实际上，正如在《传统理论与批判理论》的"跋"中，霍克海默所指出的那样，所谓批判理论"是以马克思的政治经济学批判为基础的"[①]。在《启蒙辩证法》1947年版的"导论"和1969年版的"说明"中，霍克海默和阿多诺也两次专门致谢了波洛克为他们的理论转型所提供的坚实的政治经济学基础。因此，《启蒙辩证法》是法兰克福学派在政治经济学批判基础上，对当代资本主义新发展进行全面分析，进而实现批判理论结构转型的一种理论成果。因此，有学者着手揭示了这条非常重要但又往往被忽视的理论线索。既有的研究成果主要体现在两个方面：一是以法兰克福学派史为时间线，梳理了亨里克·格罗斯曼、弗里德里希·波洛克等政治经济学家在不同历史时期对批判理论的创建所发挥的思想作用；二是进一步在理论上抽丝剥茧，阐述波洛克等人之于批判理论重要性的具体内涵。研究发现，政治经济学批判对资本主义经济结构转型的分析，改变了批判理论对资本主义的理解方式，从而推动了批判理论的逻辑转型。特别是依据波洛克的国家资本主义学说，法兰克福学派的其他成员对国家资本主义社会的政治法律结构、文化形式、社会心理等进行了深入分析，揭示了工具理性和非工具理性在历史哲学层面上的本质区别，推进了霍克海默等人对工具理性的批判。

第二，重新审视"启蒙"概念，探索启蒙的界限。作为《启蒙辩证法》批判对象的"启蒙"概念成为学者们关注的焦点。有学者从主体与客体的关系视角，重新梳理了西方思想史中不同的启蒙观。传统的观点认为启蒙哲学代表着主体哲学在现代西方的兴起，但《启蒙辩证法》认为，在对理性的追逐和人的主体地位的树立中，人的自我持存与自我毁灭并存，自我牺牲与欺诈导致了主体的分裂。霍克海默和阿多诺甚至在书中直言："启蒙在为现实社会

---

① [德]马克斯·霍克海默：《批判理论》，李小兵译，重庆出版社1989年版，第230页。

服务的过程中，逐步转变成为对大众的彻头彻尾的欺骗”[①]，启蒙运动导致了主体的衰弱，人类文明不仅没有进步，反而退步了。这些论述是否意味着他们全盘否定了启蒙、拒斥一切形而上学、否定任何同一性？霍克海默和阿多诺是后现代主义的同路人吗？这些问题成为考察《启蒙辩证法》的新视角。通过研究，大部分学者都认同，《启蒙辩证法》要反思和批判的启蒙是那种以普遍真理自居、否定一切他者、不能容忍任何特殊真理的激进启蒙。相对地，霍克海默等人主张的是一种合理的、辩证的积极启蒙观，是要将启蒙从盲目统治的绝境中解放出来。因此，霍克海默和阿多诺不会接受具有虚无主义色彩的激进启蒙概念，同样也与后现代主义思路划清了界限。

第三，反思文化工业，揭示资本主义统治形式的变化。对文化工业及其意识形态功能的分析构成了《启蒙辩证法》非常重要的部分，正是通过考察文化对社会发展的影响、文化和工业社会生产的关系等问题，霍克海默和阿多诺完成了对资本主义社会发展状况的诊断和批判。作为当代资本主义文化生产的一种标准化模式，文化工业被视为启蒙理性的产物，导致了被霍克海默和阿多诺称之为“大众欺骗”的结果。他们指出：“文化工业取得了双重胜利：它从外部祛除了真理，同时又在内部用谎言把真理确立起来。”[②]有学者分析了文化工业的实质，认为文化工业表面上是一种娱乐产业，但实际上它消解了艺术与生活的距离，使得艺术沦为资本主义再生产体系的一个部分。文化工业提供的产品让人们获得了工具理性提供的虚假快乐，即征服自然的快乐。同样，文化产品的流行也没有给予人以真正的艺术享受，而是施加了更为广泛和深层的控制。沿着这一方向，有学者结合垄断资本主义阶段的特点，从意识形态方面强调文化工业的统一性与政治统一性的联系。通过发展文化工业，借助工业技术不断地模仿、复制文化产品，资本主义社会得以使统治合理性的内容渗透到人们的私人生活及心理本性之中，以达到思维统治的同一化。在垄断条件下，大众文化具有了强制的同一性，大众的思想被禁锢在文化工业制造的密闭空间之中，资本主义的意识形态渗透逐步取代了传统的镇压统治方式。

---

① [德]马克斯·霍克海默、西奥多·阿多诺：《启蒙辩证法：哲学断片》，渠敬东、曹卫东译，上海人民出版社 2003 年版，第 40 页。

② [德]马克斯·霍克海默、西奥多·阿多诺：《启蒙辩证法：哲学断片》，渠敬东、曹卫东译，上海人民出版社 2003 年版，第 32 页。

四、文本节选

Preface（1944 and 1947）

...Our work was to adhere, at least thematically, to the traditional disciplines: sociology, psychology, and epistemology.

The fragments we have collected here show, however, that we had to abandon that trust. While attentive cultivation and investigation of the scientific heritage—especially when positivist new brooms have swept it away as useless lumber—does represent one moment of knowledge, in the present collapse of bourgeois civilization not only the operations but the purpose of science have become dubious. The tireless self-destruction of enlightenment hypocritically celebrated by implacable fascists and implemented by pliable experts in humanity compels thought to forbid itself its last remaining innocence regarding the habits and tendencies of the *Zeitgeist*. If public life has reached a state in which thought is being turned inescapably into a commodity and language into celebration of the commodity, the attempt to trace the sources of this degradation must refuse obedience to the current linguistic and intellectual demands before it is rendered entirely futile by the consequence of those demands for world history.

...

The aporia which faced us in our work thus proved to be the first matter we had to investigate: the self-destruction of enlightenment. We have no doubt—and herein lies our *petitio principii*—that freedom in society is inseparable from enlightenment thinking. We believe we have perceived with equal clarity, however, that the very concept of that thinking, no less than the concrete historical forms, the institutions of society with which it is intertwined, already contains the germ of the regression which is taking place everywhere today. If enlightenment does not assimilate reflection on this regressive moment, it seals its own fate. By leaving consideration of the destructive side of progress to its enemies, thought in its headlong rush into pragmatism is forfeiting its sublating character, and therefore its relation to truth. In the mysterious willingness of the technologically educated masses to fall under the spell of any despotism, in its self-destructive affinity to nationalist paranoia, in all this uncomprehended senselessness the weakness of contemporary theoretical understanding is evident.

We believe that in these fragments we have contributed to such understanding by showing that the cause of enlightenment's relapse into mythology is to be sought not so much in the nationalist, pagan, or other modern mythologies concocted specifically to cause such a relapse as in the fear of truth which petrifies enlightenment itself. Both these terms, enlightenment and truth, are to be understood as pertaining not merely to intellectual history but also to current reality. Just as enlightenment expresses the real movement of bourgeois society as a whole from the perspective of the idea embodied in its personalities and institutions, truth refers not merely to rational consciousness but equally to the form it takes in reality. The loyal son of modern civilization's fear of departing from the facts, which even in their perception are turned into clichés by the prevailing usages in science, business, and politics, is exactly the same as the fear of social deviation. Those usages also define the concept of clarity in language and thought to which art, literature, and philosophy must conform today. By tabooing any thought which sets out negatively from the facts and from the prevailing modes of thought as obscure, convoluted, and preferably foreign, that concept holds mind captive in ever deeper blindness. It is in the nature of the calamitous situation existing today that even the most honorable reformer who recommends renewal in threadbare language reinforces the existing order he seeks to break by taking over its worn-out categorial apparatus and the pernicious power-philosophy lying behind it. False clarity is only another name for myth. Myth was always obscure and luminous at once. It has always been distinguished by its familiarity and its exemption from the work of concepts.

...

The first essay, the theoretical basis of those which follow, seeks to gain greater understanding of the intertwinement of rationality and social reality, as well as of the intertwinement, inseparable from the former, of nature and the mastery of nature. The critique of enlightenment given in this section is intended to prepare a positive concept of enlightenment which liberates it from its entanglement in blind domination.

The critical part of the first essay can be broadly summed up in two theses: Myth is already enlightenment, and enlightenment reverts to mythology. These theses are worked out in relation to specific subjects in the two excurses. The first traces the dialectic of myth and enlightenment in the *Odyssey*, as one of the earliest representative documents of bourgeois Western civilization. It focuses primarily on the concepts of sacrifice and renunciation, through which both the difference between and the unity of mythical nature and enlightened mastery of nature become apparent. The second excursus is concerned with Kant, Sade, and Nietzsche, whose works represent the implacable consummation of enlightenment. This section shows how the subjugation of everything natural to the sovereign subject culminates in the domination of what is blindly objective and natural. This tendency levels all the antitheses of bourgeois thought, especially that between moral rigor and absolute amorality.

The section "The Culture Industry" shows the regression of enlightenment to ideology which is graphically expressed in film and radio. Here, enlightenment consists primarily in the calculation of effects and in the technology of production and dissemination; the specific content of the ideology is exhausted in the idolization of the existing order and of the power by which the technology is controlled. In the discussion of this contradiction the culture industry is taken more seriously than it might itself wish to be. But because its appeal to its own commercial character, its confession of its diminished truth, has long since become an excuse with which it evades responsibility for its lies, our analysis is directed at the claim objectively contained in its products to be aesthetic formations and thus representations of truth. It demonstrates the dire state of society by the invalidity of that claim. Still more than the others, the section on the culture industry is fragmentary.

The discussion, in the form of theses, of "Elements of Anti-Semitism" deals with the reversion of enlightened civilization to barbarism in reality. The not merely theoretical but practical tendency toward self-destruction has been inherent in rationality from the first, not only in the present phase when it is emerging nakedly. For this reason a philosophical prehistory of anti-Semitism is sketched. Its "irrationalism" derives from the nature of the dominant reason and of the world corresponding to its image. ...

——Max Horkheimer and Theodor W. Adorno, *Dialectic of Enlightenment: Philosophical Fragments*, Stanford University Press, 2002, pp. xiv - xix.

The Concept of Enlightenment

Enlightenment, understood in the widest sense as the advance of thought, has always aimed at liberating human beings from fear and installing them as masters. Yet the wholly enlightened earth is radiant with triumphant calamity. Enlightenments program was the disenchantment of the world. It wanted to dispel myths, to overthrow fantasy with knowledge. Bacon, "the father of experimental philosophy," brought these motifs together ... .

... Now we govern nature in opinions, but we are thrall unto her in necessity: but if we would be led by her in invention we should command her by action.

Although not a mathematician, Bacon well understood the scientific temper which was to come after him. The "happy much" between human understanding and the nature of things that he envisaged is a patriarchal one: the mind, conquering superstition, is to rule over disenchanted nature. Knowledge, which is power, knows no limits, either in its enslavement of creation or in its deference to worldly masters. Just as it servers all the purposes of the bourgrois economy both in factories and on the battlefield, it is at the disposal of entrepreneurs regardless of their origins. Kings control technology no more directly than do merchants: it is as democratic as the economic system with which it evolved. Technology is the essence of this knowledge. It aims to produce neither concepts nor images, nor the joy of understanding, but method, exploitation of the labor of others, capital. The "many things" which, according to Bacon, knowledge still held in store are themselves mere instruments: the radio as a sublimated printing press, the dive bomber as a more effective from of artillery, remote control as a more reliable compass. What human beings seek to learn from nature is how to use it to dominate wholly both it and human beings. Nothing else counts. Ruthless toward itself, the Enlightenment has eradicated the last remnant of its own self-awareness. Only thought which does violence to itself is hard enough to shatter myths. Faced by the present triumph of the factual mentality, Bacon's nominalist credo would have smacked of metaphysics and would have been convicted of the same vanity for which he criticized scholasticism. Power and knowledge are synonymous. ...

——Max Horkheimer and Theodor W. Adorno, *Dialectic of Enlightenment: Philosophical Fragments*, Stanford University Press, 2002, pp. 1 - 2.

But the myths which fell victim to the Enlightenment were themselves its products. The scientific calculation of events annuls the account of them which thought had once given in myth. Myth sought to report, to name, to tell of origins—but therefore also to narrate, record, explain. This tendency was reinforced by the recording and collecting of myths. From a record, they soon became a teaching. ... The awakening of the subject is bought with the recognition of power as the principle of all relationships. In face of the unity of such reason the distinction between God and man is reduced to an irrelevance, as reason has steadfastly indicated since the earliest critique of Homer. In their mastery of nature, the creative God and the ordering mind are alike. Man's likeness to God consists in sovereignty over existence, in the lordly gaze, in the command.

Myth becomes enlightenment and nature mere objectivity. Human beings purchase the increase in their power with estrangement from that over which it is exerted. Enlightenment stands in the same relationship to things as the dictator to human beings. He knows them to the extent that he can manipulate them. The man of science knows things to the extent that he can make them. Their "in-itself" becomes "for him." In their transformation the essence of things is revealed as always the same, a substrate of domination. This identity constitutes the unity of nature. ...

...

As a totality set out in language and laying claim to a truth which suppressed the older mythical faith of popular religion, the solar, patriarchal myth was itself an enlightenment, fully comparable on that level to the philosophical one. But now it paid the price. Mythology itself set in motion the endless process of enlightenment by which, with ineluctable necessity, every definite theoretical view is subjected to the annihilating criticism that it is only a belief, until even the concepts of mind, truth, and, indeed, enlightenment itself have been reduced to animistic magic. ... Just as myths already entail enlightenment, with every step enlightenment entangles itself more deeply in mythology. Receiving all its subject matter from myths, in order to destroy them, it falls as judge under the spell of myth. It seeks to escape the trial of fate and retribution by itself exacting retribution on that trial. In myths, everything that happens must atone for the fact of having happened. It is no different in enlightenment: no sooner has a fact been established than it is rendered insignificant. The doctrine that action equals reaction continued to maintain the power of repetition over existence long after humankind had shed the illusion that, by repetition, it could identify itself with repeated existence and so escape its power. But the more the illusion of magic vanishes, the more implacably repetition, in the guise of regularity, imprisons human beings in the cycle now objectified in the laws of nature, to which they believe they owe their security as free subjects. The principle of immanence, the explanation of every event as repetition, which enlightenment upholds against mythical imagination, is that of myth itself. The arid wisdom which acknowledges nothing new under the sun, because all the pieces in the meaningless game have been played out, all the great thoughts have been thought, all possible discoveries can be construed in advance, and human beings are defined by self-preservation through adaptation—this barren wisdom merely reproduces the fantastic doctrine it rejects: the sanction of fate which, through retribution, incessantly reinstates what always was. Whatever might be different is made the same. That is the verdict which critically sets the boundaries to possible experience. The identity of everything with everything is bought at the cost that nothing can at the same time be identical to itself. Enlightenment dissolves away the injustice of the old inequality of unmediated mastery, but at the same time perpetuates it in universal mediation, by relating every existing thing to every other. It brings about the situation for which Kierkegaard praised his Protestant ethic and which, in the legend cycle of Hercules, constitutes one of the primal images of mythical violence: it amputates the incommensurable. Not merely are qualities dissolved in thought, but human beings are forced into real conformity. The blessing that the market does not ask about birth is paid for in the exchange society by the fact that the possibilities conferred by birth are molded to fit the production of goods that can be bought on the market. Each human being has been endowed with a self of his or her own, different from all others, so that it could all the more surely be made the same. But because that self never quite fitted the mold, enlightenment throughout the liberalistic period has always sympathized with social coercion. The unity of the manipulated collective consists in the negation of each individual and in the scorn poured on the type of society which could make people into individuals. The horde, a term which doubtless is to be found in the Hitler Youth organization, is not a relapse into the old barbarism but the triumph of repressive *égalité*, the degeneration of the equality of rights into the wrong inflicted by equals. The fake myth of fascism reveals itself as the genuine myth of prehistory, in that the genuine myth beheld retribution while the false one wreaks it blindly on its victims. Any attempt to break the compulsion of nature by breaking nature only succumbs more deeply to that compulsion. That has been the trajectory of European civilization. Abstraction, the instrument of enlightenment, stands in the same relationship to its objects as fate, whose concept it eradicates: as liquidation. Under the leveling rule of abstraction, which makes everything in nature repeatable, and of industry, for which abstraction prepared the way, the liberated finally themselves become the "herd" (*Trupp*), which Hegel identified as the outcome of enlightenment.

——Max Horkheimer and Theodor W. Adorno, *Dialectic of Enlightenment: Philosophical Fragments*, Stanford University Press, 2002, pp. 5 - 9.

In the enlightened world, mythology has permeated the sphere of the profane. Existence, thoroughly cleansed of demons and their conceptual descendants, takes on, in its gleaming naturalness, the numinous character which former ages attributed to demons. Justified in the guise of brutal facts as something eternally immune to intervention, the social injustice from which those facts arise is as sacrosanct today as the medicine man once was under the protection of his gods. Not only is domination paid for with the estrangement of human beings from the dominated objects, but the relationships of human beings, including the relationship of individuals to themselves, have themselves been bewitched by the objectification of mind. Individuals shrink to the nodal points of conventional reactions and the modes of operation objectively expected of them. Animism had endowed things with souls; industrialism makes souls into things. On its own account, even in advance of total planning, the economic apparatus endows commodities with the values which decide the behavior of people. Since, with the ending of free exchange, commodities have forfeited all economic qualities except their fetish character, this character has spread like a cataract across the life of society in all its aspects. The countless agencies of mass production and its culture impress standardized behavior on the individual as the only natural, decent, and rational one. Individuals define themselves now only as things, statistical elements, successes or failures. Their criterion is self-preservation, successful or unsuccessful adaptation to the objectivity of their function and the schemata assigned to it. Everything which is different, from the idea to criminality, is exposed to the force of the collective, which keeps watch from the classroom to the trade union. Yet even the threatening collective is merely a part of the deceptive surface, beneath which are concealed the powers which manipulate the collective as an agent of violence. Its brutality, which keeps the individual up to the mark, no more represents the true quality of people than value represents that of commodities. The demonically distorted form which things and human beings have taken on in the clear light of unprejudiced knowledge points back to domination, to the principle which already imparted the qualities of *mana* to spirits and deities and trapped the human gaze in the fakery of sorcerers and medicine men. The fatalism by which incomprehensible death was sanctioned in primeval times has now passed over into utterly comprehensible life. The noonday panic fear in which nature suddenly appeared to humans as an all-encompassing power has found its counterpart in the panic which is ready to break out at any moment today: human beings expect the world, which is without issue, to be set ablaze by a universal power which they themselves are and over which they are powerless.

——Max Horkheimer and Theodor W. Adorno, *Dialectic of Enlightenment*: *Philosophical Fragments*, Stanford University Press, 2002, pp.21－22.

The Culture Industry: Enlightenment as Mass Deception

…

Interested parties like to explain the culture industry in technological terms. Its millions of participants, they argue, demand reproduction processes which inevitably lead to the use of standard products to meet the same needs at countless locations. The technical antithesis between few production centers and widely dispersed reception necessitates organization and planning by those in control. The standardized forms, it is claimed, were originally derived from the needs of the consumers: that is why they are accepted with so little resistance. In reality, a cycle of manipulation and retroactive need is unifying the system ever more tightly. What is more mentioned is that the basis on which technology is gaining power over society is the power of those whose economic position in society is strongest. Technical rationality today is the rationality of domination. It is the compulsive character of a society alienated from itself. Automobiles, bombs, and films hold the totality together until their leveling element demonstrates its power against the very system of injustice it served. For the present the technology of the culture industry confines itself to standardization and mass production and sacrifices what once distinguished the logic of the work from that of society. These adverse effects, however, should not be attributed to the internal laws of technology itself but to its function within the economy today. Any need which might escape the central control is repressed by that of individual consciousness. The step from telephone to radio has clearly distinguished the roles. The former liberally permitted the participant to play the role of subject. The latter democratically makes everyone equally into listeners, in order to expose them in authoritarian fashion to the same programs put out by different stations. No mechanism of reply has been developed, and private transmissions are condemned to unfreedom. They confine themselves to the apocryphal sphere of "amateurs," who, in any case, are organized from above. ... An explanation in terms of the specific interests of the technical apparatus and its personnel would be closer to the truth, provided that apparatus were understood in all its details as a part of the economic mechanism of selection. Added to this is the agreement, or at least the common determination, of the executive powers to produce or let pass nothing which does not conform to their tables, to their concept of the consumer, or, above all, to themselves.

If the objective social tendency of this age is incarnated in the obscure subjective intentions of board. chairmen, this is primarily the case in the most powerful sectors of industry: steel, petroleum, electricity, chemicals. Compared to them the culture monopolies are weak and dependent. They have to keep in with the true wielders of power, to ensure that their sphere of mass society, the specific product of which still has too much of cozy liberalism and Jewish intellectualism about it, is not subjected to a series of purges. The dependence of the most powerful broadcasting company on the electrical industry, or of film on the banks, characterizes the whole sphere, the individual sectors of which are themselves economically intertwined. Everything is so tightly clustered that the concentration of intellect reaches a level where it overflows the demarcations between company names and technical sectors. The relentless unity of the culture industry bears witness to the emergent unity of politics. ... On the charts of research organizations, indistinguishable from those of political propaganda, consumers are divided up as statistical material into red, green, and blue areas according to income group.

The schematic nature of this procedure is evident from the fact that the mechanically differentiated products are ultimately all the same. That the difference between the models of Chrysler and General Motors is fundamentally illusory is known by any child, who is fascinated by that very difference. The advantages and disadvantages debated by enthusiasts serve only to perpetuate the appearance of competition and choice. It is no different with the offerings of Warner Brothers and Metro Goldwyn Mayer. But the differences, even between the more expensive and cheaper products from the same firm, are shrinking—in cars to the different number of cylinders, engine capacity, and details of the gadgets, and in films to the different number of stars, the expense lavished on technology, labor and costumes, or the use of the latest psychological formulae. The unified standard of value consists in the level of conspicuous production, the amount of investment put on show. The budgeted differences of value in the culture industry have nothing to do with actual differences, with the meaning of the product itself. The technical media, too, are being engulfed by an insatiable uniformity. Television aims at a synthesis of radio and film, delayed only for as long as the interested parties cannot agree. Such a synthesis, with its unlimited possibilities, promises to intensify the impoverishment of the aesthetic material so radically that the identity of all industrial cultural products, still scantily disguised today, will triumph openly tomorrow in a mocking fulfillment of Wagners dream of the total art work. The accord between word, image, and music is achieved so much more perfectly than in *Tristan* because the sensuous elements, which compliantly document only the surface of social reality, are produced in principle within the same technical work process, the unity of which they express as their true content. This work process integrates all the elements of production, from the original concept of the novel, shaped by its sidelong glance at film, to the last sound effect. It is the triumph of invested capital. To impress the omnipotence of capital on the hearts of expropriated job candidates as the power of their true master is the purpose of all films, regardless of the plot selected by the production directors.

——Max Horkheimer and Theodor W. Adorno, *Dialectic of Enlightenment*: *Philosophical Fragments*, Stanford University Press, 2002, pp. 95 - 98.

五、观点解读

1. 启蒙倒退为神话

《启蒙辩证法》的核心主题是“神话就是启蒙,而启蒙却倒退成了神话”。霍克海默和阿多诺认为,启蒙倒退为神话是由其知识和理性工具主义所决定的。近代以来,启蒙有两个重要命题:第一,知识就是力量,要用知识代替幻想,用理智战胜迷信;第二,技术是知识的本质,它的目的不再是生产概念和意向,而是生产剥削他人劳动的方法,即资本的方法。启蒙的这两个纲领使知识具有了操作性的特征。在知识的技术化过程中,人们实现了对世界的祛魅，放弃了对任何意义的探索。在世界的理性化过程中，启蒙最终战胜了神话。不过，霍克海默和阿多诺认为，被摧毁的神话其实正是启蒙自身的产物。因为启蒙总是把神人同形当作神话的基础，即用主体来折射自然界，而这体现了主体的觉醒，这种觉醒把权力确认为一些关系的原则，是一种新的理性同一性观念。正是在这个意义上，他们说"神话变成了启蒙"。这一结论可以从四个方面得到理解。第一，神话命定的必然性成为启蒙的内在性原则，启蒙把每一件事情都解释为必然性的再现。近代哲学，不管是唯物主义还是虚无主义，实际上都以各自的方式肯定了必然性的支配作用。第二，万物同一，摈除一切不可度量之物，这已然成为现代市场商品交换的根本原则。按照马克思的分析，商品的交换过程就是对任何商品的特殊本质加以抽离的过程，使之成为可以用货币加以度量的物，这是对商品的特殊性质的否定，使任何商品都可以通过一定的量化关系相互通约。第三，抽象同一性的前提是主体与客体的分离，而这一分离在神话中以占有者与其通过占有物而获得事物之间的距离为基础，在生活中，这以统治和劳动的分离为基础，在神话中就表现为奥德修斯对水手的支配和控制。第四，神话来源于恐惧，把令人恐惧的事物化为神圣，这是最初的分离，因为恐惧而导致的解释形成对事物的命名，但由于对事物的命名所指称的对象既是事物，又是神圣栖居的场所，这就是观念与事物分离的原初形式。启蒙作为彻底的神话，是通过现代理性工具主义的方式完成的，这也是现代技术主义占据统治地位的结果。启蒙这种技术主义在数学理性中得到最为根本的表现。数学形式主义的根据是数字，是直接事物的最抽象的形式，它坚持思维的直接性。事实取得了胜利，认识被局限于对事物的重复，思想成了同义反复。思维的机器越使生存服从于自己，那么，在重新创造生存的过程中，这种服从也就越盲目。因此，启蒙又变成了神话，并且永远不能真正认识到如何避免这一点。

2. 启蒙陷入了自我毁灭的怪圈

霍克海默和阿多诺认为，启蒙精神所造就的理性神话本质是一种极权主义统治。由于理性变成了一种不可抗拒的力量，变成了制造其他一切工具的工具，成为经济结构的辅助手段，因此，在启蒙的世界里，神话就完全世俗化了。最终启蒙精神使工业文明成为神话，导致商品拜物教的普遍存在，进而导致人的个性的丧失。不仅如此，启蒙通过控制自然最终控制了人自身，导致人被奴役。更重要的是，随着资产阶级商品经济的发展，神话中朦胧的地平线，被推论出来的理性的阳光照亮了，在强烈的阳光照耀下，新的野蛮状态的种子得到了发展壮大。新的野蛮状态的种子导致的更具灾难性的后果是，启蒙对自然的统治必然衍生出对人的统治。因为，对自然界不断加强的统治意味着人同自然的异化，同时也意味着人类对自身控制方式的变化。启蒙理性在提高了人对自然界的统治能力的同时，也增强了某些人对另一些人的统治力量。好事善行都变成了罪恶，统治和压迫则变成了美德。结果，对于统治者来说，人们变成了资料，正像整个自然界对于社会来说都变成了资料一样。启蒙并没有给人们一个自由平等的、合理的社会秩序，启蒙思想家所憧憬的理性王国在现实面前一次又一次地被击碎，原本是为了解放人的启蒙理性现在却变成了人类主体奴役自然和自我奴役的工具。通过启蒙，人的灵魂脱离了蒙昧，然而又可悲地置身于工具理性宰制之下，物欲的大众宁愿以精神的沉沦去换取外在物质利益的丰厚，因而丧失了对价值理性的追求，于是对自由的渴望以及对民主进步的向往变成人们对权威和暴政的温顺服从，以致高度发达的理性技术管理被用来实现最大规模的、最无人道的非理性目的。这样，清醒的人们看到，技术世界的理想——废除自然——即彻底控制自然又反馈到人的身上：全面的剥削作为"理想和现实的统一"在被规定为是必然永恒的自然的剥削中只能坚持剥削的本性，"即虚假的绝对，盲目的统治的原则"，并发展为一切社会形式的统治工艺学。就是说，启蒙造就了一种新的统治工艺学，并且使这种统治的工艺学排除了一切法则。新的控制，支配方式不服从理性，它嘲笑任何爱恋真理的思想，启蒙理性因此彻底放逐了解放的可能性。启蒙后的人类从一个黑暗走向另一个更大的黑暗。

3. 文化工业成为大众欺骗的启蒙

在《启蒙辩证法》中，霍克海默和阿多诺指出，由于科技的发展，文艺作品制作的手段日渐普及，在发达资本主义社会里，文艺创作转变为以建立在科学技术之上的机械化、自动化生产为前提，进行大规模成批生产和复制，即文化创造具有大工业生产的形式。面对文化工业的产品即大众文化的日益盛行，他们从四个方面进行了批判。第一，文化工业尽管表现出一种符合需求的表象，实际上仍然是由不合理的社会力量所控制的。金钱是文化工业运转的枢纽和动力，是它存在的目的和根源。商人的力量在文化工业的背后巍然屹立着，他们为自己的利益必须有意识地为广大消费者提供适宜于心理机制的作品。因此，在文化工业中艺术家必须迎合顾客的需要来创作，无所谓“自由创造”。另一方面，现在顾客并非哪一个人，而是体现为文化消费市场的大众，但这个“大众”不是量的概念，不是真正的杂多，而是丧失了个性的“常人”。要满足这些人的同样需求，就必须处处要求有同样的商品，这就决定了文化工业的产品，其类型、内容和风格日趋单调和雷同。就此而言，文化工业的产品本质上只能是一种商品而非艺术品。第二，文化工业已丧失了艺术的超越性精神，立足于世俗的基础。在大众文化中，最普及和流行的是娱乐消遣品即轻松艺术。在高度专业化和分工日细的现代社会，富余的金钱和闲暇不能使人完全改变他的社会角色，但能通过消费娱乐来松弛一下自己紧张的身心，恢复体力和精力，忘却自己的烦恼和痛苦，从而可以继续无动于衷地作为一个无意志的齿轮和工具在社会生活中有效运转。大众对娱乐的迫切需求使娱乐取代艺术成了文化工业的原则。它恰恰反映出社会已经丧失了认真的信念。在文化工业所提供的令人轻松愉快的娱乐消遣中，艺术的精神和生命已经灭亡了。第三，就艺术技巧论，所有文化工业的作品都是以完善的技术为后盾的。与古典作家相比，当代文化工业体系中的一些创作者的作品往往十分粗糙，但借助先进的技术装备，文化工业对这帮作者起到一种驯化作用。这说明，文化工业的产品，其完善都是技术使然，没有太多的艺术价值。文化工业只是使艺术品的仿造和复制批量化，使人人都能得到一个赝品。第四，文化工业中的创作必然走向程式化，程式化的创作又必然带来语言的限制。为了保障一种被称作“风格”的程式，各个创作门类都积极地为自己确定了一套规定语言。这种语言和风格上的“特色”，不仅体现在作品中，而且会由文化工业的宣传、推销而渗透到社会大众之中，使整个民族都不自觉地学会使用这种语言。这种语言只会削弱民族语言的表现力，破坏民族语言的优美和纯洁。基于上述分析，霍克海默和阿多诺认为，文化工业的存在和发展是资本主义社会衰退的标志，是一种严重的异化现象。表面上是大众在塑造大众文化，而实际上是大众被大众文化塑造。文化工业中的一切娱乐活动都是呆板无聊的，不仅剥夺了消费者的思想，也剥夺了他的感情和主体意识，使他成为一个与主体的本质相背离的物化存在。

六、进一步阅读指南

1.《马克思恩格斯全集》第 31 卷，人民出版社 1998 年版。

2.《马克思恩格斯全集》第 44 卷，人民出版社 2001 年版。

3. 习近平：《在中国科学院第二十次院士大会、中国工程院第十五次院士大会、中国科协第十次全国代表大会上的讲话》，人民出版社 2021 年版。

4. 习近平：《在中国文联十一大、中国作协十大开幕式上的讲话》，人民出版社 2021 年版。

5. 中共中央宣传部：《习近平总书记在文艺工作座谈会上的重要讲话学习读本》，学习出版社 2015 年版。

6. 习近平：《习近平谈治国理政》第三卷，外文出版社 2020 年版。

7. [德]马克斯・霍克海默：《批判理论》，李小兵等译，重庆出版社 1989 年版。

8. [德]马克斯・霍克海默：《霍克海默集》，曹卫东编选，渠东、付德根等译，上海远东出版社 2004 年版。

9. [德]马克斯・霍克海默、西奥多・阿多诺：《启蒙辩证法：哲学断片》，渠敬东、曹卫东译，上海人民出版社 2006 年版。

10. [美]马丁・杰伊：《法兰克福学派史》，单世联译，广东人民出版社 1996 年版。

11. [德]赫尔穆特・贡尼、鲁道夫・林古特：《霍克海默传》，任立译，商务印书馆 1999 年版。

12. [美]理查德・沃林：《文化批评的观念：法兰克福学派、存在主义和后结构主义》，张国清译，商务印书馆 2000 年版。

13. 尤战生：《流行的代价：法兰克福学派大众文化批判理论研究》，山东大学出版社 2006 年版。

14. 傅永军：《法兰克福学派的现代性理论》，社会科学文献出版社 2007 年版。

15. Seyla Benhabib, Wolfgang Bonss, and John McCole, ed., *On Max Horkheimer: New Perspectives*, MIT Press, 1993.

16. Peter M. R. Stirk, *Max Horkheimer*: *A New Interpretation*, Hertfordshire: Harvester Wheatsheaf, 1992.

17. Zoltán Tar, *The Frankfurt school*: *the Critical Theories of Max Horkheimer and Theodor W. Adorno*, Schocken Books, 1985.

18. Rolf Wiggershaus, *The Frankfurt School*: *Its History*, *Theories*, *and Political Significance*, translated by Michael Robertson, MIT Press, 1994.

七、问题与思考

1. 如何理解“神话就是启蒙，而启蒙却倒退成了神话”这一核心主题？

2. 启蒙为什么会走向自我毁灭？

3. 正确理解《启蒙辩证法》中的文化工业概念，为什么说文化工业使消费者成为与主体本质相背离的物化存在？

第八章　无限可能的人
——《马克思关于人的概念》选读

教学目的与要求

了解弗洛姆思想的产生背景;理解弗洛姆关于人的概念的定义,并正确评价弗洛姆对马克思哲学的人本主义解读;掌握弗洛姆的异化观,分析这种理解是否符合马克思思想发展的实际;正确认识弗洛姆的社会主义观。

一、历史背景

(一) 作者简介

1900 年,艾瑞克·弗洛姆(Erich Fromm)出生于德国美茵河畔法兰克福一个犹太商人家庭。犹太裔背景使得弗洛姆从小受到《塔木德经》和犹太祭司的教育。他早年曾学习社会学,后又专攻精神分析学,受到弗洛伊德的深刻影响。不论是在柏林精神分析学会接受的精神分析训练,抑或是在美国进行重建华盛顿精神病学校纽约分校的经历,都反复锤炼了他作为精神社会分析学家的角色。此外,他还深受法兰克福学派的影响,是法兰克福学派的主要代表人物之一。1918 年以后,他先后在法兰克福大学、海德堡大学学习法律、社会学、心理学和哲学,并于 1922 年以《犹太人的守则:论散居在外的犹太民族的社会学》一文获得海德堡大学的博士学位。随后,他回到法兰克福开始在一家地方报纸任职。1924 年后，经过严格的精神分析训练，弗洛姆成为一名职业的精神病医生，开始从事长达四十余年的精神病临床治疗工作。

和许多同时代人一样，弗洛姆在二十世纪二十年代初期开始学习、研究马克思的著作。马克思的哲学和社会主义学说对他产生了重大影响，促使他成为一名社会主义者。随着精神分析学说研究的不断深入，他逐渐形成了一种明确的想法，力图将马克思主义与精神分析学结合起来，以弥补马克思主义在微观精神领域的空白。在二十年代末三十年代初的德国左派思想界，这是一种非常流行的观点。正在形成中的法兰克福学派的许多成员都在不同程度上支持这种观念，其中也包括霍克海默和阿多诺。正因为如此，1929 年，在洛文塔尔的介绍下，弗洛姆进入社会研究所讲授精神分析学，并于 1930 年成为研究所的核心成员和社会心理学研究室主任。

作为对纳粹兴起的一种回应，霍克海默领导下的法兰克福学派在二十世纪三十年代发动了两项重要的经验性研究：权威人格分析和纳粹分析。在这两项工作中，弗洛姆及其精神分析学都发挥了显著的作用。不过，由于学术背景的原因，弗洛姆对马克思哲学的本质、它与精神分析学的关系及其结合的可能性、现实性等问题的认识，与霍克海默、阿多诺、马尔库塞等学派其他主要成员存在明显的分歧。1933 年秋，弗洛姆前往芝加哥精神分析学院讲学，最终于 1939 年 1 月正式离开社会研究所。1941 年，弗洛姆出版了《逃避自由》一书。在这本书中，他力图证明，极权主义运动吸引了渴望逃避自由的人们。现代人获得了自由，然而在内心深处却又渴望逃避自由。现代人摆脱了中世纪的束缚，却没有能够自由地在理性与爱的基础上营造一种有意义的生活，于是现代人便想以顺从领袖、民族或国家的方式，寻求新的安全感。由于这本书从社会心理学的角度对当时人们极为关注的纳粹的兴起问题给出了有说服力的解释，因此，初版之后，不断再版，并迅速流传开来，从而牢固确立了弗洛姆的思想地位。以这本书为起点，弗洛姆后来陆续出版了《自为的人》(1947)、《健全的社会》(1955)、《爱的艺术》(1956)、《马克思关于人的概念》(1961)、《在幻想锁链的彼岸》(1962)、《希望的革命》(1968)、《占有还是生存》(1976)等著作，对自己的人本主义马克思主义的社会学说进行了多方位的阐述。弗洛姆一生不断辗转，在纳粹上台后，先后在日内瓦、纽约、华盛顿、墨西哥城、瑞士等地从事研究工作。1980 年，弗洛姆在家中去世。

（二）时代背景

1. 纳粹上台与犹太人的遭遇

纳粹上台后推行的一系列政治迫害政策给包括弗洛姆在内的犹太人造成了严重影响。当时，犹太人受到极为严苛的对待，政治地位失去保障，甚至遭受虐待，作为一个“人”应有的权力被彻底剥夺。大部分犹太人的最后结局，要么是被赶往集中营，要么就是以失去财富为代价，被迫离开德国。1945年4月，希特勒战败自杀，德国纳粹政权覆灭，但是，战争留下的巨大创伤在短时间内根本无法得到修复，而且激起人们对人类发展进程的深刻思考。对于弗洛姆来说，在暴力和战争中，人性的危机和扭曲完全暴露出来，而作为受害者的经历让他对此更有感触。因此，他基于马克思主义，付诸一生以探求人的本质和自由理论，并通过对人性的思考展开对资本主义制度的批判。

2. 苏联模式“正统”地位的动摇

在苏共二十大之前，苏联在社会主义建设和反法西斯主义战争中所取得的巨大成就牢固确立了苏联马克思主义的“正统地位”。但是，这一地位随着斯大林的逝世而受到严重冲击。1956年，社会主义阵营内部发生了两个标志性事件：一个事件是赫鲁晓夫在苏共二十大上的秘密报告，斯大林被彻底否定并清算；另一个事件是苏联出兵干涉匈牙利。这两个事件在同年发生，对社会主义阵营的政治与理论造成了巨大冲击。一些西方马克思主义者开始反思苏联模式，力求重新阐释马克思主义。同时，许多西方资产阶级学者也以此作为攻击社会主义的武器。对于弗洛姆来说，赫鲁晓夫上台后的一系列做法，为他对马克思主义原理的进一步探究提供了重要反思素材，也增强了他研究马克思主义基本原理的动力。

3. 暴力成为西方政治进程的一部分

二十世纪以后，人类经历了多次大规模战争，仅仅世界大战就爆发了两次，局部战争更是接连不断。在西欧，各国虽然科技水平获得迅速提升，经济也取得长足发展，但是，社会的动荡令西方学者不断反思两个重大问题。第一，马克思主义是如何定义暴力在人类历史发展过程中的作用的。马克思主义关于人的阐述又能够在现实中起到多大的作用。第二，在一次次或大或小的暴力过程中，人的生存状况和整个西方社会的政治制度都在不断改变，暴力在这个时代仍然显得十分平常，甚至成为政治进程中一个不可缺少的部分，成为一种政治行为。正如布洛赫所说，英国革命、法国革命和美国革命开创了西方民主政治，1917 年俄国二月革命和 1918 年德国革命也被西方广泛接受。对于西方来说，建立在暴力之上的战争和民主政府已经成为一种广泛的原则，采用暴力成为一种必要的政治手段。尽管如此，马克思认为，政治暴力并不应当成为推动人类社会发展的最重要因素，因为“暴力绝不能创造出任何崭新的事物”。因此，在暴力已经成为西方政治制度一部分的情况下，人究竟应该如何发展，如何能够维持人的本质，就成为布洛赫以及相当一部分西方马克思主义者们思考的重大理论问题。

（三）思想背景

1. 人本主义马克思主义不断发展的内在需求

1923 年卢卡奇出版了《历史与阶级意识》，开启了一种既不同于第二国际正统马克思主义又不同于西方主流意识形态的新的学术思潮。在西方马克思主义的发展中，人本主义马克思主义逐渐兴起，而且影响力越来越大。不过，在二十世纪五十年代中期以前，人本主义马克思主义的发展并不像许多人想象得那样强势。伴随弗洛伊德主义和存在主义的滥觞，人本主义马克思主义最初崛起于并主要流行于德语马克思主义理论界，随着法西斯主义的上台，这些人本主义马克思主义者或流亡苏联（卢卡奇），并与苏联马克思主义达成“被迫的和解”；或流亡美国（法兰克福学派），在漠视乃至敌视马克思主义的意识形态氛围中被迫选择孤立的学院化生存。

第二次世界大战结束后，人本主义马克思主义开始获得长足发展。这在社会历史背景上首先得益于二十世纪三十年代以来的资本主义发展面临的新问题和人的存在状态的转变。一方面是对法西斯主义的反思催生了对人本身的关注；另一方面是资本主义的发展也使人的存在问题日益凸显。具体到西方马克思主义的历史变迁中：首先，流亡苏联和美国的西方马克思主义者陆续回到自己的国家,他们在战前出版、发表的那些代表作重新被发现,并在欧洲左派知识分子中间产生越来越大的影响;其次,萨特等一批法国主流知识分子公开转向人本主义马克思主义,显著壮大了后者的理论声势;最后,随着葛兰西《狱中札记》的陆续编辑出版,人们在这位受到苏共充分肯定的前意大利共产党领导人著作中同样发现了人本主义马克思主义,这为后者的传播与发展提供了某种合法性基础。历史地看,进入二十世纪五十年代中期以后,人本主义马克思主义在西方发达资本主义国家已经对苏联马克思主义的主导地位构成了实质性的挑战,特别是 1956 年苏共二十大后的赫鲁晓夫秘密报告及苏联入侵匈牙利事件则使人本主义马克思主义不仅成为西方发达资本主义国家中马克思主义的主流,而且成为东欧新马克思主义的核心议题之一。这就要求人本主义马克思主义打破以往的专题研究性质,对自己的理论主张进行完整、系统的正面阐述,既不同于苏联马克思主义的解释,又要运用马克思来批判现实资本主义的变化。正是在这种思想史背景下,弗洛姆决意为《1844 年经济学哲学手稿》的第一个美国译本撰写长篇导论。

2. 新文本的问世与青年马克思研究

1932 年,马克思的《1844 年经济学哲学手稿》在东西方同时出版。这两个版本分别被收入《马克思恩格斯全集》历史考订版第一部分第三卷和德国社会民主党人朗兹胡特和迈尔编撰的《历史唯物主义:卡尔·马克思早期著作集》。面对马克思青年时期的这一重要哲学文本,西方学界表现出了极大的热情。该著作甫一面世,当时西方马克思主义者马尔库塞和比利时社会民主党人德曼就分别发表长文,对《1844 年经济学哲学手稿》进行阐释。值得注意的是,尽管他们都热情欢呼这一文本的面世,并都认为这种人本主义体现了马克思哲学思想的本质和真正的贡献,不过,两者之间却隐藏着细微而重大的意识形态分野。马尔库塞在《历史唯物主义的基础》中,针对第二国际以及苏联正统的马克思主义解释,表明:由卢卡奇所开创的西方马克思主义因为正确理解了马克思与黑格尔、政治经济学与哲学之间的关系,从而完整准确地把握了马克思思想的人本主义本质。而德曼的《新发现的马克思》则一方面有意识地把青年马克思和《资本论》时期成熟的马克思对立起来,用前者来贬低后者,另一方面则试图把这种人本主义与伯恩斯坦基于新康德主义的修正主义结合起来，以之为当时在社会民主党内已经逐渐主流化的伦理社会主义张目。冷战兴起之后，德曼所宣扬的这种“两个马克思”观点在西方“马克思学”中得到了广泛传播，影响日增。这种情况引起了同时代西方马克思主义者们的警惕，因此，从二十世纪五十年代末期开始，不少西方马克思主义者都开始致力于对马克思思想的重新解读，以期在人本主义的基础上对马克思思想进行统一的阐释。在这个方面，弗洛姆以及同时代的美国马克思主义者杜娜叶夫斯卡娅着力最多，影响也最大。

二、篇章结构

1961 年，弗洛姆出版了《马克思关于人的概念》一书。该书是弗洛姆为马克思的《1844 年经济学哲学手稿》首次在美国出版所撰写的长篇导论。在这本篇幅并不长的著作中，弗洛姆基于自己的新弗洛伊德主义的理论立场，对青年马克思的人本主义哲学进行了极具时代气息的阐发。因此，它一经出版，即在西方学术界乃至一般知识界产生重大影响，显著增强了人们对于马克思哲学的理论兴趣，同时，也有力地推动了人本主义的马克思主义思潮在西方世界的传播与发展。它也因此牢固确立了自己在西方马克思主义哲学发展史上的重要地位。

在弗洛姆生前出版的二十余种著作中，《马克思关于人的概念》是为数不多集中讨论马克思主义哲学的，也是哲学性质最强的一部作品。在这本书中，我们一方面可以发现，弗洛姆的思想相当驳杂，其中既有精神分析学、马克思主义、存在主义的色彩，也能察觉出新康德主义和宗教神秘主义的影响；另一方面，能够清楚地发现贯穿其思想的主线：人本主义。在他看来，“它是一种把人以及人的发展、完善、尊严和自由放在中心位置上的一种思想和情感的体系”。不管就思想深刻性而言，还是就对马克思思想诠释的准确性来说，《马克思关于人的概念》在人本主义马克思主义阵营中都算不上最杰出的。但是在西方马克思主义哲学发展史上，它的重要性在于以一种个性化的方式，深入浅出地阐述了人本主义马克思主义的基本观念，从而显著推动了人本主义马克思主义在西方的传播与发展。《马克思关于人的概念》的主体内容包括前言、八章正文和一个后记。其中前言为对包括巴特摩尔翻译的《1844 年经济学哲学手稿》以及相关马克思文献英译节选部分在内的全书所做的介绍和说明，后记为 1966 年弗洛姆对 1961 年该书写作及其引发的相关争论的回应和说明。①

在前言中，弗洛姆提供了翻译介绍以《1844 年经济学哲学手稿》为代表的马克思文献的意义的概要说明，即阐释一种人本主义的马克思主义对于理解 20 世纪中叶的资本主义和社会主义的理论价值。因此，该前言不仅可以被看作是《马克思关于人的概念》一书的导论，也可以被看作人本主义马克思主义总体理论规划的说明。弗洛姆开宗明义地指出，马克思的哲学与许多存在主义者的思想一样，也代表一种抗议，抗议人的异化，抗议人失去其自身，抗议人变成物。马克思的这种哲学思想在《1844 年经济学哲学手稿》中得到了最清楚的表达，其核心是现实的人的存在问题。在弗洛姆看来，马克思所理解的人的"本性"展现在历史之中，马克思的哲学是一种抗议，相信人能够使自己得到解放，使自己的潜能得到实现。这种人本主义的哲学传统从中世纪后期的斯宾诺莎开始，经过十八世纪法国和德国的启蒙哲学家，一直延续到十九世纪，但在现代机械论世界观中被忘却了。处在这一传统中的马克思的哲学有助于解决二十世纪中期西方的社会问题。同时因为现代世界分裂为资本主义和社会主义两大阵营，一方面马克思的思想在很大程度上被误解了，另一方面理解马克思的思想也有助于分析现实社会主义的问题。因此，弗洛姆关注《1844 年经济学哲学手稿》，写作这本书的目的不仅是要更好地帮助人们理解马克思的人本主义哲学，而且希望纠正现实资本主义世界中把马克思看作魔鬼、把社会主义看作魔鬼的王国的偏颇认识。

第一章《对马克思的概念的歪曲》首先指明了人本主义马克思主义理解的批判对象，就是第二国际和苏联马克思主义以"唯物主义"的误解为基础的哲学观念。弗洛姆指出，在对马克思的形形色色的误解中，传播最广的当属对唯物主义观念的误解。在有些人看来，仿佛马克思认为人的最主要的心理动机是获得金钱与享受，这种为获得最大利润而做出的努力，构成个人生活和人类生活中的主要动力。从这种误解出发，人们进一步把马克思的社会主义天堂描述为这样一种情景：成千上万的人听命于一个拥有至高无上权力的国家官僚机构，这些人即使可能争取到平等地位，但牺牲了他们的

① 《马克思关于人的概念》一书英文版本有 1961 年、1966 年、2013 年等多个不同版本，本章选文出自 1961 年版本。

自由和个性。弗洛姆认为，对马克思的这种解释是完全错误的。马克思的学说并不认为人的主要动机就是获得物质财富，不仅如此，马克思的目标恰恰是使人从经济需要的压迫下解脱出来，以便他能够成为具有充分人性的人。马克思主要关心的事情是使人获得解放，克服异化，恢复他自己与别人以及与自然界的密切联系的能力。之所以会出现这种误解，原因有两个：一是无知，二是苏联对马克思主义的理论独占。

第二章《马克思的历史唯物主义》在第一章讨论的基础上做进一步深化，并引申出人本主义的唯物主义历史观理解，即强调人的实践和变革的历史唯物主义。弗洛姆认为，马克思的唯物主义方法包括对人的现实的经济生活和社会生活的研究，也包括对人的实际生活的方式对这种思想和感情的研究。在一系列著作，特别是《关于费尔巴哈的提纲》中，马克思清楚地表明过自己的历史唯物主义的方法和特征。对历史唯物主义之流行的错误理解认为，它是一种论述人的动力和激情的心理学，但实际上历史唯物主义根本不是如此的。它认为，人们的生产方式决定人们的思想和欲望，它并不认为人们的主要欲望就是想获得最大的物质利益。就此而言，经济就与心理的动力无关，而与生产方式有关，与主观的、心理的因素无关，而与客观的经济社会的因素有关。马克思的唯物主义历史观与那种把所谓的“物质的”或“经济的”斗争当作人的最基本的推动力的观念，没有任何共同之处。马克思与十八世纪和十九世纪的大多数作家的根本差别之一就是，他并不认为资本主义是人的本性的结果，也不认为资本主义制度下的人的动机是人的普遍的动机。马克思对资本主义的全部批判是因为资本主义把金钱和物质利益的关系变成人的主要动力，而马克思关于社会主义的概念正是指向这样一个社会，在这个社会中物质利益不再是占支配地位的。在此过程中，“劳动”构成了一个在马克思理论中起重要作用的因素。

第三章《关于意识的问题，社会结构和暴力的使用》在人本主义的历史唯物主义理解框架中，通过说明意识这一精神分析领域中高度关注的问题，来进一步阐明马克思哲学中人的存在问题，进而通过回应西方学者在“暴力”问题上对马克思的指摘，来说明其“革命的实践”概念中所包含的未来人的可能性。弗洛姆首先简要重申了马克思《关于费尔巴哈的提纲》和《德意志意识形态》中关于意识的本质、人与环境的关系的基本观点。同时在澄清“革命的实践”概念时指出：马克思看到，在社会的和政治的进程还没有做好准备的情况下，政治的暴力是不可能产生任何结果的。因此，如果暴力是完全必要的，那么只在于它能对实际上已经成熟的发展起最后一推的作用，但是它绝不能产生任何真正的新的东西。这是马克思从人的本性理解出发超越资产阶级暴力学说的伟大卓见所在。

第四章《人的本性》分“关于人性概念”和“人的自我能动性”两个部分，集中阐发了弗洛姆对马克思的人性概念和人的自我能动性学说的理解，集中体现了三个方面的特征：一是弗洛姆阐发的人本主义观念具有强烈的精神分析背景；二是这种阐发直接依赖于《1844 年经济学哲学手稿》的文本和概念梳理；三是这种阐发所直面的是二十世纪中叶的资本主义物化现实。弗洛姆认为，马克思与当代许多社会学家和心理学家不同，他不相信不存在像人的本性那样的东西，也不相信人生来就是一张白纸，任由教养在这种白纸上留下它的烙印。马克思跟这种社会学的相对主义正好相反，他认为：人作为人是一个可认识、可确定的客体；人不仅能够按照生物学、解剖学和生理学加以规定，而且能够按照心理学加以规定。在弗洛姆看来，马克思在批判地继承黑格尔哲学的基础上，建立了一种人的潜能学说，这种潜能通过人的自我能动性逐步得到实现，历史也就因此不断地被创造出来。人的这种自我实现的能动性，最集中体现在马克思对主客体关系的分析中。基于《1844 年经济学哲学手稿》中四重异化学说以及有关需要的文本分析，弗洛姆明确区分了占有和存在的差别，明确提出人的本性是一种独立、自由的自我创造。进而，要理解这种人的本性，必须将劳动概念从经济学中解放出来，复原其人类学的含义。换言之，马克思的中心思想是要使异化的、无意义的劳动变成生产的、自由的劳动，而不是使异化的劳动从私有的或“抽象的”国家资本主义那里获得更好的报酬。这实际上构成了对包括现实资本主义和社会主义在内的“工业社会”的批判。

第五章《异化》中明确将异化界定为“生产性的否定”，并在追溯异化概念的思想史渊源基础上，分析了《1844 年经济学哲学手稿》中的异化劳动和人的类本质思想，进而在同《资本论》商品拜物教分析的比较中，进一步阐发了马克思异化劳动学说的现实意义。在该部分中，弗洛姆首先简要梳理了马克思异化学说的思想史源流，从宗教的异化到近代哲学中“生产性”观念的变迁。显然，这里所说的“生产性”与马克思的“物质生产”概念已经有了明显的区别，本质是一种人的能动性和自我实现的能力。在此基础上，弗洛姆详细地阐发了《1844 年经济学哲学手稿》中的异化学说体系，以及马克思关于人的类本质和社会主义的理解。进而弗洛姆对马克思异化思想在《资本论》及其手稿中的发展，即商品拜物教理论进行了扼要的评论，其核心思想是要阐明，在马克思那里，人类的历史就是人不断发展同时不断异化的历史，他的社会主义概念就是从异化中解放出来，就是人回到他自身，就是人的自我实现。这也体现了作为西方马克思主义者的弗洛姆对现实资本主义社会的批判性分析。

第六章《马克思关于社会主义的概念》在人的创造性本质和异化分析基础上，阐述了一种人本主义的社会主义观念。弗洛姆认为：社会主义的目的是人，是“一场在社会的现实中反对毁灭爱的抵抗运动”；这种社会主义既不同于斯大林主义的社会主义，也是对现实资本主义中人的异化的抗议；这种社会主义关注人的价值，继承了救世主义、基督教千年王国、乌托邦主义和启蒙运动的传统。可以说，在弗洛姆看来，马克思所理解的社会主义是这样一种社会制度，它允许人复归到人自身，允许存在与本质之间的同一，允许克服主体和客体之间的分裂和对抗，允许对自然的人性化；它意味着这样的一个世界，在那里，人不再是许多陌生人中的一个陌生人，而是在他自己的世界中，在那里，他是自由自在的，就像在自己家里一样。这不啻为一种与存在主义一样，抗议人的异化的人本主义的宗教。

第七章《马克思的思想的连贯性》，作为人的概念、异化思想和社会主义分析的逻辑产物，以及对《1844 年经济学哲学手稿》问世以来马克思思想发展分期争论的回应，这一部分构成了我们理解弗洛姆思想，以及理解人本主义马克思主义理解的重要文本。与后来胡克所描述的“老年马克思”与“青年马克思”不同，弗洛姆认为只存在一个马克思，这个马克思就是抗议异化、关注人的潜能的马克思。针对当时非常流行的两个马克思说，当然主要是苏联马克思主义研究中出于对西方学术界“青年马克思”问题的回应而提出的马克思早期思想发展分期问题，以及以贝尔为代表的美国主流学界对马克思思想的阐发，弗洛姆指出，尽管在概念、心境和语言上出现了某些变化，不过马克思从青年时代起发展起来的哲学核心绝没有改变，因此，如果以他在早期著作中发展起来的关于人的概念为基础，就不可能理解他后来的社会主义学说以及对资本主义的批判。这实际上也构成了人本主义马克思主义在英语学界的理论宣言。

第八章《马克思其人》是关于马克思的简要人物素描。但是这种素描更多具有文学和精神分析的特征，而对马克思本身“攀登科学高峰”的历程缺乏严谨细致的分析。

在1966年所增加的全书后记中，弗洛姆叙述了自己1961年写作这本书的目的和希望，以及二十世纪六十年代人本主义思潮在东西方同时兴起的表现：东欧马克思主义研究中的人本主义倾向以及基督教人本主义思潮的兴起。弗洛姆相信，随着两者间对话的深入以及以《1844年经济学哲学手稿》为代表的马克思人本主义著作在英美的传播，一种人本主义的马克思主义将在西方逐渐深入人心。然而历史已经证明，弗洛姆的愿景并未实现。

三、研究前沿

弗洛姆是一位重要的西方马克思主义思想家，其思想观点时至今日仍然具有重要的启发意义。早在1982年，《马克思关于人的概念》就被翻译成了中文并收入《西方学者论〈一八四四年经济学—哲学手稿〉》。不过，长期以来，它并没有得到国内学界的足够重视。人们往往只把它看作一本专门阐释青年马克思哲学思想的学术著作，而没有充分意识到它的理论内涵。因此，虽然国内学界早在二十世纪八十年代就有学者对弗洛姆及其人学思想开展研究，但是直到二十一世纪以来，特别是在第二个十年，研究弗洛姆理论的成果数量才有了较为明显的提升，研究的内容也逐步涉及弗洛姆的全部思想领域，对其人本主义立场也有了全面而客观的判断。此外，除了延续相关理论研究外，学者们还注重引译国外的弗洛姆研究作品，总体呈现了全面且多层次的研究格局。

第一，从劳动异化和生产异化角度，梳理弗洛姆人本思想的批判依据。学界普遍认为，弗洛姆作为新弗洛伊德主义的代表，始终基于西方的人道主义传统理解马克思的人学思想。在《马克思关于人的概念》中，弗洛姆深刻解读了《1844年经济学哲学手稿》，对其中的“人的本质”和“异化劳动”概念展开深刻论述，按照马克思的思路，批判了自由异化、爱的异化、消费异化，这是在继承马克思方法论基础上的一种重要的理论拓展。因此，弗洛姆哲学中的“人”的逻辑与青年马克思的“异化”是同构的。不过，弗洛姆的解读虽然能够在一定程度上赋予近代西方社会文化和社会发展层面以历史唯物主义色彩，但是这种方法还是没有摆脱“非历史的抽象人性论色彩”，因而难免具有形而上学的乌托邦色彩。

第二，从道德哲学角度，分析弗洛姆人学思想的价值取向。有学者指出，弗洛姆对工人阶级内心世界的关注是塑造其价值取向的重要表现。弗洛姆认为，当时西欧工人阶级自身往往表现出“权威主义性格”，这会导致他们在实际革命中并不能够真正付诸革命实践，而是会依附于国家社会主义意识形态。这种“权威主义性格”，或者还有一些学者称之为“权威主义宗教”，会影响工人阶级的价值观。当然，弗洛姆在研究过程中，将马克思主义同流行的精神分析学说相结合的尝试，也是一种具有深远意义的马克思主义理论方法。尽管如此，有学者指出，弗洛姆虽然在形式上继承了马克思青年时期的方法论，突出了历史唯物主义中的人本思想，但是他忽视了马克思成熟时期的方法论转型，因而并没有完成对人性更加全面的考察。

第三，分析弗洛姆人学思想和人本主义的当代意义。学界对弗洛姆的理论和时代意义予以了充分肯定。有学者认为，弗洛姆的人本思想是对欧洲文化传统中的理性主义、人本主义、批判精神、救世情怀的综合，批判了权威主义、狭隘民族主义、消费主义，真正将理论研究重新聚焦到人的身上，是探索理想型社会和人的发展的基础，对探索二十一世纪人的发展问题起到了重要的启蒙作用。在社会层面，有学者认为，弗洛姆的人性理论对考察网络社会的个体化具有重要价值。另外，有学者认为，弗洛姆构建的具有人本主义色彩的生存方式理论，以人的生存方式作为起点，对西方工业社会提出了基础性批判，指出这些国家的生存方式只是注重“重占有”，过分强调社会的私有制关系，却忽视了“重存在”的理念形态才是维护人性时所真正需要的。因此，有学者认为，弗洛姆的这一观点是基于历史唯物主义的角度提出的，对我国防止出现“重占有”而不强调人民群众的历史主体地位具有重要的参照意义。

第四，从多角度出发，把握弗洛姆人本学思想的内核。除了《马克思关于人的概念》，弗洛姆的《逃避自由》《人的呼唤》《健全的社会》等作品都是反映其人本主义思想的重要作品。弗洛姆通过这些作品完整讨论了从个人到社会的自由生成逻辑。例如，“自由”是共产主义的重要特征，也是弗洛姆人本思想的核心理念，与人本理论有非常密切的理论关联。有学者认为，弗洛姆的人性异化思想就是建立在人性标准基础之上的对人的全面反思，但是忽视了马克思主义历史观的一些基本视角和方法，这令弗洛姆建构“自由”观时始终无法抓住历史发展的本质。

四、文本节选

Preface

The bulk of this volume contains an English translation of Karl Marx's main philosophical work, published for the first time in the United States. Obviously, this publication is of importance, if for no other reason than that it will acquaint the American public with one of the major works of post-Hegelian philosophy, hitherto unknown in the English-speaking world. Marx's philosophy, like much of existentialist thinking, represents a protest against man's alienation, his loss of himself and his transformation into a thing; it is a movement against the dehumanization and automatization of man inherent in the development of Western industrialism. It is ruthlessly critical of all "answers" to the problem of human existence which try to present solutions by negating or camouflaging the dichotomies inherent in man's existence. Marx's philosophy is rooted in the humanist Western philosophical tradition, which reaches from Spinoza through the French and German enlightenment philosophers of the eighteenth century to Goethe and Hegel, and the very essence of which is concern for man and the realization of his potentialities.

...

Marx's philosophy is one of protest; it is a protest imbued with faith in man, in his capacity to liberate himself, and to realize his potentialities. This faith is a trait of Marx's thinking that was characteristic of the Western mood from the late Middle Ages to the nineteenth century, and which is so rare today. For this very reason, to many readers who are infected with the contemporary spirit of resignation and the revival of the concept of original sin (in Niebuhrian or Freudian terms), Marx's philosophy will sound dated, old-fashioned, utopian and for this reason, if not for others, they will reject the voice of faith in man's possibilities, and of hope in his capacity to become what he potentially is. To others, however, Marx's philosophy will be a source of new insight and hope.

I believe that hope and new insight transcending the narrow limits of the positivistic-mechanistic thinking of social science today are needed, if the West is to emerge alive from this century of trial. ...

... The West has much to offer as a leader of such a development for the former colonial nations; not only capital and technical advice, but also the Western humanist tradition of which Marxist socialism is the upshot; the tradition of man's freedom, not only *from*, but his freedom *to*—to develop his own human potentialities, the tradition of human dignity and brotherhood. But clearly, in order to exercise this influence and in order to understand the Russian and Chinese claims, we must understand Marx's thought and must discard the ignorant and distorted picture of Marxism which is current in American thinking today. It is my hope that this volume will be a step in that direction.

...

... They refer mainly to the fact that Marx failed to see the degree to which capitalism was capable of modifying itself and thus satisfying the economic needs of industrialized nations, his failure to see clearly enough the dangers of bureaucratization and centralization, and to envisage the authoritarian systems which could emerge as alternatives to socialism. But since this book deals only with Marx's philosophical and historical thought, it is not the place to discuss the controversial points of his economic and political theory.

——Erich Fromm, *Marx's Concept of Man*, Frederick Ungar Publishing Co., 1961, pp. v–viii.

The Nature of Man

1. The Concept of Human Nature

Marx did not believe, as do many contemporary sociologists and psychologists, that there is no such thing as the nature of man; that man at birth is like a blank sheet of paper, on which the culture writes its text. Quite in contrast to this sociological relativism, Marx started out with the idea that man *qua man* is a recognizable and ascertainable entity; that man can be defined as man not only biologically, anatomically and physiologically, but also psychologically.

Of course, Marx was never tempted to assume that "human nature" was identical with that particular expression of human nature prevalent in his own society. In arguing against Bentham, Marx said: "To know what is useful for a dog, one must study dog nature. This nature itself is not to be deduced from the principle of utility. Applying this to man, he that would criticize all human acts, movements, relations, etc., by the principle of utility, *must first deal with human nature in general, and then with human nature as modified in each historical epoch*." It must be noted that this concept of human nature is not, for Marx—as it was not either for Hegel—an abstraction. It is the *essence* of man—in contrast to the various forms of his historical *existence*—and, as Marx said, "the essence of man is no abstraction inherent in each separate individual." It must also be stated that this sentence from *Capital*, written by the "old Marx", shows the continuity of the concept of man's essence (Wesen) which the young Marx wrote about in the *Economic and Philosophical Manuscripts*. He no longer used the *term* "essence" later on, as being abstract and unhistorical, but he clearly retained the notion of this essence in a more historical version, in the differentiation between "human nature in general" and "human nature as modified" with each historical period.

In line with this distinction between a general human nature and the specific expression of human nature in each culture, Marx distinguishes, as we have already mentioned above, two types of human drives and appetites: the *constant* or fixed ones, such as hunger and the sexual urge, which are an integral part of human nature, and which can be changed only in their form and the direction they take in various cultures, and the "*relative*" *appetites*, which are not an integral part of human nature but which "owe their origin to certain social structures and certain conditions of production and communication." Marx gives as an example the needs produced by the capitalistic structure of society. "The need for money," he wrote in the *Economic and Philosophical Manuscripts*, "is therefore the real need created by the modern economy, and the only need which it creates ... This is shown subjectively, partly in the fact that the expansion of production and of needs becomes an *ingenious* and always *calculating* subservience to inhuman, depraved, unnatural, and *imaginary* appetites."

Man's potential, for Marx, is a given potential; man is, as it were, the human raw material which, as such, cannot be changed, just as the brain structure has remained the same since the dawn of history. Yet, man *does* change in the course of history; he develops himself; *he* transforms himself, he is the product of history; since *he* makes his history, he is his own product. History is the history of man's self-realization; it is nothing but the self-creation of man through the process of his work and his production: "the *whole of what is called world history* is nothing but the creation of man by human labor, and the emergence of nature for man; he therefore has the evident and irrefutable proof of his *self-creation*, of his own *origins*."

2. Man's self-activity

Marx's concept of man is rooted in Hegel's thinking. Hegel begins with the insight that appearance and essence do not coincide. The task of the dialectical thinker is "to distinguish the essential from the apparent process of reality, and to grasp their relations." Or, to put it differently, it is the problem of the relationship between essence and existence. In the process of existence, the essence is realized, and at the same time, existing means a return to the essence. "The world is an estranged and untrue world so long as man does not destroy its dead objectivity and recognize himself and his own life "behind" the fixed form of things and laws. When he finally wins this *self-consciousness*, he is on his way not only to the truth of himself, but also of his world. And with the recognition goes the doing. He will try to put this truth into action, and *make* the world what it *essentially* is, namely, the fulfillment of man's self-consciousness." For Hegel, knowledge is not obtained in the position of the subject-object split, in which the object is grasped as something separated from and opposed to the thinker. In order to *know* the world, man has to *make the world his own*. Man and things are in a constant transition from one *suchness* into another; hence "a thing is for itself only when it has posited (*gesetzt*) all its determinates and made them moments of its self-realization, and is thus, in all changing conditions, always 'returning to itself'." In this process "entering into itself becomes essence." This essence, the unity of being, the identity throughout change is, according to Hegel, a process in which "everything copes with its inherent contradictions and unfolds itself as a result." "The essence is thus as much historical as ontological. The essential potentialities of things realize themselves in the same comprehensive process that establishes their existence. The essence can 'achieve' its existence when the potentialities of things have ripened in and through the conditions of reality. Hegel describes this process as the transition to actuality." In contrast to positivism, for Hegel "facts are facts only if related to that which is not yet fact and yet manifests itself in the given facts as a real possibility. Or, facts are what they are only as moments in a process that leads beyond them to that which is not yet fulfilled in fact."

The culmination of all of Hegel's thinking is the concept of the potentialities inherent in a thing, of the dialectical process in which they manifest themselves, and the idea that this process is one of active movement of these potentialities. This emphasis on the active process within man is already to be found in the ethical system of Spinoza. For Spinoza, all affects were to be divided into passive affects (passions), through which man suffers and does not have an adequate idea of reality, and into active affects (actions) (generosity and fortitude) in which man is free and productive. Goethe, who like Hegel was influenced by Spinoza in many ways, developed the idea of man's productivity into a central point of his philosophical thinking. For him all decaying cultures are characterized by the tendency for pure subjectivity, while all progressive periods try to grasp the world as it is, by one's own subjectivity, but not separate from it. He gives the example of the poet: "as long as he expresses only these few subjective sentences, he can not yet be called a poet, but as soon as he knows *how to appropriate the world for himself, and to express it*, he is a poet. Then he is inexhaustible, and can be ever new, while his purely subjective nature has exhausted itself soon and ceases to have anything to say". "Man", says Goethe, "knows himself only inasmuch as he knows the world; he knows the world only within himself and he is aware of himself only within the world. Each new object truly recognized, opens up a new organ within ourselves." Goethe gave the most poetic and powerful expression to the idea of human productivity in his *Faust*. Neither possession, nor power, nor sensuous satisfaction, Faust teaches, can fulfill man's desire for meaning in his life; he remains in all this separate from the whole, hence unhappy. Only in being productively active can man make sense of his life, and while he thus enjoys life, he is not greedily holding on to it. He has given up the greed for *having*, and is fulfilled by *being*; he is filled because he is empty; he *is* much, because he *has* little. Hegel gave the most systematic and profound expression to the idea of the productive man, of the individual who is *he*, inasmuch as he is not passive-receptive, but actively related to the world; who is an individual only in this process of grasping the world productively, and thus making it his own. He expressed the idea quite poetically by saying that the subject wanting to bring a content to realization does so by "translating itself from the night of possibility into the day of actuality." For Hegel the development of all individual powers, capacities and potentialities is possible only by continuous action, never by sheer contemplation or receptivity. For Spinoza, Goethe, Hegel, as well as for Marx, man is alive only inasmuch as he is productive, inasmuch as he grasps the world outside of himself in the act of expressing his own specific human powers, and of grasping the world with these powers.

Inasmuch as man is not productive, inasmuch as he is receptive and passive, he is nothing, he is dead. In this productive process, man realizes his own essence, he returns to his own essence, which in theological language is nothing other than his return to God.

——Erich Fromm, *Marx's Concept of Man*, Frederick Ungar Publishing Co., 1961, pp.24 - 30.

Alienation

The concept of the active, productive man who grasps and embraces the objective world with his own powers cannot be fully understood without the concept of the *negation of productivity*: *alienation*. For Marx the history of mankind is a history of the increasing development of man, and at the same time of increasing alienation. His concept of socialism is the emancipation from alienation, the return of man to himself, his self-realization.

Alienation (or "estrangement") means, for Marx, that man does not experience himself as the acting agent in his grasp of the world, but that the world (nature, others, and he himself) remain alien to him.

They stand above and against him as objects, even though they may be objects of his own creation. Alienation is essentially experiencing the world and oneself passively, receptively, as the subject separated from the object.

…

For Marx the process of alienation is expressed in work and in the division of labor. Work is for him the active relatedness of man to nature, the creation of a new world, including the creation of man himself. (Intellectual activity is of course, for Marx, always work, like manual or artistic activity.) But as private property and the division of labor develop, labor loses its character of being an expression of man's powers; labor and its products assume an existence separate from man, his will and his planning. "The object produced by labor, its product, now stands opposed to it as an *alien being*, as a *power independent* of the producer. The product of labor is labor which has been embodied in an object and turned into a physical thing; this product is an *objectification* of labor." Labor is alienated because the work has ceased to be a part of the worker's nature and "consequently, he does not fulfill himself in his work but denies himself, has a feeling of misery rather than well-being, does not develop freely his mental and physical energies but is physically exhausted and mentally debased. The worker therefore feels himself at home only during his leisure time, whereas at work he feels homeless."

Thus, in the act of production the relationship of the worker to his own activity is experienced "as something alien and not belonging to him, activity as suffering (passivity), strength as powerlessness, creation as emasculation." While man thus becomes alienated from himself, the product of labor becomes "an alien object which dominates him. This relationship is at the same time the relationship to the sensuous external world, to natural objects, as an alien and hostile world." Marx stresses two points: 1) in the process of work, and especially of work under the conditions of capitalism, man is estranged from his own creative powers, and 2) the *objects* of his own work become alien beings, and eventually rule over him, become powers independent of the producer. "The laborer exists for the process of production, and not the process of production for the laborer."

A misunderstanding of Marx on this point is widespread, even among socialists. It is believed that Marx spoke primarily of the *economic* exploitation of the worker, and the fact that his share of the product was not as large as it should be, or that the product should belong to him, instead of to the capitalist. But as I have shown before, the state as a capitalist, as in the Soviet Union, would not have been any more welcome to Marx than the private capitalist. He is not concerned primarily with the equalization of income. He is concerned with the liberation of man from a kind of work which destroys his individuality, which transforms him into a thing, and which makes him into the slave of things. Just as Kierkegaard was concerned with the salvation of the individual, so Marx was, and his criticism of capitalist society is directed not at its method of distribution of income, but its mode of production, its destruction of individuality and its enslavement of man, not by the capitalist, but the enslavement of man—worker *and* capitalist—by things and circumstances of their own making.

Marx goes still further. In unalienated work man not only realizes himself as an individual, but also as a species-being. For Marx, as for Hegel and many other thinkers of the enlightenment, each individual represented the species, that is to say, humanity as a whole, the universality of man: the development of man leads to the unfolding of his whole humanity. In the process of work he "no longer reproduces himself merely intellectually, as in consciousness, but actively and in a real sense, and he sees his own reflection in a world which he has constructed. While, therefore, alienated labor takes away the object of production from man, it also takes away his *species life*, his real objectivity as a species-being, and changes his advantage over animals into a disadvantage in so far as his inorganic body, nature, is taken from him. Just as alienated labor transforms free and self-directed activity into a means, so it transforms the species life of man into a means of physical existence. Consciousness, which man has from his species, is transformed through alienation so that species life becomes only a means for him."

——Erich Fromm, *Marx's Concept of Man*, Frederick Ungar Publishing Co., 1961, pp. 43 - 48.

Marx's Concept of Socialism

...

Quite clearly the aim of socialism is *man*. ... in which he can return to himself and grasp the world with his own powers, thus becoming one with the world. Socialism for Marx was, as Paul Tillich put it, "a resistance movement against the destruction of love in social reality."

Marx expressed the aim of socialism with great clarity at the end of the third volume of *Capital*: "In fact, the realm of freedom does not commence until the point is passed where labor under the compulsion of necessity and of external utility is required. In the very nature of things it lies beyond the sphere of material production in the strict meaning of the term. Just as the savage must wrestle with nature, in order to satisfy his wants, in order to maintain his life and reproduce it, so civilized man has to do it, and he must do it in all forms of society and under all possible modes of production. With his development the realm of natural necessity expands, because his wants increase; but at the same time the forces of production increase, by which these wants are satisfied. The freedom in this field cannot consist of anything else but of the fact that *socialized man, the associated producers, regulate their interchange with nature rationally, bring it under their common control, instead of being ruled by it as by some blind power*; they accomplish their task with the least expenditure of energy and under conditions most adequate to their human nature and most worthy of it. *But it always remains a realm of necessity*. Beyond it begins that development of human power, which is its own end, the true realm of freedom, which, however, can flourish only upon that realm of necessity as its basis."

Marx expresses here all essential elements of socialism. First, man produces in an associated, not competitive way; he produces rationally and in an unalienated way, which means that he brings production under his control, instead of being ruled by it as by some blind power. This clearly excludes a concept of socialism in which man is manipulated by a bureaucracy, even if this bureaucracy rules the whole state economy, rather than only a big corporation. It means that the individual participates actively in the planning *and* in the execution of the plans; it means, in short, the realization of political and industrial democracy. Marx expected that by this new form of an unalienated society man would become independent, stand on his own feet, and would no longer be crippled by the alienated mode of production and consumption; that he would truly be the master and the creator of his life, and hence that he could begin to make *living* his main business, rather than producing the *means* for living. Socialism, for Marx, was never as such the fulfillment of life, but the *condition* for such fulfillment. When man has built a rational, nonalienated form of society, he will have the chance to begin with what is the aim of life: the "development of human power, which is its own end, the true realm of freedom."...

For Marx, socialism (or communism) is not flight or abstraction from, or loss of the objective world which men have created by the objectification of their faculties. It is not an impoverished return to unnatural, primitive simplicity. It is rather the first real emergence, the genuine actualization of man's nature as something real. Socialism, for Marx, is a society which permits the actualization of man's essence, by overcoming his alienation. It is nothing less than creating the conditions for the truly free, rational, active and independent man; it is the fulfillment of the prophetic aim: the destruction of the idols.

...

Marx's concept of socialism is a protest, as is all existentialist philosophy, against the alienation of man; if, as Aldous Huxley put it, "our present economic, social and international arrangements are based, in large measure, upon organized lovelessness," then Marx's socialism is a protest against this very lovelessness, against man's exploitation of man, and against his exploitativeness towards nature, the wasting of our natural resources at the expense of the majority of men today, and more so of the generations to come. The unalienated man, who is the goal of socialism as we have shown before, is the man who does not "dominate" nature, but who becomes one with it, who is alive and responsive toward objects, so that objects come to life for him.

...

Socialism is the abolition of human self-alienation, the return of man as a real human being. "It is the *definitive* resolution of the antagonism between man and nature, and between man and man. It is the true solution of the conflict between existence and essence, between objectification and self-affirmation, between freedom and necessity, between individual and species. It is a solution of the riddle of history and knows itself to be this solution". For Marx, socialism meant the social order which permits the return of man to himself, the identity between existence and essence, the overcoming of the separateness and antagonism between subject and object, the humanization of nature; it meant a world in which man is no longer a stranger among strangers, but is in *his* world, where he is at home.

——Erich Fromm, *Marx's Concept of Man*, Frederick Ungar Publishing Co., 1961, pp. 58 - 68.

五、观点解读

1. 马克思主义哲学的真谛是人本主义

弗洛姆在《马克思关于人的概念》一文的序言中就指出，该书的写作目的不仅有助于更好地理解马克思的人本主义哲学，而且有助于对社会上存在的一些关于马克思思想的不合理的态度加以纠正。作者提倡深入完整地理解马克思主义，一方面他反对把青年马克思与老年马克思根本对立的说法，认为马克思自始至终都是以人本主义哲学家的形象出现的；另一方面他不赞同把马克思主义哲学看作一种经济决定论，认为用经济主义和享乐主义式的唯物主义去解释马克思的做法，抹杀了个人在历史过程中的作用。

在《马克思关于人的概念》中，弗洛姆明确指出，马克思主义就是人本主义，马克思的哲学是一种人的抗议。弗洛姆认为，要正确理解马克思的哲学，首先应当扫除的障碍就在于对唯物主义和历史唯物主义概念的曲解。在他看来，马克思是一个本体论的唯物主义者，反对机械的、"资产阶级的"唯物主义，即那种排除历史过程的、抽象的自然科学的唯物主义，主张彻底的自然主义或人本主义。弗洛姆指出，马克思的"历史唯物主义完全不是一种心理学的理论；它认为，人们的生产方式决定着人们的思想和欲望，它并不认为人们的主要欲望就是想获得最大的物质利益"①。应当说，人及其思想和利益是由客观上已经存在着的条件来决定的，而不仅局限于对金钱的欲望。弗洛姆认为，马克思的"唯物主义"完全不同于那种把物质、经济的斗争当作人最基本的驱动力的所谓唯物主义观点，马克思的哲学是对"人、现实的和完整的人"的充分肯定，"现实地生活着的人"才是历史的主体，因此马克思的历史观应当被看作人类学解释的历史观。②

应当说，弗洛姆对青年马克思的《1844 年经济学哲学手稿》的哲学理解是基本正确的，因为马克思当时的哲学努力主要是一种基于价值悬设的异

---

① [美]艾瑞克·弗洛姆:《马克思关于人的概念》,《西方学者论〈一八四四年经济学—哲学手稿〉》,复旦大学出版社 1983 年版,第 29 页

② [美]艾瑞克·弗洛姆:《马克思关于人的概念》,《西方学者论〈一八四四年经济学—哲学手稿〉》,复旦大学出版社 1983 年版,第 30 页

化史观的人学批判，它也是马克思狭义历史唯物主义基础上社会批判理论的重要观点。但若用这种偏向于主观的伦理抗议来概括马克思主义哲学的全部本质则是不恰当的。因为马克思的历史唯物主义作为一种科学的方法论，不仅是批判资本主义现实的理论武器，更是指导人们追求现实改造、走向解放的合法道路的思想武器。

2. 人的概念是马克思主义哲学的核心

在《马克思关于人的概念》一书中，弗洛姆试图证明马克思哲学的核心并不是通常所理解的唯物主义，而是人的概念。马克思所说的人是一个可认识、可确定的实体，不是一种抽象物。在弗洛姆看来，马克思关于人的概念是基于人的一种可能性潜能而确立的，即处于自由状态之下的一种创造性活动，这是人之所以为人的一般本性。虽然在不同的历史生存情境中，这种人性会以种种异化形式出现，但追求人的自我实现和自由解放始终是人类社会进步的内驱力，这也是马克思的社会主义的最高目标。

弗洛姆进一步指出，青年马克思在《1844 年经济学哲学手稿》中所阐述的人的本质的概念即使在老年马克思的作品中都依然具有连续性。为了更好地解释人的概念，马克思区分了人的两种类型的倾向和欲望：一种是不变的欲望，如人的食欲性欲；另一种是“相对的”欲望，它与一定的生产和交换的条件相关，如对货币的需要。在弗洛姆看来，前者是人的本性的组成部分，而后者则不是，由此，人的社会历史属性作为非本质的、暂时的东西被剔除出了他的理论视域。于是弗洛姆沿着他所理解的人的本质的概念，对此进行了更进一步的说明。第一，弗洛姆把潜能看作人与生俱来的永恒不变的固有本质，认为人的本质是一种内在的、给定的潜能，人的潜能是历史真正的内驱力。第二，弗洛姆援引了黑格尔、斯宾诺莎、歌德等人的观点，认为潜能作为人的本质应当是一种生产性的能力，因此，人应该内在地具有能动的生产性，即人之所以为人就在于他是生产活动的。第三，弗洛姆指出，真正的生产性活动是人的自由行动的劳动活动。自由的、作为人的自我表现的“真正的活动”就是人生产性潜能发挥出来的人的本质，是人的唯一存在目的。至此，弗洛姆认为他对人的概念进行了全面、正确的解释。

但需要指出的是，弗洛姆将青年马克思与老年马克思对人的概念的理解混同了起来，把马克思在《1844 年经济学哲学手稿》中关于人的概念的解释误认为是对人的概念的最终的科学解释，并以此作为理解马克思哲学思想的核心。这导致了他对马克思总体思想发展的错误理解。

3. 异化是生产性的否定

弗洛姆认为，马克思的异化概念即生产性的否定，离开了这一概念就无法充分理解关于能动的、生产的、以其自己的力量把握和包摄客观世界的人的概念。人类历史在马克思那里指的就是人不断发展同时又不断异化的历史。他的社会主义概念就是从异化中解放出来，就是人回归到他自身，就是人的自我实现。黑格尔是经典异化理论的创始人，在他那里人的历史同时也就是人的异化的历史。在弗洛姆看来，马克思与黑格尔一样，认为异化概念是以存在和本质的区别为基础的。弗洛姆认为，存在一种在现实历史中从来没有实现过的人的抽象本质，人的本质的丧失，即人的生存丧失了本真的生产性就是异化。异化的出现使得人在事实上没能成为他"应当"成为的那个样子。

弗洛姆指出，马克思所理解的异化过程表现在劳动和分工中，劳动本应"是人和自然的能动关系，是新世界的创造，其中包括人自身的创造"[①]，在没有异化的劳作中，人不仅作为一个个体而且作为族类的存在实现着他自身，即人的发展导致他的全部人性的显露。但随着私有财产和分工的发展，劳动发生了异化。因此，弗洛姆将马克思关于劳动异化的思想总结为："一、在劳动过程中，特别是在资本主义条件下的劳动过程，人和其自己的创造力相疏远；二、人自己的劳动对象变成了异化的存在，最后对他实行统治，变成不以他自己为转移的力量。"[②]不仅如此，异化还造成了一切人的自身价值的贬低。

客观地说，如果弗洛姆这里是对青年马克思劳动异化理论的概括，那应该说他的理论是基本准确的。但在他分析的过程中存在着一些不容忽视的问题。首先，由于弗洛姆并不熟悉经济学理论，因此他对于马克思所说的社会发展中劳动分工所形成的社会劳动和抽象劳动概念没能形成正确的认

① [美]艾瑞克·弗洛姆：《马克思关于人的概念》，《西方学者论〈一八四四年经济学—哲学手稿〉》，复旦大学出版社1983年版，第59页。

② [美]艾瑞克·弗洛姆：《马克思关于人的概念》，《西方学者论〈一八四四年经济学—哲学手稿〉》，复旦大学出版社1983年版，第60页。

识;其次,弗洛姆将马克思的异化概念看作是个人的一种主观感受,但在马克思异化理论发展的任何一个阶段,异化都不仅仅是一种主观体验或感受,而是存在论上的人的一种根本性颠倒。即使在青年马克思那里异化主要也不是能动的生产性的否定。因此,当弗洛姆试图用他所理解的马克思早期的"异化"概念来对马克思的总体理论进行解释时,就陷入了歧途。

4. 社会主义是人的异化的扬弃

弗洛姆提出:"马克思关于社会主义的概念是由他关于人的概念中引导出来的"。[①]社会主义概念在弗洛姆那里主要具有两方面的特征:第一个方面,社会主义是人的异化的扬弃。其中包含三个要点:(1) 在真正的社会主义社会中,生产异化被真正消除了;(2) 社会主义将消除人的消费异化,从而创造人的真实需要;(3) 社会主义将实现人的真正自由发展。第二个方面,社会主义是人与自然关系异化的扬弃。弗洛姆认为,马克思的社会主义的目的就是人的解放,而人的解放同人的自我实现一样处在人跟自然的生产性的相关联、相统一的过程之中。在弗洛姆看来,社会主义的最终目的就是使个人的个性得到发展。

可是弗洛姆真正的问题在于,虽然他在理论上完成了自己人本主义的理论建构,但具体如何真实地从现实中寻找革命的道路这点他从未给予过关心。事实上,在 1845 年马克思创立历史唯物主义之后,共产主义和社会主义就不再像《1844 年经济学哲学手稿》中所描述的那样,表现为一种理论逻辑的推论和价值理论判断,而成为现实的历史客观趋势的反映。相比弗洛姆,马克思更关心的是人的解放的现实道路,因此离开实践本身对马克思总体思想的解释必定只能成为一种冥想的空洞。

六、进一步阅读指南

1. [美]艾瑞克·弗洛姆:《马克思关于人的概念》,载《西方学者论〈一八四四年经济学—哲学手稿〉》,复旦大学出版社 1983 年版。

① [美]艾瑞克·弗洛姆:《马克思关于人的概念》,《西方学者论〈一八四四年经济学—哲学手稿〉》,复旦大学出版社 1983 年版,第 69 页。

2. [美]艾瑞克·弗洛姆:《自为的人:伦理学的心理探究》,万俊人译,国际文化出版公司1988年版。

3. [美]艾瑞克·弗洛姆:《健全的社会》,孙恺祥译,上海译文出版社2011年版。

4. [美]艾瑞克·弗洛姆:《逃避自由》,刘林海译,上海译文出版社2015年版。

5. [德]卡尔·马克思:《1844年经济学哲学手稿》,人民出版社2014年版。

6. [美]杜娜叶夫斯卡娅:《马克思主义与自由》,傅小平译,辽宁教育出版社1998年版。

7. 张一兵:《文本的深度耕犁(第一卷)》第3章,中国人民大学出版社2004年版。

七、问题与思考

1. 如何正确理解、评价弗洛姆对马克思哲学的人本主义解读?

2. 弗洛姆是如何理解马克思的异化学说以及马克思前后的思想发展的?他的理解是否符合马克思思想发展的实际?

3. 试析弗洛姆的社会主义观。

第九章 批判理论的社会性塑造
——《批判理论》选读

教学目的与要求

了解以霍克海默为首的法兰克福学派对于批判理论的定位及其思想史意义；正确理解批判理论与传统理论的差异，以及前者对后者的彻底批判；了解霍克海默对形而上学的批判性分析；理解霍克海默对实证主义的尖锐批判；理解霍克海默对权威特别是权威与家庭关系的批判性分析。

一、历史背景

（一）作者简介

1895年，马克斯·霍克海默（Max Horkheimer）出生于德国斯图加特附近的一个富有的犹太商人家庭。霍克海默的父亲原本希望儿子继承家里的事业，所以提前一年结束了霍克海默的高中学习生涯，让他在自己的公司中实习。1911年，霍克海默结识弗里德里希·波洛克，开始学习哲学和社会科学。第一次世界大战结束后，霍克海默先后来到慕尼黑大学、弗莱堡大学和法兰克福大学，接受了哲学、心理学和经济学等科目的学习。大学时期的霍克海默主要受到其导师科奈留斯的新康德主义的影响。1925年，霍克海默以一篇关于康德《判断力批判》的论文通过了授课资格答辩，开始担任法兰克福大学的讲师一职。1930年,霍克海默成为法兰克福大学社会研究所的第二任所长。在霍克海默的带领下,研究所的影响越来越大。1933年希特勒上台,德国的政治环境发生剧烈变化。由于研究所的许多成员拥有犹太血统,纳粹政权以"敌视国家的倾向"的罪名使研究所遭到封禁,但并未使研究所解散。研究所先后辗转日内瓦、巴黎,最后搬至美国纽约的哥伦比亚大学。在二十世纪三十年代,霍克海默进入自己创作的一个高产期,写下了《唯物主义与形而上学》《权威与家庭》《利己主义与解放运动》《传统理论与批判理论》和《极权国家》等作品。其中,尤以1937年的《传统理论和批判理论》影响最大。在这部著作中,霍克海默认为,传统形式理性主义忽视了现实的历史性构成这一特征,企图用某种一般的、内在一致的原则来描述、把握世界,从而消解了理论的批判与实践功能,客观上沦为对现实秩序的肯定和辩护。与之相对,批判理论强调的是理论对现实的干预,是"社会变革"。流亡美国期间,霍克海默与阿多诺合写了《启蒙辩证法:哲学断片》。该书初版于1944年,再版于1947年。这部作品基于法西斯主义的时代现实,对启蒙理性的工具化蜕变、文化工业等问题做出了精彩分析,从根源上批判了西方现代文明,大胆提出"启蒙倒退为神话"这一命题,使之成为西方马克思主义乃至整个现代西方思想的经典之作。1950年,霍克海默应联邦德国政府之邀返回德国,重建社会研究所。次年,霍克海默担任法兰克福大学校长,1953年卸任,并接受法兰克福市所授予的歌德奖章。1954年,他被聘为芝加哥大学的客座教授。这一时期霍克海默的主要工作是阐述对各种政治制度的思考。1960年,霍克海默正式退休,其晚年思想愈发亲近叔本华、康德、黑格尔和尼采,特别是叔本华的形而上学悲观主义,因而离历史唯物主义渐行渐远。1973年7月7日,霍克海默病逝于纽伦堡。

(二)时代背景

尽管《批判理论》正式出版于1968年,但其所选的文章集中写作发表于二十世纪三十年代到四十年代初,因此对《批判理论》一书的时代和思想背景的介绍只能从后者出发来展开。

1. 德国工人的悲惨境遇与社会主义革命的"无望"

在二十世纪三四十年代,尽管社会生产力得到了极大提高,资本主义世界工人阶级的境遇却依然悲惨，社会不公与贫富悬殊仍旧是资本主义社会的基本面貌。特别是作为第一次世界大战战败国的德国，背上了沉重的债务负担，经济发展遇到严重阻碍，一度还出现了十分恶性的通货膨胀，工人阶级的生活处境极为艰难，多次爆发大规模的工人运动，汉堡的工人甚至开展了武装起义。出于防范苏联和国际共产主义运动的需要，以及为了确保德国能够归还战争贷款，英国、美国开始为德国提供经济贷款，并促成了一定程度上有损德国主权的“道威斯计划”，使得德国经济发展有所好转。但是，1929 年又发生了资本主义发展史上波及范围最广、打击最为沉重的世界性经济危机，德国经济再次陷入严重困境。据统计，1931 年时，德国的失业率高达 25%，共有 600 万人失业，数十万德国平民冻死或饿死，数不胜数的流浪汉在街头乞讨，人民生活困苦不堪。对工人阶级悲惨命运的同情、对社会不公和贫富差距的愤慨一直是霍克海默思想的重要出发点。霍克海默同情无产阶级的处境，并将技术的不断创新看成是无产阶级持续分化的主因。在他看来，工人阶级的一部分分化为被雇佣者，从事艰辛却又乏味的工作，另一部分则成为失业者，过着地狱般的生活，完全丧失了接受教育以及组织起来的机会。更重要的是，虽然悲惨境遇引发了工人阶级持续不断的革命，但最终都因为各种各样的原因而宣告失败，甚至工人阶级自己都逐步接受了小资产阶级的意识形态，从而丧失了革命的主动性，这些现实迫使霍克海默及其带领的研究所对如何摆脱资本主义的统治、构建一个更加公正合理的社会展开批判性的理论思考。

2. 魏玛共和国的衰败与纳粹力量的不断兴起

魏玛共和国是德国结束帝制后第一次走向共和的尝试，是德国真正意义上迈出资产阶级民主代议制的第一步。第一次世界大战的战败、十一月革命的爆发和社会民主党人的妥协是魏玛共和国成立的现实背景。尽管魏玛共和国修订了在当时整个西方社会都极为先进的宪法，但是如此美好的宪法竟然建立在虚弱、分裂的社会现实之上，因而只能是“空中楼阁”。首先，共和国可以说是“先天不足”。它从一开始就是作为德意志帝国政治危机的意外产物而出现的，因其签署了对德国来说极为屈辱的《凡尔赛和约》，承接了德意志帝国政治失败的后果，遂成为德意志帝国失败的“替罪羊”。同时，魏玛共和国也是后天“发育不良”。经济上虽说中间有段短暂的恢复，但整体而言，魏玛共和国早期和晚期的经济发展都很不尽如人意。此外，政治上亦是危机四伏，强势的极左和极右翼打心底都不认同共和体制；而支持共和国并参与魏玛宪法制定的资产阶级进步政党即社会民主党、天主教中央党、人民党则各怀心思，没有团结一致捍卫共和的决心，后两个党之后更是全部转向右翼。加之共和国的政治体制存在不尽合理之处，特别是总统权力过大，拥有解散议会等权力，导致魏玛共和国在事实上走向总统独裁政治。这种独裁政治加上经济上的萧条，以及德国内部许多民众对德意志帝国时代强权政治的怀念，使得魏玛共和国在一方面表现出一定进步气息的同时，也成为野心家的野心和纳粹力量不断膨胀的乐园。经济危机让纳粹党迎来了急速扩张的黄金期。伴随着希特勒的上台，尽管名义上希特勒仍然在魏玛宪法的框架下统治国家，但魏玛共和国已经名存实亡。事实上，霍克海默以及法兰克福大学社会研究所主要成员的命运沉浮，都因其成员大多为犹太人而与纳粹力量的兴亡密切相关。在欧洲辗转流亡期间，他们也都目睹了纳粹不断扩张而引发的人间悲剧。因此，纳粹和法西斯主义上台以及走向疯狂成为霍克海默和法兰克福学派从历史唯物主义出发构建批判理论最为重要的时代背景之一，他们对启蒙倒退为神话、极权国家、权威主义人格、反犹主义等主题的分析均与这一背景有密切关联。

3. 世界日趋合理化自动化总体化

伴随着世界性经济危机的到来，当时的发达资本主义国家都出现了国家权力不断增长的迹象，无论是罗斯福新政还是法西斯主义，其共同特点是都表现为国家不断增强对经济的干预。在霍克海默和社会研究所看来，世界多数政权都表现出了“权威主义国家”的倾向，这也表明资本主义已经由垄断资本主义步入到更新的国家资本主义阶段，此时，“官僚系统已经控制了经济运行机制，而后者已经脱离了资产阶级的纯粹利润阶段”[①]。更重要的是，国家不只是介入经济生活，而是借助于科学技术、管理等手段的变革，日益强化对政治、文化、科技和日常生活的全面控制。霍克海默看到，在科学技术与大众文化的结合中，工人阶级沉溺于社会提供的休闲娱乐活动，其

① 参见[德]罗尔夫·魏格豪斯：《法兰克福学派：历史、理论及政治影响》，孟登迎等译，上海人民出版社 2010 年版，第 376 页。

革命的自发性、主动性逐步丧失，被动甚至主动屈从于官僚体系的总体权力。从社会的思维层面来说，技术理性逐渐取代个人理性成为压抑辩证理性的主要因素，世界也因此变得越来越技术化合理化自动化。也正是基于这一点，霍克海默称当时的社会为"管控社会"(the administered society)。

(三) 思想背景

1. 黑格尔的"复活"

由于德国官方对黑格尔哲学的抛弃以及科学与实证哲学的兴起，黑格尔哲学一度被打入冷宫。但是第一次世界大战之前，克罗齐和狄尔泰等哲学家重新宣扬黑格尔哲学，将之拉回到社会理论研究的中心位置。从马克思主义的视角来看，黑格尔与马克思的思想存在着十分复杂的纠葛，其中既有马克思对黑格尔哲学的阶段性贬斥，也有马克思对黑格尔哲学某些方面的重新赞赏。伴随着"正统马克思主义"的日益教条化，一些青年马克思主义者重拾高扬主体性、历史性以及辩证法精神的黑格尔哲学，将之用作批判教条主义的重要思想武器，特别是卢卡奇《历史与阶级意识》的出版，更是开一时之风气，赋予黑格尔哲学以十分激进的气息。尽管霍克海默明确驳斥了黑格尔的形而上学倾向以及绝对真理观念，但他对于理性的本质、辩证法的重要性、实体性逻辑的存在等诸方面的立场，显然受到了黑格尔的影响，以至于有人认为批判理论和卢卡奇的理论很相似，可以将两者都归类为"黑格尔式的马克思主义"。

2. 生命哲学的兴起

十九世纪晚期，以尼采、狄尔泰、柏格森为代表的生命哲学逐渐兴起，在思想领域占据了一席之地。尽管霍克海默不赞同生命哲学，认为其本质上是唯心主义的，但是他还是在一定程度上受到了这种哲学的影响。霍克海默从历史唯物主义的视域出发，将生命哲学看成"对抽象理性主义日趋强化的僵硬性以及相随而来的发达资本主义下个体存在的标准化的一种合法抗议"①。相比于晚期卢卡奇对生命哲学的批判乃至敌视，霍克海默对生命哲

---

① [美]马丁·杰伊:《法兰克福学派史》,单世联译,广东人民出版社1996年版,第59页。

学采取了一种批判性的同情姿态，甚至在某些议题上受到生命哲学的影响，或者说存在共通之处。具体而言，两者的相近性表现在反体系冲动、对抽象理性主义的批判性反思、对现实个体的生命力的强调等诸多方面。当然，生命哲学整体上过于强调主观性和内在性，而忽视了对社会历史性和物质性层面的探讨；过于强调非理性的方面，容易造成否定理性的极端印象，正如霍克海默的判断，其归根结底仍然属于一种唯心主义哲学。

3. 实证主义的强势崛起

随着自然科学技术的发展，传统的本体论哲学以及思辨理性观念不断受到质疑，以孔德为代表的实证主义的影响不断扩大。实证主义注重感觉经验，注重厘清哲学与科学的关系，并力图将哲学溶解于科学之中，以黑格尔为代表的传统哲学则被看成是形而上学而被打倒。值得一提的是，与社会研究所同时流亡到美国的，就有在当时作为实证主义最新流派的维也纳小组——他们的学说被称为逻辑实证主义。受到十九世纪以来实证主义传统的影响，以及来自维特根斯坦《逻辑哲学论》思想的启示，维也纳学派提出了一系列有别于传统的见解。他们的核心主张有两点：一是拒斥形而上学，只承认经验是知识唯一可靠的来源；二是认为只有运用逻辑分析，才可最终解决传统哲学的问题。由于逻辑实证主义的观点与以实用主义为代表的美国本土哲学传统较为接近，所以其在美国的理论影响远远超过了社会研究所。实证主义的事实拜物教与逻辑中心主义是霍克海默以及社会研究所不能接受到，故此，社会研究所的核心成员自二十世纪三十年代以来持续对逻辑实证主义展开批判，在二十世纪六十年代以阿多诺和波普尔的“实证主义争论”走向高潮。

二、篇章结构

《批判理论》的德文版正式出版于 1968 年，该书收录了霍克海默在二十世纪三十年代写作的代表性文章。这些文章除了《权威与家庭》之外，都来源于社会研究所的官方刊物《社会研究杂志》。1972 年，《批判理论》英文版出版，新收录了《哲学的社会功能》《艺术和大众文化》，这两篇文章来自社会研究所二十世纪四十年代初在美国创办的《哲学和社会科学研究》。中文版的《批判理论》主要译自英文版，因此，我们主要以英文版为基础介绍该书的篇章结构。该书主要收录了《科学及其危机札记》《唯物主义与形而上学》《权威与家庭》《对宗教的思考》《对形而上学的最新攻击》《传统理论与批判理论》《跋》《哲学的社会功能》《艺术与大众文化》等9篇文章。

《科学及其危机札记》指出，科学作为生产力和生产手段无疑对于改善社会生活有着重要贡献，但是当代科学陷入了一种实用主义的、片面的、与人的实际需求相脱节的知识状态，有着重大的局限。整体而言，科学知识的这种不合理状态与其所处的社会条件，即同时具有垄断和无政府状态的全球性经济结构有着深刻的内在联系。只有通过克服当代科学知识中存在着的拜物教根基，通过认识那些决定所有思维的具体历史环境，当前的危机和混乱状态才能得到克服。因此，只有发展出一种能够正确认识当下社会境况的理论，并在这种理论的指导下克服当前的科学危机，打破科学的意识形态功能，才能将科学重新与人的现实需求匹配起来，实现其社会功能。唯其如此，科学才能对必将到来的社会变革发挥积极作用。

《唯物主义与形而上学》提出，要把唯物主义从仅仅作为唯心主义的反义词以及对非物质存在的简单否定中解救出来。以生命哲学、存在主义哲学为代表的近代唯心主义抨击当代唯物主义是一种形而上学，却不知自己也陷入某种形而上学的态度之中。此处霍克海默对形而上学的定义是，相信在世界的背后有着某种终极性的存在基础。真正的唯物主义因此不能被理解为一种建立在物质本体论基础上的、永远主张经济基础第一性原则的新型经济形而上学。霍克海默认为，在资本主义社会中，经济作为决定性要素这一点并不是永恒的，其同样会随着历史条件的变化而改变。霍克海默还对那种把唯物主义提高为绝对主义的知识论倾向展开了批判。这种倾向认为唯物主义认识论能够穷尽对现实的解释，其背后实际上是统治世界的隐秘欲望，从霍布斯一元论的唯物主义到今天的某些唯物主义理论都展现了这种对自然的操纵性、统治性的态度。而反过来那种相对主义的唯物主义，比如实证主义，放弃对事物本质的探寻而声称自己“只关注那些事物本身实际给予我们的东西”[①]，同样是存在问题的。就此而言，唯心主义积极强调理性认识的能动性方面反倒是值得肯定与坚持的。因此，霍克海默提

① [德]马克斯·霍克海默：《批判理论》，李小兵等译，重庆出版社1989年版，第35页。

出，真正的唯物主义将人及其所处的世界看成主客体相互作用的辩证的永恒过程，人能够依靠一种辩证的唯物主义或者一种唯物主义的辩证法去努力洞察现实世界的秩序，它关注的是当代"社会的经济理论"，并依靠自己的实践推动社会不断变革，以促进一个更加公正合理的新社会的到来。

《权威与家庭》分三个部分探讨了"文化、权威与家庭"三个主题。文章首先论述了文化在考察现代社会中的重要性。霍克海默考察了中国的祖先崇拜以及印度种姓制度，对作为一种文化心理因素在社会—经济原因消失后仍然发挥作用的现象展开了分析，证明文化在受经济基础决定性影响的同时，也存在着相对独立性。因此，霍克海默指出，在分析权威的运作机理时，除了要考察当时的社会—经济要素，也不能忘了文化心理因素。文章的第二部分论述了资产阶级世界权威的发展历史。资产阶级在反对传统的过程中发展出了崇尚自由独立的反权威主义，然而在资本主义的现实生活中又存在着日益增长的、对非理性的社会—经济秩序的异化权威的服从。当然，这不等于霍克海默赞同无政府主义，恰恰相反，在霍克海默看来，无政府主义和权威国家主义是同一个文化时代的产物。文章第三部分集中考察了家庭，充分论述了家庭特别是父亲权威在资本主义发展进程中的演变。霍克海默提出，如果说在自由主义时代，父亲享有权威有其客观的社会基础，那么随着资本主义的发展，孩子越来越受到家庭之外的社会机制的影响，父亲权威在家庭中不断衰落和瓦解，更多发挥着意识形态的功能。当今时代的问题是家庭更多地被政府进行技术操纵，而要走出这样的困境，只有对整个社会进行改造才有可能。

《对宗教的思考》是一篇很短的文章，该文指出，宗教的存在在其积极的意义上反映了人类对尘世命运的不满以及对一种神圣正义的渴望。因此，霍克海默认为，在当代，这种积极的能量仍然存在，但必须去除掉它们受限的宗教形式，在社会实践中改造为创造性的力量，否则，纯粹精神层面的抵抗也不过是极权国家机器中的一个齿轮罢了。

《对形而上学的最新攻击》主要是对逻辑实证主义关于形而上学的批判提出了反批判。霍克海默认为，在洛克、休谟等早期代表人物那里，经验主义坚持个体感知的重要性，并且肯定主体在认识事物时存在着的能动因素；启蒙运动期间，经验主义专注于运用理性来理智地洞察世界，同样具有瓦解社会统治秩序的历史进步性。然而，作为现代经验主义代表的逻辑实证主义，只承认知觉证实了的反复出现的事实，而将“那些产生于人的历史能动性的新形式”排除在理性思考之外。因此，这种事实拜物教的态度在实质上放弃了反思，其结果只能是“把事实绝对化并把现存秩序实体化”[①]。逻辑经验主义“放弃了个人观察的标准，并打算绝对严格、单纯地依靠系统的逻辑完善性，依靠记录句子”[②]。因此，霍克海默提出，在看待社会现实时，逻辑实证主义的这一态度是极其天真的，它不可能进行任何总体性的思考以及提出任何批判性的意见，因而在实质上必然成为现实社会秩序的拥护者与顺从者。

《传统理论与批判理论》是霍克海默明确对批判理论与传统理论的差别进行系统阐述的一篇文章。该文指出，传统理论总是试图用某种一般的、内在一致的原则来描述世界，从柏拉图到胡塞尔乃至重视经验和实证的英美科学皆是如此，其导致的结果是，传统理论更多追求的是纯粹知识，而不是行动。批判理论则反对传统理论的纯知识目标及其对理论与实践的割裂，批判理论的根本目标指向的是变革现实社会。因而，批判理论强调运用辩证逻辑去考察作为人类活动对象和产物的社会，强调社会研究中的历史内容、内在矛盾与对立，并探索社会历史变革的可能性，而消除社会的不公正，创造一种可能的人类美好未来，正是依赖于对现存社会的科学批判。此外，区别于经验主义和实证主义，批判理论追求运用构造性思维实现对当代社会矛盾和未来可能性的总体分析，但是又从根本上拒绝任何形而上学的抽象。

《跋》选自《社会研究杂志》第 6 卷第 3 期。该文主要强调了批判的社会理论与哲学之间的紧密关联。批判的社会理论强调从经济出发开展研究的首要性，但是反对经济主义。批判的社会理论的核心目标恰恰是运用哲学的辩证思维去关注人类社会如何才能走出现实的“经济主义”困境。

《哲学的社会功能》一文指出，关于哲学，以往的哲学家们并没有得出任何一致性的结论。霍克海默眼中的哲学试图去解决那些科学没有涉及或者无意识涉及的难题，哲学与现实总保持着某种紧张关系，哲学的真正社会功能在于它对流行的东西进行批判，并在这种批判中探寻合乎理性的人类生

---

① [美]马丁·杰伊：《法兰克福学派史》，单世联译，广东人民出版社 1996 年版，第 75 页。

② [德]马克斯·霍克海默：《批判理论》，李小兵等译，重庆出版社 1989 年版，第 154 页。

存组织形态。

《艺术和大众文化》一文指出，在历史上艺术曾经保存着个性、自律与自由，但是在现代社会，人类已经丧失了构造出一个不同于他生存世界的另一世界的能力，也就是说已经丧失了艺术的能力。究其原因，乃是因为经济环境发生了深刻变化，“对投资在每部影片上的可观资本的快速周转的经济要求，阻止着对每件艺术作品内在逻辑的追求——即艺术作品本身的自律需要”①。

三、研究前沿

自 1989 年《批判理论》中译本出版以来，国内学界便对这一收录霍克海默二十世纪三四十年代的代表性作品的文集展开了研究。2004 年，《霍克海默集》的出版更是极大推动了国内学界对霍克海默的相关研究。但是整体而言，相较于阿多诺、马尔库塞等人，霍克海默的研究仍然较为冷门，这与其在法兰克福学派中的领袖地位是极不相称的。而且这些年来，对霍克海默的研究主要集中在启蒙辩证法、批判理论等主题上，而对其他主题，比如实证主义批判、唯物主义等关注则较为有限，这些为今后一段时间的霍克海默研究留下了理论空间。整体而言，近年来关于霍克海默《批判理论》的研究在以下三个方面展现出了一些新的动向，值得我们关注。

第一，深入霍克海默思想形成过程中去研究批判理论。这里主要涉及两个方面，一是独特的时代背景对霍克海默批判理论形成发展的影响，二是回到霍克海默自身学术经历的演进。就前一个方面而言，学界认为，霍克海默批判理论的时代背景既区别于马克思所处的自由资本主义时代，也区别于列宁、卢卡奇、卢森堡等人所处的帝国主义危机以及第二国际教条主义盛行的时代，而是处于资本主义大危机直至极权资本主义不断兴起的时代。这一时代背景促使霍克海默批判理论的主题和范式发生了转变。而从个人思想发展来看，国内有学者关注到霍克海默对其导师新康德主义者科内利乌斯的继承、批判与超越的过程，也研究了霍克海默早期对以黑格尔、康德为代表的德国观念论的吸收、批判与扬弃的思想转变历程。这些研究对于

① [德]马克斯·霍克海默:《批判理论》，李小兵等译，重庆出版社 1989 年版，第 273 页。

学界理解霍克海默批判理论的形成及其内涵具有重要价值。

第二，对霍克海默批判理论的哲学基础、思想内涵等展开了进一步研究。近年来，有学者认为，霍克海默批判理论是以实践的唯物主义作为其哲学基础的，批判理论要做的正是以一种唯物主义的实践哲学为基点，从批判社会问题入手，在理论与实践的关联中，反思社会问题的深层根源，为运用马克思主义解决时代问题指明现实路径。而霍克海默对形而上学和实证主义的双重批判同样是以实践的唯物主义作为其方法论根基的。从思想内涵上看，近年来有学者分别从文化、科技伦理、权威主义批判、极权主义现实批判、实证主义批判等角度对霍克海默批判理论展开了具体研究。

第三，在批判理论的大语境下对霍克海默批判理论作专题研究或比较研究。有学者研究了法兰克福学派从批判理论到后批判理论的发展进程，将以霍克海默等为代表的第一代批判理论家界定为批判理论的第一发展阶段，此时的批判理论确定了批判理论的基本纲领，并“致力于批判理论构建与工业文明批判”。有学者对霍克海默批判理论对整个法兰克福学派理论建构的引领作用进行了探讨，认为作为“精神领袖”，霍克海默的思想领导作用体现在“破旧”与“立新”两个方面：“破旧”是指他发挥自己的哲学史专长，对实证主义进行了系统批判；“立新”则既指他确立了“批判理论”新观念，也指他为了落实“哲学与社会科学的联盟”而实施的“独裁”领导。还有学者近年来对霍克海默的批判理论与其他批判理论做了比较研究。例如，与阿多诺 1969 年去世前几个月写下的《关于批判理论的要点说明》进行比较研究；将其对于批判理论的界定同晚年福柯对批判哲学的阐释之间进行比较研究，等等。

四、文本节选

Materialism and Metaphysics

If positivism agrees with almost every other philosophy against materialism, this is due, it must be admitted, not only to the differences already noted but also to the materialist doctrine on pleasure. We have tried to show that according to materialism a man's actions do not proceed with necessity from some ultimate and absolute position on reality. To ground his decisions the materialist must, of course, appeal to more or less general criteria, but he does not ignore the fact that, given the determinative factors he has adduced, similar decisions can be expected only in similar psychic situations. These situations themselves have their social and individual conditioning factors, they have a historical dimension, and therefore one cannot deduce, simply from a valid piece of knowledge and without considering the present psychic state of the agent, that a certain action will necessarily follow.

This materialist view has the negative significance that it rejects a metaphysically grounded morality. But in addition it has always meant to materialists that man's striving for happiness is to be recognized as a natural fact requiring no justification. The extent to which a naïve, economically oriented psychology can interpret this striving as a desire for satisfaction of gross material needs has been expounded in detail in the works of Erich Fromm. The structure of needs in various forms of society, in particular social groups, and in individuals is changeable and can be explained only in relation to a specific time and a concrete situation. The known and unknown devotees of the materialist outlook have for centuries given up their freedom and their lives in the struggle for the most varied goals, but especially in solidarity with suffering men. They prove that a concern for personal physical well-being is no more closely associated with this kind of thinking than with any other. In rejecting the illusions of idealist metaphysics they have surrendered every hope of an individual reward in eternity and, with it, an important selfish motive operative in other men.

Repeated attempts to interpret such selfless dedication to the causes of humanity as a contradiction to materialist convictions lack every philosophical justification. What leads to such misunderstandings is the simplistic psychology which lies behind most doctrines that profess an absolute morality. Therefore materialism today says more accurately that all men strive for happiness, not for pleasure, and also that men keep their eyes not so much on pleasure as on what brings them pleasure. Even in simple matters each man is accustomed, as Hegel says of the so-called wise man, "to concern oneself with the matter itself and not with enjoyment, that is, not with the constant reflection on the relation to oneself as an individual, but with the matter as a matter." Materialism refuses, however, to distinguish between happiness and pleasure, because the satisfaction of desire, unlike "higher" motives, requires no reasons, excuses, or justifications. Justification may indeed be quite appropriate in a particular society for particular actions, but only to a particular authority and not because of some unconditional order of things. To say that men are determined by "elementary reactions of pleasure and pain" is perhaps not a very suitable psychological description, but it does accurately indicate a fact at which the materialist, unlike the idealist, is not scandalized. Although even some otherwise idealist philosophers such as Hegel fully agree with materialism here, this point, combined with the lack of an interpretation of the world in its totality, is a reason why otherwise mutually opposed philosophies agree in reducing materialism to the obviously untenable metaphysical thesis of the exclusive reality of matter and in then easily refuting it.

Contemporary materialism is not principally characterized by the formal traits which oppose it to idealist metaphysics. It is characterized rather by its content: the economic theory of society. Only when the formal traits are abstracted from this content do they emerge as distinguishing marks, such as are regarded as important today, for classifying the philosophical views of the past. The various materialist doctrines, therefore, are not examples of a stable and permanent idea. The economic theory of society and history arose not out of purely theoretical motives, but out of the need to comprehend contemporary society. For this society has reached the point where it excludes an ever larger number of men from the happiness made possible by the widespread abundance of economic forces. In this context is formed the idea of a better reality which will emerge from the presently prevailing state of affairs, and this transition becomes the theme of contemporary theory and practice. Materialism does not lack ideals, then; its ideals are shaped with the needs of society as a starting point and are measured by what is possible in the foreseeable future with the human forces available. But materialism does refuse to see these ideals as the foundation of history and therefore of the present as well, as though they were ideas with an existence independent of man. The efforts of idealism in this direction do more honor to history than to the idea. For ideals can become moving forces, in so far as men try to turn them from mere, even if justified, ideas into reality. But history has never ceased till now to be a record of struggles. Even with a view to success in realizing its ideals, materialism refuses to relate "what has happened and its happening now, the unique, accidental, momentary event ... to an overall context of value and meaning," as cultural history does. It can therefore hardly be understood by the latter, any more than by metaphysics generally.

——Max Horkheimer, *Critical Theory*: *Selected Essays*, Continuum Publishing Corporation, 2002, pp. 43 - 46.

Authority and the Family

In philosophy this state of affairs finds expression in the abstractness of the concept of the individual, that basic concept of modern thought. The abstractness emerges clearly in Leibniz especially: the individual is a self-enclosed, metaphysical center of power, separated from the rest of the world, an absolutely isolated monad which is made self-dependent by God. Its destiny, according to Leibniz, lies within its own determination, and its stages of development, its happiness or unhappiness, depend on its own internal dynamism. It is responsible for itself; what it is and what befalls it depend on its own will and God's decree. Such a separation of individual from society and nature (closely connected with the other philosophical dualisms of thought and being, substance and appearance, body and spirit, sense and understanding) turns the concept of the free individual, which is the bourgeois answer to the Middle Ages, into an almost metaphysical essence. The individual is to be handed over to himself. His dependence on the social conditions of real existence is forgotten and he is regarded, even in the days of absolutism but especially after its collapse, as sovereign.

Because the individual was regarded as wholly isolated and complete in himself, it could seem that the dismantling of the old authorities was the only thing required if he was to exercise his full potential. In reality, the liberation meant, before all else, that the majority of people were delivered up to the fearful exploitation of the factory system. The self-dependent individual found himself confronted with an external power to which he must accommodate himself. According to the theory, the individual was not to acknowledge the judgment of any human authority as binding upon him without first subjecting it to the test of reason. In fact, he now stood alone in the world and must adapt himself or perish. The network of relationships itself became authoritative. The Middle Ages had connected the earthly order of things with God's decree and to that extent regarded it as meaningful. In the modern period, on the contrary, all real situations are brute facts which do not embody any meaning but are simply to be accepted. It is evident that class distinctions were not from God; it is not yet recognized that they did arise out of the human process of work. These distinctions and the relations connected with them appear to the sovereign individual, the metaphysical substance of bourgeois thought, to be something alien;

they appear to be a self-contained reality, another principle confronting the knowing and acting subject. Bourgeois philosophy is dualist by its very nature, even when it takes the form of pantheism. When it attempts to bridge the gap between self and world by means of thought and to present nature and history as the expression, embodiment, or symbol of the human essence, it is already acknowledging reality as a principle which has its own rights and is not to be regarded as dependent on man and changeable at his will but as meaningful being that must be interpreted and read like a "cryptogram." Authorities are allegedly done away with and then reappear philosophically in the form of metaphysical concepts. Philosophy at this point is only a reflection of what has happened in society. Men have been freed from the limitations of the old, divinely sanctioned property system. The new one is regarded as natural, as the manifestation of a thing-in-itself which is beyond discussion and eludes human influence. Here, then, is a philosophical system in which the individual is conceived, not in his involvement with society and nature, but abstractly and as a purely intellectual essence, a being which must now think of the world and acknowledge it as an eternal principle and perhaps as the expression of his own true being. Precisely in such a system is the imperfection of the individual's freedom mirrored, his powerlessness amid an anarchic inhuman reality which is rent by contradictions.

The proud claim that no authority is to be recognized unless it can justify itself to reason proves to be a flimsy one when the categories of such awareness are subjected to internal analysis. The seeming validity of the claim can be shown to derive in two ways from the underlying social reality. It springs in every case out of the obscurity of the production process in a bourgeois society, but acquires a different meaning in the life of each of the two social classes involved. The independent entrepreneur is regarded in a free-trade economy as independent in his decisions. What wares he produces, what kind of machines he uses, how he combines the talents of men and machines, where he decides to build his factory: all this seems to depend on his free decision, on his breadth of vision and creative energy. The importance assigned to genius and to qualities of leadership in modern economic and philosophical literature derives from the situation just described. "I insist ... emphatically on the importance of genius, and the necessity of allowing it to unfold itself freely both in thought and practice," says John Stuart Mill, and he adds the widespread complaint that society does not allow genius enough free play. This enthusiasm for genius, which has since become a characteristic of the average man's consciousness, could help increase the influence of the great economic leaders because in the present system economic projects are largely a matter of divination, that is, of hunches. For the small-scale businessman the situation today is still what it was for the whole class of businessmen during the liberal period. In his planning he may indeed draw on earlier experience and find assistance in his own psychological sensitivity and his knowledge of the economic and political scene. But when all is said and done, the real decision on the value of his product and thus of his own activity depends on the market and necessarily has an irrational element, since the market in turn depends on the working of conflicting and uncontrollable forces. The manufacturer in his planning is as dependent as any medieval artisan on the needs of society; in that respect he is no freer, but the lack of freedom is not brought home to him, as it was to the artisan, by the wishes of a limited and set body of customers or in the form of a demand for service by a lord of the manor. The manufacturer's dependence is expressed, instead, in the salableness of his wares and the profit he seeks, and shows its power over him when he balances his accounts at the end of the business year. The exchange value of the product also determines its practical value to the user, inasmuch as the material composition of the goods being sold is in a measure predetermined by the raw materials needed, the machinery of production which must be kept in repair, and the men required to run the machines. In other words, the value of the wares expresses ascertainable relations between material realities. But in the present order this connection between value and society's needs is mediated not only by calculable psychic and political factors but also by a sum-total of countless uncontrollable events.

The classical period of this state of affairs passed with liberalism. In the present age, marked as it is by the struggles of great monopolies rather than, as formerly, by the competition of countless individuals, the individual capacity to make correct guesses about the market, to calculate and speculate, has been replaced by the extensive mobilization of whole nations for violent confrontations. But the small businessman passes on his own difficulties, in intensified form, to the leaders of the industrial trusts. And if he himself must continue to maneuver amid oppressive circumstances in order not to go under, then such leaders, he thinks, must be geniuses to stay on top of the heap. They may learn from personal experience that what they must develop in themselves is not the spiritual qualities of their predecessors but the ruthless steadfastness required if an economic and political oligarchy is to rule the modern masses. In any event, these leaders do not consider social reality to be clear and comprehensible. On the one hand, the population of their own country and all the hostile power-groups make their presence felt as dangerous natural forces which must be restrained or cleverly manipulated. On the other, the mechanisms of the world market are no less perplexing than more limited forms of competition are, and the leaders accept and even promote the belief of their class that to be a master of the economy takes the instincts of genius. They too experience society as a self-contained and alien principle, and freedom for them essentially means that they can adapt themselves to this reality by active or passive means, instead of having to deal with it according to a uniform plan. In the present economic system society appears to be as blind as subrational nature. For men do not use communal reflection and decision to regulate the process by which they earn their living in association with others. Instead, the production and distribution of all the goods needed for life take place amid countless uncoordinated actions and interactions of individuals and groups.

——Max Horkheimer, *Critical Theory: Selected Essays*, Continuum Publishing Corporation, 2002, pp. 77 - 81.

The Latest Attack on Metaphysics

It becomes apparent that the two elements of logical empiricism are only superficially connected. Notwithstanding some innovations—for example, the theory of types, the value of which, despite the great amount of ingenuity expended upon them, is doubtful—symbolic logic is identical with formal logic on essential points. Consequently, what is open to objection in the one is equally objectionable in the other. "Form" is an abstraction derived from a material of conceptions, judgments, and other theoretical constructions restricted in respect to kind and extent. If one logical doctrine claims to be logic as such, it therewith abandons formalism, for its statements then acquire material meaning and lead to far-reaching philosophical consequences. Characteristically, however, modern logic does not know this, and its ignorance is what distinguishes it from the material logic of Aristotle and Hegel which it so bitterly attacks. On the other hand, if any type of logic refrains from claiming universality (the claim is, however, historically associated with the very name of logic), by explicitly prohibiting its propositions from being given a normative cast, or, worse yet, by denying that any critical conclusions may be drawn from them, it loses the philosophical, and especially the antimetaphysical character which it took on in empiricism.

In any case, logic is in conflict with empiricism; in fact, logic and mathematics have always constituted unsolved difficulties for empirical systems. The attempts of John Stuart Mill and Ernst Mach to deduce logical propositions from dubious psychological data were manifest failures. Hume had the wisdom not to attempt such deduction of mathematical and related propositions. For this very reason, however, the evident relations of ideas exist side by side with empirical facts in his works in such a way that their interrelations do not become clear. For Berkeley, mathematics was a plague next only to materialism, as the *Analyst* and other writings demonstrate. He openly and unwaveringly opposed his empiricism to the developments of modern science and declared himself for the Bible and good common sense, without the benefit of modern mathematics. In fact, he seriously endangered the beginnings of modern mathematics. The rigid separation of sensuous and rational knowledge, inherent in all empiricism, asserted itself in a familiar way in Berkeley's philosophical career—he passed from empiricism to Platonism. Readers of Locke's *Essay*, after being instructed in empiricism in the first three books, have always been amazed at the surprising turn taken in the fourth. Morality and mathematics are represented as independent of experience, yet valid for it. The basic works of the earlier empiricist doctrine contain the same contradiction between the empirical conception of science and the rational elements to be found in it as is contained in the more modern variety which brings together the two extremes of this contradiction in the very name it assumes.

When modern formalistic logic encounters theoretical constructs which, as a whole, or in their separate parts, do not fit into its conception of thought, it does not call the universality of its own principles into question, but challenges the refractory object, whatever its constitution or qualities may be. The followers of this system say that it is wrong to regard thinking as a "means of knowing something that must have unconditional validity at all times and in all parts of the world." They constantly refuse to accord any "executive power" to thinking. At the same time, however, they demand that all thinking should conform to empirical criteria.

——Max Horkheimer, *Critical Theory: Selected Essays*, Continuum Publishing Corporation, 2002, pp. 172 - 174.

Traditional and Critical Theory

We must go on now to add that there is a human activity which has society itself for its object. The aim of this activity is not simply to eliminate one or other abuse, for it regards such abuses as necessarily connected with the way in which the social structure is organized. Although it itself emerges from the social structure, its purpose is not, either in its conscious intention or in its objective significance, the better functioning of any element in the structure. On the contrary, it is suspicious of the very categories of better, useful, appropriate, productive, and valuable, as these are understood in the present order, and refuses to take them as nonscientific presuppositions about which one can do nothing. The individual as a rule must simply accept the basic conditions of his existence as given and strive to fulfill them; he finds his satisfaction and praise in accomplishing as well as he can the tasks connected with his place in society and in courageously doing his duty despite all the sharp criticism he may choose to exercise in particular matters. But the critical attitude of which we are speaking is wholly distrustful of the rules of conduct with which society as presently constituted provides each of its members. The separation between individual and society in virtue of which the individual accepts as natural the limits prescribed for his activity is relativized in critical theory. The latter considers the overall framework which is conditioned by the blind interaction of individual activities (that is, the existent division of labor and the class distinctions) to be a function which originates in human action and therefore is a possible object of planful decision and rational determination of goals.

The two-sided character of the social totality in its present form becomes, for men who adopt the critical attitude, a conscious opposition. In recognizing the present form of economy and the whole culture which it generates to be the product of human work as well as the organization which mankind was capable of and has provided for itself in the present era, these men identify themselves with this totality and conceive it as will and reason. It is their own world. At the same time, however, they experience the fact that society is comparable to nonhuman natural processes, to pure mechanisms, because cultural forms which are supported by war and oppression are not the creations of a unified, self-conscious will. That world is not their own but the world of capital.

Previous history thus cannot really be understood; only the individuals and specific groups in it are intelligible, and even these not totally, since their internal dependence on an inhuman society means that even in their conscious action such individuals and groups are still in good measure mechanical functions. The identification, then, of men of critical mind with their society is marked by tension, and the tension characterizes all the concepts of the critical way of thinking. Thus, such thinkers interpret the economic categories of work, value, and productivity exactly as they are interpreted in the existing order, and they regard any other interpretation as pure idealism. But at the same time they consider it rank dishonesty simply to accept the interpretation; the critical acceptance of the categories which rule social life contains simultaneously their condemnation. This dialectical character of the self-interpretation of contemporary man is what, in the last analysis, also causes the obscurity of the Kantian critique of reason. Reason cannot become transparent to itself as long as men act as members of an organism which lacks reason. Organism as a naturally developing and declining unity cannot be a sort of model for society, but only a form of deadened existence from which society must emancipate itself. An attitude which aims at such an emancipation and at an alteration of society as a whole might well be of service in theoretical work carried on within reality as presently ordered. But it lacks the pragmatic character which attaches to traditional thought as a socially useful professional activity.

In traditional theoretical thinking, the genesis of particular objective facts, the practical application of the conceptual systems by which it grasps the facts, and the role of such systems in action, are all taken to be external to the theoretical thinking itself. This alienation, which finds expression in philosophical terminology as the separation of value and research, knowledge and action, and other polarities, protects the savant from the tensions we have indicated and provides an assured framework for his activity. Yet a kind of thinking which does not accept this framework seems to have the ground taken out from under it. If a theoretical procedure does not take the form of determining objective facts with the help of the simplest and most differentiated conceptual systems available, what can it be but an aimless intellectual game, half conceptual poetry, half impotent expression of states of mind? The investigation into the social conditioning of facts and theories may indeed be a research problem, perhaps even a whole field for theoretical work, but how can such studies be radically different from other specialized efforts? Research into ideologies, or sociology of knowledge, which has been taken over from the critical theory of society and established as a special discipline, is not opposed either in its aim or in its other ambitions to the usual activities that go on within classificatory science.

In this reaction to critical theory, the self-awareness of thought as such is reduced to the discovery of the relationship that exists between intellectual positions and their social location. Yet the structure of the critical attitude, inasmuch as its intentions go beyond prevailing social ways of acting, is no more closely related to social disciplines thus conceived than it is to natural science. Its opposition to the traditional concept of theory springs in general from a difference not so much of objects as of subjects. For men of the critical mind, the facts, as they emerge from the work of society, are not extrinsic in the same degree as they are for the savant or for members of other professions who all think like little savants. The latter look towards a new kind of organization of work. But in so far as the objective realities given in perception are conceived as products which in principle should be under human control and, in the future at least, will in fact come under it, these realities lose the character of pure factuality.

——Max Horkheimer, *Critical Theory*: *Selected Essays*, Continuum Publishing Corporation, 2002, pp.206 - 209.

The Social Function of Philosophy

Since Plato, philosophy has never deserted the true idealism that it is possible to introduce reason among individuals and among nations. It has only discarded the *false* idealism that it is sufficient to set up the picture of perfection with no regard for theway in which it is to be attained. In modern times, loyalty to the highest ideas has been linked, in a world opposed to them, with the sober desire to know how these ideas can be realized on earth.

Before concluding, let us return once more to a misunderstanding which has already been mentioned. In philosophy, unlike business and politics, criticism does not mean the condemnation of a thing, grumbling about some measure or other, or mere negation and repudiation. Under certain conditions, criticism may actually take this destructive turn; there are examples in the Hellenistic age. By criticism, we mean that intellectual, and eventually practical, effort which is not satisfied to accept the prevailing ideas, actions, and social conditions unthinkingly and from mere habit; effort which aims to coordinate the individual sides of social life with each other and with the general ideas and aims of the epoch, to deduce them genetically, to distinguish the appearance from the essence, to examine the foundations of things, in short, really to know them. Hegel, the philosopher to whom we are most indebted in many respects, was so far removed from any querulous repudiation of specific conditions, that the King of Prussia called him to Berlin to inculcate the students with the proper loyalty and to immunize them against political opposition. Hegel did his best in that direction, and declared the Prussian state to be the embodiment of the divine Idea on earth. But thought is a peculiar factor. To justify the Prussian state, Hegel had to teach man to overcome the onesidedness and limitations of ordinary human understanding and to see the interrelationship between all conceptual and real relations. Further, he had to teach man to construe human history in its complex and contradictory structure, to search out the ideas of freedom and justice in the lives of nations, to know how nations perish when their principle proves inadequate and the time is ripe for new social forms. The fact that Hegel thus had to train his students in theoretical thought, had highly equivocal consequences for the Prussian state. In the long run, Hegel's work did more serious harm to that reactionary institution than all the use the latter could derive from his formal glorification. Reason is a poor ally of reaction. A little less than ten years after Hegel's death (his chair remained unoccupied that long), the King appointed a successor to fight the "dragon's teeth of Hegelian pantheism," and the "arrogance and fanaticism of his school."

We cannot say that, in the history of philosophy, the thinkers who had the most progressive effect were those who found most to criticize or who were always on hand with so-called practical programs. Things are not that simple. A philosophical doctrine has many sides, and each side may have the most diverse historical effects. Only inexceptional historical periods, such as the French Enlightenment, does philosophy itself become politics. In that period, the word philosophy did not call to mind logic and epistemology so much as attacks on the Church hierarchy and on an inhuman judicial system. The removal of certain preconceptions was virtually equivalent to opening the gates of the new world. Tradition and faith were two of the most powerful bulwarks of the old regime, and the philosophical attacks constituted an immediate historical action. Today, however, it is not a matter of eliminating a creed, for in the totalitarian states, where the noisiest appeal is made to heroism and a lofty *Weltanschauung*, neither faith nor *Weltanschauung* rule, but only dull indifference and the apathy of the individual towards destiny and to what comes from above. Today our task is rather to ensure that, in the future, the capacity for theory and for action which derives from theory will never again disappear, even in some coming period of peace when the daily routine may tend to allow the whole problem to be forgotten once more Our task is continually to struggle, lest mankind become completely disheartened by the frightful happenings of the present, lest man's belief in a worthy, peaceful and happy direction of society perish from the earth.

——Max Horkheimer, *Critical Theory*: *Selected Essays*, Continuum Publishing Corporation, 2002, pp. 270 - 272.

五、观点解读

1. 唯物主义不是形而上学

将唯物主义和唯心主义这两种世界观和思维方式的对立看作哲学史中最具决定性的主题，是二十世纪三十年代欧洲思想界的普遍认知，无论是正统马克思主义还是西方流行的生命哲学都持有类似的观点。但是，这种普遍的认知往往将唯物主义和唯心主义的对立看成两种形而上学意向的冲突，这显然是一种误解。之所以出现这种误解，是因为人们没有以正确的方式去研究唯物主义理论与实践，比如狄尔泰就认为唯物主义是一种形而上学。狄尔泰此处所采用的就是一种流行的、粗俗的唯物主义观念："唯物主义因而被归结为这样一个简单的论断：唯有物质及其运动才是真实的"，"唯物主义或是被人们理解为一种试图把任何精神事物，尤其是意识和理性看作纯属虚幻的企图"，"或是被人们理解为借助人为假定和对未来科学发现大成问题的寄托而把精神东西剥离物质过程的企图"[①]。于是，持有唯心主义立场的学者因此批判唯物主义者根本无法解释意识和精神现象。霍克海默要做的就是清算这种关于唯物主义的庸俗看法，而强调要在实践的、社会的、充分肯定精神和理性自主性的基础上理解唯物主义，唯物主义不是形而上学。形而上学的特点是纠缠于实现对于存在或世界的整体认知，找到世界背后永恒的根据。形而上学家将具体事物的知识看成普遍知识的一个特例，唯物主义者对世界的理解与此不同。唯物主义者首先肯定事物的真实性，也试图找到事物背后的根据，但是唯物主义者将对事物的认知置于实践的、社会的、历史的具体境况中加以理解，一旦社会历史条件发生变化，那么事物本身以及对于事物的认知都会随之改变。形而上学家因为坚守那些永恒原则，因而倾向于将包含冲突与斗争的所有现实解释成一种为了实现某种神圣的终极目的必要过程。唯物主义者反对这种表面上神圣化现实，实际上却走向保守的态度，他们追求对现实存在的不合理社会秩序的斗争与改变。此外，区别于庸俗的唯物主义者对想象未来的拒绝，也区别于形而上学家对于未来的"神学化"设定，真正的唯物主义者既不拒斥对未来的想象，也不是先在地设定一个完美的未来，而是在对现实社会秩序的批判性认知中、基于人类目前已经达到的现实条件，寻找一种可能的美好未来，并且通过一种可以落地的行动规划在现实中实现它。唯物主义者不会消极无力地等待，也不会只在精神、内心的世界寻求某种虚假的慰藉。一句话，唯物主义者追求的是变革社会、变革世界。

---

① [德]马克斯·霍克海默：《批判理论》，李小兵等译，重庆出版社 1989 年版，第 12 页。

2. 权威是盲目的、卑下的屈从之基础

对权威以及权威主义人格的研究是法兰克福学派在二十世纪三十年代研究的重要内容，该研究直到今天仍然有着广泛的影响。霍克海默敏锐地意识到，权威是历史的一条核心范畴，“它在集团和个体所有的生活中以及世界的各个领域中都起着决定性作用”[①]。特别是由于极权主义国家形式的逐步兴起，权威正在成为当时历史学家概念构制中的主导性范畴。既有的研究往往倾向于给权威下一个一般性的定义，而霍克海默认为，“权威是盲目的和卑下的屈从之基础”，从主观上看，人因其“在作出自身决断时的心理惰性和无能为力”而选择屈从；从客观上看，对权威的屈从源自“受限制和无价值的生活条件的延续不绝”[②]。然而，抽象的定义很容易陷入内容上的空泛，重要的是在特定历史时期结合特定实践的一历史的任务发展出活生生的社会理论。所以霍克海默认为，首先应当在具体的历史中研究权威以及反权威的特定形式。在人类社会早期，权威的存在有其现实基础，为了更好延续群体的生存发展，权威是一种必要。但是随着人类生活条件的不断改善，对权威的服从，特别是隐藏在权威之下的各种奴役就成为完全不必要乃至必须加以超越的了。资产阶级是在反对传统权威的斗争中兴起的，无论是伏尔泰、康德还是费希特都明显表现出对于权威以及屈从于权威的不屑。然而，资产阶级在不断上升进而占据主导地位的过程中，先是摒除权威，继而很快又以某种形而上学的方式使之复活。新的财产制度、自由竞争的经济体制等等都被看成是自然而然的、神圣不可侵犯的存在。在这种新权威之下，隐藏着的是无数底层人民的苦难与被奴役的现实。在自由主义市场经济之下，“生活所需的所有产品的生产和分配，都发生于无数毫不相关的活动中以及个体和集团毫无沟通的相互作用中”[③]。人们不能把握自己的命运，因为他们依赖于“非理性的社会条件”。参与市场竞争的个人会普遍感觉到，社会现实是一种高高在上的盲目力量。盲目的经济必然性成为自由资本主义社会最高的权威。而伴随着危机的出现，极权主义国家权

① ［德］马克斯·霍克海默：《批判理论》，李小兵等译，重庆出版社 1989 年版，第 66 页。

② ［德］马克斯·霍克海默：《批判理论》，李小兵等译，重庆出版社 1989 年版，第 68 页。

③ ［德］马克斯·霍克海默：《批判理论》，李小兵等译，重庆出版社 1989 年版，第 79 页。

威的实现成为可能。只要国家能够给大众带来经济利益，那么听从权威国家的任何号令就没有什么不妥。霍克海默对人们摆脱资产阶级社会的权威作出了一些设想，这就是“让权威摆脱唯我主义的利益和压榨”。只有出现一种“更高的社会形式”，此时“工作的管理职能和实施职能不再与富殷和贫困分别联系”，那么就“不再有社会阶级之间的分别”，人们将自由摆脱资本主义时期的抽象个体形态，而成为“只受自然界及其必然性限制”的“具体人联合劳动的真正自由”①，只有此时，一种崭新的积极的权威形态才会重生。

3. 作为传统理论对立面的批判理论

“批判理论”或者准确地说“批判的社会理论”是“传统理论”的否定或直接对立面。而所谓“传统理论”，在霍克海默这里，是指近代资产阶级哲学，特别是他刚刚批判过的实证主义传统。试图用自然科学的方法研究社会历史问题、日益数学符号化，是“传统理论”的突出特征：“就这种关于理论的传统看法所表现出的倾向而言，它趋向于纯数学的符号系统。在其理论要素、命题的组成部分中，经验对象的名称变得越来越少，而数学符号却在日益猛烈增长。逻辑演算的合理化已经达到这样的程度，以至理论形成至少在大多数自然科学领域里变成了数学建构的事情。”②霍尔海默指出，“批判理论”在三个方面与“传统理论”构成直接对立或否定。第一，与资本主义生产方式的关系及对资本主义制度的态度不同。作为资本主义生产方式早期发展阶段的自发产物，“传统理论”并不清楚“科学真正的社会功能”，“不谈理论对于人类生活中意味着什么，而只谈理论在它由于历史原因而产生于其中的孤立领域中意味着什么”③，最终以不同的哲学形式表达了对现存的资本主义制度的顺从、接受和肯定。作为资本主义生产方式高度发展阶段的反思性产物，“批判理论”重新把握了理论应当具有的社会功能，超越了对“永恒逻各斯”的虚幻追求，始终把“对合理生活条件的关心”作为推动自身发展的动力，并因此拒绝相信“现存社会为其成员提供的行为准则”，认为“简单地接受解释是不诚实的；批判地接受支配着社会生活的范畴，同时就

① ［德］马克斯·霍克海默：《批判理论》，李小兵等译，重庆出版社 1989 年版，第 93 页。

② ［德］马克斯·霍克海默：《批判理论》，李小兵等译，重庆出版社 1989 年版，第 183 页。译文参照英文版略有改动。

③ ［德］马克斯·霍克海默：《批判理论》，李小兵等译，重庆出版社 1989 年版，第 189 页。

包含着对这些范畴的判决"[①]。第二,理论主体及其理论活动的性质不同。在"传统理论"的语境下,个人与自己身处其中的社会是分离的,接受"传统理论"的人把这种分离看作是绝对的甚至是先验的,因而否定改变、改造社会的可能性;选择"批判理论"的人则把这种分离看作相对的,认为"由个人活动之间的盲目作用决定的整个社会结构(现存的劳动分工和阶级划分)是一个起源于人类活动的函数,因而是一个能够有计划地决定并合理地规定目标的对象"[②],即肯定社会是可以而且应当改变的。因此,在前者那里,价值与研究、知识与行动、理论与实践是截然分离的,而在后者那里,则是有机统一的。用马克思的话说,两者的不同在于,哲学家们只是用不同的方式解释世界,而问题在于改变世界。第三,逻辑结构不同。"传统理论"和"批判理论"都通过定义普遍的概念,进而从普遍概念中推出关于真实关系的陈述,并将之描述为必然的。不过,"传统理论"的概念是抽象的、非历史的,而"批判理论"则明确地把建立在简单商品交换关系基础上的资本主义社会作为自己概念的现实起源,并宣布这些概念是非普遍的,即主要适用于现代资本主义社会。不仅如此,由于"传统理论"坚持理论与实践的截然分离,所以,它主张的必然性是排除主体实践的,因而它所追求的"必然"和"自由"其实都是同一个东西,即"实际上的顺从";而"批判理论的必然性概念本身就是一个批判概念,它以自由为前提,即使这种自由还不存在",即肯定主体在实现必然过程中的作用:"今天,在既存社会形式向未来社会形式转变过程中,人类将第一次成为有意识的主体,并将主动地规定自己的生活方式"[③]。

六、进一步阅读指南

1. [德]马克斯·霍克海默:《批判理论》,李小兵等译,重庆出版社1989年版。

2. [德]马克斯·霍克海默:《霍克海默集》,曹卫东编选,渠东、付德根

① [德]马克斯·霍克海默:《批判理论》,李小兵等译,重庆出版社1989年版,第199页。译文参照英文版略有改动。

② [德]马克斯·霍克海默:《批判理论》,李小兵等译,重庆出版社1989年版,第198页。

③ [德]马克斯·霍克海默:《批判理论》,李小兵等译,重庆出版社1989年版,第219、221页。

等译，上海远东出版社 2004 年版。

3. ［德］马克斯·霍克海默、西奥多·阿多诺：《启蒙辩证法：哲学断片》，渠敬东、曹卫东译，上海人民出版社 2006 年版。

4. ［美］马丁·杰伊：《法兰克福学派史》，单世联译，广东人民出版社 1996 年版。

5. ［德］罗尔夫·魏格豪斯：《法兰克福学派：历史、理论及政治影响》，孟登迎等译，上海人民出版社 2010 年版。

6. ［德］赫尔穆特·贡尼、鲁道夫·林古特：《霍克海默传》，任立译，商务印书馆 1999 年版。

7. ［美］理查德·沃林：《文化批评的观念：法兰克福学派、存在主义和后结构主义》，张国清译，商务印书馆 2000 年版。

8. 王凤才：《从批判理论到后批判理论（上）——对批判理论三期发展的批判性反思》，《马克思主义与现实》2012 年第 6 期。

9. 张亮：《霍克海默与法兰克福学派的理论创新道路》，《学术月刊》2016 年第 5 期。

10. Seyla Benhabib, Wolfgang Bonss, and John McCole, eds., *On Max Horkheimer: New Perspectives*, MIT Press, 1993.

11. Peter M. R. Stirk, *Max Horkheimer: A New Interpretation*, Harvester Wheatsheaf, 1992.

12. Zoltán Tar, *The Frankfurt School: the Critical Theories of Max Horkheimer and Theodor W. Adorno*, Schocken Books, 1985.

13. Rolf Wiggershaus, *The Frankfurt School: Its History, Theories, and Political Significance*, trans. Michael Robertson, MIT Press, 1994.

14. John Abromeit, *Max Horkheimer and the Foundations of the Frankfurt School*, Cambridge University Press, 2011.

15. David Held, *Introduction to Critical Theory: Horkheimer to Habermas*, Polity Press, 2013.

七、问题与思考

1. 如何理解霍克海默的唯物主义思想?

2. 霍克海默为什么要对权威这一范畴做历史唯物主义的考察?

3. 霍克海默是如何展开对批判理论的建构的?霍克海默的批判理论超越传统理论的地方在哪里?

第十章　存在主义马克思主义的扛鼎之作
——《辩证理性批判》选读

教学目的与要求

了解萨特试图综合存在主义与马克思主义的历史和理论背景；掌握萨特“存在主义的马克思主义”的人学辩证法和历史辩证法的理论逻辑；理解前进—逆溯的方法；理解萨特对总体性和总体化的区分；了解实践—惰性概念，明确萨特和马克思的异化理论之间的逻辑差别。

一、历史背景

（一）作者简介

1905年，让-保罗·萨特(Jean-Paul Sartre)出生于法国巴黎一个小资产阶级家庭，童年在外祖父母家度过，受到良好教育。1915年，萨特考入亨利中学，学习成绩优异，期间受到叔本华、尼采等人哲学的影响。1924年到1928年间，萨特在具有现代法兰西思想家摇篮之称的巴黎高等师范学校攻读哲学。1929年，他在全国大中学教师资格考试中获得第一名，并结识了一同应试、获得第二名的波伏娃。1933年，萨特赴德留学，悉心研读胡塞尔、海德格尔等人的哲学著作，并在此基础上逐步形成了自身的存在主义哲学思想体系。1934年，萨特回到巴黎，陆续发表《论自我的超越性》《想象》

《情绪理论初探》等现象学著作。第二次世界大战爆发后,萨特应征入伍,次年被俘虏,在战俘营中度过了 10 个月的铁窗生涯。在此期间,萨特大量阅读克尔凯郭尔、黑格尔和海德格尔等人的著作。战争与现实使萨特的思想发生了巨大的变化,他从战前对政治的漠不关心转向了对社会现实的关注,并主张利用文字干预生活。1941 年冬,为了反对法西斯主义,萨特和梅洛-庞蒂、德桑第、波伏娃等人共同建立了名为"社会主义与自由"的知识分子抵抗组织,并为法国共产党领导的地下刊物《法兰西文学报》撰稿。1943 年,《存在与虚无》正式出版,该书奠定了萨特的无神论存在主义哲学体系的基本内涵和根本基调,也奠定了萨特在战后法国哲学家中的领袖地位。1945 年 10 月,他在布鲁塞尔做了《存在主义是一种人道主义》的演讲,接着和梅洛-庞蒂、阿隆、波伏瓦等人一起创立《现代》杂志,从而在法国知识界声名鹊起。1946 年,萨特在《现代》杂志上发表了《唯物主义与革命》一文,开启了与法国共产党的漫长争论。1950 年初,在梅洛-庞蒂的影响下,萨特和法国共产党越走越近,尽管仍然相互批评,但萨特在政治上逐渐成为法国共产党的同路人。1955 年 9 月,萨特和波伏瓦应邀到中国访问。1956 年开始,萨特对法国共产党的态度重新变得复杂化。在苏联军队入侵匈牙利时,萨特谴责了苏联军队和对干涉表示支持的法国共产党领导人,并与法国共产党决裂,但在政治倾向上仍然持有左翼立场。1957 年,《现代》杂志发布了匈牙利问题专期,萨特写了《斯大林的幽灵》一文反对苏联干涉。但他又认为,苏联仍然是血肉筑成的社会主义。存在主义和马克思主义之间到底是什么关系?到底如何看待苏联的社会主义?在 1960 年出版的《辩证理性批判》中,萨特试图给出答案。1964 年,萨特获得诺贝尔文学奖,但他拒绝领取,理由是他不接受一切官方给予的荣誉。此后萨特更加积极地投身到左翼社会活动中去。1968 年 5 月,萨特在五月风暴中坚定地站在造反学生一边。20 世纪 70 年代之后,萨特的身体状况逐渐糟糕,在完成《家庭白痴》后停止了写作。1975 年,在接受《新观察家》周刊采访时,萨特声称自己不是马克思主义者,而是自由社会主义者。1980 年 4 月 15 日,萨特病逝于巴黎,享年 74 岁,数万群众自发聚集为他送葬,表达悼念之情。

（二）时代背景

1. 美苏冷战

第二次世界大战结束后，世界并没有迎来人们期盼已久的“永久和平”。社会主义阵营和自由主义阵营为了共同对抗法西斯主义而一度建立起来的坚实联盟，随着战争硝烟的散去以及共同敌人的不复存在而迅速瓦解。资本主义和共产主义作为两个阵营分道扬镳，人类由此进入了美苏两个超级大国长期对峙的冷战时期。美苏之间由于相互恐慌而陷入一场疯狂的军事竞赛，这使得整个时代的人都生活在冷战和核战争随时爆发的阴影之下。就这样，战后法国政治和意识形态领域的斗争也因为两大阵营的冷战形势而变得空前激烈。第二次世界大战之后，世界政治迅速分化为亲共和反共两大阵营。反共阵营的领头羊美国在资本主义阵营内部不断驱逐、削弱共产党的力量，例如，1948 年的意大利选举，如果当时意大利共产党获胜的话，美国甚至计划出兵予以干预。与此同时，苏联也将各种非共产主义的因素从其阵营内基本清除，并在其势力范围内建立起统一的共产党一党执政的国家（芬兰除外）。[①] 不过从政治领域来看，法国却是战后西方发达资本主义阵营里最独树一帜的国家，无论从官方还是民间层面看，法国都没有形成一边倒的亲美反共态势。从国家决策来看，以戴高乐将军为首的法国时常与美国的号令唱反调，特别是 1960 年之后，随着原子弹技术的研制成功，戴高乐在北约等一系列政治军事议题上都表现出鲜明的独立性。另外，由于法国共产党在抗击纳粹的抵抗运动中发挥的中坚作用（这与整个法国在第二次世界大战期间对纳粹的投降主义形成了强烈对照），法国共产党在第二次世界大战后一度成为议会第一大党，再加上法国独特的激进的知识分子传统，即便冷战爆发使得法国共产党被驱逐出法国政府，左翼力量也仍然在相当长的时间里在法国政治和思想舞台上占据着重要位置。此外，作为一个老牌帝国主义国家，第二次世界大战之后，法国仍然在北非拥有大量殖民地，轰轰烈烈的殖民地独立运动也深刻影响着法国国内

---

① ［英］艾瑞克·霍布斯鲍姆：《极端的年代：1914—1991》上，郑明萱译，江苏人民出版社 1998 年版，第 356—357 页。

的政治形势。[①] 而左翼因为其反帝国主义的本性决定了他们大多支持殖民地的独立运动。值得一提的是，萨特的《辩证理性批判》正是写于阿尔及利亚战争期间。因此，一个悖论性的现象是，身处资本主义阵营中的法国，其经济快速发展的"黄金三十年"也是左翼知识分子最为辉煌的三十年，而萨特无疑是左翼知识分子群体中最为璀璨的一颗明珠。就此而言，萨特代表了一个时代。

2. 发达工业社会的来临

尽管大国战争特别是核战争的疑云始终笼罩在世界上空，亚洲、非洲、拉丁美洲等美苏对抗的前沿地区也热战不断，但一个出乎意料的事实是：由于美苏之间保持着一种表面冷战、实质"冷和"的默契，以及美国由于提防苏联而对友好国家做出的援助之举，反而使得第二次世界大战结束后，美国之外的老牌发达资本主义国家迎来了一段长达近三十年的稳定期，这一形势直到20世纪70年代资本主义阵营爆发经济危机才被打破。[②] 就法国来说，在马歇尔计划的支持下，法国很快完成经济复苏，并在1975年之前保持了年均5%的工业生产增长幅度，以至于有学者用"黄金三十年"来描述第二次世界大战结束后的法国经济发展过程。尽管资本主义处于最好的黄金时代，但是萨特对资本主义社会的物化现实，以及资本主义的发达是建立在其他地区受剥削受压迫的基础之上这一事实有着十分清晰的认知，因而《辩证理性批判》也对相关主题多次予以分析。也正是在这个意义上，波斯特认为，萨特思想尤其是《辩证理性批判》在很大程度上预示了后来的1968年五月革命，或者说使得五月风暴"这一社会事件可以被理解"。[③]

---

① [法]让-弗朗索瓦·西里奈利：《20世纪的两位知识分子：萨特与阿隆》，陈伟译，江苏人民出版社2001年版，第257—258页。

② [英]艾瑞克·霍布斯鲍姆：《极端的年代：1914—1991》上，郑明萱译，江苏人民出版社1998年版，第341、387页。

③ [美]马克·波斯特：《战后法国的存在主义的马克思主义：从萨特到阿尔都塞》，张金鹏等译，南京大学出版社2015年版，第354页。

(三) 思想背景

1. 法国知识界的"左""右"之争

冷战使得法国知识分子在政治立场上走向分野与分化，大多数知识分子被迫选择一个亲美或亲苏的立场。知识分子往往需要在其政治立场的背后找到一个理论上的支撑点，因此，左右政治之争也随之引发了左右理论之争。要理解萨特的《辩证理性批判》，就要理解萨特在其试图给予政治立场奠基的理论立场，以及他对与其相对的政治立场背后的理论立场的回应。萨特的政治立场从根本上说是第三条道路，其反美和反资本主义的立场是一贯的，但是对法国共产党和苏联也不是绝对的支持，尽管有过亲苏和亲共的时候，但是那时他也依然是以独立知识分子的姿态来保持与法国共产党和苏联的合作关系。也因此，萨特在理论上遭到两面夹击。"左"边是来自亨利·穆然、列斐伏尔、伽罗蒂等为代表的法国共产党人的理论攻击。穆然深入抨击了萨特《存在与虚无》里糟糕的本体论，认为萨特"从作为意向性意识的主观唯心主义观点出发定义自为，而从客观唯心主义观点出发定义自在"，这是一种双重的唯心主义，"马克思主义与这个唯心主义的新近变种之间不可能存在和解"[①]。与穆然从理论上展开对萨特的批判不同，列斐伏尔以一种马克思主义的方式给予萨特的存在主义以重击。他着手揭开存在主义的社会根源，认为存在主义只是一种由"资产阶级知识分子的世界连同它的私有化意识、它的抽象文化、它的孤立、它对实践的蔑视、它与生活的分离、它平庸的而又暧昧的社会地位"所引起的"内在神经衰弱症，一种精神分裂症"。尽管承认构建一种意识哲学对于马克思主义的必要性，但整体上，列斐伏尔认为"存在主义的绝望与焦虑概念"正是"对资本主义条件下的内在矛盾的正确描述"，但由于它没有考虑真实的历史，因而不能发现历史的理性，只能提供一种非理性主义的所谓"个体完全自由"的"伪解决方案"。[②]

---

① [美]马克·波斯特：《战后法国的存在主义的马克思主义：从萨特到阿尔都塞》，张金鹏等译，南京大学出版社 2015 年版，第 106 页。

② [美]马克·波斯特：《战后法国的存在主义的马克思主义：从萨特到阿尔都塞》，张金鹏等译，南京大学出版社 2015 年版，第 107、112 页。

尽管这些来自左翼的批评声音可能一时未能得到萨特完全的接受，但的确刺激萨特认识到自己理论上的缺点，从而促动萨特在自己的著作尤其是《辩证理性批判》中来解决这些问题。对萨特的批判还有来自“右”边的，其最重要的代表则是萨特青年时期的好友雷蒙·阿隆。在萨特向马克思主义靠拢的思想演进过程中，阿隆几乎在萨特思想发展的每个阶段都对萨特（同时也对梅洛-庞蒂）做出了批判性的回应。而且阿隆是法国知名的理论家，他的批判是萨特不得不加以重视的。1956 年，梅洛-庞蒂发表与萨特彻底决裂和清算的《辩证法的历险》之后，阿隆也对该书进行了回应，写作了《辩证法的冒险和挫折》。该文对梅洛-庞蒂给予萨特的指责进行了驳斥，不过这也不能说阿隆是对萨特哲学做了辩护，事实上，他只是强调梅洛-庞蒂的批评并不公正，并且他自己的哲学往往也犯有与萨特同样的错误。阿隆在该文中指出，萨特哲学的一个明显问题是，“把主观意义当作无条件有效的意义”，“由于长期坚持历史判断的不确定性，萨特最终在主体性（或计划）中寻找确定性”，对于研究真实的社会历史来说，这种态度可以称得上是极其无知的。阿隆反讽地问：“不分析基本材料就能理解整个社会的人属于哪一个另类？”[①]尽管阿隆的政治和学术立场是自由主义和实证主义的，却不能不承认他对萨特的批判是入木三分的，这些都敦促萨特从理论上予以有力回应。

2. 存在主义与结构主义、后结构主义之争

存在主义、结构主义与后结构主义是第二次世界大战之后在法国思想界交替出现的主流思潮。萨特作为存在主义 3H 一代的中坚人物，自然处于存在主义与结构主义、后结构主义之争的中心位置，再加上萨特哲学中存在的某些鲜明的“缺陷”，因而理所当然地成为结构主义和后结构主义集火的首要对象。以萨特和梅洛-庞蒂为代表的现象学存在主义的一代，无论如何对主体性加以限定，但始终是将“主体性”置于他们整个哲学的核心位置。当他们经历了第二次世界大战以及冷战的局势之后，又增加了关于历史研究的分量，梅洛-庞蒂在相当长的时间内致力于构建一种历史现象学，萨特

① [法]雷蒙·阿隆：《想象的马克思主义》，姜志辉译，上海世纪出版集团 2007 年版，第 48、53 页。

同样如此，始终致力于使存在主义能够更好地成为理解以及介入社会历史的学说。存在主义哲学家们主要是通过不断增加黑格尔特别是辩证法在其现象学构建中的分量来实现这一点的。然而，法国思想本身固有的科学主义传统，加上从人类学、语言学等领域发展出来的一些方法论结合在一起，形成了一股风靡一时的、后来可以被称为结构主义的思潮。虽然对于是否存在一股可以称之为结构主义的流派，或者到底什么是结构主义，学界并没有形成定论，但是知识界在反对现象学存在主义哲学家们的主体、历史以及辩证法方面形成了某种一致局面则是没有争议的。他们反对现象学存在主义的理论和方法工具则是结构、语言、系统、科学等。在他们看来，现象学存在主义哲学坚持主体、崇尚辩证法，这些归根结底是崇尚一种同一性的强制，而这一切归根结底的源头是德国古典哲学，尤其是黑格尔。法国哲学由此从3H一代走向了以尼采、马克思、弗洛伊德、索绪尔等为思想源头的"怀疑一代"。"由此，对现象学意识和同一性逻辑的双重攻击都聚在了反对一般主体的一个旗帜之下进行"，现在哲学关心的是"无主体的超越领域"。[①] 列维-斯特劳斯、阿尔都塞、福柯等结构主义、后结构主义思想大师们一个接一个地对萨特发起了猛攻，而萨特不得不以某种方式与他们进行论战。因此，萨特的《辩证理性批判》无疑需要放在存在主义与结构主义以及后结构主义的争论中才能被理解。

3. 萨特早期哲学的困境

萨特在进入《辩证理性批判》写作之前已经是一位思想相对成熟的哲学家，其思想以体系的形式集中体现在《存在与虚无》之中。因此，其哲学体系的巨大转换意味着他不只是要回答时代问题和政治问题，也是原初的哲学体系存在缺陷需要调整，或者说他需要解决当初思想中的一些困境和难题。加里·古廷甚至认为《辩证理性批判》是"萨特的存在主义向社会领域的延伸"[②]。萨特早期的存在主义在关于世界存在的本体论问题、关于自我和他人之间关系的伦理学问题，以及在如何看待社会历史问题上，都有难以克服的困境，他的早期哲学也无法让他真正有效地、具体地"介入"真实的社会历

① [法]文森特·德贡布：《当代法国哲学》，王寅丽译，新星出版社2007年版，第105页。

② [美]加里·古廷：《20世纪法国哲学》，辛岩译，江苏人民出版社2004年版，第157页。

史之中。这些都促使着萨特去构建一种新的理论。

二、篇章结构

《辩证理性批判》共分两卷。第 1 卷写于 1957—1960 年，法文版于 1960 年 4 月在巴黎正式出版，标题为“关于实践的集合体的理论”。《辩证理性批判》第 1 卷，除去一篇简短的序言外，一共包括 3 个部分，第 1 部分题为“方法问题”，该部分既和后面的部分相关，又独立成篇。第 2 部分是第 1 卷全书的“引论”。第 3 部分篇幅最大，是第 1 卷的正文。正文又分为两大部分，其中第 1 部分标题为“从个体实践到实践-惰性（practico-inert）”；第 2 部分标题为“从群体（groups）到历史”。

在“方法问题”中萨特提出的问题是：今天我们是否有方法来创立一种构成的和历史的人学？萨特认为，这种人学在马克思主义哲学的内部找到了它的位置，他试图用存在主义来“补充”马克思主义，并确定建构这种人学的方法。“方法问题”共有 3 个小节。第 1 小节题为“马克思主义和存在主义”，从标题可以看出，此小节试图探讨马克思主义和存在主义两者之间的关系。萨特认为，在当前的历史实践条件下，马克思主义是我们时代不可超越的哲学。但是“现代的”马克思主义由于理论和实践的脱离而停滞了，变得不再关心现实的人和经验，而只有存在主义去研究具体的人和具体经验，因此，有必要用存在主义来补充马克思主义。第 2 小节题为“中介问题和辅助学科”，萨特认为，教条主义的马克思主义患了一种“病”，它常常以某种先在的现成的概念体系去座架历史现实，“把人类生活的一切具体规定性委诸偶然性而加以抛弃”，用普遍去代替具体，用僵化的词句取代活生生的现实。要拯救这种“病症”，就需要摆脱原先教条式的方法论，而只有通过“存在主义”的中介，同时借助“精神分析学和微观社会学”这两个辅助学科的方法，马克思主义才有可能重新与具体的现实生活相链接。第 3 小节题为“前进-逆溯方法”，此节中萨特不满于传统马克思主义的方法，而从正面提出了自己的方法论逻辑。具体说来，人学方法论中的前进法主张个人总是处于一定的社会历史结构之中，传统的马克思主义由于过于强调这一方法以致自身僵化；而逆溯法则是对个人生存的微观研究，存在主义注重从具体的物质条件、工具状况以及现实的实践这些角度来探究具体的总体化过程；整体来看，前进-逆溯的方法就是以一种总体化的要求来对个人、集团和历史现象进行差别性的研究。

作为《辩证理性批判》第1卷的导言，“引论”部分至关重要，它共分为两小节，标题分别为“教条的辩证法和批判的辩证法”和“对批判经验的批判”。该段文本中，萨特紧接着“方法问题”更为直接地阐述其创作《辩证理性批判》的理论意图。他首先认为，实证主义理性和分析理性都存在一定的弊端，它们常以一种先验的、构成性的理性统一性来面对世界，而无法理解这种“统一性”其实依赖于人类的现实活动。尽管分析理性和实证理性可以去分析事物，但是它们无从理解自身，要探索历史的可能性只有经由辩证理性才有可能。马克思通过批判地继承黑格尔发现了辩证理性，却由于他更多地倾向于政治经济学的研究，而没有从纯粹哲学理论的角度将这种辩证理性深化。随之而来的不幸是，以恩格斯的自然辩证法为代表的现代的马克思主义，堕落成为一种外在性的、超验的辩证唯物主义。因此，萨特认为，有必要在理论上充分探讨辩证理性的内涵，并考察这种理性的范围和界限。区分总体性和总体化是萨特对于西方马克思主义的一大理论贡献。萨特认为，总体性作为过去行动的残余是一种被动的、惰性的自在之在，是想象行为的相关存在；而总体化则是实现总体的、开放着的辩证运动，个体的实践是总体化的唯一基础。萨特认为，历史并不是受动的个人和死去的总体性的关系，而是一定条件下实践的个人和总体化运动之间的关系，而辩证法就是“由总体化的个体的一种多元复合性操纵的各种具体总体化之总体化”。然而，仅仅明白历史的起点是个体的实践远远不够，还必须研究这一实践通向人类集合体的各种形式、结构及其可理解性。“引论”部分关于实践-惰性理论的探讨也有一些新意，萨特认为，个人实践在与物打交道的过程中、在一定的集合体中必然被扭转为一种异化的实践，形成“实践-惰性”领域。惰性存在既是一种客观的、消极的外在性存在，又是“历史的惰性动力，它是创新的唯一可能的基础”。

《辩证理性批判》第1卷第1部分标题为“从个体实践到实践-惰性”。在此部分中，萨特主要描述了作为历史辩证运动基础的源动性的个体实践如何在“物质”(matter)和“群集”(collectives)中扭转为一种“实践-惰性”的过程。萨特首先从存在论的立场出发假想式地讨论了“作为总体化的个体实践”。萨特认为，生命体处于一种永恒性的缺失和匮乏(scarcity)之中，正是“需要”(need)作为一种“否定之否定”使生命体周围的物质世界获得一种消极的统一,而个体则可以通过具有意向性的实践行动“将物质环境扭转到真实的总体化”进程之中。萨特在本体论意义上将“匮乏”定义为人的存在的异化基础,个人之真实存在从一开始就必然受制于外在的历史性给定物的惰性总体,每一代人留给后人的总会是一个匮乏的原初存在基础。这种匮乏的惰性总体一方面永无休止地否定着人们的劳动实践,在时间性的机制中使人类的一切实践成果惰性化为“物”;另一方面也包含着积极的可能性,正是由于匮乏之无,个人存在之谋划得以被激起。萨特于此处再次提及“定形物对人本身的统治”(“实践-惰性”理论),自在存在的自然“物性”和马克思意义上的“物化的社会关系”都可以被看作萨特所定义的“定形物”,它们使实践在对象化的活动中被异化。该部分的最后,萨特描述了一种消极的人类集合体——群列(series)。所谓的“群列”主要是指日常生活中自然形成的人与人之间的外在性的集合关系,萨特分别以大城市中的街道、广场、公共汽车、无线电台和自由市场为例来描述这种无处不在的集合关系。这种实践-惰性场既在场又不在场,人与人之间由于他性的、外在的因素构成一种消极的、被总体化了的系列,在“系列”中人们维持着一种间接和冷漠的关系。无疑,这种消极的统一性以不在场的方式渗透于每个个体实践之中。

《辩证理性批判》第1卷第2部分标题为“从群体到历史”。由于种种原因,这段长达400多页的文字非常杂乱,很多地方的论证既没有历史佐证也缺乏逻辑支撑。该部分讲述了群体之间的冲突、和解与历史的关系。在萨特那里,群列只是消极的、散裂的、被动性的统一体,个人在群列之中只是无力的、离散的存在;而群体与群列则不同,它是人们为了抵抗物质性的被动制约而建构起来的一种有机结构。在群体中,人们开始联合起来形成共同的实践,群体是对群列那种纯粹个人外在的共在状态的克服。根据群体的内在构成逻辑,萨特主要描述了四种形态的群体形式,分别是聚合群体(the fused group)、法令群体(the statutory group)、组织(organization)和机构(institution)。聚合群体是群体的初级形态,区别于群列的纯粹外在的物质性统一,它是在一定的共有目标或者在外部敌对实践压力驱动下集合起来的外部群体,依靠人们相互传染的希望和激情来维持,由于尚未被过度的制度化,个人的自由在这种群体中更容易被保留,但也是由于同样的原因,聚合群体的存在是非常不稳定的。萨特认为1789年法国巴黎攻占巴士底狱的人群就是聚合群体的最好例证。群体要实现自身的稳定，就不断通过誓愿、法令、组织以及机构等新的方法和形态来达到维持自身的目的，在这种流变之中，群体越来越僵化从而呈现出惰性特征，个人在其中的自由越来越被淹没。在分析了群体的流变过程和不同形态之后，萨特将其理论目光放到唯一的真正具有战斗性和行动力的社会群体——工人阶级身上。萨特认为，工人阶级在现实的历史中经历了从外部群列到组织再到机构化的过程，从纯粹的被动性逐步走向了组织化、体制化乃至官僚化。萨特通过对不同的人类集合体的分析认为，作为真正意义上的历史主体的工人阶级"既不是一种纯粹的战斗性，也不是一种纯粹的被动性分散，更不是一种纯粹机构化了的机构。它是种种不同实践形式之间的一种复杂的运动关系"。工人阶级必须在同资产阶级的阶级斗争中不断形成对历史的自觉的总体化的理解，通过一种自由的、生成性的共同实践来推动历史的真实进步。遗憾的是，萨特这里的逻辑是无法自洽的，因为他所理解的社会历史是一系列人类主体目的性行动不断失败的过程，生成性的个人实践最终必然堕入结构性的、惰性的群体之中而被异化。由此，萨特的历史哲学被深深地打上了悲观主义的烙印。

《辩证理性批判》的第2卷延续了第1卷所探讨的问题，标题为"历史的可理解性"。按照萨特的最初计划，它至少由两个主要部分组成：一部分讨论共时性的(synchronic)总体化，另一个部分讨论历时性的(diachronic)总体化。萨特打算通过两个主要实例来阐释共时性的总体化：(1)革命之后的俄国社会：管理型社会；(2)资产阶级的民主制社会：非管理型社会，萨特称之为"散裂的(disunited)社会"。但是在文本之中，只有第一个例子被全面地涉及，计划中的其他部分只是很零散地出现在纲要性的附录之中。在对历史的研究中，萨特不断扩大自己的阅读范围，不断修正自己的概念和方法，但最终也没有形成一个完整的体系，被迫放弃了第2卷的出版。

三、研究前沿

晚期萨特因其写作风格和术语的极度个人化，其著作颇为晦涩难解，尤其是《辩证理性批判》的第2卷又是萨特在身体状况不太稳定的状况下完成的，这也给《辩证理性批判》的解读带来了特别的困难。目前国内学界对《辩证理性批判》的解读主要集中在第1卷，关于第2卷的研究则几近空白，有待未来填补。

第一，对存在主义与马克思主义结合成败做出评判。学界普遍认为，存在主义对萨特理解马克思主义的影响是十分巨大的。萨特认为，我们仍然处在马克思的"时代"，自命为对马克思主义超越的哲学不过是对马克思主义的"重复"或者"重新发现"，但是马克思主义在现实的发展中停滞了，而且出现了人学的空场，这就为存在主义补充马克思主义提供了理由。在萨特看来，现实的马克思主义出现了理论与实践的"脱离"。这种"脱离"的出现是因为苏联在特殊的历史条件下，为了保证其安全和发展过度追求"集团的整体性"的结果，因而产生了"马克思主义的唯心主义"，其具体的方法就是"概念化"和"走极端"，而"活的马克思主义"不应该是这样的，它反对孤立地、抽象地处理事实，而将许多同时产生的事实置于一个"整体的高度的统一"中进行思考，去探求事物内部的彼此联系着的相互关系。于是萨特试图创建一种辩证的、历史的人学，从而填补教条主义马克思主义那里的人学空场。虽然有少部分学者认为，萨特用存在主义对马克思主义的补充有其理论价值，但更多学者认为，萨特对马克思主义的存在主义补充陷入了一种抽象的思辨，而没有深入到真实的社会历史之中，因而不可避免地走向了失败。

第二，对晚期萨特的辩证法思想展开重点研究。学界关注的焦点主要是萨特的人学辩证法、历史辩证法。按照萨特的说法，"人学辩证法"是建立在个人、集合体以及群体实践基础上的总体化运动，个人总体化的实践是整个社会历史总体化进程的根基。在总体化的实践进程中，一方面我们被社会总体化，另一方面社会也被我们总体化。批判萨特"人学辩证法"的观点认为，在萨特这里，匮乏是其根本动力，反抗是人性的开端，个体活动是唯一真实的实践，这与马克思主义的历史唯物主义有着重大差别。但也有学者认为，如果我们想立足当代中国建构马克思主义的"人学"，那么萨特提出的关于研究具体社会状态以及各社会层次相互作用的要求就是无法回避的，他提出的方法和解决途径也有重要参考价值。萨特的"历史辩证法"是学界关注的另一个重要问题。这里着重讨论的问题有"一种总体化的历史如何可能"，以及历史是否以及如何表现为人类实践的主动性辩证过程与实践向惰性状态不断复归的反辩证法之间“永恒轮回”问题。因此，尽管我们可以批判萨特的历史哲学带有形而上学的色彩，但是他对历史的本体论式的思考是我们看待历史时所无法回避的。

第三，在后现代的视域中重思萨特。众所周知，《辩证理性批判》问世的时候也是存在主义在法国迅速被结构主义代替的时候，同时也是法国思想在二十世纪六十年代转折的开始。不管是作为推崇的对象还是作为批判的对象，萨特都像一个风向标一样屹立在二十世纪下半叶的法国。表面上看，后来的结构主义和后结构主义都是在对萨特主体性哲学的批判中“上位”的。但实际上，萨特哲学一方面坚守着主体的绝对性，但另一面他对“反思前的我思”的思考，对意识的纯粹虚无性的确认，也隐藏着对主体性的消解。因此，萨特可以被看作后现代思潮的先驱，或者说他的哲学构成了法国哲学从现代通向后现代的桥梁。此外，还有学者从后现代地理学家苏贾对萨特空间哲学的论述出发，探讨了《辩证理论批判》中蕴藏着的一种基于彻底的实践辩证法之上的空间本体论与社会空间理论及其理论价值，就此而言，存在主义马克思主义也是历史唯物主义空间理论的重要思想资源。

四、文本节选

Dialectical Monism

Everything we established in *The Problem of Method* follows from our fundamental agreement with historical materialism. But as long as we present this agreement merely as one option among others we shall have achieved nothing, and our conclusions will remain conjectural. I have proposed certain methodological rules; but they cannot be valid, in fact they cannot even be discussed, unless the materialist dialectic can be assumed to be true. It must be proved that a negation of a negation can be an affirmation, that conflicts—within a person or a group—are the motive force of History, that each moment of a series is *comprehensible* on the basis of the initial moment, though *irreducible* to it, that History continually effects totalisations of totalisations, and so on, before the details of an analytico-synthetic and regressive-progressive method can be grasped.

——Jean-Paul Sartre, *Critique of Dialectical Reason Volume One*, trans. Alan Sheridan-Smith, Verso, 2004, p. 15.

The Domain of Dialectical Reason

If dialectical Reason is to be possible as the career of all and the freedom of each, as experience and as necessity, if we are to display *both* its total translucidity (it is no more than ourself) and its untranscendable severity (it is the unity of everything that conditions us), if we are to ground it as the rationality of *praxis*, of totalisation, and of society's future, if we are then to *criticise* it as analytical Reason has been criticised, that is to say, if we are to determine its significance, then we must realise the situated experience of its apodicticity *through ourselves*. But let it not be imagined that this experience is comparable to the "intuitions" of the empiricists, or even to the kind of scientific experiments whose planning is long and laborious, but whose result can be observed instantaneously. The experience of the dialectic is itself dialectical: this means that it develops and organises itself on all levels. At the same time, it is the very experience of living, since to live is to act and be acted on, and since the dialectic is the rationality of *praxis*. It must be *regressive* because it will set out from lived experience (*le vécu*) in order gradually to discover all the structures of *praxis*. However, we must give notice that the investigation we are undertaking, though in itself historical, like any other undertaking, does not attempt to discover the movement of History, the evolution of labour or of the relations of production, or class conflicts. Its goal is simply to reveal and establish dialectical rationality, that is to say, the complex play of *praxis* and totalisation.

——Jean-Paul Sartre, *Critique of Dialectical Reason Volume One*, trans. Alan Sheridan-Smith, Verso, 2004, p. 39.

Totality and Totalisation

If, indeed, anything is to appear as the synthetic unity of the diverse, it must be a developing unification, that is to say, an activity. The synthetic unification of a habitat is not merely the labour which has produced it, but also the activity of inhabiting it; reduced to itself, it reverts to the multiplicity of inertia. Thus totalisation has the same statute as the totality, for, through the multiplicities, it continues that synthetic labour which makes each part an expression of the whole and which relates the whole to itself through the mediation of its parts. But it is a *developing* activity, which cannot cease without the multiplicity reverting to its original statute. This act delineates a practical field which, as the undifferentiated correlative of *praxis*, is the formal unity of the ensembles which are to be integrated; within this practical field, the activity attempts the most rigorous synthesis of the most differentiated multiplicity. Thus, by a double movement, multiplicity is multiplied to infinity, each part is set against all the others and against the whole which is in the process of being formed, while the totalising activity tightens all the bonds, making each differentiated element both its immediate expression and its mediation in relation to the other elements. On this basis, it is easy to establish the intelligibility of dialectical Reason; it is the very movement of totalisation. Thus, to take only one example, it is within the framework of totalisation that the negation of the negation becomes an affirmation. Within the practical field, the correlative of *praxis*, every determination is a negation, for *praxis*, in differentiating certain ensembles, excludes them from the group formed by all the others; and the developing unification appears *simultaneously* in the most differentiated products (indicating the direction of the movement), in those which are less differentiated (indicating continuities, resistances, traditions, a tighter, but more superficial, unity), and in the conflict between the two (which expresses the present state of the developing totalisation). The new negation, which, in determining the less differentiated ensembles, will raise them to the level of the others, is bound to eliminate the negation which set the ensembles in antagonism to each other. Thus it is only within a developing unification (which has already defined the limits of its field) that a determination can be said to be a negation and that the negation of a negation is necessarily an affirmation. If dialectical Reason exists, then, from the ontological point of view, it can only be a developing totalisation, occurring where the totalisation occurs, and, from the epistemological point of view, it can only be the accessibility of that totalisation to a knowledge which is itself, in principle, totalising in its procedures. But since totalising knowledge cannot be thought of as attaining ontological totalisation as a new totalisation of it, dialectical knowledge must itself be a moment of the totalisation, or, in other words, totalisation must include within itself its own reflexive retotalisation as an essential structure and as a totalising process within the process as a whole.

——Jean-Paul Sartre, *Critique of Dialectical Reason Volume One*, trans. Alan Sheridan-Smith, Verso, 2004, p.46 - 47.

The Plan of this Work

If our critical investigation actually yields positive results, we shall have established *a priori*—and not, as the Marxists *think* they have done, *a posteriori*—the heuristic value of the dialectical method when applied to the human sciences, and the necessity, with any fact, provided it is *human*, of reinserting it within the developing totalisation and understanding it on this basis. Thus the critical investigation will always present itself as a double investigation: *if* totalisation exists, the investigation will supply us with, *on the one hand* (and in the regressive order), all the *means* brought into play by the totalisation, that is to say the partial totalisations, detotalisations and retotalisations in their functions and abstract structures and, *on the other hand*, it must enable us to see how these forms dialectically generate one another in the full intelligibility of *praxis*. Moreover, in so far as our investigation proceeds from the simple to the complex, from the abstract to the concrete, from the constituting to the constituted, we must be able to settle, without reference to concrete history, the incarnations of individual *praxis*, the formal structural conditions of its alienation and the abstract circumstances which encourage the constitution of a common *praxis*. This leads to the principal divisions of this first volume: *the constituent dialectic* (as it grasps itself in its abstract translucidity in individual *praxis*) finds its limit within its own work and is transformed into an *anti-dialectic*. This anti-dialectic, or dialectic against the dialectic (dialectic *of passivity*), must reveal *series* to us as a type of human gathering and alienation as a mediated relation to the other and to the objects of labour in the element of seriality and as a serial mode of coexistence. At this level we will discover an equivalence between alienated *praxis* and worked inertia, and we shall call the domain of this equivalence the *practico-inert*. And we shall see the group emerge as a second type of dialectical gathering, in opposition both to the *practico-inert* and to impotence. But I shall distinguish, as will be seen, between the constituted dialectic and the constituent dialectic to the extent that the group has to constitute its common praxis through the individual *praxis* of the agents of whom it is composed. Therefore, if there is to be any such thing as totalisation, the intelligibility of constituted dialectical Reason (the intelligibility of common actions and of *praxis*-process) must be based on constituent dialectical reason (the abstract and individual *praxis* of man at work). Within the context of our critical investigation, we shall be able at this point to define the limits of dialectical intelligibility and, by the same token, the specific meaning of totalisation. It may then appear that realities such as class, for example, do not have a unique and homogeneous kind of being, but rather that they exist and they create themselves on all levels at once, through a more complex totalisation than we expected (since the anti-dialectic must be integrated and totalised, but not destroyed, by the constituted dialectic which, in turn, can totalise only on the basis of a constituent dialectic).

At this level, it will become evident that the regressive investigation has reached bedrock. In other words, we shall have grasped our individual depth in so far as, through the movement of groups and series, our roots reach down to fundamental materiality. Every moment of the regress will seem more complex and general than the isolated, superficial moment of our individual *praxis*, yet from another point of view, it remains completely abstract, that is, it is still no more than a *possibility*. Indeed, whether we consider the relations between group and series formally, in so far as each of these ensembles may produce the other, or whether we grasp the individual, within our investigation, as the practical ground of an ensemble and the ensemble as producing the individual in his reality as historical agent, this formal procedure will lead us to a dialectical circularity. This circularity exists; it is even (for Engels as much as for Hegel) characteristic of the dialectical order and of its intelligibility. But the fact remains that reversible circularity is in contradiction with the irreversibility of History, as it appears to investigation. Though it is true in the abstract that groups and series can indifferently produce each other, it is also true that historically a particular group, through its serialisation, produces a given serial ensemble (or conversely) and that, if a new group originated in the serial ensemble, then, whatever it might be, it would be irreducible to the serial ensemble. Moreover, such a regressive investigation, though it brings certain conflicts into play, only reveals our underlying structures and their intelligibility, without revealing the dialectical relations between groups and series, between different series or between different groups.

Thus, dialectical investigation in its regressive moment will reveal to us no more than the static conditions of the possibility of a totalisation, that is to say, of a history. We must therefore proceed to the opposite and complementary investigation: by progressively recomposing the historical process on the basis of the shifting and contradictory relations of the formations in question, we shall experience History; and this dialectical investigation should be able to show us whether the contradictions and social struggles, the communal and individual *praxis*, labour as producing tools, and tools as producing men and as regulator of human labour and human relations, etc., make up the unity of an intelligible (and thus directed) totalising movement. But above all, though these discoveries have to be made and consolidated in relation to these particular examples, our critical investigation aims to recompose the intelligibility of the historical movement within which the different ensembles are defined by their conflicts. On the basis of synchronic structures and their contradictions, it seeks the diachronic intelligibility of historical transformations, the order of their conditionings and the intelligible reason for the irreversibility of History, that is to say, for its direction. This synthetic progression, though merely formal, must fulfil several functions: by recomposing instances in terms of process, it must lead us, if not to the absolute concrete, which can only be individual (*this* event at *this* date of *this* history), at least to the absolute system of conditions for applying the determination "*concrete* fact" to the fact of *one* history.

In this sense it could be said that the aim of the critical investigation is to establish a structural and historical anthropology, that the regressive moment of the investigation is the basis of the intelligibility of sociological Knowledge (without prejudging any of the individual components of this Knowledge), and that the progressive moment must be the basis of the intelligibility of historical Knowledge (without prejudging the real individual unfolding of the totalised facts). Naturally, the progression will deal with the same structures as those brought to light by regressive investigation. ...

——Jean-Paul Sartre, *Critique of Dialectical Reason Volume One*, trans. Alan Sheridan-Smith, Verso, 2004, p. 66 - 69.

五、观点解读

1. 应当用存在主义来“补充”马克思主义

按照萨特自己的说法，他的理论目标是建构一种既是历史的又是结构的人学，要实现这一宏旨，则必须用他的存在主义来“补充”马克思主义。正是基于萨特对马克思主义和存在主义关系的明确探讨，许多学者将以萨特晚期思想为代表的马克思主义理论称之为“存在主义的马克思主义”。众所周知，萨特是著名的存在主义哲学家，探讨的是存在论意义上个人的生存和意识结构的问题，那么他是如何接受马克思主义的呢？萨特自我分析道，促使其接受马克思思想的原因在于受到马克思主义的现实——一个“巨大的阴郁的团体”即工人阶级存在的触动。萨特首先强调，马克思主义是我们时代不可超越的哲学，那些所谓对马克思主义的“超越”，最多不过是对马克思思想的“重新发现”而已，甚至还达不到马克思的水准。黑格尔承认总体性和辩证法，克尔凯郭尔则强调人的存在的特殊性，他们的思想在萨特看来各自既有合理性又存在弊端，而只有马克思真正超越了他们，因为马克思主义既“肯定了人的存在的特殊性”，又“在其客观的现实性中掌握了具体的人”。同时，萨特无条件地承认历史唯物主义的这一前提，即物质生活的生产方式决定着社会生活、政治生活以及一般精神生活的过程，只有在此基础上，我们才能真正地理解历史和现实。既然如此，存在主义为什么还能保持它的独立性呢？萨特说这是因为马克思主义哲学在其发展的过程中僵化、停滞了，它已经堕落为“一种唯意志主义的唯心主义”。因为马克思主义哲学的理论和实践之间已经相互脱离了，“实践变成一种无原则的经验主义，而理论则变成一种纯粹的和僵硬的知识”。“当代的”马克思主义既放弃了对“人的真理”的追寻，也放弃了对具体经验的研究。在萨特看来，存在主义是“接近现实的唯一的具体道路”，因此它可以成为马克思主义中的一块“飞地”，以便可以具体地研究现实的人和经验，从而创造一种兼具历史性和生成性的人学。

2. 将前进—逆溯法作为历史的结构的人学的方法论

萨特不满于传统马克思主义的方法论，并从正面提出了自己的方法论逻辑，即前进-逆溯的方法。萨特承认马克思的这一理论断言：人们在一定的环境条件之中创造着自己的历史。但是教条的马克思主义将这一原理僵化为一种机械的历史决定论，而个人则被惰性化为“一个被动的产物，是一堆条件反射的总和”，萨特对这两者一一驳斥。首先，萨特从个人与历史的关系的角度批判了历史决定论，他认为历史绝不是一个机械的、拥有固定轨道的必然性过程，不可还原的个人实践才是历史创造的真正原动；当然，历史也绝不是主体可以随意加以控制的对象，历史常常具有不透明的特征，进行具体实践的个人“在整个和客观的结果中认不出他们的行动的意义”。其次，萨特也反对将人看作完全被动的“物”，人的存在论的规定性在于，他是一种可以通过“谋划”来实现对既定条件超越的存在，这可以说是萨特存在主义哲学借以补充马克思主义的根基所在。因而辩证法和历史研究关注的对象就不仅仅是历史总体，也应该同时关注构成历史总体的个人及其实践；不能只是关注宏观的社会结构，而忽视个人的存在；不能只是将个人消融在社会结构之中，而忽视个人的实践对于历史的总体化进程的作用；不能只是单向度地从社会历史总体去涵盖个人，而应该双向度地考察社会历史总体化和个人实践之间的辩证关系。这种双向度的研究方法就是前进—逆溯法。具体说来，前进法强调个人在一定的社会历史结构中的定位，它将人或事件放到历史的总体之中去考察并以此去规定其意义；而逆溯法则是对个人生存的微观研究，它探求具体的生存条件、工具条件以及它们与个人的具体谋划相互结合作用的方式。从整体来看,前进—逆溯法就是以一种总体化的要求来对个人、群体和历史现象进行差别性的研究。只有在前进法与逆溯法之间不断地“双向往复”中,我们才得以探究真实的而非抽象的历史,才能使我们理解的历史总体化进程更加丰富和具体。

3. 用批判的辩证法取代教条的辩证法

萨特首先是通过对实证理性和分析理性的批判来引出辩证理性的。在萨特眼中,实证理性和分析理性都存在一定的弊端,它们常常以一种先验的、构成性的理性统一性来面对世界,从而不能理解这种“统一性”其实依赖于人类现实的实践活动。只有辩证理性才能真正合理地理解历史,它认识到辩证法既是一种方法,又是一种客体中的运动。黑格尔尽管第一次创立了辩证理性及其逻辑结构,但这一鲜活的历史辩证法被窒息在绝对精神复归自身的运动之中;只有马克思才真正发现了一种既是生成的、又是现成的辩证法。然而,现代的马克思主义堕落成为一种外在性的、超验的辩证唯物主义,无论是自然对象还是人类社会事实都成了一种僵死了的客体。在此,恩格斯的自然辩证法成了萨特口诛笔伐的首要对象,自然辩证法将人作为“外来的附加成分”从自然规律中排除掉了,自然界的运动的本质被恩格斯抽象为著名的三大规律。在斯大林主义那里,辩证法的这一客观规律和决定论特征不仅存在于自然界中,还延伸到社会和历史之中。辩证法已经不再关心自己的时代,也不再更新自己的理论议题,而是宣告自己已经拥有了全部真理,一切新生的事件、行动和经验只不过进一步证实了辩证唯物主义的抽象图式,真实的历史进程和人的具体实践不过是必然规律的表征。在萨特看来,这种脱离了实践的“客观认识”是一种“伪客观”,离开了人和具体经验的辩证法实则是一种外在的、教条的辩证法。区别于试图囊括一切的教条的辩证法,萨特认为有必要重新寻求一种批判的辩证法。这种辩证法首先明确意识到自身的界限:(1) 辩证法不能脱离物性的周围世界,它必须“在马克思主义的真实物质世界里完成”,主体“和物质世界以及和他人的外在性关系”始终在唯一的外在性世界中在场;(2) 辩证法不能超越真实的、偶然的经验,它总是存在于“直接的、日常的经验”中;(3) 辩证法始终不能脱离具体的主体而存在,它总是在沉思理性或实践活动的内在性中显现自身。辩证法自身处于一种不断的总体化运动之中,我们既不能通过对事物现象的归纳总结出这种辩证法，也无法在纯粹意识之中去发现它，因为它存在于现实的社会历史生活之中。萨特认为存在着两种相互缠绕着的辩证法：一方面，批判的辩证法总是处于一定的先在的条件之中，具有必然性因素，可以称之为"现成的辩证法"；另一方面，还存在着一种"生成的辩证法"，个体或群体的具体的"总体化"现实地建构着历史本身。因此，辩证法并不去外在地规定一切具体的事物和经验，相反，它既包含在任何经验之中，又超越了一切具体的经验。[①] 辩证理性不是固定不变的，它作为实践的一个契机在实践中显示自身，内在地包含着对自身的批判和超越。

4. 从一种实存主义的实践论出发重构辩证法

萨特主张，社会历史生活建基于特定历史条件下的人的实践活动之上，特定条件下的人的具体实践活动构成了整个社会历史的源动力，是社会历史得以生产和再生产的基础。一切现实中实存的社会关系、社会结构等，也都是由处于这些关系和结构中的人的实践活动（不管是自觉的、无意识的还是被迫的）所维系的。既然辩证法无法抽离具体的社会历史而存在，而具体社会历史的演进又是以人的实践活动为源动力，那么辩证法就和实践密切相关。一方面，对社会历史存在的理解，其实质就是特殊的实践活动，一种带有认知和解释功能的实践；另一方面，实践的结构从根本上决定了辩证法的特性。萨特所理解的实践是一种目的性的谋划，这一谋划正是人类的创造性所在。借助于谋划，主体的实践活动得以进行：主体与它内在地否定或总体化了的客观性发生关联，将自己谋划的内在性外化为一种被客观化了的主观性，而此前的客观性则借助于主体的实践活动而演变为一种包含了主观性的新的客观实在。因此，计划、主观、实践等等就作为客观性与客观性之间的环节而存在。那么实践和谋划是如何发生的呢？萨特认为，这种谋划表现为依照某个面向未来的目标对过去以及当下处境的总体把握，从而确定主体的行动计划。由此，实践本身的逆溯和前进性质得以表现出来。按照萨特的理解，实践的逆溯性表现为在行动中总是包含着对过去的物质性条件的回溯，表现为主体能够将我们当下的生活，将我自己、我身边的人以及我的整个环境纳入一种客观进行着的综合性的统一之中。实践的前进

① 让-保罗·萨特：《辩证理性批判（上）》，林骧华等译，安徽文艺出版社 1998 年版，168 页。

性则表现为，人是有目的的存在，是始终朝向未来的可能性的存在，人始终走在自己的前面来对当下的自己和世界进行规定、统筹和超越。萨特对实践的实存主义解释直接决定了其对辩证法的看法：没有必要将辩证法神秘化，从根本上说它就是主体在实践过程中对于周围世界和社会历史的辩证理解，它逆溯性地对当下处境和状况加以统一性的认知，而前进性地根据现实条件和主体目标而识别并生成历史的可能未来。而从时间性的角度来说，实践本身是一个创造性的时间化过程，在时间化的实践活动中，人与周围世界以及人与人之间的关系得以编织和演化，历史也得以展开。在此意义上，萨特强调辩证法始终是共时性和历时性的统一，始终努力在共时性的复杂结构中寻求一个历史性的方向。用萨特自己的说法，辩证法应当"以共时性结构及其矛盾为基础，寻找对历史变化的历时性可理解性"，"寻找它的方向"①。

六、进一步阅读指南

1. [法]让-保罗・萨特：《辩证理性批判》，林骧华等译，安徽文艺出版社 1998 年版。

2. [法]雷蒙・阿隆：《想象的马克思主义》，姜志辉译，上海世纪出版集团 2007 年版。

3. [美]弗雷德里克・詹姆逊：《马克思主义与形式》，钱佼汝，李自修译，百花洲文艺出版社 1997 年版。

4. [美]A.丹图：《萨特》，安延明译，工人出版社 1986 年版。

5. [法]贝尔纳・亨利・列维：《萨特的世纪——哲学研究》，闫素伟译，商务印书馆 2005 年版。

6. 张一兵：《文本的深度耕犁(第一卷)》第 5 章，中国人民大学出版社 2004 年版。

7. 王时中：《实存与共在：萨特历史辩证法》，中国社会科学出版社 2007

① 让-保罗・萨特：《辩证理性批判(上)》，林骧华等译，安徽文艺出版社 1998 年版，第 203 页，译文有所改动。See Jean-Paul Sartre, *Critique of Dialectical Reason*, *Volume One*, trans. Alan Sheridan-Smith, Verso, 2004, p. 68.

年版。

8. 汪帮琼:《萨特本体论思想研究》,学林出版社 2006 年版。

9. 刘怀玉、王赛:《改革开放新时期存在主义马克思主义在中国学术界的理论旅行——以萨特为例》,《理论探讨》2019 年第 5 期。

10. Jean-Paul Sartre, *Search for a Method*, Alfred A. Knopf, 1963.

11. Jean-Paul Sartre, *Critique of Dialectical Reason*, *Volume One*: *Theory of Practical Ensembles*, trans. Alan Sheridan-Smith, Verso, 2004.

12. Jean-Paul Sartre, *Critique of Dialectical Reason*, *Volume Two* (*unfinished*): *The Intelligibility of History*, trans. Quintin Hoare, Verso, 1991.

13. Joseph S. Catalano, *A Commentary on Jean-Paul Satre's Critique of Dialectical Reason Volume One*, *Theory of Practical Ensembles*, The University of Chicago Press, 1986.

14. Mark Poster, *Existential Marxism in Postwar France*: *From Sartre to Althusser*, Princeton University Press, 1975.

七、问题与思考

1. 萨特为什么想要用存在主义来“补充”马克思主义?

2. 在萨特眼中,马克思主义的方法论存在着哪些缺陷?他是如何改造马克思主义的方法论的?

3. 萨特是如何从他的实存主义的实践论出发去重构唯物主义辩证法的?

4. 如何理解萨特的异化概念和马克思的异化概念之间的联系和差别?

第十一章　新实证主义马克思主义的奠基与发展——《卢梭和马克思》和《马克思主义和黑格尔》选读

教学目的与要求

重点把握平等主义自由的内涵,准确理解德拉-沃尔佩关于马克思和卢梭关系的阐述;全面评估德拉-沃尔佩对马克思哲学革命实质的理解,掌握马克思主义是"道德领域中的伽利略主义"的科学内涵;准确理解"物质辩证法"的含义,把握科莱蒂关于辩证唯物主义与黑格尔哲学关系的论述;重点掌握社会生产关系理论,客观评估科莱蒂对马克思哲学革命的诠释。

一、历史背景

(一) 作者介绍

1895 年,加尔维诺·德拉-沃尔佩(Galvano Della-Volpe)出生于意大利波伦亚附近的伊莫拉,1920 年毕业于波伦亚大学,先在本地的一所高级中学教历史和哲学,1929 年回到波伦亚大学任现代哲学史讲师,经过几轮竞争,于 1938 年获得了墨西拿大学哲学史教授的职位。总体来看,德拉-沃尔佩转向马克思主义经历了一个相当漫长的过程。在 1920 年代,他主要研究金蒂雷和克罗齐,力图将二者的观点调和起来,1930 年代转向休谟研究,1940 年初又开始研究卢梭,并成为一名地道的卢梭主义者。也是在后者的影响下，德拉-沃尔佩对马克思的政治和哲学思想产生了浓厚兴趣，并于1944年在西西里参加了意大利共产党，开始着手翻译马克思的早期著作《黑格尔法哲学批判》和《1844年经济学哲学手稿》，并撰写了《关于人类解放的马克思主义理论》(1945)、《共产主义的自由》(1946)和《关于实证人道主义的理论》(1947)等论文，阐述了马克思这两部著作的基本思想。正是在这时，德拉-沃尔佩才真正成为一名马克思主义者。1950年，他出版了《作为实证科学的逻辑学》一书，率先开启了将实证主义与马克思主义嫁接起来的理论先河，为后来整个学派的发展奠定了理论基础。在这一著作中，他从哲学史上寻找到一系列的参照系：亚里士多德、伽利略、逻辑实证主义。用亚里士多德的同一律来诠释马克思的唯物主义，以此来反对黑格尔的辩证矛盾观，把马克思的唯物主义打扮成亚里士多德同一律的变种；用伽利略的实验方法来诠释马克思的实践概念，把马克思的历史唯物主义解释为伽利略的"实验实践模式"，把马克思装扮为伽利略的嫡系传人；用逻辑实证主义的实证原则来论证马克思哲学的"科学性"，由此建构了一种完全不同于黑格尔先验逻辑学的实证科学。1957年，德拉-沃尔佩出版了《卢梭和马克思》，这是他多年来关于卢梭和马克思思想研究的一次汇总，也是他最具影响力的一部作品。1960年，德拉-沃尔佩出版了《趣味批判》，对历史唯物主义美学做了深入、系统的探讨，并提出了一套研究诗歌和艺术的社会逻辑方法。由于德拉-沃尔佩与意共领导人存在重要分歧，1962年，意共内部发生了一场理论争论，德拉-沃尔佩受到了全方位的批判，《社会》杂志也被解散。为了反驳意共对自己的批判，他先后写下了《论辩证法》(1962)、《历史辩证法的关键》(1964)、《现时代的辩证法》(1965)等论文，但在反驳的过程中，他也意识到了自己的理论缺陷，并向正统的辩证唯物主义做出了让步和妥协，最明显的例证就是，在出版《作为实证科学的逻辑学》的第3版时，他将书名改成了《作为历史科学的逻辑学》。1965年，德拉-沃尔佩从墨西拿大学退休，1967年出版了《当代思想批判》，对阿尔都塞的结构主义马克思主义提出了严厉批判。1968年，德拉-沃尔佩在罗马去世。

1924年，卢西奥·科莱蒂(Lucio Colletti)出生于意大利罗马，父亲是一位银行官员。他早年深受克罗齐和金蒂雷唯心主义思想的影响，是一位地道的唯心主义者。1949年，科莱蒂取得了自己的博士学位，主要内容就是研究克罗齐的逻辑学。由于深受列宁《唯物主义和经验批判主义》的影响，科莱蒂转向马克思主义，并于1950年加入意大利共产党，1957年在意共创办的《社会》杂志中担任编辑工作，从而受到他的老师德拉-沃尔佩的较大影响。1958年起，科莱蒂先后担任罗马大学讲师、高级讲师和教授的职务，主要从事哲学理论的教学和研究工作。1962年，《社会》杂志被解散，在此之后，科莱蒂与意共领导人的分歧进一步加剧。1964年，他退出意大利共产党，潜心从事理论研究。从60年代后期起，科莱蒂的思想有了一定的变化，开始反思德拉-沃尔佩的缺陷，并从理论上进一步修正和完善了他的学说。这些新思考在下述著作和论文中都得到了集中体现：《马克思主义和黑格尔》(1969)、《意识形态和社会》(1969)(1972年英文版译为《从卢梭到列宁》)、《一篇政治和哲学的访谈录》(1974)、《矛盾和对立：马克思主义和辩证法》(1975)、《〈卡尔·马克思早期著作〉导言》(1975)、《政治哲学札记》(1975)等。具体而言，这种继承和发展主要表现在五个方面：(1) 在对待辩证唯物主义的态度上，科莱蒂更加激进。他认为，所有的辩证唯物主义都只不过是黑格尔"物质辩证法"的内在同谋，是一种没有认识到自身性质的唯心主义的神学。(2) 在唯物主义认识论上，他利用康德的"真正对立"理论，重新诠释了无矛盾原理，提出了思维与存在的异质性原则，把后者当作所有唯物主义认识论和科学认识论的基本纲领。(3) 德拉-沃尔佩整个哲学更多地停留在认识论—方法论之中，而科莱蒂则突破了他老师的局限，充分挖掘了马克思生产关系理论的科学内涵，弥补了德拉-沃尔佩的不足之处。(4) 德拉-沃尔佩认为，马克思始终是沿着亚里士多德的无矛盾原理和伽利略的实验方法前进的，黑格尔的辩证矛盾观在马克思那里毫无价值。但科莱蒂通过对马克思后期经济学著作的研究，认识到了德拉-沃尔佩的错误之处，从中发掘了辩证矛盾的科学意义，揭示了马克思政治经济学批判的科学内涵，恢复了马克思哲学的批判性。(5) 继承了德拉-沃尔佩关于马克思与卢梭政治哲学关系的分析，进一步深化了对这一问题的研究。1980年，科莱蒂出版了《意识形态的终结》一书。在这一著作中，他的立场发生了根本变化，开始公开批判马克思主义，倒向了传统自由主义的怀抱。2001年，科莱蒂因心脏病逝世。

(二) 时代背景

1. 苏共二十大和匈牙利事件

1956年,苏联共产党第二十次代表大会在莫斯科克里姆林宫召开。在非正式会议上,时任苏共中央第一书记的赫鲁晓夫做了题为《关于个人崇拜及其后果》的报告,也就是通常所说的“秘密报告”。在这份报告中,赫鲁晓夫尖锐批判了对斯大林的个人崇拜,并对斯大林的执政时期进行了全盘否定。这份报告引起了巨大的震动,这次大会也成为苏共党史和国际共产主义运动史上的一次重大历史事件。同年十月,“匈牙利事件”爆发。受苏共二十大影响,匈牙利劳动人民党内外要求批判领导人拉科西·马加什的情绪日益强烈。匈牙利的学生和知识分子走上街头,试图以游行的方式呼吁摆脱苏联控制和走符合匈牙利特点的社会主义道路。随后事态逐渐失去控制,发生了流血事件。苏联先后两次派遣军队进入布达佩斯进行军事活动,最终平息骚乱。这两起事件都严重损害了苏联共产党的信誉和威望,在欧洲各个国家的共产党及其他工人运动组织中造成了极大的破坏性影响。

2. 意大利共产党的政治危机

意大利共产党是欧洲的一个重要的左翼政党,成立于1921年,葛兰西曾经担任总书记,在反对墨索里尼法西斯政权的过程中获得了意大利人民的支持。苏共二十大的召开和匈牙利事件的爆发,使得各国共产党陷入一种混乱,而在意大利共产党内部则演变为党内的理论、政治和信仰危机。如科莱蒂所说,对大部分意共知识分子而言,赫鲁晓夫对斯大林的谴责以及匈牙利事件,导致了一场理论和政治的大灾难。在政治层面,曾一度成为本国最大政党的意大利共产党元气大伤,组织力量和群众影响力被极大削弱。在理论层面,许多意共知识分子出现了疏离和脱离政治的趋向,选择退出意大利共产党。留在党内的少数知识分子为了使意大利共产党从这场危机中走出来,主张以一种全新的方式来阅读马克思的著作,建构一种既不同于苏俄辩证唯物主义也不同于西方马克思主义的马克思哲学,以重塑意大利共产党的理论信仰。

(三) 思想背景

1. 新实证主义马克思主义

要理解德拉-沃尔佩的《卢梭和马克思》以及科莱蒂的《马克思主义和黑格尔》,我们首先要了解什么是新实证主义马克思主义。新实证主义马克思主义学派是西方马克思主义的一个重要分支,在地域上主要局限于意大利。它大致兴起于二十世纪五十年代,衰落于 1965 年,创始人是德拉-沃尔佩,主要成员包括科莱蒂(哲学和方法论)、J. 彼特拉奈拉(政治经济学)、马里奥·罗西(哲学史)、V.切罗尼(法哲学)、梅尔格尔(哲学史)、马佐内(哲学史)、穆索利诺(美学)等等,他们基本上都是德拉-沃尔佩的学生,因此,这一流派也被称为德拉-沃尔佩学派。但严格说来,它还算不上是一个真正的学术流派,如 R.A.戈尔曼所说:"所谓德拉-沃尔佩学派实际上仅仅是几个注重和发展德拉-沃尔佩思想的个人,而并不是一个有组织的集团。"①

1956 年,苏共二十大和匈牙利事件的爆发引起了意大利共产党内部的理论和政治危机。在这种特定背景,德拉-沃尔佩等人的学说迎合了当时的政治需要,产生了重大影响,成为党内众多知识分子的救命稻草,逐渐弥补了他们心灵上的空缺,使他们从信仰危机中走了出来。但是,到了二十世纪六十年代初期,意大利共产党感觉到,他们"已经成功地从 1956 年的骚乱中恢复了过来,已经赢得了这场政治斗争的胜利,并且也已经同苏联的辩证唯物主义和斯大林主义正统划清了界限"②,在理论上也日趋成熟。在此情况下,意共于 1962 年召开了一次党内讨论,最终结果是,这一学派被定性为党内的"分裂主义者",而他们的理论中心即《社会》杂志也被宣告解散,于是,新实证主义马克思主义逐渐丧失了在党内的优先权,慢慢地衰落了。1964 年,科莱蒂退出意大利共产党,1965 年德拉-沃尔佩退休,这一学派最终名存实亡。

---

① [美]罗伯特·戈尔曼主编:《"新马克思主义"传记辞典》,赵培杰等译,重庆出版社 1990 年版,第 220 页。

② John Fraser, *An Introduction to the Thought of Galvano della Volpe*, Lawrence and Wishart, 1977, p. 26.

2. 清除马克思主义中的黑格尔主义要素

在新实证主义马克思主义看来，黑格尔哲学代表了整个形而上学的传统，因此，要想维护马克思主义的科学性，就必须要宣称马克思与黑格尔的彻底决裂，从马克思主义中彻底清除掉一切黑格尔的杂质。立足于此，德拉-沃尔佩等人对苏俄辩证唯物主义和以卢卡奇为代表的西方马克思主义做出了尖锐批判。一方面，他们指出，以普列汉诺夫、列宁为代表的辩证唯物主义者虽然力图强调马克思哲学与黑格尔哲学之间的本质差异，突出马克思哲学的革命意义，但由于他们过分强调马克思与黑格尔之间的继承关系，这就使他们所有的努力都付诸东流，结果，所有苏俄马克思主义者都引以为自豪的"辩证唯物主义"实际上只不过是黑格尔唯心主义的一种变种。另一方面，德拉-沃尔佩和科莱蒂又指出，卢卡奇的研究完全是建立在黑格尔思辨的主—客体同一之上的，这就把马克思主义重新拉回到了纯粹哲学的镜像之中，进而沦为一种抽象的思辨的理性推演。在这里，马克思成为黑格尔的一个幻象。因此，与其说辩证唯物主义与西方马克思主义存在本质差异，还不如它们是同一个黑格尔传统的两极。于是，他们认为，为了真正理解马克思思想的真谛，就必须要正本清源，清除掉苏俄辩证唯物主义以及西方马克思主义从黑格尔思想中拿过来并附加给马克思的东西。于是他们倡导一种新的解释模式，提出"第三条道路"，彻底否认马克思与黑格尔之间的任何继承关系，反对任何黑格尔主义化的马克思主义。

3. 反对抽象的人本主义

第二次世界大战之前，人本主义马克思主义思潮几乎占据了西方马克思主义的全部舞台，而新实证主义马克思主义就是在反对这种人本主义解读模式的背景下产生的，因此，它也构成了西方马克思主义从人本主义向科学主义转变的重要环节，并与以阿尔都塞为代表的结构主义马克思主义一起，共同构成了科学主义马克思主义的两条路径。但与阿尔都塞不同，新实证主义马克思主义没有那么彻底，他们并不像后者那样力图否定一切人本主义，而只是反对那种以抽象的、形而上学的方法来追寻人道主义的做法。新实证主义马克思主义认为，只要从经验方法来论证人本主义，那么这种人本主义就不再是思辨的、抽象的形而上学了，而是转变为一种实证的、科学的人本主义了。

二、篇章结构

《卢梭和马克思》是德拉-沃尔佩的一部论文集，首次出版于1957年，截至1964年，前前后后共出版了四次，在意大利理论界产生了广泛而又持久的影响。但由于版本不同，收录的文章也存在较大差异。1957年首次出版时，主要包括三篇论文：《对卢梭的抽象的人的批判》(1957)、《现代民主制度发展中的平等主义自由问题，或活着的卢梭》(1954)和《社会主义和自由》(1956)；并附有一份论马克思1843年到1859年的方法论著作的材料，题目是《为一种关于经济学和道德科学的一般唯物主义方法论辩护》，包括三篇论文：《关于1843年和1844年的哲学遗著》(1955)、《关于〈哲学的贫困〉(1847)》(1956)、《关于〈政治经济学批判〉导言(1857)和〈政治经济学批判〉序言(1859)》(1957)。1962年出版第三版时，增加了《说明》(1961)一文。1964年出版第四版时，又增加了四个附录：《再论社会主义的合法性》(1964)、《孟德斯鸠和伏尔泰的博爱主义与卢梭博爱主义之比较》(1962)、《马克思主义对卢梭的批判》(1963)、《我们和宪法》(1962)。除此之外，意大利文版还收录了其他五篇论文，分别是《关于伦理学的五个片断》《评逻辑实证主义》《亚里士多德》《没有唯心主义的辩证法》和《方法概论》。1979年，这一著作被译成英文出版，依据的稿本是1964年的第四版。不过，在翻译过程中，译者删除了后面的五篇论文。

从内容上看，这部著作可以分为两大部分：一是政治论文，主要阐述自由、民主、平等、法和人道主义等问题，其主旨是阐述卢梭与马克思政治哲学思想的内在联系及其本质差异，突显卢梭自由观在当代社会生活中的重大现实意义。具体而言：《对卢梭的抽象的人的批判》从马克思的商品生产和价值理论出发，系统评述了洛克的劳动权利理论、康德的道德律令学说和卢梭的社会契约论的理论贡献与不足之处。德拉-沃尔佩指出，与洛克、康德的自由主义理论不同，卢梭在《论人类不平等的起源和基础》中提出了一种全新的理论，即平等主义的自由学说，并力图在《社会契约论》中探讨实现这种自由的方式，这是卢梭在政治哲学上的一个重要贡献。然而，由于方法论的不彻底性，导致他并没有真正解决这一问题，最终像洛克和康德一样，陷入基督教的抽象人崇拜之中。在他看来，要真正解决这一问题，就必须摆脱抽象的或唯意志论的理性主义方法，采用马克思列宁主义的科学方法即具体的或唯物主义的理性主义方法。《现代民主制度发展中的平等主义自由问题；或活着的卢梭》和《社会主义和自由》两篇论文，重点阐述了卢梭提出来的平等主义自由的科学内涵及其当代意义。德拉-沃尔佩指出，现代自由和民主具有两个灵魂：一是公民自由，这是由议会民主制度建立的，并由洛克、孟德斯鸠、洪堡、康德和贡斯当系统论述的自由主义的自由；一是平等主义的自由，它是由社会主义民主制度确立的，在理论上首先由卢梭提出，后被马克思、恩格斯、列宁继承下来并系统阐发。在他看来，公民自由实际上就是资产阶级的自由，它的根本目的是保护私有财产；而平等主义的自由则意味着，每个人都有权利要求他的个人能力得到社会的承认，这是一种社会正义，即更大更有效的、大多数人的自由。德拉-沃尔佩指出，卢梭虽然最先提出了这一理论，但由于方法的不彻底性，因而未能真正解决这一问题。而马克思、恩格斯和列宁则从历史唯物主义和阶级斗争入手，克服了卢梭的缺陷，实现了对这一问题的全面继承和发展。特别是随着俄国十月革命的胜利，这一学说逐渐从一种理论走向实践，开创了将公民自由与平等主义自由结合起来的新局面。《说明》和四篇附录分别从不同的角度，进一步补充、概括和总结了前面提出的论点。

第二部分是哲学论文，主要包括三篇论文，重点探讨了马克思方法论革命的实质及其发展过程，系统诠释了马克思的唯物辩证法与黑格尔唯心辩证法的根本差异。针对这一问题，在 1950 年的《作为实证科学的逻辑学》中，德拉-沃尔佩就做出了细致分析。在那里，他首先从亚里士多德和伽利略入手，引出无矛盾原理和实验方法，系统论述了它们的唯物主义意义；然后，通过对马克思唯物辩证法的实证诠释："特殊对象的特殊逻辑"就是唯物主义的无矛盾原理，唯物辩证法是一种"哲学—历史的或社会学—唯物主义"，特别是将"抽象上升到具体"的方法解释为"具体—抽象—具体"的方法论循环，实现了马克思的哲学方法与伽利略实验方法的同质性证明，系统论证了马克思主义作为"道德领域中的伽利略主义"的革命意义；最后，他把马克思和伽利略的方法放大为所有知识、科学（自然科学和社会科学）所共有的唯一方法，并以此为基础，试图将人类史与自然史统一起来，建构一种大写的历史科学。从思想发展脉络来看，这三篇论文分别是对这一著作的补充和完善，在总体思路和观点上，没有什么太大变化。

科莱蒂的《马克思主义和黑格尔》出版于1969年，1973年被译成英文，在西方学术界产生了重要反响。单纯从书名来看，这一著作似乎与柯尔施的《马克思主义和哲学》一样，要探讨马克思主义哲学史上的一个核心问题，即马克思主义和黑格尔之间的关系问题。然而，不同的是，他们的结论却是相反的：通过对马克思主义发展史的细致考察，柯尔施充分肯定了马克思主义与黑格尔之间的批判继承关系；但由于深受德拉-沃尔佩的影响，科莱蒂则走向了另一面，彻底否定二者之间的继承关系，并在《马克思主义和黑格尔》中做出了全面、系统的分析。

从篇章结构来看，这部著作共包括十二章。

第一章题为《黑格尔和“物质辩证法”》，着重分析了黑格尔唯心辩证法的内在本质。科莱蒂指出，黑格尔的中心主题就是论证哲学与唯心主义的内在同一性。为了做到这一点，黑格尔彻底抛弃了唯物主义和科学思维的理智原则，发明了一套将有限转为无限的思辨方法。科莱蒂将其命名为“物质辩证法”，并认为它构成了黑格尔整个哲学的方法论基础，也是他唯心主义性质的集中体现。然而，在科莱蒂看来，更加可悲的是，后来所有的辩证唯物主义者都没认识到这种辩证法的唯心主义性质，反而将它当作高级唯物主义和新科学的重要标志，不能不说是一种极大的扭曲。也是在此基础上，科莱蒂得出结论说，就其实质而言，辩证唯物主义所建构出来的唯物辩证法，只不过是黑格尔物质辩证法的翻转，二者在本质上是内在同构的。

第二章是《黑格尔和斯宾诺莎》，旨在通过二者的比较分析，进一步阐述黑格尔物质辩证法的本质。科莱蒂指出，在黑格尔看来，斯宾诺莎对绝对的论证在形式上是完善的，但他的最大缺陷在于没有引入否定和矛盾性，致使绝对成为一个脱离有限而单独存在的孤立体，陷入一种独断论之中，没有把唯心主义贯彻到底。也是在斯宾诺莎停止的地方，黑格尔引入了物质辩证法，打破了有限与无限的绝对界限，实现了存在与思维、实体与主体的辩证统一，开创了一种全新的形而上学。

第三章《辩证唯物主义和黑格尔》，意在从谱系学入手，系统揭示辩证唯物主义对黑格尔哲学误读的起源。科莱蒂指出，正是恩格斯把黑格尔的“物质辩证法”引入到唯物主义之中，创立了辩证唯物主义，因此，恩格斯才是这种误读的罪魁祸首，要为近一个世纪的误读负全责。在他看来，恩格斯在以下两个方面误读了黑格尔：一方面，他没有理解黑格尔"物质辩证法"的本意，错误地把科学方法（无矛盾原理）判定为形而上学，把黑格尔的"物质辩证法"当作"新科学"的标准；另一方面，他误解了黑格尔哲学的性质，机械地将其划分为革命的方法与保守的体系，成了贻害后世的原始毒瘤。而后来的所有辩证唯物主义者，居然没有一个认识到恩格斯的错误，反而把它当作绝对真理，一味地遵从下去。

第四章题为《黑格尔和"反映论"》。科莱蒂强调到，黑格尔哲学在本质上完全是一种唯心主义，而他的方法恰恰是与后者内在一致的。然而，在后来的发展中，黑格尔的哲学性质被二元化了，成为唯心主义—唯物主义的矛盾统一体。接下来，科莱蒂分别以卢波里尼、卢卡奇、列宁、科耶夫、马尔库塞为例，详细论证了这一问题。

第五章《黑格尔和怀疑主义》，旨在考察黑格尔对两种怀疑主义的批判与超越，进一步论证黑格尔反理智的立场。科莱蒂指出，在哲学史上，存在两种怀疑主义：一是以皮浪为代表的古代怀疑主义，一是以休谟为代表的现代怀疑主义。对于前者，黑格尔给予高度肯定，认为它开创了一种消除有限物质的辩证法，将哲学或唯心主义定义为一种反理智的形而上学；然而，它的缺陷在于没有把对有限的否定表述为一种肯定过程，也就是说，没有把这种否定逻辑转化为一种本体论，把实体转化为主体本身。对于后者，黑格尔完全持一种拒斥态度，认为它重新陷入科学、唯物主义和经验主义的理智传统之中，是彻底反哲学的。也是在此基础上，科莱蒂重申了黑格尔哲学的反理智、反科学的本性。

第六章《对物质的怀疑主义和对理性的怀疑主义》，旨在通过对黑格尔与康德的比较分析，重新诠释划分唯心主义和唯物主义的标准。科莱蒂指出，黑格尔的"物质辩证法"实际上是建立在"思维与存在的同质性"之上的。在他这里，思维与存在的关系其实就是思维与自身的关系，它们不仅是同一的，更是同质的。对此，科莱蒂愤怒地评价道，思维与存在的同一，只是表示思维与自身的同一，这种同一性戕害了存在外在于思维的特征，在本质上，只不过是唯心主义所虚构出来的幻象，是一种泯灭唯物主义的神学。因此，在科莱蒂看来，要恢复批判的唯物主义，最根本的要义就是打破思维与存在的同质霸权，恢复"唯物主义的原则：思维与存在的异质性"，而这一点恰恰是康德的重要贡献。在《纯粹理性批判》中，他提出了思维与存在的异质性原则，为后来的唯物主义奠定了方法论基础。也是在此基础上，科莱蒂总结到，区分唯心主义和唯物主义的标准，绝不是恩格斯所说的思维与存在何为第一性的问题，而是思维与存在究竟是同一的还是异质的。

第七章《卡西尔论康德和黑格尔》。在这一章中，科莱蒂以新康德主义者恩斯特·卡西尔为例，系统评述了他对康德和黑格尔哲学的认知。科莱蒂指出，卡西尔的重要贡献在于，揭示了两位哲学家对思维与存在关系认识的本质区别，肯定了康德的重要贡献。但他的缺陷在于，完全停留在知识论的层面上来探讨这一问题，并没有从根本上系统论述马克思主义与康德、黑格尔之间的关系。

第八章《康德、黑格尔与马克思》，旨在揭示马克思与康德之间的理论继承关系。在科莱蒂看来，马克思与康德的关系类似于马克思与卢梭的关系，是一个极其重要却鲜有论述的重大问题。他指出，如果说卢梭是马克思政治思想的来源，那么，康德则是马克思哲学思想的债权人。接下来，他通过对《黑格尔法哲学批判》《〈1857—1858 年经济学手稿〉导言》《资本论》等文本的详细分析，认为马克思彻底批判了黑格尔关于思维与存在的同质性的观点，继承了康德关于思维与存在的异质性的分析，这一点不仅构成了马克思唯物主义理论的指导原则，而且也是他后期政治经济学批判的指导纲领。也是在此基础上，科莱蒂得出结论说，作为一种科学，马克思哲学恰恰是沿着康德的道路前进的，只有站在康德的肩膀上，才能更好地理解马克思唯物主义的科学性；也只有立足于康德，才能真正彰显马克思方法论革命的全部意义。

第九章《黑格尔和雅各比》。在这一章中，科莱蒂比较分析了黑格尔和雅各比思想的异同。在他看来，他们的理论目标是一致的，都是为了摧毁科学的理智思维，建构一种理性的形而上学：科学始终被视为是一种抽象的知识，相反，只有哲学才是具体的。但他们对二者的称谓却是相反的：黑格尔把科学和理智称为唯物主义，把哲学称为唯心主义；相反，雅各比则把科学和理智称为唯心主义，把哲学称为实在论。

第十章《从伯格森到卢卡奇》，在这部分中，科莱蒂以物化理论为轴心，系统分析了现代西方哲学、西方马克思主义和辩证唯物主义对科学与理智的批判，力图从根本上诠释马克思物化批判理论的真实内涵。科莱蒂指出，像黑格尔一样，后来的现代西方哲学家包括伯格森、文德尔班、李凯尔特、席美尔等都批判了科学和理智思维，认为后者是导致物化的根源，从而将物化批判与科学批判等同了起来，这一点在卢卡奇的《历史与阶级意识》中得到了充分体现。科莱蒂评价到，卢卡奇的重要贡献在于，他将物化批判视为资本主义批判的核心，首次恢复了被正统辩证唯物主义遗忘的物化批判理论，彰显了马克思哲学的批判性；但他的缺陷在于，完全扭曲了马克思物化批判理论的真实内涵。科莱蒂强调，在马克思看来，资本主义物化的根源并不在于科学和理智，而是在于资本主义的雇佣劳动制度，因此，要扬弃物化，单纯地依靠观念，即黑格尔意义上的思辨的主客体同一，是根本行不通的，相反，必须彻底推翻资本主义的现实本身，才有可能。也是基于此，科莱蒂总结道，与其说，西方马克思主义与辩证唯物主义的区别是实践哲学与理论哲学的区别，还不如说二者是黑格尔传统内部的两种对立思潮。

第十一章《"社会生产关系"概念》。在这里，科莱蒂反思了德拉-沃尔佩的理论缺陷，认为后者完全把马克思的哲学革命局限在认识论和方法论层面，窒息了马克思哲学的生命力。他指出，实际上，社会生产关系理论才是马克思哲学革命的突破口，也正是从这一理论出发，马克思才真正超越了德国古典哲学，创立了自己的历史唯物主义。首先，科莱蒂分析了康德、黑格尔、费尔巴哈关于人的本质的理解缺陷，然后从劳动和生产入手，诠释了马克思对德国古典哲学的超越，由此引出了生产关系理论，并基于《1844 年经济学哲学手稿》《雇佣劳动与资本》《1857—1858 年经济学手稿》和《资本论》，系统分析了马克思生产关系理论的形成和发展过程。不过，他最终认为，在那么多文本中，最为重要的一部著作，既不是《雇佣劳动与资本》，也不是《资本论》，而是《1844 年经济学哲学手稿》。

第十二章《"资产阶级—基督教"社会的理念》，旨在从生产关系入手，全面阐发马克思政治经济学批判和拜物教批判理论的革命意义。科莱蒂指出，在资产阶级社会中，资本成为统治一切的抽象逻辑，致使人们错误地把社会关系投射出来的物象，当成自然之物，从而出现了拜物教和异化现象。而黑格尔的物质辩证法，只不过是这种颠倒现实的一种观念反映，因此，要真正超越黑格尔，就必须深入"资产阶级—基督教"社会的经济—政治制度之中，将对物质辩证法的批判同对资本的批判结合起来，实现对资产阶级社会的总体批判，这才是马克思政治经济学批判和拜物教批判理论的革命意义。

三、研究前沿

德拉-沃尔佩的《卢梭和马克思》与科莱蒂的《马克思主义和黑格尔》是新实证主义马克思主义的代表作。虽然这一学派的存在时间及其理论影响力的持续时间并不算长，但依旧在西方马克思主义发展史上划下了一道弧光。从既有研究状况来看，国内学者主要关注以下三个方面。

第一，考察卢梭与马克思的思想联系，重新评价德拉-沃尔佩和科莱蒂对马克思政治理论的理解。在《卢梭和马克思》中，德拉-沃尔佩强调了马克思政治理论与卢梭思想之间的联系，为马克思的政治理论研究添加了新的思想线索。沿着这个方向，有学者以西方马克思主义对卢梭的政治哲学解读为中心，在对阿尔都塞和朗西埃等人进行比较分析后，阐述了德拉-沃尔佩的理论贡献，认为他对卢梭的民主政治哲学做出了"近马克思主义"的理解。有学者围绕政治自由、平等主义自由与社会主义合法性等主题，阐述了德拉·沃尔佩政治哲学的理论主题与价值向度。还有学者评述了科莱蒂在这一问题上的观点，强调马克思政治理论与卢梭在思想上有着质性的差异。

第二，追溯思想渊源，探求新实证主义马克思主义方法论之"新"。西方马克思主义的一个显著特征是不断从传统的欧洲哲学思想中寻找马克思主义的哲学渊源，德拉-沃尔佩和科莱蒂也是如此。国内学者着重考察了他们的思想来源问题。通过阅读文本和考察思想史可以发现，德拉-沃尔佩对马克思思想的解释主要是上溯到了亚里士多德、伽利略和休谟，而科莱蒂则把这一传统上溯至康德。两者虽然侧重点不一样，但实际上都受到了现代逻辑实证主义的影响，尝试用实证的自然科学方法来研究和论证马克思的哲学。也正因为如此，他们在吸收西方哲学传统时有所选择：德拉-沃尔佩重新引入亚里士多德的无矛盾原理和伽利略的试验方法，力图恢复形式与内容、理性与事实的均衡关系，而科莱蒂关注的是康德的"真正对立"理论。只不过，这种把马克思辩证法完全作科学化和实证化的理解，割裂了马克思辩证法与黑格尔辩证法真实的内在联系，因而导致马克思的辩证法丧失了批判性和革命性。在思考导致这一缺陷的原因时，有学者认为，这是德拉-沃尔佩的两面性——在理论上反叛辩证唯物主义，但是在政治上又绝对地服从于"辩证唯物主义"当权者——造成的。

第三，展开对比分析，总体评价德拉-沃尔佩和科莱蒂的理论得失。随着国内学者研究视野的拓展，对不同思想流派进行差异比较成为学术研究的一种重要方式。有学者对新实证主义马克思主义与结构主义马克思主义进行了比较分析，认为两者存在三个方面的差异。首先，虽然它们都主张马克思与黑格尔之间的彻底决裂，但在决裂时间、决裂方式以及决裂后果上存在明显分歧。其次，在方法论上，前者是经验实证主义，后者是反经验主义，二者是完全对立的。最后，在人本主义问题上，前者承认历史主体的存在，只反对抽象的人本主义，并主张用实证的方法来证明马克思人本主义的科学性；而后者不仅否认历史主体的存在，而且彻底反对一切人本主义。也有学者分析了新实证主义马克思主义与同属于意大利传统的自治主义，提出两者在反对正统马克思主义和早期西方马克思主义解读路径方面是一致的，并且也都拒绝承认马克思与黑格尔之间存在任何继承关系，试图从根基上彻底终结一切辩证法。但两者又存在区别：前者是科学主义与马克思主义外在嫁接的理论产物，而后者则是意大利工人主义实践与后结构主义相融合的内在结果；前者将《黑格尔法哲学批判》视为反辩证法的“圣经”，而后者则选择了《政治经济学批判大纲》，因此，这两条路径虽然具有一定的积极价值，但也存在不可避免的理论缺陷，在一定程度上扭曲了马克思哲学方法论的内在本质。

四、文本节选

The Marxist Critique of Rousseau

1. In the *Critique of the Gotha Programme*, quoted and discussed by Lenin in *State and Revolution* (V, 3-4), Marx says as follows:

> “Equal right” [of each to the equal product of social labour] we certainly do have here [i.e. in the first phase of communism], but it is *still* a “Bourgeois right”, which like every right, *implies inequality*. Every right is an application of an *equal* measure to *different* people who in fact are not like, are not equal to one another. That is why “equal right” is a violation of equality and an injustice. In fact, everyone, having performed as much

social labour as another, receives an equal share of the social products. [...] But people are not alike: one is strong, another is weak. [...] With an equal performance of labour, and hence an equal share in the social consumption. Marx concludes "one will in fact receive more than another, one will be richer than another, and so on. To avoid all these defects, right would have to be unequal rather than equal." The first phase of communism, therefore, cannot yet provide justice and equality [...]; but the *exploitation* of man by man will have become impossible because it will be impossible to seize the *means of production* [...] and make them private property. [...] The vulgar economists [...] constantly reproach the socialists with forgetting the inequality of people and with "dreaming" of eliminating this equality. Such a reproach, as we see, only proves the extreme ignorance of the bourgeois ideologists.

Marx not only most scrupulously takes account of the *inevitable inequality of men*, but he also takes into account the fact that the mere conversion of the means of production into the common property of the whole of society (commonly called socialism) *does not remove* the defects of distribution and the inequality of "bourgeois right".

Now, Rousseau in the *Discours sur l'origine, et les fondements de l'inégalité parmi les hommes* (1755) had posed the problem of the "inevitable" inequality of men in these terms:

I conceive of *two kinds* of *inequality* in the human species: one which I term *natural* or *physical*, because it is established by nature, and which consists in the differences of ages, health, bodily strength, and the qualities of mind and spirit [or inequality *of* men]; the other, which one can call *moral* or *political* [or inequality *between* men], because it rests on a kind of convention and is established, or at least legitimated, by the agreement of men. This consists of the different privileges which some enjoy to the disadvantage of others: as by being richer, more respected, more powerful than the rest, or even by making themselves obeyed [...] From this exposition, it follows that [moral or political] inequality [Rousseau

> concludes at the end of the *Discours*, after covering the whole of human prehistory and history], being almost non-existent in the state of nature ["a state which ... perhaps has never existed"], draws its strength and growth from the development of our faculties and the progression of the human mind, and finally becomes established and legitimate by the institution of property and the laws. It follows again that *moral inequality*, legitimated only by positive law. is *contrary to natural law* [that is, to ideal law, imposed by pure reason] *each time it does not coincide in the same proportion with physical inequality* [i. e. natural inequality of strength and qualities, or merits]—a distinction which sufficiently clarifies what one should think of that kind of inequality which is found among all civilized peoples; since it is manifestly contrary to the law of nature [i. e. against reason], however one defines it, that a child should give orders to an old man, that an idiot direct a wise person, and that a handful of men gorge on luxuries while the hungry multitude lacks the necessities of life.

But, before looking at the last implications of this famous conclusion to the *Discours*, let us see the Marxist solution to the difficulty expounded above, in the Marx—Lenin text—that, given the inequality or diversity of men, right should be not equal but unequal, a difficulty which can now be defined as of the (anti-levelling) egalitarian-Rousseauan variety. And so, in the first phase of communist society (usually called socialism)—Lenin's text goes on—"bourgeois right" is not abolished in its entirety, but only in part, only in proportion to the economic revolution so far attained, i.e. only in respect of the means of production [...] However, it persists as far as its other part is concerned; it persists in the capacity of regulator (determining factor) in the distribution of products and the allotment of labour among the members of society. The socialist principle, "He who does not work shall not eat," is already realised; the other socialist principle, "An equal amount of [social] products for an equal amount of [social] labour", is also already realised. But this is not yet communism, and it does not yet abolish "bourgeois right", which give *unequal* individuals in return for *unequal* (really unequal) amounts of labour, *equal* amounts of products [...]

Marx continues and concludes:

> In a higher phase of communist society, after the enslaving subordination of the individual to the division of labour and with it also the antithesis between mental and physical labour have vanished, after labour has become not only a livelihood but life's prime want, after the productive forces have increased with the all-round development of the individual, and *all the springs of co-operative wealth flow more abundantly*—only then can the narrow horizon of bourgeois right be crossed in its entirety and society inscribe on its banners: From each according to his ability, to each according to *his needs*!

And the following conclusions of Engels in *Anti-Dühring* (III, 2) are in agreement:

> The possibility of *assuring for each* member of society, by *means of socialized production*, an *existence not only fully sufficient* materially, and becoming day and day more full, but an existence guaranteeing to all the free development and exercise of their physical and *mental faculties*—this possibility is now and for the first time here, but it is here.

Let us return to Rousseau to see the solution he provides to the difficulty of establishing a *proportional comparison* between the inequality and diversity of men and inequality between them (or the whole of the civil differences set up and administered by society)—a difficulty, as shown, reformulated by Marx and Lenin as the necessity of unequal right, given the inevitable inequality of men, and thus resolved by their scientific criterion of a communist society.

Rousseau, therefore, explains to us that "wealth, nobility or rank, power and *personal merit* [the latter '*origin* of all the *other* qualities'] being the chief distinctions [or 'kinds of inequality'] by which one is measured in society, I could show that the agreement or conflict of these different forces [i. e. personal merit and other qualities] is the surest indication of a state well or badly set up." And in fact it is finally made clear in the last footnote to the *Discours* that "the *ranks* of the citizens should be regulated [...] according to the *real services* ['*proportional* to their [unequal] *talents* and their *strengths*'] which they give to the state."

This means that for Rousseau the solution of the problem of an effective universal equality (not only for the bourgeois) requires the unlimited, universal application of the criterion of merit and personal conditions. This is the "talent" or merits (of which no human being as such is wholly bereft) as the origin of all the other (social) qualities, and also the "strengths" of which he speaks, the very conditions of existence of the human person (age, health, etc.). It requires, in other words, an equality based on the social recognition of the unequal or different capacities and potentialities of all men, without exception.

This solution involves, therefore, the building of a new society, a democratic one, to surpass not only the society of those privileged under absolutism, but also bourgeois society itself as based in effect on the merits-rights of the possessors. For it is obvious that the recognition of *every* person, on which the institution of a real equality, for all, depends, can only be of a social nature. This follows not only because it presupposes materially, *de facto*, the regulation of questions of "rank" or civil order, but also and above all because (as a question of law, or of value) "*distributive* justice would be *opposed* even to that *rigorous equality* of the *state of nature*, if that should be practicable in a civil society". (And cf., still in the *Discours*, the following lively protest against those, the majority, who gravely misunderstand the Rousseauan critique of society: "What then! Must societies be destroyed, get rid of what is yours and mine, and go back to live in the forests with the bears? This is a conclusion after my opponents, who I should like to warn, as much as to leave them with the shame of drawing it.")

Consider, therefore, this final appeal of Rousseau to distributive justice (the opposite, be it remembered, of commutative or exchange justice) this modern summons back to the chief ethico-political, Aristotelian category, with the aim of counterposing the superiority of *social* equality, to *natural* equality itself. The first is based on the civil rank of each citizen, calculated according to his real services, i. e. proportional to the talents and strength which he gives to society. The second is the rigorously perfect equality of the mythical state of nature, which, if practicable in civil society, Rousseau implies, would be unjust and hence self-contradictory, given its anarchic indifference to the original, different value of every human individual, every person.

From these series of texts by Lenin—Marx, Engels, and Rousseau, we can infer that the meticulous attention bestowed by Marxism-Leninism on the problem of the economic-proportional recognition by (communist) society of the inequalities or differences of individuals and their capacity and need expresses, on a new historical level, the continuity and development of the anti-levelling egalitarian thought of Rousseau. It seems difficult, in other words, to deny that across the chasm of method which separates the metaphysical idealism and humanitarian moralism, the natural-law moralism, of Rousseau on the one hand, from the historical materialism of the criterion of class struggle on the other, lies the major problem posed by Rousseau. That is, that "everything depends on not destroying the natural man [the *free* individual] in adapting him to society" (*La Nouvelle Héloïse*, V, 8), and it is this problem which the supreme scientific hypothesis of the conclusive phase of communism re-formulates in order to solve it. (This leaves aside-the question, which we shall see later, of the historical knowledge Marxism-Leninism had of its debt to Rousseau's egalitarianism.)

In this context, one can conclude as follows: 1. that scientific socialism is capable of resolving by its *materialist* method the problem of an *equality* both *universal* and *mediating* of *persons* which was discovered by the humanitarian *moralist* Rousseau, with his egalitarian-anti-levelling conception of the human person. I. e. a social recognition of the unequal merits and potentialities of all men through their respective proportional services rendered by each to the state; 2. that, in this ultimate concern for the human person by scientific socialism, is revealed, certainly, the Christian legacy chiefly transmitted to it by Rousseau (but how changed by him!). The difference between the heir and the bestower of the legacy consists on one hand in the first's joining the value of the person and his destiny to *history*, that is, to an institution such as a sufficiently unitary society which prevents any centrifugal movement by individuals and classes who may be parasitic and exploitative of man.

The second, Rousseau, however, joins the value of the person and his destiny to an *extra-historical*, theological investiture ("I tell you, in the name of *God* that it is the *part* [i.e. the human *individual*] which is greater than the whole [i.e. than the human *race*]", *Emile*, IV). And yet this can only *justify a partial*, *bourgeois* solution to the problem of a social, truly democratic, recognition of the merits and needs of each person, given that the *sacred-a priori* of the human person can justify only an *abstract*, frustrated individualism, and consequently the kind of semi-anarchic and impotent society which is bourgeois, liberal society.

2. After this, we have still to examine the conscious disposition of the founders of scientific socialism towards Rousseau and his work.

For Marx's attitude, observe the following characteristic and significant aspects.

(1) As against Hegel's conservative opinion, that "the sovereignty of the people is one of those confused notions which are rooted in the *wild* idea of the people", Marx retorts that "the 'confused notions' and

the 'wild idea' are here exclusively Hegel's" (the posthumously published *Critique of Hegel's Philosophy of Law* [1843].). And in the same work, pervaded wholly by the typical Rousseauan idea of popular sovereignty, the people "represented" in the liberal state is defined by Marx as "people in miniature" (as the "estate edition" of civil society).

(2) However, in *On the Jewish Question* (1844) Marx offers us only as an ("excellent") picture of the bourgeois "abstraction of political man" the famous passage in the *Contrat social* (II, 7) in which is clearly visible the democrat Rousseau's attempt to integrate "natural", abstractly independent, man into the social body, and thus to transform the individual-whole, or solitary individual of nature, into the individual-part which is the citizen, social man. Rousseau in fact says: "He who would care to undertake to institute a people must feel himself in a condition to change human nature, so to say; to transform each individual, who, by himself, is a perfect, solitary whole, into a part of a larger whole, from which this individual may receive in some manner his life and being", etc. Thus is explained (though not justified) how, making a judgement of Rousseau as a political writer at the beginning of the *Introduction* (1857), (published posthumously) and in the *Grundrisse* (1857 - 8, published posthumously), Marx sees in Rousseau only the worshipper of natural law, who "brings naturally independent, autonomous subjects into relation and connection by contract", simply as an "anticipation of 'civil society'". However, the *Contrat social* would simply return to the Robinsonades of the eighteenth century, a critique of which, indeed, begins the *Introduction* of 1857.

3. In *Capital* (I. Chap. 30), on the other hand, Marx openly employs a (moralistic) criticism of the rich in his analysis of the expropriation of the "multitude of small producers" by the "great manufactories", to be found in Rousseau's *Discours sur l'écommie politique* which, quoted by Marx, runs as follows: "I shall allow you, *says the capitalist*, the honour of serving me, provided you give me the

little you have left for the trouble I take to give you orders." However, it is also true that this quotation-tribute by Marx is far indeed from doing justice to the deep democratic (egalitarian) inspiration which, as we know, he received from Rousseau. For, thanks to the correction made by Marx replacing Rousseau's "rich"—a term of generic sociological moralism—with the specifically materialist term 'capitalist', the quotation is clearly transformed into a new, socialist form. And compare the crucial substitution, in Marx-Engels's *German Ideology* of "*necessary* association", i.e. union "on the basis of (*material*) conditions", in the place of "by no means an *arbitrary* one, such as is expounded for example in the *Contrat Social*. However, regarding the *Contrat* one must at least observe that, even when its contractualist natural law theory is destroyed, its enormous influence on Marx himself has still to be explained. This influence is transmitted through its criteria of "sovereign popular will", of the "sovereign" which "can be represented only by itself", etc.—as we have seen. The influence thereafter, too, bears on the whole historical development of socialism, from the Paris Commune of 1870 to the Soviet socialist state (with its "democratic centrality").

4. In the cited *Critique of the Gotha Programme*, we find almost at the beginning that Rousseau is evoked as a kind of typical example of a semi-utopian, semi-rhetorical sociologist. Therefore, with the intention of scolding the inconsequentially and superficiality of the Lassallean authors of the Gotha Programme, Marx writes as follows:

> According to the first proposition [of the programme], labour was the source of all wealth and all culture; therefore no society is possible without labour. Now we learn, conversely, [in the second proposition] that no "useful" labour is possible without society. One could just as well have said that only in society can useless and even socially harmful labour become a branch of gainful occupation, that only in society can one live by being idle,

etc. — *in short, one could just as well have copied the whole of Rousseau.*

From this it is clear that this Rousseau who wrote the *Discours sur les sciences et les arts* and other comparable texts, Rousseau the rhetorical, *minor* critic of society, became for Marx, in the *literary* passion of his political polemic, neither more nor less than the *whole* Rousseau. (Cf. Rousseau's "This is how luxury, dissoluteness and slavery have been for the whole of time the bane of the pretentious efforts we have made to escape from the happy ignorance in which eternal wisdom had placed us.") Naturally, Marx's oversight is the more singular and remarkable because it occurs in that work of his most imprinted with the philosophical spirit of Rousseau the *major* critic of societies and of their inequalities and injustices, as seen above. This is at once a profound and unconscious contradiction.

No less contradictory and embarrassing than Marx's is the attitude of Engels towards Rousseau, though it emerges as more interesting and significant because of the historical sense of the complex problem of egalitarianism shown by Engels.

The relevant texts by Engels can be arranged as follows:

1. The judgements on the *Contrat social* which, sometimes, do strict justice to that theoretical masterpiece of modern democracy, as when Engels says that 'the *Contrat social* of Rousseau came into being, and only could come into being, as a democratic bourgeois republic' (*Socialism: Scientific and Utopian*, 1,1877, and *Anti-Dühring*, Introduction, 1878), or that Rousseau "with his republican *Contrat social* indirectly overcomes the constitutional Montesquieu" (letter to Mehring, 14 July 1893). And sometimes, on the other hand, the judgements are below the level of truth and justice, as when Engels, for example, includes the *Contrat* indiscriminately in his condemnation of the abstract 'state based upon reason' and concludes in the manner of Hegel that, the *Contrat* "had found its realisation in the Reign of Terror" (*Socialism* ... etc., 1).

2. The general judgement on the egalitarian idea is one which is formally, theoretically, correct to the following extent: he postulates that "since the French bourgeoisie, from the great revolution on, brought civil equality to the forefront, the French proletariat has answered blow for blow [the '*proletarische Konsequenzzieherei*'] with the demand for social, economic equality". He ends by saying that "the real content of the proletarian demand for equality" is the demand for the *abolition of classes*, and that "Any demand for equality which goes beyond that, of necessity passes into absurdity" (*Anti-Dühring*, I, 10). (Cf. the *Vorarbeiten* of the *Anti-Dühring*: "The equality of the bourgeoisie [abolition of class *privileges*] is very different from that of the proletariat [abolition of the classes themselves]".) Yet this is a judgement which, if it is combined with the significance attributed by Engels himself to the influence of Rousseauan thought in the egalitarian movement, is shown to be lacking and defective in its historical reflections, since all that Engels *tells* us about the egalitarian Rousseau is the generic phrase that the idea of equality has "especially thanks to Rousseau played a theoretical ... role" (*Anti-Dühring*). This is said despite the frank Rousseauan accents, those of the *greater* egalitarian-anti-levelling Rousseau, which we find in the critique by Engels of Dühring's abstract egalitarianism. There, for example, "what interests us is [Dühring's] admission that, as a result of the moral equality between men, equality has vanished once more" (ibid.).

If it is true that in the *Vorarbeiten* cited here (but only in them) there is an attempt to clarify that the "bourgeois side" of egalitarianism was formulated in a manner "*on behalf of all humanity*" by Rousseau, it is equally true that Engels immediately adds that "As was the case with all demands of the bourgeoisie, so here too the proletariat cast a fateful shadow beside it and drew its *own conclusions* [*Babeuf*]." This is the same as saying that the only, or chief, conclusions drawn by the revolutionary proletariat from Rousseau's egalitarianism must have been the egalitarian, levelling and utopian corollaries of a Babeuf, that bad caricature of a hack (cf. for example the "equal and honest mediocrity" of Babeuf beside the *Contrat social*, II, 11). All these are things which can explain but not justify the final judgement of the *Vorarbeiten* (and left there), that the principle of equality (defined here as "there must be no privileges") is "essentially negative" and that "Because of its lack of positive content and its off-hand rejection of the entire past it is just as suitable for proclamation by a great revolution, 1789 – 1796, as for the later blockheads engaged in manufacturing systems."

3. The specific judgement of the *Discours* on inequality, a judgement apparently very comprehensive and generous, is based on an attempted historical-dialectical analysis of some basic elements of the *Discours*. For example, "For the poet it is gold and silver, but for the philosopher iron and corn, which have civilized man [*human individuals*] and ruined the human race", and which concludes as follows:

> Each new advance of civilization is at the same time a new advance of inequality [*among* men, or civil, political: cf. above, para. 1]. [...] And so inequality once more changes into equality; not, however, into the former natural equality of speechless primitive men, but into the higher equality of the social contract. The oppressors are oppressed. It is the negation of the negation [see Hegel]. Already in Rousseau, therefore, we find not only a line of thought which corresponds exactly to the one developed in Marx's *Capital* [sic], but also point by point a whole series of the same dialectical turns of speech as Marx used: processes which in their nature are antagonistic, contain a contradiction; transformation of one extreme into its opposite; and finally, as the kernel of the whole thing, the negation of the negation (*Anti-Dühring*, I, 13: cf. *Socialism*, etc., 1).

Here it can be seen that Engels's tendency to search everywhere, indiscriminately, for precedents for the dialectic of historical materialism on die one hand concedes *too much* to Rousseau by placing him alongside Marx as regards historical method, but on the other hand he concedes *too little*. In this case, Rousseau's original research into equality is passed over—that of the reconciliation of the two types of inequality (of which only one, that of civil or political inequality is here taken up by Engels), and thus his specific (anti-levelling) egalitarianism is dissolved into a game of antitheses and syntheses—of inequality and equality—both generic and schematic, revealing the heavy Hegelian residue in Engels' conception of the dialectic of historical materialism. Hence, finally, this judgement of the *Discours* by Engels is re-attached, by its historical deficiency, to his general judgement of the egalitarian idea, reproduced above.

It seems to me that this is sufficient evidence of the confused knowledge the founders of scientific socialism had of their historical debt to Rousseau. (That this confused knowledge can be perpetuated in Soviet socialist culture is shown, for example in the *Introduction* by Vyshinsky, to the *Law of the Soviet State* (New York: Macmillan, 1948), where in a four-line footnote, compared with more than a page devoted to Kant-Kelsen, one finds the following: "J.-J, Rousseau [...] an ideologist of the radical petty bourgeoisie. His famous *Du contrat social*, wherein his views as to public law are developed, exerted an enormous influence on the development of the bourgeois liberal-democratic theory of the state as the incarnation of the general will." For the rectification of the grave historical error which restricts the influence of the criterion of "general will" and its implicit "popular sovereignty" to the bourgeois state, see our remarks on *national*-popular, *bourgeois* sovereignty above—*Clarifications*, 5, 4 and 5, and also the note at the end of II, 7, for documentation of those elements of Rousseauan *direct democracy*, present in the Soviet constitution of 1936.

This historical debt, finally, can he expressed as follows: that the Rousseauan theorems of anti-levelling egalitarianism, mediating of persons, should be numbered among the essential historical and intellectual premises of the concept-model of abolition of classes in a-society of free (because equal) persons, such as the communist society set out hypothetically in the *Critique of the Gotha Programme*, in *Anti-Dühring*, and in *State and Revolution*. In this concept-model is expressed, therefore, together with the perfect "proletarian [egalitarian] answer blow by blow," of which Engels spoke, that *positive* (Rousseauan) content of the egalitarian principle, which Engels disputed in the *Vorarbeiten* of *Anti-Dühring*.

——Galvano della Volpe, *Rousseau and Marx*, trans. John Fraser, Lawrence and Wishart, 1978, pp. 138 - 150.

The *Introduction* (1857) and the *Preface* (1859) to *the Critique of Political Economy*

(The movement towards the solution of the problem of an analytic dialectic)

The *Introduction* (1857) to the *Contribution to the Critique of Political Economy* (1859) was discovered by Karl Kautsky in 1902 in Marx's archives, in the so-called *Nachlass*, and published by him in the issues of *Neue Zeit* for the 7th, 14th and 21st March 1903. It was republished in 1907 (again by Kautsky in the second edition of the *Contribution*), and finally in 1939 by the Russian editors who have given us a critically edited text of the fragmented and difficult manuscript (see now: K. Marx, *Grundrisse der Kritik der politischen Öekonomie* (Berlin: Dietz, 1953). In the (1859) *Preface* to the *Contribution*, which we shall discuss later, *Marx* had referred, however, to a "general introduction" "drafted" by him and "omitted" on the grounds that it can be "confusing to anticipate results which still have to be substantiated", and that the reader who wishes to follow him "will have to decide *to advance from the particular to the general*".

Let us at once notice that this generic *scientist's* scruple, that of proceeding from the particular to the general, from facts to ideas and not (one-sidedly) vice versa, was to be finally argued out, explained, and developed in the omitted *Introduction* in Chapter 3, devoted to the "method of political economy". This scruple has no importance in itself, with respect to this methodological chapter which specifically interests us, but rather as regards the other chapters of concrete research, devoted to "production"—chapters on the other hand not themselves without illuminating methodological insights. In short, the fact remains that the 1857 *Introduction* is a work that stands by itself, with its own authority, precisely in that Marx gives us there a "brilliant sketch"—as the most recent editors put it—of the "methodical principles" of the application of the materialist dialectic to political economy, as well as basic concepts of historical materialism. We already know from the above conclusions something of the meaning of the logico-materialist analysis of method, which is the subject of this essay. Now we have to follow this analysis through its most incisive points.

If, for example, says Marx halfway through the chapter, we take the economic category of *production*, in its general aspect, we must realise that its *general* or common character, revealed by comparative analysis, is *articulated* and complex, and is *diversified* in numerous specific instances. Some of these elements are common to all periods, others only to a few. Certain characteristics will be common to the most modern period as well as the most ancient—they are characteristics without which no production could be undertaken. But just as the more developed languages have laws and characteristics in common with those less developed, and it is precisely the departure from the common, or general, which constitutes their "development", so "general" characteristics must be "separated out" (*gesondert*) so that in the name of "unity", uniformity, or generality, the "essential" or specific "difference" should not be forgotten.

Marx points out here how only a rigorous, scientific analysis of the general and the particular, and the "separating out" of general characteristics, not confusing them with specifics, can avoid that "forgetfulness" of the latter because of, or in favour of, the former. In short, only thus can one avoid the prevalence of the general over the specific which is the norm for the abstract synthesis of the *a priori*, the norm of *hypostases*.

The supposed "profundity" of economists lies in this forgetting, when they set out to prove the "eternity and harmoniousness of the existing social relations." They explain that *no* production is possible without an *instrument of production*, "even if this instrument is only the hand", or, even if without past, stored-up labour, "it is only the facility gathered together and concentrated in the hand of the savage by repeated practice". And they explain capital as a "general, eternal, natural relation". This is true *if* we leave out the "specific character" which makes stored-up labour a "capital" in the *modern* sense.

They tend, in short, to "confuse and eliminate all *historical* differences", the *specific* ones, when they formulate their "general human laws". Thus (cf. John Stuart Mill, for example) they "present *production* [...] as encased in eternal natural laws independent of history, at which opportunity bourgeois relations [of production] are then quietly *smuggled in* [*ganz unter der Hand* ... untergeschoben] as the *inviolable* natural laws on which society *in the abstract*", in *general*, "is founded". So, they fall continually into "tautologies". "All production is appropriation of nature on the part of an individual within and through a *specific* form of *society*. In this sense it is a tautology to say that property (appropriation) is a precondition of production [appropriation]. But it is altogether ridiculous to *leap* [*Sprung*] from that to a specific form of property, e. g. private [modern, bourgeois] property."

Marx here wishes to tell us: (1), that the conclusion is ridiculous, since it is useless to define the determinate, specific, historical form of property, bourgeois property, by saying that as property, appropriation, it is a precondition of production or appropriation. This falls into a real tautology, or logical inversion. (2), that this tautological, and hence, from a cognitive point of view, *sterile* conclusion is none other than the result and *punishment* of a *hypostasis*. Precisely by having endowed the most *generic* concept of production as appropriation of nature with a powerful presence in *reality*, through the *a priori* method, it thus assumes and consumes within itself modern, bourgeois production *as well*, *so transcending* its *specific* characteristics. It has, in short, as Marx says, *smuggled in*, or replaced the specific meaning of bourgeois relations of production with the generic and unchanging conception of production, preconceived thus as the natural, eternal law of economic society *in the abstract*.

Hence, *metaphysical smuggling*, or *a priori replacement*, in favour of the generic, or most abstract, against the specific or most concrete *in the definition of the latter*, indeed shows us, clearly the wrong, twisted structure of those arguments about the "metaphysics of political economy" (see the *Poverty of Philosophy*, as discussed in the previous section). This is the structure and method of a mystifying dialectic which, we know, by reducing the specific or concrete to a mere "allegorical" or symbolic manifestation of the Idea (with a capital letter), or the generic, finishes with tautologies or logical inversions which are confirmation of a *fraudulent*, hence *undigested*, non-mediated specific, or concrete quality. This fraudulent presence indeed involves nonetheless a presence of the concrete, but note the critical postulate of matter in the first section, and later the discussion of the "evaporation" of concrete representation in *a priori* definition.

It is therefore necessary, Marx continues, to follow a "scientifically correct method". That means above all *proceeding* to *abstractions* (without which there is neither thought nor knowledge of any kind) *starting from* the "*concrete*" (*das Konkrete*), from the "real subject", in this case an historical "*determinate* society". The *Robinsonades* with which even today bourgeois economists amuse themselves—Robbins for example—are thus for Marx only "conceits", inspired by natural law theory. That is, "Production by an isolated individual outside society—a rare exception which may occur when a civilized person in whom the social forces are already dynamically present is cast by accident into the wilderness—is as much of an absurdity as is the development of language without individuals living together and talking to each other."

However, while the "concrete" is the effective starting point of observation and understanding it appears, nonetheless, *in our thought* as a process of syntheses, as a "result" and "not as a point of departure". The concrete is concrete because, in fact, it is "the concentration of many determinations, hence *unity* of the *diverse*". If, in order to examine the whole social process of production, we start from population as its basis, without really bearing in mind the "classes", i.e. the concrete, historical elements which compose it, like wage labour, capital, etc., and the corresponding implications, we start from "a *chaotic* conception of the whole". We arrive, by a step-by-step analysis, at increasingly simple concepts. In this, we proceed from an "imaginary" (*vorgestellten*) concrete to *abstractions* even *less complex* (*immer dünere Abstrakta*), to *genericity* (*Allegemeinheiten*), in order to reach the most simple abstractions, such as the division of labour, money, value, etc. This is the method pursued by bourgeois political economy: "Along the first path the full conception *was evaporated* [*verflüchtigt*] to yield an abstract [in the pejorative sense] determination [*zu abstrakter Bestimmung*]."

This determination—be it noted—is *not* "empty", as the Kantian criticism of abstract rationalism would have it. Rather, the definition is *full of a "chaotic"*, confused, *undigested concrete*, or non-mediated "*bad* empiricism" (see the first section, and earlier in this one). As we know, this abstract definition, weakened by its own *a priori* element, is converted into a real *tautology*—or one *of the real* or its *content* (the *punishment* mentioned above). Hence the "evaporation" of concrete representation does not refer for Marx to its being emptied as representation, but to the "chaotic", "imaginary", *undifferentiated* character of its *content*. That is, what *evaporates* in the abstract, *a priori* definition, is the *cognitive value* of representation, *not its content*. This presence, or rather permanence, of the content, the concrete, matter, in the concept, come what may and however distorted (that is, as fraudulent content, hence chaotic, undifferentiated, or vulgar, non-mediated empiricism) may be expressed, explained, as we know, by the positive circle of matter and reason revealed by the *materialist* critique of the *a priori* and the corresponding critical postulate of matter (cf. the first chapter).

However, Marx continues, when we reach the simplest abstractions, such as the division of labour, exchange value, etc., "From there the journey would have to be *retraced* [*rückwärts*] until I had arrived at the population again," and "this time not as the chaotic conception of a whole, but as a rich totality [unity] of many determinations and relations". In other words, Marx means that if the totality is thus examined in terms of its *historical character*, we are in this way following the *correct method*, by which "abstract definitions [no longer in the pejorative sense, not *a priori*, but now based on the continual 'return' to the *concrete* as such, or unity-diversity] lead towards a reproduction of the *concrete* by way of *thought*," (and we know that without definitions or abstractions there is no thought or knowledge of any kind). In this way, Hegel "fell into the illusion of conceiving the real as the product of thought concentrating itself". Whereas "the method of *rising* [*aufzusteigen*] from the abstract to the concrete is the only way in which thought appropriates the concrete [or real], reproduces it as a concept in the mind [*geistig*]", being the real, or concrete in fact, "the subject, [specific] society" is the "presupposition" from which we start and this "must always be kept in mind".

Consequently, the correct method can be represented as a *circular* movement from the concrete or real to the abstract of ideal, and thence back to the former (cf. the positive circle of matter-reason, discussed above). In other words, correct method consists, with logical precision, in a continual, invariable *historical explanation of abstractions* or (in particular) economic *categories*—if their truth, as we have seen, is in *inverse relation* to the *simplification* or *generic* abstraction of their *content*. It is the correct method, as Marx writes, to the extent that "the path of *abstract* thought, *rising* from the simple to the *combined*, [or specific, concrete] would correspond to the *real historical* process". One can see this clearly in the correct, scientific elaboration of the basic category of *labour*.

Labour, says Marx, seems "a quite simple category", a general one, and as an idea in this sense, as *labour in general*, is very *ancient*. "Nevertheless, when it is economically conceived in this simplicity, "labour" is as *modern* a category as are the relations which create this *simple* abstraction."

This actually means that this category is certainly an *abstraction*, but *historical*, *not a priori*. That is, it *summarizes* the economic, practical and theoretical "progress" made after that "commercial and manufacturing activity", in which the source of wealth was transferred from the thing, money, to subjective activity such as commercial or manufacturing labour, up to the "Physiocratic system" which pointed to its source in "agricultural labour". Finally, it led up to Adam Smith who discovered it in "simple labour" or "labour in general". From this we have not only the character of activity as creative of wealth, but also the general character of the object defined as wealth, or "the product as such, but labour as past, objectified labour".

Now, "it might seem that all that had been achieved thereby was to discover the abstract expression for the simplest and most ancient [economic] relation in which human beings—*in whatever society*—play the role of producers". And "this is correct in one respect. Not in another." It is true that "*Indifference* towards any specific kind of labour *presupposes* a *very developed* totality of real kinds of labour, of which no single one is any longer predominant." Thus, "*the most general* abstractions arise *only* in the midst of the *richest possible concrete development*, where one thing appears as common to *many*, to all. Then it ceases to be thinkable in a particular form alone."

On the other hand:

> this *abstraction* of *labour as such* is not merely the mental product of a concrete totality of labours. Indifference towards specific labours *corresponds* to a *form of society* in which individuals can with ease transfer from one labour to another, and where the specific kind is a matter of chance for them, hence of indifference. Not only the category labour, but labour in reality has here become the means of creating wealth in general, and has ceased to be organically linked with particular individuals in any specific form. Such a state of affairs is at its most *developed* in the most *modern*, form of existence of *bourgeois society*—in the United States. Here, then, for the first time, the point of departure of modern economics, namely the abstraction of the category of "labour", "labour as such", labour pure and simple [*tout court*] becomes true in practice.

The economist Sweezy says: "It is important to realize that the reduction of all labour to a common denominator, so that units of labour can be compared with and substituted for one another, added and subtracted, and finally totalled up to form a social aggregate, is not an arbitrary abstraction [...]. It is rather, as Lukács correctly observes, an abstraction 'which belongs to the essence of capitalism'." So, as Marx concludes,

> the *simplest abstraction*, then, which modern economics places at the head of its discussions, and which expresses an immeasurably ancient relation valid in all forms of society (cf. the possible objection earlier, that ["it might seem that all that had been achieved thereby, etc."]) nevertheless achieves practical *truth* as an *abstraction* (*nur in dieser Abstraktion*) only as a category of the *most modern society*. This example of "labour" shows strikingly how even the *most abstract categories*, despite *their validity*—precisely because of their abstractness—for all epochs, are nevertheless, in the *specific character* of this *abstraction* (*in der Bestimmtheit dieser Abstraktion*), themselves likewise a product of historic relations, and possess their *full validity only for* and *within* these relations.

And now we shall see another example of a basic *abstract* or *historic determination*, or a "reproduced" *unity of diversity*—called *capital*.

Naturally, this *historical explanation of the categories* or economic abstractions, which forms the *concrete-abstract-concrete circle*, does not mean in fact that one should adopt them "in the same sequence as-chat in which they were historically decisive." This would be "unfeasible" [*untubar*] and "wrong" [*falsch*]. For "their *sequence* is *determined* rather by their *relation to one another in bourgeois society*, which is *precisely the opposite* of that *which seems to be their natural order* or which corresponds to [chronological] historical development". Thus, "(t)he point is *not* the historical position of the economic relations in the *succession* of different forms of society." *Even less* is their sequence "*in the idea*" (*Proudhon*)—and as Hegel meant still more profoundly (see previous chapter) —but "(r)ather their *order within* [*um ihre Gliederung innerhalb*] modern *bourgeois society*".

Now, what exactly is the meaning of the Marxist rejection not only and not so much of the "sequence [of economic categories] in the idea" (a rejection incontestable now after all that has gone before, and especially after the *Poverty of Philosophy*), but also of their "natural sequence", the historico-chronological kind? What does the subsequent reference to their "organic connection" within "modern bourgeois society" mean, i.e. the reference to the sequence and order determined *by* their reciprocal relations in modern society (this latter order which is, we repeat, "precisely the opposite" of their natural order)? The *logical* method of Marx in his critique of political economy says the entry in the *Great Soviet Encyclopedia*, "is none other than the *historical* method, *only freed from the historical forms* [really: chronological] and all *disturbing accidents* [i. e. irrationality]". We add that the *real* question is that of not *confusing Marx's* method with *Hegel's* (which indeed comes out too free of historical accidents, disturbing or otherwise, even though it is claimed to be the method of historical dialectics!). This is the problem of seeing *how the essential historicity* of the economic categories *may be reconciled* with the *non-chronological* nature of their order (or "inverse" order). This problem is simply the resolving development of the question of the concrete-abstract-concrete circle, that of the method of *determinate* or *historical abstraction*, hence the *scientific* abstraction. Let us examine this.

A decisive direction is given us already by the arguments made above on the *historical* formation of the *most modern* and also *general* category of labour. Here one sees that only as secondary to the latest, modern-historical character of *labour pure and simple* do the other (former!) historical characteristics of labour acquire a meaning which is *no longer historically bounded* nor chronologically fixed. In short, in the conceptual *synthesis*, represented by the abstraction of labour pure and simple, the different historical characteristics of labour are exchanged into conceptual forms, and hence take on a unitary, general meaning, losing their restricted, particularist, merely analytical, historico-chronological meaning—*without*, on the other hand, losing their specificity or meaningful *analytical power*, derived from their historicity or historical *necessity*. These are not fanciful characteristics!

From this is derived a *synthesis* which is also an *analysis*. This is the so-called historical or determinate abstraction in which real historicity and the ideal (non-chronological order) are reconciled. Of course, we have still to investigate further the *subordination* of former historical characteristics to the last historical characteristic, which is the principle of the formation of the historical or determinate abstraction as *synthesis-analysis*. This subordination, let us say at once, does not, cannot, mean anything other than the inclusion of those former characteristics in a nexus or concept whose formation can only be inspired by the latest, or *present*, historical characteristic, by, that is, *its problematic*.

Marx says:

> The so-called historical presentation of development is founded, as a rule, on the fact that the latest form regards the previous ones at steps leading up to itself, and, since it is only rarely and only under quite specific conditions able to *criticise itself* [*sich selbst zu kritisieren*] [...] it always conceives them *one-sidedly*. The Christian religion was able to be of assistance in reaching an *objective* [not one-sided] understanding of earlier mythologies only when its own *self-criticism* [*Selbstkritik*] had been accomplished to a certain degree, so to speak, *δυνάμει* (potentially) ...

that is, to become a history of religions.

Likewise, bourgeois economics arrived at an *understanding* [i.e. at an objective understanding] of feudal, ancient, oriental economics only after the *self-criticism of bourgeois society* had begun. Insofar as the bourgeois economy did not mythologically identify itself altogether with the past [through those *a priori* projections of categories, whether into the past or the future, which characterize hypostases], its critique of the previous economies, notably of feudalism, with which it was engaged in direct struggle, resembled the critique which Christianity "levelled against paganism, or also that of Protestantism against catholicism. [...]" Hence, modern "bourgeois society" "*for science as well*" by no means begins at the point where one can speak of it *as such* (the last two emphases are Marx's).

Let us move on to the formation of another basic determinate, or historical, abstraction, *capital*, typically brought into being by the latest or *present* historical characteristic of capital. That is, the abstraction is brought about by the *problematic* of capital, emerging from the *self-criticism* of society and *bourgeois* economics. In the medieval economy, says Marx, capital, except for that in the shape of money, has, in its form as traditional productive instrument, a landed-proprietary character. However, "In bourgeois society it is the opposite", where "Agriculture more and more becomes merely a branch of industry and is entirely dominated *by* capital". Dominated, that is, by the dominant element "the *social*, historically created element", where, if "Ground rent *cannot be understood without* capital ... capital can *certainly be understood without ground rent*". Therefore, this element, capital, "must form the *starting-point as well as the finishing-point*, and must be *dealt with before* landed property" (and only "After both have been examined in particular (should) their interrelation be examined.").

Here one sees in fact *how* the *meaning of the relation* between former economic categories, those of the past, or "historical" (medieval landed property and corresponding capital), and the subsequent categories of modern society (rent and corresponding capital), is determined by an "*inverse*" *order* from that of the *chronological* order of categories. In other words, the order is not: landed property—capital, but capital—landed property. Thus the *reverse* order, or ideal, or value order, of the categories, which forms the meaning of the relation between past and modern, is determined by the *modern* or *actual* historical necessity of understanding and resolving the problematic of the phenomenon of *rent*. This is the "organic connection" of relations and economic categories "within modern bourgeois society" discussed earlier. This procedure demands for this purpose that capital must be the "starting-point and the finishing-point", and be investigated "before" landed property, *reversing* the (empirical) chronological order.

This is the substance of the 1857 *Einleitung*. The text, if we are not mistaken, allows us the following conclusions, when expounded more deeply, and consistently with the methodological principles Marxism - Leninism has uncovered, in *Capital* above all: (1) That an *objective*, not one-sided, *understanding* of its historical *precedents*, and hence of its resulting problems (e.g. rent), may be achieved by economics only to the extent that it is capable of *self-criticism*, and also aware of the *problematic* nature of its *own* categories. This presupposes (a) that it has acquired an *historical consciousness* of the *given concrete* or subject, that is, of *modern* bourgeois *society*, *contemporary* society, a consciousness lacking in bourgeois political economy. We have seen in the *Poverty of Philosophy* that in the perspective of bourgeois economy "there has been history, but there is no longer any", regarding as "natural" or "eternal" the specific institutions of that economy. (b) that it therefore be found from the start rooted without *a priori* or dogmatism on the very terrain of the concrete or experience, like every science worthy of the name. It should properly be found on the terrain of historico-*material*, *social* demands—the opening, or first movement of the above-mentioned circle from the concrete to the abstract. (2) That, consequently, it should formulate abstractions, for an objective understanding of its problems. Their nature as *syntheses*, a synonym for abstraction, concept, or category, *should be inseparable* from that of *analysis*, in that one is concerned positively to evaluate their historical *precedents*, and bring out the conceptual *connection* with their *consequences* or present and problematic historical features, and resolve these.

However, this must be done in such a way that the *ideal* or reverse order which the concepts thus assume does not lead to the total loss of their specificity or meaningful analytic quality, along with their restricted, isolated, in short merely analytical or historico-chronological reference. For the former is their historical appositeness and necessity. Such specificity or analytical equality is essential, since without it a *progressive*, synthetic-dialectical orientation is not even possible. This last is characteristic of concepts, is composed of them, and imprints on them the reverse, ideal, or rational order, or in short their connection with their consequences.

By this procedure *abstractions*, *syntheses*, or *unities*, are indeed formed, but as *specific*, analytical, ones, or those of *diversity*. These are, in short, abstractions in which the historico-*rational* demand may be satisfied as a demand in turn as function of the historico-*material* imperative, from which were started out. This is delineated jointly by the first and second movement—from concrete to abstract and *vice versa*—of the above methodological circle. It is a delineation, therefore, of the reconcilability (in the determinate abstraction) of historicity and intellectuality, or rationality. (3) Finally, as the *normativeness* inherent in the objectivity or rationality of the determinate abstraction—not a categorical or absolute normativeness, but only a *hypothetical* one—it is precisely expressive of *historico*-rational demands, and also of rational-*functional* ones (reason as function of matter and also the other way round). Thus, this hypothetical-normativeness cannot be *verified*, or acquire truth-value and become law-reality, save in and through historical (not abstract!) *materiality*, that of *practical* economic and social *experience*.

This is again depicted by the methodical circle in its second and final movement of *return* from abstract to concrete, which *thus closes the circle*. This was rigorously expressed by Lenin in *Materialism and Empirio-criticism* in these words: that

> inasmuch as the *criterion of practice*, i.e. the *course of development* of all capitalist countries in the last few decades, *proves* only the objective *truth* of Marx's whole social and economic theory in general, and not merely of one or other of its parts, formulations, etc., it is clear that to talk here of the "dogmatism" of the Marxists is to make an unpardonable concession to bourgeois economics.

A concession, that is, to a really dogmatic economics, in so far as it was speculative or contemplative. For the decisive category of *practice*, never forget the second *Thesis on Feuerbach* where the following appears:

> The question whether *objective truth* can be attributed to human thinking is not a question of theory but is a practical question. Man must *prove the truth*, i.e. [...] the *this-worldliness* of his *thinking* in *practice*. The dispute over the reality or non-reality of *thinking which is isolated from practice* is a purely scholastic question.

The foregoing conclusions show us schematically the significance of that *scientific*, i.e. *analytic*, *dialectics*, of economics and the *moral* disciplines in general, towards which Marx was working from the *Poverty of Philosophy*, and from the anti-*a priori* polemic of the *Critique of the Hegelian philosophy of public law*. This dialectic is one of determinate or historical abstractions, criticizing and dissolving from within the speculative dialectic, or dialectic of generic, indeterminate *a priori* abstractions, wrong, mystified, and inconclusive—since as we well know, it ends up in tautologies of fact.

Now, the methodological importance of the scientific dialectic (symbolized in the concrete-abstract-concrete circle, or circle of matter and reason, induction and deduction) is little short of revolutionary. It means that any *knowledge* worthy of the name is *science*, hence not mere knowledge or contemplation. It means there is only *one* science because there is *only one* method, *one* logic. The *materialist* logic of modern, experimental science, it is understood, has taken science away from that more or less mathematizing Platonism, which is the philosophical background of science theoretically expressed by every bourgeois scientist from Galileo to Einstein. Hence, though the *techniques* which formulate laws certainly differ, as experience and reality differ—from the law of physics to that of economics and of morality,—the *method*, the *logic*, whose symbol is the above-mentioned circle, does not change. (Even though, for example, mathematics enters as an essential constitutive element in the formal elaboration of the laws of physics in general, on the other hand it can only be employed as an auxiliary instrument in the elaboration of economic and social laws and so forth.)

We know already from Marx in the *Economic and Philosophic Manuscripts* that

> *History* itself is a *real* part of *natural history*—of nature developing into men. Natural science will in time incorporate into itself the science of man, just as the science of man will incorporate into itself natural science [that is, it will adopt its experimental method and have an historico-practical method in the historico-dialectical sense].

And as Zhdanov puts it in his famous *Speech* on the history of Western philosophy:

> The unique character of the *development* of philosophy resides in the fact that from it, as the scientific knowledge of nature and science developed, the *positive sciences branched off* one after another. Consequently the domain of *philosophy* [or speculation] was continually *reduced on account of the development of the positive sciences* (I might add that the process has not ended even up to the present time). This *emancipation* of the natural and social sciences from the aegis of

[speculative] philosophy constitutes a *progressive* process, for the natural and social sciences as well as *for philosophy itself*.

This means, finally, that the very progress of human knowledge permits us to affirm the *unity* not only of scientific logic, but also the *scientific* unity of *logic*, and, in short, the *unity of logic*. Thus, it is no longer permissible to propose a "philosophical" logic distinct from that of "science". Philosophy as *science of man*, to use the expression in the way Marx mentioned earlier, is no longer "science" in the metaphorical, groundless, misleading sense in which it is used, for example, in formulas such as "philosophy as science of the spirit". These are only synonyms for "metaphysics", "speculation", etc. Rather, it is in this specific sense of *history-science* or *materialist science of history* in which we indeed find, in the 1857 *Einleitung*, the first appearance, in outline, of an *epistemological-scientific* foundation of economics as science.

This can well be described as the *moral Galileanism* specific to Marxism: that is, that the traditional "moral sciences" are really, and without exception, sciences in the most strict sense. We speak of *Galileanism* intentionally, to make a distinction between historical materialism and its method, both as regards *idealism* and its hypostases, and also, no less important, *positivism* and its idolatry of "facts" and related Baconian repugnance towards *hypotheses* and ideas. Our journey with Marx in the period 1843 - 1857 has led us, in fact, from the critique of the *hypostases* of Hegelian speculative philosophy to positive theoretical knowledge of the *hypotheses* of *Capital proved* therein, or turned into economic and social *laws*, as Lenin had correctly seen in *Materialism and Empirio-criticism* (1908).

If in conclusion we turn briefly to the *Vorwort* or *Preface* (two years later than the *Einleitung* of 1857), its well known philosophical content regarding the structure-superstructure relation are significantly revealing after what has gone before—especially the methodological

Introduction of 1857. Let us recall the basic feature of its content, Marx says in reference to his "critical re-examination of the Hegelian philosophy of law":

> My inquiry led me to the conclusion that neither legal relations nor political forms could be comprehended whether by themselves or on the basis of a so-called general] development of the human mind, but that on the contrary they originate in the material conditions of life [...]. The totality of these relations of production constitutes the economic *structure* of society, the real foundation, on which arises a legal and political *superstructure* and to which correspond definite forms of social consciousness. The mode of production of material life conditions the general process of social, political, and intellectual life [...]. At a certain stage of development, the material productive forces of society come into conflict with the existing relations of production or—this merely expresses the same thing in legal terms—with the property relations within the framework of which they have operated hitherto. From forms of development of the productive forces these [property] relations turn into their fetters. Then begins an era of social revolution. The changes in the economic foundation lead sooner or later to the transformation of the whole immense superstructure. In studying such transformations it is always necessary to distinguish between the material transformation of the economic conditions of production, which can be determined with the precision of natural science, and the legal, political, religious artistic or philosophic—in short, *ideological* forms in which [*worin*] men become conscious of this conflict and *fight it out*.

Now, besides the purely philological observation that refers to his *re-examination* of Hegelian legal philosophy as the determining factor in the methodological considerations recorded above, Marx certainly also means to make reference to the relevant *Contribution to the Critique of Hegel's Philosophy of Law*—as well as to the *Introduction to the Critique of Hegel's Philosophy of Law*, published in 1844 and cited here. The

Critique, as we know from the first section, is directly concerned with questions of logic and method. Apart from this one must point out, as part of the historical-systematic element, that the conception of method symbolized in the 1857 *Introduction* by the concrete-abstract-concrete circle allows us more than a strict and general *logical* view of the *structure-superstructure relation*. It also allows us to single out and define, in that *consciousness*, mentioned above at the end of the passage quoted from the *Preface*, the *decisive criterion* of *practice* as *moral* criterion, or criterion of *action*. This *closes* the circle by *verifying* the hypotheses, but is also an *intellectual* or technical criterion where the economico-social (etc.) *law* is proclaimed, into which the now-verified hypothesis is converted by practical experience, by action.

Marxists, Sweezy has stressed, are not only "criticizing" the capitalist system, in that they have recognized its historical and hence transitory character. Rather, its critical, and hence its "intellectual", position is also "*morally* relevant", as compared with a "critical position regarding the *solar* system, whatever its imperfections". It is also morally relevant "since human action is itself *responsible* for the changes the *social* system experiences and will experience".

Thus the *second thesis on Feuerbach* is clearly explained in all its methodologically revolutionary significance.

——Galvano della Volpe, *Rousseau and Marx*, trans. John Fraser, Lawrence and Wishart, 1978, pp. 186 - 203.

Hegel and "Dialectic of Matter"

...

The dialectic of matter is all here. The finite is infinite, the Real is *Rational*. In other words, the determinate or real object, the exclusive "this right here", no longer exists; what exists is *Reason*, the Idea, the logical *inclusion* of opposites, the "this together with that". On the other hand, once being is reduced to thought, thought, in its turn, *is*; i. e., the logical unity of opposites comes to exist and becomes incarnate in a real object. Everything is itself and its opposite, "it is" and "it is not". This contradiction puts it in motion, in other words, causes it to die as thing so that it may be reborn as thought or infinity. As Hegel says: "Everything finite has this characteristic: that it sublates itself." On the other hand, "if", as Marx says, "one finds in logical categories the substance of all things, one imagines one has found in the logical formula of movement the *absolute method*, which not only explains all things, but also implies the movement of things". In other words, the real object is resolved into its *logical* contradiction—this is the first movement; in the second movement the logical contradiction becomes, in its turn, *objective and real*. The philosopher is by now a perfect Christian. What distinguishes one from the other, as Marx says, is only this: that "the Christian, in spite of logic, has only one incarnation of the *Logos*", whereas "the philosopher has never finished with incarnations".

If we open Book 2 of Hegel's *Science of Logic*, we will find the "dialectic of matter" stated in plain terms. Concluding his critique of the principle of identity and non-contradiction, Hegel emphasizes that, contrary to this principle, one must affirm that "*everything is inherently contradictory*, and in the sense that this law in contrast to the others expresses rather the truth and the essential nature of things". It is "one of the fundamental prejudices of logic as hitherto understood and of ordinary thinking, that contradiction is not so characteristically essential and immanent a determination as identity". Nevertheless, "if it were a question of grading the two determinations and they had to be kept separate, then contradiction would have to be taken as the profounder determination and more characteristic of essence. For as against contradiction, identity is merely the determination of the simple immediate, of dead being; but contradiction is the root of all movement and vitality; it is only in so far as something has a contradiction within it that it moves, has an urge and activity".

On the other hand, just as everything is contradictory, so *logical* contradiction, in its turn, exists and is real. Hegel continues: "... Contradiction is usually kept aloof from things, from the sphere of being and of truth generally; it is asserted that *there is nothing that is contradictory*", as if contradictions were just "a contingency, a kind of abnormality and a passing paroxysm of sickness". But, "now as regards the assertion that *there is* no contradiction, that it does not exist, this statement need not cause us any concern; an absolute determination of essence must be present in every experience, in everything actual, as in every notion ... Further, (the contradiction) is not to be taken merely as an abnormality which only occurs here and there, but is rather the negative as determined in the sphere of essence, the principle of all self-movement, which consists solely in an exhibition of it. External, sensuous motion itself is contradiction's immediate existence. Something moves, not because at one moment it is here and at another there, but because in this 'here', it at once is and is not. The ancient dialecticians must be granted the contradictions that they pointed out in motion; but it does not follow that therefore there is no motion, but on the contrary, that motion is *existent* contradiction itself."

And Hegel concludes: "Similarly, internal self-movement proper, *instinctive urge* in general, ... is nothing else but the fact that something is, in one and the same respect, *self-contained and* deficient, *the negative of itself*. Abstract self-identity is not as yet a livingness, but the positive, being in its own self a negativity, goes outside itself and undergoes alteration. Something is therefore alive only in so far as it contains contradiction within it, and moreover is this power to hold and endure the contradiction within it."

One finds all of this in the *Science of Logic*. However one may choose to evaluate the two pages cited above, it is a fact that the birthplace of *dialectical materialism* is to be found here. Even if one chooses to leave open the question of what a "dialectic of matter" could possibly mean, it remains an incontrovertible fact that the first "dialectician of matter" was Hegel; the first and—let us add—also the only one, since after him there has been mere mechanical transcription.

Identity is only the determination of the mere immediate, of *dead being*; whereas contradiction is the root of movement and vitality. This is Hegel and, at the same time, it is also *Anti-Dühring*. "So long as we consider things as static and lifeless, each one by itself, alongside of and after each other," Engels tell us, "it is true that we do not run up against any contradictions in them. ... But the position is quite different as soon as we consider things in their motion, their change, their life, their reciprocal influence on one another. Then we immediately become involved in contradictions. Motion itself is a contradiction: even simple mechanical change of place can only come about through a body at one and the same moment of time being both in one place and in another place, being in one and the same place and also not in it. And the continuous assertion and simultaneous solution of this contradiction is precisely what motion is."

For the *Science of Logic*, something is alive only in so far as it contains within itself contradictions, or only in so far as it is itself and the negative of itself at one and the same time. In *Anti-Dühring*, similarly, "life consists just precisely in this—that a living thing is at each moment itself and yet something else. Life is therefore also a contradiction which is present in things and processes themselves, and which constantly asserts and solves itself; and as soon as the contradiction ceases, life too comes to an end, and death steps in."

Two conceptions that ought to be, it seems, totally different from one another, two authors that we would expect to find the very antithesis of one another—Hegel, the idealist, and Engels, the materialist—define in the same way both reality and that which seems to them abstract or devoid of reality.

I hope the reader will permit me the citation of another text: "Everything that surrounds us may be viewed as an instance of Dialectic. We are aware that everything finite, instead of being stable and ultimate, is rather changeable and transient; and this is exactly what we mean by that Dialectic of the finite, by which the finite, as that which in itself is other than itself, is forced beyond its own immediate or natural being to turn suddenly into its opposite. ... All things, we say—that is, the finite world as such—are doomed (*zu Gericht gehen*); and in saying so, we have a vision of Dialectic as the universal and irresistible power before which nothing can stay however secure and stable it may deem itself. Power, as one of God's determinations, does not, it is true, exhaust the depth of the divine nature or the Notion of God; but it certainly represents an essential moment in all religious consciousness. ... We find traces of its (the Dialectic's) presence in each of the particular provinces and phases of the natural and the spiritual world. Take as an illustration the motion of the heavenly bodies. At this moment the planet stands in this spot, but implicitly it is the possibility of being in another spot; and that possibility of being otherwise the planet brings into existence by moving. Similarly the 'physical' elements prove to be Dialectical. The process of meteorological action is the exhibition of their Dialectic. It is the same dynamic that lies at the root of every other natural process, and, as it were, forces nature beyond itself."

This is subheading of the *Encyclopedia*, or rather, its *Zusatz* (additional remark). In fact, when Plekhanov, in his *Essays in the History of Materialism*, arrives finally at the place where he has to indicate what the "dialectic" is for Marx, he cannot find anything better to do than, first, to quote and transcribe extensively from this paragraph (with the exception, of course, of the reference to God and religion), and, then, to summarize its most important conclusion as follows: "The essence of everything finite lies in the fact that it cancels itself and passes into its opposite." In other words, everything is, once again, self-contradictory, everything is itself and the negative of itself, in one and the same respect.

We will conclude the presentation of texts by returning to the page of the *Logic* cited above: "... Identity is merely the determination of the simple immediate, of dead being; but contradiction is the root of all movement and vitality; it is only in so far as something has a contradiction within it that it moves, has an urge and activity." When Lenin arrived at this page during the course of his reading of the *Logic*, he feverishly noted down, as if overcome by irresistible sympathy for the argument: "movement and '*self*-movement' ... 'change', 'movement and vitality', 'the principle of all self-movement', 'impulse (*Trieb*)' to 'movement' and 'activity'—the opposite to '*dead Being*'—who would believe that this is the core of 'Hegelianis', of abstract and abstruse ... Hegelianism? This core had to be discovered, understood, *hinüberretten* (rescued), laid bare, refined, which is precisely what Marx and Engels did."

We shall leave Marx aside. It is a fact that Lenin, as well as Engels, sees in this page of the *Logic* the "kernel" worth saving from Hegel's philosophy, the breaking through of a genuine realism in contradiction to the system's "shell" and to the "mystique of the Idea". The firm belief that dominates him at this point is what he elevated into a criterion for all of his readings of Hegel: "I am in general trying to read Hegel materialistically: Hegel is materialism which has been stood on its head (according to Engels)—that is to say, I cast aside for the most part God, the Absolute, the Pure Idea, etc."

The page from Hegel that we are presently considering is at the beginning of Remark 3 to Chapter 2, C of Book 2, in the *Science of Logic*. Before taking leave of this passage, I should like to reproduce the remarks with which Hegel concludes this *Zusatz* and which Lenin, in accordance with his "criterion", neglected to transcribe and comment upon: "Finite things, therefore, in their indifferent multiplicity are simply this, to be contradictory and *disrupted within themselves and to return into their ground*. As will be demonstrated later, the true inference from a finite and contingent being to an absolutely necessary being does not consist in inferring the latter from the former as from a being that *is and remains the ground*; on the contrary, the inference is from a being that, as is also directly implied in *contingency*, is only in a state of collapse and is *inherently self-contradictory*; or rather, the true inference consists in showing that contingent being in its own self withdraws into its ground in which it is sublated, and further, that by this withdrawal it posits the ground only in such a manner that it rather makes itself into a positedness. In ordinary inference, the *being* of the finite appears as ground of the absolute; because the finite is, therefore the absolute is. But the truth is that the absolute is, because the finite is the inherently self-contradictory opposition, because it is *not*. In the former meaning, the inference runs thus: the being of the finite is the being of the absolute; but in the latter, thus: the non-being of the finite is the being of the absolute."

The "reading" given by Lenin of these pages rests, as one can see, on a basic misinterpretation. He "tried" to read Hegel "materialistically" precisely at the place where the latter was ... negating matter. Haunted by the famous propositions of *Anti-Dühring* and led astray by the very method that he had laid down for himself—which meant a lapse of attention wherever Hegel talks about God—Lenin did not realize that Remark 3 to Chapter 2, which opens with the statement that "everything is inherently contradictory" and proceeds in the way shown above, bears upon one precise topic: the problem of proving the existence of God.

The question which Hegel is discussing here is the same one which we take as our starting-point: the logical inconsistency introduced into philosophy by the principle of non-contradiction; the impossibility of realizing the"principle" of idealism while employing the method of the "intellect" or, as stated in this case, "ordinary inference". The understanding or intellect, which separates the finite from the infinite, does not succeed, as Hegel says, in putting an end to the finite. The consequence is the contradiction into which the so-called cosmological proofs for the existence of God fall. The latter, in fact, naturally take as "their point of departure a *Weltanschauung* which views the world as an aggregate of contingent facts", and therefore as a mass of worthless things; except that they take this point of departure as a "solid foundation" that has to "remain and be left in the purely empirical form" that it had before. "The relation between the beginning and the conclusion to which it leads has a purely affirmative aspect, as if we were only reasoning from one thing which *is* and continues to *be*, to another thing which also is", with the consequence that the world, which is what is created, becomes, in their syllogism, the "major premiss", whereas God, who is the creator and therefore foremost, becomes instead the minor premiss. The effect becomes the cause, and the cause effect. Thus, as Hegel states, Jacobi was able to make the "justified criticism that thereby one sought to establish conditions (i.e. the world) for the unconditional (*das Unbedingte*); that the infinite (God) was in this way represented as the dependent and derivative".

In other words, the"understanding" shores up the finite. Keeping it from *passing over* into its opposite—if the finite, as Hegel says, were "touched ... by the infinite, it would be annihilated" —the understanding turns the finite into a "fixed being" that is and remains solidly grounded. The dialectic of matter, however—i.e., the dialectical conception of the finite, the conception of the finite as "ideal", and therefore *idealism* (in so far as it leads the finite to destroy itself and thus eradicates any materialistic grounding) —this dialectic of matter realizes for the first time the "principle" of philosophy, i.e. God, enabling Him to prevail in a coherent fashion as the unconditional and the absolute. In "ordinary inference" and reasoning, the being of the finite is made "absolute"; i. e., the finite is regarded as a reality that subsists independently or for itself. With the mode of reasoning followed by philosophy or idealism, however, the dialectical conception of matter enables one to state that, precisely "because the finite is the inherently self-contradictory opposition, because it is not, ... the absolute is". The first case, in which the finite "remains" and is a "fixed being", is the kingdom of death: "fixed being", says Hegel, is "*dead being*"; it is matter that has not been transvalued into and as Spirit. The second case, the "passage" or "movement" by which the finite negates "itself" passing over into the "other", is termed *living being* (*vitalità*), precisely in the same sense that for the Christian death is the beginning of the true life, which commences when one passes from the here and now over to the beyond.

The meaning and function of the "dialectic of matter" in Hegel's thought is that (in his own words): "It certainly constitutes an essential moment of all religious consciousness." However, the meaning that the dialectic of matter has in Engels and Lenin is, as is well known, quite different: it represents for them the most advanced and developed form of *materialism*. One might presume at this point that, under the common name, there must lie *two* different conceptions. In reality, this hypothesis must be dismissed. The lengthy comparison of texts which we have indulged in, and the others that we will present below, prove, it seems to us, two things: (a) that all the basic propositions of the "dialectic of matter" were originally formulated by Hegel; (b) that dialectical materialism has confined itself to transcribing those propositions from his texts. Since the authors of dialectical materialism, in the process of recopying them, have made clear that they understood these statements to imply a materialist stance *already in Hegel's text*, the conclusion must be drawn (I believe) that they simply committed an error of interpretation. An error which by now lies at the basis of almost a century of theoretical Marxism.

——Lucio Colletti, *Marxism and Hegel*, NLB, 1973, pp.20 - 27.

The Concept of the "Social Relations of Production"

...

Our main aim is to arrive at an explanation of the concept of "social relations of production"—a concept which Marxists have always taken for granted, when in point of fact it is the most difficult of all. Previously articulated in *The German Ideology*, this concept has its clearest and most fundamental formulation in Marx's essay (still an "early writing") on *Wage-Labour and Capital*. "In the process of production, human beings work not only upon nature, but also upon one another. They produce only by working together in a specified manner and reciprocally exchanging their activities. In order to produce, they enter into definite connections and relations to one another, and only within these social connections and relations does their influence upon nature (*ihre Einwirkung auf die Natur*) operate, i.e., does production take place."

A paraphrasing of this concept gives us some of the formulae encountered above. (a) Man's relationship to nature is at the same time man's relationship to his fellow man; i.e. production is intersubjective communication, *a social relationship*. (b) The relationship of man to his fellow man, on the other hand, is established for the purpose *of producing*, i.e. in view of and as a function of man's action and effect on nature. Formulated more concisely, the concept means these two things: first, that in order for me to relate to an object, I must also relate to other men, since the object itself is actually a *human objectification* ("the sensuous world ... is not a thing given direct from all eternity, ... but the product of industry and of the state of society"); which then means that the relationship of the species "man" with other species is actually a relationship within his own species, i. e. that the *generic* (or inter-species) relationship is actually a relationship *specific* to man. Second, that in order to relate to other men, I must relate to the natural *object* itself, taken precisely with regard to its otherness or heterogeneity of species—for man's being is *nature* (one need only remember Marx's remark that 'a being which does not have its nature outside itself is not a *natural* being'). In other words, man does not have a being of his own, but has as his own being that of others; thus the *specific* relation (man's relationship to other men) implies the *generic* relationship of man to the other natural beings different from him.

The reader who has some familiarity with Marx's writings knows that the propositions just mentioned are the same ones that are the focus of the *Economic and Philosophical Manuscripts*; and that it is precisely these concepts which make this text by far and away the most tortuous and obscure of Marx's works. There, work is defined as man's *self*-production, not only in the sense that the product of labour is an objectification of the worker (and therefore the result of a work of transformation by which nature has been adapted and made to conform to our needs and our aims); but also in the opposite sense that in the work process man *adapts himself* to nature, and his idea is the *means* which enables him to respect the specificity of the materials with which he is working—i. e. it enables him to deal with the *object* of labour in terms of that which it truly *is*. In both cases, work is man's self-reproduction (both as "creativity" and as "adaptation"), precisely for the reason stated above. In the first case, because man's relation to objective otherness is actually a manifestation (through objectivity) of his relationship to other men. In the second case, because man's relation to other men and therefore to his own species or to himself implies—since man is a being that has "his" nature "outside himself"—that, in order to relate to himself, he must relate to a *being* that is *other* than human.

All of historical materialism is here *in nuce*, if one looks closely. The impossibility of separating "economics" from "society", "nature" from "history", "production" from "social relationships", "material" production from the production "of ideas"—if the roots of the concept are not here, then where are they? In Marx's words: "... The identity of nature and man appears in such a way that the restricted relation of men to nature determines their restricted relation to one another, and their restricted relation to one another determines men's restricted relation to nature ... ". On the other hand, just as the expansion of the first relationship is also an expansion of the second, so the opposite is true. From that follows the consequence that "a certain mode of production, or industrial stage, is always combined with a certain mode of co-operation, or social stage" and vice versa; to the point that "this mode of co-operation is itself a 'productive force'".

Historical materialism and the "logic" of *Capital* itself are rooted here. Since man, in the process of producing, produces *himself*—both in the sense that he produces his relationship with other men, i.e. with his own species, and in the sense that he produces his relationship with natural objectivity and therefore with the tools and materials of his work—one can understand not only the inter-relation that exists between all the categories of *Capital*, but also the "cyclicity" or principle of self-movement which presides over the process of capitalist accumulation. "Capitalist production, therefore, under its aspect of a continuous connected process, of a process of reproduction, produces not only commodities, not only surplusvalue, but it also produces and reproduces the *capitalist relation*; on the one side the *capitalist*, on the other the *wage-labourer*."

This is precisely what Marx discovered for the first time and elaborated in the 1844 *Manuscripts*. The manuscript on 'alienated labour'—which is the veritable rebus of this entire work—develops the circularity and interdependence of the following relationships: (a) that "the relationship of the worker to the *product of labour* as an alien object which dominates him" is at the same time "the relationship of the worker to his own activity as something alien"; (b) that "since alienated labour: (1) alienates nature from man; and (2) alienates man from himself, from his own active function, his life activity; so it alienates him from the *genus*"; (c) that this "genus", i.e. the "specific essence of man", is just as much external nature ("his own body, as well as external nature") as it is other men; for, as Marx says, "what is true of man's relationship to his work, to the product of his work and to himself, is also true of his relationship to other men, to their labour and to the objects of their labour". Thus, he concludes, "through alienated labour, therefore, man not only produces his relation to the object and to the process of production as to alien and hostile men; he also produces the relation of other men to his production and his product, and the relation between himself and other men".

Let us attempt to put this in more linear terms. In positive terms (i.e. apart from the question of alienation), the network of relationships referred to above is already present in the concept of *work* itself. Work is both causality and finalism, material causality and ideal causality; it is (if we invert the actual order) man's action and effect on nature and at the same timenature's action and effect on man. This accounts for a twofold characteristic of the product of labour (and of objectivity in general), which it may be useful to bring out again. (a) The product of labour is the objectification of my ideas, i. e. of my needs and my conscious objectives; (b) it is a simple changing of "the forms of matter", so that "in the process of production, man can only work as nature works", i. e. the object can only be handled in accordance with its particular specificity and so with respect to and in conformity with its own particular nature (one commands nature, Bacon would say, only by obeying her). With reference to this twofold character of objectivity, the function of the *idea* is also twofold. It is both a subjective goal that man pursues, and therefore praxis or ideology; and it is a function of truth, i.e. a *means* for recognizing and dealing with the object in accordance with the yardstick best-suited to it—and therefore a means of escaping from anthropomorphism and giving an objective dimension to human practice. Marxism is not—one should be clear on this point—either pragmatism or a *Wissensoziologie* (sociology of knowledge); it is the first theory of "situated thought", but it is also a theory of thought as *truth*.

This argument, which in Marx assumes various forms, is developed (e.g.) in the second section of his *Introduction* of 1857 in terms of the production-consumption relationship. (a) Consumption creates production. It creates production in that 'consumption produces production by creating the need for *new* production, i.e. by providing the ideal, inward, impelling cause which constitutes the prerequisite of production. Consumption furnishes the impulse for production as well as its object (ideal or interior), which plays in production the part of its guiding aim. It is clear that while production furnishes the material object of consumption, consumption posits the object of production in an *ideal* form, as its inner image, its need, its impulse and its purpose. It furnishes the object of production in its subjective form. No needs, no production. But consumption reproduces the need. (b) "In its turn, production furnishes: first, consumption with its material, its object. Consumption without an object is not consumption, hence production works in this direction by producing consumption; but second, it is not only the object that production creates for consumption. It gives consumption its determinacy, its character, its finish. For the object is not simply an object in general, but a determinate object, which is consumed in a determinate manner mediated in its turn by production. Hunger is hunger: but the hunger that is satisfied with cooked meat eaten with fork and knife is a different kind of hunger from the one that devours raw meat with the aid of hands, nails, and teeth. Not only the object of consumption, but also the manner of consumption is produced by production, and not just objectively but also subjectively. Production thus creates the consumers. Third, production not only supplies the need with material, but supplies the material with a need." Consumption, in fact, "as a moving spring is itself mediated by its object. The need for it which consumption experiences is created by its perception of the product. The object of art, as well as any other product, creates a public capable of artistic appreciation and aesthetic enjoyment. Production thus produces not only an object for the subject, but also a subject for the object".

On the one hand, then, the object is the idea itself objectified; what consumption"posits in an ideal form", production posits *in re*. On the other hand, this "ideal, interior cause" is mediated by the object previously consumed; i. e. the idea is determined by the perception of the object. In conclusion and once again: finalism and causality.

Here is still another variation on the same theme, before we go on to take the bull by its horns. "Man's musical sense is only awakened by music. The most beautiful music has no meaning for the nonmusical ear, is not an object for it, because my object can only be the confirmation of one of my own faculties. It can only be so for me in so far as my faculty exists for itself as a subjective capacity, because the meaning of an object for me extends only as far as the sense extends (only makes sense for an appropriate sense). For this reason, the *senses* of social man are *different* from those of non-social man. In other words, objective sensuous nature is, in reality, my own subjective sensitivity itself. *Esse est percipi*. There is no consciousness of the object that is not self-consciousness. What I see of the world is what my ideas predispose me to see. My relationship to nature is conditioned by the level of socio-historical development." ... Their restricted relation to one another determines men's restricted relation to nature' (here is the point of departure for moving in the direction of a historicization of the sciences of nature themselves).

On the other hand, if "it is only when objective reality everywhere becomes for man in society the reality of human faculties, human reality, and thus the reality of his own faculties, that all *objects* become for him the *objectification of himself*, ... objects (which) confirm and realize his individuality, ... are *his own* objects, i. e. man *himself* becomes the object", just *how* it is that these objects "become his own depends upon *the nature of the object*". As Marx explains it: "When real, corporeal man" posits objects, "the *positing* is not the subject of this act but the subjectivity of *objective* faculties whose action must also, therefore, be *objective*"; which means that man "creates and establishes *only objects*, *because* (he) is established by objects, and because (he) is fundamentally *natural*"; and, in short, that "in the act of establishing (he) does not descend from (his) 'pure activity' to the *creation of objects*; (his) *objective* product simply confirms (his) *objective* activity, (his) activity as an objective, natural being".

The reader with a developed taste for the reasoning process will understand that the essential outlines of historical materialism are already here in embryo—that is under the heavy cover of this incredible language. The further developments of the analysis, i. e. its detailed articulation, must of course be sought in *Capital*. However, the essential role of the 1844 *Manuscripts* (that reef on which a whole generation of French existentialist "Marxists" foundered) is that it is precisely in them that the original key to unlocking the meaning of the concept of "social relations of production" can be found—the key to this real *summa* of Marx's theoretical revolution. Marx writes: "... The history of *industry* ... is an *open* book of the *human faculties*, and a human *psychology* which can be sensuously apprehended. This history has not so far been conceived in relation to human *nature*, but only from a superficial utilitarian point of view, since in the condition of alienation it was only possible to conceive real human faculties and *the acts of man as a generic being* (*menschliche Gattungsakte*) in the form of general human existence, as religion, or as history in its abstract, general aspect as politics, art and literature, etc." On the other hand, this psychology, i.e. the world of projects and *ideas* that lies behind industry is as little subjective and anthropomorphic as can be imagined—precisely because the knowledge that sustains that practice is not metaphysical, i.e. not the dreams of clairvoyants, but *science*, i.e. the recognition of the objective world. "Of course, animals also produce. They construct nests, dwellings, as in the case of bees, beavers, ants, etc. But they only produce what is strictly necessary for themselves or their young. They produce only in a single direction, while man produces universally. They produce only under the compulsion of direct physical needs, while man produces when he is free from physical need and only truly produces in freedom from such need. Animals produce only themselves, while man reproduces the whole of nature. The products of animal production belong directly to their physical bodies, while man is free in face of his product. Animals construct only in accordance with the standards and needs of the species (Marx himself uses the term 'species') to which they belong, while man knows how to produce in accordance with the standards of every species and knows how to apply the appropriate standard to the object."

To conclude: Historical materialism reaches its point of culmination in the concept of "social relations of production". This concept, in turn, had its first and decisive elaboration in the 1844 *Manuscripts*, in the form of the concept of man as a "generic natural being".

——Lucio Colletti, *Marxism and Hegel*, NLB, 1973, pp.226–234.

五、观点解读

1. 马克思是卢梭政治思想的继承人

德拉-沃尔佩指出，在政治哲学方面存在一个长久被忽视的问题，即马克思与卢梭之间的思想渊源问题，这致使马克思的政治思想一直处于晦暗不明的处境。为了进一步明晰、深化对马克思政治哲学的理解，他以自由和平等观为核心，写出了《卢梭和马克思》这一著作，力图全面揭示二者之间的继承关系。在德拉-沃尔佩看来，卢梭在政治哲学方面的贡献主要集中于三点：第一，他区分了两种"不平等"：自然不平等和社会不平等。前者是自然的、天生的；后者是人类历史发展的产物，并随着私有制和法律的建立而根深蒂固，这种不平等是不合理的，必须要予以扬弃。第二，提出了不同于"公民自由"的"平等主义自由"。德拉-沃尔佩指出，所谓公民的自由是由洛克、孟德斯鸠等人提出来的，是为了保护私有财产权的资产阶级式的自由；而卢梭提出来的自由则与此不同，它不是为了保护资产阶级私有权利，而是为了每个个体成员的自由，这是一种更大的自由，是人民主权式的自由，德拉-沃尔佩将其称为"平等主义的自由"。第三，揭示了资产阶级拉平式的平等与真正平等之间的本质差异。资产阶级的平等实际上是把同样的平等标准分别应用于不同的人身上，从而得出来的空洞的形式主义的平等，它是完全建立在抹杀个人的自然生理不平等之上的，因而是一种不顾一切个体差别的拉平式的平等，在其背后掩盖的是一种真正的政治不平等。而真正的平等绝不是资产阶级这种拉平式的平等，而是建立在尊重每个个体差异之上的：既然每个个体在自然生理上都是不平等的，这就意味着，真正的平等应当是一种不平等，因此，社会应当按照每个人的自然生理上的差异以及他对社会的实际贡献来赋予个体应有的平等，在两种不平等之间寻求一个相称的综合。

德拉-沃尔佩进一步指出，虽然马克思、恩格斯、列宁从来没有公开承认他们对卢梭平等理论的继承，但不可否认，他们之间的传承关系已经渗透进他们政治著作的字里行间。首先，在《黑格尔法哲学批判》中，德拉-沃尔佩指出，马克思在反对黑格尔君主专制时所倡导的真正"民主制"，实际上就是来源于卢梭，由此将这一著作判定为卢梭主义的延续，是"一部自始至终渗透着典型的卢梭人民主权思想的著作”。其次，通过对《哥达纲领批判》的文本分析，德拉-沃尔佩指出，卢梭关于两种平等的学说，成为支配马克思《哥达纲领批判》的核心思想，因此，《哥达纲领批判》无疑是一部典型的卢梭主义的著作。再次，不论是恩格斯的《反杜林论》还是列宁的《国家与革命》，在平等观上都像马克思一样继承了卢梭的观点。基于此，德拉-沃尔佩得出结论说，马克思扬弃了卢梭的道德主义和唯意志论的抽象方法，在唯物主义的基础上更好地解决了卢梭的问题；但无论如何，必须承认，马克思、恩格斯、列宁关于平等主义自由的论述完全承袭于卢梭。然而，德拉-沃尔佩进一步提出，马克思、恩格斯并没有对卢梭的贡献做出合理的评价。马克思把卢梭界定为一个二三流的社会批评家和自然法崇拜者。而恩格斯一方面在方法论上将卢梭与马克思相提并论，忽视了二者的本质差异；另一方面，又借助于黑格尔的“否定之否定”方法来评价卢梭的两种不平等理论，将其视为一种反题、合题的文字游戏，完全抹杀了卢梭在这一问题上的重要贡献，也充分暴露了他思想中的黑格尔主义遗迹。

2. 马克思主义是“道德领域中的伽利略主义”

在德拉-沃尔佩看来，马克思哲学革命主要表现为一种方法论变革，即对黑格尔思辨辩证法的超越。基于这一视角，他将马克思的方法论革命划分为三个阶段：首先，是《黑格尔法哲学批判》和《1844 年经济学哲学手稿》，这是马克思科学辩证法的初步形成期；其次，是《哲学的贫困》，这是马克思科学辩证法的创立期；最后，是《〈政治经济学批判〉导言》(1857)(以下简称《导言》)和《〈政治经济学批判〉序言》(1859)，这是马克思方法论变革的彻底完成，而《资本论》只不过是这一方法的具体运用。他指出，《黑格尔法哲学批判》之所以重要，是因为通过对黑格尔思辨逻辑的批判，马克思颠覆了黑格尔从思维到存在的神秘主义路线，恢复了经验存在的本体地位，初步创立了一种与它相对立的“科学辩证法”，后者最主要的体现，就是主谓颠倒方法和“特殊对象的特殊逻辑”。这一点在《1844 年经济学哲学手稿》中得到了进一步的阐发。德拉-沃尔佩进一步指出，如果说《黑格尔法哲学批判》是马克思科学辩证法的最初形态，那么，到了《哲学的贫困》，这一方法最终趋于成熟。他说，在后一著作中，马克思站在唯物主义的立场之上，对黑格尔的先验辩证法进行了彻底清算，用一种“哲学—历史的或社会学—唯物主义”

的概念取代黑格尔的哲学—思辨的概念，实现了与黑格尔的彻底决裂，完成了方法论的根本变革。在分析完《哲学的贫困》之后，德拉-沃尔佩就过渡到1857年的《导言》，认为这是马克思方法论革命的彻底完成。在这里，他集中阐述了自己对马克思从抽象上升到具体的方法的理解。通过对《导言》的研究，可以发现，在马克思看来，这一方法实际上只是思维用来把握具体的认识方法，而不是一种实证方法。然而，德拉-沃尔佩恰恰误解了这一点，将其诠释为具体—抽象—具体的方法论循环：a.具体，既定事实；b.抽象，在具体之上进行理性假设；c.具体，回到事实，以证明假设的有效性；d.证实途径，实践或实验。[①] 在自然科学中，向具体的回归，是伽利略的实验方法；而在社会科学中，则是马克思的实践逻辑。也是基于此，德拉-沃尔佩得出结论说，马克思的方法论与伽利略的实验方法是内在同质的。马克思在哲学和道德科学中所完成的事情，恰是伽利略在自然科学中所完成的事情，于是，传统意义上的"道德科学"或哲学已经不再是形而上学的天下了，而是转化为伽利略意义上的最严格的科学。也是以此为由，德拉-沃尔佩把马克思主义称为"道德领域中的伽利略主义"。

3. 物质辩证法：黑格尔哲学与辩证唯物主义的共同本质

德拉-沃尔佩虽然在理论上痛恨苏联的辩证唯物主义，但是迫于当时的政治压力，他又不得不服从于辩证唯物主义。与之相比，科莱蒂则彻底得多。他认为，要彻底终结辩证唯物主义的统治霸权，就必须搞清楚辩证唯物主义与黑格尔思辨辩证法的内在关系。在这里，科莱蒂独创了一个概念来命名黑格尔辩证法的本质，即"物质辩证法"。那么，何谓物质辩证法呢？科莱蒂认为，它包含三个环节：第一，存在转化为思维，这是有限物质转化为观念的运动。第二，观念化身为具体物质的过程，绝对理念为了能够继续存在下去，就不能仅仅迷恋于优美的天国，还必须沉降到世俗之中，使有限转化为绝对的化身。第三，辩证矛盾的动力机制，只有对立双方的矛盾运动，才能实现这种过渡，最终达到思维与存在的同一性。科莱蒂指出，这种物质辩证法是黑格尔全部哲学的方法论本质，他正是借助于这种方法，才彻底根除唯物主义，恢复形而上学的本性，把唯心主义的原则贯彻到底的。那么，辩

① Galvano della Volpe, *Logic as a Positive Science*, NLB, 1980, p. 163, pp. 178－179.

证唯物主义所倡导的“唯物辩证法”又是什么呢？科莱蒂通过对恩格斯、普列汉诺夫、列宁著作的分析指出，在他们那里，“唯物辩证法”都被理解为三个环节：第一，具体物体转化为“物质”的过程。世界统一于物质，后者是世界的本原，一切具体物质形态都是“物质”的化身。第二，“物质”必须世俗化为具体的存在物。第三，矛盾动力机制，一切运动的源泉就在于事物自身的内在矛盾。对此，科莱蒂指出，从表面上看，唯物辩证法似乎与黑格尔的“物质辩证法”存在本质差别，但实则不然，他们根本不明白，空洞地谈论物质和空洞地谈论观念实际上是一回事，“说一个物体是物质的，这仍旧什么都没说。物质本身并没有具体化，它只是一个种的属性，是任何物共同的属性…… 我们应当大声地明确地说：物质就其自身而言只是一个概念，一句废话。”①因此，所谓的“物质辩证法”其实就是观念的辩证法，而“唯物辩证法”也只不过是这种观念辩证法的变形。基于此，科莱蒂得出结论说：“所有‘辩证唯物主义’的物质辩证法与我们在黑格尔的著作中所发现的‘物质辩证法’是完全同质的”②，前者从头到尾都不过是后者的机械的手抄本。然而，具有讽刺意味的是，那些辩证唯物主义者却不愿意承认这种共谋性，而是高调地把它当作唯物主义的高级原理。结果可想而知，被所有辩证唯物主义当作唯物主义最先进、最高级的东西，正是黑格尔唯心主义所宣扬的“物质辩证法”。辩证唯物主义究其一生都在同黑格尔的唯心主义做斗争，然而到最后才发现自己用来抗争黑格尔的武器恰恰就是黑格尔本人的，这不能不说是辩证唯物主义的悲哀，这也透露出辩证唯物主义者极度脆弱的心灵。科莱蒂对辩证唯物主义的控诉也达到了极点。

4. 社会生产关系理论是马克思哲学革命的根本体现

科莱蒂认为，德国古典哲学的最大缺陷就在于没有科学解决人的问题。由于康德不理解劳动和生产的意义，导致他无法诠释人的本质，最终不得不又求助于唯灵论，陷入二元论之中。在他这里，人的问题被绕了过去。相反，黑格尔虽然看到了劳动的作用，但他仅仅把劳动理解为一种精神劳动，致使人被淹没在上帝的光环之中，成为一个哑谜。在他这里，人的问题又被

① Lucio Colletti, *From Rousseau to Lenin*, Monthly Review Press, 1972, p. 5.

② Lucio Colletti, *Marxism and Hegel*, NLB, 1973, pp. 50 - 51.

诓了过去。虽然费尔巴哈恢复了人的感性原则，但是由于他像康德和黑格尔一样不理解劳动和生产的意义，致使人沦为一个虚无缥缈的空壳。在他这里，人的问题再次被敷衍了过去。而马克思恰恰在这一问题上实现了对德国古典哲学的全面超越。科莱蒂指出，马克思从劳动和生产出发，一方面，揭示了人与自然的内在统一；另一方面，揭示了人与人之间的主体间性关系。这双重维度共同构成了马克思社会生产关系理论的科学内涵，同时也从根本上揭示了人的本质属性，即自然性与社会性的辩证统一。基于此，科莱蒂指出，正是借助于社会生产关系理论，马克思彻底颠覆了德国古典哲学的人学观，将人从形而上学的襁褓中解放了出来，实现了对后者的全面超越。以此为由，他批判了德拉-沃尔佩从认识论来解读马克思哲学革命的做法，并从生产关系理论入手，重新诠释了马克思哲学革命的历程。具体而言，主要表现为三个阶段：首先，是《1844年经济学哲学手稿》，这是社会生产关系理论的起点；其次，是《德意志意识形态》和《雇佣劳动与资本》，在这里，马克思提出了最清楚的、最完备的生产关系概念；最后，是《1857—1858年经济学手稿》和《资本论》，在这些著作中，马克思建立了生产关系再生产理论，标志着生产关系理论的彻底成熟。从这一逻辑来看，科莱蒂似乎更加看重后期的文本，但实际上并非如此，在他看来，最为重要的一个文本，既不是《雇佣劳动与资本》，也不是《资本论》，而是《1844年经济学哲学手稿》。就像他在结论中强调的那样，如果说历史唯物主义在"社会生产关系"概念中达到了顶点，那么，反过来，这一概念则在《1844年经济学哲学手稿》中以"类的自然存在"的形式，首次得到了决定性的阐述。

六、进一步阅读指南

1.《马克思恩格斯选集》第2卷，人民出版社2012年版。

2.《马克思恩格斯选集》第3卷，人民出版社2012年版。

3. 习近平：《决胜全面建成小康社会　夺取新时代中国特色社会主义伟大胜利》，人民出版社2017年版。

4. 习近平：《在纪念马克思诞辰200周年大会上的讲话》，人民出版社2018年版。

5. 习近平：《辩证唯物主义是中国共产党人的世界观和方法论》，《求是》2019 年第 1 期。

6. 习近平:《在庆祝中国共产党成立 100 周年大会上的讲话》,人民出版社 2021 年版。

7. [意]德拉-沃尔佩:《趣味批判》,王柯平等译,光明日报出版社 1990 年版。

8. [意]卢西奥·科莱蒂:《〈卡尔·马克思早期著作〉导言》,张战生等译,《马克思主义研究参考资料》1985 年第 11 期。

9. [意]卢西奥·科莱蒂:《一篇政治和哲学的访谈录》,《西方马克思主义批判文选》,新左派评论编,徐平译,台湾远流出版事业股份有限公司 1994 年版。

10. [美]安·史密斯:《黑格尔主义和马克思:对科莱蒂的批判》,载《马克思主义研究资料》1987 年第 3 辑。

11. 俞吾金、陈学明:《国外马克思主义哲学流派新编》,复旦大学出版社 2002 年版。

12. 王维、庞景君:《20 世纪西方的马克思主义思潮》,首都师范大学出版社 1999 年版。

13. Galvano della Volpe, *Logic as a Positive Science*, NLB, 1980.

14. Lucio Colletti, *From Rousseau to Lenin*. Monthly Review Press, 1972.

15. Lucio Colletti, "Marxism and the Dialectic", *NLR*, 93, September-October, 1975.

16. John Fraser, *An Introduction to the Thought of Galvano della Volpe*, Lawrence and Wishart, 1977.

七、问题与思考

1. 德拉-沃尔佩是如何理解马克思与卢梭之间的关系的?

2. 为什么说马克思主义是"道德领域中的伽利略主义"?

3. 什么是物质辩证法? 科莱蒂如何理解辩证唯物主义与黑格尔哲学的关系?

4. 为什么说社会生产关系理论是马克思哲学革命的核心?

第十二章 “结构主义的马克思主义”的发轫之作——《保卫马克思》选读

教学目的与要求

掌握“认识论断裂”观念；了解阿尔都塞对马克思思想发展过程的认识及“总问题”的转换；正确理解马克思主义是“理论上的反人本主义”命题；掌握阿尔都塞对于“颠倒”概念的理解；正确认识历史是一个无主体过程命题；了解阿尔都塞关于伪历史时间和反历史主义的思想。

一、历史背景

（一）作者介绍

1918 年，路易・阿尔都塞（Louis Althusser）出生于法属殖民地阿尔及利亚首都阿尔及尔附近的一个小镇。其祖上原本定居于法国北部的阿尔萨斯省，由于法国在普法战争后将阿尔萨斯等地割让给德国，因不愿生活在德国人的统治下而移民至此。阿尔都塞的母亲有良好的文化修养，注重子女的教育，希望自己的子女能够回到法国本土发展。阿尔都塞从小勤奋好学，1924—1936 年，他先后在阿尔及尔和马赛读完小学和初中。为了能够考入巴黎高等师范学校，1936—1939 年，他又在里昂的一所中学补习，最终于1939 年夏季顺利进入巴黎高师。

就在阿尔都塞考入巴黎高师不久，第二次世界大战爆发。他应征入伍，后不幸被俘，在德军战俘营中度过了五年时间。在战俘营中，他的肉体和精神都受到严重折磨，从而留下了精神病的病根（从1947年起，他就不得不开始接受电击治疗）。期间，他偷偷地做了些笔记，记录自己在战俘营中的日常生活、心理体验和一些偶思。从这些笔记中可以看出，他这一时期的思想具有天主教神秘主义的特征。不过，也正是在这一期间，他接触到了马克思主义和共产主义思想。

第二次世界大战结束后，阿尔都塞重新回到巴黎高师继续自己的学业，后在科学哲学家、结构主义的先驱之一加斯东·巴歇拉尔的指导下从事高等研究资格论文的写作，题目是《黑格尔哲学中的内容概念》。1948年，他通过法国哲学教师资格考试，资格论文也顺利通过答辩，随即留校任教。在写作《黑格尔哲学中的内容概念》一文时，阿尔都塞还是一名虔诚的天主教徒，积极参加天主教改革运动。不过，该文已经明显地表现出马克思主义特别是青年马克思的思想影响。这种新的思想倾向的浮现一方面体现了法国当时总体思想状况的影响，另一方面也是阿尔都塞个人情感生活发生重大变化的一个积极结果：1945年底或1946年初，他在里昂经人介绍认识并爱上了一名参加过抵抗运动的坚定的女共产党人——埃莱娜·露高台安，正是在后者的影响下，他朝着马克思主义迈出了决定性的一步。于是，1948年，阿尔都塞有些出人意料地突然加入法国共产党，并开始将研究方向从德国古典哲学转向马克思主义哲学。不过，天主教改革派思想的影响并没有一下子就消失，事实上，直到二十世纪五十年代前半期，他都还是一个天主教俱乐部的成员。

1948年以后，阿尔都塞一直在巴黎高师教授哲学。他热心教学工作，在培养学生方面花费了大量心血。二十世纪六十年代以后在法国乃至整个世界哲学界叱咤风云的许多法国思想家都曾是他的学生，如福柯、德里达、布尔迪厄、巴里巴尔、马歇雷、巴迪欧等。不过，他本人在整个五十年代的研究工作倒不是非常引人注目，除了1959年出版了《孟德斯鸠：政治与历史》外，几乎没有其他论文和著述。然而，正是在这个不为人所知的沉潜时期，他对同时代人的一系列方法论研究成果进行吸收和改造，基本完成了“结构主义马克思主义”的思想建构。这些同时代人的方法论研究成果主要有：第一，由巴歇拉尔等开创的法国科学认识论传统，特别是其中的“认识论断裂”

学说；第二，结构主义的基本观念；第三，拉康在实现结构主义转型之后提出的症候阅读方法。

作为一名哲学家，阿尔都塞当然也对斯大林主义有所不满。不过，与大多数同时代人不同，他的不满主要不集中在斯大林主义的政治方面，而是集中在它的理论方法，即它的教条主义和经济决定论，以及它对马克思主义者健全而自由的理论思考的压制。对于他来说，苏共二十大的冲击远比斯大林主义的冲击大。因为他认为，人本主义马克思主义此后的流行与泛滥表明，马克思主义的正统已经受到资产阶级意识形态的污染与威胁，而他有责任对这种意识形态局面进行干预，以探索马克思主义理论与非马克思主义意识形态之间的界限。正是基于这种考虑，从 1960 年开始，他陆续发表了一系列论文，就马克思思想的本质、马克思与黑格尔的关系、马克思早期著作与后期著作的关系等在当时具有重大现实意义的理论问题阐发了自己的见解。同时，他还主持了一个关于《资本论》的研讨班，和青年学生一起研读《资本论》。1965 年，他将自己的相关论文以《保卫马克思》之名结集出版，同月之内，他与几位青年合作者共同完成的《读〈资本论〉》也出版发行。一时间，这两本书在法国知识界特别是青年学生中间产生巨大反响。“结构主义马克思主义”就此正式登上历史舞台。

1968 年五月风暴期间，阿尔都塞因病在外地疗养。不过，他却和萨特一起成为激进学生的精神领袖。五月风暴结束后，阿尔都塞完成了《论再生产》的长篇手稿，其中“意识形态与意识形态国家机器”部分于 1970 年公开发表。在这篇长文中，他对个体改变社会结构的能力与界限进行了严肃深入的探讨，指出现代资本主义国家已经形成了一种双重统治体制，即强制性压迫和意识形态教化共同构成的“恩威并重”的社会网络。

二十世纪七十年代以后，法国以及巴黎高师的学术氛围都发生改变，阿尔都塞中断了在巴黎高师的研讨班，将精力主要投入法国共产党内的理论斗争，先后出版了《列宁和哲学及其他论文集》（1968）、《答 L. 刘易斯》（1972）、《自我批评文集》（1974）等著作，就 1965 年以来所发生的一系列重大理论问题进行了回顾、总结和答辩。1975 年，为了申请法国国家博士学位，他向皮卡迪大学提交了《要成为马克思主义哲学家容易吗?》一文，对自己从事马克思主义哲学研究的过程与方法、理论和政治实践的不可分离性等问题进行了总结和反思。

1980年11月16日，阿尔都塞精神病发作，在无意识中将相濡以沫四十年的妻子掐死，随后被送进精神病院，被迫离开巴黎高师和法国理论界。尽管法国司法部后来并没有对他提出起诉，但他事实上被判处了与世隔绝的“死刑”。此后，他的精神状态时好时坏，并不时想起当年杀妻的恐怖场景，一直忍受着巨大的灵魂折磨。1985年，他完成自传《来日方长》(死后出版)。1990年10月22日，他因心脏病发作在巴黎去世。

(二) 时代背景

1. 苏共二十大后的复杂意识形态格局

第二次世界大战结束后，在世界范围内形成了一个以苏联为核心的社会主义阵营。对于马克思主义而言，这应当是一件好事。然而，由于苏联不仅没有对斯大林主义进行及时的反思调整，反而继续强力推行，从而导致教条主义日益严重，并在包括处理国际共产主义运动内部关系等在内的一系列内政外交问题上出现重大失误。在这种情况下，欧美左派阵营对苏联社会主义和斯大林主义的消极负面情绪不断积累。更严重的是，苏共二十大后，赫鲁晓夫以非科学的方式对待斯大林，对斯大林的所谓种种“暴虐行为”进行了“揭露”。于是，斯大林在一夜之间从“伟大的无产阶级领袖”被妖魔化成了法西斯主义式的暴君。这种“非斯大林主义化”运动一方面导致斯大林主义的理论破产，另一方面为各种资产阶级思潮向马克思主义的进攻和渗透打开了方便之门。结果，马克思主义理论界一下子失去了方向感，为了与“非人的”斯大林主义划清界限，人们纷纷诉诸人性、人的本质，于是，人本主义马克思主义在大繁荣的同时出现了泛化的趋势。“有些马克思主义哲学家，为了让别人起码能听得下去，不得不把自己乔装改扮起来——他们这样做完全出自自然的本能，而不怀有任何策略的考虑——他们把马克思装扮成胡塞尔、黑格尔或提倡伦理和人道主义的青年马克思，而不惜冒弄假成真的危险。”①

---

① [法]路易·阿尔都塞：《保卫马克思》，顾良译，商务印书馆2010年版，第9页。

2. 在意识形态领域保卫马克思的需要

由于过去学界都以公开发表的马克思恩格斯著作来理解马克思主义，使得二十世纪三十年代马克思生前未公开发表的早期著作《1844 年经济学哲学手稿》被翻译介绍到法国之后，其中的人本主义思想、异化问题、人的概念一下子成为学界研究的热点。结果是，比起《资本论》中的科学严谨的晚期马克思形象，许多学者更热衷于接受《1844 年经济学哲学手稿》中洋溢着人性伦理光辉的青年马克思形象。在此时的巴黎，马克思主义被大肆宣传为一种关于人本主义与异化的哲学，这促使苏东和部分欧洲共产党学者站出来为马克思主义辩护。不过，面对《1844 年经济学哲学手稿》这一新公开的青年马克思文本，他们采取了另一种非科学的方式保卫马克思，即试图用《资本论》的科学思想来反注《论犹太人问题》等早期著作，在青年马克思身上寻找晚期马克思的影子。这场意识形态领域的论战促使阿尔都塞着手重新客观地审视马克思恩格斯的著作，寻找非目的论式的马克思主义哲学史研究方法，真正发起保卫马克思的思想战斗，驳斥将马克思主义解读为异化理论的人本主义马克思主义的泛滥思潮。

（三）思想背景

1. 二十世纪五十年代末六十年代初法国马克思主义的理论图景

虽然社会主义和共产主义运动历史悠久，不过，法国在马克思主义理论方面却相当“贫困”。因此，自成立以后，法国共产党在理论上长期追随斯大林主义。随着法国共产党内一些青年哲学家不断成长，这种状况逐渐引起了他们的不满，并力图改变这种状况。在这个方面，列斐伏尔迈出了第一步。二十世纪三十年代早中期，他与其他人合作编译出版了马克思包括《1844 年经济学哲学手稿》在内的一些早期著作以及列宁的《哲学笔记》。在此过程中，他的思想发生了巨大变化。在 1939 年出版的《辩证唯物主义》一书中，他把批判的矛头直指斯大林主义的辩证唯物主义和历史唯物主义体系，认为马克思一生都没有放弃人道主义，辩证唯物主义其实就是人道主义。列斐伏尔对马克思主义哲学的这种人本主义解读在当时的法国理论界产生了巨大影响，不过却在法国共产党内受到批评。这迫使列斐伏尔本人在之后相当长的时间里不得不以游击战的方式进行理论研究。相反，他的这种思路在法国共产党之外却得到了自觉的延续。在理论上，第二次世界大战结束后，萨特和梅洛-庞蒂等存在主义者开始向马克思主义靠拢。他们批评斯大林主义是一种排斥人的经济决定论，主张用存在主义来补充马克思主义，使人重新回到马克思主义中去。这种"存在主义马克思主义"在二十世纪五十年代成为法国马克思主义理论界的主导声音。在学术上，以马克西米安·吕贝尔为代表的西方"马克思学"家竭力抬高青年马克思的人本主义异化理论，把人的概念作为理解马克思思想的核心线索，指责斯大林主义歪曲了马克思的思想，认为现行所谓的马克思主义实际上和马克思的学说关系甚少。在上述思潮和学术潮流的共同作用下，二十世纪五十年代以后的法国共产党在理论上实际上已经危机重重。非斯大林主义运动的发生则使这种危机爆发了出来。1956 年，列斐伏尔出版《马克思主义的当前问题》一书，重申自己早已有之的思想，主张复兴马克思主义，回到马克思真正的人道主义那里去。他因此被法国共产党开除出党。但是，自此以后，人本主义马克思主义思潮在法国共产党内逐渐泛滥开来。一个具有标志性意义的事件是：一向被认为是斯大林主义者的法国共产党政治局委员加罗第也很快与斯大林主义决裂，转到了人本主义马克思主义立场上。

2. 存在主义与结构主义的此消彼长

《保卫马克思》出版后，不仅在法国国内产生了巨大影响，而且很快漂洋过海在整个欧美都产生了巨大影响。之所以会如此，一个不可忽视的思想史背景就是二十世纪六十年代思想界正在发生着的存在主义与结构主义的此消彼长。作为二十世纪四大哲学主流之一的结构主义，其源头应当追溯到索绪尔的结构主义语言学。不过，真正使结构主义产生巨大的跨学科影响的其实是法国人类学家克劳德·列维-斯特劳斯。1945 年，列维-斯特劳斯出版《语言学的结构分析与人类学》一书，第一次将结构主义语言学的研究成果运用到人类学上。此后，他还出版了一系列相关研究成果，逐渐引起了其他学科对结构主义的高度重视，进入六十年代以后，结构主义渗透到了人文社会科学的许多重要学科领域。与此同时，随着丰裕社会的来临，第二次世界大战后一直占据主导地位的存在主义哲学的基本理念同变化了的社会现实开始发生冲突，人们逐渐对"个人""存在""自我意识"等存在主义范畴失去了原先的热情和兴趣。正是在这种背景下，以客观的结构为中心的结构主义作为存在主义的否定物乘势而起，在存在主义的退潮声中，在大西洋两岸开辟了一个新的结构主义时代。

二、篇章结构

《保卫马克思》的法文版包含一篇序言、一篇关于术语和论文出处的说明以及 8 篇论文。在题为《今天》的长篇序言中，阿尔都塞首先对自己为什么写作这些论文、为什么反对人本主义马克思主义进行了说明，进而简要叙述了自己每一篇论文的由来及基本观点。

《费尔巴哈的“哲学宣言”》发表于《新评论》1960 年 12 月期。在这篇论文中，阿尔都塞对费尔巴哈 1839—1845 年期间发表的那些最重要的论著进行了分析评论。阿尔都塞认为，之所以将费尔巴哈的理论称为“哲学宣言”，一方面是由于他的理论发现将使人从枷锁下解放出来，使人成为名副其实的自由、平等、博爱的真正的人，另一方面也是由于他的思想对于那些在十九世纪四十年代陷于“德意志贫困”和新黑格尔主义哲学的矛盾中不能自拔的激进青年知识分子来说更是宣告未来道路的宣言，阿尔都塞强调，这一切都只是在哲学的范围内发生的哲学宣言。但是哲学事件有时也可以同时是历史事件。在历史意义上来看，费尔巴哈作为青年黑格尔运动理论危机的见证人和当事人，在此期间的作品不仅属于一个特定的历史阶段，且起到了历史作用，特别是对马克思青年时期的思想起到了渗透性的影响。另外，从理论意义上讲，通过阅读并对照费尔巴哈与马克思理论之间的联系与分歧，可以更为准确地理解到马克思的理论革命正是要把马克思的理论思想从旧因素（黑格尔哲学和费尔巴哈哲学）那里解放出来，并把它建立在一个新因素的基础上，马克思与费尔巴哈的决裂意味着他采纳了一个新的总问题。而这可以从阅读马克思成熟时期的著作和了解马克思同费尔巴哈决裂的原因两种方法去加以领会。

在原发表于《思想》杂志 1961 年 3、4 月合刊的《论青年马克思（理论问题）》一文中，阿尔都塞从政治、理论和历史三个方面来研究马克思青年时期的著作。在政治问题上，阿尔都塞认为关于马克思青年时期著作的辩论首先是一场政治辩论。双方提出两个论点：认为青年马克思不是马克思，或断言青年马克思就是马克思。对此阿尔都塞给予了批判。在理论问题上，他认为人们在研究青年马克思的著作时，往往表现为源泉论或提前论，始终在这套老观点中悄然起作用的三个理论前提则分别是：分析性前提，目的论前提，全部意识形态历史都在意识形态内部进行。从根本上说，其最显著的特点就在于它是一种折中主义的方法。为了对青年马克思的著作进行马克思主义的研究，就必须同这三个前提决裂，并运用马克思关于思想发展的理论原则去研究课题。阿尔都塞指出，必须承认哲学家也有自己的青年时代，必须了解相关思想产生和发展时所处的意识形态环境，揭示这一思想的内在整体即思想的总问题，才能认识这一思想的发展。从历史问题看，就涉及“全部意识形态历史都在意识形态内部进行”这一前提，即“马克思的道路”的问题。阿尔都塞认为，马克思从一个偶然开端出发，越过幻觉的重重障碍，才终于突破了沉重的意识形态的襁褓。绝不能说“青年时期的马克思属于马克思主义”，应该说青年马克思的确在向着马克思主义发展，但这要以马克思努力回溯自己的哲学根基为代价，要对德国历史所灌输给他的种种幻觉做英勇战斗为代价，以全神贯注地发现被这些幻觉所掩盖的现实为代价。

《矛盾与多元决定(研究笔记)》发表于《思想》1962 年 12 月期。在这篇文章中阿尔都塞所想要表达的是，所谓“对黑格尔的颠倒”这种说法并不适用于马克思，至少不适用于已脱离了“人本学”阶段的马克思。阿尔都塞首先认为，马克思与黑格尔之间的真正不同应该体现在辩证法的实质中，即在它的规定性和特有结构中得到反映。所谓对辩证法的“颠倒”，在马克思那里并不是要用相同的方法去研究不同对象的性质，而是从辩证法本身去研究辩证法的性质。接着，围绕列宁“最薄弱环节”的理论，阿尔都塞从矛盾论的角度对马克思与黑格尔的不同进行讨论。阿尔都塞指出，在马克思那里矛盾在本质上是多元的，一切矛盾在历史事件中都以多元决定的形式出现，这与黑格尔的徒具多元外表的简单矛盾相比具有特殊性。继而，阿尔都塞进一步从历史观角度出发，反对把马克思的历史观看作对黑格尔的“颠倒”的说法。因为假若这一说法成立，原本在黑格尔那里政治因素和意识形态因素是经济因素的本质的提法，到了马克思那里经济因素就会成为政治和意识形态因素的全部本质，这必将把历史的辩证法彻底地降低为产生一些生产方式的辩证法，即把马克思主义降低为经济主义或技术主义。阿尔都塞总结认为，在马克思主义的历史研究中，必须对理论有一个精确的认识，以摆脱“颠倒”的概念及由此产生的种种混乱。

《皮克罗剧团、贝尔多拉西和布莱希特（关于一部唯物主义戏剧的笔记）》发表于 1962 年 12 月的《精神》。阿尔都塞对《我们的米兰》这部与众不同的剧本进行了讨论，认为剧本所具有的那种不对称的和批判的潜在结构，与布莱希特的剧本一样，存在着两种相互分离、互无关系、同时并存、交错进行但又永不会合的时间形式，还存在着由局部的、单独的、似乎凭空出现的辩证法做总结的真实世界。因此人们就能用有待人们承认的、令人困惑不解的现实对意识的幻觉、对虚假的辩证法进行真正的批判，因为这种现实正是意识和辩证法的底蕴。阿尔都塞认为，当剧作者不再用自我意识的形式来表达剧本的意义和潜在意义时，他推翻了传统戏剧的总问题。剧作者希望用间离效果在观众和演出之间建立一种批判的和能动的关系。从剧本方面看，其本身的潜在结构产生了观众同演出之间的距离；从观众意识来看，就首先要把妨碍思考观众意识的两个传统公式，即自我意识和感情共鸣否定掉。在阿尔都塞看来，戏剧的目的就是要触犯自我承认这一不可触犯的形象，动摇静止不动的、神秘的幻觉世界，使剧本在观众中产生和发展出一种尚未完成的新意识，创造出新观众，由他们在生活中把演出演完。

《卡尔·马克思的〈1844 年手稿〉（政治经济学与哲学）》发表于 1963 年 2 月的《思想》。阿尔都塞对艾·波蒂热利版本的《1844 年手稿》法文版在著作界和评论界的重大意义给予了毫不吝啬的赞扬。阿尔都塞认为，《1844 年手稿》的写作体现了马克思第一次接触政治经济学之后的理论成果，同时也是哲学同政治经济学的一次接触。这种哲学仍然有费尔巴哈总问题的痕迹，始终为是否从费尔巴哈退到黑格尔那里而犹豫不决。这部作品对于研究马克思的思想发展具有十分重要的意义。阿尔都塞赞同波蒂热利要求确定一个全新的、严格的研究方法的做法，同时认为新译本对于马克思主义者具有双重的理论意义，不仅关系到马克思的思想形成和转变，而且还给了马克思主义关于意识形态的理论一个运用和验证其方法的最好机会。在评论中阿尔都塞提出，在哲学对即将成为绝对独立的内容的绝对统治方面，离马克思最远的马克思正是离马克思最近的马克思，即最接近转变的那个马克思。阿尔都塞同时认为，对于马克思青年时期的著作可以从政治角度和理论角度进行阅读，应设计出“另一种方法”来解释马克思思想的形成过程。

《关于唯物辩证法(论起源的不平衡)》发表于 1963 年 8 月的《思想》,阿尔都塞针对外界对自己的批评,着重阐发了自己关于马克思辩证法的特殊性的观点。阿尔都塞所希望表达的观点是:"马克思对黑格尔辩证法的'颠倒'究竟颠倒了什么?把马克思的辩证法和黑格尔的辩证法区分开来的特殊性究竟是什么?"是一个理论问题,而他所要进行的工作就是对马克思主义实践已经对之做出的解答进行理论的阐述,使真理的存在真正得到认识。阿尔都塞首先定义了实践、理论概念。他将理论区分为"理论"和理论两种,前者是关于社会形态发展的马克思主义科学,即历史唯物主义;后者则是一般实践的理论,即唯物辩证法。而关于对实践解答的理论阐述这一问题就与理论(即辩证法)相关。阿尔都塞认为,理论能够说明科学的道理和目标,批判意识形态的各种假面具,并作为世界上最好的方法论为科学指引方向,这是一种真正的唯物辩证法,绝对不同于所谓颠倒了的黑格尔的辩证法。其次,阿尔都塞从理论实践和政治实践两个方面,研究了马克思主义辩证法与其本身所参与的实践之间的关系。阿尔都塞认为,辩证法是一种方法,而不是一种解释既成事实的理论,"颠倒""合理的内核"概念绝不是一种真正的认识。接着,阿尔都塞就理论实践的过程进行了叙述,分析了马克思主义辩证法相较于黑格尔辩证法的特殊性,认为"颠倒"引起的是意识形态的混淆,对意识形态的颠倒是无法成为科学的。之后,阿尔都塞的视线转落在了矛盾的特殊性上。在他看来,"特殊性"是认识的特殊性,由于辩证法"是研究对象的本质自身中的矛盾",为了抓住这一核心就需要对矛盾的特殊性进行解释,于是问题最终回到了马克思辩证法相比黑格尔辩证法具有特殊性的问题上。阿尔都塞指出,与黑格尔矛盾的简单性不同,马克思主义的矛盾的特殊性的原因就在于其多元决定性,而矛盾不平衡发展的法则就是马克思主义的实践的要害。至此,阿尔都塞认为,在马克思主义矛盾的特殊性这个定义中,他认识到了马克思主义辩证法的本质。

在《马克思主义和人道主义》中,阿尔都塞表达了他关于人道主义的本质是意识形态的观点,同时阿尔都塞希望将意识形态和科学理论给予清晰的划分。阿尔都塞从"社会主义人道主义"这个概念出发,区分了"阶级人道主义"和"社会主义个人人道主义"两种形式。阿尔都塞认为这个词汇包含着理论的不平衡性:即在马克思的思想中,"社会主义"是个科学的概念,而"人道主义"则是意识形态的概念。因此他针对人道主义展开研究。从马克思的思想发展来看，在青年马克思那里，人的哲学是其理论基础，但自1845年起，马克思就同一切把历史和政治归结为人的本质的理论彻底决裂。应当说这一决裂是和马克思的科学发现浑然一体的。以往哲学的全部领域和阐述都建立在人性这个总问题的基础上。而马克思确立了一个新的总问题，用实践的辩证唯物主义和历史唯物主义取代了旧有的理论假定。在阿尔都塞看来，马克思否认人道主义是理论，把它作为意识形态来加以认识，因此他从意识形态的角度出发，论证了人道主义存在的必要性，并进一步指出社会主义人道主义的论题就是根据当时苏联出现的一些问题而提出的。但阿尔都塞真正所要说明的是，虽然社会主义人道主义已经被提上了议事日程，但这一意识形态存在的合理性绝对不能作为缺失理论的补充去解决实际问题，意识形态和科学理论是不能相混淆的。因为马克思的哲学最为宝贵之处就在于它是一种批判的和革命的理论。阿尔都塞提醒马克思主义者："一切策略必定建立在战略的基础上，而一切战略必定建立在理论的基础上。"①

在《关于"真正的人道主义"的补记》中，阿尔都塞进一步指出，实现"真正的人道主义"的转移，不仅是从抽象到具体的位置移动，而且是基本概念的根本转移。在马克思用以思考的概念中，以理论概念出现的不再是人的概念或人道主义的概念，而是生产方式、生产力、上层建筑等崭新的概念。人道主义的口号没有理论价值但有实际指示的价值，应避免用任何只具有实际职能的字眼去不恰当地代替理论职能，而应使这些字眼在完成其实际职能的同时，从理论场所中消失。

三、研究前沿

《保卫马克思》是阿尔都塞的一部论文集，收录了他在1960—1965年间发表的不同文章。其中，为了击退在法国思想界泛滥的人本主义马克思主义思潮，阿尔都塞基于马克思的著作在《保卫马克思》中重新阐释了马克思的思想发展历程。为此，阿尔都塞借用了结构主义思潮的认识论断裂、问题式等概念，强调马克思的理论出发点不是抽象的人及其本质，相反，在《德意

① [法]路易·阿尔都塞：《保卫马克思》，顾良译，商务印书馆2010年版，第239页。

志意识形态》一书中创立历史唯物主义之后，马克思便与既往的人本主义话语决裂，并指认历史是无主体的客观过程。由此，《保卫马克思》催生了风靡一时的结构主义马克思主义思潮，并在国内学界得到了长久且多元的关注。

第一，探究《保卫马克思》在马克思主义思想史中的重要作用。在国内研究中，《保卫马克思》被视为反对人本主义马克思主义的西方马克思主义经典著作，开创了结构主义马克思主义思潮。为此，国内学界高度肯定了在特定历史背景下《保卫马克思》的重要理论意义，认为它重新解读了马克思恩格斯前后期的著作，并指出马克思思想发展过程中存在着从意识形态阶段向科学阶段的"认识论断裂"，马克思主义是捅破了人道主义意识形态襁褓后的科学，是"历史无主体"的"理论上的反人道主义"。这为回应当时甚嚣尘上的"青年马克思""马恩对立"等重大理论问题提供了重要理论依据，也基于马克思恩格斯著作提供了非教条主义的马克思主义思想发展叙事。不过，国内学者也指出，在《保卫马克思》中，阿尔都塞的解读明显受到了当时结构主义思潮的影响，导致其对马克思主义思想发展的阐释带有独断论的色彩，忽视了马克思前后期思想发展的理论关联性。

第二，对《保卫马克思》的理论概念、思想判断的专题研究。国内学者详细阐释了《保卫马克思》中的关键概念与判断，特别是对"认识论断裂""问题式""多元决定论""意识形态"等进行了详细论述。一方面，国内学者对阿尔都塞的概念与判断进行了热烈讨论，特别是关于 1845 年前后马克思思想发展中是否存在两个完全不同的思想问题式、法国科学认识论与阿尔都塞的"认识论断裂"的关联与差异、"多元决定"对一元决定论的理论创造等。另一方面，国内学者也集中探讨了《保卫马克思》中阿尔都塞对马克思主义思想的独特判断，如"理论上的反人道主义""历史无主体"等。学者普遍认为，这些判断是阿尔都塞为了反击以人道主义歪曲理解马克思主义而做，从而以意识形态与科学之分捍卫马克思主义的科学性质，但也存在独断和形而上学之嫌，影响了其思想观点的科学性。此外，也有学者仔细辨析了阿尔都塞所说的反人道主义与马克思主义的人文关怀、历史无主体与马克思主义的主体理论等之间的关系。

第三，对《保卫马克思》的方法论探讨。通过《保卫马克思》，阿尔都塞不仅击退了"青年马克思"、人本主义马克思主义的思潮，其独特的马克思主义研究方法也为结构主义马克思主义奠定了基础，并引起了众多思想回响。

对此，国内学界对阿尔都塞在《保卫马克思》中留下的丰富思想遗产进行了阐释。比如，部分学者认为，在《保卫马克思》中，阿尔都塞提出了多元决定的马克思主义辩证法，从而改变了人们对马克思主义经济决定论的理解，以免将马克思主义理解为经济主义或技术主义。也有学者探究了《保卫马克思》关于科学认识过程的方法论内容，认为阿尔都塞的“认识论断裂”“多元决定论”和“结构性因果关系”为科学认识提供了理论前提，并赋予了理论实践以真理性的内在标准。

四、文本节选

Introduction: Today

...

Of course, the quotation in which Marx himself attests to and locates this break “(we resolved ... to settle accounts with our erstwhile philosophical conscience”) in 1845 at the level of *The German Ideology*, can only be treated as a declaration to be examined, and falsified or confirmed, not as a proof of the existence of the break and a definition of its location. The examination of the status of this declaration called for a theory and a method—the *Marxist theoretical concepts* in which the reality of theoretical formations in general (philosophical ideologies and science) can be considered must be applied to Marx himself. Without a theory of the history of theoretical formations it would be impossible to grasp and indicate the specific difference that distinguishes two different theoretical formations. I thought it possible to borrow for this purpose the concept of a “*problematic*” from Jacques Martin to designate the particular unity of a theoretical formation and hence the location to be assigned to this specific difference, and the concept of an “*epistemological break*” from Gaston Bachelard to designate the mutation in the theoretical problematic contemporary with the foundation of a scientific discipline. That one of these concepts had to be constructed and the other borrowed does not imply at all that either is arbitrary or foreign to Marx, on the contrary, it can be shown that both are present and active in Marx's scientific thought, even if this presence is most often in the practical state. These two concepts provided me with the indispensable theoretical minimum authorizing a pertinent analysis of the process of the theoretical transformation of the Young Marx, and leading to some precise conclusions.

Let me summarize here in extremely abbreviated form some of the results of a study which took several years and to which the pieces I am presenting here bear only partial witness.

(1) There is an unequivocal "*epistemological break*" in Marx's work which does in fact occur at the point where Marx himself locates it, in the book, unpublished in his lifetime, which is a critique of his erstwhile philosophical (ideological) conscience: *The German Ideology*. *The Theses on Feuerbach*, which are only a few sentences long, mark out the earlier limit of this break, the point at which the new theoretical consciousness is already beginning to show through in the erstwhile consciousness and the erstwhile language, that is, as *necessarily ambiguous and unbalanced concepts*.

(2) This "*epistemological break*" concerns conjointly *two distinct theoretical disciplines*. By founding the theory of history (historical materialism), Marx simultaneously broke with his erstwhile ideological philosophy and established a new philosophy (dialectical materialism). I am deliberately using the traditionally accepted terminology (historical materialism, dialectical materialism) to designate this double foundation in a single break. And I should point out two important problems implied by this exceptional circumstance. Of course, if the birth of a new philosophy is simultaneous with the foundation of a new science, and this science is the science of history, a crucial theoretical problem arises: by what necessity of principle should the foundation of the scientific theory of history *ipso facto* imply a theoretical revolution in

philosophy? This same circumstance also entails a considerable practical consequence: as the new philosophy was only implicit in the new science it might be tempted to *confuse itself with it*. *The German Ideology* sanctions this confusion as it reduces philosophy, as we have noted, to a faint shadow of science, if not to the empty generality of positivism. This practical consequence is one of the keys to the remarkable history of Marxist philosophy, from its origins to the present day. I shall examine these two problems later.

(3) This "*epistemological break*" divides Marx's thought into two long essential periods: the "ideological" period before, and the scientific period after, the break in 1845. The second period can itself be divided into two moments, the moment of Marx's theoretical transition and that of his theoretical maturity. To simplify the philosophical and historical labours in front of us, I should like to propose the following provisional terminology which registers the above periodization.

(a) I propose to designate the works of the earlier period, that is, everything Marx wrote from his Doctoral Dissertation to the *1844 Manuscripts* and *The Holy Family* by the already accepted formula: *Marx's Early Works*.

(b) I propose to designate the writings of the break in 1845, that is, the *Theses on Feuerbach* and *The German Ideology* which first introduce Marx's new problematic, though usually still in a partially negative and sharply polemical and critical form, by a new formula: *the Works of the Break*.

(c) I propose to designate the works of the period 1845—1857 by a new formula: *the Transitional Works*. While it is possible to assign the crucial date of the works of 1845 (the *Theses on Feuerbach* and *The German Ideology*) to the break separating the scientific from the ideological, it must be remembered that this mutation could not produce immediately, in *positive* and *consummated* form, the new theoretical problematic which it inaugurated, in the theory of history as well as in that of philosophy. In fact, *The German Ideology* is a commentary, usually a negative and critical one, on the different forms of the ideological problematic Marx had rejected. Long years of *positive* study and elaboration were necessary before Marx could produce, fashion and establish a conceptual terminology and systematics that were adequate to his revolutionary theoretical project. That is why I propose to designate the works written between 1845 and the first drafts of *Capital* (around 1845—1857), that is, the *Manifesto*, the *Poverty of Philosophy*, *Wages*, *Price and Profit*, etc., as the *Works of Marx's Theoretical Transition*.

(d) Finally, I propose to designate all the works after 1857 as *Marx's Mature Works*. This gives us the following classification:

1840—1844: the Early Works.

1845: the Works of the Break.

1845—1857: the Transitional Works.

1857—1883: the Mature Works.

(4) The period of Marx's Early Works (1840—1945), that is, the period of his ideological works, can itself be subdivided into two moments:

(a) the liberal-rationalist moment of his articles in *Die Rheinische Zeitung* (up to 1842).

(b) the communalist-rationalist moment of the years 1842—1845.

As my essay on "Marxism and Humanism" briefly suggests, the presupposition of the works of the first moment is a problematic of Kantian-Fichtean type. Those of the second moment, on the contrary, rest on Feuerbach's anthropological problematic. The Hegelian problematic inspires one absolutely *unique* text, which is a rigorous attempt to "invert" Hegelian idealism, in the *strict* sense, into Feuerbach's pseudo-materialism: this text is the *1844 Manuscripts*. Paradoxically, therefore, if we exclude the Doctoral Dissertation, which is still the work of a student, the Young Marx *was never strictly speaking a Hegelian*, except in the *last* text of his ideologico-philosophical period; rather, he was first a Kantian Fichtean, then a Feuerbachian. So the thesis that the Young Marx was a Hegelian, though widely believed today, is in general a myth. On the contrary, it seems that Marx's one and only resort to Hegel in his youth, on the eve of his rupture with his "erstwhile philosophical conscience", produced the prodigious "abreaction" indispensable to the liquidation of his "disordered" consciousness. Until then he had always kept his distance from Hegel, and to grasp the movement whereby he passed from his *Hegelian university studies* to a Kantian-Fichtean problematic and thence to a Feuerbachian problematic, we must realize that, far from being close to Hegel, Marx moved *further and further away from* him. With Fichte and Kant he had worked his way back to the end of the eighteenth century, and then, with Feuerbach, he regressed to the heart of the theoretical past of that century, for in his own way Feuerbach may be said to represent the "ideal" eighteenth-century philosopher, the synthesis of sensualist materialism and ethico-historical idealism, the real union of Diderot and Rousseau. It would be difficult not to speculate that Marx's sudden and total last return to Hegel in that genial synthesis of Feuerbach and Hegel, the *1844 Manuscripts*, might not have been an explosive experiment uniting the substances of the two extremes of the theoretical field which he had until then frequented, that this extraordinarily rigorous and conscientious experiment, the most extreme test of the "inversion" of Hegel ever attempted might not have been the way Marx lived practically and achieved his own transformation, in a text which he *never published*. Some idea of the logic of this prodigious mutation is given by the extraordinary theoretical tension of the *1844 Manuscripts*, for we know in advance the paradox that the text of the last hours of the night is, theoretically speaking, the text the furthest removed from the day that is about to dawn.

(5) The *Works of the Break* raise delicate problems of interpretation, precisely as a function of their place in the theoretical formation of

Marx's thought. Those brief sparks, the *Theses on Feuerbach*, light up every philosopher who comes near them, but as is well known, a spark dazzles rather than illuminates: nothing is more difficult to locate in the darkness of the night than the point of light which breaks it. One day we will have to show that these eleven deceptively transparent theses are really riddles. As for *The German Ideology*, it offers us precisely a thought in a state of rupture with its past, playing a pitiless game of deadly criticism with all its erstwhile theoretical presuppositions: primarily with Feuerbach and Hegel and all the forms of a philosophy of consciousness and an anthropological philosophy. But this new thought so firm and precise in its interrogation of ideological error, cannot define itself without difficulties and ambiguities. It is impossible to break with a theoretical past at one blow: in every case, words and concepts are needed to break with words and concepts, and often the old words are charged with the conduct of the rupture throughout the period of the search for new ones. *The German Ideology* presents the spectacle of a reenlisted conceptual reserve standing in for new concepts still in training ... and as we usually judge these old concepts by their bearing, taking them at their word, it is easy to stray into a positivist conception (the end of all philosophy) or an individualist-humanist conception (the subjects of history are "real, concrete men"). Or again, it is possible to be taken in by the ambiguous role of the *division of labour*, which, in this book, plays the principal part taken by alienation in the writings of his youth, and commands the whole theory of *ideology* and the whole theory of science. This all arises from its proximity to the break, and that is why *The German Ideology* alone demands a major critical effort to distinguish the suppletory theoretical *function* of particular concepts from the concepts themselves. I shall return to this.

(6) Locating the break in 1845 is not without important theoretical consequences as regards not only the relation between Marx and Feuerbach, but also the relation between Marx and Hegel. Indeed,

Marx did not first develop a systematic critique of Hegel after 1845; he had been doing so since the beginning of the second moment of his Youthful period, in the *Critique of Hegel's Philosophy of Right* (1843 Manuscript), the *Introduction to a Critique of Hegel's Philosophy of Right* (1843), the *1844 Manuscripts* and *The Holy Family*. But the *theoretical principles* on which this critique of Hegel was based are *merely* a reprise, a commentary or a development and extension of the admirable critique of Hegel repeatedly formulated by Feuerbach. It is a critique of Hegelian philosophy as *speculative* and *abstract*, a critique appealing to the concrete-materialist against the abstract-speculative, i.e. a critique which remains a prisoner of the idealist problematic it hoped to free itself from, and therefore a critique which belongs by right to the theoretical problematic with which Marx broke in 1845.

——Louis Althusser, *For Marx*, trans. Ben Brewster, Verso, 2005, pp.32 - 37.

Marxism and Humanism

In 1845, Marx broke radically with every theory that based history and politics on an essence of man. This unique rupture contained three indissociable elements.

(1) The formation of a theory of history and politics based on radically new concepts: the concepts of social formation, productive forces, relations of production, superstructure, ideologies, determination in the last instance by the economy, specific determination of the other levels, etc.

(2) A radical critique of the *theoretical* pretensions of every philosophical humanism.

(3) The definition of humanism as an *ideology*.

This new conception is completely rigorous as well, but it is a new rigour: the essence criticized (2) is defined as an ideology (3), a category belonging to the new theory of society and history (1).

This rupture with every *philosophical* anthropology or humanism is no secondary detail; it is Marx's scientific discovery.

It means that Marx rejected the problematic of the earlier philosophy and adopted a new problematic in one and the same act. The earlier idealist ("bourgeois") philosophy depended in all its domains and arguments (its "theory of knowledge", its conception of history, its political economy, its ethics, its aesthetics, etc.) on a problematic of *human nature* (or the essence of man). For centuries, this problematic had been transparency itself, and no one had thought of questioning it even in its internal modifications.

This problematic was neither vague nor loose; on the contrary, it was constituted by a coherent system of precise concepts tightly articulated together. When Marx confronted it, it implied the two complementary postulates he defined in the Sixth Thesis on Feuerbach:

(1) that there is a universal essence of man;

(2) that this essence is the attribute of "*each single individual*" who is its real subject.

These two postulates are complementary and indissociable. But their existence and their unity presuppose a whole empiricist-idealist world outlook. If the essence of man is to be a universal attribute, it is essential that *concrete subjects* exist as absolute givens; this implies an *empiricism of the subject*. If these empirical individuals are to be men, it is essential that each carries in himself the whole human essence, if not in fact, at least in principle; this implies an *idealism of the essence*. So empiricism of the subject implies idealism of the essence and vice versa. This relation can be inverted into its "opposite"—empiricism of the concept/idealism of the subject. But the inversion respects the basic structure of the problematic, which remains fixed.

In this type-structure it is possible to recognize not only the principle of theories of society (from Hobbes to Rousseau), of political economy (from Petty to Ricardo), of ethics (from Descartes to Kant), but also the very principle of the (pre-Marxist) idealist and materialist "theory of knowledge" (from Locke to Feuerbach, via Kant). The content of the human essence or of the empirical subjects may vary (as can be seen from Descartes to Feuerbach); the subject may change from empiricism to idealism (as can be seen from Locke to Kant): the terms presented and their relations only vary within the invariant type-structure which constitutes this very problematic: *an empiricism of the subject always corresponds to an idealism of the essence (or an empiricism of the essence to an idealism of the subject)*.

By rejecting the essence of man as his theoretical basis, Marx rejected the whole of this organic system of postulates. He drove the philosophical categories of the *subject*, of *empiricism*, of the *ideal essence*, etc., from all the domains in which they had been supreme. Not only from political economy (rejection of the myth of *homo economicus*, that is, of the individual with definite faculties and needs as the *subject* of the classical economy); not just from history (rejection of social atomism and ethico-political idealism); not just from ethics (rejection of the Kantian ethical idea); but also from philosophy itself: for Marx's materialism excludes the empiricism of the subject (and its inverse: the transcendental subject) and the idealism of the concept (and its inverse: the empiricism of the concept).

This total theoretical revolution was only empowered to reject the old concepts because it replaced them by new concepts. In fact Marx established a new problematic, a new systematic way of asking questions of the world, new principles and a new method. This discovery is immediately contained in the theory of historical materialism, in which Marx did not only propose a new theory of the history of societies, but at the same time implicitly, but necessarily, a new "philosophy", infinite in its implications. Thus, when Marx replaced the old couple individuals/human essence in the theory of history by new concepts (forces of production, relations of production, etc.), he was, in fact, simultaneously proposing a new conception of "philosophy". He replaced the old postulates (empiricism/idealism of the subject, empiricism/idealism of the essence) which were the basis not only for idealism but also for pre-Marxist materialism, by a historico-dialectical materialism of *praxis*: that is, by a theory of the different specific *levels of human practice* (economic practice, political practice, ideological practice, scientific practice) in their characteristic articulations, based on the specific articulations of the unity of human society. In a word, Marx substituted for the "ideological" and universal concept of Feuerbachian "practice" a concrete conception of the specific differences that enables us to situate each particular practice in the specific differences of the social structure.

So, to understand what was radically new in Marx's contribution, we must become aware not only of the novelty of the concepts of historical materialism, but also of the depth of the theoretical revolution they imply and inaugurate. On this condition it is possible to define humanism's status, and reject its *theoretical* pretensions while recognizing its practical function as an ideology.

——Louis Althusser, *For Marx*, trans. Ben Brewster, Verso, 2005, pp. 227 - 229.

五、观点解读

1. 马克思的思想存在着"认识论断裂"

阿尔都塞关注的核心问题是如何重新理解马克思主义。面对人本主义马克思主义的泛滥，他希望通过构建一种全新的理论结构和提问方法，还马克思哲学以本来面貌。他反对将马克思主义人本主义化的哲学倾向，认为马克思的著作本身就是科学，不能把科学与意识形态相混淆。他试图构建一种全新的解释学，对马克思主义哲学史做出不同解释，并提出了断裂说：认为马克思在1845年写下的《关于费尔巴哈的提纲》和《德意志意识形态》中，思想发生了一次重要的“认识论断裂”，即意识形态和科学两种不同问题式之间的截然决裂。马克思采纳了一个新的总问题，根本否定了他以前曾经拥有过的意识形态问题式，并试图将自己的理论思想建立在这个新因素的基础上。在阿尔都塞看来，马克思思想发生的这一“断裂”是不可逆转的，它是一个持续的“断裂”，不是一个瞬间、立即完成的质变，而只是一个开创科学活动过程的开端。他概括了“断裂”所包含的三个“不可分割的理论方面”：一是“确定人道主义为意识形态”；二是“彻底批判任何哲学人道主义的理论要求”；三是“制定出在崭新概念基础上的历史理论和政治理论”。阿尔都塞认为，前两点具有革命性的否定意义，宣告了意识形态旧问题式的死亡；后一点则具有肯定意义，意味着科学问题式的新生，即马克思主义历史科学的诞生。通过说明“认识论断裂”的问题，阿尔都塞指出，马克思的思想存在着一个从意识形态向马克思主义科学（即历史唯物主义）的过渡，他否定了被人本学派倍加推崇的《1844年经济学哲学手稿》的地位，认为其是青年马克思意识形态框架发展的最高阶段，更重要的是他对人本主义的马克思诠释学从根基上给予了彻底的批判。应当说，阿尔都塞正确地捕捉到马克思主义哲学理论中存在的重要逻辑断裂。但我们也需清楚地认识到，阿尔都塞的分析忽略了历史发展的复杂性，且抛弃了马克思主义理论发展的实践本质，这使得马克思复杂的思想进程被他独断地曲解为一种意识形态与科学的线性替代过程。在阅读阿尔都塞作品时需要对此十分注意。

2. 马克思主义是“理论上的反人本主义”

阿尔都塞根据自己对马克思主义思想发展进程的理解，提出了一个响亮的口号：马克思主义是“理论上的反人本主义”。而1845年以前尚未与费尔巴哈决裂的青年马克思则被他指认为“理论上的人本主义”，即非科学的意识形态。在此处，“理论”是指一定的系统的整体世界观，用阿尔都塞的话来说即某种理论框架的整体结构（问题式）。阿尔都塞认为，马克思主义最重要的原则就是要拒绝理论逻辑意义上的人本主义，反对一切主体哲学。

青年马克思的“理论上的人本主义”的整体理论基础是人的类本质，与以往哲学一样，其思想的全部领域和阐述都建立在人性这个总问题的基础上。在阿尔都塞看来，这是资产阶级意识形态的人本主义问题式，这种人本主义哲学绝不可能是马克思主义的科学。到了 1845 年之后，马克思确立了一个新的总问题，用实践的辩证唯物主义和历史唯物主义取代了旧有的理论假定。马克思不再把人的本质当作理论基础，一举抛弃了旧的人本主义哲学理论框架，把作为一种总体理论框架的人本主义看作了意识形态，从理论上拒绝了人本主义，建立了科学的历史唯物主义。阿尔都塞认为，为了坚持马克思主义的科学立场，就必须反对理论上的人本主义立场。当然，还需指出的是，阿尔都塞在反对把马克思主义看成是理论上的人本主义的同时，也承认人本主义作为意识形态存在的必要性。客观地说，阿尔都塞把青年马克思时期的思想看作“理论人本主义”是很有见地的；但我们也必须看到其理论的片面性，阿尔都塞无法看到，虽然马克思不再从人本主义的理论逻辑出发来研究现实，但这并不意味着马克思从此就不再关心人，实际上解放全人类、建立自由人的联合体是马克思终生追求的人道主义理想。

3. 历史是一个无主体过程

阿尔都塞力图证明的观点是：历史是一个没有主体或目的的过程。他指出，人本主义哲学的前提是主体，所以人本主义的历史观是把历史看成一个有主体的过程。主体哲学应当是资产阶级意识形态在哲学上的表现形式。在阿尔都塞看来，马克思在《1844 年经济学哲学手稿》中还认为历史的主体是异化过程的历史。但也正是在这部仍处于人本主义理论问题式的作品中，马克思引进了黑格尔哲学，从而实现了其主体哲学的一次“爆炸”。阿尔都塞认为，黑格尔的历史是作为没有主体的异化过程或没有主体的辩证过程被思考的，在其哲学的总体逻辑中不存在一个异化过程的主体，而绝对理念作为一个大写的主体则应被理解为辩证法。阿尔都塞指出，在这一点上，马克思选择性地接受了黑格尔，在马克思的历史科学中，历史就成了一个无主体的过程，而在历史中起作用的辩证法并不来自任何主体。进一步说，在历史唯物主义的理论视域中，既没有作为开端的逻辑起源，也没有本真的逻辑主体，具体存在的个人与群体并不是历史的主体，个人在历史中充当的是使过程具体化的角色。阿尔都塞进一步解释说，“历史作为一个没有主体或目的的过程，‘人们’在其中作为受到社会关系制约的一些主体的这个既定条件是阶级斗争的产物。因为历史在主体这个名词的哲学意义上，并不具有一种主体，只有一种‘原动力’，这就是阶级斗争”。[①] 阿尔都塞认为，1845年后，马克思用“过程”代替了主体，并声称方法或本身是绝对的过程的概念是世上唯一绝对的东西。在阿尔都塞看来，方法就是一切，无主体就是过程；这也是与他对于“过程的概念是科学的”，而“主体的概念是意识形态的”这一判断是相符合的。

4. 纠正“历史主义的误解”

阿尔都塞认为，马克思建立了一门全新的历史科学，但他反对传统研究对马克思历史概念的理解，特别是反对历史主义的伪历史概念。我们知道，阿尔都塞一方面反对传统的人道主义，认为历史是一个无主体的过程；另一方面他又反对传统的历史主义，认定历史绝不是平滑、连续的历时性过程。人们通常认为马克思是通过批判古典经济学以及整个资产阶级意识形态的非历史性（也就是说将资本主义看成一种永恒的、固定不变的制度）而确立自己的历史规定的，并常常将马克思与古典经济学的关系看成一种类似于黑格尔与古典哲学的关系。在阿尔都塞看来，对马克思历史概念的这种解释存在着一种“历史主义的误解”，这种误解的根源在于黑格尔的历史性时间概念。在阿尔都塞看来，黑格尔的历史性时间具有两个特征：一是“时间的同质的连续性”，绝对观念有多少环节，时间的连续性就被分割成多少个历史时期；二是“时间的同时性或者历史的在场范畴”，也就是说黑格尔的历史性时间都从属于绝对精神的最高存在，因而所有的历史时间都是观念总体的共时性逻辑存在，历时性本质上处于一种共时性之中。阿尔都塞认为，当代的大多数历史学家仍然处在黑格尔式的历史时间的模式之下，而马克思的历史概念和时间概念与黑格尔并不相同，要建立起马克思主义的历史时间的概念，就需要理解马克思主义关于社会总体性的概念。在阿尔都塞看来，马克思的整体概念与黑格尔不同，它不是一种思辨的统一性，而是由各种复杂层次和环节之间构成和被构成的整体的统一性。而历史就是一种

① ［法］路易·阿尔都塞：《自我批评文集》，杜章智、沈起予译，台湾远流出版公司1990年版，第118页。

被构成的、正在生成的总体结构，它可以被表述为不同层次的有机整体的结构，一方面，各个环节和各种关系在整体中的共同存在受到占统治地位的结构次序的支配；另一方面，这种被构成的总体结构不是一种绝对同质同构的专制系统，每一层次（子结构）都具有自己相对的自主性，此处阿尔都塞明显在批判正统马克思主义的经济决定论。因此，历史时间的概念指涉的不是传统历史主义的那种连续性的、同质的伪历史时间性，而是一定的社会历史整体的结构；同时，区别于黑格尔哲学将所有具体的历史和时间都纳入绝对观念的强制的共时性本质之中，在阿尔都塞所理解的马克思那里，不同层次的历史和时间在一定的总体结构中在保持着相对自主的独立性的同时，又相互作用。

六、进一步阅读指南

1. 习近平：《习近平谈治国理政》第二卷，外文出版社 2017 年版。

2.《习近平新时代中国特色社会主义思想三十讲》，学习出版社 2018 年版。

3. [法]路易・阿尔都塞：《保卫马克思》，顾良译，商务印书馆 2010 年版。

4. [法]路易・阿尔都塞、[法]艾蒂安・巴里巴尔：《读〈资本论〉》，李其庆、冯文光译，中央编译出版社 2001 年版。

5. [法]路易・阿尔都塞：《列宁和哲学》，杜章智、沈起予译，台湾远流出版事业股份有限公司 1990 年版。

6. [日]今村仁司：《阿尔都塞：认识论的断裂》，朱建科译，河北教育出版社 2001 年版。

7. 陈越编：《哲学与政治：阿尔都塞读本》，吉林人民出版社 2003 年版。

8. 张一兵：《问题式、症候阅读与意识形态：关于阿尔都塞的一种文本学解读》，中央编译出版社 2003 年版。

9. 孟登迎：《意识形态与主体建构：阿尔都塞意识形态理论》，中国社会科学出版社 2002 年版。

10. 黄继锋：《阿尔都塞与马克思》，安徽人民出版社 2003 年版。

11. 庞晓明：《结构与认识：阿尔都塞认识论思想解析》，中国社会科学出版社 2006 年版。

12. 朱晓慧:《哲学是革命的武器:阿尔都塞意识形态理论》,学林出版社 2007 年版。

13. Alex Callinicos, *Althusser's Marxism*, Pluto, 1976.

14. Simon Clarke, et al., *One Dimensional Marxism*, Alison & Busby, 1980.

15. Ted Benton, *The Rise and Fall of Structural Marxism, Althusser and His Influence*, Macmillan, 1984.

16. Gregory Elliott, *Althusser: The Detour of Theory*, Brill, 2006.

七、问题与思考

1. 什么是“认识论断裂”? 阿尔都塞是如何运用这一观念来认识、评价马克思思想发展过程的?

2. 阿尔都塞为什么认为马克思主义是“理论上的反人本主义”?

3. 历史在何种意义上是一个无主体的过程?

4. 什么是伪历史时间? 阿尔都塞为什么认为马克思的历史科学是反历史主义的?

第十三章　意识形态批判的里程碑
——《意识形态与意识形态国家机器》选读

教学目的与要求

了解阿尔都塞意识形态国家机器概念出现的历史和理论背景；把握意识形态国家机器的概念内涵；理解意识形态国家机器的观点与《保卫马克思》和《读〈资本论〉》的思想关联；能够对马克思、阿尔都塞及其他西方马克思主义者的意识形态批判理论进行比较分析。

一、历史背景

（一）作者介绍

1918 年，路易·阿尔都塞（Louis Althusser）出生于阿尔及利亚，国籍为法国，并于 1932 年回到法国。阿尔都塞在进入巴黎高等师范学院学习时，由于正值第二次世界大战期间德国入侵法国，因而应召入伍，但随后被德军俘虏。在集中营期间，阿尔都塞接触到共产主义，并于 1945 年战争结束后重返巴黎高等师范学院，1948 年获哲学博士学位并留校任教，同年加入法国共产党。法国五月风暴后，阿尔都塞开始系统研究资本主义再生产问题，一直在撰写《论再生产》手稿。根据阿尔都塞自己的计划，他准备撰写两卷本的著作，第一卷讨论资本主义生产关系的再生产，第二卷探讨资本主义社会形态中的阶级斗争。但是阿尔都塞最终并没有全部完成这一计划，只是围绕第一卷留下了《论再生产》的手稿，《意识形态与意识形态国家机器》就是从这部手稿中择取出来，并为引发讨论而发表的。在这篇文章中，阿尔都塞推进了自己的意识形态批判理论，提出并集中阐发了"意识形态国家机器"（法语简写 AIE 或英语简写 ISA）概念。这是阿尔都塞运用结构主义方法，吸收弗洛伊德和拉康精神分析、葛兰西意识形态领导权等观点，对马克思恩格斯以及西方马克思主义意识形态批判理论的改造和发展。1990 年，阿尔都塞去世后，《论再生产》手稿经过整理于 1995 年在法国大学出版社出版，2014 年翻译成英文在威尔索出版社出版。（人物生平详见上一章）

（二）时代背景

1. 资本主义的新变化与西方马克思主义的立场分化

二十世纪西方马克思主义的兴起、发展和转型与资本主义世界的发展状况紧密联系。阿尔都塞有关意识形态国家机器的思考，本身也是应运而生。众所周知，西方发达国家在第二次世界大战之后，进入一个普遍繁荣的黄金时期。对于这一黄金时期，理论家们从不同角度出发展开了分析，创造了"福特制资本主义""福利国家制度""消费社会"等观点。这些不同的观点共同指涉了这样一些事实：首先，资本主义进入一个高速发展阶段，资本主义生产和再生产过程将资本内部的对抗性因素保持在一个相对稳定的范围。其次，与这样一种相对稳定的高速发展相契合，资本主义社会改变了十九世纪"自由放任""守夜人政府"的形态，并且经过两次世界大战已经宣称远离了"帝国主义"和"极权主义"，资本主义国家机器开始以一种更加隐蔽的方式服务于资本主义生产方式的运转。最后，在特定资本主义国家内部，阶级矛盾得到缓解，更进一步，在这样一种资本主义再生产过程中，通过以教育、消费为中心的一系列机制，劳动力、消费者的角色被更加紧密地结合在一起。较之卢卡奇写作《历史与阶级意识》的时代，不仅无产阶级丧失了革命性，而且无产阶级本身被卷入资本再生产的过程之中，成为资本再生产的一个特定环节。

2. 法国社会的激烈动荡

1968年在法国爆发的五月革命是由多方面因素共同造成的。第二次世界大战之后，西方各国经济全面恢复，各项社会事业也持续开展。但是到了二十世纪六十年代，经济发展逐渐放缓，民众的不满开始积累，而商品经济和消费社会也不断引发民众的反感情绪。这些因素导致全社会的经济与文化之间存在极大的鸿沟。同时，高校大学生人数迅速增长，这一人群对既有的教育制度普遍持有异议；到了1968年5月，各种矛盾交织在一起，共同导致了这次社会运动。五月风暴持续时间长、牵涉群体数量多，并一直持续到同年6月，最多的一天有超过1 000万名工人参与罢工。五月革命对阿尔都塞和整个法国社会产生了深远影响。在阿尔都塞及其同事和学生看来，五月风暴的爆发，作为一个历史性事件，呼唤马克思主义者以马克思主义哲学的方法为武器，应对资本主义世界的新变化：这就是要理解法国资本主义社会形态中生产关系再生产的结构，并在这一结构秘密的破解中发现新的阶级斗争形式。经过这场运动，法国的人文社会科学界发生了深刻的变化，学者之间产生了明显的立场对立，全社会对革命性作品的需求也更加急迫。

（三）思想背景

1. 从《读〈资本论〉》到“意识形态国家机器”

众所周知，《资本论》作为马克思一生思想的集大成，不仅包含对资本主义生产方式以及资产阶级政治经济学的批判，而且蕴含了丰富的哲学思想。但是在马克思出版《资本论》之后的很长一段时间里，这部著作都只是被当作一部经济学的作品来看待。这在很大程度上是因为十九世纪下半叶实证主义的兴起，以至马克思的思想不仅在资产阶级学者眼中，甚至在第二国际的理论家看来，都是一种实证的社会科学。马克思主义的理论就是唯物史观或历史唯物主义，马克思主义理论家的一项重要工作就是为其寻求哲学的内核。这种情况到了列宁写作《哲学笔记》之后才有所改观。二十世纪六十年代，随着对列宁的《哲学笔记》研究热的出现，《1857—1858年经济学手稿》的出版和传播，以及对《资本论》第一版的重新关注，《资本论》中的哲学考察成为苏联和欧美马克思主义理论家共同关注的热点话题。当然，如上所述对于《资本论》中哲学问题的关注，在现实层面上同二十世纪中叶资本主义的变迁和福特制资本主义的发展直接相关。在二十世纪六十年代的德国，就曾经出现了讨论资本逻辑和国家理论、《资本论》物化批判与马克思主义辩证法的学术潮流。而在苏联，所谓的"六十年代一代"也大都以讨论《资本论》、辩证法和马克思主义认识论著称。在此过程中，阿尔都塞"读《资本论》"的研讨班及其成果，不仅介入而且直接推动了这一学术潮流的发展。同时，《意识形态与意识形态国家机器》一文的写作，本身可以说就是作为《资本论》中的马克思主义哲学探索的一项副产品。

2. 结构主义、精神分析与意识形态领导权

在西方左翼理论看来，面对资本主义世界发生的一系列新变化，资本主义意识形态批判的任务和主题也应进行调整。例如，资本主义物化批判被进一步推进到日常生活批判和消费社会批判；资本主义国家理论除了强调阶级压迫外，更加注重国家在资本主义生产过程中的作用和角色；从寻求重建作为历史总体性主体的无产阶级，转向对个人异化状态的批判等。其中，一个核心议题就是对于"主体"概念的反思，特别是经过人本主义思潮的洗礼，开始从寻求建构历史主体的可能性转向反思主体自身存在的问题。根据《意识形态与意识形态国家机器》，构成阿尔都塞写作这一文本的主要理论背景有：结构主义思潮、弗洛伊德—拉康精神分析以及葛兰西的意识形态领导权思想。

作为一种发轫于语言学之中的哲学思潮，结构主义在20世纪中叶的法国成为一门"显学"。不仅在语言学、文学和哲学，而且在人类学、社会学、历史学等领域中都成为一种主导性的理论方法。在《保卫马克思》和《读〈资本论〉》中，我们已经知道：阿尔都塞运用结构主义的方法，批判了作为资产阶级意识形态的人本主义历史主义观点，并且区分了马克思哲学发展中存在的从意识形态向科学"问题式"的转变，或者说"断裂"。在此基础上，通过发现《资本论》中的"症候阅读"来说明作为科学理论生产方式的马克思主义哲学。在这篇长文中，阿尔都塞坚持了这一方法，并运用它来阐释马克思的资本主义再生产理论和哲学方法，进而在此过程中，提出了"意识形态国家机器"的概念。可以说，结构主义理论构成了阿尔都塞"意识形态国家机器"理

论的总问题式。

为了实现“意识形态国家机器”从资本主义再生产的宏观层面向资本主义社会形态中个人存在状态的有效过渡，阿尔都塞借用了同时代人拉康的精神分析理论资源来建构其意识形态批判理论。从二十世纪三十年代开始，精神分析理论便同西方马克思主义的发展纠结在一起。如果说法兰克福学派的理论代表，如弗洛姆、马尔库塞等人主要借用的是弗洛伊德的理论，那么阿尔都塞之后的法国激进哲学家，主要遵循的是拉康的思想。拉康对精神分析理论的主要贡献在于：第一，发展了镜像主体的理论；第二，实现了对“无意识”背后结构秘密的剖析，这一发现被称为精神分析的“新大陆”；第三，通过建构“镜像阶段”“象征阶段”和“实在”理论，发现了主体本身作为一种不可能性的症候的存在机制。“意识形态国家机器”理论中“将个人传唤为主体”的分析直接受到了拉康的影响。

与结构主义和精神分析不同，很难说阿尔都塞是葛兰西主义的一员，更准确的说法可能是前者受到了后者的启发，或者说二者面对共同的理论难题。这就是在一个变化了的资本主义社会形态中，如何通过意识形态领域的斗争实现无产阶级的革命。葛兰西主要面对的是二十世纪上半叶法西斯主义的兴起，无产阶级同资产阶级争夺意识形态领导权的斗争。而阿尔都塞则是在二十世纪中叶，在福特制资本主义条件下，无产阶级如何摆脱资本主义意识形态钳制的问题。此外，二者的方法论构架也存在截然的差别。即便如此，在国家理论、意识形态分析以及市民社会分析层面，对于传统马克思主义理论中基础和上层建筑关系的新的探索上，葛兰西都启发或者说影响了阿尔都塞。

二、篇章结构

作为杂志上发表的一篇长文，《意识形态与意识形态国家机器》本身篇幅并不长，主要包括五部分内容和一篇附记。这五部分内容先后完成于1969 年 1—4 月，附记写于 1970 年 4 月。分别是：

Ⅰ　关于生产条件再生产

　　生产资料再生产

　　劳动力再生产

Ⅱ　基础和上层建筑

Ⅲ　国家

从描述性理论到理论本身

马克思主义国家理论

意识形态国家机器

Ⅳ　关于生产关系再生产

Ⅴ　关于意识形态

意识形态没有历史

意识形态是个人与其实在生存条件的想象关系的“表述”

论点1:意识形态是个人与其实在生存条件的想象关系的“表述”

论点2:意识形态具有一种物质的存在

意识形态把个人传唤为主体

一个实例:基督教意识形态

附记

具体说来。

“Ⅰ　关于生产条件再生产”是《意识形态与意识形态国家机器》非常重要的导引部分,尽管在既有的研究中对这一部分的关注并不多。实话说,“生产条件再生产”这个表述是有问题的,因为在《资本论》中马克思所谈的就是物质生产和再生产。结合后来出版的《论再生产》,我们有理由相信:这一部分是对马克思主义哲学方法和生产方式的一篇简短但又十分关键的导论。在一开始,阿尔都塞就强调,不能孤立地看待生产,因为这是一种经验主义的日常意识。从马克思主义或者说结构主义的方法来看,任何一个社会形态都是由主导性的生产方式所决定的,而生产条件的再生产本身就包括生产力的再生产和生产关系的再生产两个方面。在接下来的部分中,阿尔都塞分两个小的要点集中讨论了生产力再生产问题。

第一个要点是“生产资料的再生产”。与开篇相类似,阿尔都塞首先批判了一般经济学家,或者说一般的资本家所理解的生产资料再生产,认为这只是在企业水平上分析再生产的结果,而非再生产的条件和机制。根据马克思对于资本主义生产方式的分析,特别是两大部类的区分,生产资料的再生产内在包含资本流通关系以及剩余价值的实现。

第二个要点是“劳动力的再生产”。基于马克思的分析，阿尔都塞的分析从劳动力再生产的价值量，即工资出发，认为工资不仅取决于生物学的需要，而且取决于历史决定的最低需要。此外，劳动力还必须运用技能，也就是在社会技术分工中，获得某种本领，胜任某种工作岗位。而这必须在生产过程之外获得。更进一步，在结构主义的立场上，阿尔都塞提出劳动力的再生产只有通过意识形态使得工人服从现存秩序规范，才有可能获得本领和技能。这就引出了需要进一步讨论的问题：再生产不能离开生产关系的分析，要说明生产关系又离不开对社会的理解。

“Ⅱ 基础和上层建筑”选取了马克思主义理论中一个经典的理论隐喻来说明问题。阿尔都塞首先强调，社会的整体不等于黑格尔意义上的总体，必须理解社会中的不同层面和诉求。更进一步，针对基础和上层建筑这一空间隐喻，或者说地形学隐喻，在马克思主义发展史上所遭遇的理论挑战，即如何理解上层建筑的相对独立性和反作用，阿尔都塞强调从再生产出发来理解这一隐喻，他认为：从实践和生产的观点出发和从再生产的观点出发，对于法律、国家和意识形态的分析将会产生巨大的区别，而如果不采取再生产的观点就不可能提出（并解答）这些问题。

“Ⅲ 国家”中阿尔都塞选择以马克思主义的国家理论来说明从再生产观点出发所展开的分析。在这部分的一开始，阿尔都塞就首先借用马克思自己，特别是《路易·波拿巴的雾月十八日》中提出的“国家机器”概念来加以说明。作为理论展开，阿尔都塞进一步区分为三个小的要点。

第一个要点说明“从描述性理论到理论本身”的推进。也就是说，阿尔都塞强调空间隐喻或地形学隐喻都不过是一种“描述性的理论”，是所有理论的第一个阶段，或者说理论发展的过渡阶段。之所以强调这一区分，是为了说明马克思主义国家理论中，从国家向国家机器概念过渡的重要性。换言之，只有通过国家机器的概念才能以结构主义的方式理解国家在资本主义再生产过程中的作用，或者说是在资本主义再生产过程中定义国家。

第二个要点是“马克思主义国家理论”。在这里，阿尔都塞进一步强调了国家政权与国家机器的区别，并认为马克思主义国家理论中已经包含了国家机器的思想，但因其仍然是描述性的，所以需要做进一步补充理论的发展。

这就是第三个要点中提出的“意识形态国家机器”概念，这也是《意识形态与意识形态国家机器》中最为核心的概念。阿尔都塞认为，为了将马克思主义经典作家在实践中认识到的复杂性用理论表达出来，推进国家理论，不仅必须考虑国家政权与国家机器的区分，还必须考虑到另一种现实，即意识形态国家机器。意识形态国家机器与镇压性国家机器“运用暴力”发挥功能不同，前者“运用意识形态”发挥功能。也正是在这一部分，阿尔都塞强调了列宁和葛兰西的观点，任何一个阶级如果不在掌握政权的同时对意识形态国家机器行使其领导权，那么它的政权就不会持久。为了进一步说明意识形态国家机器的作用方式，阿尔都塞接下来探讨了“生产关系的再生产”和“意识形态”两个问题。

“Ⅳ　关于生产关系再生产”中阿尔都塞明确提出：生产关系的再生产是通过国家政权在国家机器——（镇压性）国家机器和意识形态国家机器两方面——中的运用来保证的。他再次提到当代资本主义社会形态中存在多种意识形态国家机器：教育的、宗教的、家庭的、政治的、工会的、传播的、“文化的”等等。紧接着，阿尔都塞专门讨论了从前资本主义时期到资本主义时期，占统治地位的意识形态国家机器的变化是从教会转变为教育的（学校）。结合当时的社会历史情境以及阿尔都塞的学术研究工作，我们可以认为：阿尔都塞之所以在教育的意识形态国家机器上着墨颇多主要有两个原因：一是五月风暴的发生，凸显了教育在资本主义意识形态国家机器中的重要性；二是阿尔都塞本人与其同事正在从事一项围绕“教育形式”和“教育机器”的学术研究规划。

“Ⅴ　关于意识形态”是《意识形态与意识形态国家机器》中影响最大，也为后来学者关注最多的一个部分。阿尔都塞首先在回顾意识形态的思想史历程之中，提出了一个看起来“离经叛道”的观点——意识形态是一种现实，进而尝试建构一种“意识形态一般”的理论说明。

为了说明“意识形态一般”，阿尔都塞借用马克思的说法，提出了“意识形态没有历史”的观点。但是，他认为自己的观点与《德意志意识形态》中那个实证论的、历史主义的论点有着根本不同。因为意识形态的特殊性在于被赋予了一种结构和功能，变成了一种在阶级社会的历史中无所不在的现实。显然，这种观点受到了弗洛伊德梦的解析中关于“无意识是永恒的”命题的影响。在我们看来：“意识形态一般”之所以是没有历史的、永恒的，就在于它是一种结构性、功能性存在，反映的是阶级社会中（毋宁说资本主义社会形态中)生产关系再生产的结构机制。

为了进一步讨论意识形态的结构和功能,阿尔都塞提出:"意识形态是个人与其实在生存条件的想象关系的'表述'"。作为其展开,包括两个相互呼应的论点。

"论点1:意识形态表现了个人与其实际生存条件的想象关系。"为了说明这一论点,阿尔都塞首先回顾了十八世纪机械论和神学、费尔巴哈哲学到马克思对意识形态的分析,指出:正是人们与他们的生存条件的关系的想象性质才构成了全部意识形态中一些想象性歪曲的基础。意识形态中表述出来的东西,不是个人生存的实在关系的体系,而是这些个人同自己身处其中的实在关系所建立的想象的关系。显然,这一判断既有《德意志意识形态》的影子,但也更多是受到了《资本论》商品拜物教批判的影响。

作为上述论点的展开,阿尔都塞接着提出了"论点2:意识形态具有一种物质的存在",即一种意识形态总是存在于某种机器当中,存在于这种机器的时间或各种实践当中。这种存在就是物质的存在。这种物质性存在并不是指"实物性"的物质存在,而是指社会关系,包括想象关系就具有客观物质的存在。阿尔都塞认为,对于意识形态来说,表述的想象性歪曲取决于个人与自身生存条件的想象关系,归根结底取决于他们与生产关系和阶级关系的想象关系。为了说明这一点,阿尔都塞紧接着谈到了观念和物质行为,特别是实践和仪式之间的关系。这一点在后文基督教意识形态的实例中得到了充分的展开。对于这一观点,我们可以认为:阿尔都塞之所以强调意识形态具有一种物质的存在,除了受到《资本论》中商品形式分析的影响外,更直接地来自结构主义的启发。意识形态国家机器作为一种维持资本主义再生产的结构性、功能性存在,其虚假性来源于个人与其生存条件之间的想象关系,而这种想象关系本身又是由生产关系再生产的整体所决定的。

在此基础上,阿尔都塞得出了自己的"中心论点":"意识形态把个人传唤为主体,没有不借助于主体并为了这些主体而存在的意识形态"。这也是阿尔都塞挪用拉康精神分析理论最为集中的一个片段。他以一种拉康式的口吻提出,"主体之所以是构成所有意识形态的基本范畴,只是因为所有意识形态的功能(这种功能定义了意识形态本身)就在于把具体的个人'构成'为主体"。首先,所有意识形态都通过主体这个范畴发挥功能,把具体的个人呼唤或传唤为具体的主体。由于意识形态是永恒的,个人从来都是主体。

为了说明这样一个看似悖论的结论，阿尔都塞紧接着以基督教意识形态为例展开了分析。

在“一个实例：基督教意识形态”中，阿尔都塞借用宗教意识形态提供了一种对于意识形态作用机制的精细分析。特别需要注意的是，阿尔都塞提到了大写主体(Subject)与小写主体(subject)的镜像关系，即把个人传唤为主体(s)的是一个独一的、中心的、作为他者的主体(S)的“存在”为前提的。所有意识形态的结构都是反射的镜像结构，而且还是一种双重反射的结构。因此，“意识形态一般”的秘密就是，意识形态复制的镜像结构同时保障着：(1)把个人传唤为主体(s)；(2)他们对主体(S)的臣服；(3)主体(s)与主体(S)的相互承认，主体间的相互承认，以及主体最终的自我承认；(4)绝对保证一切都确实是这样——“就这样吧”。换言之，在意识形态国家机器中，个人被传唤为(自由的)主体(s)，为的是能够自由地服从主体(S)的诫命，能够(自由地)接受这种臣服的地位。显然这一表述是十分精彩的，并且这一结构机制在阿尔都塞《论再生产》中有关劳动过程的说明中也已经初步触及了。但令人遗憾的是，在表述这一理论的过程中，阿尔都塞选择了自己熟悉的宗教意识形态作为例证，没有将其同马克思的政治经济学批判完全对接起来。

在“附记”中，阿尔都塞提出了在《意识形态和意识形态国家机器》中有待解决的难题：一是实现生产关系再生产的全过程的难题；二是特定社会形态中存在的各种意识形态的阶级性质的难题。二者都共同触及了如何处理阶级斗争观点的问题，而这恰恰是阿尔都塞没有完成的那一卷的内容。

三、研究前沿

意识形态问题研究是阿尔都塞研究中的一个重要问题。我国学界早在二十世纪八十年代就开始研究或引译阿尔都塞的作品。从研究的数量来看，到二十一世纪有了较大幅度的上升；从研究的层次来看，应当说，阿尔都塞的相关问题研究始终都受到国内前沿学者和学科的高度重视，体现在成果的发表层次、研究的质量及产生的理论影响等各个方面。国内阿尔都塞研究的重要意义不仅体现在思想和文本解读上，还体现在引申出对西方马克思主义一系列突破性的解读模式创新，以及对历史唯物主义的新阐释方式。当然，学者们对阿尔都塞的开放式解决也造成了一定的立场分歧。就《意识形态和意识形态国家机器》这一著作的研究来说，国内相关研究也出现了理论性和应用性相结合的重要特点。

第一，对意识形态内涵的专门研究。有学者认为，阿尔都塞将经济、政治与意识形态共同作为人类社会的三类实践，并且认为三部分是相互联系的，体现出了鲜明的实践性和革命性立场。还有学者从历史的角度阐述阿尔都塞意识形态理论发展的阶段性特征，在第一阶段，阿尔都塞是将意识形态作为一种整体性的概念或者是一种新的实体，其本身的存在目的不是作为一种科学，而是要促使人民进行政治实践；在第二阶段，阿尔都塞从国家机器出发，将意识形态本质定义为资本主义社会关系的生产和再生产。因此，有学者指出，意识形态国家机器同暴力国家机器有着内在区别，前者凭借隐匿着的微观权力，进而以意识形态的独特方式发挥对人的思想和行为的操控作用，具有更加深层的规约性和渗透性。

第二，对阿尔都塞研究视角和总体立场的批判性研究。有学者提出，阿尔都塞的意识形态国家机器理论是以社会再生产为出发点而形成的，是通过生产力与生产关系再生产、社会基本矛盾学说、国家理论等角度，形成的现实批判理论体系。有学者还将阿尔都塞的意识形态理论解构成多重意蕴，包括本质上作为一种人们对周围世界的无意识体验、认同幻觉和合法性认知等等，从认识论角度揭示了阿尔都塞批判资本主义意识形态的路径。还有学者认为，阿尔都塞尝试从多角度论述意识形态理论，对意识形态的阐释具有突出贡献，但是也存在着一些问题，比如，阿尔都塞对意识形态的分析过程仍然在一定程度上受制于资产阶级的思维模式，对意识形态与政治关系的解释缺乏辩证张力，等等。

第三，对阿尔都塞意识形态国家机器理论研究方法的反思。有学者认为，要准确把握阿尔都塞的研究视角就要采用特殊的视角，对阿尔都塞的研究不能停留在具体的理论成果上，而是要关注其理论前提，比如，从“症候阅读法”入手，把握其作品的深层理论问题式；从西方马克思主义发展史的角度，分析阿尔都塞意识形态国家机器理论的理论创新和历史定位；通过比较研究，阐释意识形态国家机器理论的重要意义，等等。

第四，对《意识形态和意识形态国家机器》及意识形态理论的应用价值的研究。有学者指出，阿尔都塞的意识形态国家机器理论是对马克思强制性国家机器理论的重要补充，充分继承了马克思的意识形态理论，进一步为认知资本主义生产关系的再生产提供了重要认知基础，也为进一步研究国家问题提供了重要的视角。还有学者提出，阿尔都塞充分意识到教育在意识形态工作中的重要地位，这对当前思想政治理论教育和捍卫马克思主义主流意识形态工作有重要的借鉴意义。

四、文本节选

Infrastructure and Superstructure

On a number of occasions I have insisted on the revolutionary character of the Marxist conception of the "social whole" insofar as it is distinct from the Hegelian "totality". I said (and this thesis only repeats famous propositions of historical materialism) that Marx conceived the structure of every society as constituted by "levels" or "instances" articulated by a specific determination: the *infrastructure*, or economic base (the "unity" of the productive forces and the relations of production) and the *superstructure*, which itself contains two "levels" or "instances": the politico-legal (law and the State) and ideology (the different ideologies, religious, ethical, legal, political, etc.).

Besides its theoretico-didactic interest (it reveals the difference between Marx and Hegel), this representation has the following crucial theoretical advantage: it makes it possible to inscribe in the theoretical apparatus of its essential concepts what I have called their *respective indices of effectivity*. What does this mean?

It is easy to see that this representation of the structure of every society as an edifice containing a base (infrastructure) on which are erected the two "floors" of the superstructure, is a metaphor, to be quite precise, a spatial metaphor: the metaphor of a topography (*topique*). Like every metaphor, this metaphor suggests something, makes some thing visible. What? Precisely this: that the upper floors could not "stay up" (in the air) alone, if they did not rest precisely on their base.

Thus the object of the metaphor of the edifice is to represent above all the "determination in the last instance" by the economic base. The effect of this spatial metaphor is to endow the base with an index of effectivity known by the famous terms: the determination in the last instance of what happens in the upper "floors" (of the superstructure) by what happens in the economic base.

Given this index of effectivity "in the last instance", the "floors" of the superstructure are clearly endowed with different indices of effectivity. What kind of indices?

It is possible to say that the floors of the superstructure are not determinant in the last instance, but that they are determined by the effectivity of the base; that if they are determinant in their own (as yet undefined) ways, this is true only insofar as they are determined by the base.

Their index of effectivity (or determination), as determined by the determination in the last instance of the base, is thought by the Marxist tradition in two ways: (1) there is a "relative autonomy" of the superstructure with respect to the base; (2) there is a "reciprocal action" of the superstructure on the base.

We can therefore say that the great theoretical advantage of the Marxist topography, i. e. of the spatial metaphor of the edifice (base and superstructure) is simultaneously that it reveals that questions of determination (or of index of effectivity) are crucial; that it reveals that it is the base which in the last instance determines the whole edifice; and that, as a consequence, it obliges us to pose the theoretical problem of the types of "derivatory" effectivity peculiar to the superstructure, i. e. it obliges us to think what the Marxist tradition calls conjointly the relative autonomy of the superstructure and the reciprocal action of the superstructure on the base.

The greatest disadvantage of this representation of the structure of every society by the spatial metaphor of an edifice, is obviously the fact that it is metaphorical: i.e. it remains *descriptive*.

It now seems to me that it is possible and desirable to represent things differently. NB, I do not mean by this that I want to reject the classical metaphor, for that metaphor itself requires that we go beyond it. And I am not going beyond it in order to reject it as outworn. I simply want to attempt to think what it gives us in the form of a description.

I believe that it is possible and necessary to think what characterizes the essential of the existence and nature of the superstructure *on the basis of reproduction*. Once one takes the point of view of reproduction, many of the questions whose existence was indicated by the spatial metaphor of the edifice, but to which it could not give a conceptual answer, are immediately illuminated.

My basic thesis is that it is not possible to pose these questions (and therefore to answer them) *except from the point of view of reproduction*.

I shall give a short analysis of Law, the State and Ideology *from this point of view*. And I shall reveal what happens both from the point of view of practice and production on the one hand, and from that of reproduction on the other.

——Louis Althusser, *Essays on Ideology*, Verso, 1984, pp.8-10.

The State Ideological Apparatuses

...

In fact, i.e. in their political practice, the Marxist classics treated the State as a more complex reality than the definition of it given in the "Marxist theory of the State", even when it has been supplemented as I have just suggested. They recognized this complexity in their practice, but they did not express it in a corresponding theory.

I should like to attempt a very schematic outline of this corresponding theory. To that end, I propose the following thesis.

In order to advance the theory of the State it is indispensable to take into account not only the distinction between *State power* and *State apparatus*, but also another reality which is clearly on the side of the (repressive) State apparatus, but must not be confused with it. I shall call this reality by its concept: *the ideological State apparatuses*.

What are the ideological State apparatuses (ISAs)?

They must not be confused with the (repressive) State apparatus. Remember that in Marxist theory, the State Apparatus (SA) contains: the Government, the Administration, the Army, the Police, the Courts, the Prisons, etc., which constitute what I shall in future call the Repressive State Apparatus. Repressive suggests that the State Apparatus in question "functions by violence"—at least ultimately (since repression, e.g. administrative repression, may take non-physical forms).

I shall call Ideological State Apparatuses a certain number of realities which present themselves to the immediate observer in the form of distinct and specialized institutions. I propose an empirical list of these which will obviously have to be examined in detail, tested, corrected and re-organized. With all the reservations implied by this requirement, we can for the moment regard the following institutions as Ideological State Apparatuses (the order in which I have listed them has no particular significance):

- the religious ISA (the system of the different Churches),
- the educational ISA (the system of the different public and private 'Schools'),
- the family ISA,
- the legal ISA,
- the political ISA (the political system, including the different Parties),
- the trade-union ISA,

– the communications ISA (press, radio and television, etc.),

– the cultural ISA (Literature, the Arts, sports, etc.).

I have said that the ISAs must not be confused with the (Repressive) State Apparatus. What constitutes the difference?

As a first moment, it is clear that while there is *one* (Repressive) State Apparatus, there is a *plurality* of Ideological State Apparatuses. Even presupposing that it exists, the unity that constitutes this plurality of ISAs as a body is not immediately visible.

As a second moment, it is clear that whereas the unified—(Repressive) State Apparatus belongs entirely to the *public* domain, much the larger part of the Ideological State Apparatuses (in their apparent dispersion) are part, on the contrary, of the *private* domain. Churches, Parties, Trade Unions, families, some schools, most newspapers, cultural ventures, etc., etc., are private.

We can ignore the first observation for the moment. But someone is bound to question the second, asking me by what right I regard as Ideological *State* Apparatuses, institutions which for the most part do not possess public status, but are quite simply *private* institutions. As a conscious Marxist, Gramsci already forestalled this objection in one sentence. The distinction between the public and the private is a distinction internal to bourgeois law, and valid in the (subordinate) domains in which bourgeois law exercises its "authority". The domain of the State escapes it because the latter is "above the law": the State, which is the State *of* the ruling class, is neither public nor private; on the contrary, it is the precondition for any distinction between public and private. The same thing can be said from the starting-point of our State Ideological Apparatuses. It is unimportant whether the institutions in which they are realized are "public" or "private". What matters is how they function. Private institutions can perfectly well "function" as Ideological State Apparatuses. A reasonably thorough analysis of any one of the ISAs proves it.

But now for what is essential. What distinguishes the ISAs from the (Repressive) State Apparatus is the following basic difference: the Repressive State Apparatus functions "by violence", whereas the Ideological State Apparatuses *function* "*by ideology*".

I can clarify matters by correcting this distinction. I shall say rather that every State Apparatus, whether Repressive or Ideological, "functions" both by violence and by ideology, but with one very important distinction which makes it imperative not to confuse the Ideological State Apparatuses with the (Repressive) State Apparatus.

This is the fact that the (Repressive) State Apparatus functions massively and predominantly *by repression* (including physical repression), while functioning secondarily by ideology. (There is no such thing as a purely repressive apparatus.) For example, the Army and the Police also function by ideology both to ensure their own cohesion and reproduction, and in the "values" they propound externally.

In the same way, but inversely, it is essential to say that for their part the Ideological State Apparatuses function massively and predominantly *by ideology*, but they also function secondarily by repression, even if ultimately, but only ultimately, this is very attenuated and concealed, even symbolic. (There is no such thing as a purely ideological apparatus.) Thus Schools and Churches use suitable methods of punishment, expulsion, selection, etc., to "discipline" not only their shepherds, but also their flocks. The same is true of the Family. ... The same is true of the cultural IS Apparatus (censorship, among other things), etc.

Is it necessary to add that this determination of the double "functioning" (predominantly, secondarily) by repression and by ideology, according to whether it is a matter of the (Repressive) State Apparatus or the Ideological State Apparatuses, makes it clear that very subtle explicit or tacit combinations may be woven from the interplay of the (Repressive) State Apparatus and the Ideological State Apparatuses?

Everyday life provides us with innumerable examples of this, but they must be studied in detail if we are to go further than this mere observation.

Nevertheless, this remark leads us towards an understanding of what constitutes the unity of the apparently disparate body of the ISAs. If the ISAs "function" massively and predominantly by ideology, what unifies their diversity is precisely this functioning, insofar as the ideology by which they function is always in fact unified, despite its diversity and its contradictions, *beneath the ruling ideology*, which is the ideology of "the ruling class". Given the fact that the "ruling class" in principle holds State power (openly or more often by means of alliances between classes or class fractions), and therefore has at its disposal the (Repressive) State Apparatus, we can accept the fact that this same ruling class is active in the Ideological State Apparatuses insofar as it is ultimately the ruling ideology which is realized in the Ideological State Apparatuses, precisely in its contradictions. Of course, it is a quite different thing to act by laws and decrees in the (Repressive) State Apparatus and to "act" through the intermediary of the ruling ideology in the Ideological State Apparatuses. We must go into the details of this difference—but it cannot mask the reality of a profound identity. To my knowledge, *no class can hold State power over a long period without at the same time exercising its hegemony over and in the State Ideological Apparatuses*. I only need one example and proof of this: Lenin's anguished concern to revolutionize the educational Ideological State Apparatus (among others), simply to make it possible for the Soviet proletariat, who had seized State power, to secure the future of the dictatorship of the proletariat and the transition to socialism.

This last comment puts us in a position to understand that the Ideological State Apparatuses may be not only the *stake*, but also the *site* of class struggle, and often of bitter forms of class struggle. The class (or class alliance) in power cannot lay down the law in the ISAs as easily as it can in the (repressive) State apparatus, not only because the former ruling classes are able to retain strong positions there for a long time, but also because the resistance of the exploited classes is able to find means and occasions to express itself there, either by the utilization of their contradictions, or by conquering combat positions in them in struggle.

Let me run through my comments.

If the thesis I have proposed is well-founded, it leads me back to the classical Marxist theory of the State, while making it more precise in one point. I argue that it is necessary to distinguish between State power (and its possession by ...) on the one hand, and the State Apparatus on the other. But I add that the State Apparatus contains two bodies: the body of institutions which represent the Repressive State Apparatus on the one hand, and the body of institutions which represent the body of Ideological State Apparatuses on the other.

But if this is the case, the following question is bound to be asked, even in the very summary state of my suggestions: what exactly is the extent of the role of the Ideological State Apparatuses? What is their importance based on? In other words: to what does the "function" of these Ideological State Apparatuses, which do not function by repression but by ideology, correspond?

——Louis Althusser, *Essays on Ideology*, Verso, 1984, pp. 16 - 22.

On the Reproduction of the Relations of Production

I can now answer the central question which I have left in suspense for many long pages: *how is the reproduction of the relations of production secured*?

In the topographical language (Infrastructure, Superstructure), I can say: for the most part, it is secured by the legal-political and ideological superstructure.

But as I have argued that it is essential to go beyond this still descriptive language, I shall say: for the most part, it is secured by the exercise of State power in the State Apparatuses, on the one hand the (Repressive) State Apparatus, on the other the Ideological State Apparatuses.

What I have just said must also be taken into account, and it can be assembled in the form of the following three features:

1. All the State Apparatuses function both by repression and by ideology, with the difference that the (Repressive) State Apparatus functions massively and predominantly by repression, whereas the Ideological State Apparatuses function massively and predominantly by ideology.

2. Whereas the (Repressive) State Apparatus constitutes an organized whole whose different parts are centralized beneath a commanding unity, that of the politics of class struggle applied by the political representatives of the ruling classes in possession of State power, the Ideological State Apparatuses are multiple, distinct, "relatively autonomous" and capable of providing an objective field to contradictions which express, in forms which may be limited or extreme, the effects of the clashes between the capitalist class struggle and the proletarian class struggle, as well as their subordinate forms.

3. Whereas the unity of the (Repressive) State Apparatus is secured by its unified and centralized organization under the leadership of the representatives of the classes in power executing the politics of the class struggle of the classes in power, the unity of the different Ideological State Apparatuses is secured, usually in contradictory forms, by the ruling ideology, the ideology of the ruling class.

Taking these features into account, it is possible to represent the reproduction of the relations of production in the following way, according to a kind of "division of labour".

The role of the repressive State apparatus, insofar as it is a repressive apparatus, consists essentially in securing by force (physical or otherwise) the political conditions of the reproduction of relations of production which are in the last resort *relations of exploitation*. Not only does the State apparatus contribute generously to its own reproduction (the capitalist State contains political dynasties, military dynasties, etc.), but also and above all, the State apparatus secures by repression (from the most brutal physical force, via mere administrative commands and interdictions, to open and tacit censorship) the political conditions for the action of the Ideological State Apparatuses.

In fact, it is the latter which largely secure the reproduction specifically of the relations of production, behind a "shield" provided by the repressive State apparatus. It is here that the role of the ruling ideology is heavily concentrated, the ideology of the ruling class, which holds State power. It is the intermediation of the ruling ideology that ensures a (sometimes teeth-gritting) "harmony" between the repressive State apparatus and the Ideological State Apparatuses, and between the different State Ideological Apparatuses.

We are thus led to envisage the following hypothesis, as a function precisely of the diversity of ideological State Apparatuses in their single, because shared, role of the reproduction of the relations of production.

Indeed we have listed a relatively large number of ideological State apparatuses in contemporary capitalist social formations: the educational apparatus, the religious apparatus, the family apparatus, the political apparatus, the trade-union apparatus, the communications apparatus, the "cultural" apparatus, etc.

But in the social formations of that mode of production characterized by "serfdom" (usually called the feudal mode of production), we observe that although there is a single repressive State apparatus which, since the earliest known Ancient States, let alone the Absolute Monarchies, has been formally very similar to the one we know today, the number of

Ideological State Apparatuses is smaller and their individual types are different. For example, we observe that during the Middle Ages, the Church (the religious ideological State apparatus) accumulated a number of functions which have today devolved on to several distinct ideological State apparatuses, new ones in relation to the past I am invoking, in particular educational and cultural functions. Alongside the Church there was the family Ideological State Apparatus, which played a considerable part, incommensurable with its role in capitalist social formations. Despite appearances, the Church and the Family were not the only Ideological State Apparatuses. There was also a political Ideological State Apparatus (the Estates General, the *Parlement*, the different political factions and Leagues, the ancestors or the modern political parties, and the whole political system of the free Communes and then of the *Villes*). There was also a powerful "proto-trade union" Ideological State Apparatus, if I may venture such an anachronistic term (the powerful merchants' and bankers' guilds and the journeymen's associations, etc.). Publishing and Communications, even, saw an indisputable development, as did the theatre; initially both were integral parts of the Church, then they became more and more independent of it.

In the pre-capitalist historical period which I have examined extremely broadly, it is absolutely clear that *there was one dominant Ideological State Apparatus, the Church*, which concentrated within it not only religious functions, but also educational ones, and a large proportion of the functions of communications and "culture". It is no accident that all ideological struggle, from the sixteenth to the eighteenth century, starting with the first shocks of the Reformation, was *concentrated* in an anti-clerical and anti-religious struggle; rather this is a function precisely of the dominant position of the religious ideological State apparatus.

The foremost objective and achievement of the French Revolution was not just to transfer State power from the feudal aristocracy to the merchant-capitalist bourgeoisie, to break part of the former repressive State apparatus and replace it with a new one (e. g., the national popular Army) but also to attack the number-one Ideological State Apparatus: the Church. Hence the civil constitution of the clergy, the confiscation of ecclesiastical wealth, and the creation of new ideological State apparatuses to replace the religious ideological State apparatus in its dominant role.

Naturally, these things did not happen automatically: witness the Concordat, the Restoration and the long class struggle between the landed aristocracy and the industrial bourgeoisie throughout the nineteenth century for the establishment of bourgeois hegemony over the functions formerly fulfilled by the Church: above all by the Schools. It can be said that the bourgeoisie relied on the new political, parliamentary-democratic, ideological State apparatus, installed in the earliest years of the Revolution, then restored after long and violent struggles, for a few months in 1848 and for decades after the fall of the Second Empire, in order to conduct its struggle against the Church and wrest its ideological functions away from it, in other words, to ensure not only its own political hegemony, but also the ideological hegemony indispensable to the reproduction of capitalist relations of production.

That is why I believe that I am justified in advancing the following Thesis, however precarious it is. I believe that the ideological State apparatus which has been installed in the *dominant* position in mature capitalist social formations as a result of a violent political and ideological class struggle against the old dominant ideological State apparatus, is the *educational ideological apparatus*.

This thesis may seem paradoxical, given that for everyone, i.e. in the ideological representation that the bourgeoisie has tried to give itself and the classes it exploits, it really seems that the dominant ideological State apparatus in capitalist social formations is not the Schools, but the political ideological State apparatus, i. e. the regime of parliamentary democracy combining universal suffrage and party struggle.

However, history, even recent history, shows that the bourgeoisie has been and still is able to accommodate itself to political ideological State apparatuses other than parliamentary democracy: the First and Second Empires, Constitutional Monarchy (Louis XVIII and Charles X), Parliamentary Monarchy (Louis-Philippe), Presidential Democracy (de Gaulle), to mention only France. In England this is even clearer. The Revolution was particularly "successful" there from the bourgeois point of view, since unlike France, where the bourgeoisie, partly because of the stupidity of the petty aristocracy, had to agree to being carried to power by peasant and plebeian "*journées révolutionnaires*", something for which it had to pay a high price, the English bourgeoisie was able to "compromise" with the aristocracy and "share" State power and the use of the State apparatus with it for a long time (peace among all men of good will in the ruling classes!). In Germany it is even more striking, since it was behind a political ideological State apparatus in which the imperial Junkers (epitomized by Bismarck), their army and their police provided it with a shield and leading personnel, that the imperialist bourgeoisie made its shattering entry into history, before "traversing" the Weimar Republic and entrusting itself to Nazism.

Hence I believe I have good reasons for thinking that behind the scenes of its political Ideological State Apparatus, which occupies the front of the stage, what the bourgeoisie has installed as its number-one, i. e. as its dominant ideological State apparatus, is the educational apparatus, which has in fact replaced in its functions the previously dominant ideological State apparatus, the Church. One might even add: the School-Family couple has replaced the Church-Family couple.

Why is the educational apparatus in fact the dominant ideological State apparatus in capitalist social formations, and how does it function?

For the moment it must suffice to say:

1. All ideological State apparatuses, whatever they are, contribute to the same result: the reproduction of the relations of production, i.e. of capitalist relations of exploitation.

2. Each of them contributes towards this single result in the way proper to it. The political apparatus by subjecting individuals to the political State ideology, the "indirect" (parliamentary) or "direct" (plebiscitary or fascist) "democratic" ideology. The communications apparatus by cramming every "citizen" with daily doses of nationalism, chauvinism, liberalism, moralism, etc, by means of the press, the radio and television. The same goes for the cultural apparatus (the role of sport in chauvinism is of the first importance), etc. The religious apparatus by recalling in sermons and the other great ceremonies of Birth, Marriage and Death, that man is only ashes, unless he loves his neighbour to the extent of turning the other cheek to whoever strikes first. The family apparatus ... but there is no need to go on.

3. This concert is dominated by a single score, occasionally disturbed by contradictions (those of the remnants of former ruling classes, those of the proletarians and their organizations): the score of the Ideology of the current ruling class which integrates into its music the great themes of the Humanism of the Great Forefathers, who produced the Greek Miracle even before Christianity, and afterwards the Glory of Rome, the Eternal City, and the themes of Interest, particular and general, etc. nationalism, moralism and economism.

4. Nevertheless, in this concert, one ideological State apparatus certainly has the dominant role, although hardly anyone lends an ear to its music: it is so silent! This is the School.

It takes children from every class at infant-school age, and then for years, the years in which the child is most "vulnerable", squeezed between the family State apparatus and the educational State apparatus, it drums into them, whether it uses new or old methods, a certain amount of "know-how" wrapped in the ruling ideology (French, arithmetic, natural history, the sciences, literature) or simply the ruling ideology in its pure state (ethics, civic instruction, philosophy). Somewhere around the age of sixteen, a huge mass of children are ejected "into production": these are the workers or small peasants. Another portion of scholastically adapted youth carries on: and, for better or worse, it goes somewhat further, until it falls by the wayside and fills the posts of small and middle technicians, white-collar workers, small and middle executives, petty bourgeois of all kinds. A last portion reaches the summit, either to fall into intellectual semi-employment, or to provide, as well as the "intellectuals of the collective labourer", the agents of exploitation (capitalists, managers), the agents of repression (soldiers, policemen, politicians, administrators, etc.) and the professional ideologists (priests of all sorts, most of whom are convinced 'laymen').

Each mass ejected *en route* is practically provided with the ideology which suits the role it has to fulfil in class society: the role of the exploited (with a "highly-developed" "professional", "ethical", "civic", "national" and a-political consciousness); the role of the agent of exploitation (ability to give the workers orders and speak to them: "human relations"), of the agent of repression (ability to give orders and enforce obedience "without discussion", or ability to manipulate the demagogy of a political leader's rhetoric), or of the professional ideologist (ability to treat consciousnesses with the respect, i.e. with the contempt, blackmail, and demagogy they deserve, adapted to the accents of Morality, of Virtue, of "Transcendence", of the Nation, of France's World Role, etc.).

Of course, many of these contrasting Virtues (modesty, resignation, submissiveness on the one hand, cynicism, contempt, arrogance, confidence, self-importance, even smooth talk and cunning on the other) are also taught in the Family, in the Church, in the Army, in Good Books, in films and even in the football stadium. But no other ideological State apparatus has the obligatory (and not least, free) audience of the totality of the children in the capitalist social formation, eight hours a day for five or six days out of seven.

But it is by an apprenticeship in a variety of know-how wrapped up in the massive inculcation of the ideology of the ruling class that the *relations of production* in a capitalist social formation, i.e. the relations of exploited to exploiters and exploiters to exploited, are largely reproduced. The mechanisms which produce this vital result for the capitalist regime are naturally covered up and concealed by a universally reigning ideology of the School, universally reigning because it is one of the essential forms of the ruling bourgeois ideology: an ideology which represents the School as a neutral environment purged of ideology (because it is ... lay), where teachers respectful of the "conscience" and "freedom" of the children who are entrusted to them (in complete confidence) by their "parents" (who are free, too, i.e. the owners of their children) open up for them the path to the freedom, morality and responsibility of adults by their own example, by knowledge, literature and their "liberating" virtues.

I ask the pardon of those teachers who, in dreadful conditions, attempt to turn the few weapons they can find in the history and learning they "teach" against the ideology, the system and the practices in which they are trapped. They are a kind of hero. But they are rare and how many (the majority) do not even begin to suspect the "work" the system (which is bigger than they are and crushes them) forces them to do, or worse, put all their heart and ingenuity into performing it with the most advanced awareness (the famous new methods!). So little do they suspect it that their own devotion contributes to the maintenance and nourishment of this ideological representation of the School, which makes the School today as "natural", indispensable-useful and even beneficial for our contemporaries as the Church was "natural", indispensable and generous for our ancestors a few centuries ago.

In fact, the Church has been replaced today *in its role as the dominant Ideological State Apparatus* by the School. It is coupled with the Family just as the Church was once coupled with the Family. We can now claim that the unprecedentedly deep crisis which is now shaking the education system of so many States across the globe, often in conjunction with a crisis (already proclaimed in the *Communist Manifesto*) shaking the family system, takes on a political meaning, given that the School (and the School Family couple) constitutes the dominant Ideological State Apparatus, the Apparatus playing a determinant part in the reproduction of the relations of production of a mode of production threatened in its existence by the world class struggle.

——Louis Althusser, *Essays on Ideology*, Verso, 1984, pp.22-31.

On Ideology

When I put forward the concept of an Ideological State Apparatus, when I said that the ISAs "function by ideology", I invoked a reality which needs a little discussion: ideology.

It is well known that the expression "ideology" was invented by Cabanis, Destutt de Tracy and their friends, who assigned to it as an object the (genetic) theory of ideas. When Marx took up the term fifty years later, he gave it a quite different meaning, even in his Early Works. Here, ideology is the system of the ideas and representations which dominate the mind of a man or a social group. The ideologico-political struggle conducted by Marx as early as his articles in the *Rheinische Zeitung* inevitably and quickly brought him face to face with this reality and forced him to take his earliest intuitions further.

However, here we come upon a rather astonishing paradox. Everything seems to lead Marx to formulate a theory of ideology. In fact, *The German Ideology* does offer us, after the *1844 Manuscripts*, an explicit theory of ideology, but ... it is not Marxist (we shall see why in a moment). As for *Capital*, although it does contain many hints towards a theory of ideologies (most visibly, the ideology of the vulgar economists), it does not contain that theory itself, which depends for the most part on a theory of ideology in general.

I should like to venture a first and very schematic outline of such a theory. The theses I am about to put forward are certainly not off the cuff, but they cannot be sustained and tested, i.e. confirmed or rejected, except by much thorough study and analysis.

——Louis Althusser, *Essays on Ideology*, Verso, 1984, p.32.

五、观点解读

1. 再生产与意识形态国家机器

无论是从文本写作还是理论逻辑上来看，意识形态国家机器概念的提出都同再生产紧密联系在一起。1969 年，阿尔都塞准备撰写两卷本的著作，分别论述资本主义生产关系的再生产和阶级斗争。《意识形态与意识形态国家机器》一文就是从先期完成的手稿中抽出来，加以修改发表的。阿尔都塞后来进一步写作、修订，但只是在他去世后，这部手稿才由雅克·比岱整理出版。就该文逻辑展开来说，阿尔都塞首先讨论的是生产条件的再生产，并在从生产力再生产向生产关系再生产的过渡中，为了说明问题，引入了经济基础和上层建筑、国家以及意识形态国家机器的讨论。而关于意识形态的详尽分析，也可以看作对生产关系再生产得以保障的结构和机制的分析的逻辑展开。尽管在从再生产分析向意识形态国家机器说明的展开中，阿尔都塞有意识地运用了结构主义方法、借鉴了弗洛伊德-拉康的精神分析理论，并回应了葛兰西的意识形态领导权问题。

在马克思的著作中并没有直接谈及再生产与意识形态的关系问题。这在很大程度上是与不同时期马克思著作写作的具体指向有关。在集中讨论意识形态问题的《德意志意识形态》和《路易·波拿巴的雾月十八日》中，情况分别是，前者中马克思主要是在批判“德意志意识形态”中确立自己的理论方法，从物质生产和再生产出发分析生产方式、所有制形式，进而说明上层建筑。因此，尽管物质生产和再生产本身是关联在一起的，但马克思关注的是历史唯物主义方法的制订，而非具体的意识形态分析。在后者那里，马克思具体分析了作为资产阶级统治工具的法兰西“帝国”，提出了国家机器的概念，并涉及资本主义再生产的问题，但因主要为政治讨论，并未展开。只是到了《资本论》中，马克思才全面探讨了资本主义再生产问题，并在此基础上批判了资本主义社会中的物化和拜物教现象，虽然没有专门提意识形态，却为意识形态批判奠定了科学的基础。

阿尔都塞身处二十世纪中叶，面对福特制资本主义（消费社会）的滥觞，站在结构主义立场上反思现代主体，吸收马克思列宁主义国家理论以及当时《资本论》研究成果，选择从再生产出发回应困扰当时左翼学者的一个关键问题：意识形态，并提出了具有里程碑式意义的意识形态国家机器概念。在此过程中，需要注意的问题有三：第一，实践和生产观点与再生产观点之间的区别，在阿尔都塞看来只有从后者出发才能看清意识形态国家机器的作用方式。这显然是由阿尔都塞从结构主义出发反对人本主义的理论立场所决定的。第二，无论在生产资料的再生产、劳动力的再生产还是生产关系的再生产中，阿尔都塞都坚持了一种结构主义的整体观点，自觉反对作为资本主义意识形态的经验主义，并且为了说明问题，还区分了描述性理论和理论本身的差别。第三，意识形态国家机器概念的提出可以看作意识形态和国家机器两个概念的“连接”，而国家机器概念是从再生产分析向意识形态批判过渡的重要逻辑环节。较之马克思恩格斯的时代，阿尔都塞运用这个概念着力强调了意识形态的微观作用机制。

2. 意识形态没有历史

这是基于马克思恩格斯《德意志意识形态》中的判断得出的一个颇具创新性的诠释。在《德意志意识形态》中，只有物质生产方式才有自己的历史，也就是说，只有物质生产方式的变化才能产生真正的历史变迁，而法、国家、意识形态等上层建筑本身是没有历史的。换言之，马克思恩格斯意在强调：对于国家和意识形态等问题的争论，应当回到真正历史之中的物质生产方式中去，才能得到科学的理解。阿尔都塞一方面遵循了马克思恩格斯的观点,认为意识形态是没有自身的历史的;但另一方面,他更加强调了意识形态,或者说"意识形态一般"具有一种自身的作用机制,在阶级社会的历史中,意识形态是永恒的。这里所说的没有历史的、永恒的意识形态,并不是指意识形态的内容,而是指意识形态的形式。这一观点的得出受到了弗洛伊德精神分析的影响。在阿尔都塞看来,正如无意识是没有历史的一样,意识形态也是没有历史的。这种意识形态的形式分析开启了后来以齐泽克为代表的当代激进哲学意识形态批判的先声。

3. 意识形态是具有一种物质的存在

意识形态国家机器或者说意识形态具有物质实在的观点。这一点看起来是对经典马克思主义观点的背叛,但是考虑到马克思主义哲学的历史发展以及德国古典哲学的历史语境,我们有理由相信:在马克思那里,意识形态本身也是一种客观存在,而阿尔都塞之所以强调"物质实在"则与其对斯宾诺莎唯物主义的推崇有关。如前所述,在马克思恩格斯的著作中,意识形态主要是被作为观念上层建筑来看待的,而历史唯物主义第一次在人类历史上提出,需要从物质生产过程出发来理解意识形态的存在方式。尽管传统马克思主义研究经常援引恩格斯晚年书信中提到的"归根结底"和意识形态"相对独立性"的说法来分析意识形态的特征。但是考虑到马克思的《资本论》,包括《德意志意识形态》中对资产阶级社会形态的分析,意识形态批判必须同资本主义生产方式,尤其是资本主义社会形态中的物化批判结合起来加以理解。在这个意义上,我们有理由相信阿尔都塞的观点是对马克思主义的一种继承和发展。当然,这种发展带有强烈的结构主义特征。

这一特征集中表现在阿尔都塞所提出的"意识形态是个人与其实在生存条件的想象关系的'表述'"的观点上。在阿尔都塞看来,意识形态中表述出来的,并不是个人生存的实在关系的体系,而是这些个人同自己身处其中的实在关系所建立的想象的关系。而意识形态作为一种机制或者说一种形式,是对这些想象关系的表述。由此,意识形态的颠倒和虚假的特征,就不是由意识形态本身作为一种观念存在的属性所决定的,而是由这些想象关系本身的颠倒和虚假的特征所决定的。在这一过程中,个人同其实在生存条件的想象关系的观点,受到了结构主义的直接影响。我们知道:结构主义对于符号能指和所指关系的界定中,专门强调了能指之间的关系对于所指的规定作用，而在阿尔都塞看来，意识形态的作用就在于保障这种能指关系对所指的规定性。只不过这种保障作用并不是首先通过压制性的国家机器来完成的，而是通过传唤性的意识形态国家机器来实现的。这就涉及对主体的分析，而这本身就是结构主义和精神分析共同的主题。

4. 意识形态把个人传唤为主体

“意识形态把个人传唤为主体，没有不借助于主体并为了这些主体而存在的意识形态”，这是《意识形态与意识形态国家机器》中最核心的论点。根据阿尔都塞对意识形态国家机器的分析，我们不难理解这里所说的意识形态本身就是这样一种将个人传唤为主体的机制。但是接下来需要我们仔细分析的就是个人和主体这两个概念。

在中文语境中个人似乎并不是一个特殊的概念。但是回顾现代思想史，我们可以发现：个人，或者说个体这个概念是一个现代的发明。在现代哲学的意义上，应当说是莱布尼茨的单子论最先表达了个体的含义，即最小不可分割的单位，但同时个体的存在依赖于个体之间的反身关系。在《1857—1858年经济学手稿》的导言中，马克思专门以鲁滨逊为例，讨论了作为现代市民社会产物的个人。因此，当我们理解阿尔都塞所说的意识形态把个人传唤为主体时，首先必须注意他所说的不是一般意义上的人类或人，也非法权、宗教意义上的人格，而是在现代资产阶级社会中得到充分展现的现代个人。同样，主体这个概念也是一个“晚近的发明”。阿尔都塞在以基督教意识形态为例展开的分析中，专门提到了两种主体：小写的主体(subject)，或者说个人被传唤为主体；大写的主体(Subject)，即作为他者、独立存在的主体。这样两种主体之间的纠结和相互承认，本身不仅贯穿于基督教教义(三位一体、道成肉身)之中，而且直接体现在资本主义生产方式之中，回顾一下《资本论》中有关商品价值形式以及物化分析的段落，就会发现，这样一种小写主体与大写主体之间的相互承认，本身的确构成了资本主义社会再生产的形式秘密。

然而，一方面，阿尔都塞的分析并没有立足于马克思的政治经济学批判而展开，而主要是借助于对宗教仪式在基督教意识形态中的作用来展开的，这在很大程度上可能得益于阿尔都塞早年的天主教背景；另一方面，这种分析的框架主要来自拉康的精神分析理论，尤其是其中有关主体镜像承认、小写主体与大写主体之间相互承认的分析。在阿尔都塞看来，把个人传唤为小写主体的是以一个独一的、中心的、作为他者的大写主体的“存在”为前提的。所有意识形态的结构都是一种双重反射的结构，意识形态复制的镜像结构同时保障着：(1) 把个人传唤为小写主体；(2) 他们对大写主体的臣服；(3) 小写主体与大写主体的相互承认，主体间的相互承认，以及主体最终的自我承认；(4) 绝对保证一切都确实是这样——“就这样吧”。显然，这样一种“意识形态一般”的形式说明是十分精彩的，但这更像是一张 CT 的纵切扫描图，个人、小写主体、大写主体之间承认的机制到底是如何展开的，这仍有待于进一步的分析。沿着这一路向，不少阿尔都塞的学生们转向了对拉康的持续援引，这是不无道理的。

六、进一步阅读指南

1. 《马克思恩格斯文集》第 9 卷，人民出版社 2009 年版。

2. 习近平：《决胜全面建成小康社会　夺取新时代中国特色社会主义社会伟大胜利》，人民出版社 2017 年版。

3. 习近平：《在党史学习教育动员大会上的讲话》，人民出版社 2021 年版。

4. 习近平：《习近平谈治国理政》第三卷，外文出版社 2020 年版。

5. [法]路易・阿尔都塞：《列宁和哲学》，杜章智译，台湾远流出版事业股份有限公司 1990 年版。

6. 陈越主编：《哲学与政治：阿尔都塞读本》，吉林人民出版社 2003 年版。

7. [斯]斯拉沃热・齐泽克等：《图绘意识形态》，方杰译，南京大学出版社 2002 年版。

8. 张一兵：《问题式、症候阅读与意识形态：关于阿尔都塞的一种文本学解读》，中央编译出版社 2003 年版。

9. Louis Althusser, *Essays on Ideology*, Verso, 1984.

10. Louis Althusser, *On the Reproduction of Capitalism: Ideology and Ideological State Apparatuses*, Verso, 2014.

七、问题与思考

1. 如何理解意识形态国家机器这一概念?
2. 意识形态是一种观念还是物质实在?
3. 意识形态、国家、个人、主体之间的关系是怎样的?
4. 比较说明马克思与阿尔都塞意识形态概念的异同。

第十四章　发达工业社会之激进的意识形态批判
——《单向度的人》选读

教学目的与要求

了解发达工业社会是如何压制了人们思想中的否定性、批判性和超越性维度，使社会成为单向度的社会，人成为单向度的人；正确理解科学技术是如何实现了对人的意识形态的控制；理解肯定性思维是怎样一步步在与否定性思维的对抗中取得胜利；掌握语言的"治疗"概念。

一、历史背景

（一）作者介绍

1898年，赫伯特·马尔库塞（Herbert Marcuse）出生于柏林一个犹太富商家庭。第一次世界大战期间，他在德军中服役，1917年加入德国社会民主党的多数派，在1918年的柏林革命中，他曾是革命士兵委员会的成员。但是，在1919年德国社会民主党参与杀害了罗莎·卢森堡和卡尔·李卜克内西后，他愤然退党，并从此退出了一切有组织的政治活动。1918年初，他开始在柏林大学攻读博士学位。1919年复员后，他转到弗赖堡大学继续攻读学位，并于1922年以《论德国艺术家小说》一文获得哲学博士学位。此后，他在柏林从事图书销售业务。1927年，海德格尔出版《存在与时间》一书，给德国哲学界带来巨大震动。在此背景下，马尔库塞于 1928 年重返弗赖堡，在海德格尔的指导下从事教职论文的写作，从而真正开始了自己的学术生涯。

作为一名西方马克思主义者，马尔库塞接受了卢卡奇在《历史与阶级意识》中所指明的方向，把扬弃物化意识、重新恢复无产阶级的阶级意识作为马克思主义哲学的历史使命。但是，究竟应当如何去完成这一历史使命呢？和同时代其他西方马克思主义者一样，马尔库塞也并不是十分清楚。《存在与时间》的出现则使马尔库塞发现了一种可能性：通过引入海德格尔的基础本体论，建构一种具有当代性的马克思主义历史理论，以达成马克思主义哲学的历史使命。正是怀着这个目的，马尔库塞重新回到了弗赖堡，以期在海德格尔的直接指导下，建构出一种海德格尔式的马克思主义。1932 年，马尔库塞完成了自己的教职论文《黑格尔的本体论和历史性理论》，以一种比较含蓄的学术化形式勾画出了自己的海德格尔式的马克思主义的理论蓝图。但令马尔库塞没有想到的是，海德格尔以沉默表示反对，最终导致教职论文未能获得通过。1932 年底，马尔库塞离开弗赖堡，并于次年加入霍克海默领导的法兰克福大学社会研究所。纳粹上台后，他前往瑞士任教一年。1934 年，他前往美国，与已经转移到哥伦比亚大学的社会研究所会合，直到 1942 年底加入美国战略情报局。

在 1933 年加入社会研究所之初，马尔库塞还是在努力综合马克思和海德格尔，致力于海德格尔式的马克思主义的建构。这在他当年发表的《论经济学劳动概念的哲学基础》一文中得到了体现。不过，他很快就放弃了这种努力，转而和霍克海默、阿多诺等一起投身于批判理论的建构，从而成为法兰克福学派早期批判理论的主要缔造者之一。1941 年，他出版了《理性与革命——黑格尔和社会理论的兴起》一书，针对将黑格尔国家哲学视为法西斯主义的理论先导这一错误的流行观点提出批判，着力证明黑格尔哲学是法国大革命在德国的理论表达，而马克思主义哲学则是黑格尔哲学的革命性的继承人。

1942 年底，马尔库塞加入美国战略情报局，任高级研究员。次年，他转到秘密服务局，在其中的中欧部从事分析研究工作直到第二次世界大战结束。1945 年秋，秘密服务局解散后，他转到美国国务院的中欧局继续从事情报分析工作。1951 年，在冷战氛围愈演愈烈的情况下，他最终离开政府部门，重新开始自己的学术生涯。二十世纪五十年代早期，他先后在哥伦比亚大学、哈佛大学短期任教，1954 年至 1967 年任教于布兰迪斯大学，1967 年以后任教于加利福尼亚大学圣地亚哥分校。

二十世纪五十年代初，当马尔库塞重新开始自己的学术生涯时，美国保守的整体化趋势已经日渐明显了。在这种状态下，原本就与美国现实相距遥远的社会主义革命似乎变得根本不可能了。严酷的现实虽然让马尔库塞感到悲观，但他并没有放弃革命理想，而是以一种积极的姿态进行理论探索，寻找新的可能性。正是在这个背景下，他发现了弗洛伊德精神分析学说的批判潜能，进而以其中的爱欲学说为结合点，将精神分析与马克思主义相结合，提出了一种全新的爱欲解放论。他的这种新理论在 1954 年出版的《爱欲与文明——对弗洛伊德思想的哲学探讨》中得到系统阐发。

在完成新的批判理论工具的建构后，马尔库塞将目光转向了对现实的批判。1958 年，他出版了《苏联马克思主义》一书，对苏联的理论和实践进行了批判，批评后者已经背离了马克思的原初设想，而 1964 年的《单向度的人——发达工业社会意识形态研究》则体现了马尔库塞对发达资本主义社会的基本批判立场。《单向度的人》之后，马尔库塞陆续发表了《压抑的容忍》(1965)、《关于解放的论文》(1969)、《反革命和造反》(1972)等一系列著名论文，就发达资本主义条件下新左派政治学的建构进行了不断探索，同时为各种新生社会运动进行了积极的辩护。他也因此成为 20 世纪 60 年代学生运动的精神导师之一。

进入二十世纪七十年代以后，欧美的学生运动逐渐退潮，发达资本主义社会重新归于稳定。在这种背景下，马尔库塞进行了新的理论反思，并像阿多诺一样回到美学，认为美学形式中包含巨大的解放潜能，能够在革命不再可能的条件下发挥保存革命意识、体现革命立场的独特作用。他的这些思想在 1979 年出版的《美学之维》中得到了表达。1979 年 7 月，马尔库塞在应邀前往联邦德国讲学的途中逝世，享年 81 岁。

(二) 时代背景

1. 战后发达资本主义国家科学技术的快速发展

第二次世界大战结束后，处于和平环境下的发达资本主义国家的经济、社会得到快速恢复和发展，科学技术在社会发展中的作用更加凸显。但是与此同时，科学技术对人的生活的控制力度也不断增大，特别是在马尔库塞所处的美国这个世界上科学技术最为发达的国家，科学技术的强大力量更是对马尔库塞产生了巨大的冲击。科学技术在当时已经不仅仅是生产力的重要组成因素，而且也成为一种越来越重要的统治手段。随着科学技术统治的不断加强，马尔库塞、哈贝马斯等人愈发认识到人类社会正在迎来新的形态，人被科学技术严重异化，后者已经具备了一种广泛而深刻的影响力和统治力。在此背景下，包括马尔库塞在内的西方马克思主义者们纷纷寻求人的自由的重新回归，开展了一系列深刻的理论探寻之路。

2. 战后美国社会运动和学生运动的勃兴

第二次世界大战后，美国一跃成为头号资本主义强国。经济的高速发展使得美国率先进入丰裕社会。但是，在政治上和文化上，二十世纪五十年代的美国却极为保守。这种状况的出现固然和麦卡锡主义的盛行有关，但归根结底则是因为资本主义的整体化趋势压制了人们的批判性思维能力，成为一种单向度的人。具体地说，当时的美国已经处于热核战争阴云的笼罩下，但是，美国国内却弥漫着一种万事如常、人人安分的气氛。任何对核试验和维持第二次世界大战时期的那种征兵制的怀疑都被主流意识形态斥之为异端。正是在这种保守的整体化趋势中，马尔库塞完成了《爱欲与文明》一书，以一种乐观的方式表明了自己对当代资本主义发展的悲观主义判断。不过，二十世纪五十年代末以后，美国的文化氛围和政治氛围却发生了剧烈变化：在民权运动和反战运动等社会运动的激励下，新左派学生运动不断高涨，以文化大拒绝这种形式表达了对资本主义的不满。这虽然不足以让马尔库塞改变对解放前景的悲观主义判断，不过，也确实让他看到了某种真实的希望。正因如此，他才会在《单向度的人》中高度评价了文化大拒绝的历史性意义，并把它视为进行资本主义替代选择的一种可能手段。

（三）思想背景

1. 法兰克福学派的理论进展

在法兰克福学派批判理论的早期发展中，霍克海默、阿多诺和马尔库塞是最重要的三个思想核心。二十世纪四十年代末，霍克海默和阿多诺与社会研究所一起返回德国，马尔库塞则选择继续留在美国。此后，他们的理论道路出现了明显分化。就在《单向度的人》出版两年后，自二十世纪五十年代起就逐渐取代霍克海默成为学派理论旗手的阿多诺也于 1966 年出版了自己最重要的著作《否定的辩证法》。可是，在随后爆发的学生运动中，这两个人和这两本书的遭遇却截然不同：《单向度的人》名重一时，而《否定的辩证法》却陷于被人遗忘的角落；马尔库塞被新左派学生奉为与马克思、毛泽东并列的三个“M”之一，而阿多诺却遭到新左派女学生的弑父式的攻击，不久后就因心脏病突发遽然离世。从共同的立场出发，马尔库塞究竟是如何达到《单向度的人》的呢？这不仅需要追溯马尔库塞的个人思想史，而且需要分析战后发达资本主义国家的发展趋势及其在美国和欧洲这两个不同语境中的同与异。

2. 战后西方主流社会科学思潮的分化

第二次世界大战后，发达资本主义国家在许多方面都发生了重大变化。这些变化究竟是如何发生的？它们将带来什么样的后果？关于这个问题，在大多数同时代理论者还只满足于对结果的分析与批判时，作为法兰克福学派中后期政治经济学理论的主要提供者——波洛克就敏锐地发现，这种变化实际上是源于当代资本主义生产本身的发展，即自动化的普及。为此，在 1956 年出版的《自动化的经济和社会后果研究》一书中，他详细探讨了自动化的发展历程及其不同的经济社会后果，最终指明，这种新的资本主义生产组织方式已经发展到如此程度，以至于它可以将全社会整合为一个整体，最终，从肉体到精神，个人都不再能够脱离社会的控制。① 波洛克的研究实际上提出了一个重大问题，即在工人阶级已不再能够自发地形成革命意识、发动革命战争的条件下，革命是否可能？以及如何可能？面对这个不可回避的重大问题，马尔库塞和阿多诺实际上都是悲观的，即认为革命在很大程度上已经不再可能，但是，他们并没有因此像加缪、梅洛-庞蒂等人那样转向右派，而是坚持批判立场，探索不可能的可能。不仅如此，他们还不约而同

① Friedrich Pollock, *Automation: A Study of Its Economic and Social Consequences*, Blackwell, 1957.

地将目光转向了哲学，把重新恢复否定性作为使不再可能的革命重新变得可能的前提和关键。但他们最终的差异在于，马尔库塞选择了文化大拒绝这种更加激进因而也显得更为积极的革命战略，而阿多诺则选择了韬光养晦的“冬眠”战略，在激进的新左派学生看来，这无疑是保守的甚至是阻碍革命的。马尔库塞和阿多诺之所以会选择这两种截然不同的战略，原因有很多，但关键在于他们所处的资本主义语境存在差异。

二、篇章结构

《单向度的人》发表于 1964 年，是马尔库塞最负盛名的作品之一。正文由“单向度的社会”“单向度的思想”和“进行替代性选择的机会”三个部分组成。马尔库塞认为，当代工业社会是一个新型的极权主义社会，因为它成功地压制了这个社会中的反对派和反对意见，压制了人们内心中的否定性、批判性和超越性的向度，从而使这个社会成了单向度的社会，使生活于其中的人成了单向度的人。

第一部分题为“单向度的社会”，包含四个章节：《控制的新形式》《政治领域的封闭》《不幸意识的征服：压抑性的俗化趋势》《话语领域的封闭》。马尔库塞系统阐发了“单向度的社会”形成的内在根源及其表现方式。

马尔库塞认为，由于技术的进步，一种舒服、平稳、合理而又民主的不自由在发达的工业文明中流行开来。在工业社会这样一个极权主义社会中，原本作为工业社会的形成时期和早期阶段十分重要的权利和自由两大因素，现在却正在丧失其传统的理论基础和内容。发达的工业文明构建出了一种不合理的合理性，有效地抑制了人们对自由的需要。同时，社会控制更多地以技术的形式进一步潜化到人们的生活内部，使人们原本作为理性的批判力量的内心向度屈从于异化的社会存在，从而无法认清自己真实的生活状态。由于意识形态本身就内嵌在生产过程之中，伴随着工业产品在人群中的广泛传播，一种新的生活方式被普及开来，这种生活方式具有内在地阻碍自身发生新的质变的特性，由此便出现了一种单向度的思想和行为模式。与此同时，技术的合理性展示出其政治特性，使社会完全成为一个凝固的生活系统，使一切真正的对立一体化。

首先是政治经济领域的一体化。在当代工业社会中，“极权主义”已不仅是一种恐怖的政治协作，而且也是一种非恐怖的经济技术协作，很难再出现那种可以有效地反对社会整体的局面。机器成了任何以机器生产程序为基本结构的社会的最有效的政治工具。劳动阶级也逐步发生转变，他们的身体、大脑甚至灵魂都逐步被物所支配，其职业自主权也逐渐被机器剥夺，劳工开始“自愿地一体化”，丧失了他们的否定性和革命性，最终沦为一种工具的、物的存在。从表面上看，在资本主义社会的发达阶段，社会是受到压制的多元系统，但其实质是一种具有意识形态欺骗性的所谓多元化，并且借助统治阶级长期对战争威胁的宣扬促生出一种凝聚力来遏制社会变革，使奴役状态永恒化、使政治经济一体化。同时发生的是文化思想领域的一体化。“高层文化”中的对立性因素和超越性因素正在被清除，使之屈从于流行在当代工业社会发达地区的俗化趋势，丧失了大部分真理，不再具有同现实相区别的另一向度。双向度的文化被消除，各种“文化价值”则被全部纳入已确立的秩序，被大规模地复制和显示。超越现实的理想现在却被现实所同化、超越，艺术异化也同其他否定方式一道屈从于技术合理性的进程，在话语领域中则出现了新型的顺从主义。

在此社会制度下，一个单向度的交流领域被建立起来。该领域的语言便是统一性和一致性的证明，它有步骤地鼓励肯定性思考和行动，并步调一致地攻击超越性批判观念，同时通过统治阶级对语言的概念和命题等的全面转译，使其所指的内容不再具有张力，被局限在一个封闭的范围内，使得人们的思想本身及其功能和内容也正在发生势不可挡的物化。

第二部分“单向度的思想”由第五、六、七三个章节构成，分别题为：《否定性的思维：被击败了的抗议逻辑》《从否定性思维到肯定性思维：技术合理性和统治的逻辑》《肯定性思维的胜利：单向度的哲学》。在这一部分里，马尔库塞着重讨论了原初那种矛盾的、双向度的思维模式沦为单向度的肯定性思维模式的过程。

双向度的思维模式存在于前工业文明之中，主要是指在现实和试图把握现实的思想之间存在着一种对立的结构，在这种模式下，对现实的认同和对现实的抗议以辩证的方式结合在一起，理论理性和实践理性本身既存在维持既有现实状态的倾向，同时也会成为一种对现实具有否定性和破坏性的力量。而到了工业文明之后，认同“既有的现实便是合理的”肯定性思维模式击败了具有破坏性力量的否定性思维，占据了人们思想领域的统治地位。

第五章追溯了前工业文明的思维方式，并着重比较了柏拉图的辩证逻辑和亚里士多德的形式逻辑之间的异同。在发达的工业文明到来之前，稳定的趋势同理性的破坏性要素、肯定性思维的力量同否定性思维的力量在相互对抗的张力中发展。在古希腊哲学的传统中，思想的抽象和社会现实之间既有着紧密的联系，也始终保持着特定的距离。哲学并不认同既有的现实，它所追求的真理代表着一种比现实更高的真实性，为真理而斗争实际上就是在对现实的破坏中去拯救本质的"存在"。柏拉图就是这种辩证逻辑的代表，他的哲学构造了一个超越现实之上的纯粹的理念王国，现实和哲学的理念之间存在着永恒性的辩证运动。到了亚里士多德那里发展出了形式逻辑，这种逻辑试图为思维规则制定一种普遍有效性，形式取代了内容。马尔库塞将形式逻辑看作通往科学思维道路的第一阶段。在马尔库塞看来，形式逻辑由于强调形式的本质作用，而将具体的现实内容和历史内容抽离了出去，沦为对形式和现象的纯粹肯定性；而辩证逻辑的对象是真实具体的实在，它对现实的历史内容保持着一种开放性态度，思维的结构和现实的历史之间也维持着一种辩证的统一关系，从而保存了思维的批判性和否定性向度。

第六章阐释了在科学技术的推动下，肯定性思维在与否定性思维的对抗中如何占据了上风。在发达工业社会中，一方面，科学精神消解着主客体间的对抗关系；另一方面，科学逐渐变成技术，在技术作用下，物质和科学的"中立"特征把客观现实同流行于社会中的意识联系起来，由于这一中立性是通过当时社会并为了社会而确立的，在此意义上中立性成为一种肯定性。此外，在政治意图对技术的渗透下，技术合理性一方面使统治权力合法化，另一方面使人的不自由合理化，科学-技术的合理性和操纵一起被熔接成一种新型的社会控制形式，技术成为物化的重要工具。由此，肯定性的思维一步步走向了胜利。

第七章通过对语言分析的论述表明了肯定性思维的胜利。对于思想来说，它的再限定有助于精神操作同社会现实中的操作相协调，其目的是治疗。反过来讲，当思想不再超越既是纯公理的又是与既定话语和行为领域共存的概念框架时，它便与现实处于同一水平上了。因此，语言分析提出要对思想和言语中的形而上学的成分进行治疗，其立场被限制在与否定性思维不相容的立场。分析从两个方面进行：一方面，经验主义对普通行为领域自我强加的限制有助于产生一种内在的肯定态度，这种预先就受到制约的分析使它得出的"中立观点"会屈从于肯定性思维的力量；另一方面，实证主义把各种形而上学、先验论和唯心主义当作蒙昧主义的落后思想方式来加以反对，在科学对现实的理解和改造下，在社会变成工业社会和技术社会的同时，实证主义在社会中证明理论与实践、真理与事实的一致。哲学思维和语言领域同日常思维和语言领域间存在着不可归约的差别。哲学概念以事实和意义的一种向度为目的"从外部"来解释日常话语的原子化的词组或语词，具有对抗性的、超越的力量；但语言分析所使用的素材是一种"净化了的"单向度的语言，它的"治疗"使不同的、对立的意义相互隔离，具有意义的、容易引起争议的历史向度却被迫保持缄默。语言分析这种治疗方式的胜利表明了肯定性思维方式的胜利。

第三部分"进行替代性选择的机会"包括《哲学的历史承诺》《解放的大变动》《结论》三个章节。在这一部分里，马尔库塞希望重拾哲学的思想历史作用，使否定性力量与肯定性力量间能再次以一种张力的形式推进历史发展。

马尔库塞首先讨论了分析哲学对普遍性概念的理解。他认为，分析哲学排除了普遍性概念的形而上学的、模糊的特征，把经过剪裁和整理的现象当成了现实，逃避了它们本应负有的"否定性"责任。但事实上，马尔库塞所认同的普遍概念是从具体的实体中抽象而来，又能够表达实体的潜在可能性，普遍性从观念上把握着种种既在现实中实现、又在现实中受到阻碍的可能性。马尔库塞进一步指出，普遍概念的客观有效性的根基在于各个主体的"谋划"行为和共同世界之间的相互作用。从客观向度看，主体的"谋划"总是处于一种共同的特定社会结构和工具世界之中；从主观向度看，作为历史实践的谋划本身具有超越性，它试图超越已确立的总体，去创造一种更高的合理性。在厘清以上思路后，马尔库塞又重新回到了对肯定性思维的探讨上。

首先，马尔库塞认为在肯定性的思维模式占统治地位的社会中，否定性要素被肯定性要素吸收，否定特征仅被理解为发展过程中不能避免的副产品出现。否定性与肯定性"愉快"地结合在一起，获得了一种虚假的和谐，进而具有一种意识形态功能。

其次，马尔库塞回顾了科学技术、形而上学与艺术间的关系史。早期的三者间存在着对抗而又补充的关联，形而上学是一切学科的根基，艺术是从感性出发超越现实的一种可能性领域，早期科学的发展借鉴了很多形而上学和艺术要素。但到了工业文明的发达阶段，科学技术理性进一步发展，科学与形而上学、艺术的传统关系发生了颠倒。由于科学技术可以设计和规定一种自由地、和平地存在的可能现实，其形而上学特征和情感特征就彻底丧失了，科学技术的合理性取得了彻底的统治性地位。

至此，马尔库塞得出结论：技术的进步造成了一个新的极权主义社会，并使抗议的传统方式失去了作用。但马尔库塞仍旧坚持批判的否定性功能，他将希望寄托在了生活在社会最底层的被剥削者身上，认为他们从外部对现存制度的打击才有可能终结这个单向度的极权世界。

三、研究前沿

马尔库塞在《单向度的人》等作品中，深刻阐述了发达工业社会中以“单向度”为显著特征的系列弊病，对现代文明中的科学技术、人之生存境况、文化观念和思维方式等方面进行了全面诊断，实现了对现代文明的总体性哲学反思。自二十世纪八十年代西方马克思主义传入我国以来，国内学界始终保持着对马尔库塞思想的关注，研究不断走向深入，多维度、全方面地考察和评价了马尔库塞的思想。总体来看，相关研究呈现出成果数量较多，主题分布宽泛，研究质量不断提升等特点，聚焦的问题主要是在以下三个方面。

第一，进一步深化对马尔库塞发达工业社会批判的研究。在描述发达工业社会时，马尔库塞提出了当代社会中被控制、被利用的“虚假需要”问题。学者们就马尔库塞所说的“虚假需要”的内涵、作用机制展开了热烈讨论。有学者强调，必须基于弗洛伊德的学说去理解、考察马尔库塞的需要理论；有学者认为，马尔库塞对“虚假需要”的揭示，凸显了消费时代中人类生活方式和思维方式的彻底变化，刻画了消费时代带来的社会危机和精神生态困境；也有学者批判马尔库塞的需要理论始终停留在抽象的人性需要理论，缺少历史唯物主义的基本视角。同时，学者们关注到了马尔库塞对“肯定文化”的批判，一方面将其与霍克海默等人的文化工业批判联系起来进行研究，另一方面则拓展其内涵，进一步论述发达工业社会中文化的社会统治功能，批判其同一化和片面化的消极特征。

第二，全面讨论马尔库塞技术理性批判的本质、内涵及其当代发展与价值。马尔库塞对现代科学技术的批判构成了他对发达工业社会分析的重要维度，他敏锐地发现了当代科学技术的政治功能，揭示了科学技术作为政治统治合法性的意识形态工具新特征，因而他的科学技术观、"技术理性"概念内涵与技术异化等观点获得了学界越来越多的关注。学界相关研究主要集中在三个方面。其一，立足于文本分析，完整展示马尔库塞技术批判理论的全貌。有学者仔细分析了《单向度的人》《爱欲与文明》等作品，从语言学、存在论和价值论等多重角度进行考察，认为马尔库塞理解的技术实质上是一种控制体系，而这种控制的根源在于对技术的形而上学使用。有学者则指出，马尔库塞对科学技术的论述不单单只包含通过表明科技的异化来批判发达工业社会这样的否定意义，还包括了建构未来自由社会的"新技术与科学"的积极内涵，第二，通过比较分析，凸显马尔库塞关于现代科学技术观点的意义和价值。在法兰克福学派内部，有关科学技术的讨论一直存在，马尔库塞与霍克海默、阿多诺和哈贝马斯等人的观点既有共通之处，也保留了自己的独特性。有学者甄别了《启蒙辩证法》中的"工具理性"与马尔库塞的"技术理性"概念的异同；也有学者研究了马尔库塞与哈贝马斯科学技术观的差别，指出二者在解释造成技术异化的原因以及克服技术异化的途径等问题上的分歧；还有学者认为马尔库塞是将海德格尔的技术现象学转变成了技术社会批判理论。第三，紧跟理论动态，介绍马尔库塞技术批判理论的当代发展与更新，讨论了芬伯格等国外学者对马尔库塞的继承与发展。总的来看，国内学者们都不赞成马尔库塞技术统治论表现出来的悲观主义态度，但肯定了其对当代社会中技术统治现象的解释与分析。

第三，探寻马尔库塞的新感性理论，反思马尔库塞对人的解放问题的思考。出于对人们生存状况的担忧，马尔库塞一直力图找到一条突破困境的解放道路，提出了新感性、无压抑性新文明、解放美学等思想，在欧美左派发展史中产生过非常大的影响。基于"爱欲"理论，马尔库塞从心理分析的角度观察现代文明，认为现代文明是限制人的生物本能充分发展的一种压抑性文明，必须彻底解放爱欲才能建设非压抑性文明。对此，就什么是"爱欲"、如何建构爱欲文化、基于爱欲的未来文明何以可能等问题，国内学者们展开了丰富讨论。有学者分析了马尔库塞"压抑性心理机制",对其压抑与反压抑的动力机制做出了系统阐释,并结合现代人深层次的异化和文化危机论证其合理性。此外,通过对马尔库塞关于艺术与审美功能论述的考察,学者们一方面在学理上阐述了这一思想的历史起源、内在逻辑和现实影响,另一方面也从马克思主义基本立场给予了批判性回应,指明这一思想片面强调艺术、审美的功能,忽视了现实原则和技术理性的统治,是在审美幻觉中对现存社会的想象性批判,这种艺术审美救世主义丝毫未触及资本主义制度的根源,是一种新形式的乌托邦。

四、文本节选

Conclusion

The advancing one-dimensional society alters the relation between the rational and the irrational. Contrasted with the fantastic and insane aspects of its rationality, the realm of the irrational becomes the home of the really rational—of the ideas which may "promote the art of life." If the established society manages all normal communication, validating or invalidating it in accordance with social requirements, then the values alien to these requirements may perhaps have no other medium of communication than the abnormal one of fiction. The aesthetic dimension still retains a freedom of expression which enables the writer and artist to call men and things by their name—to name the otherwise unnameable.

The real face of our time shows in Samuel Beckett's novels; its real history is written in Rolf Hochhut's play *Der Stellvertreter*. It is no longer imagination which speaks here, but Reason, in a reality which justifies everything and absolves everything—except the sin against its spirit. Imagination is abdicating to this reality, which is catching up with and overtaking imagination. Auschwitz continues to haunt, not the memory but the accomplishments of man—the space flights; the rockets and missiles; the "labyrinthine basement under the Snack Bar"; the pretty electronic plants, clean, hygienic and with flower beds; the poison gas which is not really harmful to people; the secrecy in which we all participate. This is the setting in which the great human achievements of science, medicine, technology take place; the efforts to save and ameliorate life are the sole promise in the disaster. The willful play with fantastic possibilities, the ability to act with good conscience, *contra naturam*, to experiment with men and things, to convert illusion into reality and fiction into truth, testify to the extent to which Imagination has become an instrument of progress. And it is one which, like others in the established societies, is methodically abused. Setting the pace and style of politics, the power of imagination far exceeds *Alice in Wonderland* in the manipulation of words, turning sense into nonsense and nonsense into sense.

The formerly antagonistic realms merge on technical and political grounds—magic and science, life and death, joy and misery. Beauty reveals its terror as highly classified nuclear plants and laboratories become "Industrial Parks" in pleasing surroundings; Civil Defense Headquarters display a "deluxe fallout-shelter" with wall-to-wall carpeting ("soft"), lounge chairs, television, and Scrabble, "designed as a combination family room during peacetime (sic!) and family fallout shelter should war break out." If the horror of such realizations does not penetrate into consciousness, if it is readily taken for granted, it is because these achievements are (a) perfectly rational in terms of the existing order, (b) tokens of human ingenuity and power beyond the traditional limits of imagination.

The obscene merger of aesthetics and reality refutes the philosophies which oppose "poetic" imagination to scientific and empirical Reason. Technological progress is accompanied by a progressive rationalization and even realization of the imaginary. The archetypes of horror as well as of joy, of war as well as of peace lose their catastrophic character.

Their appearance in the daily life of the individuals is no longer that of irrational forces—their modern avatars are elements of technological domination, and subject to it.

In reducing and even canceling the romantic space of imagination, society has forced the imagination to prove itself on new grounds, on which the images are translated into historical capabilities and projects. The translation will be as bad and distorted as the society which undertakes it. Separated from the realm of material production and material needs, imagination was mere play, invalid in the realm of necessity, and committed only to a fantastic logic and a fantastic truth. When technical progress cancels this separation, it invests the images with its own logic and its own truth; it reduces the free faculty of the mind. But it also reduces the gap between imagination and Reason. The two antagonistic faculties become interdependent on common ground. In the light of the capabilities of advanced industrial civilization, is not all play of the imagination playing with technical possibilities, which can be tested as to their chances of realization? The romantic idea of a "science of the Imagination" seems to assume an ever-more-empirical aspect.

The scientific, rational character of Imagination has long since been recognized in mathematics, in the hypotheses and experiments of the physical sciences. It is likewise recognized in psychoanalysis, which is in theory based on the acceptance of the specific rationality of the irrational; the comprehended imagination becomes, redirected, a therapeutic force. But this therapeutic force may go much further than in the cure of neuroses. It was not a poet but a scientist who has outlined this prospect.

…

Imagination has not remained immune to the process of reification. We are possessed by our images, suffer our own images. Psychoanalysis knew it well, and knew the consequences. However, "to give to the imagination all the means of expression" would be regression. The mutilated individuals (mutilated also in their faculty of imagination) would organize and destroy even more than they are now permitted to do. Such release would be the unmitigated horror—not the catastrophe of culture, but the free sweep of its most repressive tendencies. Rational is the imagination which can become the *a priori* of the reconstruction and redirection of the productive apparatus toward a pacified existence, a life without fear. And this can never be the imagination of those who are possessed by the images of domination and death.

To liberate the imagination so that it can be given all its means of expression presupposes the repression of much that is now free and that perpetuates a repressive society. And such reversal is not a matter of psychology or ethics but of politics, in the sense in which this term has here been used throughout: the practice in which the basic societal institutions are developed, defined, sustained, and changed. It is the practice of individuals, no matter how organized they may be. Thus the question once again must be faced: how can the administered individuals—who have made their mutilation into their own liberties and satisfactions, and thus reproduce it on an enlarged scale—liberate themselves from themselves as well as from their masters? How is it even thinkable that the vicious circle be broken?

Paradoxically, it seems that it is not the notion of the new societal *institutions* which presents the greatest difficulty in the attempt to answer this question. The established societies themselves are changing, or have already changed the basic institutions in the direction of increased planning. Since the development and utilization of all available resources for the universal satisfaction of vital needs is the prerequisite of pacification, it is incompatible with the prevalence of particular interests which stand in the way of attaining this goal. Qualitative change is conditional upon planning for the whole against these interests, and a free and rational society can emerge only on this basis.

The institutions within which pacification can be envisaged thus defy the traditional classification into authoritarian and democratic, centralized and liberal administration. Today, the opposition to central planning in the name of a liberal democracy which is denied in reality serves as an ideological prop for repressive interests. The goal of authentic self-determination by the individuals depends on effective social control over the production and distribution of the necessities (in terms of the achieved level of culture, material and intellectual).

Here, technological rationality, stripped of its exploitative features, is the sole standard and guide in planning and developing the available resources for all. Self-determination in the production and distribution of vital goods and services would be wasteful. The job is a technical one, and as a truly technical job, it makes for the reduction of physical and mental toil. In this realm, centralized control is rational if it establishes the preconditions for meaningful self-determination. The latter can then become effective in its own realm—in the decisions which involve the production and distribution of the economic surplus, and in the individual existence.

In any case, the combination of centralized authority and direct democracy is subject to infinite variations, according to the degree of development. Self-determination will be real to the extent to which the masses have been dissolved into individuals liberated from all propaganda, indoctrination, and manipulation, capable of knowing and comprehending the facts and of evaluating the alternatives. In other words, society would be rational and free to the extent to which it is organized, sustained, and reproduced by an essentially new historical Subject.

At the present stage of development of the advanced industrial societies, the material as well as the cultural system denies this exigency. The power and efficiency of this system, the thorough assimilation of mind with fact, of thought with required behavior, of aspirations with reality, militate against the emergence of a new Subject. They also militate against the notion that the replacement of the prevailing control over the productive process by "control from below" would mean the advent of qualitative change. This notion was valid, and still is valid, where the laborers were, and still are, the living denial and indictment of the established society. However, where these classes have become a prop of the established way of life, their ascent to control would prolong this way in a different setting.

And yet, the facts are all there which validate the critical theory of this society and of its fatal development: the increasing irrationality of the whole; waste and restriction of productivity; the need for aggressive expansion; the constant threat of war; intensified exploitation; dehumanization. And they all point to the historical alternative: the planned utilization of resources for the satisfaction of vital needs with a minimum of toil, the transformation of leisure into free time, the pacification of the struggle for existence.

But the facts and the alternatives are there like fragments which do not connect, or like a world of mute objects without a subject, without the practice which would move these objects in the new direction. Dialectical theory is not refuted, but it cannot offer the remedy. It cannot be positive. To be sure, the dialectical concept, in comprehending the given facts, transcends the given facts. This is the very token of its truth. It defines the historical possibilities, even necessities; but their realization can only be in the practice which responds to the theory, and, at present, the practice gives no such response.

On theoretical as well as empirical grounds, the dialectical concept pronounces its own hopelessness. The human reality is its history and, in it, contradictions do not explode by themselves. The conflict between streamlined, rewarding domination on the one hand, and its achievements that make for self-determination and pacification on the other, may become blatant beyond any possible denial, but it may well continue to be a manageable and even productive conflict, for with the growth in the technological conquest of nature grows the conquest of man by man. And this conquest reduces the freedom which is a necessary *a priori* of liberation. This is freedom of thought in the only sense in which thought can be free in the administered world—as the consciousness of its repressive productivity, and as the absolute need for breaking out of this whole. But precisely this absolute need does not prevail where it could become the driving force of a historical practice, the effective cause of qualitative change. Without this material force, even the most acute consciousness remains powerless.

No matter how obvious the irrational character of the whole may manifest itself and, with it, the necessity of change, insight into necessity has never sufficed for seizing the possible alternatives. Confronted with the omnipresent efficiency of the given system of life, its alternatives have always appeared utopian. And insight into necessity, the consciousness of the evil state, will not suffice even at the stage where the accomplishments of science and the level of productivity have eliminated the utopian features of the alternatives—where the established reality rather than its opposite is utopian.

Does this mean that the critical theory of society abdicates and leaves the field to an empirical sociology which, freed from all theoretical guidance except a methodological one, succumbs to the fallacies of misplaced concreteness, thus performing an ideological service while proclaiming the elimination of value judgments? Or do the dialectical concepts once again testify to their truth—by comprehending their own situation as that of the society which they analyze? A response might suggest itself if one considers the critical theory precisely at the point of its greatest weakness—its inability to demonstrate the liberating tendencies *within* the established society.

The critical theory of society, was, at the time of its origin, confronted with the presence of real forces (objective and subjective) *in* the established society which moved (or could be guided to move) toward more rational and freer institutions by abolishing the existing ones which had become obstacles to progress. These were the empirical grounds on which the theory was erected, and from these empirical grounds derived the idea of the liberation of *inherent* possibilities—the development, otherwise blocked and distorted, of material and intellectual productivity, faculties, and needs. Without the demonstration of such forces, the critique of society would still be valid and rational, but it would be incapable of translating its rationality into terms of historical practice. The conclusion? "Liberation of inherent possibilities" no longer adequately expresses the historical alternative.

The enchained possibilities of advanced industrial societies are: development of the productive forces on an enlarged scale, extension of the conquest of nature, growing satisfaction of needs for a growing number of people, creation of new needs and faculties. But these possibilities are gradually being realized through means and institutions which cancel their liberating potential, and this process affects not only the means but also the ends. The instruments of productivity and progress, organized into a totalitarian system, determine not only the actual but also the possible utilizations.

At its most advanced stage, domination functions as administration, and in the overdeveloped areas of mass consumption, the administered life becomes the good life of the whole, in the defense of which the opposites are united. This is the pure form of domination. Conversely, its negation appears to be the pure form of negation. All content seems reduced to the one abstract demand for the end of domination—the only truly revolutionary exigency, and the event that would validate the achievements of industrial civilization. In the face of its efficient denial by the established system, this negation appears in the politically impotent from of the "absolute refusal"—a refusal which seems the more unreasonable the more the established system develops its productivity and alleviates the burden of life. ...

...

But if the abstract character of the refusal is the result of total reification, then the concrete ground for refusal must still exist, for reification is an illusion. By the same token, the unification of opposites in the medium of technological rationality must be, *in all its reality*, an illusory unification, which eliminates neither the contradiction between the growing productivity and its repressive use, nor the vital need for solving the contradiction.

But the struggle for the solution has outgrown the traditional forms. The totalitarian tendencies of the one-dimensional society render the traditional ways and means of protest ineffective—perhaps even dangerous because they preserve the illusion of popular sovereignty. This illusion contains some truth: "the people," previously the ferment of social change, have "moved up" to become the ferment of social cohesion. Here rather than in the redistribution of wealth and equalization of classes is the new stratification characteristic of advanced industrial society.

However, underneath the conservative popular base is the substratum of the outcasts and outsiders, the exploited and persecuted of other races and other colors, the unemployed and the unemployable. They exist outside the democratic process; their life is the most immediate and the most real need for ending intolerable conditions and institutions. Thus their opposition is revolutionary even if their consciousness is not. Their opposition hits the system from without and is therefore not deflected by the system; it is an elementary force which violates the rules of the game and, in doing so, reveals it as a rigged game. When they get together and go out into the streets, without arms, without protection, in order to ask for the most primitive civil rights, they know that they face dogs, stones, and bombs, jail, concentration camps, even death. Their force is behind every political demonstration for the victims of law and order. The fact that they start refusing to play the game may be the fact which marks the beginning of the end of a period.

Nothing indicates that it will be a good end. The economic and technical capabilities of the established societies are sufficiently vast to allow for adjustments and concessions to the underdog, and their armed forces sufficiently trained and equipped to take care of emergency situations. However, the spectre is there again, inside and outside the frontiers of the advanced societies. The facile historical parallel with the barbarians threatening the empire of civilization prejudges the issue; the second period of barbarism may well be the continued empire of civilization itself. But the chance is that, in this period, the historical extremes may meet again: the most advanced consciousness of humanity, and its most exploited force. It is nothing but a chance The critical theory of society possesses no concepts which could bridge the gap between the present and its future; holding no promise and showing no success, it remains negative. Thus it wants to remain loyal to those who, without hope, have given and give their life to the Great Refusal.

At the beginning of the fascist era, Walter Benjamin wrote:

> *Nur um der Hoffnungslosen willen ist uns die Hoffnung gegeben.*
>
> It is only for the sake of those without hope that hope is given to us.

——Herbert Marcuse, *One-Dimensional Man*, Routledge, 1964, pp.251 - 261.

五、观点解读

1. 科学技术实现了对人的意识形态统治

马尔库塞关于整部作品的论题是：当代社会是一个新型的极权主义社会，这个社会成功地压制了其反对派及反对意见，压制了思维的否定性、批判性和超越性的向度，使得整个社会成为单向度的社会，生活于其中的人也成为单向度的人。而造成这个社会极权主义性质的原因则主要在于科学技术的进步。在发达的工业社会中，科学丧失了其“中立性”的历史传统，并在很大程度上成为技术的代名词。科学技术与社会、政治联系在一起，作为一个系统来发挥着作用，在此基础上，先前对立的领域也被结合在了一起。科学技术在发展的过程中，一步步地以技术合理化的方式完成了对人的意识形态统治：首先，科学技术在参与对自然的改造来供给人们生活资料的同时，以技术化控制的形式反过来为人对人的统治提供了概念和工具；其次，它消除了私人与公众、个人需要与社会需要之间的对立，成为社会控制和社会团结的新的、更有效的、更令人愉快的形式；最后，它逐步渗透到人们的思想层面，通过构建一个新的物化价值准则，使其成为一种控制人们思想的意识形态。

马尔库塞认为，在工业社会中，当个体的意识同加于其身上的存在相一致并从中得到了自己发展的满足时，异化的观念就产生了；当这种一致化成为现实时，就构成了异化的更高阶段。此时，异化了的主体也就被异化了的存在所吞没了，同时合理的“虚假意识”也就变成了真实的意识。在当代，劳动的科学管理和科学分工一方面大大提高了政治、经济、文化事业的生产率；另一方面，这一“合理”的事业所产生出的思维和行为的范型又为其对终极目的的破坏、对人民的压制进行辩护。技术的合理性保护了统治的合法性，它和操纵一起被转化成为一种新的社会控制形式。这种技术的控制似乎真正体现了有益于整个社会集团和社会利益的理性，一切矛盾似乎都成了不合理的，而一切对抗似乎都不可能了。在现代工业社会新型的极权主义之下，一种单向度的思想和行为模式便出现了。

2. 肯定性思维对否定性思维的胜利

在《单向度的人》中，马尔库塞认为，要对现代工业社会中极权主义的合理性问题加以讨论，就有必要对理性本身进行认真的分析。在理性的历史性发展过程中，顺从主义和意识形态特征被看作肯定性思维方式，而思辨和乌托邦特征被看作否定性思维方式。马尔库塞试图论证的观点是：在技术和前技术阶段，都共同拥有着一些表现西方传统连续性的、有关人和自然的基本概念，在这种连续性的范围内，来自不同途径的各种思想方式相互抵触，致使稳定的趋势与理性的破坏性要素之间、肯定性思维的力量与否定性思维的力量之间相互冲突，这种状态一直持续到发达的工业文明产生之前，但在此之后伴随着科学技术的推动作用，单向度的现实达成了对各种矛盾的同化，思想由原初的那种矛盾的、双向度的思维模式沦为单向度的肯定性思维模式。

在马尔库塞看来，理性早先除了具有认识现实、维持现实的肯定性力量之外，还具有颠覆性的功能，即“否定性的力量”。如黑格尔所说：“如果理性是主客体的共同名称，它是作为对立面的综合而存在的共同特征。因此，本体论包含了主客体间的紧张关系；它充满了具体性。理性的现实则是这种紧张关系在自然、历史和哲学中的表现。”这种理性所认同的真理是一种价值准则，为真理而战就是从破坏中进行拯救，以达到其本应所是的现实。这个概念实际上反映了这样一种世界的存在：这个世界的现实存在与理念世界具有一些不符之处，因此常受到否定性、破坏性因素的威胁，但同时它又是一个朝着最终目标进行构建的完整系统。这种自身包含对抗性的世界在多大程度上支配着哲学范畴的发展，哲学也就在多大程度上生存于一个双向度的领域之中。而到了发达工业社会，极权主义的技术合理性领域就成为理性观念演变的最新成果。在科学技术的作用下，先前那些否定的、超越性的力量同已确立的制度呈现出一种一体化趋势，似乎在创造一种新的社会结构。从现实层面上来说，伴随着政治意图对技术的不断渗透，科学技术的合理性成为新型的社会控制形式的主导力量，技术成为物化的重要工具，社会以单向度的路径不断发展；从思想层面上讲，语言分析利用其“治疗”作用把不同的、对立的意义相互隔离，取消了思想层面的对抗性，将人们的思维单一化。理性的颠覆性功能被取消，肯定性思维一步步走向胜利。

3. 辩证逻辑与形式逻辑的比对

马尔库塞希望通过对柏拉图的辩证逻辑和亚里士多德的形式逻辑进行比对，来回到哲学思想的起源中去认清否定性思想与肯定性思想之间的对抗性关系。在古希腊哲学中，真理与现实存在处于一种具有张力的关系之中。理性具有区分真和假的认知功能，真理起着价值标准的作用，世界以及与之相关的哲学都处在一种具有对抗性的双向度领域。对于起源于辩证法的哲学来说，它的论域也就与一种对抗性现实相对应。但与科学思想的作用不同，哲学的价值准则并没有引导人们去组织社会、改造自然，它试图从有限世界出发来构造一种具有自由本质的所谓"现实"。有限的存在不是真正的实在，存在方式是从潜能到具体、到现实的飞跃这样一种充满了否定的运动方式。进一步讲，哲学把历史、现实丢在后面不去掌握，但同时又使真理安然地居于历史现实之上。在这里，真理的本体论概念就处于那种可作为前技术合理性范型的逻辑的中心。而在技术性谋划的实施过程中，双向度话语领域的合理性得到了发展。

在柏拉图的辩证法里，"存在""一和多"等术语在方法论上是开放的、多义的、不完全确定的。它们有一个开放的视域和完整的意义领域，这一领域在交流过程中自身逐步构造起来，没有被封闭。各命题在对话中被提出并得到发展和检验。而交流者在参与对话的过程中，又同时进入一种新的话语向度，话语表达着他的自由。术语有许多意义，它们的逻辑发展是对现实进程或事情本身的反应。在柏拉图的理论中，思想的法则辩证了现实的法则，辩证法思想和既定现实之间是矛盾的，真正的判断不是从现实的角度，而是从展望现实覆灭的角度来判断这种现实，在这种覆灭中达到其自身的真理。但在亚里士多德的形式逻辑里，哲学的抽象性避开了人们生活于其中的世界，思想的两种向度似乎不再相互妨害了。思想对它的对象漠不关心，思想的主体成了主观性的纯粹而又普遍的形式，一切特殊之处都从形式中被清除出去了。

4. 语言分析是对形而上学"幽灵"的治疗

形式逻辑应当是通往科学思维漫长道路上的第一阶段，之后在技术合理化对思维方式的调整下，思维走向了更高程度的抽象和数学化。对思想的再限定有助于精神操作与社会现实中的操作相协调，即所谓的"治疗"。语言分析的出现就是要治疗出没于思想和言语中的令人混淆的形而上学"幽灵"，排除或至少暴露其中暧昧、幻想和怪癖的成分。其宗旨是揭露超验的概念，参照系是语词的日常用法、流行的使用状况。它的立场与那些在同流行话语和行为领域的对立甚至矛盾中来详述其概念的思维方式，即否定性思维方式是不能相容的。分析所使用的大量素材的语言是一种净化了的语言，但被净化掉的不仅是"非正统"的语言，也包括那些表达内容与社会所提供的内容不符的表达方式。语言分析学者把净化了的语言当作完成的事实，原封不动地加以接受并把语言同它没有表达的东西隔离开来。因此语言分析实际上是从普通语言在谈论中所展示的东西出发来进行抽象的，是一种基于放大的语言原子、言语片段上的抽象。

哲学概念以事实和意义的一种向度为目的，从“外部”解释日常话语的原子化的词语，试图理解日常话语的根本意义；语言分析则从物化领域之内来揭示和澄清日常话语。后者将判断性思维片面地转译为肯定性思维，把普遍概念转译成更为精确、明晰的操作术语和行为术语。在转译的欺骗性下，经过剪裁和整理的现象就被当成了现实。特殊的哲学向度被忽略了，哲学思维的历史连续性也消失殆尽。在此基础上，一种新的肯定的意识形态被建立起来。语言不再是私人的，多向度的语言被转变成单向度的语言，不同的、对立的意义相互隔离，那些引起争议的历史向度被抹杀，社会矛盾呈现出虚假的和谐。

六、进一步阅读指南

1. [美]赫伯特·马尔库塞：《单向度的人——发达工业社会意识形态研究》，刘继译，上海译文出版社 2008 年版。

2. [美]赫伯特·马尔库塞：《爱欲与文明》，黄勇、薛民译，上海译文出版社 2008 年版。

3. [美]赫伯特·马尔库塞：《现代文明与人的困境》，李小兵等译，上海三联书店 1989 年版。

4. [美]理查德·沃林：《海德格尔的弟子：阿伦特、勒维特、约纳斯和马尔库塞》，张国清、王大林译，江苏教育出版社 2005 年版。

5. [美]阿拉斯代尔·麦金太尔：《马尔库塞》，邵一诞译，中国社会科学出版社 1989 年版。

6. 李忠尚：《第三条道路——马尔库塞和哈贝马斯的社会批判理论研究》，学苑出版社 1994 年版。

7. 陆俊：《马尔库塞》，湖南教育出版社 1999 年版。

8. 程巍：《否定性思维：马尔库塞思想研究》，北京大学出版社 2001 年版。

9. 范晓丽：《马尔库塞批判的理性与新感性思想研究》，人民出版社 2007 年版。

10. 郑春生:《拯救与批判——马尔库塞与六十年代美国学生运动》,上海三联书店 2009 年版。

11. Douglas Kellner, *Herbert Marcuse and the Crisis of Marxism*, University of California Press, 1984.

七、问题与思考

1. 如何正确理解单向度社会中合理性与不合理性之间的关系?
2. 肯定性思维以何种方式取得了对否定性思维的胜利?
3. 如何理解语言分析对形而上学"幽灵"的治疗作用?

第十五章　西方马克思主义哲学的逻辑终结——《否定的辩证法》选读

教学目的与要求

了解《否定的辩证法》一书的写作形式和特点，了解阿多诺之所以采取这一写作方式的深层原因；理解“否定的辩证法”的理论建构，掌握阿多诺是如何完成对同一性、本体论以及主体哲学的批判的；正确认识阿多诺的“否定的辩证法”在西方马克思主义哲学中的逻辑地位。

一、历史背景

（一）作者介绍

1903年，西奥多·阿多诺（Theodor W. Adorno）出生于美因河畔法兰克福的一个犹太富商家庭。在歌唱家母亲和钢琴家姨妈的影响下，他从小就接受了专业的音乐训练，表现出了很高的音乐天赋。与此同时，他也表现出了很强的哲学思辨能力。15岁时，他便在社会批判家和电影理论家克拉考尔的指导下开始阅读《纯粹理性批判》。1921年，阿多诺进入法兰克福大学，学习哲学、心理学、社会学和音乐学等。当时盛行的新康德主义思潮和布洛赫、罗森茨威格、本雅明等人的犹太乌托邦主义思想对阿多诺影响颇深。此外，阿多诺和当时已经形成的西方马克思主义运动建立了密切的联系，他对主客体关系、第一哲学的本质和个别性的乌托邦等问题已有了明显的西方马克思主义式的认识。而这些也成为贯穿阿多诺思想发展的基本问题。1924年，阿多诺以论文《胡塞尔现象学中物和思的先验性》获得哲学博士学位。

1925年，阿多诺师从伯尔格学习新音乐。伯尔格是现代主义音乐大师勋伯格的学生。这对阿多诺来说是一个很好的机会，他有可能成为一名自己向往已久的新音乐家。然而，阿多诺在维也纳的新音乐生涯并不顺利，因为他对于理论的严肃态度总是让老师们感到不可思议。于是，1927年他重返法兰克福从事哲学研究。不过，勋伯格无调式音乐的理念和方法却深刻地影响了阿多诺的思想发展。阿多诺更加强调原先便已重视的客体的重要性、否定性和个别性等因素，这使他与同时代其他强调辩证法主体向度的西方马克思主义者拉开了微妙而重要的距离。

1927年，阿多诺向他的博士论文指导老师科奈留斯教授提交了一篇评论弗洛伊德无意识学说的教职资格论文，但遭到拒绝，因为此时的阿多诺思想中已经有了明显的、让科奈留斯不能接受的西方马克思主义的痕迹。在此后的四年中，阿多诺一方面继续进行音乐社会学方面的创作，另一方面则开始在西方马克思主义的土壤中培育他命名为"崩溃的逻辑"的哲学种子。此时，对他影响最大的是刚刚出版了《德国悲剧的起源》的本雅明。在1931年获得通过的题为《克尔凯郭尔：审美对象的建构》的教职资格论文中，他批判了克尔凯郭尔的存在哲学。由于克尔凯郭尔被视为海德格尔思想的先驱，所以这也是阿多诺对海德格尔哲学的第一次间接性批判。在1931年题为"哲学的现实性"的就职演讲和1932年的"自然历史观念"讲演中，阿多诺提出了如下观点，即具有现实性的马克思主义哲学将从海德格尔止步的地方生发出来，它就是从本雅明的自然理念观念中升华出来的"崩溃的逻辑"。值得注意的是，这一时期阿多诺暂时搁置了他的"崩溃的逻辑"。作为一名正在形成中的法兰克福学派成员，他自觉接受了霍克海默所倡导的批判理论，遵守他们共同的思想旨向。

1933年纳粹上台之后，阿多诺开始了流亡生涯。他发自内心地不愿意离开欧洲，所以，作为权宜之计，他最初选择到牛津大学攻读博士学位。但形势的发展迫使他于1938年前往美国，与霍克海默等人会合。在美国，阿多诺成为学派的核心成员。除了参与学派组织的一些大型经验性研究外，阿多诺最重要的工作就是与霍克海默合作《启蒙辩证法》。该书阐明了他们对资本主义的历史哲学判断。与此同时，隐匿在阿多诺思想中的“崩溃的逻辑”开始获得了日益主题化的发展。

1949年，阿多诺随社会研究所回迁德国，出任法兰克福大学哲学和社会学教授。由于霍克海默出任法兰克福大学校长，大部分精力转向行政工作，所以，二十世纪五十年代以后，阿多诺成为学派的主要理论旗手和研究所的实际负责人。1958年，阿多诺正式出任所长。期间，《最低限度的道德》(1951)、《棱镜》(1955)、《认识论的元批判》(1956)、《黑格尔：三篇研究》(1963)等著作陆续出版。此外，还有大量的音乐社会学论述面世，它们都具有强烈的哲学化形式。值得注意的是，阿多诺和霍克海默对战后德国的政治形势做出了悲观主义的判断，并开始有意识地放弃早期批判理论跨学科的研究传统。二十世纪六十年代，作为德国社会学界的领导人之一，阿多诺参与甚至主导了三场著名的论战，即1961年以后与波普尔等进行的旷日持久的实证主义论战、1964年前后关于韦伯社会学的争论和1968年前后关于“晚期资本主义还是工业社会”的争论。

在二十世纪六十年代初，阿多诺开始准备写就一部正面论述自己哲学思想的著作，以充分阐释他酝酿多年的“崩溃的逻辑”。1964年，先期出版的《本真性的行话》是阿多诺先行清算当时德国思想界流行“行话”而剧烈膨胀产生的额外产物。1966年，真正凝结他一生哲学思考的《否定的辩证法》面世。在《否定的辩证法》之后，阿多诺进入了《美学理论》一书的创作，并完成了全部手稿。不料，1968年学生运动来临了，他与激进的左派学生发生了尖锐的冲突。1969年4月，三位左派女学生赤裸上身冲上阿多诺的讲台，以弑父般的举动对他进行了羞辱。阿多诺愤然停课，前往瑞士度假。在瑞士，他继续修改《美学理论》的手稿，乐观地计划于1970年出版，但同年8月，一场突如其来的心脏病夺走了他的生命。

(二) 时代背景

1. 冷战阴云下联邦德国的意识形态状况

当时的德国处于冷战最前沿，政治和意识形态控制比美国都要严厉的多。在二十世纪五十年代的美国，尽管麦卡锡主义的白色恐怖已经泛滥开来，对美国左派产生了很大影响，但这种影响并没有大到让马尔库塞等人感觉有必须掩盖、隐藏自己的左派立场的程度；而与此同时，身处德国的霍克海默和阿多诺却不得不做出决定，彻底隐匿学派的马克思主义立场以确保研究工作得以继续。作为对抗社会主义阵营的桥头堡，联邦德国内部建立起了非常严厉的意识形态管控机制，虽然经济实现了快速发展，但是政治体制却远不如西方声称的那样“自由”与“民主”。许多学者尝试探索社会主义和资本主义之外的“第三条路”，既要体现德国的政治体制相对整个西方的特殊性，还要注意不能走向资本主义或者社会主义。阿多诺最终发现，整个联邦德国的政治文化和意识形态环境并不利于马克思主义的发展。

2. 联邦德国工人运动热情的冷却

第二次世界大战结束后，联邦德国的经济快速发展，为普遍提高社会的生活水平奠定了重要基础。二十世纪五十年代开始，联邦德国同其他发达资本主义国家同步开始建设现代福利国家制度，在一定程度上提升了民众的生活水平，这就给无产阶级运动带来了现实问题，一方面是政治环境的变化，让联邦德国国内的无产阶级斗争逐渐远离政治层面。当时，工会组织已不再把政治斗争作为首要目标，而是以争取经济利益、建立经济秩序作为出发点。工会的领导权基本由资产阶级掌控，虽然依然会选择和社会民主党等左翼政党展开联合斗争，但是，斗争的目标往往是争取更多的经济权力，而非政治权力。另一方面是工人阶级革命主体意识不断丧失，造成革命运动的动力不足。全社会实现充分就业后，社会民众暂时放下了生计焦虑，在一定程度上享受到了经济社会发展带来的红利。同其他欧洲国家类似，到了二十世纪六十年代之后，联邦德国的工人运动慢慢走向平静，资本主义的民主选举体制得到全面推行和稳固。

（三）思想背景

1. 对德国传统哲学的批判与自我重建

作为对当代哲学保持高度关切的表现，多年以来，阿多诺与霍克海默一直在法兰克福大学共同主持一个黑格尔哲学研讨班。他们研究黑格尔始终怀有一种自我反思的态度。1956 年是黑格尔去世 125 周年，阿多诺直接针对海德格尔在《林中路》（*Holzwege*）中所阐扬的对黑格尔的存在主义解读，[①]陆续公开了他的研究成果。对于黑格尔，他的基本看法是：虽然黑格尔已经死去，但他的哲学依旧活着，因为其本质是资本主义社会的自我意识。黑格尔哲学的现实性即在于其能够经验异质性的否定的辩证法，但这种辩证法的力量源泉并不在于抽象的否定概念自身，而在于被引入黑格尔哲学中来的经验的历史自身。[②]

如果以一种目的论的眼光来看待阿多诺对黑格尔等人的研究，那就会很自然地得出一个结论："否定的辩证法"至少在二十世纪五十年代中期就形成了，因为在那个时候，同一性和非同一性观念这两个"否定的辩证法"的基本构件已经大致成熟了。可要是我们搁置这种成见，就会看到：在本质上，它们是阿多诺在一个总体稳定的力场中，对"启蒙辩证法"的既有理论空间进行拓展的结果，是"崩溃的逻辑"的另外两个过渡性形态。但是，在另一方面，阿多诺对"崩溃的逻辑"的理论探索趋于完成之时，也就是"崩溃的逻辑"终结之日。因为他身处的理论力场发生了一次重大的方向性调整：他原本要求促进哲学的现实化、取消哲学、瓦解哲学，但之后认为要在"修正了的辩证法观念"的基础上建构一种批判的否定的哲学。"否定的辩证法"就此在"崩溃的逻辑"的成熟之处破茧而出，迎来自己本义的历史。

2. 与胡塞尔现象学、海德格尔存在论哲学的直接对话

早在二十世纪三十年代，阿多诺就明确指出，从胡塞尔到海德格尔的当代哲学主流的基本问题就是反对唯心主义。胡塞尔哲学是"一个从内部摧毁唯心主义的尝试，一个以意识根据去击穿先验分析之墙、同时又试图尽可能完成这一分析的尝试"，但是，"本质学说被认为是胡塞尔反唯心主义的最后一击，但它揭示自身为唯心主义的顶点：纯粹本质。它似乎是驱除了任何主观构成的客观性，其实却不过就是它的抽象性中的主观性、思维的纯粹功

---

① 参见海德格尔《黑格尔的经验概念》，载[德]马丁·海德格尔《林中路》，孙周兴译，上海译文出版社 1999 年版。

② Theodor W. Adorno, *Hegel: Three Studies*, trans. Shierry Weber Nicholsen, The MIT Press, 1993.

能、康德意识统一意义上的‘我思’”。[①] 就此而论，现象学已经为自身的解体做好了准备。以舍勒为中介，当代哲学发展到海德格尔阶段的时候，客观理念和客观存在的问题被纯粹主观的问题取代了。二十世纪三十年代以后阿多诺的哲学思想发展是始终围绕着与海德格尔的对话展开的，在这个意义上，它与海德格尔哲学的关系犹如马克思哲学与黑格尔哲学的关系，它需要在从内在颠覆海德格尔哲学之后重建哲学的现实性，所以，《否定的辩证法》的第一部分就是对海德格尔哲学的批判，“否定的辩证法”正是在这个基础上得以展开的。

3. 伯明翰学派的大众文化关怀及争鸣

在《否定的辩证法》完成之前，尽管德国的社会运动已经如火如荼，但其规模和展现出来的变革力量远远达不到同时期美国的水平，这更加深了阿多诺的悲观情绪。当时联邦德国的社会运动在实际开展过程中，遇到了文化理论和现实的双重障碍。在文化方面，随着工业化进程的加快，工业文明展现出越拉越大的影响力。但这也引发了一部分理论者对文化工业的反思，并且力图重新回归到大众的文化关怀之中。阿多诺与同时代的伯明翰学派的根本区别在于立场和视角的差异：阿多诺站在精英主义的立场上，自上而下地审视文化，因此，他更多地看到的是无法摆脱的控制；而伯明翰学派则从大众的立场出发，自下而上地审视问题，找到了摆脱控制的信心。伯明翰学派是二十世纪六十年代发源于英国伯明翰大学的一场思潮，以霍加特、霍尔为代表。该学派以大众文化和大众生活为研究对象，审视各种文化媒介发挥的意识形态作用。伯明翰学派开辟了大众文化探索的一条新路，后来，阿多诺带领法兰克福学派，同伯明翰学派之间开展了文化工业与大众文化之争。

二、篇章结构

《否定的辩证法》的正文有四个部分。在长篇导论中，阿多诺对“否定的

---

① Theodor W. Adorno, “Husserl and the Problem of Idealism”, *The Journal of Philosophy*, Volume XXXVII, No. 1, 1940, p. 6, p. 18.

辩证法"进行了预备性阐述。在第一部分"与本体论的关系"中，他通过批判、颠覆海德格尔哲学，表明"否定的辩证法"是拒斥任何本体论的；继而在第二部分"否定的辩证法：概念和范畴"中，他对"否定的辩证法"进行了正面阐发，重点突出其反对第一哲学、反对主体客体二元对立构架和反对同一性逻辑的根本立场。第三部分"模式"在很大程度上是一种附录，包含了阿多诺二十世纪三十年代对康德道德哲学与资产阶级自由观念的关系、黑格尔的世界历史学说与马克思的自然社会历史理论的关系的思考，以及他作为一名犹太思想家对形而上学问题的独特理解。在正文之前的序言中，阿多诺简要说明了创作的因缘和全书的结构，并预判了各方面对该书的可能反应。

在导论中，阿多诺开宗明义地指出，原本应当在改造世界的过程中实现自身、消灭自身的哲学，因为错过了改造世界的机会而被迫幸存。在现时代，各种具体科学试图迫使哲学重新成为一门具体科学，而哲学必须打破这种朴素性。今天，各种理论都躲不开市场的同一性逻辑的控制，而真正的辩证法必须要突破这种同一性，去经验非同一性。但在现实中，黑格尔的唯心主义辩证法占据了主导地位，其目的就是在主体的立场上去调和主体与客体。历史地看，哲学真正感兴趣的东西是非概念性、个别性和特殊性，但是，在形而上学传统中，它们却被作为暂时的、无意义的东西打发掉了。占据主导地位的唯心主义辩证法本质上就是同一性的辩证法，是事物的虚假状态的本体论。概念不能被视为一种自给自足的总体，它本身就是现实的因素，因此，必然要涉及非概念物。哲学的反思就是要确保概念中的非概念物。只有意识到，概念总是和非概念纠缠在一起并以后者为基础，概念才能获得觉醒，哲学才有摆脱无限性的幻象的可能。所以，哲学需要摆脱的是唯心主义而不是哲学思辨本身。真正的思辨是让思想获得自由，以服从主体表现自身的迫切要求。在这个意义上，哲学的自由就是呼喊出自身不自由的能力。如果人们对这种表现要求过多，哲学就会退化为世界观；如果对此没有任何要求，哲学就成了具体的科学。真正的思辨也是反体系的，因为笛卡尔和斯宾诺莎之后的各种体系都是不真实的。它们以市场逻辑为根据，表现出了一种狂躁的病症，反对思想的一切内容并力图在思想中将这些内容蒸发掉。批判体系的目的并非要简单地消灭体系，而是为了摆脱唯心主义体系赋予先验主体的融贯性力量。因为唯心主义排除了一切异质的存在物，把体系规定为纯粹的生成、纯粹的过程，最终陷入总体与无限的二律背反。这种背反本质上是对资本主义社会二律背反的模仿。否定的辩证法被人指责是令人眩晕的。之所以会出现这种眩晕，是因为认识将自身完全消失地投射到了对象上。它的出现恰恰是可靠认识的标志。摆脱体系的同一性强制后，思想将从具体的事物出发进行哲学思考，就此把握到的真理将因为其时间性的内容而是脆弱的。不过，否定的辩证法并不因此而是相对主义的。相对主义源于资产阶级个人主义的意识形态，体现了资产阶级的怀疑主义。它终将因为自己的狭隘性而粉碎。同时，否定的辩证法也不是绝对主义的。相信从稳固性和直接性中能够跳出一个未被破坏的整体，这实际上是一种唯心主义的怪想。对于否定的辩证法而言，直接性不是它的基础而只是它的一个要素。不仅如此，否定的辩证法还是反对精英主义的，因为哲学的经验并不是少数人的特权。经验客体重要的是反对近代以来的定量化倾向，公正地对待客体的质的要素，重视个别性、特殊性和偶然性，使非同一性摆脱同一性思维中抽象的总体方法的束缚。当代的存在主义力图摆脱概念拜物教，但它们终究没有脱离唯心主义的束缚。

第一部分“与本体论的关系”延续导论结尾提出的话题，对海德格尔的存在主义特别是基础本体论进行了深入的内在批判。该部分有两章。第一章《本体论的需要》阐明，海德格尔颠覆了传统本体论，但其本身保留着隐性的本体论需要，其本质仍然是同一性哲学。阿多诺指出，尽管曾有政治劣迹，但是，海德格尔哲学重新成为德国的时尚，成为盛行一时的“行话”。海德格尔唤醒了对存在的崇拜，但存在已经被社会生活的生产和再生产破坏了。就其实质而言，海德格尔是企图凭借威胁存在的东西来拯救存在，因此，他的哲学具有一种非批判的肯定性质。通过把历史的第一性确立为存在的本体论在先性，海德格尔动摇了传统的人类中心主义。但是，海德格尔并没有甚至也无意解决人被物化的第二自然所奴役这个问题，毋宁说他通过排除人的中心地位并使人意识自己的无能为力，而强化了第二自然的魔力。在谈论存在的时候，海德格尔放弃了胡塞尔的范畴观，而诉诸范畴观方面所谓更高贵的尊严，即好古癖的教义学。据此，海德格尔既规避了主观化的形而上学也规避了客观化的形而上学的衰亡，但是，返回古希腊并没有解决问题，海德格尔的存在学说归根结底还是一种本质学说。它以为脱离了科学，但实际上不过是把科学的东西当作本质，从而使科学失去了本体论所能给予它们的东西。海德格尔把内容的缺失、认识的空洞转化为了深刻的标志,通过这种手法,他将许诺被存在超越的存在物原本不动地隐藏在了存在之中。因此,他的存在论归根结底还是一种失去经验内容的先验本质论。海德格尔将存在置于不能被思考被操作的神秘位置,其本质是一种既机智又令人绝望的暴力行为。面对现实的不自由,海德格尔也试图反抗,但是,他在形而上学上所故意做出的无家可归和无法无天的姿态,不过是从意识形态的角度对现有秩序进行了辩护。从某种意义上讲,海德格尔也反对物化,不过,在马克思揭示观念的现实本质的地方,海德格尔却将物化现实变成了一种观念,并作为神圣的命运让人们接受。最终,阿多诺认为,海德格尔存在哲学的本质是以幻想的联系取代真实的现实关系的意识形态,只有超越他所幻想的不变性,形而上学的曙光才可能出现在地平线上。

第一部分第二章"存在与实存"是阿多诺对海德格尔存在哲学的内在批判。阿多诺肯定,海德格尔的存在哲学是以对存在的物化的批判为先决条件的,但是,他的存在并不是对现实统治的本性进行批判的自我反思。这种存在脱离了任何实存,或者说,海德格尔拿走了给予存在的任何东西。海德格尔的秘密在于系动词的本体化,即用一般的语法形式代替了具体内容,把系动词的存在状态的性能改变成本体论的性能、存在的一种存在方式。这实际上是过分地把中介延伸为一种非对象性的客观性,使得"是"脱离其意义根源,抽象化和一般化为具有本体论功能的"存在"。于是,存在成了优先于主体和客体的"至高无上的概念",任何理性的思考都撼动不了它的优先性和超然性地位。究其本质,这是以功能性的存在本体取代传统同一性哲学僵化的实体性本体。海德格尔本人曾经达到了对同一性中非同一性的辩证认识的边界,但是,他的存在概念本身并没有贯彻这一点,因此这个存在本身还是一种同一性。他的先验是一种绝对化的内在性。海德格尔对哲学的理解是深刻的,但是他不恰当地抬高了哲学的那种悬而未决性,从而通过滥用荷尔德林的思想,为时代的贫困贡献出了一种幻想超越时代的思想的贫困。同义反复是海德格尔言说存在时采取的一种基本战略,因为他只有通过这种仪式化的重复行为才能言说存在这种完全不确定的东西。正是通过这种理论上的绕弯子,海德格尔战胜了其他本体论者,使没有存在物就没有存在这一事实变成了一种形式,存在物的存在具有了存在的本质,最终是真理变成了非真理,存在物进入了本质。就此而言,海德格尔的本体论是一种把无意义的东西当作意义来赞美的新神话。当他根据现实的基本陈述来建构自己的本体论时,对于正在遭受苦难的人来说,这种本体论就是一种纯粹的恐怖。海德格尔哲学归根结底还是一种人本学,而一切人本学都是不可能的,因为人把几千年来所承受的残缺不全当作他的社会遗产吃力地拖着向前走,如果仅仅靠他现在的状况来破译他的本质是不可能的。和存在概念一样,海德格尔的主体概念也是模糊的。不仅如此,他还抽象地拔高了主体的地位,而事实上,主体中真实的东西表现在与非主体本身的东西的关系中,绝不表现在对主体方式的自夸的确证中。最后,海德格尔对历史的处理也是自相矛盾的:一方面,他把历史变成历史性,结果,抵制物化的认识并没有使僵化的事物流动起来并使人们意识到历史,反而,此在特有的"我属性"阻碍了任何社会性视角的产生,现实的社会历史内容被摒除在外,基础本体论完全丧失了社会批判的视角;另一方面,他把历史本体论化,使得人们不加审视地把存在的力量归结为历史的力量,从而证明服从历史形势是合理的,即导致对权力的赞同。存在不能对统治的本性进行批判的自我反思,这导致的是对现存的非批判和顺从,在这个意义上,基础本体论具有了意识形态的功能,它培养了大众的奴隶性思维,使得统治和支配深入大众的思想和心理层面,造成了大众整体被奴役的状态以及更为可悲的、对这种被奴役状态的非反思、麻木甚至耽溺于此而不能自拔。

在实现对海德格尔存在哲学的内在批判后,阿多诺在第二部分"否定的辩证法:概念和范畴"中对自己的哲学理念进行了正面阐发。他开宗明义地指出,自己的目的就是要把非同一性、存在物、事实性设定为真正的"第一"。因为任何一般概念的基本特性在决定性的存在物面前分解了,所以任何总体性哲学都是不值得期待的。康德以降的哲学都力图走近事物本身,但是,它们所言说的存在物概念并不是事物本身,而不过是存在概念虚假的影子。之所以如此,是因为在它们那里,主体概念和存在概念合二为一了,结果主体看到的存在不过是它自身的投影。正是这种同一性原则促使黑格尔反对纯粹的存在物,最终背离了自己所确立的辩证法的基本精神。事实上,青年黑格尔派和马克思都已经看到了超越这种同一性辩证法的方向,即转向非同一性,进而怀疑同一性、瓦解同一性。但后来的马克思主义者并没有能够认识这一思路的重要性。阿多诺认为,这种同一性辩证法并不是单纯的思想产物,而是对市场经济过程中商品交换原则的复制。反对同一性辩证法就是要回到非同一性的事物本身，承认矛盾的客观性。而客观的矛盾性并不只是表示在我们的判断之外仍存在的存在物，还标志着被判断的东西之中的某种东西。他者对同一性的抵抗是辩证法的力量所在，而星丛则是非同一性的存在形式。作为否定的辩证法的基本范畴，星丛首先意味着解构主体和客体之间的二元对立关系，恢复两者的相互构成关系；其次是在现象和本质的非同一性矛盾中重新定位两者的关系，依靠事物所是和应当是之间的矛盾来认识本质；最后是确认中介的客观性。在简要勾勒出否定的辩证法的基本面貌后，阿多诺在同一性哲学和否定的辩证法的比较视野中对一些基本问题进行深化讨论。首先是主体的先验性问题。阿多诺指出，先验的一般性的根源其实并不在于个人主体，而在于等价交换的商品原则。摆脱主体第一性的幻象的途径不是让客体占据主体曾经的位置，而是恢复客体的优先性。客体确实是被中介的，但是，它更是在先的。客体绝不是主体的思想产物，而是贯穿同一性的非同一性。其次是物化、异化问题。厌恶客体的优先性是费希特之后德国哲学的一种常态。之所以如此，是因为他们力图超越商品及其主观反思形式即物化意识。作为虚假的客观性，物化只是资本主义经济关系总体的副现象，异化则是对物化现实的主观意识。成熟时期马克思的物化、异化理论的实质是扬弃"为利润而生产"，从而在人的自由状态和人的天然的直接性之间做出了正确的区分。而卢卡奇则在对物化、异化的批判中走向了史前状态的浪漫主义美学。最后是否定的辩证法和唯物论的关系问题。只有在转向客体之后，辩证法才成为唯物主义的。通过把进入认识过程的客体精神化，同一性哲学确立了主体的第一性，可是，肉身要素作为认识的非纯粹认识部分是不可还原的。这并不是说要重新回到庸俗唯物主义的立场上。因为马克思所创立的历史唯物主义本质上是对整个唯心主义以曲解的方式选择的现实的批判。这种批判的任务就是判断主体和客体的份额及其动力。黑格尔把精神确立为主体和客体的统一，而其实质不过是一个主体。不仅如此，这个主体还像它的现实原型社会劳动一样，容易把同化个人劳动的一般劳动美化为一种自然，但却忽视了个人。现实存在的唯物主义在反对唯心主义的过程中用物质欲望取代精神，重新和神学走到了一起。而坚持历史唯物主义基本精神的否定辩证法追求的则是将精神从处在实现状态的物质需要的第一性中解放出来。因为只有当物质的渴望被平息时，精神才会被驯服，才能成为它唯一许诺的东西。

第三部分“模式”的写作目的是要确证否定的辩证法在具体的学科领域中的实际存在。它由三章组成。在第一章“自由:实践理性总批判”中,阿多诺借助对康德道德哲学的批判性反思,阐发了自己对自由问题的理解。他的基本思想是认为自由实际上是市场经济过程的自发产物,资产阶级意识形态刻意制造了个人的绝对自由的假象,而作为社会的存在物,个人既是自由的也是不自由的;更重要的是,在资产阶级社会中,自由已经走向了自己的反面,成为内在的服从;在这种真实的不自由中谈论自由只能是主体式的精神分裂症,它只是更严重地把人拉进自然的魔法中。在第二章“世界精神与自然历史——有关黑格尔的题外话”中,阿多诺揭示了黑格尔世界精神概念的秘密,指出它的本质是资本主义社会总体性,资本主义社会中的个人都处于这种虚假同一性的魔法控制之中;不仅如此,这种总体性过程还内在地生成了颠倒的资产阶级意识形态,从而把自身的历史规律神秘化为一种非历史的、永恒的自然历史过程。第三章“关于形而上学的沉思”展示了阿多诺对死亡的形而上学思考。在这个问题上,他的基本观点是:第一,纳粹对犹太人的大屠杀与资产阶级的同一性原则是一致的,它证明同一性哲学原理就是死亡;第二,奥斯维辛集中营的出现表明同一性原则已经将人变成了鬼怪,变成了幽灵世界的一部分,而人们的自觉意识却没有意识到它的存在,在此之后,如果不经历变革,艺术乃至神学都失去了存在的权利;第三,奥斯维辛集中营既证明了资产阶级文化的彻底失败,也昭示了反抗和批判的重要性,正因为如此,人类才重新获得了希望。

三、研究前沿

作为法兰克福学派的核心人物,阿多诺也是国内学界研究的一个热点人物。不过,这种热潮与对其他法兰克福学派重要成员的研究相比显得稍晚,特别是国内学界对《否定的辩证法》的研究也是经历了一个较为曲折的阶段。起初,由于一系列原因,国内学者并没有真正对这部著作产生太多的兴趣;只是从二十一世纪开始,该著作才陆续得到了学者们的深度挖掘,形成了较多的重要成果。尽管如此,研究的相对迟滞并没有影响研究的水平,相反,阿多诺的系统性研究成果一经推出就产生了巨大的影响。时至今日,国内学界对阿多诺及其《否定的辩证法》的研究已经达到了相当的理论深度，更是当前学者们进行哲学思考的重要素材，相关研究也得到了国家重大项目在内的各类别经费的资助，大量研究成果得以在权威平台发表出版。

第一，从对《否定的辩证法》的误解到再认识。1993 年，阿多诺的哲学名著《否定的辩证法》中译出版后，却遭到国内学界的长期冷遇，寂寥地躺在图书馆的角落里。为什么会如此呢？首先，该书名为《否定的辩证法》，但出乎国内读者意料的是，其核心思想更多涉及本体论、认识论，而非辩证法！其次，极具颠覆性的“否定的辩证法”矛头直指卢卡奇《历史与阶级意识》中的总体性辩证法，对于当时的中国学界来说，总体性辩证法尚未能完全理解和把握，就更不用说“否定的辩证法”了。再次，《否定的辩证法》的文本原本就抗拒读者的同一性理解方式，加之中译本质量欠佳，更加让人有读天书之感。最后，当时的欧美学界几乎一边倒地批评“否定的辩证法”，认为它是“一个巨大的失败”，[①]“阿多诺自觉地追随勋伯格的模式，企图在哲学内部发动一场革命，实际上却屈从了同样的命运，他反体系的原则本身已变成一种体系。……当否定的辩证法成为总体的时候，哲学也将趋向静止，因而二十世纪六十年代的新左派批评阿多诺把批判理论引向死胡同是公正的。”[②]不过，进入二十一世纪以后，在一些学者的带领之下，国内学界最终通过自己的努力，重新发现了《否定的辩证法》的学理价值，对其理论形成、实质及其思想史意义形成了更完整更深刻的认识。

第二，基于《否定的辩证法》的特点寻求解读路径。《否定的辩证法》向来被学界认为是一部不可迻译、不可理解的天书。原因有三。第一，为了维护自己作为客体的尊严，拒绝任何廉价收买其思想的企图，阿多诺采用了极为独特的“反体系”文本形式，刻意地设置了大量理解障碍。第二，《否定的辩证法》里充斥着诸多思想家的“幽灵”。读者会发现，这里既有康德、黑格尔、马克思、恩格斯、柏格森、胡塞尔、海德格尔、席勒、本雅明等哲学家，还有我们可能不大熟悉的诗人贝克特、作曲家舍恩和卡尔·克劳斯等。阿多诺假定，读者对他们的思想了如指掌，因此在很多情况下他也就无须说明地直接与这些思想家进行对话和论战，或者针对他们的某一些论题或表述直接

---

① [美]弗雷德里克·詹姆逊：《马克思主义与形式》，李自修译，百花洲文艺出版社 1995 年版，第 46 页。

② Susan Buck-Morss, *The Origin of Negative Dialectics, Theodor W. Adorno, Walter Benjamin, and the Frankfurt Institute*, The Free Press, 1977, pp. 189 - 190.

批判。这对读者而言，无疑是一大挑战，只有对这些思想家都非常了解的人才能从容地跟上阿多诺的脚步。第三，最重要的是，面对《否定的辩证法》的具体理论“废墟”，绝大多数研究者都习惯于以非历史的方式来对待之，而没有意识到《否定的辩证法》具有一个非常漫长的历史形成过程。因此，有学者呼吁，只有深入《否定的辩证法》的创作过程之中，方能获得打开该书的钥匙。在这一呼吁之下，国内学界逐渐摆脱陈旧判断，寻找到了正确解读该书的路径和方法。

第三，多领域、多视角开展解读研究。阿多诺的学术成长和研究生涯始终同艺术、政治、哲学、文化等领域有着密切的联系，其著作中充满了形式与立场的巨大张力，这也推动国内学界从不同领域开展对包括《否定的辩证法》在内的相关著作的研究。不过，正是阿多诺本身的哲学家身份令国内学者对他的研究不论是从哪一个角度出发，最终往往都上升到哲学思考。同时，由于阿多诺及《否定的辩证法》所处的特殊历史语境，在对其进行研究的过程中衍生出来的与西方存在主义哲学和西方马克思主义相关的比较性对话性思考，也成为研究中的一个重要特色。学者们结合现代工业文明、西方马克思主义的终结、从黑格尔至今的美学发展史及其与现代性的遭遇、文化的大众化、与哈贝马斯交往行动理论等不同形态历史唯物主义解读的比较分析等角度，扩充了《否定的辩证法》的理论外延。因此，从一定意义上来说，学者们借助阿多诺及其《否定的辩证法》的研究对西方当代哲学文化理论形式进行了全面深刻的反思，同时也实现了对西方马克思主义发展状况和趋势的当代诊断与总结。

四、文本节选

Dialectics Not a Standpoint

No theory today escapes the marketplace. Each one is offered as a possibility among competing opinions; all are put up for choice; all are swallowed. There are no blinders for thought to don against this, and the self-righteous conviction that my own theory is spared that fate will surely deteriorate into self-advertising. But neither need dialectics be muted by such rebuke, or by the comitant charge of its superfluity, of being a method slapped on outwardly, at random. The name of dialectics says no more, to begin with, than that objects do not go into their concepts without leaving a remainder, that they come to contradict the traditional norm of adequacy. Contradiction is not what Hegel's absolute idealism was bound to transfigure it into: it is not of the essence in a Heraclitean sense. It indicates the untruth of identity, the fact that the concept does not exhaust the thing conceived.

Yet the appearance of identity is inherent in though itself, in its pure form. To think is to identity. Conceptual order is content to screen what thinking seeks to comprehend. The semblance and the truth of thought entwine. The semblance cannot be decreed away, as by avowal of a being-in-itself outside the totality of cogitative definitions. It is a thesis secretly implied by Kant and mobilized against him by Hegel—that the transconceptual "in itself" is void, being wholly indefinite. Aware that the conceptual totality is mere appearance, I have no way but to break immanently, in its own measure, through the appearance of total identity. Since that totality is structured to accord with logic, however, whose core is the principle of the excluded middle, whatever will not fit this principle, whatever differs in quality, comes to be designated as a contradiction. Contradiction is nonidentity under the aspect of identity; the dialectical primary of the principle of contradiction makes the thought of unity the measure of heterogeneity. As the heterogeneous collides with its limit it exceeds itself.

Dialectics is the consistent sense of nonidentity. It does not begin by taking a standpoint. My thought is driven to its own inevitable insufficiency, but my guilt of what I am thinking. We are blaming the method for the fault of the matter when we object to dialectics on the ground (repeated from Hegel's Aristotelian critics on) that whatever happens to come into the dialectical mill will be reduced to the merely logical form of contradiction, and that (an argument still advanced by

Croce) the full diversity of the noncontradictory, of that which is simply differentiated, will be ignored. What we differentiate will appear divergent, dissonant, negative for just as long as the structure of our consciousness obliges it to strive for unity: as long as its demand for totality will be its measure for whatever is not identical with it. This is what dialectics holds up to our consciousness as a contradiction. Because of the immanent nature of consciousness, contradictoriness itself has an inescapably and fatefully legal character. Identity and contradiction of thought are welded together. Total contradiction is nothing but the manifested untruth of total identification. Contradiction is nonidentity under the rule of a law that affects the nonidentical as well.

——Theodor W. Adorno, *Negative Dialectics*, trans. E.B. Ashton, Routledge, 2004, pp.4 - 6.

"Peephole Metaphysics"

Wherever a doctrine of some absolute "first" is taught there will be talk of something inferior to it, of something absolutely heterogeneous to it, as its logical correlate. *Prima philosophia* and dualism go together. To escape from this, fundamental ontology must try to avoid defining what comes first to it. What was first to Kant, the synthetic unity of apperception, suffered the same fate. To Kant, every definition of the object is an investment of subjectivity in unqualitative diversity—regardless of the fact that the defining acts, which he takes for spontaneous achievements of transcendental logic, will adjust to a moment which they themselves are not; regardless of the fact that we can synthesize only what will allow and require a synthesis on its own. The active definition is not something purely subjective; hence the triumph of the sovereign subject which dictates its laws to nature is a hollow triumph. But as in truth subject and object do not solidly confront each other as in the Kantian diagram—as they reciprocally permeate each other, rather—Kant's degrading of the thing to a chaotic abstraction also affects the force that is to give it form.

The spell cast by the subject becomes equally a spell cast over the subject. Both spells are driven by the Hegelian fury of disappearance. The subject is spent and impoverished in its categorical performance; to be able to define and articulate what is confronts, so as to turn it into a Kantian object, the subject must dilute itself to the point of mere universality, for the sake of the objective validity of those definitions. It must cut loose from itself as much as from the cognitive object, so that this object will be reduced to its concept, according to plan. The objectifying subject contracts into a point of abstract reason, and finally into logical noncontradictoriness, which in turn means nothing except to a definite object. The absolute First remains necessarily as undefined as that which confronts it; no inquiry into something concrete and precedent will reveal the unity of abstract antithesis. Instead, the rigidly dichotomical structure disintegrates by virtue of either pole's definition as a moment of its own opposite. To philosophical thought, dualism is given and as inescapable as the continued course of thinking makes it false. Transmission—"mediation"—is simply the most general and inadequate way to express this.

Yet if we cancel the subject's claim to be first—the claim which surreptitiously keeps inspiring ontology—that which the schema of traditional philosophy calls secondary is no longer secondary either. It is no longer subordinate in a twofold sense. Its disparagement was the obverse of the trivium that all entity is coloured by the observer, by his group or species. In fact, cognition of the moment of subjective mediation in the objective realm implies a critique of the notion that through that realm we get a glimpse of the pure "in-itself", a forgotten notion lurking behind that trivium. Except among heretics, all Western metaphysics has been peephole metaphysics. The subject—a mere limited moment—was locked up in its own self by that metaphysics, imprisoned for all eternity to punish it for its deification. As through the crenels of a parapet, the subject gazes upon a black sky in which the star of the idea, or of Being, is said to rise. And yet it is the very wall around the subject that casts its shadow on whatever the subject conjures: the shadow of reification, which a subjective philosophy will then helplessly fight again. Whatever experience the word "Being" may carry can only be expressed in configurations of entities, not by allergies to entity; otherwise the philosophical substance becomes the poor result of a process of subtraction, not unlike the one-time Cartesian certainty of the subject, the thinking substance.

There is no peeping out. What would lie in the beyond makes its appearance only in the materials and categories within. This is where the truth and the untruth of Kantian philosophy divide. It is true in destroying the illusion of an immediate knowledge of the Absolute; it is untrue in describing this Absolute by a model that would correspond to an immediate consciousness, even if that consciousness were the *intellectus archetypes*. To demonstrate this untrue ... in its equation of subjectively mediated truth with the subject-in-itself—as if the pure concept of the subject were the same as Being.

——Theodor W. Adorno, *Negative Dialectics*, trans. E. B. Ashton, Routledge, 2004, pp. 138 - 140.

On the Dialectics of Identity

As the thinker immerses himself in what faces him to begin with, in the concept, and as he perceives its immanently antinomical character, he clings to the idea of something beyond contradiction. The antithesis of thought to whatever is heterogeneous to thought is reproduced in thought itself, as its immanent contradiction. Reciprocal criticism of the universal and of the particular; identifying acts of judgment whether the concept does justice to what it covers, and whether the particular fulfills its concept—these constitute the medium of thinking about the nonidentity of particular and concept.

And not of thinking only. If mankind is to get rid of the coercion to which the form of identification really subjects it, it must attain identity with its concept at the same time. In this, all relevant categories play a part. The barter principle, the reduction of human labor to the abstract universal concept of average working hours, is fundamentally akin to the principle of identification. Barter is the social model of the principle, and without the principle there would be no barter; it is through barter that nonidentical individuals and performances become commensurable and identical. The spread of the principle imposes on the whole world an obligation to become identical, to become total. But if we denied the principle abstractly—if we proclaimed, to the greater glory of the irreducibly qualitative, that parity should no longer be the ideal rule—we would be creating excuses for recidivism into ancient injustice. From olden times, the main characteristic of the exchange of equivalents has been that unequal things would be exchanged in its name, that the surplus value of labor would be appropriated. If comparability as a category of measure were simply annulled, the rationality which is inherent in the barter principle—as ideology, of course, but also as a promise—would give way to direct appropriation, to force, and nowadays to the naked privilege of monopolies and cliques.

When we criticize the barter principle as the identifying principle of thought, we want to realize the ideal of free and just barter. To date, this ideal is only a pretext. Its realization alone would transcend barter. Once critical theory has shown it up for what it is—an exchange of things that are equal and yet unequal—our critique of the inequality within equality aims at equality too, for all our skepticism of the rancor involved in the bourgeois egalitarian ideal that tolerates no qualitative difference. If no man had part of his labor withheld from him any more, rational identity would be a fact, and society would have transcended the identifying mode of thinking. This comes close enough to Hegel. The dividing line from him is scarcely drawn by individual distinctions. It is drawn by our intent: whether in our consciousness, theoretically and in the resulting practice, we maintain that identity is the ultimate, that it is absolute, that we want to reinforce it—or whether we feel that identity is the universal coercive mechanism which we, too, finally need to free ourselves from universal coercion, just as freedom can come to be real only through coercive civilization, not by way of any "Back to nature."

Totality is to be opposed by convicting it of nonidentity with itself—of the nonidentity it denies, according to its own concept. Negative dialectics is thus tied to the supreme categories of identitarian philosophy as its point of departure. Thus, too, it remains false according to identitarian logic: it remains the thing against which it is conceived. It must correct itself in its critical course—a course affecting concepts which in negative dialectics are formally treated as if they came "first" for it, too. It is one thing for our thought to close itself under compulsion of the form which nothing can escape from, to comply in principle, so as immanently to deny the conclusive structure claimed by traditional philosophy; and it is quite another thing for thought to urge that conclusive form on its own, with the intent of making itself "the first."

In idealism, the highly formal identity principle had, due to its formalization, an affirmative substance. This is innocently brought to light by terminology, when simple predicative sentences are called "affirmative." The copula says: It is so, not otherwise. The act of synthesis, for which the copula stands, indicates that it shall not be otherwise—else the act would not be performed. The will to identity works in each synthesis. As an a priori task of thought, a task immanent in thought, identity seems positive and desirable: the substrate of the synthesis is thus held to be reconciled with the I, and therefore to be good. Which promptly permits the moral desideratum that the subject, understanding how much the cause is its own, should bow to what is heterogeneous to it.

Identity is the primal form of ideology. We relish it as adequacy to the thing it suppresses; adequacy has always been subjection to dominant purposes and, in that sense, its own contradiction. After the unspeakable effort it must have cost our species to produce the primacy of identity even against itself, man rejoices and basks in his conquest by turning it into the definition of the conquered thing: what has happened to it must be presented, by the thing, as its "in-itself." Ideology's power of resistance to enlightenment is owed to its complicity with identifying thought, or indeed with thought at large. The ideological side of thinking shows in its permanent failure to make good on the claim that the non-I is finally the I: the more the I thinks, the more perfectly will it find itself debased into an object. Identity becomes the authority for a doctrine of adjustment, in which the object—which the subject is supposed to go by—repays the subject for what the subject has done to it.

The subject is to see reason against its reason. The critique of ideology is thus not something peripheral and intra-scientific, not something limited to the objective mind and to the products of the subjective mind. Philosophically, it is central: it is a critique of the constitutive consciousness itself.

——Theodor W. Adorno, *Negative Dialectics*, trans. E. B. Ashton, Routledge, 2004, pp. 146 - 148.

Constellation

The unifying moment survives without a negation of negation, but also without delivering itself to abstraction as a supreme principle. It survives because there is no step-by-step progression from the concepts to a more general cover concept. Instead, the concepts enter into a constellation. The constellation illuminates the specific side of the object, the side which to a classifying procedure either a matter of indifference or a burden.

The model for this is the conduct of language. Language offers no mere system of signs for cognitive functions. Where it appears essentially as a language, where it becomes a form of representation, it will not define its concepts. It lends objectivity to them by the relation into which it puts the concepts, centered about a thing. Language thus serves the intention of the concept to express completely what it means. By themselves, constellations represent from without what the concept has cut away within: the "more" which the concept is equally desirous and incapable of being. By gathering around the object of cognition, the concepts potentially determine the object's interior. They attain, in thinking, what was necessarily excised from thinking.

The Hegelian usage of the term "concrete"—according to which the thing itself is its context, not its pure selfhood—takes note of this; and yet, for all the criticism of discursive logic, that logic is not ignored. But Hegelian dialectics was a dialectics without language, while the most literal sense of the word "dialectics" postulates language; to this extent, Hegel remained an adept of current science. He did not need language in an emphatic sense, since everything, even the speechless and opaque, was to him to be spirit, and the spirit would be the context. That supposition is past salvaging. Instead, what is indissoluble in any previous thought context transcends its seclusion in its own, as nonidentical. It communicates with that from which it was separated by the concept. It is opaque only for identity's claim to be total; it resists the pressure of that claim. But as such it seeks to be audible. Whatever part of nonidentity defies definition in its concept goes beyond its individual existence; it is only in polarity with the concept, in staring at the concept, that it will contract into that existence. The inside of nonidentity is its relation to that which it is not, and which its managed, frozen self-identity withholds from it. It only comes to in relinquishing itself, not in hardening—this we can still learn from Hegel, without conceding anything to the repressive moments of his relinquishment doctrine.

The object opens itself to a monadological insistence, to a sense of the constellation in which it stands; the possibility of internal immersion requires that externality. But such an immanent generality of something individual is objective as sedimented history. This history is in the individual thing and outside it; it is something encompassing in which the individual has its place. Becoming aware of the constellation in which a thing stands is tantamount to deciphering the constellation which, having come to be, it bears within it. The *chorismos* of without and within is historically qualified in turn. The history locked in the object can only be delivered by a knowledge mindful of the historic positional value of the object in its relation to other objects by the actualization and concentration of something which is already known and is transformed by that knowledge. Cognition of the object in its constellation is cognition of the process stored in the object. As a constellation, theoretical thought circles the concept it would like to unseal, hoping that it may fly open like the lock of a well-guarded safe-deposit box: in response, not to a single key or a single number, but to a combination of numbers.

——Theodor W. Adorno, *Negative Dialectics*, trans. E.B. Ashton, Routledge, 2004, pp.162 - 163.

The Object's Preponderance

Carried through, the critique of identity is a groping for the preponderance of the object. Identitarian thinking is subjectivistic even when it denies being so. To revise that kind of thinking, to debit identity with untruth, does not bring subject and object into a balance, nor does it raise the concept of function to an exclusively dominant role in cognition; even when we merely limit the subject, we put an end to its power. Its own absoluteness is the measure by which the least surplus of nonidentity feels to the subject like an absolute threat. A minimum will do to spoil it as a whole, because it pretends to be the whole.

Subjectivity changes its quality in a context which it is unable to evolve on its own. Due to the inequality inherent in the concept of mediation, the subject enters into the object altogether differently from the way the object enters into the subject. An object can be conceived only by a subject but always remains something other than the subject, whereas a subject by its very nature is from the outset an object as well. Not even as an idea can we conceive a subject that is not an object; but we can conceive an object that is not a subject. To be an object also is part of the meaning of subjectivity; but it is not equally part of the meaning of objectivity to be a subject.

...

... Mediation of the object means that it must not be statically dogmatically hypostatized but can be known only as it entwines with subjectivity; mediation of the subject means that without the moment of objectivity it would be literally nil. An index of the object's preponderance is the impotence of the mind—in all its judgments as well as, to this day, in the organization of reality. The negative fact that the mind, failing in identification, has also failed in reconcilement, that its supremacy has miscarried, becomes the motor of its disenchantment.

The human mind is both true and a mirage: it is true because nothing is exempt from the dominance which it has brought into pure form; it is untrue because, interlocked with dominance, it is anything but the mind it believes and claims to be. Enlightenment thus transcends its traditional self-understanding: it is demythologization—no longer merely as a *reductio ad hominem*, but the other way round, as a *reductio hominis*, an insight into the delusion of the subject that will style itself an absolute. The subject is the late form of the myth, and yet the equal of its oldest form.

——Theodor W. Adorno, *Negative Dialectics*, trans. E.B. Ashton, Routledge, 2004, pp.183 – 186.

After Auschwitz

We cannot say any more that the immutable is truth, and that the mobile, transitory is appearance. The mutual indifference of temporality and eternal ideas is no longer tenable even with the bold Hegelian explanation that temporal existence, by virtue of the destruction inherent in its concept, serves the eternal represented by the eternity of destruction. One of the mystical impulses secularized in dialectics was the doctrine that the intramundane and historic is relevant to what traditional metaphysics distinguished as transcendence—or at least, less gnostically and radically put, that it is relevant to the position taken by human consciousness on the questions which the canon of philosophy assigned to metaphysics. After Auschwitz, our feelings resist any claim of the positivity of existence as sanctimonious, as wronging the victims; they balk at squeezing any kind of sense, however bleached, out of the victims' fate. And these feelings do have an objective side after events that make a mockery of the construction of immanence as endowed with a meaning radiated by an affirmatively posited transcendence.

... the visible disaster of the first nature was insignificant in comparison with the second, social one, which defies human imagination as it distills a real hell from human evil. Our metaphysical faculty is paralyzed because actual events have shattered the basis on which speculative metaphysical thought could be reconciled with experience. Once again, the dialectical motif of quantity recoiling into quality scores an unspeakable triumph. The administrative murder of millions made of death a thing one had never yet to fear in just this fashion. There is no chance any more for death to come into the individuals' empirical life as somehow conformable with the course of that life. The last, the poorest possession left to the individual is expropriated. That in the concentration camps it was no longer an individual who died, but a specimen—this is a fact bound to affect the dying of those who escaped the administrative measure.

Genocide is the absolute integration. It is on its way wherever men are leveled off—"polished off," as the German military called it—until one exterminates them literally, as deviations from the concept of their total nullity. Auschwitz confirmed the philosopheme of pure identity as death. The most far out dictum from Beckett's *End Game*, that there really is not so much to be feared any more, reacts to a practice whose first sample was given in the concentration camps, and in whose concept—venerable once upon a time the destruction of nonidentity is ideologically lurking. Absolute negativity is in plain sight and has ceased to surprise anyone. Fear used to be tied to the *principium individuationis* of self-preservation, and that principle, by its own consistency, abolishes itself. What the sadists in the camps foretold their victims, "Tomorrow you'll be wiggling skyward as smoke from this chimney," bespeaks the indifference of each individual life that is the direction of history. Even in his formal freedom, the individual is as fungible and replaceable as he will be under the liquidators' boots.

...

Spellbound, the living have a choice between involuntary ataraxy—

an esthetic life due to weakness—and the bestiality of the involved. Both are wrong ways of living. But some of both would be required for the right *désinvolture* and sympathy. Once overcome, the culpable self-preservation urge has been confirmed, confirmed precisely, perhaps, by the threat that has come to be ceaselessly present. The only trouble with self-preservation is that we cannot help suspecting the life to which it attaches us of turning into something that makes us shudder: into a specter, a piece of the world of ghosts, which our waking consciousness perceives to be nonexistent. The guilt of a life which purely as a fact will strangle other life, according to statistics that eke out an over whelming number of killed with a minimal number of rescued, as if this were provided in the theory of probabilities—this guilt is irreconcilable with living. And the guilt does not cease to reproduce itself, because not for an instant can it be made fully, presently conscious.

This, nothing else, is what compels us to philosophize. And in philosophy we experience a shock: the deeper, the more vigorous its penetration, the greater our suspicion that philosophy removes us from things as they are—that an unveiling of the essence might enable the most superficial and trivial views to prevail over the views that aim at the essence. This throws a glaring light on truth itself. In speculation we feel a certain duty to grant the position of a corrective to common sense, the opponent of speculation. Life feeds the horror of a premonition: what must come to be known may resemble the down-to-earth more than it resembles the sublime; it might be that this premonition will be confirmed even beyond the pedestrian realm, although the happiness of thought, the promise of its truth, lies in sublimity alone.

If the pedestrian had the last word, if it were the truth, truth would be degraded. The trivial consciousness, as it is theoretically expressed in positivism and unreflected nominalism, may be closer than the sublime consciousness to an *adaequatio rei atque cogitationis*; its sneering mockery of truth may be truer than a superior consciousness, unless the formation of a truth concept other than that of *adaequatio* should succeed. The innervation that metaphysics might win only by discarding itself applies to such other truth, and it is not the last among the motivations for the passage to materialism. We can trace the leaning to it from the Hegelian Marx to Benjamin's rescue of induction; Kafka's work may be the apotheosis of the trend. If negative dialectics calls for the self-reflection of thinking, the tangible implication is that if thinking is to be true—if it is to be true today, in any case—it must also be a thinking against itself. If thought is not measured by the extremity that eludes the concept, it is from the outset in the nature of the musical accompaniment with which the SS liked to drown out the screams of its victims.

——Theodor W. Adorno, *Negative Dialectics*, trans. E.B. Ashton, Routledge, 2004, pp.361 - 365.

五、观点解读

1. 哲学是一种非体制化的异质性经验

阿多诺认为，哲学的真谛就是要逃脱概念拜物教的罗网，去寻求一种来自人的生命深处的异质性经验。所谓概念拜物教是指传统形而上学的概念观用虚假的本体、自给自足的物化和强制的同一性和总体性来掩盖实际上的非本体性、不完整性和非同一性。阿多诺认为，概念的觉醒，即人们摆脱概念拜物教的同一性奴役，是一味哲学的解毒剂。因为概念拜物教的本质是一种由绝对本质导引出来的虚假的无限性，概念拜物教正是通过这种绝对无限性将世界还原为命题和同一的抽象本质。与此相对，阿多诺主张一种“否定的辩证法”，它要努力使自己沉浸在和哲学相异的事物中，但又避免把这些事物放置在先验的范畴中；也就是说，要“紧紧地坚持异质的东西”。传统哲学认为自己拥有一个无限的对象，并靠此信念成了一种有限的、结论性的哲学。而实际上，“任何客体都不能完全被认识，知识不必提出一个总体的幻象”。真正的哲学不再轻言无限，它的实质就存在于非概念化、非图式化的对象的多样性之中，“哲学将真正献身于这些对象，而不是用它们作为一面重新理解自己的镜子，把自身的形象误作为具体化”。真正的哲学将和异质的东西紧密联系在一起，是“以概念为中介的完全不可还原的经验”。进而，阿多诺强调，真正的哲学一定是反体系的。必须认识到，阿多诺所反对的体系并不是一般的哲学表述体系，而是本体论意义上的哲学逻辑体系，其原型是现实中的“被管理的世界”。就像现实中的商品交换体制吞没一切那样，这种体系也“凶残”地将一切思想同一化。“体系的形式对世界是合适的，世界的实质逃避人类思维的统治，统一和一致同时是一种被平息的、不再对抗状态向统治性的、压抑性的思维坐标的纯粹投射”。但是，哲学的体系从一开始就是自相矛盾的，它们的基础被它们自身的不可能性永恒纠缠。换句话说，凝固化的哲学体系的现实基础却是变动不居的社会运动，它造成形而上学构架永存幻想的不可能性。所以，“每一种体系都注定在下一种体系手中被消灭”。最终，体系遭遇自身的界限，于是就出现了唯心主义哲学无法摆脱的内在本质即总体和无限的二律背反。阿多诺认为，这种体系的二律背反正是资产阶级现实社会二律背反的真实映照。资本主义为了保存自身、保持同样，必须不断扩展、进步，必须不断推进它的边界，然而这又导致了它不尊重任何界限，不能保持同样；也就是说资本同一性的扩张运动的结果必然是产生遭遇非同一性。一旦资本主义达及一个顶点，一旦在它自身之外不再有可利用的非资本主义领域，其自身的概念和存在就会自我消亡。

2. 商品交换是同一性逻辑的社会模式

《否定的辩证法》建立在对同一性逻辑的批判与否定基础之上。那么，同一性究竟是什么呢？根据阿多诺自己的说明，作为西方哲学史中源远流长的一个范畴，同一性有四种意思：首先是个人意识的统一性；其次是在一切合理的本质上同样合法的东西即作为逻辑普遍性的思想；再次是每一思想对象与自身的等同，即 A = A；最后是认识论中主体和客体的和谐一致。最后一种才是阿多诺所要批判和否定的同一性。他指出，同一性总是以一种服从统治的自足性为前提，并成为迄今为止的一切理性形式的深层逻辑，是意识形态抵抗真正启蒙的同谋。这种同一性逻辑之所以能够形成，原因在于：首先，它是伴随人类中心主义而生的。在人类中心主义的强权话语中，同一性思维“使自然的奴役长存下去”“使每一种不等同的事物相等同”；其次，在任何一种文化体系中概念的内在要求都是：试图始终不变地建立秩序，并以这种不变性来反对它所包含的东西的变化；最后，它是交换原则这一社会事实在思想中的反映，因为交换原则把人类劳动还原为社会平均劳动时间的抽象的一般概念，因而从根本上与同一化原则相类似。简言之，商品交换是同一性原则的社会模式。阿多诺指出，在现代商品社会中，借助于工具理性的扩张，同一性逻辑已经实现了对人的彻底控制，以致每一个人在进入社会结构的时候，其角色的“逻辑归类的技术”必然深嵌着“操纵”和“消除本质差别”的强制。最终结果是，它通过诉诸技术生产力而忽视了社会的生产关系，仿佛只有这些生产力的状况决定着社会的形态。在阿多诺看来，启蒙之后那种为生产而生产的实践冲动是同一性逻辑暴力的现实基础。由此，他表示应当反对实践，以打破为生产而生产的魔咒。

3. 真正的辩证法是对非同一性的自觉

阿多诺认为，真正的辩证法不是追求同一性，而是怀疑一切同一性。它在本质上是一种关注作为对象的事物本身的特质即非同一性的认识。在阿多诺的视域中，非同一性不是简单的拒绝和破坏，而是一种基于同一性、内在于同一性自身逻辑中的非同一性和差异性，即矛盾统一之中不可调和的差异性。作为同一性中的异质性，非同一性是一种客观的矛盾，是他者对同一性的永远的抵抗，它并不因为反对抽象的同一性而将与观念一般相对立的个别变成一种形而上学的最终之物。在这种真正的辩证法中，主体与客体、主体与主体、主体与类、意识与存在、概念与经验、技术与价值等原本处于二元对立之中的关系，都变成了一种平等的、非奴役的关系，这种关系就是星丛。星丛实际上是阿多诺从本雅明那里借用过来的一个术语。“星丛不应该被还原为某一种本质，在这个星丛中内在地存在的东西本身不是本质。”通过星丛这个术语或者更确切地说这个意象，阿多诺着重强调了非同一性关系是一种消除了所有奴役关系之后的全新伙伴关系。例如，在主体和客体的星丛中，主体和客体是一种平等的相互中介、相互构成的关系，其实质是事物之间、主体和客体之间以及主体和主体之间有差别的平等交往。

又如，在本质和想象的星丛中，本质和现象不再是凝固的、现成的反映关系，而都处于历史性的生成过程中，对本质的认识是通过事物所是的样子和它们应当是的样子之间的矛盾来完成的。

4. 没有同一性原则就不会有奥斯维辛集中营

这是身为犹太人的阿多诺对纳粹屠犹事件的形而上学反思和批判。阿多诺指出，与人类历史上曾经发生过的各种基于自然原因或社会原因的大屠杀不同，纳粹通过管理手段实施了对数百万犹太人的大屠杀，从而使得死亡变成了一件在样子上并不可怕的事情。并且，在集中营中死掉的也不再是个人，而是样品。这种事情为什么会发生以及它究竟意味着什么？阿多诺指出，这实际上是西方文明几千年来追求的同一性原则的最终结果。“奥斯维辛集中营证实纯粹同一性的哲学原理就是死亡！”因为“种族灭绝是绝对的同一化”，这是与资产阶级文明的同一性原则一致的。所以说，没有同一性原则就不会有奥斯维辛集中营。当为了实现种族“存在”的高贵同一性，大量非同一性的“存在者”式的人们“被干掉”时，死去的不再是个人，而只是等待实验的样品。在那里，“个人经验生命的死亡再也不能像是与生命过程相符合的事情”，生与死的神性均荡然无存。同时死去的还有一切在过去形而上学沉思中使人的形而上学之思、人的生存从自然中超拔出来的神圣的本质性东西。

六、进一步阅读指南

1. [德]西奥多·阿多诺:《否定的辩证法》，张峰译，重庆出版社 1993 年版。

2. [德]洛伦茨·耶格尔:《阿多诺:一部政治传记》，陈晓春译，上海人民出版社 2007 年版。

3. [美]弗雷德里克·詹姆逊:《晚期马克思主义》，李永红译，南京大学出版社 2008 年版。

4. [日]细见和之:《阿多诺:非同一性哲学》，谢海静等译，河北教育出版社 2002 年版。

5. 张一兵:《无调式的辩证想象——阿多诺〈否定的辩证法〉的文本学

解读》,三联书店 2001 年版。

6. 张亮:《"崩溃的逻辑"的历史建构:阿多诺早中期哲学思想的文本学解读》,中央编译出版社 2003 年版。

7. 赵海峰:《阿多诺"否定的辩证法"研究》,黑龙江人民出版社 2003 年版。

8. 谢永康:《形而上学的批判与拯救:阿多诺否定辩证法的逻辑和影响》,江苏人民出版社 2008 年版。

9. Theodor W. Adorno, *Negative Dialectics*, trans. E. B. Ashton, Routledge, 2004.

10. Theodor W. Adorno, *Problems of Moral Philosophy*, ed. Thomas Schröder, trans. Rodney Livingstone, Polity Press, 2000.

11. Theodor W. Adorno, *Against Epistemology: A Metacritique Studies in Husserl and the Phenomenological Antinomies*, trans. Willis Domingo, B. Blackwell, 1982.

12. Brian O'Connor, *Adorno's Negative Dialectic: Philosophy and the Possibility of Critical Rationality*, MIT Press, 2004.

13. Willem van Reijen, *Adorno: An Introduction*, trans. Dieter Engelbrecht, Pennbridge Books, 1992.

14. Susan Buck-Morss, *The Origin of Negative Dialectics: Theodor W. Adorno, Walter Benjamin and The Frankfurt Institute*, The Free Press, 1977.

七、问题与思考

1. 阿多诺是如何批判海德格尔本体论的存在哲学的?

2. 如何理解马克思对于阿多诺"否定的辩证法"的理论影响?

3. 如何理解和评价"星丛"概念?

4. 在何种意义上,阿多诺的《否定的辩证法》标志着西方马克思主义的逻辑终结?

第十六章　从意识形态的重建到历史唯物主义的重构
——《通往理性的社会》和《交往与社会进化》选读

教学目的与要求

对哈贝马斯的理论发展逻辑有一个总体性的认识，弄清哈贝马斯在法兰克福学派发展中所起到的作用；对比马尔库塞的理论，了解哈贝马斯所说的科学技术与意识形态之间的关系；掌握科学技术已成为"第一生产力"的概念；理解科学技术已成为统治的合法性基础的理论根源；准确理解、客观评价哈贝马斯对历史唯物主义的重建。

一、历史背景

(一) 作者介绍

1929年，尤尔根·哈贝马斯(Jürgen Habermas)出生于德国的杜塞尔多夫，成长于科隆附近的小镇古默斯堡。他的父亲和祖父都是纳粹的支持者，而他本人也在第二次世界大战后期成为一个纳粹青年组织的成员。第二次世界大战结束后，他方才意识到自己曾长期生活于其中的德意志第三帝国犯下了严重的政治罪行。通过收听纽伦堡审判、观看有关纳粹集中营的纪录片，他的思想受到极大震动，最终，对纳粹问题的反思成为推动其早期思想发展的一种重要动力。

哈贝马斯在上大学之前就读过不少马克思的著作，同时，在美国占领军主导的再教育下，他比较多地接受了民主主义的理念。1949年至1954年，他分别在哥廷根、苏黎世、波恩的几所大学学习哲学、历史、心理学、文学和经济学等。由于可以理解的历史原因，他的哲学教授们都曾是纳粹的支持者或者顺应者。这让他感到焦躁不安。1953年，海德格尔未经修改和做任何说明就出版了1935年的演讲稿《形而上学导论》。这使哈贝马斯感到非常震惊，因为这说明海德格尔未对自己支持纳粹的行径进行任何反思。他随即发表了一篇评论对海德格尔进行了批评。而这一事件的后果是：一方面，哈贝马斯意识到哲学和政治绝不是彼此隔绝的两个领域；另一方面，他对以海德格尔哲学为代表的德国现代哲学和德国现实本身失去了信心，认为从其中并不能寻找到自己所渴望的规范性价值取向。

在博士论文写作期间，哈贝马斯阅读了《历史与阶级意识》，其中那种将马克思主义传统运用于对现代社会的分析与批判的独特理论道路让他感到耳目一新。不过，此时对他影响最大的还是洛维特的《从黑格尔到尼采》一书，因为正是该书激起了他对青年黑格尔派和青年马克思的关注，继而完成了题为《绝对性与历史——论谢林思想的二重性》的博士论文。

博士毕业后，哈贝马斯获得一份奖学金，专门从事与意识形态概念有关的研究。期间，他阅读了《启蒙辩证法》，觉得似乎这就是自己所寻找的哲学与政治的统一形式。由于机缘巧合，阿多诺邀请哈贝马斯到社会研究所工作，随后于1956年秋季成为阿多诺的助手。进入研究所以后，哈贝马斯比较系统地阅读了早期批判理论的一些著作，特别是本雅明和马尔库塞的作品，以及以韦伯和涂尔干为代表的现代社会学经典，其思想发生了巨大变化，政治性日益明显。这引起了霍克海默的忧虑和不满，因为自从返回德国后，霍克海默对德国的政治局势始终保持警惕，竭力掩饰法兰克福学派既有的激进理论立场。最终，霍克海默通过反对哈贝马斯在法兰克福大学取得教职，迫使哈贝马斯于1959年辞职离开社会研究所。离开社会研究所后，哈贝马斯致力于《公共领域的结构转型》一书的创作，后于1961年12月获得马堡大学的教职资格，并于1962年7月出任海德堡大学教授。

1962年，哈贝马斯的《公共领域的结构转型》一书出版。该书一经出版即成为一部广受好评的学术畅销书，30年间重印达17次之多。1963年，哈贝马斯出版了《理论与实践》论文集。该文集收录了他在1961年前后创作的一些有关哲学史的论文。1961 年以后,哈贝马斯和阿多诺一起参加了与波普尔等人的实证主义论战,从意识形态批判角度对实证主义进行了批判。这场论战显著促进了哈贝马斯的思想发展。1965 年,哈贝马斯回到法兰克福大学接任霍克海默空缺出来的教职。在就职仪式上,他发表了题为"认识与兴趣"的演讲。以这篇演讲为基础,1968 年,他出版了《认识与兴趣》一书,通过对德国古典哲学以来认识论思想史的批判性反思,指出认识并不是纯生理的或纯理性的活动,而是一种具有强烈社会性的特殊范畴,是人类维持自身生存的工具和创造新生活的手段,因此,彻底的认识论必然是一种社会理论。同一时期,他还出版了《通往理性的社会》和《交往与社会进化》等论文集,均产生了巨大反响,从而牢固确立了哈贝马斯作为西方马克思主义思想家的理论地位。之后,由于与左派学生的尖锐矛盾,哈贝马斯被迫于 1971 年离开法兰克福大学,前往慕尼黑的普朗克学会任职。

二十世纪七十年代以前,哈贝马斯不仅是法兰克福学派的一员,而且还实质性地推动了批判理论的后期发展;二十世纪七十年代以后,法兰克福学派最终成为历史,而哈贝马斯也日益偏离学派的既有立场,在新的综合创新过程中开创出了一个新的理论流派。虽然这个可以用哈贝马斯的名字来命名的新流派与法兰克福学派具有直接的渊源关系,但它与后者存在质的区别,因为它在本质上是一种非马克思主义的思潮,尽管是一种影响巨大的非马克思主义思潮。时至今日,哈贝马斯依旧活跃在西方理论舞台之上。二十一世纪以来,哈贝马斯对地区冲突、欧盟一体化、民族主义、难民问题、世界和平等问题保持了高度关注。

(二) 时代背景

1. 欧洲工潮的复兴

从二十世纪六十年代开始,欧洲各主要资本主义国家内部的工人运动再次兴起,这一系列工潮发生的根本原因是当时欧洲经济的发展进入了新的阶段。第二次世界大战后,在马歇尔计划的刺激下,欧洲经济得到恢复与发展,社会生产活动再次进入繁荣阶段。同时,在现代福利国家制度建立的前提下,民众的生活水平得到整体提升。但是,这种繁荣非但没有完全解决资本主义社会的固有矛盾,反而诱发了严重的社会问题。经济发展在推动工人就业率达到高峰后，随即出现了大量工人失业的现象，福特制生产方式遭遇严重危机。[①] 另外，美国当时经济发展过热造成的通货膨胀问题借助布雷顿森林体系而转嫁给欧洲国家，导致物价上涨，也引发了欧洲社会的强烈不满。这一时期的工人运动主要有三个特点：第一，爆发范围广。这场工人运动涉及英国、法国、联邦德国、意大利、荷兰等大部分欧洲发达国家，且每一个国家中参与运动的人数之多也是第二次世界大战后从未有过的。第二，爆发具有持续性。在近二十年的时间里，欧洲各国先后爆发了数次连续的工人运动，且每次的运动规模都会较前次更大，持续时间也更长。可见，欧洲工人运动呈现出明显的传播性，也说明工人运动成为当时欧洲工人热衷采用的政治表达方式。第三，影响十分深远。这一系列的工人运动产生了深刻的社会影响，对当时欧洲的经济发展、政治进程、文化理论、艺术形式等都产生了深远的影响，直接促成了西方左派政治和理论的又一次全面发展。

2. 1968 年德国学生抗议活动

欧洲的工人运动波及德国。其中，要论对法兰克福学派和哈贝马斯产生最直接影响的，当属青年学生运动。当时，德国的青年学生深受左翼思潮影响，掀起了一场具有浓厚左倾色彩的学生运动，这一运动波及了德国的主要高校，产生了深远影响。应当讲，在整个二十世纪六十年代，哈贝马斯都是作为一名激进的西方马克思主义者活跃在德国思想舞台之上的。他的思想对德国的学生运动影响颇大。但是，当 1968 年学生抗议运动的高潮来临时，这种关系却发生了微妙的变化。就哈贝马斯个人来说，他深受德国传统哲学的影响，在遇到激进的学生左翼思潮时，便表现出与后者格格不入的立场。因此，当哈贝马斯拒绝加入学生的运动，并且试图制止时，理所当然地招致了学生的强烈不满。左派学生们不仅宣布他是“文化革命的叛徒”，而且一度占领了他领导的社会研究所。当然，学生们的攻击和时局的变化非但没有改变哈贝马斯日渐保守的倾向，而且还进一步推动他展开对交往理性及其他规范性社会理论的考察。现在看来，正是这种经历促使哈贝马斯

---

① 张亮、孙乐强等：《21 世纪国外马克思主义哲学若干重大问题研究》，人民出版社 2020 年版，第 50 页。

反思自己的理论立场，在政治上和理论上不断退却，最终放弃了自己早期坚持的西方马克思主义立场，转而成为资本主义制度合法性的论证者和捍卫者。

（三）思想背景

1. 法兰克福学派的形成与发展

作为一个学派，法兰克福学派正式形成的起点应当从 1931 年 1 月霍克海默出任社会研究所所长开始算起。在就职仪式上，霍克海默发表了具有纲领性的就职演讲“社会哲学的目前形势和社会研究所的任务”，除了重申所长专制这一组织原则外，他把卢卡奇和柯尔施所重新发现的、马克思开辟的哲学发展之路，提炼为“哲学和社会科学的联盟”这句口号，并确立为学派今后的主要任务。[①] 正是在这一口号的激励下，整个二十世纪三十年代，霍克海默、阿多诺、马尔库塞等都不同程度地转向社会科学，和学派其他成员一起，投身于哲学与政治经济学、现代社会学和社会理论、精神分析、音乐学、文学理论等的联盟，从而在对国家社会主义、权威主义、纳粹主义、大众文化等各种新的重大现实问题进行跨学科研究的过程中，创立批判理论这一具有深远影响的马克思主义哲学当代形态。社会研究所重返德国后，出于对德国政治形势的恐惧和警惕，霍克海默和阿多诺在如何对待自己所开创出来的这种跨学科传统问题上显得非常保守，他们不仅拒绝再版包括《启蒙辩证法》在内的早期著作，而且将研究所二十世纪三十年代出版的刊物锁进箱子放在地下室里，不愿让青年一代去阅读。而他们自己的理论创作也采取了更加哲学化的形式。不管后来政治和理论立场发生了怎样的变化，必须承认正是哈贝马斯继承并发展了早期批判理论的跨学科研究传统，很好地推动了批判理论在二十世纪六十年代的发展。不仅如此，在偏离西方马克思主义之后，哈贝马斯的全部理论创新实际上也都还是通过继续这种研究传统而完成的。

---

① Max Horkheimer, “The Present Situation of Social Philosophy and the Tasks of an Institute for Social Research”, in Max Horkheimer, *Between Philosophy and Social Science: Selected Early Writings*, The MIT Press, 1993, pp. 1 - 15.

2. 结构主义的重要影响

按照哈贝马斯自己的说法，他也曾受到结构主义的影响。但一方面他不满足于静时态的分析，而格外推崇皮亚杰发生学的结构主义；另一方面人类学中的结构主义观点为其“类的历史”分析提供了新的资源。以戈德利尔为代表，哈贝马斯借助这些研究论证了“社会劳动”并不足以区分不同生产方式的进化，而只能用来区分人类社会与动物世界的观点，以及人类社会的发展主要表现为社会一体化形式的改变，而社会一体化形式在很大程度上又同包含生产实践和道德意识两方面的内在学习机制相关联的观点。也就是说，正是二十世纪上半叶结构主义人类学的发展，为哈贝马斯提供了一种新的理论视角：搁置物质生产方式，从文化机制、心理结构、象征关系等范畴出发，来理解人类历史的发展。而这恰恰也是同时期萨林斯、鲍德里亚等人做的工作。只不过，哈贝马斯借此专门强调了包含符号相互作用在内的“交往理论”的重要性。而符号相互作用的行动理论，主要是在二十世纪上半叶的语言学和心理学研究中被提出的，其主要代表人物是哈贝马斯经常提起的 G. H. 米德。米德的《心灵、自我与社会》论证了个人主体（自我）形成过程中，社会符号互动的作用。

二、篇章结构

《通往理性的社会》是尤尔根·哈贝马斯 1969 年 8 月出版的一本重要论文集，1987 年英译本面世。全书正文部分包含六篇文章。第一篇为《民主中的大学：大学的民主化》。哈贝马斯认为，大学应当在科学研究的同时，注重培养学生的政治素养。具体地说，首先，大学应当保证学生能够在各自专业领域中获得高水平的教育；其次，大学应当注重维持自身的一种文化传统，为学生创造一种浓厚的社会政治氛围；最后，随着时代的发展，大学对自身的定位已经越来越模糊，特别是在政治方面。这是大学亟待需要改正的一个状况。随着第二次世界大战的结束，欧洲迎来了一个特殊阶段：既需要维护其政治传统，同时又需要重新构建一个新型的民主模式。这赋予了大学独特而重要的社会政治功能。在此，哈贝马斯呼吁一种新的政治理性的到来。

第二篇为《德意志联邦共和国的学生抗议》。哈贝马斯充分意识到了当时学生运动已经成为一种非常重要的社会政治活动。其中包括以下几个特点:第一,学生将他们自身定义为国家未来的精英阶层,应当肩负重大的责任;第二,学生不仅仅将他们的政治抱负放在大学之中,还放在整个社会中;第三,学生对旧的社会有着切身的体会,家庭成长就是一个很重要的方式。哈贝马斯对学生运动的态度并不是十分积极。他认为,学生运动并没有鲜明的政治特征,他们对国家经济生活知之甚少,对资本主义制度的一系列政治体制也缺乏了解。因此,学生还不能够成为国家政治生活的决策者。哈贝马斯进而引申到对当时整个德国新左派的评论。与学生运动一样,新左派所开展的一系列社会运动只是他们参与社会政治的一种方式,一种潮流。但要在发达国家政治体制中占有一席之地的可能性已经越来越小。

第三篇为《德国的运动:一个批判性的分析》。哈贝马斯在这一篇文章中对德国的政治运动进行了专门的思考。在文章的第一部分,哈贝马斯阐述了这篇文章的主要意图。首先,是深层分析"大拒绝"的内在缘由和产生机制。哈贝马斯认为,这是资本主义世界内部新型民主产生的一种标志;其次,是分析当时德国的政治进程与理性的关系。他指出,政治运动已经和大众伦理紧密联系在一起,这源于社会财富生产的日益繁荣;最后,是对官僚治理模式的分析。随着民众对于自由的呼声不断提高,这种执政模式必将一去不复返。在第二部分中,哈贝马斯对帝国主义的发展进行了考察。他认为,虽然马克思的反帝国主义理论能够为当代的运动者,特别是学生们提供借鉴,但是,这种影响是建立在误解的基础之上的。因为现今所谓的联合的世界是一个虚假的幻想。因此,要将全世界的无产阶级联合起来并不现实。第三部分,哈贝马斯对新无政府主义进行了考察。新无政府主义的出现是阶级关系发生变化的一个表现。就当时来看,社会运动进入了一个高潮期,主题是人们为了争取各项权益。但是哈贝马斯认为这些运动与马克思笔下的那种革命运动是截然不同的,因为民众在参与政治请愿时更加倾向于表达一种诉求,而不是直接推翻现实。第四部分,哈贝马斯关于文化革命的讨论。这一部分是前一部分的延续。因为哈贝马斯认定现今的政治运动已完全不同于马克思的暴力革命,而是采取了一种更加和平的方式进行。因此,"文化革命"就成为一个良好的政治表达方式。或者说,今后的政治革命会随着社会和文化的多元化而具有多种多样的表达方式,具备更加突出的思想性特征。在接下去的部分，哈贝马斯又将视线转移到大学上来。因为大学是理性和文化的聚集地，因此，大学应当在政治运动中扮演至关重要的角色。

第四篇为《科技进步与社会生活》。哈贝马斯在这一部分初步探讨了科学进步给人们的生活世界带来的可能影响。一方面是科学方法能够改变社会生产过程；另一方面是科学方法能够改变人的行为特征。他认为，随着生产和社会进程的发展，人类对于历史和自身的认识也会不断发生改变。同时，由权力所构成的社会理性系统会越来越深刻地影响社会的整体变迁。而我们需要注意的，就是通过对政治权力进行理性思考，不断创造出新的决策理论，摆脱社会对人越来越明显的束缚作用。

第五篇为《政治科学化与公共立场》。这一篇是上一篇的延续。哈贝马斯认为，虽然政治的科学化并没有成为现实，但是这已经成为一种趋势。现今的人类需要正确认识理性的重要性。在科学技术的作用日益明显的情形下，人类的理性会随之发生何种变化，又当如何驾驭科学技术给社会造成的巨大影响，是一个非常棘手的问题。哈贝马斯认为其中最为关键的是科学对公共决策的影响。在这一过程中，交往仍然会扮演十分重要的纽带作用，因为它可以使所有个体共同参与到政治决策中去，将大众的理性集合起来，帮助实现大众相对于科技发展的主体性作用。哈贝马斯称之为大众“政治意志的启蒙”。

第六篇为《作为“意识形态”的技术与科学——纪念 H. 马尔库塞诞辰 70 周年》。它既是对全书其他文章中所提观点的进一步发挥，也是同马尔库塞的科技进步观的辩论，是全书篇幅最长的一章。在马尔库塞看来，技术理性也许本身就是意识形态。技术理性的运用，甚至其本身就是(对自然和人的)统治，而科学技术同意识形态一样，具有明显的工具性和奴役性，起着统治人和奴役人的社会功能。哈贝马斯不赞成马尔库塞的观点。他认为在现今资本主义国家中，由于国家干预活动的增加保障了资本主义制度的稳定性，以及科学研究和技术之间的相互依赖使科学成了第一位的生产力这两种趋势，破坏了制度框架(相互作用)和目的理性活动(劳动)的子系统的原有格局，这使得运用马克思根据自由资本主义社会所提出的政治经济学的重要条件消失了。因此哈贝马斯将科技进步作为“新的坐标系”，希望以此对社会的不断合理化、科技进步作为生产力和意识形态的双重功能这两个论点进行重新评价。首先，哈贝马斯认为在传统社会，由于制度框架具有"优越性"，因此只要目的理性活动的子系统的发展保持在文化传统的合法的和有效的范围内，"传统的"社会就能存在下去；但在资本主义社会中，制度框架逐渐丧失了在生产力面前的传统的"优越性"，其提供的统治的合法性不再得自于文化传统，而是从社会劳动的根基上获得的。其次，在资本主义社会中，科学、技术及其运用逐渐结成一个体系，技术和科学成为第一位的生产力，并形成了技术统治论的意识。但这种意识一方面没有那种看不见的迷惑人的力量，另一方面这种意识把辩护的标准非政治化，并继而同目的理性活动的子系统的功能紧密联系在一起，是一种难以抗拒的"隐形的意识形态"。哈贝马斯认为，这种技术统治论的意识虽然也发挥着使人们安于眼下生活、阻止他们思考和议论社会的基本问题的作用，但它已完全没有了传统的意识形态的压抑和奴役人的功能。因此，哈贝马斯反对马尔库塞在科技进步面前所表现的悲观主义，并对青年学生在悲观理论指导下所采取的极端行动持保留态度。

《交往与社会进化》一书共包括五章，第一章为"什么是普遍语用学"，共包括两节内容。在第一节中，哈贝马斯讨论了言语的有效性基础。他认为，任何进行交往活动的人一旦要使用语言和行为，就需要符合一定的要求，并且这种判断的标准是可以被识别的。在如何界定言语的"对象领域"的讨论中，他指出，不论是从逻辑学、语言学还是语言分析哲学出发对语言进行考察，应当存在着一个共同的目标，那就是从规范分析的角度澄清语言的具体应用过程。另外，在合理重建言语程序时，哈贝马斯运用了"交往性经验或理解"分析了话语的产生过程与意义。在第一节的最后，哈贝马斯提出重建语言学的程序：将人的前理论认识转换为客观的、明晰的知识。在第二节中，哈贝马斯系统讨论了普遍语用学，包括言语行为的标准形式、言语的双重结构、有效性的交往的具体要求等等。

第二章为"道德发展与自我同一性"，一共包括四节。第一节中哈贝马斯以阿多诺和马尔库塞为例，讨论了同一性本身的相关特征，并以人的自由为起点，尝试用社会行为理论解释自我同一性的辩证概念。在第二节中，哈贝马斯考察了同一性的内在机制。分别包括主体学习过程、主体言说和行为能力的分离过程、主体言说和行为能力的危机支配原则、主体言说和行为能力的独立性特征、言说和行为主体的连贯性要求，以及外在结构与内在结构的转换机制。在第三节中，哈贝马斯具体考察了交往行为的发生机制，并探讨了交往与道德意识的内在联系，指出道德是体现每一个人交往行为同一性的内在决定因素。在第四节中，哈贝马斯在第三节基础之上，进一步讨论了交往行为与道德冲突机制。他指出，作为交往个体，每一个人都有不同于其他个体的特质，当这种特质遇到同一性要求时，就会出现冲突。此时，就要正确处理好人的自由与自律的关系。

第三章和第四章收录了哈贝马斯重建历史唯物主义最为核心的文章。第三章"历史唯物主义与规范结构的发展"共计五个小节。在第一节中哈贝马斯明确表述了重建的立场："重建是把一种理论拆开，用新的形式重新加以组合，以便更好地达到这种理论所确立的目标。"以及理解这一重建的三个要点：决定论、规范理论、交往理论。在第二节和第三节中，哈贝马斯专门讨论了交往理论对历史唯物主义的贡献，并明确提出自我发展与社会进化存在共同的意识结构。第四节的分析中，哈贝马斯认为，规范结构有其内在的历史，并区分了生产活动和实践两种形式，后者是交往的行动和目的合理的行动。在第五节，哈贝马斯回应了交往理论可能遭受的两种误解：一是唯心主义的指责，二是被看作一种抽象的逻辑分析；并且将历史唯物主义看作一种全面的进化理论。最后一节论述了进化理论在历史哲学中的范围，包含了对全书逻辑构架的概要说明。本章第一节和第五节可以看作哈贝马斯重建历史唯物主义的理论宣言，而第二、三、四节则分别从"交互主体""自我同一性""规范结构"三个角度集中论述了重建的基础——交往理论。

第四章"走向历史唯物主义的重建"第一节主要讨论了"社会劳动"这一范畴。哈贝马斯认为，"社会劳动"不能充分表达人类生活的再生产形式，只适用于区分人和动物，而不适用于区分人类生活方式的再生产，必须关注个人的动机、社会角色和象征性的相互作用的复杂关系。紧接着在第二节有关"类的历史"的讨论中，哈贝马斯对生产方式概念进行了一种过度诠释。尽管哈贝马斯也强调生产方式概念是重建类的历史的钥匙，但是他更加强调了总体社会形式，并强调立足生产力和社会交往形式可以为制度存在做辩护。作为这一观点的展开，第三节专门讨论了经济基础和上层建筑、生产力和生产关系这些历史唯物主义的基本范畴。哈贝马斯立足"学习能力"和"交往行动理论"得出了这样的结论：人类不仅在对于生产力的发展具有决定性作用的、技术上可以使用的知识领域中进行学习，而且也在对于相互作用的结构具有决定性作用的道德-实践意识的领域中进行学习。交往行动的规则遵循自身的逻辑。有鉴于此，第四节中进而强调正确理解“类的历史”，必须在反对技术决定论及其新形式的同时，认真磨砺生产方式这把“尚未充分打磨的钥匙”。这就需要在生产方式基础上，形成高度抽象的社会组织原则，包括个人学习能力的获得(个人在同生活世界的象征性结构融为一体时，才能获得学习能力)以及学习水平的制度化等。这也是第五节讨论的内容。第六节作为例证，专门讨论了阶级社会的形成，以及阶级社会中以学习过程或者说交往理论为视角，社会进化的阶段性特征既包括生产力，也包括社会一体化水平。最后一节主要是同结构主义、生物学模式的新进化论、系统论的功能主义三种社会理论的批判性对话。值得注意的是，哈贝马斯在行文最后提出，历史唯物主义的进步标准是，同社会一体化的形式的完善相联系的生产力的发展意味着学习能力在两个方面的进步：客观化知识中的进步和道德-实践洞察力中的进步。

第五章为“现代国家中的合法化问题”，包括五节内容。第一节中，哈贝马斯对合法性进行了详细定义，认为合法性意味着某种政治秩序被认可的价值。合法性概念主要被运用在政治学当中，它决定了社会同一性原则能够在社会中得到广泛认可。在第二节，哈贝马斯讨论了合法化的内在结构。他认为，在当今社会，只有以自由、和平为基础达成的一致才具有真正的合法性力量。因此，在强权政治下的同一性往往是大众没有理智地接受而造成的结果。在第三节中，哈贝马斯分析了现代国家的合法性问题。他将国家结构分为内在和外在两个方面。内在是指国家的经济系统分化方式，外在则指世界经济形势。而国家的合法化则是内在与外在得到相对平衡的结果。在第四节，哈贝马斯讨论了三个议题，首先是现今导致合法化问题的一个基本冲突，即工人运动对权力的反抗。其次是这一问题得到解决的限制因素，包括国家与经济的目标冲突、世界市场的发展和民族意识的枯竭。最后是合法化消解的两个阶段，分别是分配矛盾的尖锐化，以及人们自身对于幸福的追求。在第五节中，哈贝马斯讨论了研究合法化问题的意义，那就是可以帮助重构个人的道德意识和认知。

三、研究前沿

哈贝马斯是法兰克福学派的核心人物之一。国内关于哈贝马斯的相关研究始终是西方马克思主义研究中一个十分重要的组成部分，也对国内相关领域产生了重要的学术影响。从研究的数量来看，国内对哈贝马斯的研究起步于二十世纪七十年代，相关成果数量在所有西方马克思主义者研究成果中相对较多；从研究成果的层次来看，国内学者对哈贝马斯的专题研究得到各级杂志刊物的广泛刊载，也得到了各级项目的资助，体现出哈贝马斯研究在国内得到了较高的重视；从研究的影响来看，国内相关研究的下载量、引用率等，都保持了较高水准。其中，哈贝马斯的"交往、交往理性、社会进化理论研究"最为多见，相关成果也呈现出较为完善的研究结构和较为宽阔的研究视野。

第一，关于哈贝马斯与法兰克福学派关联的研究。在对哈贝马斯进行思想史定位时，很多学者都习惯性地称他为法兰克福学派第二代的代表人物。这实际上是一种似是而非的论断。因为自二十世纪七十年代以后，哈贝马斯实际上逐渐偏离了法兰克福学派传统的西方马克思主义立场，最终形成了一种中间偏右的全新理论立场，并在 1981 年出版的《交往行为理论》中得到了公开展示。此后，尽管哈贝马斯还是哈贝马斯，但他再也不是所谓法兰克福学派的第二代批判理论家，而成了一种全新的、非西方马克思主义的理论思潮的开创者。随着学界对哈贝马斯研究的不断深入，这一观点已经得到越来越多学者的认可。

第二，对哈贝马斯交往理论的专题与比较研究。作为哈贝马斯的代表性观点以及整个理论体系的主要基石，交往理论研究是理解哈贝马斯基本政治、社会立场的起点，也是把握其马克思主义基本立场发生转向的内在机制的重要理论基础。学者普遍认为，哈贝马斯的交往理论所提供的交往间性，为其讨论其他主题——包括对交往主体的不对称性而导致的平等问题，并由此而引发的对诸如教育过程在内的很多现实问题的思考等——提供了重要的空间。同时，还有众多学者聚焦哈贝马斯交往理论与其他观点立场的比较，比如实用主义、马克思实践哲学、杜威教育观、儒学中的关系构建体系等，并且引申出其与古典实用主义和现象学关系的讨论。同时，哈贝马斯的交往理论在政治领域还形成了另一种重要的话语体系,即商谈政治。这一观点在西方当代民主政治话语中具有极高的代表性。学者们所持的总体立场是,商谈政治是哈贝马斯为交往理论所做的一种现实性的弥补,目的是要让后者能够持续运作,是交往理论的现实运用。有学者认为,这种商谈政治和交往理论在现实中有一定的借鉴意义,但是同我国当前的协商民主还存在着本质性的差别。

第三,对哈贝马斯社会进化理论的专题研究。学界在研究该专题时,往往是同其重建历史唯物主义的尝试结合起来分析的。这一研究涉及对马克思主义历史观的重新把握。学界普遍认为,分析哈贝马斯的社会进化理论同样要从交往理性出发。哈贝马斯是将交往理性和学习机制作为社会进化的内在动力,中间蕴含着结构主义的立场与方法。这意味着必须将哈贝马斯的历史观同唯物史观划清界限。同时,哈贝马斯将马克思哲学中的"劳动"概念曲解为一种工具理性行为,从而丧失了对社会发展实践的准确理解,这也是他放弃马克思主义社会进化理论的重要原因和诱因。

四、文本节选

Technology and Science as "Ideology"

In our context it is relevant that despite considerable differences in their level of development, civilizations, based on an economy dependent on agriculture and craft production, have tolerated technical innovation and organizational improvement only within definite limits. One indicator of the traditional limits to the development of the forces of production is that until about three hundred years ago no major social system had produced more than the equivalent of a maximum of two hundred dollars per capita per annum. The stable pattern of a precapitalist mode of production, preindustrial technology, and premodern science makes possible a typical relation of the institutional framework to subsystems of purposive-rational action. For despite considerable progress, these subsystems, developing out of the system of social labor and its stock of accumulated technically exploitable knowledge, never reached that measure of extension after which their "rationality" would have become an open threat to the authority of the cultural traditions that legitimate political power. The expression "traditional society" refers to the circumstance that the institutional framework is grounded in the unquestionable underpinning of legitimation constituted by mythical, religious or metaphysical interpretations of reality—cosmic as well as social—as a whole. "Traditional" societies exist as long as the development of subsystems of purposive-rational action keep within the limits of the legitimating efficacy of cultural traditions. This is the basis for the "superiority" of the institutional framework, which does not preclude structural changes adapted to a potential surplus generated in the economic system but does preclude critically challenging the traditional form of legitimation This immunity is a meaningful criterion for the delimitation of traditional societies from those which have crossed the threshold to modernization.

...

The permanent regulation of the economic process by means of state intervention arose as a defense mechanism against the dysfunctional tendencies, which threaten the system, that capitalism generates when left to itself. Capitalism's actual development manifestly contradicted the capitalist idea of a bourgeois society, emancipated from domination, in which power is neutralized. The root ideology of just exchange, which Marx unmasked in theory, collapsed in practice. The form of capital utilization through private ownership could only be maintained by the governmental corrective of a social and economic policy that stabilized the business cycle. The institutional framework of society was repoliticized. It no longer coincides immediately with the relations of production, i. e. with an order of private law that secures capitalist economic activity and the corresponding general guarantees of order provided by the bourgeois state. But this means a change in the relation of the economy to the political system: politics is no longer *only* a phenomenon of the superstructure. If society no longer "autonomously" perpetuates itself through self-regulation as a sphere preceding and lying at the basis of the state—and its ability to do so was the really novel feature of the capitalist mode of production—then society and the state are no longer in the relationship that Marxian theory had defined as that of base and superstructure. Then, however, a critical theory of society can no longer be constructed in the exclusive form of a critique of political economy. A point of view that methodically isolates the economic laws of motion of society can claim to grasp the overall structure of social life in its essential categories only as long as politics depends on the economic base. It becomes inapplicable when the "base" has to be comprehended as in itself a function of governmental activity and political conflicts. According to Marx, the critique of political economy was the theory of bourgeois society only as *critique of ideology*. If, however, the ideology of just exchange disintegrates, then the power structure can no longer be criticized *immediately* at the level of the relations of production.

…

I do not even think that the model of a technologically possible surplus that cannot be used in full measure within a repressively maintained institutional framework (Marx speaks of "fettered" forces of production) is appropriate to state-regulated capitalism. Today, better utilization of an unrealized potential leads to improvement of the economic-industrial apparatus, but no longer *eo ipso* to a transformation of the institutional framework with emancipatory consequences. The question is not whether we completely *utilize* an available or creatable potential, but whether we *choose* what we want for the purpose of the pacification and gratification of existence. Rut it must be immediately noted that we are only posing this question and cannot answer it in advance. For the solution demands precisely that unrestricted communication about the goals of life activity and conduct against which advanced capitalism, structurally dependent on a depoliticized public realm, puts up a strong resistance.

A new conflict zone, in place of the virtualized class antagonism and apart from the disparity conflicts at the margins of the system, can only emerge where advanced capitalist society has to immunize itself, by depoliticizing the masses of the population, against the questioning of its technocratic background ideology: in the public sphere administered through the mass media. For only here is it possible to buttress the concealment of the difference between progress in systems of purposive-rational action and emancipatory transformations of the institutional framework, between technical and practical problems. And it is necessary for the system to conceal this difference. Publicly administered definitions extend to *what* we want for our lives, but not to *how* we would like to live if we could find out, with regard to attainable potentials, how we *could* live.

Who will activate this conflict zone is hard to predict. Neither the old class antagonism nor the new type of underprivilege contains a protest potential whose origins make it tend toward the repoliticization of the desiccated public sphere. For the present, the only protest potential that gravitates toward the new conflict zone owing to identifiable interests is arising among certain groups of university, college, and high school students. Here we can make three observations:

1. Protesting students are a privileged group, which advances no interests that proceed immediately from its social situation or that could be satisfied in conformity with the system through an augmentation of social rewards. The first American studies of student activists conclude that they are predominantly not from upwardly mobile sections of the student body, but rather from sections with privileged status recruited from economically advantaged social strata.

2. For plausible reasons the legitimations offered by the political

system do not seem convincing to this group. The welfare-state substitute program for decrepit bourgeois ideologies presupposes a certain status and achievement orientation. According to the studies cited, student activists are less privatistically oriented to professional careers and future families than other students. Their academic achievements, which tend to be above average, and their social origins do not promote a horizon of expectations determined by anticipated exigencies of the labor market. Active students, who relatively frequently are in the social sciences and humanities, tend to be immune to technocratic consciousness because, although for varying motives, their primary experiences in their own intellectual work in neither case accord with the basic technocratic assumptions.

3. Among this group, conflict cannot break out because of the extent of the discipline and burdens imposed, but only because of their quality. Students are not fighting for a larger share of social rewards in the prevalent categories: income and leisure time. Instead, their protest is directed against the very category of reward itself. The few available data confirm the supposition that the protest of youth from bourgeois homes no longer coincides with the pattern of authority conflict typical of previous generations. Student activists tend to have parents who share their critical attitude. They have been brought up relatively frequently with more psychological understanding and according to more liberal educational principles than comparable inactive groups. Their socialization seems to have been achieved in subcultures freed from immediate economic compulsion, in which the traditions of bourgeois morality and their petit-bourgeois derivatives have lost their function. This means that training for switching over to value-orientations of purposive-rational action no longer includes fetishizing this form of action. These educational techniques make possible experiences and favor orientations that clash with the conserved life form of an economy of poverty. What can take shape on this basis is a lack of understanding

in principle for the reproduction of virtues and sacrifices that have become superfluous—a lack of understanding why despite the advanced stage of technological development the life of the individual is still determined by the dictates of professional careers, the ethics of status competition, and by values of possessive individualism and available substitute gratifications: why the institutionalized struggle for existence, the discipline of alienated labor, and the eradication of sensuality and aesthetic gratification are perpetuated. To this sensibility the structural elimination of practical problems from a depoliticized public realm must become unbearable. However, it will give rise to a political force only if this sensibility comes into contact with a problem that the system cannot solve. For the future I see *one* such problem. The amount of social wealth produced by industrially advanced capitalism and the technical and organizational conditions under which this wealth is produced make it ever more difficult to link status assignment in an even subjectively convincing manner to the mechanism for the evaluation of individual achievement. In the long run therefore, student protest could permanently destroy this crumbling achievement-ideology, and thus bring down the already fragile legitimating basis of advanced capitalism, which rests only on depoliticization.

——Jürgen Habermas and Jeremy J. Shapiro, *Toward a Rational Society: Student protest, Science, and politics*, Beacon Press, 1970, pp. 94 - 122.

Historical Materialism and the Development of Normative Structures

...

In contexts of social action, the rationalization of means and the choice of means signifies a *heightening of productive forces*, that is, a socially significant implementation of knowledge, with the help of which we can improve the technical outfitting, organizational deployment, and qualifications of available labor power. Marx saw in this process the motor of social development. It is of course necessary to distinguish more precisely among (a) the rationality structures and (if appropriate) developmental logic of the knowledge that can be transposed into technologies, into strategies or organizations, and into qualifications; (b) the mechanisms that can explain the acquisition of this knowledge, the corresponding learning processes; and (c) the boundary conditions under which available knowledge can be implemented in a socially significant way. Only these three complexes of conditions together can explain rationalization processes in the sense of the development of productive forces. However, there is now the further question of whether *other* rationalization processes are just as important or even more important for the explanation of social evolution. In addition to the development of the forces of production, Marx regarded social movements as important. But in conceiving of the organized struggle of oppressed classes as itself a productive force, he established between the two motors of social development—technical-organizational progress on the one hand and class struggle on the other—a confusing, in any event an inadequately analyzed, connection.

In contradistinction to purposive-rational action, *communicative action* is, among other things, oriented to observing intersubjectively valid norms that link reciprocal expectations. In communicative action, the validity basis of speech is presupposed. The universal validity claims (truth, rightness, truthfulness), which participants at least implicitly raise and reciprocally recognize, make possible the consensus that carries action in common. In strategic action, this background consensus is lacking; the truthfulness of expressed intentions is not expected, and the norm—conformity of an utterance (or the rightness of the norm itself) is presupposed in a different sense than in communicative action—namely, contingently. One who repeatedly makes senseless moves in playing chess disqualifies himself as a chess player; and one who follows rules other than those constitutive of chess is not playing chess. Strategic action remains indifferent with respect to its motivational conditions, whereas the consensual presuppositions of communicative action can secure motivations. Thus strategic actions must be institutionalized, that is, embedded in inter-subjectively binding norms that guarantee the fulfillment of the motivational conditions. Even then we can distinguish the aspect of purposive-rational action—in Parsons' terminology, the task aspect—from the framework of normatively guided communicative action. In purposive-rational action it is supposed only that each subject is following preferences and decision maxims that he has determined for himself—that is, monologically, regardless of whether or not he agrees therein with other subjects. When, therefore, a strategic action system (e. g., war) makes it necessary for several subjects to agree in certain preferences (and to the extent that this agreement is not guaranteed in fact by the interest situations), purposive-rational action has somehow to be bound or institutionalized (e. g., in the framework of the Hague Convention). Institutionalization again means the organization of consensual action resting on inter subjectively recognized validity claims.

…

System problems express themselves as disturbances of the reproduction process of a society that is normatively fixed in its identity. Whether problems arise which overload the adaptive capacity of a society is a contingent matter; when problems of this type do arise, the reproduction of the society is placed in question—unless it takes up the evolutionary challenge and alters the established form of social integration that limits the employment and development of resources. *Whether* this alteration—which Marx describes as an overthrow of the relations of production—is actually possible, and *how* it is developmental-logically possible, cannot be read off the system problems; it is rather a question of access to a new learning level. The solution to the problems producing the crisis requires (a) attempts to loosen up the existing form of social integration by embodying in new institutions the rationality structures already developed in world views, and (b) a milieu favorable to the stabilization of successful attempts. Every economic advance can be characterized in terms of institutions in which rationality structures of the next higher stage of development are embodied—for example, the royal courts of justice, which, early in the development of civilization, permitted administration of justice at the *conventional* level of moral consciousness; or the capitalist firm, rational administration of the state, and bourgeois norms of civil law, which, at the beginning of the modern period, organized morally neutral domains of strategic action according to *universalistic* principles. Previously sociologists talked only of an "institutionalization of values," through which certain value orientations receive binding force for actors. When I now attempt to grasp evolutionary learning processes with the aid of the concept of "the institutional embodiment of structures of rationality," it is no longer a question of making orienting contents binding but of opening up *structural possibilities for the rationalization of action*.

——Jürgen Habermas, *Communication and the Evolution of Society*, Beacon Press, 1979, pp. 117 - 122.

Toward a Reconstruction of Historical Materialism

Only twice did Marx express himself connectedly and fundamentally on the materialist conception of history; otherwise he used this theoretical framework, in the role of historian, to interpret particular historical situations or developments—unsurpassedly in *The Eighteenth Brumaire of Louis Bonaparte*. Engels characterized historical materialism as a guide and a method. This could create the impression that Marx and Engels saw this doctrine as no more than a heuristic that helped to structure a (now-as-before) narrative presentation of history with systematic intent. But historical materialism was not understood in this way—either by Marx and Engels or by Marxist theoreticians or in the history of the labor movement. I shall not, therefore, treat it as a heuristic but as a theory, indeed as a theory of social evolution that, owing to its reflective status, is also informative for purposes of political action and can under certain circumstances be connected with the theory and strategy of revolution. The theory of capitalist development that Marx worked out in the *Grundrisse* and in *Capital* fits into historical materialism as a *subtheory*.

In 1938 Stalin codified historical materialism in a way that has proven of great consequence; the historical-materialist research since undertaken has remained largely bound to this theoretical framework. The version set down by Stalin needs to be reconstructed. My attempt to do so is also intended to further the critical appropriation of competing approaches—above all of neoevolutionism and of structuralism. Of course, I shall be able to make plausible only a few viewpoints from which such a re-construction might be attempted with some hope of success.

I would like first to introduce and consider critically some basic concepts and assumptions of historical materialism; I shall then point out certain difficulties that arise in applying its hypotheses and advance and illustrate an (abstract) proposal for resolving them; finally, I shall see what can be learned from competing approaches.

I

...

At a level of description that is unspecific in regard to the human mode of life, the exchange between the organism and its environment can be investigated in the physiological terms of material-exchange processes. But to grasp what is specific to the human mode of life, one must describe the relation between organism and environment at the level of labor processes. From the physical aspect the latter signify the expenditure of human energy and the transfer of energies in the economy of external nature; but what is decisive is the sociological aspect of the goal-directed transformation of material according to *rules of instrumental action*.

…

Means of subsistence are produced only to be consumed. The distribution of the product of labor is, like the labor itself, socially organized. In the case of rules of distribution, the concern is not with processing material or with the suitably coordinated application of means, but with the systematic connection of reciprocal expectations or interests. Thus the distribution of products requires rules of interaction that can be set intersubjectively at the level of linguistic understanding, detached from the individual case, and made permanent as recognized norms or *rules of communicative action*.

We call a system that socially regulates labor and distribution an *economy*. According to Marx, then, the economic form of reproducing life is characteristic of the human stage of development.

The concept of social labor as the *form of reproduction of human life* has a number of connotations. It is critical of the most basic assumptions of the modern philosophy of the subject or reflection. The statement—"As individuals express their life, so they are. What they are, therefore, coincides with *what* they produce and *how* they produce"—can be understood, according to the first of the *Theses on Feuerbach*, in the sense of an epistemologically oriented *pragmatism*, that is, as a critique of a phenomenalism of any sort, empiricist or rationalist, which understands the knowing subject as a passive, self-contained consciousness. The same statement has *materialist* connotations as well; it is directed equally against theoretical and practical idealism, which assert the primacy of the spirit over nature and that of the idea over the interest. Or consider the statement: "But the essence of man is no abstraction inhering in each single individual. In its actuality it is the ensemble of social relationships." Here Marx, schooled in the Hegelian concept of objective spirit, declares war on the methodological individualism of the bourgeois social sciences and on the practical individualism of English and French moral philosophy; both set forth the acting subject as an isolated monad.

…

Ⅱ

Marx links the concept of social labor with that of the *history of the species*. This phrase is intended in the first place to signal the materialist message that in the case of a single species natural evolution was continued by other means, namely, through the productive activity of the socialized individuals themselves. In sustaining their lives through social labor, men produce at the same time the material relations of life; they produce their society and the historical process in which individuals change along with their societies. The key to the reconstruction of the history of the species is provided by the concept of a *mode of production*. Marx conceives of history as a discrete series of modes of production, which, in its developmental-logical order, reveals the direction of social evolution. Let us recall the most important definitions.

A *mode of production* is characterized by a specific state of development of productive forces and by specific forms of social intercourse, that is, relations of production. The *forces of production* consist of (1) the labor power of those engaged in production, the producers; (2) technically useful knowledge insofar as it can be converted into instruments of labor that heighten productivity, that is, into technologies of production; (3) organizational knowledge insofar as it is applied to set labor power efficiently into motion, to qualify labor power, and to effectively coordinate the cooperation of laborers in accord with the division of labor (mobilization, qualification, and organization of labor power). Productive forces determine the degree of possible control over natural processes. On the other hand, the *relations of production* are those institutions and social mechanisms that determine the way in which (at a given stage of productive forces) labor power is combined with the available means of production. Regulation of access to the means of production, the way in which socially employed labor power is controlled, also determines indirectly the distribution of socially produced wealth. The relations of production express the distribution of social power; with the distributional pattern of socially recognized opportunities for need satisfaction, they prejudge the *interest structure* of a society. Historical materialism proceeds from the assumption that productive forces and productive relations do not vary independently, but form structures that (a) correspond with one another and (b) yield a finite number of structurally analogous stages of development, so that (c) there results a series of modes of production that are to be ordered in a developmental logic. (The handmill produces a society of feudal lords, the steam mill a society of industrial capitalists.)

...

Marx judged social development not by increases in complexity but by the stage of development of productive forces and by the maturity of the forms of social intercourse. The development of productive forces depends on the application of technically useful knowledge; and the basic institutions of a society embody moral-practical knowledge. Progress in these two dimensions is measured against the two universal validity claims we also use to measure the progress of empirical knowledge and of moral-practical insight, namely, the truth of propositions and the rightness of norms. I would like, therefore, to defend the thesis that the criteria of social progress singled out by historical materialism as the development of productive forces and the maturity of forms of social intercourse can be systematically justified. I shall come back to this.

Ⅲ

...

The development of productive forces can then be understood as a problem-generating mechanism that *triggers but does not bring about* the overthrow of relations of production and an evolutionary renewal of the mode of production. But even in this formulation the theorem can hardly be defended. To be sure, we know of a few instances in which system problems arose as a result of an increase in productive forces, overloading the adaptive capacity of societies organized on kinship lines and shattering the primitive communal order—this was apparently the case in Polynesia and South Africa. But the great endogenous, evolutionary advances that led to the first civilizations or to the rise of European capitalism were not conditioned but followed by significant development of productive forces. In these cases the development of productive forces could not have led to an evolutionary challenge.

It is advisable to distinguish between the potential of available knowledge and the implementation of this knowledge. It seems to be the case that the mechanism of not-being-able-not-to-learn (for which Moscovici has supplied intuitive support) again and again provides surpluses that harbor a potential of technical-organizational knowledge utilized only marginally or not at all. When this cognitive potential is drawn upon, it becomes the foundation of structure-forming social divisions of labor (between hunters and gatherers, tillers and breeders, agriculture and city craftsmen, crafts and industry, and so on). The endogenous growth of knowledge is thus a necessary condition of social evolution. But only when a new institutional framework has emerged can the as-yet unresolved system problems be treated with the help of the accumulated cognitive potential; from this there *results* an increase in productive forces. Only in this sense can one defend the statement that a social formation is never destroyed and that new, superior relations of production never replace older ones "before the material conditions for their existence have matured within the framework of the old society."

Ⅷ

…

> I argue that if we investigate by normal scientific methods the way in which the existence of ethical beliefs is involved in the causal nexus of the world's happenings, we shall be forced to conclude that the function of ethicizing is to mediate the progress of human evolution, a progress which now takes place mainly in the social and psychological sphere. We shall also find that this progress, in the world as a whole, exhibits a direction which is as well or ill denned as the concept of physiological health. Putting these two points together we can define a criterion, which does not depend for its validity on any recognition by a preexisting ethical belief.

But if the biological wisdom of any ethics singled out by evolution is expressed in the fact that it promotes the evolution and the learning ability of social systems, then we have to presuppose (a) that we know how social evolution can be measured, and (b) that we regard social evolution as good. Waddington starts from the idea that these presuppositions have been adequately clarified within biology because (a) the directional criterion of natural evolution is supposed to hold for social evolution as well, and (b) with the reproduction of life, health is posited as an objective value. Even if (a) were unproblematic, there is in (b) a naturalistic fallacy: the biologist is in no way forced to adopt as his own preference the observed tendency to self-maintenance inherent in organic life—unless it be through the fact that he is himself a living being. But in the objectivating attitude of the knowing subject he can ignore this fact.

The situation is somewhat different in the case of the normative foundation of linguistic communication, upon which, as theoreticians, we must always (already) rely. In adopting a theoretical attitude, in engaging in discourse—or for that matter in any communicative action whatsoever—we have always (already) made, at least implicitly, certain presuppositions, under which alone consensus is possible: the presupposition, for instance, that true propositions are preferable to false ones, and that right (i. e., justifiable) norms are preferable to wrong ones. For a living being that maintains itself in the structures of ordinary language communication, the validity basis of speech has the binding force of universal and unavoidable—in this sense transcendental—presuppositions. The *theoretician* does not have the same possibility of choice in relation to the validity claims immanent in speech as he does in relation to the basic biological value of health. Otherwise he would have to deny the very presuppositions without which the theory of evolution would be meaningless. If we are not free then to reject or to accept the validity claims bound up with the cognitive potential of the human species, it is senseless to want to "decide" for or against reason, for or against the expansion of the potential of reasoned action. For these reasons I do not regard the choice of the historical-materialist criterion of progress as arbitrary. The development of productive forces, in conjunction with the maturity of the forms of social integration, means progress of learning ability in both dimensions: progress in objectivating knowledge and in moral-practical insight.

——Jürgen Habermas, *Communication and the Evolution of Society*, Beacon Press, 1979, pp. 130 - 177.

五、观点解读

1. 科技已成为“第一位的生产力”

在全书的前言中，哈贝马斯就明确指出，他所写文章的内容是对马尔库塞提出的以下论点的辩论，即“技术的解放力量—物的工具化—转而成了解放的桎梏，成了人的工具化”。马尔库塞将技术理性的概念等同于意识形态，认为技术本身就是对自然和人的统治，而政治统治的压迫与科学技术的“合理性”实现了特有的融合。对此哈贝马斯认为，在当下的资本主义社会中，由于科学研究和技术之间的相互依赖关系日益密切，使科学本身成为“第一位的生产力”。他将科技进步作为新的坐标系，来对社会的不断合理化与科技进步的制度化的关系进行重新判断。一方面，从生产力的角度看，科技作为第一位的生产力，其直接结果便是社会物质财富的高度丰富、人民生活水平的大幅提高，这使得阶级差异和对抗也随之消失；另一方面，从意识形态的角度看，哈贝马斯不赞成将科技进步所起的社会功能同传统的意识形态所起的社会功能相提并论，他认为技术统治论的意识是一种“隐形的意识形态”，它虽然也发挥着使人们安于眼下生活、阻止他们思考和议论社会的基本问题的作用，但它已完全没有了传统的意识形态的压抑和奴役人的功能。因此他对科技在社会的作用持肯定乐观的态度。此外，哈贝马斯指出，十九世纪末以来，作为晚期资本主义的特点之一的技术的科学化的趋势取得了惊人的发展，科学、技术及其运用结成了一个体系。在这个过程中，科技在国家的军事领域和民用商品生产部门中都发挥了重要作用，科技的进步大幅提高了劳动生产率，成为决定经济发展的第一位的生产力。哈贝马斯认为，此时科技的进步已成为一种独立的剩余价值来源，与之相比较，马克思将生产者的劳动作为剩余价值来源的学说就显得过时了。因此，哈贝马斯认为，自己在提出科技已成为第一生产力的时候，事实上一方面反对了马尔库塞对科技的悲观主义态度，另一方面也是在新的历史条件下对马克思剩余价值学说的超越。

2. 科技成为统治的合法性基础

哈贝马斯认为，科学与技术在当今社会成为第一位的生产力的同时，也成为统治的合法性的基础。哈贝马斯指出，十九世纪的后 25 年，先进的资本主义国家中出现了两大发展趋势：科学和技术之间的相互依赖关系日益密切并使科学发展成为第一位的生产力；国家干预活动的增强保障了资本主义制度的稳定性。这两种趋势破坏了制度框架（相互作用）和目的理性活动（劳动）的子系统的原有格局，并使统治的合法性地位获得加强。从第一个趋势来看，哈贝马斯并不赞同马尔库塞认为技术的特征是政治的说法，在他看来，技术世界的机械系统"本身"对于政治目的来说仍然是中立的。同时，由于科学技术成为第一位的生产力，生产力的发展更多地取决于科技进步而非生产关系的变化，因此生产力与生产关系之间的矛盾得到了缓解，与马克思的观点不同，哈贝马斯认为生产力不再是解放的潜力，也不再能引起解放运动了。从第二个趋势看，由于科技的发展使得国家的行政调节变得活跃起来，在二者的相互作用下，统治的合法性得到更进一步加强。首先，技术的进步动摇了制度框架在生产力面前的"优越性"，资本主义的生产方式使革新本身制度化了，这种生产方式不仅提出了统治的合法性问题，而且也解决了统治的合法性问题，且这种合法性是"从社会劳动的根基上"获得的；其次，国家通过干预对经济发展做出持续性的调整，使得马克思提出的公平交换的基本意识形态实际上被补偿纲领所替代，国家通过补偿把群众的忠诚同保障私人资本增值的形式联结在一起，虽然阶级对立仍然存在，但其冲突被削弱了；最后，第一位的生产力已经成了统治的合法性的基础，这种新的合法性形式丧失了意识形态的旧形式，这种技术统治的意识在镇压有限交往的基础上，制定了"使愿望得以实现"和"使补偿得到满足"的标准，比之旧式的意识形态范围更加广泛，且更令人难以抗拒。但需要说明的一点是，哈贝马斯也认为技术统治意识的意识形态的核心是实践和技术的差别的消失，是失去了权利的制度框架和目的理性活动的独立系统之间的新格局的反映，它把辩护的标准与共同生活的组织分离开来，把辩护的标准非政治化，代之而来的是把辩护的标准同目的理性活动的子系统的功能联系在一起。新的意识形态损害了由日常语言交往所决定的社会化和个体化的形式联系在一起的兴趣。因此对新的意识形态的反思，必须与历史上既定的阶级利益（阶级兴趣）脱钩，并把正在形成的类的利益关系（兴趣关系）显示出来。

3. 重建历史唯物主义

自二十世纪七十年代以来，重建历史唯物主义的理论呼声就不绝于耳，其中影响最大、争论最多的莫过于哈贝马斯用交往行动理论改造生产方式的理论诉求。但哈贝马斯到底是怎样理解历史唯物主义的，这一重建的含义到底是什么，其思想资源和理论方法仍然需要我们审慎地加以对待。

我们可以发现：哈贝马斯所理解的历史唯物主义主要是第二国际以来在苏联斯大林主义中教条化的历史唯物主义观念。在哈贝马斯看来，这种历史唯物主义的不足主要表现在三个方面：一是虽然关注历史的发展和进化，但是作为一种全面进化的理论，对于社会总体进化的机制理解不准确，无法提供对“复合社会”的充分分析；二是马克思从生产方式出发分析人类历史演进的阶段，虽然提供了一把“钥匙”，却是一把“尚未充分打磨的钥匙”，不够抽象，无法分析总体的社会组织化原则；三是在这样一种社会一体化形式中，历史唯物主义缺乏对如个人、社会之间的复杂互动关系的理解和说明。有鉴于此，哈贝马斯提出“重建历史唯物主义”的口号。这种重建不是在原有基础上的修修补补，而是一种理论的“重构”。如其自述，“我们所说的重建是把一种理论拆开，用新的形式重新加以组合，以便更好地达到这种理论所确立的目标。这是对待一种在某些方面需要修正，但其鼓舞人心的潜在力量仍旧（始终）没有枯竭的理论的一种正常态度，我认为，即使对马克思主义者来说，也是正常的态度”。

可以说，哈贝马斯的重建是一种彻底的理论重构，并且无论是从其自身的思想历程还是文本的逻辑展开来看，以交往行动理论来重建历史唯物主义已经从根本上溢出了马克思的生产方式理论。之所以运用交往理论来重建历史唯物主义，哈贝马斯主要的思想资源和方法论构架是，第一，对韦伯所提出的、在西方马克思主义形成发展中扮演重要角色的合理化概念的继承和运用。与卢卡奇、霍克海默颠倒使用合理化，提出物化概念不同，哈贝马斯将法兰克福学派对物化、同一性的批判重新翻转为符合社会一体化形式的建构。第二，为了实现这一建构，哈贝马斯强调自我同一性与集体的理性同一性之间共同的意识结构。支撑这一论述的是三种理论资源：其一是法兰克福学派通过弗洛伊德精神分析理论，对极权主义意识形态以及资本主义社会中人格结构的分析；其二是皮亚杰的认识发生论和米德的符号相互作用的行动理论；其三是法兰克福学派有关市民社会史及资产阶级社会理论的考察，特别是黑格尔自我意识哲学的考察。第三，为了说明二十世纪下半叶资本主义的新变化，尤其是在国家、意识形态领域的新情况，哈贝马斯提出在作为基础的生产方式之外，讨论包含内在学习机制的社会一体化形式的理论诉求。

也正是在这个意义上，哈贝马斯特别强调交往行动理论对于历史唯物主义重建的理论意义。但是这样一种重建在很大程度上同时标志着哈贝马斯开始告别马克思主义。正如哈贝马斯自己所言，首先，这一重建的基础并非是对现实资本主义的批判，而是对现实社会制度的辩护；其次，这一重建回避了马克思主义理论中最为核心的问题之一，阶级对抗和剩余价值，而只是在搁置生产方式的基础上，片面强调交往理性在规范结构中的作用，因而被很多左翼学者所批评；最后，尽管交往理论确实对扭转传统马克思主义研究中的教条主义具有积极意义，但是交往理论与生产方式之间的内在关联并未得到科学的说明，甚至于后来出现了交往范式对生产方式替代的情况。

4. 自我的同一性

尽管交往行动理论是哈贝马斯重建历史唯物主义的核心理论范式，但是这一理论本身并非仅仅是孤立地强调用“交往范式”来取代“生产范式”，构成其理论基础的是对现代“主体”概念的反思。就此而言，与“自我同一性”确立直接相关的“学习能力”的概念是理解“交往理论”和“重建历史唯物主义”的重要逻辑环节。在此过程中，首先涉及对主体概念的重新思考。正如哈贝马斯所提到的，“从黑格尔经过弗洛伊德直到皮亚杰，一种观点得到了发展：主体和客体的形成是相辅相成的；主体只有在同它自身的客观世界的比较中，并且通过他自身的客观世界的建设才能清楚地认识自己，这种非主体的东西一方面是皮亚杰诉说的‘客体’——认识上对象化了的和实际上能够占有的实在；另一方面是弗洛伊德所说的‘客体’：交往所开拓的和认同所保证的相互作用领域”。也就是说，作为现代哲学中的一个核心范畴，“主体”本身不是抽象不变的，在不同的理论构架中承担不同的角色。而“主体”本身的意识结构又构成了联结个体自我同一性与社会一体化形式的中介。这样一种“主体”，就不是简单的“主客体”二元关系中的“主体”，而是一种不断“发生的”与抽象的社会组织原则相关的主体。这种主体的显著特征就是

"交互主体",这一主体的确立,本身既意味着自我同一性的确立,又意味着集体同一性的确立。而这一过程,在重建历史唯物主义过程中被哈贝马斯描述为一个"学习过程",同时也是个人同生活世界的象征性结构融为一体的过程。

5. 从劳动到交往:历史唯物主义的重建范式

根据哈贝马斯自己的表述,似乎在马克思的历史唯物主义中,更多关注的是物质生产和社会劳动,而对交往问题缺乏足够的重视。受哈贝马斯的影响,不少关注马克思和马克思主义的学者也接受了一种观点:物质生产方式分析不足以应对当代资本主义的新变化,因而应当为历史唯物主义分析增加交往的内容。但是这种观点存在三个值得注意的地方。

第一,哈贝马斯所针对的主要是第二国际以来,特别是在斯大林式的马克思主义解释中存在的将历史唯物主义教条化的理解。在这种理解中,生产力和生产关系的总和构成生产方式,生产方式作为基础,与竖立其上的法、国家和意识形态等上层建筑相对应,并在归根结底的意义上起决定作用。生产力包括劳动力、劳动工具和劳动对象三个要素,而生产关系包括生产资料所有制的形式、人们在生产中的地位和相互关系、产品分配的形式等。这种理解本身没有问题,但是将其抽象地运用于人类历史的发展就会产生一系列难题。在哈贝马斯的时代,主要表现为,一方面,随着资本主义发展,工具理性或科学技术越发呈现出意识形态的特征,同时法、道德领域呈现出新的规范结构;另一方面,随着人类学历史学研究的进展,提出了传统历史唯物主义无法直接解释的问题,即文化象征结构在社会同一性中的作用。

第二,尽管存在上述问题,但是我们不能简单宣判历史唯物主义缺乏交往的维度,或者说不足以构成科学的理论方法。回到马克思恩格斯的理论探索过程中去,我们可以看到,历史唯物主义理论中生产和交往的维度本身是内在关联在一起的,而马克思恩格斯恰恰是透过一定生产方式基础上的交往及其形形色色的意识形态外壳,才真正发现了社会历史的内在结构和动力,即物质生产和再生产过程的。在确立历史唯物主义一般原则的《德意志意识形态》中,马克思恩格斯受制于古典政治经济学和德国古典哲学的话语表述方式,仍然使用了"交往形式"的概念。但非常明确的是,这种交往形式本身是同一定的生产方式，即一定的劳动分工的方式结合在一起的，并且构成了一定“市民社会”的基础“所有制形式”。也就是说，历史唯物主义中并不是缺乏“交往”的理论维度，而是这种维度被内蕴于一定的物质生产方式分析中加以理解。在《资本论》中，这一理论维度得到了更加深刻的阐发，即资本主义生产和再生产过程中，与生产力相对应的生产关系及其在社会形态中的转型和再现方式，得到了更加深刻的阐发。在这个意义上，并不是生产方式概念不够抽象，而是哈贝马斯不能理解抽象的生产方式概念，以至于为了获得对现代资本主义社会的理解，而有意无意走了“交往行动理论”这一逻辑捷径。

第三，基于上述分析，交往行动理论并不是对历史唯物主义的补充或重建，而更多是一种告别或宣判。这一点在哈贝马斯自身的思想发展历程中也得到了现实的印证。但无论如何，哈贝马斯在提出这一理论过程中所运用的复杂理论资源，所折射出来的资本主义现实变化都是值得我们认真关注的。

六、进一步阅读指南

1. [德]尤尔根·哈贝马斯:《作为“意识形态”的技术与科学》，李黎、郭官义译，学林出版社 1999 年版。

2. [德]尤尔根·哈贝马斯:《重建历史唯物主义》，郭官义译，社会科学文献出版社 2000 年版。

3. [德]尤尔根·哈贝马斯:《交往与社会进化》，张博树译，重庆出版社 1989 年版。

4. [美]托马斯·麦卡锡:《哈贝马斯的批判理论》，王江涛译，华东师范大学出版社 2010 年版。

5. [美]洛克莫尔:《历史唯物主义:哈贝马斯的重建》，孟丹译，北京师范大学出版社 2009 年版。

6. 张亮、孙乐强:《21 世纪国外马克思主义哲学若干重大问题研究》，人民出版社 2020 年版。

7. Jürgen Habermas, *Zur Rekonstruktion Des Historischen Materialismus*, Suhrkamp Verlag, 1976.

8. Jürgen Habermas, *Communication and the Evolution of Society*, Beacon Press, 1979.

七、问题与思考

1. 如何理解哈贝马斯关于科学技术已成为“第一位的生产力”的命题?
2. 哈贝马斯为什么认为科技已经成为合法性的基础?
3. 哈贝马斯为什么重建历史唯物主义?
4. 如何理解自我的同一性?
5. 如何理解哈贝马斯的交往范式理论?

第三版后记

2010 年，本教材的第一版《西方马克思主义哲学原著选读》作为“马克思主义哲学实验教材”丛书之一由北京师范大学出版社出版，次年入选江苏省高等学校精品教材。2015 年入选江苏省高等学校重点教材(修订教材)建设项目后，编写组于 2016 年完成《西方马克思主义哲学原著选读(第二版)》的修订工作，改由南京大学出版社出版。2021 年，本教材再次入选江苏省高等学校重点教材(修订教材)建设项目，编写组随即启动面向一线教师的调研，并根据调研结果开展了以下四个方面的修订工作：第一，将书名调整为《西方马克思主义原著选读(第三版)》；第二，将各章的“历史背景”细化为“作者介绍”“时代背景”“思想背景”三个部分；第三，增加了国内相关研究状况的述评总结；第四，对“进一步阅读指南”进行了充实和优化。今后，编写组将持续倾听来自教学一线师生的意见和建议，不断做好修订工作，努力建成导向正确、质量一流、适宜性强的新时代精品教材。

本教材的第三版修订工作由张亮、孙乐强主持完成，参与修订的有陈硕、张晓、孔智键、刘冰菁、赵立，陈硕、张晓协助主编完成了统稿和定稿工作。第二版修订工作由张亮主持完成，参与修订的有孙乐强、冯潇、周嘉昕、陈硕、杨丽婷、田明、张晓，孙乐强、冯潇协助主编完成了修改和统稿工作，张晓承担了英文选文部分的编辑工作。第一版编写由张亮与冯潇、夏凡、陈硕共同完成，冯潇、陈硕协助完成了审校工作，陈鹏协助完成了许多事务性工作。

本教材的历次立项和出版均得到南京大学本科生院(原教务处)的大力支持，在此特致谢忱！

本教材第二、三版的修订出版工作得到南京大学出版社社长金鑫荣教授的支持，特致谢忱！施敏博士为两次修订出版提供了大量帮助和便利，在此一并表示感谢！

编写组

2022 年 5 月 20 日

图书在版编目(CIP)数据

西方马克思主义原著选读 / 张亮，孙乐强主编. —3 版. — 南京 ：南京大学出版社，2022.9
ISBN 978-7-305-26063-6

Ⅰ. ①西… Ⅱ. ①张… ②孙… Ⅲ. ①西方马克思主义-高等学校-教材 Ⅳ. ①B089.1

中国版本图书馆 CIP 数据核字(2022)第 147816 号

出版发行 南京大学出版社
社　　址 南京市汉口路 22 号　　邮　编 210093
出 版 人 金鑫荣

书　　名 西方马克思主义原著选读(第 3 版)
主　　编 张　亮　孙乐强
副 主 编 陈　硕　张　晓
责任编辑 施　敏

照　　排 南京南琳图文制作有限公司
印　　刷 南京京新印刷有限公司
开　　本 787×960 1/16 印张 33.25 字数 528 千
版　　次 2022 年 9 月第 3 版 2022 年 9 月第 1 次印刷
ISBN 978-7-305-26063-6
定　　价 88.00 元

网址：http://www.njupco.com
官方微博：http://weibo.com/njupco
官方微信号：njupress
销售咨询热线：(025) 83594756